THE EARLY HISTORY OF INDIA

THE EARLY HISTORY OF INDIA

FROM 600 B.C. TO THE MUHAMMADAN CONQUEST

INCLUDING THE INVASION OF ALEXANDER THE GREAT

VINCENT A. SMITH

EDITED BY

S. M. EDWARDES, C.S.I., C.V.O.

GYAN

Published by

GYAN

Gyan Publishing House
5, Ansari Road
Daryaganj, New Delhi-110002
Phone: 011-47034999, 9811692060
E-mail: books@gyanbooks.com

Distribution Network
gyanbooks.com
India, USA, Canada, UK, Australia, France

ISBN: 978-81-212-8716-6 (PB)
First Published, 1904

2nd Impression 2023

Printed at: Gyan Press, Delhi.

THE EARLY HISTORY OF INDIA
Author: vincent A. Smith

THE EARLY HISTORY OF INDIA

ROCK-CUT ELEPHANT ABOVE THE ASOKA INSCRIPTION AT DHAULI, ORISSA

THE EARLY HISTORY OF INDIA

FROM 600 B.C. TO THE MUHAMMADAN CONQUEST

INCLUDING THE INVASION OF ALEXANDER THE GREAT

BY

VINCENT A. SMITH

M.A. (DUBL. ET OXON.); F.R.A.S., F.R.N.S., LATE OF THE INDIAN CIVIL SERVICE;
AUTHOR OF 'ASOKA, THE BUDDHIST EMPEROR OF INDIA',
'A HISTORY OF FINE ART IN INDIA AND CEYLON', ETC.

FOURTH EDITION, REVISED BY

S. M. EDWARDES, C.S.I., C.V.O.

LATE OF THE INDIAN CIVIL SERVICE

OXFORD
AT THE CLARENDON PRESS

PREFACE TO FOURTH EDITION

THE task of revising this history for a fourth edition was entrusted to me in accordance with the wish of the author, who realized that he would not be spared to complete the work himself. For one who has not devoted the greater portion of a lifetime to careful study of the problems involved, the task has been by no means easy. Fortunately, however, I was furnished with notes on various points recorded by Dr. Vincent A. Smith before his death; and with these and the help of reports, papers and essays on Indian history and antiquities, which have appeared in various publications since 1914, I have endeavoured to the best of my ability to bring the work up to date.

The excavations carried out at Taxila by the Archaeological Department of the Government of India, and the researches of Indian scholars like Messrs. R. D. Banerji, K. P. Jayaswal, D. R. Bhandarkar and others, have necessitated the preparation of several additional notes, as well as chronological and other amendments in the text and appendices of various chapters.

As regards the problem of the origin of the Pallavas, which the author perforce left unsolved in the third edition, I have included in the text a theory advanced by a scholar of Colombo, based upon a tradition embodied in ancient Tamil literature. His suggestion as to the original connexion of the dynasty with Ceylon, which formed the gist of an article in the *Indian Antiquary* of April 1923, should be compared with a valuable paper on 'The Origin and Early History of the Pallavas of Kanchi' by Professor S. Krishnaswami Aiyangar, which appeared in the *Journal of Indian History* (Vol. II, Part I) for November 1922. I much regret that a copy of the article, which Professor Aiyangar kindly sent to me, arrived too late to admit of my quoting or embodying his conclusions in this edition. Those, however, who are interested in the early history of South India will do well to acquaint themselves with the Professor's view of the problem, based as it is upon prolonged research and careful reasoning.

It remains to add that the Index of the work has been revised and slightly enlarged, and that a few necessary alterations have been made in the maps and illustrations.

S. M. E.

EXTRACT FROM PREFACE TO FIRST EDITION

THE plan and limitations of this book have been explained so fully in the Introduction that little more need be said by way of preface. The room for difference of opinion on many of the subjects treated is so great that I cannot expect my views on controverted points to meet with universal acceptance; and the complexity of my undertaking forbids me to hope that positive errors, justly open to censure, have been avoided altogether; but I trust that critics will be prepared to concede the amount of indulgence which may be granted legitimately to the work of a pioneer.

The devotion of a disproportionately large space to the memorable invasion of Alexander the Great is due to the exceptional interest of the subject, which, so far as I know, has not been treated adequately in any modern book.

The presentation of cumbrous and unfamiliar Oriental names must always be a difficulty for a writer on Indian history. I have endeavoured to secure reasonable uniformity of spelling without pedantry. The system of transliteration followed in the notes and appendices is substantially that used in the *Indian Antiquary*; while in the text long vowels only are marked where necessary, and all other diacritical signs are discarded.

Vowels have values as in Italian ; except the short *a*, which is pronounced like *u* in *but*, when with stress, and like *A* in *America*, when without stress. The consonants are to be pronounced as in English ; and *ch*, consequently, is represented in French by *tch*, and in German by *tsch* ; similarly, *j* is equivalent to the French *dj* and the German *dsch*. The international symbol *c* for the English *ch*, as in *church*, which has been adopted by the Asiatic Societies, may have some advantages in purely technical publications ; but its use results in such *monstra horrenda* as *Cac* for *Chach*, and is unsuitable in a work intended primarily for English and Indian readers.

CONTENTS

ILLUSTRATIONS

MAPS AND PLANS

[1] Dr. P. Gardner exhibited to the Philological Society in 1915 a photograph of a colossal statue of Alexander found at Cyrene by the Italians, which he thought would be considered in future as the best portrait. He pointed out that the Tivoli herm is partly restored and is in bad condition. The herm is probably intended for Alexander but it is not wholly certain that the head belongs to the inscribed pedestal, or that the inscription is contemporaneous.

CONTENTS OF PLATE OF INDIAN COINS (1) IN THE BRITISH MUSEUM

No.	*King.*	*Obverse.*	*Reverse.*	*Reference.*
1	Sophytes.	Head of the king r., in close-fitting helmet, bound with wreath; wing on cheek-piece.	ΣΩΦΥΤΟΥ Cock r.; above, caduceus.	Gardner, *Catal. of Greek and Scythic Kings of Bactria and India*, Pl. I, 3.
2	Eukratides.	Bust of the king r., diademed, and wearing helmet (*kausia*), adorned with ear and horn of bull, and crest.	ΒΑΣΙΛΕΩΣ ΜΕΓΑΛΟΥ ΕΥΚΡΑΤΙΔΟΥ The Dioskouroi charging r., holding long lances and palms.	ibid., Pl. V, 7.
3	Menander.	ΒΑΣΙΛΕΩΣ ΣΩΤΗΡΟΣ ΜΕΝΑΝΔΡΟΥ Bust of the king r., diademed.	Not figured.	ibid., Pl. XI, 7.
4	Hermaios.	ΒΑΣΙΛΕΩΣ ΣΩΤΗΡΟΣ ΕΡΜΑΙΟΥ Bust of the king r., diademed.	Not figured.	ibid., Pl. XV, 4.
5	Kadphises I.	ΧΟΡΑΝϹΥ ΖΑΟΟΥ ΚΟΖΟΛΑ ΚΑΔΑΦΕϹ. Head of the king r., diademed, and closely resembling that of Augustus.	Not figured.	ibid., Pl. XXV, 5.
6	Gondophares.	Greek legend imperfect. ΒΑϹΙΛΕΟΝ .... ΥΝΔΟΦΕΡ ... Bust of the king r., diademed.	Not figured.	ibid., Pl. XXII, 11.
7	Sivalakura of Āndhra dynasty.	*Raño Mādhariputasa Sivalakurasa.* Strung bow, with arrow fixed.	Not figured.	Cunningham, *Coins of Ancient India*, p. 109.
8	Kadphises II.	ΒΑϹΙΛΕΥϹ ΟΟΗΜΟ ΚΑΔΦΙϹΗϹ. Bust of king emerging from clouds; helmet and diadem; Greek chlamys; club ? in r. hand.	Kharoshṭhī inscription, *maharajasa*, &c. Śiva and Indian bull.	Gardner, op. cit., Pl. XXV, 7.
9	Kanishka.	Standing king in Turki costume, with spear and sword. Legend in modified Greek characters. ΡΑΟΝΑΝΟΡΑΟ ΚΑΝΗΡΚΙ ΚΟΡΑΝΟ (? Ρ to be read *sh*).	ΑΡΔΟΧΡΟ Female deity with cornucopiae.	Gardner, op. cit., Pl. XXVI, 6.
10	Samudragupta.	King seated, playing lyre. Legend, *mahārājādhirāja śrī Samudraguptah*; on footstool, *si*.	Not figured.	*J.R.A.S.*, 1889, Pl. I, 5.
11	Samudragupta.	Horse, standing before altar and sacrificial post. Legend imperfect; between horse's legs, *si*.	Not figured.	ibid., 4.
12	Chandra-gupta II, Vikramāditya.	King shooting lion. Legend, *mahārājādhirāja śrī*.	Goddess seated on lion. Legend, *Śrī Siṁha Vikramah*.	ibid., Pl. II, 6.
13	Kīrttivarman Chandella.	Legend, *śrīmat Kīrttivarmma-deva*.	Four-armed goddess, seated.	Cunningham, *Coins of Mediaeval India*, Pl. VIII, 12.
14	A Pāṇḍya king.	Two fishes under an umbrella, with other symbols.	Legend uncertain.	Elliot, *Coins of Southern India*, Pl. III, 129.
15	Rājarāja Choḷa.	Standing king.	Seated figure. Legend, *Rājarāja*.	ibid., Pl. IV, 165.
16	A Pallava chief.	Lion r.	Vase on stand.	ibid., Pl. II, 49.
17	A Chera king.	Seated figure, corrupted.	Bow and umbrella.	ibid., Pl. III, 128.

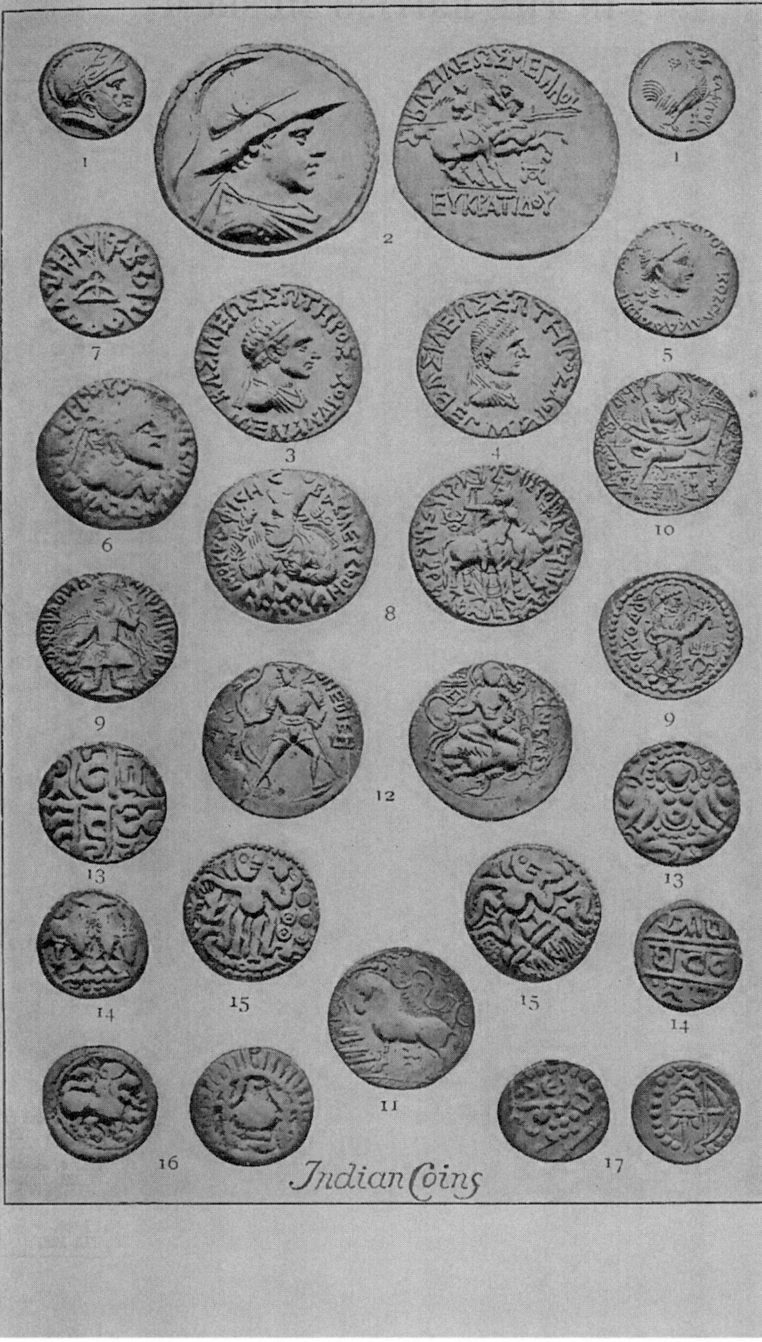

Indian Coins

CHAPTER I

I. INTRODUCTION

Elphinstone and Cowell on the Hindu period.

THE illustrious Elphinstone, writing in 1839, observed that in Indian history 'no *date* of a public event can be fixed before the invasion of Alexander; and no *connected* relation of the national transactions can be attempted until after the Mahometan conquest'. Professor Cowell, when commenting upon this dictum, twenty-seven years later, begged his readers to bear it in mind during the whole of the Hindu period; assigning as his reason for this caution the fact that 'it is only at those points where other nations came into contact with the Hindus, that we are able to settle any details accurately.'[1]

Although the first clause of Elphinstone's proposition, if strictly interpreted, still remains true—no date in Indian history prior to Alexander's invasion being determinable with absolute precision—modern research has much weakened the force of the observation, and has enabled scholars to fix a considerable number of dates in the pre-Alexandrine history of India with approximate accuracy, sufficient for most purposes.

Results of modern research.

But when the statement that a connected narrative of events prior to the Muhammadan conquest cannot be prepared is examined in the light of present knowledge, the immense progress in the recovery of the lost history of India made during the last seventy years becomes apparent. The researches of a multitude of scholars working in various fields have disclosed an unexpected wealth of materials for the reconstruction of ancient Indian history; and the necessary preliminary studies of a technical kind have been carried so far that the accumulated and ever-growing stores of knowledge can be sorted and arranged with advantage. It now appears to be practicable to exhibit the results of antiquarian

[1] Elphinstone, *History of India*, ed. Cowell, 5th ed., p. 11.

studies in the shape of a 'connected relation'; not less intelligible to the ordinary educated reader than Elphinstone's narrative of the transactions of the Muhammadan period.

Political history. The first attempt to present such a narrative of the leading events in Indian political history for eighteen centuries was made in the first edition of this book, which, even in its now much expanded form, is still designedly confined for the most part to the relation of political vicissitudes. A sound framework of dynastic annals must be provided before the story of Indian religion, literature, and art can be told aright. Although religious, literary, and artistic problems are touched on very lightly in this volume, the references made will suffice, perhaps, to convince the reader that the key is often to be found in the accurate chronological presentation of dynastic facts.

East and West. European students, whose attention has been mainly directed to the Graeco-Roman foundation of modern civilization, may be disposed to agree with the German philosopher in the belief that 'Chinese, Indian, and Egyptian antiquities are never more than curiosities';[1] but, however well founded that opinion may have been in Goethe's day, it can no longer command assent. The researches of orientalists during the last hundred years have established many points of contact between the ancient East and the modern West; and no Hellenist can now afford to profess complete ignorance of the Babylonian and Egyptian culture which forms the bedrock of European institutions. Even China has been brought into touch with Europe; while the languages, literature, art, and philosophy of the West have been proved to be connected by innumerable bonds with those of India. Although the names of even the greatest monarchs of ancient India are at present unfamiliar to the general reader, and awaken few echoes in the minds of any save specialists, it is not unreasonable to hope that an orderly presentation of the ascertained facts of ancient Indian history may be of interest to a larger circle than that of professed orientalists, and that,

[1] *The Maxims and Reflections of Goethe*, No. 325, in Bailey Saunders's translation.

as the subject becomes more familiar to the reading public, it will be found no less worthy of attention than better known departments of historical study. A recent Indian author justly observes that 'India suffers to-day in the estimation of the world more through that world's ignorance of the achievements of the heroes of Indian history than through the absence or insignificance of such achievements'.[1] The following pages may serve to prove that the men of old time in India did deeds worthy of remembrance, and deserving of rescue from the oblivion in which they have been buried for so many centuries.

Alexander the Great. The section of this work which deals with the invasion of Alexander the Great may claim to make a special appeal to the interest of readers trained in the ordinary course of classical studies; and the subject has been treated accordingly with much fulness of detail. The existing English accounts of Alexander's marvellous campaign, among which that of Thirlwall, perhaps, is entitled to the highest place, treat the story as an appendix to the history of Greece rather than as part of that of India, and fail to make full use of the results of the labours of modern geographers and archaeologists. In this volume the campaign is discussed as a memorable episode in the history of India, and an endeavour has been made to collect all the rays of light from recent investigation and to focus them upon the narratives of ancient authors.

The author's aim. The author's aim is to present the story of ancient India, as far as practicable, in the form of a connected narrative, based upon the most authentic evidence available; to relate facts, however established, with impartiality: and to discuss the problems of history in a judicial spirit. He has striven to realize, however imperfectly, the ideal expressed in the words of Goethe:—

'The historian's duty is to separate the true from the false, the certain from the uncertain, and the doubtful from that which cannot be accepted. . . . Every investigator must before all things look upon himself as one who is summoned

[1] C. N. K. Aiyar, *Sri Sancharacharya, his Life and Times*, p. iv.

to serve on a jury. He has only to consider how far the statement of the case is complete and clearly set forth by the evidence. Then he draws his conclusion and gives his vote, whether it be that his opinion coincides with that of the foreman or not.' [1]

The application of these principles necessarily involves the wholesale rejection of mere legend as distinguished from tradition, and the omission of many picturesque anecdotes, mostly folk-lore, which have clustered round the names of the mighty men of old in India.

Value of tradition. The historian of the remote past of any nation must be content to rely much upon tradition as embodied in literature, and to acknowledge that the results of his researches when based upon traditionary materials, are inferior in certainty to those obtainable for periods of which the facts are attested by contemporary evidence. In India, with very few exceptions, contemporary evidence of any kind is not available before the time of Alexander ; but critical examination of records dated much later than the events referred to can extract from them testimony which may be regarded with a high degree of probability as traditionally transmitted from the sixth or, perhaps, the seventh century, B. C.

Necessity for criticism. Even contemporary evidence, when it is available for later periods, cannot be accepted without criticism. The flattery of courtiers, the vanity of kings, and many other clouds which obscure the absolute truth, must be recognized and allowed for. Nor is it possible for the writer of a history, however great may be his respect for the objective fact, to eliminate altogether his own personality. Every kind of evidence, even the most direct, must reach the reader, when presented in narrative form, as a reflection from the mirror of the writer's mind, with the liability to unconscious distortion. In the following pages the author has endeavoured to exclude the subjective element so far as possible, to make no statement of fact without authority, and to give the authority, that is to say, the evidence, for every fact alleged.

But no obligation to follow authority in the other sense

[1] *The Maxims and Reflections of Goethe*, Nos. 453, 543.

of the word has been accepted, and the narrative often assumes a form apparently justified by the evidence, although opposed to the views stated in well-known books by authors of repute. Indian history has been too much the sport of credulity and hypothesis, inadequately checked by critical judgement of evidence, or verification of fact; and 'the opinion of the foreman', to use Goethe's phrase, cannot be implicitly followed.

Unity of India.

Although this work purports to relate the Early History of India, the title must be understood with certain limitations. India, encircled as she is by seas and mountains, is indisputably a geographical unit, and, as such, is rightly designated by one name. Her type of civilization, too, has many features which differentiate it from that of all other regions of the world, while they are common to the whole country, or rather sub-continent, in a degree sufficient to justify its treatment as a unit in the history of the social, religious, and intellectual development of mankind.[1]

But the complete political unity of India under the control of a paramount power, wielding unquestioned authority, is a thing of yesterday, barely a century old.[2] The most notable of her rulers in the olden time cherished the ambition of universal Indian dominion, and severally attained it in a greater or less degree. Not one of them, however, attained it completely, and this failure involves a lack of unity in political history which renders the task of the historian difficult.

The same difficulty besets the historian of Greece still more pressingly; but, in that case, with the attainment of unity the interest of the history vanishes. In the case of India the converse proposition holds good, and the reader's interest varies directly with the degree of unity attained; the details of Indian annals being insufferably wearisome except when generalized by the application of a bond of political union.

[1] See Radhakumud Mookerji, M.A., *The Fundamental Unity of India* (from Hindu sources), Longmans, Green & Co. 1914.

[2] It may be dated from 1818, at the close of the Pindārī and Marātha wars of the Marquis of Hastings.

Predominant dynasties.

A political history of India, if it is to be read, must necessarily tell the story of the predominant dynasties, and either ignore, or relegate to a very subordinate position, the annals of the minor states. Elphinstone acted upon this principle in his classic work, practically confining his narrative to the transactions of the Sultans of Delhi and their Moghal successors. The same principle has been applied in this book, attention being concentrated upon the dominant dynasties which, from time to time, have aspired to or attained paramount power.

Twice, in the long series of centuries dealt with in this history, the political unity of all India was nearly attained; first, in the third century B. C., when Asoka's empire extended almost to the latitude of Madras; and again, in the fourth century after Christ, when Samudragupta carried his victorious arms from the Ganges to the borders of the Tamil country. Other princes, although their conquests were less extensive, yet succeeded in establishing, and for a time maintaining, empires which might fairly claim to rank as paramount powers. With the history of such princes the following narrative is chiefly concerned, the affairs of the minor states being either slightly noticed, or altogether ignored.

Supremacy of the north.

The paramount power in early times, when it existed, invariably had its seat in Northern India—the region of the Gangetic plain lying to the north of the great barrier of jungle-clad hills which shut off the Deccan from Hindustan. That barrier may be defined conveniently as consisting of the Vindhyan ranges, using that term in a wide sense; or may be identified, still more compendiously, with the river Narmadā, or Nerbudda, which falls into the Gulf of Cambay, and flows between the Vindhyan and Sātpura ranges.[1]

[1] Mr. Pargiter holds that a careful examination of the names of rivers and mountains in Canto 57 of the *Mārkaṇḍeya Purāṇa* indicates that in ancient times the name Vindhya was confined to the eastern part of the range to the north of the Narmadā, extending from about Bhopāl to Bihār, the more western part of the range along with the Aravallis (Aṛāvalā) being included under the term Pāripātra (*J. R. A. S.*, 1894, p. 258). Modern writers apply the term Vindhya to the whole range north of the river.

The researches of Dr. Fleet, Professor Kielhorn, and many other patient scholars have revealed in outline much of the history of the kingdoms of the Deccan plateau lying between the Narmadā on the north and the Krishnā and Tungabhadra on the south, from the sixth century after Christ. But the details are mainly of local interest and can never attract the attention of the outer world to the same degree as can the history of the northern empires, constantly in touch with that world.

Early history of the Deccan.

The ancient kingdoms of the far south, although rich and populous, inhabited by Dravidian nations not inferior in culture to their Aryan rivals in the north, were ordinarily so secluded from the rest of the civilized world, including Northern India, that their affairs remained hidden from the eyes of other nations; and, native annalists being lacking, their history, previous to the year 800 of the Christian era, has almost wholly perished. Except on the rare occasions when an unusually enterprising sovereign of the north either penetrated or turned the forest barrier, and for a moment lifted the veil of secrecy in which the southern potentates lived enwrapped, very little is known concerning political events in the far south during the long period extending from 600 B.C. to A.D. 800. To use the words of Elphinstone, no 'connected relation of the national transactions' of Southern India in remote times can be written; and an early history of India must, perforce, be concerned mainly with the north.

Isolation of the far south.

Although it is still as true as it was when the first edition of this book was published, that an exact chronological narrative of the purely political history of the Tamil kingdoms of Southern India previous to A.D. 800 cannot be written at present, and it is possible that such a history cannot be written at any time, I must not be understood to mean that the early history of the South is either wholly inaccessible or devoid of interest. On the contrary, I believe that, if we can be content to dispense with precise chronology, materials exist for the reconstruction in no small measure of the history of Dravidian institutions, and that a history of that kind, when worked out by scholars

The non-Aryan element.

adequately skilled in the languages, literatures, and customs of the Dravidian peoples, will be of essential service to the historian of India as a whole, and will enable the student of the development of Indian civilization to see his subject in true perspective.

Attention has been concentrated too long on the North, on Sanskrit books, and on Indo-Aryan notions. It is time that due regard should be paid to the non-Aryan element.

This book being deliberately confined almost exclusively to the summary presentation of the political history of India, I am precluded from following out the suggested line of research, but I cannot refrain from quoting certain observations of an eminent Indian scholar, prematurely deceased, which seem to me worthy of serious consideration, and are as follows :—

India Proper in the South.

'The attempt to find the basic element of Hindu civilization by a study of Sanskrit and the history of Sanskrit in Upper India is to begin the problem at its worst and most complicated point. India, south of the Vindhyas—the Peninsular India—still continues to be India Proper. Here the bulk of the people continue distinctly to retain their pre-Aryan teatures, their pre-Aryan languages, their pre-Aryan social institutions. Even here, the process of Aryanization has gone indeed too far to leave it easy for the historian to distinguish the native warp from the foreign woof. But, if there is anywhere any chance of such successful disentanglement, it is in the South ; and the farther South we go the larger does the chance grow.

The scientific historian of India, then, ought to begin his study with the basin of the Krishna, of the Cauvery, of the Vaigai, rather than with the Gangetic plain, as it has been now long, too long, the fashion.'[1]

When the ideal Early History of India, including institutions as well as political vicissitudes, comes to be written on a large scale, it may be that the hints given by the learned Professor will be acted on, and that the historian will begin with the South. But the time is not yet ripe for such revolutionary treatment of the subject, and at present I must follow the old fashion.

[1] The late Prof. Sundaram Pillai, as quoted in *Tamilian Antiquary*, No. 2 (1908), p. 4.

An attempt to present in narrative form the history of the ancient dominant dynasties of Northern India is, therefore, the primary purpose of this work. The story of the great southern kingdoms, being known too imperfectly to permit of treatment on the same scale, necessarily occupies less space; while the annals of the innumerable minor states in every part of the country seldom offer matter of sufficient general interest to warrant narration in detail. In the fourteenth chapter, the reader will find a condensed account of the more salient events in the story of the principal mediaeval kingdoms of the north; and the two succeeding chapters are devoted to an outline of the fortunes of the kingdoms of the Deccan tableland and the Peninsula, so far as they are known, from the earliest times to the Muhammadan invasion at the beginning of the fourteenth century. **Scope of this work.**

The time dealt with is that extending from the commencement of the historical period in 650 or 600 B.C. to the Muhammadan conquest, which may be dated in round numbers as having occurred in A.D. 1200 in the north, and a century later in the south. The earliest political event in India to which an approximately correct date can be assigned is the establishment of the Saisunāga dynasty of Magadha about 642 B.C., a few years before the beginning of 'the sixth century—that wonderful century—a cardinal epoch in human history, if ever there was one'.

II. SOURCES OF INDIAN HISTORY

The sources of, or original authorities for, the early history of India may be arranged in four classes. The first of these is tradition, chiefly as recorded in native literature; the second consists of those writings of foreign travellers and historians which contain observations on Indian subjects; the third is the evidence of archaeology, which may be subdivided into the monumental, the epigraphic, and the numismatic; and the fourth comprises the few works of native contemporary, or nearly contemporary, literature which deal expressly with historical subjects. **Four sources.**

Tradition only in earliest period.

For the period anterior to Alexander the Great, extending from 600 B. C. to 326 B. C., dependence must be placed almost wholly upon literary tradition, communicated through works composed in many different ages, and frequently recorded in scattered incidental notices. The purely Indian traditions are supplemented by the notes of the Greek authors, Ktēsias, Herodotus, the historians of Alexander, Megasthenes and others.

The Kashmīr Chronicle.

The Kashmīr Chronicle, composed in the twelfth century, which is in form the nearest approach to a work of regular history in extant Sanskrit literature, contains a large body of confused ancient traditions, which can be used only with much caution. It is also of high value as a trustworthy record of local events for the period contemporary with, or slightly preceding, the author's lifetime.[1]

The Sanskrit epics.

The great Sanskrit epics, the Mahābhārata and Rāmāyana, while of value as traditional pictures of social life in the heroic age, do not seem to contain matter illustrating the political relations of states during the historical period.

Incidental notices.

Linguistic specialists have extracted from the works of grammarians and other authors many incidental references to ancient tradition, which collectively amount to a considerable addition to historical knowledge. Such passages from Sanskrit and Prākrit literature, so far as they have come to my notice, have been utilized in this work; but some may have escaped attention.

Jain books.

The sacred books of the Jain sect, which are still very imperfectly known, also contain numerous historical statements and allusions of considerable value.[2]

[1] *Kalhaṇa's Rājataraṅginī, a Chronicle of the Kings of Kaśmīr*, translated with an Introduction, Commentary, and Appendices, by M. A. Stein (2 vols., Constable, 1900). This monumental work is as creditable to the enterprise of the publishers as it is to the industry and learning of the translator, who has also produced a critical edition of the text.

[2] Some of the leading Jain texts have been translated by Prof. Hermann Jacobi (*S. B. E.*, vols. xxii, xlv). For full information on all publications relating to Jainism see Dr. A. Guérinot's fine work, *Essai de Bibliographie Jaina, répertoire analytique et méthodique des travaux relatifs au Jainisme* (Paris, Leroux, 1906; pp. 568), and the supplement to it, entitled 'Notes de Bibliographie Jaina' (*J. As.*, Juillet-Août 1909). The reader may also consult Barodia, *History and Literature of Jainism*, Bom-

Jātaka stories.

The Jātaka, or Birth stories, and other books of the Buddhist canon, include many incidental references to the political condition of India in the fifth and sixth centuries B.C., which although not exactly contemporary with the events alluded to, certainly transmit genuine historical tradition.[1]

Pāli chronicles of Ceylon.

The chronicles of Ceylon in the Pāli language, of which the *Dīpavaṁsa*, dating probably from the fourth century after Christ, and the *Mahāvaṁsa*, about a century and a half later in date, are the best known, offer several discrepant versions of early Indian traditions, chiefly concerning the Maurya dynasty. These Sinhalese stories, the value of which has been sometimes overestimated, demand cautious criticism at least as much as do other records of popular and ecclesiastical tradition.[2]

The Purāṇas.

The most systematic record of Indian historical tradition is that preserved in the dynastic lists of the Purāṇas. Five out of the eighteen works of this class, namely, the Vāyu, Matsya, Vishṇu, Brahmānda, and Bhāgavata contain such lists. The Brahmānda and the Vāyu, as well as the Matsya, which has large later additions, appear to be the earliest and

bay, 1909; and Mrs. Sinclair Stevenson's works, especially *The Heart of Jainism*, Oxford University Press, 1915. Jagmanderlal Jaini's *Outlines of Jainism*, Cambridge University Press, 1916, is an authoritative work. A good summary of the early history of Jainism in English is given by Dr. Hoernle in his presidential address to the Asiatic Society of Bengal (*Proc. A. S. B.*, 1898, pp. 39–53). Bühler's tract *Ueber die indische Secte der Jaina* (1887) was ed. and transl. by Burgess (1903), with many errors in the rendering (*Z. D. M. G.*, 1906, p. 384).

[1] A complete translation of the Jātakas, initiated by the late Prof. Cowell, and executed by Dr. W. H. D. Rouse and other scholars, has been published (Cambridge 1895–1907, and Index 1913). For a theory as to the date of the collection see Rhys Davids's *Buddhist India*, pp. 189–208.

[2] For a favourable view of the Ceylon chronicles see Rhys Davids's *Buddhist India*; and, on the other side, Foulkes, 'The Vicissitudes of the Buddhist Literature of Ceylon' (*Ind. Ant.* xvii, 100); 'Buddhaghosa' (ibid. xix, 105); Taw Sein Ko, 'Kalyāni Inscriptions' (ibid. xxii, 14); V. A. Smith, *Asoka, the Buddhist Emperor of India*, 3rd ed. 1920. The *Mahāvaṁśa* exists in more recensions than one; but that ordinarily quoted is the one translated by Turnour, whose version has been revised by Wijesimha. The latest version is that by Prof. Geiger and Mrs. Bode (*J. Pāli Text Soc.*, 1912). Mr. John Still's *Index to the Mahawansa* (Colombo, 1907), is useful. The *Dīpavaṁśa* has been translated by Prof. Oldenberg. See Geiger, *Dīpavaṁśa und Mahāvaṁśa* (Leipzig, Böhme, 1905; Engl. transl. in *Ind. Ant.*, 1906, p. 153).

most authoritative. Theory required that a Purāṇa should deal with 'the five topics of primary creation, secondary creation, genealogies of gods and patriarchs, reigns of various Manus, and the histories of the old dynasties of kings'. The last named of the five topics is the only one which concerns the historian.[1] Modern European writers have been inclined to disparage unduly the authority of the Purānic lists, but closer study finds in them much genuine and valuable historical tradition.

Darius, Ktēsias, Herodotus.

The earliest foreign notice of India is that in the inscriptions of the Persian king, Darius, son of Hystaspes, at Persepolis and Naksh-i-Rustam, the latter of which may be referred to the year 486 B.C.[2] Herodotus, who wrote late in the fifth century, contributes valuable information concerning the relation between India and the Persian empire, which supplements the less detailed statements of the inscriptions. The fragments of the works of Ktēsias of Knidos, who was physician to Artaxerxes Mnemon in 401 B.C., and amused himself by collecting travellers' tales about the wonders of the East, are of very slight value.[3]

Officers of Alexander, and envoys.

Europe was practically ignorant of India until the veil was lifted by Alexander's operations and the reports of his officers. Some twenty years after his death the Greek ambassadors sent by the kings of Syria and Egypt to the court of the Maurya emperors recorded careful observations on the country to which they were accredited, which have been partially preserved in the works of many Greek and

[1] Macdonell, *Hist. of Sanskrit Literature*, p. 301. The Vishṇu Purāṇa was translated by H. H. Wilson, whose version was improved and annotated by Hall. The relative dates of the different Purāṇas, as stated by Bhandarkar in *Early Hist. of the Dekkan*, 2nd ed., p. 162 (*Bombay Gazetteer* (1896), vol. i, part ii) are corrected by the more recent researches of Mr. Pargiter, for which see App. A at the end of this chapter.

[2] Rawlinson, *Herodotus*, vol. ii, p. 403; iv, 207.

[3] Translated by McCrindle in *Ind. Ant.* x, 296; the translation was also published separately at Calcutta in 1882. All the pre-Alexandrine notices of India are laboriously collected and discussed by Wilhelm Reese in *Die griechischen Nachrichten über Indien bis zum Feldzuge Alexanders des Grossen*, a pamphlet of 106 pages including bibliography, Teubner, Leipzig, 1914. The notices include scraps from Aristotle, who seems to have used Hecataeus and Ktēsias. Herodotus seems to rest on Hecataeus and Skylax.

Roman authors. The fragments of Megasthenes are especially valuable.[1]

Arrian, a Graeco-Roman official of the second century after Christ, wrote a capital description of India, as well as an admirable critical history of Alexander's invasion. Both these works being based upon the reports of Ptolemy son of Lagos, and other officers of Alexander, and the writings of the Greek ambassadors, are entitled to a large extent to the credit of contemporary documents, so far as the Indian history of the fourth century B.C. is concerned. The works of Quintus Curtius and other authors, who essayed to tell the story of Alexander's Indian campaign, are far inferior in value; but each has merits of its own.[2] **Arrian, and others.**

The philosophical romance, composed in honour of Apollonios of Tyana by Philostratos 'the Athenian' about A.D. 215–18 at the request of the empress Julia Domna, professes to give minute and interesting details of the observations made by the hero of the book in the course of a tour through north-western India, which according to Professor Petrie took place in the cold season of A.D. 43–4. If the details recorded could be trusted this account would be invaluable, but so much of the story is obviously fiction that few statements by the author can be accepted with confidence. Although it is not certain that Apollonios visited India at all, he had access to correct information on certain points, which has been confirmed by modern researches.[3] **Apollonios of Tyana.**

[1] Edited by Schwanbeck, Bonn, 1846; translated by McCrindle, 1877.

[2] Most of the Greek and Roman notices of India have been collected, translated, and discussed by McCrindle in six useful books, published between 1882 and 1901, and dealing with (1) Ktēsias, (2) *Indika* of Megasthenes and Arrian, (3) *Periplus of the Erythraean Sea*, (4) Ptolemy's Geography, (5) Alexander's Invasion, and (6) Ancient India, as described by other classical writers. The latest version of the *Periplus* is that by W. H. Schoff (1912).

[3] Concerning the credibility of the tale see Priaulx, *The Indian Travels of Apollonius of Tyana*, &c. (Quaritch, 1873, a very rare book); Prof. Flinders Petrie, *Personal Religion in Egypt before Christianity*, 1909; the two translations of the work of Philostratos published by Prof. Phillimore and F. C. Conybeare in 1913; V. A. Smith's paper 'The Indian Travels of Apollonius of Tyana' (*Z. D. M. G.*, 1914); and Marshall, *A Guide to Taxila* (Calcutta, 1918), pp. 15, 91.

Chinese historians.

The Chinese 'Father of history', Ssŭ-ma-ch'ien, 'the Herodotus of China', who completed his work about 100 B.C., is the first of a long series of Chinese historians, whose writings throw much light upon the early annals of India. The accurate chronology of the Chinese authors gives their statements peculiar value.[1]

Fa-hien, Chinese pilgrim.

The stream of Chinese Buddhist pilgrims who continued for several centuries to visit India, which they regarded as their Holy Land, begins with Fa-hien (Fa-hsien); who started on his travels in A.D. 399, and returned to China fifteen years later. The book in which he recorded his journeys has been preserved complete, and translated once into French, and four times into English. It includes a very interesting and valuable description of the government and social condition of the Gangetic provinces during the reign of Chandra-gupta II, Vikramāditya.[2] He visited Ceylon in A.D. 412 during the reign of Buddhadāsa.[3] Several other pilgrims left behind them works which contribute something to the elucidation of Indian history, and their testimony will be cited in due course.

Hiuen Tsang.

The prince of pilgrims, the illustrious Hiuen Tsang, whose fame as Master of the Law still resounds through all Buddhist lands, deserves more particular notice. His travels, described in a work entitled *Records of the Western World*, which has been translated into French, English, and German, extended from A.D. 629 to 645, and covered an enormous area, including almost every part of India, except the extreme south. His book is a treasure-house of accurate information, indispensable to every student of Indian antiquity, and has done more than any archaeological discovery to render

[1] Chavannes has published five volumes, out of nine, 47 chapters out of 130, of a translation of Ssŭ-ma-ch'ien. The French sinologists have been specially active in exploring the Chinese sources of Indian history, and several of their publications will be cited in later chapters. For the chronology, the work entitled *Synchronismes chinois*, by Le P. Mathias Tchang, S. J. (Chang-Hai, 1905), is very useful.

[2] In order to prevent confusion, the name of Chandragupta Maurya is printed without the hyphen, and that of Chandra-gupta I and II of the Gupta dynasty with it.

[3] He thus preceded Buddhaghosha's visit by some seventy years (Ayrton in *The Ceylon Antiquary and Literary Register*, Oct. 1915, p. 98).

possible the remarkable resuscitation of lost Indian history which has been recently effected. Although the chief historical value of Hiuen Tsang's work consists in its contemporary description of political, religious, and social institutions, the pilgrim has increased the debt of gratitude due to his memory by recording a considerable mass of ancient tradition, which would have been lost but for his care to preserve it. The *Life of Hiuen Tsang*, composed by his friend Hwui-li, contributes many details supplemental to the narrative in the *Records*,[1] though not quite so trustworthy.

Alberūnī. The learned mathematician and astronomer, Alberūnī, almost the only Muhammadan scholar who has ever taken the trouble to master Sanskrit, essentially a language of idolatrous unbelievers, when regarded from a Muslim point of view, entered India in the train of Mahmūd of Ghaznī. His work, descriptive of the country, and entitled 'An Enquiry into India' (*Taḥḳīḳ-i-Hind*), which was finished in A. D. 1030, is of high value as an account of Hindu manners, science, and literature; but contributes comparatively little information which can be utilized for the purposes of political history.[2]

Marco Polo. The visit of the Venetian traveller, Marco Polo, to Southern India in A. D. 1294–5 just comes within the limits of this volume.[3]

Muhammadan historians. The Muhammadan historians of India are valuable authorities for the history of the conquest by the armies of Islam; and the early Muslim travellers throw much light upon the condition of the mediaeval Hindu kingdoms.[4]

[1] See Appendix B, *The Chinese Pilgrims*, at the end of this chapter.

[2] Edited and translated by Sachau. Raverty points out that the title of Alberūnī's work is *Taḥḳīḳ-*, not *Tārīkh-i-Hind* (*J. A. S. B.*, 1872, part I, p. 186 note). The author's full designation was Abū-Rihān, Muhammad, son of Ahmad; but he became familiarly known as the *Ustād*, or Master, Bū-Rihān, surnamed Al-Bērūnī (ibid.).

[3] M. Cordier brought out a new edition of Yule's version in 1903.

[4] The works of both the historians and the travellers are most conveniently consulted in Elliot and Dowson's *History of India as told by its own Historians*, 8 vols., 1867–77; a valuable work, although not free from errors, many of which have been corrected by Raverty in various publications. Bayley and Dowson's *History of Gujarāt*, 1886 (only one volume published), is a supplement to the general collection. See also Abū Turāb's *History of Gujarāt*, ed. Denison Ross, published by A. S. B., 1909; and Wilberforce-Bell's *The History of Kāthiāwād*, London, 1916.

Monumental evidence.

The monumental class of archaeological evidence, considered by itself and apart from the inscriptions on the walls of buildings, while it offers little direct contribution to the materials for political history, is of high illustrative value, and greatly helps the student in realizing the power and magnificence of some of the ancient dynasties. The stratification or orderly succession of the layers of ruined buildings, when systematically observed, as it has been by Sir J. H. Marshall, may be made to yield conclusive testimony concerning the relative dates of dynasties and stages of civilization.

Inscriptions.

Unquestionably the most copious and important source of early Indian history is the epigraphic; and the accurate knowledge of many periods of the long-forgotten past which has now been attained is derived mainly from the patient study of inscriptions during the nineteenth and twentieth centuries. The great majority of inscriptions are commemorative, dedicatory, or donative. The first and second classes comprise a vast variety of records, extending from the mere signature of a pilgrim's name to an elaborate panegyrical poem in the most artificial style of Sanskrit verse; and for the most part are incised on stone. The third class, the donative inscriptions, or grants, on the other hand, are mostly engraved on plates of copper, the favourite material used for permanent record of conveyances.

Curious inscriptions.

Pre-eminent among inscriptions of a special character are Asoka's edicts, or sermons on stone, which form a class by themselves; no other sovereign having imitated his practice of engraving ethical exhortations on the rocks. Equally peculiar is the record on tables of stone of two Sanskrit plays at Ajmēr and of a third at Dhār. Also at Dhār on the pillars of the Bhoja Sāla, an old grammar-school, *c.* A. D. 1150, are two curious inscriptions—one 'a chart of the Sanskrit alphabet', the other a table of verbal terminations from the *Katantra*. They are engraved *Sarpabandha*, 'in the form of intertwining serpents with their bodies twisted lengthwise and cross-wise, leaving oblong spaces within for letters.'[1]

[1] *A. S. Prog. Rep. W. I.*, 1917–18, p. 36.

PIPRĀWĀ INSCRIBED VASE CONTAINING RELICS OF BUDDHA

(. . . *salilanidhane budhasa bhagavate* . . .)

A fragmentary inscription at Chitor, on the great tower, is part of a treatise on architecture.[1] At Kuḍimiyāmalai in the Pudukoṭṭai State is a rock inscription, apparently of the seventh century, containing the score of music for the *vīṇā*.[2] One of the oddest of these legacies from the past is a slab in Jain temple No. 1 at Deogarh, containing specimens of 18 dialects (*bhāshā*) and 18 scripts, Maurya, Dravidian, &c.[3]

Southern inscriptions.

The south of India is peculiarly rich in inscriptions of almost all kinds, both on stone and copper, some of which attain extraordinary length. The known southern inscriptions number several thousands, and many must remain for future discovery. But these records, notwithstanding their abundance, are inferior in interest to the rarer northern documents, by reason of their comparatively recent date. No important southern inscription earlier than the Christian era is known, except the Mysore and Maski editions of Asoka's Minor Rock Edicts and the brief dedications of the Bhattiprolu caskets.[4] The records prior to the seventh century after Christ are few.

Oldest inscriptions.

The oldest northern document was supposed at one time to be the dedication of the relics of Buddha at Piprāwā, which was believed to date from about 450 B. C., but more recent criticism has thrown doubt upon that theory.[5] At present the oldest extant inscription is the Sohgaura copper plate from the Gorakhpur district, which is tentatively assigned to a date about fifty years prior to Asoka. This document, which is concerned with government storehouses, needs further elucidation.[6] The number of documents prior to the Christian era is much more considerable in the north than in the south. Few records of the third century after Christ

[1] Kielhorn, *Bruchstücke indischer Schauspiele in Inschriften zu Ajmere* (Berlin, 1901); Hultzsch, *Archaeol. S. of India, Annual Report*, 1903–4, p. 240; *Progr. Rep. Archaeol. S. W. I.*, 1903–4, pp. 40, 58.

[2] *Ep. Ind.*, xii, 226.

[3] See *Heart of Jainism*, p. 274; *Prog. Rep.* N. Circle, 1917–18, p. 10.

[4] *Ep. Ind.*, ii, 323. A few pre-Christian records of little importance exist in Ceylon, and in India brief inscriptions are found in caves in the Arcot region.

[5] Barth., *J. des Savants*, Oct. 1906; *Ind. Ant.*, 1907, pp. 117–24.

[6] See *Proc. A. S. B.*, 1894 and Bühler (*Vienna Or. J.*, vol. x (1896), p. 138).

have survived, but, if the scheme of Kushān chronology adopted in this work is approximately correct, those of the second century may be described as numerous.

Work remaining.

Although much excellent work has been done, infinitely more remains to be done before the study of Indian inscriptions can be considered as exhausted; and the small body of unselfish workers at the subject is in urgent need of recruits, content to find their reward in the interest of the work itself, the pleasure of discovery, and the satisfaction of adding to the world's knowledge.[1]

Numismatics.

The numismatic evidence as a whole is more accessible than the epigraphic. Many classes of Indian coins have been discussed in special treatises, and compelled to yield their contributions to history; while a general survey completed by Prof. Rapson enables the student to judge how far the muse of history has been helped by her numismatic handmaid.

From the time of Alexander's invasion coins afford invaluable aid to the researches of the historian in every period; and for the Bactrian, Indo-Greek, and Indo-Parthian dynasties they constitute almost the sole evidence.[2]

[1] See Fleet's article in *Ind. Ant.*, 1901, p. 1, and his chapter 'Epigraphy' in 'The Indian Empire', vol. ii of *Imperial Gazetteer*, 1908. It is impossible to give a complete list of the publications in which Indian inscriptions appear. The properly edited records will be found mostly in the *Indian Antiquary*, *Epigraphia Indica*, *South Indian Inscriptions*, and Dr. Fleet's *Gupta Inscriptions*; but documents, more or less satisfactorily edited, will be met with in almost all the voluminous publications on Indian archaeology. Mr. Lewis Rice has published notices of thousands of southern documents in *Epigraphia Carnatica* and other works, summarized in *Mysore and Coorg from the Inscriptions* (Constable, 1909). Prof. Kielhorn's and Prof. Lüders's *Lists*, with *Supplements* in *Ep. Ind.*, v, vii, viii, and x are invaluable.

[2] Some of the principal modern works on ancient Indian numismatics are:—Rapson, *Indian Coins* (Strassburg, 1898); and *Catalogue of the Coins of the Andhra Dynasty, &c., in the British Museum*, 1908; Cunningham, *Coins of Ancient India* (1891); *Coins of Mediaeval India* (1894); Von Sallet, *Die Nachfolger Alexanders des Grossen in Baktrien und Indien* (Berlin, 1879); P. Gardner, *The Coins of the Greek and Scythic Kings of Bactria and India in the British Museum* (1886); V. A. Smith, 'Andhra History and Coinage' (*Z.D.M.G.*, 1902, 1903); *Catalogue of Coins in the Indian Museum*, vol. i (1906); Elliot, *Coins of Southern India* (1885); R. B. Whitehead, *Catalogue of the Panjab Museum, Lahore, Indo-Greek Coins* (1914); J. Allan, *Catalogue of the Coins of the Gupta Dynasties and Śasānka, King of Gauḍa*, with 24 plates, Catal. of Indian Coins in the British Museum; London, 1914. Minor

Contemporary literature.

The fourth class of materials for, or sources of, early Indian history, namely, contemporary, or nearly contemporary, native literature of an historical kind, is of limited extent, comprising, in addition to the Kashmīr chronicle (*ante*, p. 10), and local annals of Nepāl and Assam, a few works in Sanskrit and Prākrit, with certain poems in Tamil. None of these works is pure history ; they are all of a romantic character, and present the facts with much embellishment.[1]

The best-known composition of this class is that entitled 'The Deeds of Harsha' (*Harsha-Charita*), written by Bāna, about A.D. 620, in praise of his master and patron, King Harsha of Thānēsar and Kanauj, which is of high value, both as a depository of ancient tradition, and a record of contemporary history, in spite of obvious faults.[2] A similar work called 'The Deeds of Vikramānka', by Bilhana, a poet of the twelfth century, is devoted to the eulogy of a powerful king who ruled a large territory in the south and west between A.D. 1076 and 1126.[3] A valuable poem entitled *Rāmacharita*, dealing with the Pāla kings of Bengal, discovered in 1897, was published in 1910 ;[4] and several compositions, mostly by Jain authors, besides that of Bilhana, treat of the history of the Chalukya dynasties of the west.[5] The earliest of the Tamil poems alluded to is believed to date from the first or second century of the Christian era. These compositions, which include epics and panegyrics on famous kings of the south, appear to contain a good deal of historical matter.[6]

publications are too numerous to specify. The early essays by James Prinsep and other eminent scholars are now mostly obsolete.

[1] There are many historical and semi-historical manuscripts in the Mackenzie Collection, of various ages. See *Descriptive Catalogue* by H. H. Wilson (1828 ; and Madras reprint, 1882).

[2] Translated by Cowell and Thomas (*Or. Transl. Fund, N. S.*, published by R. As. Society, 1897).

[3] Ed. by Bühler with English Introduction in Bombay Sanskrit Series, No. xiv, 1875, and fully described and criticized in *Ind. Ant.*, v (1876), pp. 317, 324 ; xxx (1901), p. 12.

[4] *Memoirs A. S. B.*, vol. iii (1910), pp. 1–56.

[5] *Proc. A. S. B.*, 1901, p. 26 ; G. H. Ojha, *Early History of the Solankīs*, part I, p. 2 ; Ajmēr, 1907 ; in Hindī.

[6] Analysed by Mr. V. Kanakasabhai Pillai (*Ind. Ant.*, xviii, 259 ; xix, 329 ; xxii, 141). See *The Tamils Eighteen Hundred Years Ago* by same author ; Madras, 1904 : S. K. Aiyangar, *Ancient India* (1911) ; *The Beginnings of South Indian History*, Madras, 1918 ; M. Srinivasa Aiyangar, *Tamil Studies*, first series, Madras, 1914 ; and many articles in *The Tamilian Antiquary* and other periodicals.

Chronological difficulties.

The obstacles which prevented for so many years the construction of a continuous narrative of Early Indian History are due not so much to the deficiency of material as to the lack of definite chronology referred to by Elphinstone and Cowell. The rough material is not so scanty as has been supposed. The data for the reconstruction of the early history of all nations are necessarily meagre, largely consisting of bare lists of names supplemented by vague and often contradictory traditions which pass insensibly into popular mythology. The historian of ancient India is fairly well provided with a supply of such lists, traditions, and mythology ; which, of course, require to be treated on the strict critical principles applied by modern students to the early histories of both western and eastern nations. The application of those principles in the case of India is not more difficult than it is in Babylonia, Egypt, Greece, or Rome. The real difficulty is the determination of fixed chronological points. A body of history must be supported upon a skeleton of chronology, and without chronology history is impossible.

Numerous eras.

The Indian nations, in so far as they maintained a record of political events, kept it by methods of their own, which are difficult to understand, and until recently were not at all understood. The eras used to date events are not only different from those used by other nations, but very numerous and obscure in their origin and application. Cunningham's *Book of Indian Eras* (1883) enumerates more than a score of systems which have been employed at different times and places in India for the computation of dates ; and his list might be considerably extended. The successful efforts of several generations of scholars to recover the forgotten history of ancient India have been largely devoted to a study of the local modes of chronological computation, and have resulted in the attainment of accurate knowledge concerning most of the eras used in inscriptions and other documents.[1]

[1] The late Professor Kielhorn, Professor Jacobi, Mr. R. Sewell, and Dr. J. F. Fleet have done specially valuable service in this department, and many other scholars have made valuable contributions to knowledge. Among Indian students of the subject Diwān L. D. Swamikannu Pillai is pre-eminent.

Armed with these results, it is now possible for a writer on Indian history to compile a narrative arranged in orderly chronological sequence, which could not have been thought of before the close of the nineteenth century.

Greek synchronisms.

For a long time the only approximately certain date in the early history of India was that of the accession of Chandragupta Maurya, as determined by his identification with Sandrakottos, the contemporary of Seleukos Nikator, according to Greek authors. The synchronism of Chandragupta's grandson, Asoka, with Antiochos Theos, grandson of Seleukos, and four other Hellenistic princes, having been established subsequently in 1838, the chronology of the Maurya dynasty was placed upon a firm basis, and is no longer open to doubt in its main outlines.

With the exception of these two synchronisms, and certain dates in the seventh century after Christ, determined by the testimony of the Chinese pilgrim, Hiuen Tsang, the whole scheme of Indian chronology remained indeterminate and exposed to the caprice of every rash guesser.

Gupta era.

A great step in advance was gained by Fleet's determination of the Gupta era, which had been the subject of much wild conjecture. His demonstration that the year 1 of that era is A. D. 319–20 fixed the chronological position of a most important dynasty, and reduced chaos to order. Fa-hien's account of the civil administration of the Gangetic provinces at the beginning of the fifth century thus fell into its place as an important historical document illustrating the reign of Chandra-gupta II, Vikramāditya, one of the greatest of Indian kings. Most of the difficulties which continued to embarrass the chronology of the Gupta period, even after the announcement of Fleet's discovery in 1887, have been removed by M. Sylvain Lévi's publication of the synchronism of Samudragupta with King Meghavarna of Ceylon (*c.* A. D. 352–79).

Āndhra synchronism.

A connected, although imperfect, history of the Āndhra dynasty has been rendered possible by the establishment of synchronisms between the Āndhra kings and the Western satraps.

Northern chronology settled; except Kushān.

In short, the labours of many scholars have succeeded in tracing in firm lines the outline of the history of Northern India from the beginning of the historical period to the Muhammadan conquest, with one important exception, that of the Kushān or Indo-Scythian period, the date of which, to the extent of about forty years, is still open to discussion. The system of Kushān chronology adopted in this volume has much to recommend it, and is sufficiently supported to serve as a good working hypothesis. If it should ultimately secure general acceptance, the whole scheme of North Indian chronology may be considered as settled, although many details will remain to be filled in.

Southern chronology.

Much progress has been made in the determination of the chronology of the Southern dynasties, and the dates of the Pallavas, a dynasty the very existence of which was unknown to European students until 1840, have been worked out with special success.

Feasibility of 'connected relation'.

The foregoing review will, I trust, satisfy my readers that the attempt to write 'a connected relation of the national transactions' of India prior to the Muhammadan conquest is justified by an adequate supply of material facts and sufficient determination of essential chronological data.

APPENDIX A

The Age of the Purāṇas.

Wilson's erroneous date.

H. H. Wilson, misunderstanding certain passages in the Purāṇas as referring to the Muhammadans, enunciated the opinion that the *Vishṇu Purāṇa* was composed in or about A. D. 1045. The error, excusable in Wilson's time, unfortunately continued to be repeated frequently, although refuted by patent facts many years ago.[1] The persistent repetition of Wilson's mistake renders it desirable to bring together a few easily intelligible and decisive proofs that the Purāṇas are very much older than he supposed.

Evidence of Albērūnī.

Albērūnī, who wrote his scientific account of India in A. D. 1030, gives a list of the eighteen Purāṇas 'composed by the so-called Rishis', and had actually seen three of them, namely parts of the *Matsya, Āditya, and Vāyu.* He also gives a variant list of the

[1] e. g., it recurs in the latest, 22nd, edition of Sir W. Hunter's book, *A Brief History of the Indian People*, 1897, p. 103.

eighteen works, as named in the *Vishṇu Purāṇa.*[1] It is, therefore, certain that in A. D. 1030 the Purāṇas were, as now, eighteen in number, and were regarded as coming down from immemorial antiquity when the mythical Ṛishis lived.

Bāṇa.

Bāṇa, the author of the *Harsha-Charita*, or panegyric on King Harsha, who wrote about A. D. 620, carries the proof of the antiquity of the Purāṇas four centuries further back. When he went home to his village on the Sōn river, in the country now known as the Shāhābād District, he listened to Sudṛishti, who read 'with a chant' the *Purāṇa* described as *pavanaprokta* which may be identified with either the *Vāyu* or the *Brahmāṇḍa.*[2] Dr. Führer believed that he could prove the use by Bāṇa of the *Agni, Bhāgavata,* and *Mārkaṇḍeya Purāṇas,* as well as the *Vāyu.*[3]

Ancient Bengal MS.

Independent proof of the existence of the *Skanda Purāṇa* at the same period is afforded by a Bengal manuscript of that work, 'written in Gupta hand, to which as early a date as the middle of the seventh century can be assigned on palaeographical grounds.'[4]

'Questions of Milinda.'

The Purāṇas in some form were well known to the author of the 'Questions of Milinda' (*Milindapanha*) as ancient sacred writings grouped with the Vēdas and epic poems. Book I of that work, in which the first reference occurs, is undoubtedly part of the original composition, and was almost certainly composed earlier than A. D. 300.[5]

Gupta dynasty.

Many other early quotations from, or references to, the Purāṇas have been collected by Bühler, who points out that 'the account of the future kings in the *Vāyupurāṇa, Vishṇupurāṇa, Matsyapurāṇa,* and *Brahmāṇḍapurāṇa* seems to stop with the imperial Guptas and their contemporaries'.[6] Bühler speaks of 'future kings', because all the historical statements of the Purāṇas are given in the form of prophecy, in order to maintain the appearance of great antiquity in the books, which in their oldest forms were undoubtedly very ancient.

Mr. Pargiter's results.

Mr. F. E. Pargiter in his valuable work, *The Dynasties of the Kali Age* (Clarendon Press, 1913), has succeeded in obtaining more definite results. He suggests that the *Bhavishya Purāṇa* in its early form was the original authority from which the *Matsya, Vāyu,* and *Brahmāṇḍa Purāṇas* derived their dynastic lists. The *Vāyu* and *Brahmāṇḍa* were originally one, and have become differentiated. The versions of the lists as now found in the *Matsya, Vāyu,* and *Brahmāṇḍa Purāṇas* 'grew out of one and the same original text.' But the *Matsya* version is in some respects the best of those three, notwithstanding that it includes additions of later date. The *Vishṇu* and *Bhāgavata Purāṇas* are

[1] Sachau's translation, vol. i, pp. 130, 131, 264.

[2] Cowell and Thomas, trans., p. 72.

[3] *Trans. VIth Or. Congress,* vol. iii, p. 205.

[4] *J. R. A. S.*, 1903, p. 193.

[5] *S. B. E.*, vol. xxxv, pp. 6, 247.

[6] *Ind. Ant.*, vol. xxv (1896), p. 323.

later condensed redactions, and the *Bhavishya* in its existing form, which has been freely corrupted and interpolated, is worthless for historical purposes. Those purposes are served chiefly by the *Matsya, Vāyu*, and *Brahmāṇḍa*. There are clear indications that the Sanskrit account of the dynasties as it now stands in these three works is an adaptation of older Prākrit *ślokas*, or verses; and there is some reason for suspecting that the most ancient text was originally written in the Kharoshṭhi script.

Mr. Pargiter holds that the first compilation of the historical matter may have been made in the reign of the Āndhra king, Yajñaśrī, about the end of the second century after Christ; that the first certain compilation was made in the original *Bhavishya Purāṇa* about A. D. 260; that the *Bhavishya* account was revised about A. D. 315–20 and inserted in MS. *e Vāyu*; that the same account was again revised a few years later, about A. D. 325–30, and inserted in the other *Vāyu* MSS. as well as in the *Brahmāṇḍa*, so that those *Purāṇas* have preserved the contents of the *Bhavishya* at the date last named. The *Matsya* version seems to preserve the *Bhavishya* text in a slightly earlier stage, dating from about the last quarter of the third century.

Keith traverses all Pargiter's theories, and holds that *bhavishya* simply means 'in the future'.[1] Pargiter maintains his view as to the interpretation of the word in a reply to Keith.[2] J. Kennedy discusses the historical value of the Puranic tradition, and gives Pargiter credit for weaving it into a 'consecutive and intelligible whole'.[3]

Mr. Pargiter's treatise is based on the collation of sixty-three MSS., and deserves careful study. It cites other authorities fully.

Purāṇas in fourth century B. C.

I may add that *Purāṇas* in some shape were already authoritative in the fourth century B. C. The author of the *Arthaśāstra* ranks the *Atharvaveda* and *Itihāsa* as the fourth and fifth Vedas (Bk. I, ch. 3); and directs the king to spend his afternoons in the study of *Itihāsa*, which is defined as comprising six factors, namely, (1) *Purāṇa*, (2) *Itivṛitta* (history), (3) *Ākhyāyika* (tales), (4) *Udāharaṇa* (illustrative stories), (5) *Dharmaśāstra*, and (6) *Arthaśāstra* (Bk. I, ch. 5).

APPENDIX B

The Chinese Pilgrims.

Chinese names; Fa-hien.

The transliteration of Chinese names presents such difficulties, owing to many reasons, that much variation exists in practice. The name of the first pilgrim is variously spelled as Fâ-Hien (Legge); Fa-hian (Laidlay, Beal); and Fa-Hsien (Giles and Watters). In this volume Legge's spelling has been adopted,

[1] *J. R. A. S.*, 1914, pp. 1021–31.
[2] Ibid., 1915, pp. 516–21, and pp. 141–7, 328.
[3] Ibid., 1915, pp. 507–16.

omitting the long vowel mark, which is not used by the other scholars named.

Fa-hien's work, entitled *Fo-kuo-ki* (or 'Record of Buddhistic Kingdoms'), covers the period from A. D. 399 to 414.[1]

The early French version by Messrs. Rémusat, Klaproth, and Landresse (1836) was translated into English by J. W. Laidlay, and published anonymously at Calcutta in 1848, with additional notes and illustrations, which still deserve to be consulted. French version.

Beal issued an independent version in a small volume, entitled *Buddhist Pilgrims*, published in 1869, which was disfigured by many errors. His amended and much improved rendering appeared in the first volume of *Buddhist Records of the Western World* (Trübner's Oriental Series, Boston, 1885); but the notes to the earlier version were not reprinted in full. Beal's versions.

The translation by Giles, which appeared at London and Shanghai in 1877, is intermediate in date between Beal's two versions; and the notes, which are largely devoted to incisive criticisms on the early work of Beal, contain little to help the reader who desires to study the pilgrim's observations from an Indian point of view. But Giles's scarce little volume is of value as an independent rendering of the difficult Chinese text by a highly qualified linguist. Certain errors in his work were corrected by Watters in his articles 'Fa-hsien and his English Translators', in the *China Review*, vol. viii. Giles's version.

The latest translation, that of Legge (Oxford, Clarendon Press, 1886), is on the whole the most serviceable; the author having had the advantage of using his predecessors' labours. The notes, however, leave much to be desired. The final translation of Fa-hien's *Travels*, equipped with an up-to-date commentary adequately fulfilling the requirements of both Chinese and Indian scholarship, has not yet appeared; and the production of such a work by a single writer is almost impossible. Legge's version.

The proper spelling of Hiuen Tsang's name has been the subject of considerable discussion; and the variation in practice has been, and still is, very great.[2] Name of Hiuen Tsang.

The question may be considered as settled, so far as such matters can be settled, by the ruling of Professor Chavannes that 'deux orthographes sont admissibles; ou bien l'orthographe scientifique *Hiuen-Tsang*, ou bien l'orthographe conforme à la prononciation pékinoise *Hiuen-tchoang* [=*chwâng* in English]'.[3] It must, of course, be remembered that to a French reader the

[1] M. Chavannes (*Song Yun*, p. 53) agrees with Legge and Watters that Fa-hien began his travels in A. D. 399.

[2] Hiouen Thsang (Julien and Wade), Huan Chwang (Mayers), Yuèn Chwàng (Wylie), Hiuen Tsiang (Beal), Hsüan Chwang (Legge), Hhuen Kwân (Nanjio), Yüan Chwâng (Rhys Davids). This list (*J. R. A. S.*, 1892, p. 387) might be extended. See Watters, i, 6.

[3] *Religieux éminents*, Addenda, p. 202.

initial *H* is in practice silent. Professor de Lacouperie also held that Hiuen Tsang was the best mode of spelling the name, and I have therefore adopted it. Beal's spelling, Hiuen Tsiang, which his books have made more or less familiar to English readers, is nearly the same.

Julien's and Beal's versions. M. Stanislas Julien's great work, which included a French version of both the *Life* and *Travels* of Hiuen Tsang (3 vols., Paris, 1853–8), has never been superseded; but it is now very scarce and difficult to obtain. Beal's English version of the *Travels* appeared in 1885 in the volumes already cited; and was followed in 1888 by a translation of the *Life*. The notes were supplied to a large extent by Burgess. The student of Indian history finds himself compelled sometimes to consult both the French and English versions. The commentary in both is now out of date; but the deficiencies have been supplied in considerable measure by a work compiled by Watters, entitled *On Yuan Chwang's Travels in India* (R. As. Soc., 1904–5, 2 vols.). An adequate annotated translation of the *Life* and *Travels* of Hiuen Tsang would require the co-operation of a syndicate of scholars. The first draft of his book, the *Ta Táng-Hsi-yü-chi*, 'Records of Western Lands of the Great Tàng Period', was presented to the Emperor in 646, but the book, as we have it now, was not completed until 648. It was apparently copied and circulated in MS. in its early form during the author's life, and for some time after. There are several editions, which present considerable variations in both the text and the supplementary notes and explanations. The 'Han-shan' recension, which seems to be the only one hitherto known to Western scholars, is substantially a modern Soochow reprint of an edition of the Ming period. Three other editions were consulted by Watters, who has noted the more important variant readings (*On Yuan Chwang*, ch. 1). The pilgrim's route can be traced by the help of the Itinerary and maps added by the author of this history to the second volume of Watters's book.

Inferior authority of Books x–xii. Students should not forget the fact that Bks. (*chuan*) x, xi, and xii of Hiuen Tsang's *Travels* are far inferior in authority to the earlier books. Watters's observations are as follows:—'According to the *Records* the pilgrim proceeded from Malakuṭa to Seng-ka-lo or Ceylon, but the *Life* represents him as merely hearing of that country. If we had only the *Records* we should be at liberty to believe that he proceeded to Ceylon, and returned thence to Draviḍa. But it is perhaps better to regard him as writing about Malakoṭṭa and Ceylon from information given to him in Draviḍa, and from books. There seems to be much in *Chuan* x and xi that is not genuine, and it may be observed that in certain old texts like C these two *chuan* are given without mention of Pien-chi as compiler. They are also, together with *Chuan* xii, marked by the character *yi*, meaning *doubtful*. It does not seem, therefore, to be necessary to dwell much on the curious legends and descriptions given in this part of the *Records*' (vol. II, p. 233).

Song-yun and Ū-k'ong.

The small work descriptive of the mission of Song-yun and Hwei-Săng, early in the sixth century, has been translated by Beal in the first volume of *Records*. A revised critical translation in French, fully annotated, has been published by Chavannes.[1]

The itinerary of Ū-k'ong (Ou-k'ong), who travelled in the eighth century, has been translated by Sylvain Lévi and Chavannes.[2]

Sixty pilgrims in seventh century.

The latter scholar has published (Paris, 1894) an admirably edited version of a work by I-tsing (Yi-tsing), entitled *Les Religieux éminents qui allèrent chercher la loi dans les pays d'occident*, which gives an account of no less than sixty Chinese Buddhist pilgrims who visited India in the latter half of the seventh century.

I-tsing.

I-tsing, who died in A. D. 713, at the age of seventy-nine, was himself a pilgrim of no small distinction. 'This great monk, no less famous in the Buddhist world of China than Hiuen Thsang with whom we are more familiar, was pre-eminently a scholar and the best Sanskritist amongst the Chinese pilgrims whose writings have yet reached us. His stay at the centres of learning in the Hindu colonies of Sumatra, and ten years' study at the university of Nalanda under the greatest professors of the time, gave him an intimate knowledge of the methods of the teaching of Sanskrit and the complete curriculum in vogue in those days, and enabled him to describe them in faithful detail. The unique treatment of the subject forms the thirty-fifth chapter of *The Records of Buddhist Practices in India*.'[3] His interesting work, *A Record of the Buddhist Religion as practised in India and the Malay Archipelago* (A. D. 671–95), has been skilfully translated by J. Takakusu (Oxford, Clarendon Press, 1896). This book, while invaluable for the history of Buddhism and Sanskrit literature, contributes little to the materials for political history.

[1] *Voyage de Song Yun dans l'Udyāna et le Gandhāra* (518–22 p. C.), in *Bull. de l'École Fr. d'Extrême-Orient* (Hanoi, 1903). This excellent work contains notices of many other early pilgrims, including Che-mong (Tche-mong), who quitted China in A. D. 404 only five years later than Fa-hien (p. 14); and Fa-yong, who started in A. D. 420.

[2] *Journal Asiatique*, 1895.

[3] *J. and Proc. A. S. B.*, 1911, p. 309.

CHAPTER II

THE DYNASTIES BEFORE ALEXANDER

600 B. C. TO 326 B. C.

History limited by chronology.

THE political history of India begins for an orthodox Hindu more than three thousand years before the Christian era with the famous war waged on the banks of the Jumna, between the sons of Kuru and the sons of Pāndu, as related in the vast epic known as the Mahābhārata.[1] But the modern critic fails to find sober history in bardic tales, and is constrained to travel down the stream of time much farther before he comes to an anchorage of solid fact. In order to be available for the purpose of history, events must be susceptible of arrangement in definite chronological order, and capable of being dated approximately, if not exactly. Facts to which dates cannot be assigned, although they may be invaluable for the purposes of ethnology, philology, and other sciences, are of no use to the historian. Modern research has brought to light innumerable facts of the highest scientific value concerning prehistoric India, but the impossibility of assigning dates to the phenomena discovered excludes them from the domain of the historian, whose vision cannot pass the line which separates the dated from the undated.

Beginning of historical period.

That line, in the case of India, may be drawn, at the earliest, through the middle of the seventh century B. C.; a period of progress, marked by the development of maritime commerce, and probably by the diffusion of a knowledge of the art of writing. Up to about that time the inhabitants of India, even the most intellectual races, seem to have been

[1] The epoch of the Kaliyuga, 3102 B. C., is usually identified with the era of Yudhishṭhira, and the date of the Mahābhārata war. But certain astronomers date the war more than six centuries later (Cunningham, *Indian Eras*, pp. 6–13). See Fleet, *J. R. A. S.*, 1911, p. 675; and R. Shamasastry, *Gavām Ayana* (Mysore, 1908).

generally ignorant of the art of writing, and to have been obliged to trust to highly trained memory for the transmission of knowledge.[1]

Sixteen states in N. India.

In those days vast territories were still covered by forest, the home of countless wild beasts and scanty tribes of savage men ; while regions of great extent in Northern India had been occupied for untold centuries by more or less civilized communities of the higher races who, from time to time, during the unrecorded past, had pierced the mountain barriers of the north-western frontier. Practically nothing is ascertained concerning the immigration of the possibly equally advanced Dravidian races who entered India, we know not how, where, or whence, spread over the plateau of the Deccan, and extended to the extremity of the Peninsula. Our slender stock of knowledge is limited to the fortunes of the vigorous races, speaking an Aryan tongue, who poured down from the mountains of the Hindū Kush and Pāmīrs, filling the plains of the Panjāb and the upper basin of the Ganges with a sturdy and quick-witted population, unquestionably superior to the aboriginal races of those regions. The settled country between the Himalaya mountains and the Narbadā river was divided into a multitude of independent states, some monarchies and some tribal republics, owning no allegiance to any paramount power, secluded from the outer world, and free to fight among themselves. The most ancient literary traditions, compiled probably in the fourth or fifth century B. C., but looking back to an older

[1] J. Kennedy, 'The Early Commerce of India with Babylon ; 700–330 B.C.' (*J. R. A. S.*, 1898, pp. 241–88) ; Bühler, 'Indische Palaeographie (*Grundriss Indo-Ar. Phil. und Alt.*, Strassburg, 1898) ; transl. as Appendix to *Ind. Ant.*, vol. xxxiii (1904) ; 'On the Origin of the Brāhma and Kharoṣṭhī Alphabets' (two papers, in *Sitzb. Akad. Wiss. Wien*, 1895) ; Hoernle, 'An Epigraphical Note on Palm-leaf, Paper, and Birchbark' (*J. A. S. B.*, vol. lxix, part 1, 1900). I have not seen a Dutch work by Holle, *Oud-en Nieuw-Indische Alphabetten*, Batavia, 1882, cited in *J. R. A. S.*, 1911, p. 370. The art of writing may have been introduced by merchants on the south-western coast as early as the eighth century B. C., or even before that time. The knowledge of the art seems to have gradually spread to the north, where probably it became widely known during the seventh century. But, of course, no data exist for accurate chronology. So much is clear, that writing must have been known long before the appearance of the earliest extant inscriptions in the fourth or fifth century B. C.

time, enumerate sixteen of such states or powers, extending from Gandhāra, on the extreme north-west of the Panjāb, comprising the modern districts of Peshāwar and Rāwalpindi, to Avanti or Mālwā, with its capital Ujjain, which still retains its ancient name unchanged.[1]

Religion and history. The works of ancient Indian writers from which our historical data are extracted do not ordinarily profess to be histories, and are mostly religious treatises of various kinds. In such compositions the religious element necessarily takes the foremost place, and the secular affairs of the world occupy a very subordinate position. The particulars of political history incidentally recorded refer in consequence chiefly to the countries most prominent in the development of Indian religion.

Jainism and Buddhism. The systems which we call Jainism and Buddhism had their roots in the forgotten speculations of the prehistoric past; but, as we know them, were founded respectively by Vardhamāna Mahāvīra and Gautama Buddha. Both these philosophers, who were for many years contemporary, were born, lived, and died in or near the kingdom of Magadha, the modern South Bihār. Mahāvīra, the son of a nobleman of Vaisāli, the famous city north of the Ganges, was nearly related to the royal family of Magadha, and died at Pāwā, in the modern district of Patna, within the territory of that kingdom.

Gautama Buddha, although born farther north, in the Sākya territory at the foot of the Nepāl hills,[2] underwent his most memorable spiritual experiences at Bōdh Gayā in Magadha, and spent many years of his ministry within the limits of that state. The Buddhist and Jain books, therefore, tell us much about the Vrijjian confederacy, of which Vaisāli

[1] The complete list will be found in Rhys Davids's *Buddhist India*, p. 23. The first two chapters of that work furnish full references to the Pāli texts which give information about the clans and states in the fifth and sixth centuries. Professor Rhys Davids is inclined to attribute higher antiquity to the Pāli Buddhist scriptures than some other scholars can admit.

[2] The Śākya territory, to the north of the modern Bastī and Gorakhpur Districts, was a dependency of Kosala. 'The Blessed One also is of Kosala' (Rockhill, *Life of the Buddha*, p. 114). See also Jātaka No. 465 (Cambridge transl., iv, 92).

was the capital,[1] and about Magadha, with its subordinate kingdom of Anga (Bhāgalpur).

Kosala and Kāsī.

The neighbouring realm of Kosala, the modern kingdom of Oudh, was closely connected with Magadha by many ties; and its capital Srāvastī (Savatthi), situated on the upper course of the Rāpti near the foot of the hills, was the reputed scene of many of Buddha's most striking discourses.[2]

In the sixth century B. C. Kosala appears to have occupied the rank afterwards attained by Magadha, and to have enjoyed precedence as the premier state of Upper India. It is therefore mentioned as often as the rival power. At the beginning of the historical period, the smaller kingdom of Kāsī, or Benares, apparently had lost its independence, and had been annexed by Kosala, with which its fortunes were indissolubly bound up. The lesser state owes its fame in the ancient books not only to its connexion with its powerful neighbour, but also to its being one of the most sacred spots in Buddhist church history, the scene of Buddha's earliest public preaching, where he first 'turned the wheel of the Law'.

Kings of Magadha.

The reputation for special sanctity enjoyed by both Benares and Gayā in Magadha among orthodox Brahmanical Hindus adds little to the detailed information available, which is mainly derived from the writings of Jains and Buddhists, who were esteemed as heretics by the worshippers of the old gods. But the Brahmanical Purāṇas, compiled

[1] Basāṛ or Basāṛh (N. lat. 25° 59′, E. long. 85° 8′), and the neighbouring village of Bakhirā, in the District of Muzaffarpur, situated about 27 miles a little west of north from Patna, undoubtedly represent the ancient Vaisāli (V. A. Smith, 'Vaisāli,' *J. R. A. S.*, 1902, pp. 267–88). See Bloch's 'Excavations at Basārh', *Archaeol. S. Annual Rep.*, 1903–4, pp. 81–122.

[2] It is difficult to resist the new evidence in favour of the identification of Śrāvastī with the ruins at Sahēṭh-mahēṭh in Northern Oudh, on the boundary of the Goṇḍa and Bahraich Districts, which is summarized in *J. R. A. S.*, 1909, pp. 1066–8; but the fact remains that the site does not agree with the itineraries of Fa-hien and Hiuen Tsang, who indicate a site higher up the course of the Rāptī in Nepāl, as formerly advocated by me in *J. R. A. S.*, 1898, pp. 502–31, with map, and ibid., 1900, pp. 1–24. I cannot bring myself to accept the supposed error in *both* pilgrims' accounts without some explanation. The statement that four villages known to have been near Śrāvastī can be identified with four villages in the immediate neighbourhood of Sahēṭh-Mahēṭh needs to be supported in detail.

centuries later in honour of the orthodox deities,[1] happily include lists of the Buddhist and other kings of Magadha, which had become, before the time of their compilation, the recognized centre both religious and political of India; and so it happens that the Jain, Buddhist, and Brahmanical books combined tell us much about the history of Magadha, Anga, Kosala, Kāsī, and Vaisāli, while they leave us in the dark concerning the fortunes of most other parts of India.

Śaiśunāga dynasty.

In the Purānic lists the earliest dynasty which can claim historical reality is that known as the Saisunāga, from the name of its founder Sisunāga, or Sisunāka.[2]

c. 642 B.C.

He was, apparently, the king, or Rāja, of a petty state, corresponding roughly with the present Patna and Gayā Districts; his capital being Rājagriha (Rājgīr), among the hills near Gayā. Nothing is known about his history, except the statement that he placed his son in Benares, and himself took up his abode at Girivraja near Rājagriha. The second, third, and fourth kings, likewise, are mere names.

Bimbisāra *c.* 582 B.C.

The first monarch about whom anything substantial is known is Bimbisāra, or Srēnika, the fifth of his line. He is credited with the building of New Rājagriha, the outer town to the north of the ring of hills encircling the ancient fort; and with the annexation of Anga, the small kingdom to the east, corresponding with the modern district of Bhāgalpur, and probably including Monghyr (Mungir).[3] The annexa-

[1] The oldest dynastic lists of the Purāṇas, those of the *Matsya*, probably date from the third century after Christ in their present form, and the *Vāyu* lists from the first half of the fourth century.

[2] *Śiśunāka* is the usual reading in the *Matsya* and *Vāyu Purāṇas* (Pargiter, *J. R. A. S.*, 1915, p. 146).

[3] Jacobi, *Introd.*, vol. xxii, *S. B. E.* Rājgīr is situated in N. lat. 25° 2′, E. long. 85° 26′, about NE. from Gayā, and SSE. from Patna. The very ancient town within the circle of hills is believed to have been founded by the mythical king, Jarāsandha, and was also known as Kuśāgārapura. Rājgir has numerous modern Jain shrines, and is much frequented by Jain pilgrims, who rank it with Parasnāth and Pawapari (*Mod. Rev.* Jan. 1916, p. 18). The most trustworthy account of the extensive site is that by Dr. J. H. Marshall in *Ann. Rep. A. S. India*, 1905–6, which gives references to earlier publications, and is accompanied by a good map. But the researches at this most interesting spot amount only to a preliminary reconnaissance. Thorough exploration would require the work of several seasons. The secrets of the most ancient sites in India still remain hidden, with few exceptions.

tion of Anga was the first step taken by the kingdom of Magadha in its advance to greatness and the position of supremacy which it attained in the following century; so that Bimbisāra may be regarded as the real founder of the Magadhan imperial power. He strengthened his position by matrimonial alliances with the more powerful of the neighbouring states, taking one consort from the royal family of Kosala, and another from the influential Lichchhavi clan at Vaisāli.[1] The latter lady was the mother of Ajātasatru, also called Kūnika, or Kūniya, the son who was selected as heir-apparent and crown prince. If our authorities may be believed, the reign of Bimbisāra lasted for twenty-eight years; and it is said that, towards its close, he resigned the royal power into the hands of his favourite son, and retired into private life.

Devadatta.

Orthodox Buddhist tradition affirms that Ajātasatru, weary of awaiting the slow process of nature, murdered his father by starvation, at the instigation of Devadatta, Buddha's cousin, who figures in the legends as a malignant plotter and wicked schismatic.[2] It is probable, however, that the story is the product of *odium theologicum*, or sectarian rancour, which has done so much to falsify the history of ancient India. Devadatta certainly refused to accept the teaching of Gautama, and, preferring that of 'the former Buddhas', became the founder and head of a rival sect, which still survived in the seventh century after Christ.[3]

[1] The Lichchhavis occupy a prominent place in the Buddhist ecclesiastical legends. The Jains spell the name as *Lechchhaki* (Prākrit, *Lechchhaī*) (Jacobi, *S. B. E.*, xxii, 266). For the Tibetan affinities of the Lichchhavis see *Ind. Ant.*, 1903, p. 233.

[2] Rhys Davids, *Buddhist India*, p. 14; Rockhill, *Life of the Buddha*, pp. 90, 94, from Tibetan sources.

[3] These heretics were seen by Fa-hien at Śrāvastī in or about A. D. 405. 'There are also companies of the followers of Devadatta still existing. They regularly make offerings to the three previous Buddhas, but not to Śākyamuni [*scil.* Gautama] Buddha' (*Travels*, ch. xxii, in Legge's version. All the versions agree as to the fact). In the seventh century Hiuen Tsang found three monasteries of Devadatta's sect in Karṇasuvarṇa, Bengal (Beal, *Records*, ii, 201; *Life*, p. 131). Detailed legends concerning Devadatta will be found in Rockhill's *Life of the Buddha* (see Index), and the disciplinary rules of his order on p. 87 of that work. The fact that Asoka twice repaired the *stūpa* of Kanakamuni, one of 'the previous Buddhas', proves that reverence for those saints was not

Schism has always been esteemed by the orthodox a deadly sin, and in all ages the unsuccessful heretic has been branded as a villain by the winning sect. Such, probably, is the origin of the numerous tales concerning the villanies of Devadatta, including the supposed incitement of his princely patron to commit the crime of parricide.

There seems to be no doubt that both Vardhamāna Mahāvīra, the founder of the system known as Jainism, and Gautama, the last Buddha, the founder of Buddhism as known to later ages, were preaching in Magadha during the reign of Bimbisāra, although it is difficult to reconcile traditional dates.

Death of Mahāvīra and Buddha.

The Jain saint, who was a near relative of Bimbisāra's queen, the mother of Ajātasatru, possibly passed away towards the close of Ajātasatru's reign, while the death of Gautama Buddha occurred in the earlier years of the same reign. There is reason to believe that the latter event took place in or about the year 543 B. C.[1]

Interview of Buddha with Ajātaśatru.

Gautama Buddha was certainly an old man when Ajātasatru, or Kūnika, as the Jains call him, came to the throne about 554 B. C.; and he had at least one interview with that king.[2]

One of the most ancient Buddhist documents narrates in detail the story of a visit paid to Buddha by Ajātasatru, who is alleged to have expressed remorse for his supposed crime,

incompatible with devotion to the teaching of their successor, Gautama (Nigliva Pillar inscription, in *Asoka, the Buddhist Emperor of India*, 3rd ed., p. 224). Very little is known about the teaching of 'the previous Buddhas'. Three of them seem to have been real persons, namely Krakuchanda, Kanakamuni, and Kāśyapa.

[1] For the uncertain chronology, see Appendix C at the end of this chapter.

[2] Reference may be made here to the view put forward by K. P. Jayaswal that the Parkham statue of Mathurā represents Ajātasatru or Kunika (*J. B. O. Res. Soc.* v, pp. 550–51). Brindavan C. Battacharya had previously drawn attention to the identity of character of this statue and the two 'Saisunāka statues', now in the Indian Museum, which K. P. Jayaswal identifies as those of Udaya and Nandivardhana (*J. B. O. Res. Soc.* v, pp. 402–6). K. P. Jayaswal holds that Ajātasatru died *c.* 518 B. C., and that the statue must date back to *c.* 515 B. C. The theory, if established, revolutionizes the history of Indian art and proves that the art of sculpture in stone was well matured two centuries before Asoka. V. A. Smith expressed the view that the statues in question are pre-Mauryan and executed not later than 400 B. C. (*J. B. O. Res. Soc.* v, pp. 512–18). See also ibid. vi, pp. 173 ff.

and to have professed his faith in Buddha, who accepted his confession of sin. The concluding passage of the tale may be quoted as an illustration of an ancient Buddhist view of the relations between Church and State.

'And when he had thus spoken, Ajātasatru the king said to the Blessed One: "Most excellent, Lord, most excellent! Just as if a man were to set up that which has been thrown down, or were to reveal that which is hidden away, or were to point out the right road to him who has gone astray, or were to bring a lamp into the darkness so that those who have eyes could see external forms—just even so, Lord, has the truth been made known to me, in many a figure, by the Blessed One. And now I betake myself, Lord, to the Blessed One as my refuge, to the Truth, and to the Order. May the Blessed One accept me as a disciple, as one who, from this day forth, as long as life endures, has taken his refuge in them. Sin has overcome me, Lord, weak and foolish and wrong that I am, in that for the sake of sovranty, I put to death my father, that righteous man, that righteous king! May the Blessed One accept it of me, Lord, that I do so acknowledge it as a sin, to the end that in future I may restrain myself."

'"Verily, O king, it was sin that overcame you in acting thus. But inasmuch as you look upon it as sin, and confess it according to what is right, we accept your confession as to that.

'"For that, O king, is custom in the discipline of the noble ones, that whosoever looks upon his fault as a fault, and rightfully confesses it, shall attain to self-restraint in future."

'When he has thus spoken, Ajātasatru the king said to the Blessed One, "Now, Lord, we would fain go. We are busy, and there is much to do."

'"Do, O king, whatever seemeth to thee fit."

'Then Ajātasatru the king, pleased and delighted with the words of the Blessed One, arose from his seat, and bowed to the Blessed One, and keeping him on the right hand as he passed him, departed thence.

'Now the Blessed One, not long after Ajātasatru the king had gone, addressed the brethren, and said: "This king, brethren, was deeply affected, he was touched in heart. If, brethren, the king had not put his father to death, that righteous man, and righteous king, then would the clear and

D 2

spotless eye for the truth have arisen in him, even as he sat here."

'Thus spake the Blessed One. The brethren were pleased and delighted at his words.'[1]

Comment.

It is difficult to sympathize with the pleasure and delight of the brethren. The stern and fearless reprobation of a deed of exceptional atrocity which we should expect from a great moral teacher is wholly wanting in Buddha's words, and is poorly compensated for by the politeness of a courtier. But, as stated above, it is difficult to accept the story of the parricide as historically true; and our doubts are not lessened when the Ceylonese chronicler asks us to believe that Ajātasatru was followed in due course by four other parricide kings, of whom the last was dethroned by his minister, with the approval of a justly indignant people. The fact that the history of Parthia presents a nearly exact parallel in the succession of three parricide monarchs is of little value in establishing the credibility of the Buddhist tradition.[2] Probably Ajātasatru, like many later Indian sovereigns, did not confine his royal favour to any one sect, but at different times patronized the followers of the 'former Buddhas' led by Devadatta, the adherents of Gautama's reformed Buddhism, and the Jains. Later when in consequence of Asoka's patronage Buddhism became pre-eminent in northern India,

[1] Translated from the *Sāmaññaphala Sūtra*, by Prof. Rhys Davids in *Dialogues of the Buddha*, 1899, p. 94. I have used the ordinary spelling Ajātaśatru instead of Agātasattu, as in the *Dialogues*. Throughout this work the Sanskrit forms are generally employed for the sake of uniformity. The Tibetan version of the Sūtra is translated by Rockhill (*Life*, p. 95, foll.). The visit is depicted in a bas-relief from the *stūpa* of Barhut (Bharhut, Bharaut), executed probably about 200 B.C. (Cunningham, *Stūpa of Bharhut*, pl. xvi; Rhys Davids, *Buddhist India*, p. 14, fig. 2).

[2] *Mahāvaṁśa*, ch. iv. The Parthian kings were Orodes, Phraates IV, and Phraates V (Von Gutschmid, *Geschichte Irans*, p. 116). Local Jain tradition in South Bihār ignores the accusation of parricide, and credits Kūṇika or Ajātaśatru with having 'ruled the country for eighty years according to the laws of his father', who is represented as having been a devout Jain, responsible for many buildings at Bhāgalpur and elsewhere (*Ind. Ant.*, xxxi (1902), p. 71). S. V. Venkatesvara Aiyar, consequently, disbelieves the parricide story ('The Ancient History of Magadha', *Ind. Ant.*, 1916, p. 12). He compares Ajātaśatru with Harsha and Akbar, because he is related to have patronized various forms of religion (Ibid., p. 13).

leanings towards Jainism became criminal in the eyes of ecclesiastical chroniclers, who were ready to blacken the memory of persons deemed heretical with unfounded accusations of the gravest character.

War with Kosala.

One of the chief events of Ajātasatru's reign was a war with the aged king of Kosala, whose sister was the queen of Bimbisāra. Fortune in the contest inclined, now to one side, and now to another; and on one occasion, it is said, Ajātasatru was carried away as a prisoner in chains to his opponent's capital. Ultimately peace was concluded, and a princess of Kosala was given in marriage to the king of Magadha. The facts of the struggle are obscure, being wrapped up in legendary matter from which it is impossible to disentangle them; but the probability is that Ajātasatru won for Magadha a decided preponderance over its neighbour of Kosala. It is certain that the latter kingdom is not again mentioned as an independent power, and that in the fourth century B. C. it formed an integral part of the Magadhan empire.

Conquest of Vaisāli.

The ambition of Ajātasatru, not satisfied with the humiliation of Kosala, next induced him to undertake the conquest of the country to the north of the Ganges, now known as Tirhūt, in which the Lichchhavi clan, famous in Buddhist legend, and probably of Tibetan origin, then occupied a prominent position. The invasion was successful; the Lichchhavi capital, Vaisāli, was occupied, and Ajātasatru became master of his maternal grandfather's territory.[1] It may be presumed that the invader carried his victorious arms to their natural limit, the foot of the mountains, and that from this time the whole region between the Ganges and the Himalaya became subject, more or less directly, to the suzerainty of Magadha.

Foundation of Pāṭaliputra.

The victor erected a fortress at the village of Pātali on the northern bank of the Sōn near its confluence with the Ganges

[1] According to the Jains, the mother of Ajātaśatru was Chellanā, daughter of Chetaka, Rāja of Vaisāli (Jacobi, *Introd.*, *S. B. E.*, vol. xxii). According to the Tibetan *Dulva*, she was named Vāsavī, and was the niece of Gopāla (Rockhill, *Life of the Buddha*, p. 63).

to curb his Lichchhavi opponents. The foundations of a city nestling under the shelter of the fortress were laid by his grandson Udaya. The city so founded, including settlements of various ages, not precisely on one site, was known variously as Kusumapura, Pushpapura, or Pātaliputra, and rapidly developed in size and magnificence ; until, under the Maurya dynasty, it became the capital, not only of Magadha, but of India.[1]

Massacre of the Śākyas. Buddha, as has been mentioned above, died in the reign of Ajātasatru, in the eighth year of the reign, according to the *Mahāvaṁśa*, which cannot be relied on for details.[2] Shortly before his death, Kapilavastu, his ancestral home, was captured by Virūdhaka, king of Kosala, who is alleged to have perpetrated a ferocious massacre of the Sākya clan to which Buddha belonged. The story is so thickly encrusted with miraculous legend that the details of the event cannot be ascertained, but the coating of miracle was probably deposited upon a basis of fact, and we may believe that the Sākyas suffered much at the hands of Virūdhaka.[3]

cir. 527 B. C. Darsaka. When Ajātasatru died (*cir.* 527 B. C.), he was succeeded, according to the Purāṇas, by a son named Darsaka, who was in turn succeeded by his son Udaya.[4] The Buddhist books

[1] The names Kusumapura and Pushpapura are synonymous, both meaning 'Flower-town'; *pāṭali* means 'trumpet-flower', *Bignonia suaveolens*. The story of the fortress is told in the Buddhist 'Book of the Great Decease' (*Mahāpārinibbāna Sutta*), of which the Tibetan version is summarized by Rockhill, op. cit., p. 127. The building of the city by Udaya is attested by the Vāyu Purāṇa. Asoka made Pāṭaliputra the permanent capital (Hiuen Tsang, in Beal, *Records*, ii. 85), but it was already the royal residence in the time of his grandfather, Chandragupta, when Megasthenes visited it. The sites of the capitals occupied by different kings probably were not quite identical.

[2] The Tibetan books allege that Buddha died five years after the accession of Ajātaśatru, who reigned for thirty-two years (Rockhill, *Life of the Buddha*, pp. 91, 233). All such details are unreliable, whether in the books of Ceylon or of other countries.

[3] The story is in all the books about Buddhism. Rhys Davids (*Buddhist India*, p. 11) gives references to the Pāli authorities. For the site and remains of Kapilavastu, see Mukherji and V. A. Smith, *Antiquities in the Tarāi, Nepāl* (Calcutta, 1901, being vol. xxvi, part 1, of *Archaeol. Survey Rep., Imp. Series*), and Hastings's *Encycl. of Religion and Ethics*, s. v.

[4] The name Udaya has variant forms, Udayana, Udayāśva, &c., in the Purāṇas. The Buddhists call him Udayi Bhadda (Udayibhadraka), and represent him as the son of Ajātaśatru, whose grandson he was, according to the Purāṇas (*Mahāvaṁśa*, ch. iv;

erroneously omit the intermediate name, and represent Udaya as the son and immediate successor of Ajātasatru. The reality of the existence of Darsaka, as king of Magadha, with his capital at Rājagriha, is established by the discovery of a play named *Svapnavāsavadatta*, attributed to Bhāsa, perhaps in the third century after Christ, which represents Darsaka as the contemporary of Udayana, king of Vatsa, and Mahāsena (*alias* Pradyota), king of Avanti, or Ujjain.[1]

Udaya, &c., *cir.* 503 B. C.

The reign of Udaya may be assumed to have begun about 503 B. C. The tradition that he built Pātaliputra, or more accurately, the adjoining town of Kusumapura, is all that is known about him.

Persian conquests.

If the chronology adopted in this chapter be even approximately correct, Ajātasatru's son, Darsaka, and his grandson, Udaya, must be regarded as the contemporaries of Darius, the son of Hystaspes, autocrat of the Persian Empire from 521 to 485 B. C. Darius, who was a very capable ruler, employed his officers in the exploration of a great part of Asia by means of various expeditions.

cir. 500 B. C.

One of these expeditions was dispatched at some date later than 516 B. C. to prove the feasibility of a passage by sea

Dulva, in Rockhill, *Life of the Buddha*, p. 91; Rhys Davids, *Dialogues* (1899), p. 68). The building of the city of Pāṭaliputra, or rather of 'Kusumapura, on the south bank of the Ganges, in his fourth year', by Udaya is asserted by the Vāyu Purāṇa. This statement indicates that Kusumapura, the oldest settlement, was on the bank of the Ganges, at an appreciable distance from the later capital, Pāṭaliputra, on the Sōn.

[1] The daughter of Mahāsena was queen of king Udayana, whose realm of Vatsa probably was identical with Kauśāmbī. Padmāvatī was sister of king Darśaka, and Pradyota, king of Avanti, or Mahāsena, is represented as seeking her hand for his own son (Jacobi, transl. of *Vāsavadattā* in *Intern. Monatschr. für Wissenschaft*, March, 1913). The discovery goes a long way to support the authority of the Purāṇic lists as against the muddled account of the *Mahāvaṁśa*, to which Professor Geiger does 'not hesitate to give the preference wholly and unreservedly'. The learned Professor proceeds to say: 'Again, in the Purāṇas yet another king, called Darśaka, &c., is inserted between Ajātaśatru and Udāyin. That is certainly an error. The Pāli canon indubitably asserts that Udāyibhadda was the son of Ajātaśatru and probably also his successor.' (transl. *Mahāvaṁśa*, 1912, pp. xliv, xlv). Many 'indubitable assertions', unfortunately, are not true.

As to the authenticity of the plays, including *Svapnavāsavadatta*, attributed to Bhāsa, see Max Landenau's *Bhāsa Studien* (Harrassowitz, Leipzig, 1918, 51 pp.), and paper by Bhattanātha Svamin of Kumbakonam in *Ind. Ant.*, Dec. 1916, pp. 189–95.

from the mouth of the Indus to Persia. The commander, Skylax of Karyanda in Karia, managed somehow to equip a squadron on the waters of the Panjāb rivers in the Gandhāra country, to make his way down to the ocean, and ultimately, in the thirteenth month, to reach the Red Sea. The particulars of his adventurous voyage have been lost, but we know that the information collected was of such value that, by utilizing it, Darius was enabled to annex the Indus valley, and to send his fleets into the Indian Ocean. The archers from India formed a valuable element in the army of Xerxes, and shared the defeat of Mardonius at Plataea (479 B. C.).

The Indian satrapy. The conquered provinces were formed into a separate satrapy, the twentieth, which was considered the richest and most populous province of the empire. It paid the enormous tribute of 360 Euboic talents of gold-dust, or 185 hundredweights, worth fully a million sterling, and constituting about one-third of the total bullion revenue of the Asiatic provinces. Although the exact limits of the Indian satrapy cannot be determined, we know that it was distinct from Arīa (Herāt), Arachosia (Kandahār), and Gandaria (North-western Panjāb). It must have comprised, therefore, the course of the Indus from Kālabāgh to the sea, including the whole of Sind, and perhaps included a considerable portion of the Panjāb east of the Indus. But when Alexander invaded the country, nearly two centuries later, the Indus was the boundary between the Persian empire and India, and both the Panjāb and Sind were governed by numerous native princes.[1] In ancient times the courses of the rivers were

[1] Voyage of Skylax (*Herod.* iv, 44). The *Periplus*, attributed to Skylax though really written between 338 and 335 B. C., does not treat of India (Müller, *Geogr. Graeci Minores*, vol. i, pp. xliv, 156–9). The city of Kaspatyros in the Paktyan land (Πακτυϊκὴ γῆ), from which Skylax began his voyage, is called Kaspapyros, a city of the Gandharians, by Hekataios. The site cannot be identified, and it is impossible to say which form of the name is correct. Gandhāra was the modern Peshāwar District and some adjacent territory. Kaspatyros, or Kaspapyros, has nothing to do with Kashmīr, as many writers have supposed (Stein, *Rājataraṅginī*, trans. ii. 353). For satrapies see *Herod.* iii, 88–106, especially 94. The Euboic talent weighed 57·6 lb. avoirdupois; 360 talents = 20,736 lb., which, assuming silver to be worth five shillings (quarter of

quite different from what they now are, and vast tracts in Sind and the Panjāb, now desolate, were then rich and prosperous.[1] This fact largely explains the surprising value of the tribute paid by the twentieth satrapy.

According to the Purānic lists Udaya's successors were Nandivardhana and Mahānandin, both of whom are shadowy figures, mere *nominis umbrae*.[2] The long reigns attributed to them, of forty (or forty-two) and forty-three years respectively, total eighty-three or eighty-five years, are not likely to be correct. The names of both kings, *Nandi*vardhana and Mahā*nandin*, seem to justify the inference that they were Nandas; and Mahānandin, the last of the dynasty, is said to have had by a Sūdra, or low-caste, woman a son named Mahāpadma Nanda, who usurped the throne, and so established the Nanda family or dynasty. This event may be dated in or about 413 B. C.

?470 B. C.

413 B. C.

The Nandas.

At this point all our authorities become unintelligible and incredible. According to the Purāṇas the last two kings of the Saisunāga dynasty were followed by the 'Nine Nandas', namely king Mahāpadma (eighty-eight years) and his eight sons (twelve years), of whom the first was named Sukalpa,

a sovereign) an ounce, or £4 per lb., and the ratio of silver to gold to be as 13 to 1, would be worth £1,078,272. If the Euboic talent be taken as equivalent to 78, not 70, *minae*, the figures given by Herodotus will tally. 360 gold talents = 4,680 talents of silver; the total bullion revenue for the Asiatic provinces (including a small part of Libya in Africa) was 14,560 silver talents (Cunningham, *Coins of Ancient India*, pp. 12, 14, 26, 30).

India is not included in the list of provinces in the Behistun inscription of 516 B.C., but is included in the lists in the Persepolis and Naksh-i-Rustam inscriptions. The last-named record, inscribed on the sepulchre of Darius, is the fullest (Rawlinson, *Herodotus*, vol. ii, p. 403, note; iv, 177, 207).

For the Indian contingent in Xerxes' army, clad in cotton garments, and armed with cane bows and iron-tipped cane arrows, see *Herod.* vii. 65. The fact that the Indian troops used iron in 480 B. C. is worth noting. See Prof. P. Neogi, *Iron in Ancient India*, Calcutta, 1914.

[1] Raverty, 'The Mihrān of Sind and its Tributaries' (*J. A. S. B.*, 1892, part 1, esp. pp. 301, 311, 340, 361, 375, 377, 435, 489).

[2] In the case of Nandivardhana this statement must be qualified if K. P. Jayaswal's identification of the two 'Saisunāka statues' in the Indian Museum as those of Udaya and Nandivardhana is correct (*J. B. O. Res. Soc.* v. (1919), pp. 88–106). R. D. Banerji accepts the identification as correct (ibid. v, pp. 210–15). Jayaswal dates Udaya's reign, 483–467 B.C., and Nandivardhana's reign, 449–409 B.C. His article deserves careful study.

with variants.[1] These two generations are thus supposed to have reigned for a century. It is clear that the history has somehow been falsified and that the chronology cannot be correct. The Jains, doing still greater violence to reason, extend the duration of the dynasty to 155 years, while the Buddhist Mahāvaṁsa, Dīpavaṁsa, and Asokāvadāna deepen the confusion by hopelessly muddled and contradictory stories not worth repeating. Some powerful motive, possibly *odium theologicum*, as in other cases, must have existed for the distortion of the history of the so-called 'Nine Nandas' in all forms of the tradition.[2]

Greek accounts. The Greek and Roman historians, who derived their information from either Megasthenes or the companions of Alexander, and thus rank as contemporary witnesses reported at second-hand, throw a little light on the real history. When Alexander was stopped in his advance at the Hyphasis
326 B. C. in 326 B. C., he was informed by a native chieftain named Bhagala or Bhagēla, whose statements were confirmed by Pōros, that the king of the Gangaridae and Prasii nations on the banks of the Ganges was named, as nearly as the Greeks could catch the unfamiliar sounds, Xandrames or Agrammes. This monarch was said to command a force of 20,000 horse, 200,000 foot, 2,000 chariots, and 3,000 or 4,000 elephants. Inasmuch as the capital of the Prasii nation undoubtedly was Pātaliputra, the reports made to Alexander can have referred only to the king of Magadha, who must have been one of the Nandas mentioned in native tradition.[3] The reigning king was alleged to be extremely unpopular, owing to his wickedness and base origin. He was, it is said, the son of a barber, who, having become the paramour of the queen of the last legitimate sovereign, contrived the king's death, and, under pretence of acting as

[1] Some MSS. of the Purāṇas state the length of Mahāpadma's reign as twenty-eight years only, but apparently all assert that the dynasty lasted for a hundred years.

[2] See note to p. 44, *infra*.

[3] Curtius, Bk. ix, ch. 2; Diodorus, Bk. xvii, ch. 93. The interpretation of the name Phegelas in the text of Curtius as Bhagala is due to Sylvain Lévi (*Journal As.*, 1890, p. 239). The name Bhagēlū is still often heard in Northern India. The names of the Gangaridae and Prasii are corrupted in some texts (McCrindle, *Alexander*, notes C *c* and D *d*).

guardian to his sons, got them into his power, and exterminated the royal family. After their extermination he begat the son who was reigning at the time of Alexander's campaign, and who, 'more worthy of his father's condition than his own, was odious and contemptible to his subjects.'[1]

Indian traditions.

This story confirms the statements of the Purāṇas that the Nanda dynasty was of ambiguous origin and comprised only two generations. The oldest Purāṇa brands the first Nanda, Mahāpadma, as a prince, 'urged on by prospective fortune', whose reign marked the end of the Kshatriya, or high born, kings, and the beginning of the rule of those of low degree, ranking as Sūdras. The Mahāvaṁsa, when it dubs the last Nanda by the name of Dhana or 'Riches', seems to hint at an imputation of avariciousness against the first Nanda; and the Chinese pilgrim Hiuen Tsang also refers to the Nanda Rāja as the reputed possessor of great wealth.[2]

Summary.

By putting all the hints together we may conclude with tolerable certainty that the Nanda family really was of base origin, that it acquired power by the assassination of the legitimate king, and retained possession of the throne for two generations only. The great military power of the usurpers, as attested by Greek testimony, was the result of the conquests effected by Bimbisāra and Ajātasatru, and presumably continued by their successors; but the limits of the Nanda dominions cannot be defined, nor can the dates of the dynasty be determined with accuracy. It is quite certain that the two generations did not last for a hundred and fifty-five, and improbable that they lasted for a hundred, years; but it is impossible to determine their actual duration.[3]

[1] Agrammes (Curtius, Bk. ix, ch. 2), Xandrames (Diodorus, Bk. xvii, ch. 93). All the Hindu and Greek versions of the story are collected in H. H. Wilson's Preface to the *Mudrā-Rākshasa* (*Theatre of the Hindus*, ii, pp. 129–50). The tales in the *Vṛihat-Kathā* and *Mackenzie MSS.* are mere folk-lore.

[2] The five *stūpas* near Pāṭaliputra ascribed to Asoka were attributed by another tradition to Nanda Rāja, and supposed to be his treasuries (Beal, ii. 94). In the *Mudrā-Rākshasa*, Act I, Chāṇakya speaks with contempt of the 'avaricious soul' of Nanda.

[3] The longest recorded duration for two generations of kings is found in the history of Orissa. Inscriptions establish that Choḍa-ganga reigned from 998 to 1069 Saka, equivalent approximately to A. D. 1076–1147, and that he was succeeded by four sons, who reigned until A. D. 1198. Those figures give about 122 years for

The period of ninety-one years has been assumed as fitting into a definite chronological scheme.

Rise of Chandragupta Maurya. c. 322 B. C.

However mysterious the Nine Nandas may be—if, indeed, they really were nine [1]—there is no doubt that the last of them was deposed and slain by Chandragupta Maurya, who seems to have been an illegitimate scion of the family.[2]

five reigns and two generations (M. M. Chakravarti, 'Chronology of the Eastern Ganga Kings of Orissa', *J. A. S. B.*, part I, vol. lxxii, 1903).

[1] K. P. Jayaswal interprets *nava-Nandāh* as meaning the 'new', not the 'nine Nandas'. See *J. B. O. Res. Soc.* iv. 91–5. On this supposition they must be distinguished from Kshemendra's *Pūrvanandāḥ*, the 'early' Nandas, namely Nanda(or Nandi)vardhana and Mahānanda (or -nandin). Harit Krishna Deb (ibid.) gives good reasons for believing that Chandragupta Maurya was a kinsman of the respectable early Nandas and not a Sūdra or low-caste man, like the later Nandas of ill-repute.

[2] Nanda Rāja is mentioned twice in the mutilated Prākrit inscription at Udayagiri of the Jain king of Kalinga, named Siri Khāravēla Mahāmegha-vāhana. The text of the inscription has been settled as far as possible in 1917 by R. D. Banerji and K. P. Jayaswal (*J. B. O. Res. Soc.*, vol. iii, Dec. 1917, pp. 425–507). The inscription is a record of the royal doings in peace and war for thirteen years of the reign of king Khāravela of Kalinga or Orissa, who belonged to the Cheta dynasty and was a zealous Jain. He carried his arms far westwards, even to Berar, defying the might of Sātakarni, the third Āndhra king. The inscription is dated in the year 165 or 164 of the era of 'Rājā Muriya', *scil.* Chandragupta, which began about 322 B. C. and so is equivalent to about 157 or 158 B. C. It refers to a Nanda king, probably Nandivardhana, having made a canal about 300 years before the fifth year of Khāravela (165 B. C.), and therefore in about 465 B. C. (See, however, R. C. Majumdar's Notes on the Khāravela inscription in *Ind. Ant.*, 1918, p. 223 and 1919, pp. 187–191. He dissents from the interpretation of this date. The subject requires to be still further discussed, and for the present I accept the reading of Messrs. Banerji and Jayaswal.)

Sir G. Grierson informs me that the Nandas were reputed to be bitter enemies of the Brahmans, and that their reign was therefore excluded from chronological computation by the poet Chand in the twelfth century, who used the *Ananda* ('without Nanda') form of the Vikrama era, less by ninety or ninety-one than the ordinary reckoning. The word 'nanda' seems to be used as equivalent to 'nine' (100–9 = 91). It is very probable that the Nandas were Jains and therefore hateful to the Brahmans, who would naturally regard them as unholy persons unworthy of inclusion in orthodox Hindu annals. It is unquestionable that the Nanda king dethroned by Chandragupta was a heretic in Hindu eyes, for the concluding verse of Kantilya's *Arthasāstra* (transl. by Shāma Sastri) states that 'this *Sāstra* has been made by him who from intolerance (of misrule) quickly rescued the scriptures and the science of weapons and the earth which had passed to the Nanda king'. (The text is quoted by R. K. Mukerji in Introd., p. xiii, to N. N. Law, *Studies in Ancient Hindu Polity*.) The supposition that the last Nanda was either a Jain or a Buddhist is strengthened by the fact that one form of the local tradition attributed to him the erection of the Pānch Pahārī at Patna, a group of ancient *stūpas* which might be either Jain or Buddhist.

There is no difficulty in believing the tradition that the revolution involved the extermination of all related to the fallen monarch, for revolutions in the East are not effected without much shedding of blood. Nor is there any reason to discredit the statements that the usurper was attacked by a confederacy of the northern powers, including Kashmīr, and that the attack failed owing to the Machiavellian intrigues of Chandragupta's Brahman adviser, who is variously named Chānakya, Kautilya, or Vishnugupta. But it would not be safe to rely on the details given in our only authority, a play written centuries after the events referred to; nor would there be any use in recounting the wondrous tales, mostly belonging to the world's common stock of folk-lore, which have been recorded in various books, and relate the miracles attendant upon the birth and youth of Chandragupta, the first strictly historical universal monarch of India.[1]

Accession of Chandragupta.

His accession to the throne of Magadha may be dated between 325 and 320 B. C., perhaps in 322 B. C. The dominions of the Magadha crown were then extensive, certainly including the territories of the nations called Prasii and Gangaridae by the Greeks, and probably comprising at least the kingdoms of Kosala, Tirhūt or North Bihār, and Benares, as well as Anga and Magadha proper or South Bihār. Two or three years before the revolution at Pātaliputra, Alexander had swept like a hurricane through the

[1] The *Mudrā-Rākshasa* play gives a very interesting and detailed account of the revolution. Scholars used to believe that the play dated from the seventh century (Rapson, *J.R.A.S.*, 1900, p. 535). Jacobi, observing that some MSS. substitute the name of Avantivarman for that of Chandragupta, held that it was performed before Avantivarman of Kashmīr on Dec. 2, 860 (*Vienna Or. J.*, vol. ii (1888), p. 212). But Hillebrandt, Speyer, and Tawney affirm it to be much older, and certainly anterior to the earliest recension of the *Panchatantra* and to Bhartṛihari who died in A. D. 651. It is suggested that the play may have been composed in the time of Chandragupta II, about A. D. 400. I agree with Prof. Hillebrandt that the author 'scheint auf sehr genauen Nachrichten zu fussen und sehr weit an die ursprüngliche Tradition des Hofes heranzureichen;' that is to say, that the plot is based on accurate information and ancient court tradition (reprint from *86. Jahresber. d. Schlesischen Gesellsch. für vaterl. Cultur*, July, 1908, p. 29). Prof. Tawney's remarks are in *J.R.A.S.*, 1908, p. 910. Konow is inclined to agree with Speyer and assigns the play to the fourth century (*Ind. Ant.*, 1914, p. 68). See also 'The Date of the Mudra-Rakshasa', *Ind. Ant.*, Oct. 1913, pp. 265–7.

Panjāb and Sind, and it is said that Chandragupta, then a youth, had met the mighty Macedonian.[1] Whether that anecdote be true or not, and I see no reason to doubt its truth, it is certain that the troubles consequent upon the departure of Alexander gave young Chandragupta his opportunity. He assumed the command of the native revolt against the foreigner, and destroyed most of the Macedonian garrisons. The language of our authorities seems to imply that the destruction of the Nanda royal family preceded the attack on the foreign settlements in the basin of the Indus. The revolution was not completed in a moment, it being clear that the various stages occupied at least a year. When all opposition had been crushed by force or circumvented by guile, Chandragupta, in the vigour of his early manhood, stood forth as the unquestioned master of Northern India.[2] But before the story of the deeds of Chandragupta Maurya and the descendants who succeeded him on the throne of Magadha can be told, we must pause to unfold the wondrous tale of the Indian adventure of 'Philip's warlike son'.

APPENDIX C

Chronology of the Śaiśunāga and Nanda Dynasties.

Fixed data. Although the discrepant traditionary materials available do not permit the determination with accuracy of the chronology of the Śaiśunāga and Nanda dynasties, it is, I venture to think, possible to attain a tolerably close approximation to the truth,

[1] Plutarch, *Life of Alexander*, ch. lxii. The words of Plutarch are :—'Androkottos himself, who was then but a youth, saw Alexander himself, and afterwards used to declare that Alexander could easily have taken possession of the whole country, since the king was hated and despised by his subjects for the wickedness of his disposition and the meanness of his origin' (McCrindle's transl.).

[2] 'Siquidem occupato regno, populum quem ab externa dominatione vindicaverat, ipse [*scil.* Sandracottus] servitio premebat . . . Molienti deinde bellum adversus praefectos Alexandri . . . Sic acquisito regno, Sandracottus ea tempestate, qua Seleucus futurae magnitudinis fundamenta iaciebat, Indiam possidebat' (Justin, xv. 4). The language does not state the order of events quite clearly, but the word *deinde* seems to imply that the palace revolution at Pāṭaliputra preceded the attack on Alexander's governors. In *Mudrā-Rākshasa*, Act iv, Malayaketu, the hill chieftain, observes :—

'Nine months have over us
passed since that sad day
My father perished.'

and to reconcile some of the traditions. The fixed point from which to reckon backwards is the year 322 B.C., the date for the accession of Chandragupta Maurya, which is approximately correct, with a possible error not exceeding three years. The second principal datum is the list of ten kings of the Śaiśunāga dynasty as given in the oldest historical entries in the Purāṇas, namely, those in the *Matsya* and the *Vāyu*, the general correctness of which is confirmed by several lines of evidence; the third is the revised reading (1917) of the Khāravela inscription, referred to in note 2 on p. 44 *supra*; and the fourth is the probable date of the death of Buddha.

Duration of reigns.

Although the fact that the Śaiśunāga dynasty consisted of ten kings may be admitted, neither the duration assigned by the Purāṇas to the dynasty as a whole, nor that allotted to certain reigns, can be accepted. Experience proves that in a long series an average of twenty-five years to a generation is rarely attained, and that this average is still more rarely exceeded in a series of reigns as distinguished from generations.

The English series of ten reigns from Charles II to Victoria inclusive, 1649–1901 (reckoning the accession of Charles II from the death of his father in 1649), occupied 252 years, and included the two exceptionally long reigns of George III and Victoria, aggregating 124 years. The resultant average, 25·2 years per reign, may be taken as the maximum possible, and consequently 252 years are the maximum allowable for the ten Śaiśunāga reigns. The Purānic figures of 321 (*Matsya*) and 332 (*Vāyu*) years, obtained by adding together the durations of the several reigns, may be rejected without hesitation as being incredible. The *Matsya* account concludes with the statement, 'These will be the ten Śaiśunāga kings. The Śaiśunāgas will endure 360 years, being kings with Kshatriya kinsfolk.'[1] Mr. Pargiter suggests that the figures '360' should be interpreted as '163'. If that interpretation be accepted the average length of reign would be only 16·3, and it would be difficult to make the death of Buddha (*c.* 543 B.C.) synchronize with the dates of his contemporaries, Bimbisāra and Ajātaśatru. It is probable that the dynasty lasted for more than two centuries.

Anterior limit of date.

As stated in the text, the traditional periods assigned to the Nanda dynasty of either 100 or 155 years for two generations cannot be accepted. The A-nanda mode of reckoning, used by the poet Chand, suggests 90 or 91 years as the true period. We thus get 342 (252+90) as the maximum admissible period for the Śaiśunāga and Nanda dynasties combined; and, reckoning backwards from the fixed point, 322 B.C., *the year* 664 B.C. *is found to*

[1] S. V. Venkatesvara Aiyar asserts that the real meaning of *Kshatrabandhavaḥ* ('with Kshatriya kinsfolk') is equivalent to *Kshatriyādhawaḥ*, i.e. 'Kshatriyas of a very low order' (*Ind. Ant.*, 1916, p. 11).

be the earliest possible date for Śiśunāga, the first king. But of course the true date may be, and probably is, somewhat later, because it is extremely unlikely that twelve reigns (ten Śaiśunāga and two Nanda) should have attained an average of 25·16 years.

Probable actual reigns.

The reigns of the fifth and sixth kings, Bimbisāra, or Śrēnika, and Ajātaśatru or Kūṇika, were well remembered owing to the wars and events in religious history which marked them. We may therefore assume that the lengths of those reigns were known more or less accurately, and are justified in accepting the concurrent testimony of the *Vāyu* and *Matsya* Purāṇas, that Bimbisāra reigned for twenty-eight years.

Ajātaśatru is assigned twenty-five, or twenty-seven years by different Purāṇas, and thirty-two years by Tibetan and Ceylonese Buddhist tradition. I assume the correctness of the oldest Purānic list, that of the *Matsya,* and take his reign to have been twenty-seven years. The real existence of Darśaka (erroneously called Vaṁśaka by the *Matsya*) having been established by Bhāsa's *Svapna-Vāsavadattā,* his reign may be assigned twenty-four years, as in the *Matsya.* Udaya, who is mentioned in the Buddhist books, and is said to have built Pāṭaliputra, is assigned thirty-three years by the Purāṇas, which may pass.[1]

The *Vāyu* and *Matsya* Purāṇas respectively assign eighty-five and eighty-three years to the sum of the reigns of kings nos. 9 and 10 together. These figures are improbably high, and it is unlikely that the two reigns actually occupied much more than fifty years. The figure 57 is assumed.

The evidence as far as it goes, and at best it does not amount to much, indicates that the average length of the later reigns was in excess of the normal figure. We may assume, therefore, that the first four reigns, about which nothing is known, must have been comparatively short, and did not exceed some sixty years collectively. An assumption that these reigns were longer would unduly prolong the total duration of the dynasty, the beginning of which must be dated about 642 B. C.

Traditional dates of Mahāvīra and Gautama.

The existence of a great body of detailed traditions, which are not mere mythological legends, sufficiently establishes the facts that both Mahāvīra, the Jain leader, and Gautama Buddha were contemporary to a considerable extent with one another and with the kings Bimbisāra and Ajātaśatru.[2]

[1] The subject has been re-examined by S. V. Venkatesvara Aiyar in 'The Ancient History of Magadha' (*Ind. Ant.*, 1915, pp. 41 *et seq.*). He suggests that the nine Nandas are simply the last nine Saisunāgas, and agrees that Darśaka is a real figure, and that the dynasty began about 600 B. C. He, however, rejects Kālāsoka, who may after all have been real. K. P. Jayaswal's paper on 'The Empire of Bindusāra' in *J. B. O. Res. Soc.*, vol. ii, part i, March, 1916, pp. 81–3, is well worth consultation.

[2] Jacobi, Introd., *S.B.E.*, vols. xxii, xlv; the visit of Kūṇiya (Ajātaśatru) is alluded to in § 1, p. 9, of the Jain *Uvāsaga Dasāo*

The deaths of these saints form well-marked epochs in the history of Indian religion, and are constantly referred to by ecclesiastical writers for chronological purposes. It might therefore be expected that the traditional dates of the two events would supply at once the desired clue to the dynastic chronology. But close examination of conflicting traditions raises difficulties. According to Pāli tradition Mahāvīra predeceased Buddha. But other reasons support the date 467 B. C., as advocated by Charpentier, and this fits in with the traditional date of Bhadrabāhu, who was the contemporary of Chandragupta Maurya.[1] The year 527 (528–7) B. C., the most commonly quoted date for the death of Mahāvīra, is merely one of several traditionary dates,[2] but it is supported by the evidence of the Khāravela inscription. It is impossible to reconcile wholly the Jain traditions either among themselves or with the known approximate date of Chandragupta.

Death of Buddha, 543 B. C.

The variety of dates assigned for the death of Buddha is almost past counting.[3] Diwan Bahadur L. D. Swamikannu Pillai, working from the week-days recorded for events of Buddha's life, as given by Bigaudet, finds that they suit Tuesday, April 1, 478 B. C., which, consequently, he regards as the true date of Buddha's death (*Ind. Ant.*, Oct. 1914 (vol. xliii), pp. 197–204). Three other arguments confirm the approximate date as being 487 or 486 B. C. :—

(1) The 'dotted record' kept up at Canton until A. D. 489 showed 975 dots up to that year; 975 – 489 = 486 (Takakusu, *J. R. A. S.*, 1905, p. 51).

(*Bibl. Ind.*, ed. and trans. Hoernle), and in the Buddhist *Dulva* (Rockhill, *Life of the Buddha*, p. 104). Dr. Hoernle has kindly supplied these references.

[1] Charpentier 'The Date of Mahavira', *Ind. Ant.*, 1914, pp. 175–7.

[2] Burgess, *Ind. Ant.*, ii. 139. Hoernle (ibid. xx, 360) discusses the contradictory Jain dates, and observes that although the Digambara and Śvetāmbara sects agree in placing the death of Mahāvīra 470 years before Vikrama, whose era begins in 58 B. C., the Digambaras reckon back from the birth, and the Śvetāmbaras from the accession of Vikrama. The books indicate that 551, or 543, or 527 B. C. may be regarded as the traditional date. See also ibid. ii, 368; ix, 158; xi, 245; xiii, 279; xxi, 57; and xxiii, 169, for further discussion of Jain chronology. Note especially the statements that Sthūlabhadra, ninth successor of Mahāvīra, who was *mantrin* of the ninth Nanda, died either 215 or 219 years after the death of Mahāvīra, the same year in which Nanda was slain by Chandragupta (ibid. xi, 246). This latter event having occurred in or about 322 B. C., it is clear that 527 B. C. offers a more suitable basis for calculating the date of Sthūlabhadra's death than the date 467 B. C., proposed by Charpentier. Mērutuṅga dates Pushyamitra, who came to the throne *cir.* 185 B. C., in the period 323–53 after Mahāvīra (Weber, *Sacred Lit. of the Jains*, p. 133).

[3] The variant dates for the death of Buddha given by the Chinese and other authorities are too numerous and well known to need citation. Fleet at one time held 482 B. C. to be 'the most probable and satisfactory date that we are likely to obtain' (*J. R. A. S.*, 1906, p. 667).

(2) Paramārtha, author of the *Life of Vasubandhu,* places the teachers Vrisha-gaṇa and Vindhya-vāsa, who flourished in the fifth century after Christ, as living in the tenth century after the Nirvāna (487 + 413 = 900).

(3) One form of the Khotan tradition places Dharma Asoka 250 years after the Nirvāna of Buddha, and makes him contemporary with the Chinese emperor, She-hwang-ti, the builder of the Great Wall, who came to the throne in 246 B.C., became 'universal emperor' in 221, and reigned until 210 (Sarat Chandra Dās, *J. A. S. B.*, part 1, 1886, pp. 193–203 ; Tchang, *Synchronismes chinois*).[1]

I do not believe that the date can be fixed with anything like certainty, and in opposition to the arguments in favour of 487 or 486 B.C. we now have the new reading of the Khāravela inscription which, if correct, obliges us to move back all the Saisunāga dates more than 50 years and therefore supports the Ceylon date for the death of Buddha, viz. 544 or 543 B.C. It may be argued that traditions preserved in Magadha should be more trustworthy than those recorded at a later date by monks in distant Ceylon : but there is ample evidence of the fact that Gautama Buddha was contemporary with both Bimbisāra or Srēnika and his son Ajātasatru or Kunika, and this being so, I feel compelled, until further light is thrown on the subject, to accept tentatively the earlier date, 543 B.C., based on the chronology disclosed by the Khāravela inscription.

It is impossible to fix precise dates for the pre-Maurya kings. The following table assumes the correctness of their names and order as given in the oldest Purānic lists, those of the *Matsya* and *Vāyu*, but no reliance can be placed on the recorded length of the reigns. Some may be correct, while it is certain that some are erroneous.

[1] Other forms of the Tibetan tradition are given by Sarat Chandra Das, l. c., and by Rockhill, *Life of the Buddha*, pp. 233, 237.

CHRONOLOGY (APPROXIMATE) OF ŚAIŚUNĀGA AND NANDA DYNASTIES

Serial No.	*King (Matsya Purāṇa).*	*Length of Reign. (Matsya P.)*	*Probable date of Accession.*	*Remarks.*
	ŚAIŚUNAGA DYNASTY.		B. C.	
1	Śiśunāga . . .	40 }	? 642	Originally Rājā of Kāsī or Benares.
2	Kākavarṇa . .	26 }	..	} Nothing known. Sixty years allowed for four reigns.
3	Kshemadharman	36 } 126	..	
4	Kshemajit or Kshatraujas .	24 }	..	
5	Bimbisāra. . .	28	*c.* 582	Built New Rājagṛiha; annexed Anga; contemporary with Mahāvīra and Gautama Buddha.
6	Ajātaśatru . .	27	*c.* 554	Death of Buddha, 543; built fort of Pāṭaliputra; wars with Kosala and Vaisāli; death of Mahāvīra.
7	Darśaka . . .	24	*c.* 527	See *Svapna-Vāsavadatta* of Bhāsa.
8	Udāsin or Udaya	33	*c.* 503	Built city of Kusumapura near Pāṭaliputra.
9	Nandivardhana .	40 } 83	? 470	Nothing known; reigns probably shorter in reality: 57 years allowed.
10	Mahānandin . .	43 }	..	
	Total . .	321	*c.* 229	
	Average .	32·1	22·9 (maximum possible 25·0)	The *Matsya* assigns either 360 or ? 163 (Pargiter, p. 69) to the dynasty, as a whole.
	NANDA DYNASTY.			
11 } 12 }	Mahāpadma, &c., 9; 2 generations	} 100	413	91 years allowed. Low caste heretics, hostile to Brahmans and Kshatriyas; destroyed by Chandragupta and Kautilya.
	MAURYA DYNASTY.			
13	Chandragupta .	24	322 (?325)	Date approximately correct.

CHAPTER III

ALEXANDER'S INDIAN CAMPAIGN: THE ADVANCE

April 327 B. C. Passage of Hindū Kush.

ALEXANDER THE GREAT,[1] having completed the subjugation of Bactria, resolved to execute his cherished purpose of emulating and surpassing the mythical exploits of Dionysos, Heraklcs, and Semiramis by effecting the conquest of India. Towards the close of spring in the year 327 B. C., when the sun had sufficiently melted the snows, he led his army, including perhaps fifty or sixty thousand Europeans, across the lofty Khāwak and Kaoshān passes of the Hindū Kush, or Indian Caucasus, and after ten days' toil amidst the mountains emerged in the rich valley now known as the Koh-i-Dāman.[2]

Alexandria under the Caucasus.

Here, two years earlier, before the Bactrian campaign, he had founded a town, named as usual, Alexandria, as a strategical outpost to secure his intended advance. The governor of this town, whose administration had been a failure, was replaced by Nikanor, son of Parmenion, the king's intimate friend; the population was recruited by fresh settlers from the surrounding districts; and the garrison was strengthened by a reinforcement of veterans discharged from the ranks of the expeditionary force as being unequal to the arduous labours of the coming campaign.[3]

[1] The story of Alexander's reign prior to the Indian expedition may be read best in Bury, *A History of Greece* (Macmillan, 1904).

[2] Ἐξήκοντος ἤδη τοῦ ἦρος (Arrian); i. e. late in April, or early in May. For identification of the passes see Holdich, *Report of the Pāmir Boundary Commission*, pp. 29, 30. The height of the Khāwak Pass, as marked on the India Office map of India, is 13,200 feet. The strength of the force that crossed the Hindū Kush is not known. The statement of Plutarch (*Alexander*, ch. lxvi) that his hero entered India with 120,000 foot and 15,000 horse may or may not be correct, and is open to much variety of interpretation.

[3] Alexandria 'under the Caucasus', or 'in the Paropanisadai', to distinguish it from the numerous other towns of the same name. The exact position cannot be determined, but its site *may* be marked by the extensive ruins at Opiān or Houpiān, near Chārikar, some thirty miles northward from

The important position of Alexandria, which commanded the roads over three passes, having been thus secured, in accordance with Alexander's customary caution, the civil administration of the country between the passes and the Kophēn, or Kābul, river was provided for by the appointment of Tyriaspes as satrap. Alexander, when assured that his communications were safe, advanced with his army to a city named Nikaia, situated to the west of the modern Jalālābād, on the road from Kābul to India.[1] Nikaia.

Here the king divided his forces. Generals Hephaistion and Perdikkas were ordered to proceed in advance with three brigades of infantry, half of the horse guards, and the whole of the mercenary cavalry direct to India. They were required to reach the Indus, and occupy Peukelaōtis,[2] situated in the territory now held by the Yusufzī. In all probability they marched along the valley of the Kābul river, and not through the Khyber Pass. Their instructions were couched in the spirit of the Roman maxim—'*Parcere subiectis et debellare superbos*'.[3] June or July, 327 B.C. Hephaistion and Perdikkas.

Kābul. The old identification with Bāmiān is certainly erroneous (McCrindle, *Invasion of India by Alexander the Great*, 2nd ed., p. 58, and note A; Cunningham, *Anc. Geog. India*, pp. 21–6). Von Schwarz identifies Alexandria in the Paropanisadai with Kābul (*Alexander des Grossen Feldzüge in Turkestan*, pp. 94, 101, 102).

[1] The rival opinions concerning the site of Nikaia are collected by McCrindle (op. cit. note B). I follow General Abbot, who was clearly right, as Jalālābād marks the spot where the division of the army would naturally take place. Certain local chiefs, the Sultans of Pīch, claim descent from Alexander (Raverty, *Notes on Afghanistan*, pp. 48–51). See Burnes, *Travels into Bokhara*, &c., 2nd ed., 1835, vol. iii, pp. 186–90. The other claimants to descent from Alexander are:—(1) the former Mīrs of Badakshan, superseded by a Turk dynasty about 1822; (2–5) the chiefs of Darwāz, Kulāb, Shighnān, and Wakhan; and (6–8) the chiefs of Chitrāl, Gilgit and Iskardo. The last-named fort is said to have been built by Alexander. The Tungani soldiers who garrisoned Yarkand in 1835, also claimed descent from Alexander's soldier colonists.

[2] Or Πευκελαῶτις. Grierson holds that this name and other Greek transliterations are from Paiśāchī Prākrit (*Ind. Ant.*, 1915, p. 228).

[3] The ancient road did not pass through the Khaibar (Khyber) Pass (Holdich, *The Indian Borderland*, 1901, p. 38); Foucher, *Notes sur la géographie ancienne du Gandhāra* (Hanoi, 1902, in *Bull. de l'École Fr. d'Extrême-Orient*). The Khaibar route probably was used once by Mahmūd of Ghaznī, and certainly several times by Bābur and Humāyun. In the eighteenth century, Nādir Shāh, Ahmad Shāh Abdālī, and his grandson, Shāh-i-Zamān, all passed through the Khaibar (Raverty, *Notes*, pp. 38, 73).

August, 327 B.C. Attitude of the native chiefs.

Most of the tribal chiefs preferred the alternative of submission, but one named Hasti (Astēs) ventured to resist. His stronghold, which held out for thirty days, was taken and destroyed. During this march eastward, Hephaistion and Perdikkas were accompanied by the king of Taxila, a great city beyond the Indus, who had lost no time in obeying Alexander's summons, and in placing his services at the disposal of the invader. Other chiefs on the western side of the Indus adopted the same course, and, with the help of these native potentates, the Macedonian generals were enabled to make satisfactory progress in the task of bridging the Indus, which had been committed to them by their sovereign.

August, September, 327 B.C. Alexander's flanking march.

Alexander in person assumed the command of the second corps or division, consisting of the infantry known as hypaspists, the foot guards, the Agrianian or Thracian light infantry, the archers, the mounted lancers, and the rest of the horse guards. With this force he undertook a flanking movement through the difficult hill country north of the Kābul river, in order to subdue the fierce tribes which inhabited, as they still inhabit, that region; and thus to secure his communications, and protect his army from attacks on the flank and rear. The difficulties of the operation due to the ruggedness of the country, the fierce heat of summer, the bitter cold of winter, and the martial spirit of the hillmen, were enormous; but no difficulties could daunt the courage or defeat the skill of Alexander.[1]

Details of his route unknown.

Although it is absolutely impossible to trace his movements with precision, or to identify with even approximate certainty the tribes which he encountered, or the strongholds which he captured and destroyed in the course of some five months' laborious marching; it is certain that he ascended the valley of the Kūnar or Chitrāl river for a considerable distance. At a nameless town in the hills, Alexander was

[1] 'Αλλ' οὔτε χειμὼν ἐγένετο ἐμποδὼν αὐτῷ οὔτε αἱ δυσχωρίαι . . . οὐδὲν ἄπορον 'Αλεξάνδρῳ τῶν πολεμικῶν ἦν ἐς ὅ, τι ὁρμήσειε (Arrian, *Anab.* vii, 15). Similar precautions were not required on the south of the line of march, because the hills there have 'never afforded suitable ground for the collection of fighting bodies of men in any great strength' (Holdich, *The Gates of India*, p. 95).

wounded in the shoulder by a dart; and the incident so enraged his troops that all the prisoners taken there were massacred, and the town was razed to the ground.[1]

Soon after this tragedy, Alexander again divided his forces, leaving Krateros, 'the man most faithful to him, and whom he valued equally with himself[2]', to complete the reduction of the tribesmen of the Kūnar valley; while the king in person led a body of picked troops against the Aspasians, who were defeated with great slaughter.

Second division of field-force.

He then crossed the mountains and entered the valley now called Bājauṛ, where he found a town named Arigaion, which had been burnt and abandoned by the inhabitants. It may have stood at or near the position of Nawagai, the present chief town of Bājauṛ.[3] Krateros, having completely executed his task in the Kūnar valley, now rejoined his master; and measures were concerted for the reduction of the tribes further east, whose subjugation was indispensable before an advance into India could be made with safety.

Entry into Bājauṛ.

The Aspasians were finally routed in a second great battle, losing, it is said, more than 40,000 prisoners, and 230,000 oxen. The perfection of the arrangements by which Alexander maintained communication with his remote European base is strikingly illustrated by the fact that he selected the best and handsomest of the captured cattle, and sent them to Macedonia for use in agriculture.

Final defeat of Aspasians.

A fancied connexion with Dionysos and the sacred Mount Nysa of Greek legend gave special interest to the town and

Nysa.

[1] A list of very speculative identifications of tribes and places will be found in Bellew's *Ethnography of Afghanistan*, pp. 64–76 (Woking, 1891). The guesses of Cunningham and other writers are equally unsatisfactory. I do not agree with Pincott that Alexander went as far north as Chitrāl (*J. R. A. S.*, 1894, p. 681); but at present it is not possible to determine the point at which he turned eastwards, and crossed the mountains into Bājauṛ. It is, however, certain that he used one of the regular passes, which necessarily remain unchanged, and by which alone Bājauṛ territory can be entered. Raverty describes, from native information, two routes from Kābul to Bājauṛ; and it may well be that Alexander followed the 'left-hand', or eastern one, which goes through a village named Kūz Danāhi, where two roads diverge, of which one leads to Chitrāl, and the other to the Shahr, or capital of Bājauṛ (*Notes*, pp. 112–18).

[2] Arrian, *Anab.* vii, 12.

[3] Holdich, *The Gates of India*, 1910, p. 103.

hill-state called Nysa, which was among the places next attacked.[1] An attempt to take the town by assault having failed by reason of the depth of the protecting river, Alexander was preparing to reduce it by blockade when the speedy submission of the inhabitants rendered further operations unnecessary. They are alleged to have craved his clemency on the ground that they were akin to Dionysos and the Greeks, because the ivy and vine grew in their country, and the triple-peaked mountain which overshadowed their town was no other than Mount Mēros. Alexander, who found such fancies useful as a stimulant to his home-sick troops, did not examine the evidence for the kinship with Dionysos in too critical a spirit, but was glad to accept the Nysaean appeals and to exercise a gracious clemency.

Revels. In order to gratify his own curiosity, and to give some of his best troops a pleasant holiday, he paid a visit to the mountain, probably that now known as the Koh-i-Mōr, accompanied by an adequate escort of the companion cavalry and foot guards. The chants and dances of the natives, the ancestors of the Kāfirs of the present day, bore sufficient resemblance to the Bacchanalian rites of Hellas to justify the claims made by the Nysaeans, and to encourage the soldiers in their belief that, although far from home, they had at last found a people who shared their religion and might be regarded as kinsmen. Alexander humoured the convenient delusion and allowed his troops to enjoy, with the help of their native friends, a ten days' revel in the jungles. The Nysaeans, on their part, showed their gratitude for the clemency which they had experienced by contributing a contingent of three hundred horsemen, who remained with Alexander throughout the whole period of his advance and were not sent home until October, 326 B.C., when he was about to start on his voyage down the rivers to the sea.[2]

[1] Curtius (viii, 10), places the surrender of Nysa before the siege of Massaga.

[2] Arrian, *Anab.* v, 1, vi, 2; *Curtius*, viii, 10; *Justin*, xii, 7; Plutarch, *Alex.*, ch. lviii; *Strabo*, xv, 7-9. The conjectures concerning the identity of Nysa collected in McCrindle's Note G are unsatisfactory. Sir H. T. Holdich, whose knowledge of the frontier is unsurpassed, has been more successful, and has indicated the approximate position of Nysa with

Alexander now undertook in person the reduction of the formidable nation called the Assakēnoi, who were reported to await him with an army of 20,000 cavalry, more than 30,000 infantry, and thirty elephants. Quitting the Bājauṛ territory, Alexander crossed the Gouraios (Panjkora) river, with a body of picked regiments, including, as usual, a large proportion of mounted troops, and entered the Assakenian territory, in order to attack Massaga, the greatest city of those parts and the seat of the sovereign power. This formidable fortress, probably situated not very far to the north of the Malakand Pass, but not yet precisely identified, was strongly fortified by both nature and art.[1] On the east, an impetuous mountain stream, flowing between steep banks, barred access; while, on the south and west, gigantic rocks, deep chasms,

The Assakēnoi and Massaga.

tolerable certainty. 'Elsewhere,' he writes (*Geogr. J.* for Jan., 1876), 'I have stated my reasons for believing that the Kamdesh Kafirs who sent hostages to the camp of Ghulam Haidar are descendants of those very Nysaeans who greeted Alexander as a co-religionist and compatriot, and were kindly treated by him in consequence. They had been there, in the Suwāt country bordering the slopes of the Koh-i-Mor ("Meros" of the Classics), from such ancient periods that the Makedonians could give no account of their advent; and they remained in the Suwāt country till comparatively recent Buddhist times . . . The lower spurs and valleys of the Koh-i-Mor [are] where the ancient city of Nysa (or Nuson) once stood. Apparently it exists no longer above ground, though it may be found in the maps of thirty years ago, figuring as rather an important place under its old name . . . Bacchanalian processions . . . chanting hymns, as indeed they are chanted to this day by certain of the Kafirs' (Holdich, *The Indian Borderland*, Methuen, 1901, pp. 270, 342; *The Gates of India*, 1910, p. 123). Properly speaking, Mēros was the name of a single peak of the triple-peaked mountain (τρικόρυφον ὄρος). The other summits were named Korasibiē and Kondasbē respectively (Polyainos, I, 1; p. 7 in ed. Melbar). The three peaks are visible from Peshāwar. Compare the anecdote of Conolly and his 'relatives, the Kāfirs' (Raverty, *Notes*, p. 129). Philostratos (*Apollonios*, Bk. II, ch. 9) avers that 'the inhabitants of Nysa deny that Alexander ever went up the mountain', and adds that 'the companions of Alexander did not write down the truth in reporting this'.

[1] The Greek and Roman writers spell the name variously, as Massaga, Massaka, Mazaga, and Masoga. Holdich suggests that the fortress stood at or near Matakanai (*The Gates of India*, 1910, p. 128). M. Foucher suggests Katgalla (Kātgalah), some miles farther north (*Sur la Frontière Indo-Afghane*, Paris, 1901, p. 158). Enriquez (*The Pathan Borderland*, 1910, p. 37) suggests a place called Guri as being 'the supposed Massaga'. Minglaur or Manglawar, which has been proposed as the site and in some respects is suitable, lies too much to the east. For Manglawar, see Raverty, *Notes on Afghanistan*, pp. 200, 234; Stein, *Archaeol. Tour in Bunēr*, Lahore, 1898, p. 53; Deane, *J. R. A. S.*, 1896, p. 655.

and treacherous morasses impeded the approach of an assailing force. Where natûre failed to give adequate protection, art had stepped in, and had girdled the city with a mighty rampart, built of brick, stone, and timber, about four miles (35 *stadia*) in circumference, and guarded by a deep moat (*Q. Curtius*, viii, 10). While reconnoitring these formidable defences, and considering his plan of attack, Alexander was again wounded by an arrow. The wound was not very serious, and did not prevent him from continuing the active supervision of the siege operations, which were designed and controlled throughout by his master mind.

Storm of the fortress. Commanded by such a general the meanest soldier becomes a hero. The troops laboured with such zeal that within nine days they had raised a mole level with the ground sufficient to bridge the moat, and to allow the movable towers and other engines to approach the walls. The garrison was disheartened by the death of their chief, who was killed by a blow from a missile discharged by an engine, and the place was taken by storm. Kleophis, the consort of the slain chieftain, and her infant son were captured, and it is said that she subsequently bore a son to Alexander.[1]

Massacre of mercenaries. The garrison of Massaga had included a body of 7,000 mercenary troops from the plains of India. Alexander, by a special agreement, had granted these men their lives on condition that they should change sides and take service in his ranks. In pursuance of this agreement, they were allowed to retire and encamp on a small hill facing, and about nine miles (80 *stadia*) distant from, the Macedonian camp. The mercenaries, being unwilling to aid the foreigner in the subjugation of their countrymen, desired to evade the unwelcome obligation which they had incurred, and proposed to slip away by night and return to their homes. Alexander,

[1] Arrian (*Anab.* iv, 27) speaks of 'the mother and daughter of Assakenos'. Q. Curtius (viii, 10) states that 'Assacanus, its previous sovereign, had lately died, and his mother Cleophis now ruled the city and the realm'. He adds that 'the queen herself, having placed her son, still a child, at Alexander's knees, obtained not only a pardon . . . at all events she afterwards gave birth to a son who received the name of Alexander, whoever his father may have been'. Apparently, Kleophis must have been the widow of the chief who was killed in the siege, according to Arrian.

having received information of their design, suddenly attacked the Indians while they reposed in fancied security and inflicted severe loss upon them. Recovering from their surprise, the mercenaries formed themselves into a hollow circle, with the women and children in the centre, and offered a desperate resistance, in which the women took an active part. At last, the gallant defenders were overpowered by superior numbers, and, in the words of an ancient historian, 'met a glorious death which they would have disdained to exchange for a life with dishonour.' The unarmed camp followers and the women were spared.[1]

Comment.

This incident, which has been severely condemned by various writers, ancient and modern, as a disgraceful breach of faith by Alexander, does not seem to have been, as supposed by Diodorus, the outcome of implacable enmity felt by the king against the mercenaries. The slaughter of the contingent was rather, as represented by Arrian, the tremendous penalty for a meditated breach of faith on the part of the Indians, and, if this explanation be true, the penalty cannot be regarded as altogether undeserved. While the accession of seven thousand brave and disciplined troops would have been a welcome addition to Alexander's small army, the addition of such a force to the enemy in the plains would have been a serious impediment to his advance; and he was, I think, justified in protecting himself against such a formidable increase of the enemy's strength.

Retirement of tribes to Aornos.

Alexander next captured a town called Ora or Nora, and occupied an important place named Bazira, the inhabitants of which, with those of other towns, had retired to the stronghold of Aornos near the Indus.[2] The desire of Alexander to capture this position, believed to be impregnable, was based upon military exigencies, and fired by a legend that the demi-god, Herakles, whom he claimed as an ancestor, had been baffled by the defences.

Description of Aornos.

The mountain, according to Diodorus, was washed on the

[1] Arrian, *Anab.* iv, 27; Diodorus, xvii, 84; Curtius, viii, 10.

[2] Holdich places Ora and Bazira at or near Rustam, between Mardān and the Ambēlā Pass (*The Gates of India*, p. 106). But that position seems to me to be too far south.

southern face by the Indus, the greatest of Indian rivers, which at this point was very deep, and enclosed by rugged and precipitous rocks, forbidding approach from that side. On the other sides, as at Massaga, ravines, cliffs, and swamps presented obstacles sufficient to daunt the bravest assailant. Arrian states that a single path gave access to the summit, which was well supplied with water, and comprised arable land requiring the labour of a thousand men for its cultivation. The summit was crowned by a steeply scarped mass of rock, which formed a natural citadel, and, doubtless, was further protected by art.[1]

Preliminary operations.

Before undertaking the siege of this formidable stronghold, Alexander with his habitual foresight, secured his rear by placing garrisons in the towns of Ora, Massaga, Bazira, and Orobatis, in the hills of Suwāt and Bunēr.

He further isolated the fortress by personally marching

[1] Arrian, *Anab.* iv, 28; Diodorus, xviii, 86; Curtius, viii, 11; Strabo, xv, 8. Different people will necessarily form different notions of the circuit of a mountain mass, as they include or exclude subsidiary ranges; but the estimate of Diodorus that the circuit was 100 *stadia*, or 11½ miles, probably is nearer the truth than Arrian's estimate of 200 *stadia*. On the other hand, Arrian guesses the minimum elevation as being 11 *stadia*, or nearly 6,700 feet, which is a more reasonable figure than the 16 *stadia* of Diodorus. All attempts to identify the position of Aornos have failed. The plausible identification with Mahāban was shattered by Sir M. A. Stein's exploration, as recorded in the *Report of Archaeol. Survey Work in the N. W. Frontier Province, &c.*, for 1904–5. It is difficult to believe that the Greek authors can have been mistaken in placing this fortress on the Indus. The Greek commanders were familiar with that river, which they were engaged in bridging. The Mahāban site fails to satisfy the conditions, not only for the reasons stated by Sir M. A. Stein, but also because, according to Curtius (Bk. viii, ch. 12). Alexander, after leaving Embolima, which was not far from Aornos, did not reach the Indus until he had made sixteen encampments. That statement implies a marching distance of at least 70 or 80 miles even in difficult country. I agree with Sir Bindon Blood that Aornos must be looked for on the Indus, higher up than Mahāban, and perhaps near Baio, which is beyond the sharp bend above Kotkai. We must remember that the Indus washed the *southern* face of the stronghold (see Holdich, *The Gates of India*, p. 121). I think it probable that Alexander may have marched back through the Ambēlā Pass, and then turned at or near Rustam towards the river. He must certainly have taken a wide circuit. Mr. Merk does not accept the evidence that Aornos was on the Indus, and would look for it in Suwāt (Swat) (*J. Roy. Soc. of Arts*, 1911, p. 760).

Earlier speculations on the subject will be found recorded in Appendix D of the second edition of this work. It is not now necessary to reprint that disquisition.

down into the plains, probably through the Shāhkōt Pass,[1] and receiving the submission of the important city of Peukelaōtis (Chārsadda), and the surrounding territory, now known as the Yusufzī country. During this operation he was assisted by two local chiefs. He then made his way somehow to Embolima, a small town on the Indus, at the foot of Aornos, and there established a dépôt under the command of Krateros. In case the assault should fail, and the siege be converted into a blockade, this dépôt was intended to serve as a base for protracted operations should such prove to be necessary.

Reconnaissance.

Having thus deliberately made his dispositions for the siege, Alexander spent two days in careful personal reconnaissance of the position with the aid of a small force, chiefly consisting of light-armed troops. Assisted by local guides, whose services were secured by liberal reward, Ptolemy, the son of Lagos, secured a valuable foothold on the eastern spur of the mountain, where he entrenched his men. An attempt made by the king to support him having been frustrated, this failure led to a vigorous attack by the Indians on Ptolemy's entrenchments, which was repulsed after a hard fight.

Construction of approach.

A second effort made by Alexander to effect a junction with his lieutenant, although stoutly opposed by the besieged, was successful; and the Macedonians were now in secure possession of the vantage-ground from which an assault on the natural citadel could be delivered.

The task before the assailants was an arduous one, for the crowning mass of rock did not, like most eminences, slope gradually to the summit, but rose abruptly in the form of a steep cone. Examination of the ground showed that a direct attack was impossible until some of the surrounding ravines should be filled up. Plenty of timber being available in the adjoining forests, Alexander resolved to use this material to form a pathway. He himself threw the first

[1] The ancient route, as followed by Hiuen Tsang, 'est celle qui montait de Po-lou-cha au Svât par la passe de Shahkote, l'Hatthilâr, ou "défilé des éléphants" des indigènes actuels, et le col le plus important de ces montagnes, avant qu'en 1895 les Anglais n'eussent choisi le Malakand pour y faire passer leur route stratégique du Chitrâl' (Foucher, op. cit., p. 40).

trunk into the ravine, and his act was greeted with a loud cheer signifying the keenness of the troops, who could not shrink from any labour, however severe, to which their king was the first to put his hand.

Evacuation by garrison.

Within the brief space of four days Alexander succeeded in gaining possession of a small hill on a level with the rock, and in thus securing a dominant position. The success of this operation convinced the garrison that the capture of the citadel was merely a question of time, and negotiations for capitulation on terms were begun.

The besieged, being more anxious to gain time for escape than to conclude a treaty, evacuated the rock during the night, and attempted to slip away unobserved in the darkness. But the unsleeping vigilance of Alexander detected the movement, and partially defeated their plans. Placing himself at the head of 700 picked men, he clambered up the cliff the moment the garrison began to retire and slew many.

Macedonian garrison posted.

In this way the virgin fortress, which even Herakles had failed to win, became the prize of Alexander. The king, justly proud of his success, offered sacrifice and worship to the gods, dedicated altars to Athēnē and Nikē, and built a fort for the accommodation of the garrison which he quartered on the mountain. The command of this important post was entrusted to Sisikottos (Sasigupta), a Hindu, who long before had deserted from the Indian contingent attached to the army of Bessus, the rebel satrap of Bactria, and had since proved himself a faithful officer in the Macedonian service.

Advance to Indus.

Alexander then proceeded to complete the subjugation of the Assakenians by another raid into their country, and occupied a town named Dyrta, which probably lay to the north of Aornos. This town and the surrounding district were abandoned by the inhabitants, who had crossed the Indus, and taken refuge in the Abhisāra country, in the hills between the Hydaspes (Jihlam) and Akesinēs (Chināb) rivers.[1] He then slowly forced his way through the forests

[1] Various attempts to identify Dyrta have been made without success. The position of Abhisāra, or 'the kingdom of Abisares',

down to the bridge-head at Ohind. Although the direct distance could not be great, the work of clearing a road passable for an army was so arduous that fifteen or sixteen marches were required to reach Hephaestion's camp.[1]

Opinions have differed concerning the location of the bridge over the Indus, and most writers have been inclined to place it at Attock (Atak), where the river is narrowest. But the investigations of M. Foucher have clearly established the fact that the bridge, presumably constructed of boats, must have been at Ohind or Und, 16 miles above Attock. Having arrived at the bridge-head, Alexander sacrificed to the gods on a magnificent scale, and gave his army thirty days of much needed rest, amusing them with games and gymnastic contests.[2]

Bridge at Ohind.

January 326 B.C. February 326 B.C.

At Ohind Alexander was met by an embassy from Ambhi (Omphis),[3] who had then succeeded to the throne of Taxila, the great city three marches beyond the Indus. The lately deceased king had met the invader in the previous year at Nikaia and tendered the submission of his kingdom. This

Embassy from Taxila.

was correctly defined for the first time by Sir M. A. Stein, who writes that 'Dārvābhisāra [i. e. Dārva and Abhisāra] comprised the whole tract of the lower and middle hills lying between the Vitastā (Jihlam or Hydaspes) and the Candrabhāgā (Chināb or Akesines) . . . The hill-state of Rājapurī (Rajaurī) was included in Dārvābhisāra . . . One passage would restrict the application of the term to the lower hills'. The small chieftainship of Rajaurī and Bhimbhar, the ancient Abhisāra, is now included within the limits of the Kashmīr State, as defined in recent times. Abhisāra used to be erroneously identified with the Hazāra District, which really corresponds with Uraśā, or the kingdom of Arsakes (Stein, *Rājataraṅginī*, transl., Bk. i, 180; v, 217; and McCrindle, op. cit., p. 375). The line of march from Aornos is not known.

[1] Curtius (vii, 12) is the authority for the fifteen or sixteen marches. His words are: 'Having left this pass [? Ambēlā], he arrived after the sixteenth encampment at the river Indus'.

[2] Arrian, v, 3; Diodorus, xvii, 86. The ancient road to India from the Kābul river valley followed a circuitous route through Purushapura (Peshāwar), Pushkalāvatī (Peukelaotis), Hoti Mardān, and Shāhbāzgaṛhi (Po-lu-sha of the Chinese), to Und or Ohind. The direct route to Attock has been made practicable only in modern times. Und is the pronunciation of the inhabitants of the town which is called Ohind by the people of Peshāwar and Mardān; the Sanskrit name was Udabhāṇḍapura (Cunningham, *Ancient Geography*, p. 52; Stein, *Rājat*, transl., ii, 336; Foucher, op. cit., p. 46, with maps). Raverty considers Uhand to be the correct spelling, and this form is the nearest to the Sanskrit.

[3] The restoration of the name Āmbhi is due to M. Sylvain Lévi (*Journal Asiatique* for 1890, p. 234).

tender was now renewed on behalf of his son by the embassy, and was supported by a contingent of 700 horse and the gift of valuable supplies comprising thirty elephants, 3,000 fat oxen, more than 10,000 sheep, and 200 talents of silver.

The ready submission of the rulers of Taxila is explained by the fact that they desired Alexander's help against their enemies in the neighbouring states. At that moment Taxila was at war both with the hill kingdom of Abhisāra, and with the more powerful state governed by the king whom the Greeks called Pōros, approximately coincident with the modern districts of Jihlam, Gujarāt, and Shāhpur.[1]

February or March, 326 B.C. Passage of Indus.

Spring had now begun, and the omens being favourable the refreshed army began the passage of the river one morning at daybreak; and, with the help of the Taxilan king, safely effected entrance on the soil of India, which no European traveller or invader had ever before trodden.[2]

Curious incident.

A curious incident marked the last day's march to Taxila. When four or five miles from the city Alexander was startled to see a complete army in order of battle advancing to meet him. He supposed that treacherous opposition was about to be offered, and had begun to make arrangements to attack the Indians, when Āmbhi galloped forward with a few attendants and explained that the display of force was intended as an honour, and that his entire army was at Alexander's disposal. When the misunderstanding had been

[1] Curtius, viii, 12. The country of Pōros lay between the Hydaspes (Jihlam) and the Akesinēs (Chināb), and contained 300 towns (Strabo, xv, 29). The Indian form of the name or title transcribed as Pōros by the Greeks is not known. Pūru was the name of a Vedic tribe. The guess that it might be *Paurava* is not convincing.

[2] The chronology is determined by Strabo, xv, 17, who states, on the authority of Aristoboulos, the companion and historian of Alexander, that 'they remained in the mountainous country belonging to the Aspasioi and to Assakanos during the winter. In the beginning of spring they descended to the plains and the great city of Taxila, whence they went on to the Hydaspes and the land of Poros. During the winter they saw no rain, but only snow. Rain fell for the first time while they were at Taxila'. The passage of the Indus must therefore be dated in February, or at the latest, in March, 326 B.C. Mr. Pearson notes that 'when Burnes was with Ranjit Singh at Lahore, the festival of spring was celebrated with lavish magnificence on the 6th of February' (*Ind. Ant.* 1905, p. 257). The rain at Taxila must have been due to a passing storm, because the regular rainy season does not begin before June.

removed the Macedonian force continued its advance and was entertained at the city with royal magnificence.

Taxila. Taxila, now represented by more than twelve square miles of ruins to the east and north-east of Sarai-Kala, a railway-junction twenty miles north-west of Rāwalpindī, was then one of the greatest cities of the east, and was famous as the principal seat of Hindu learning in Northern India, to which scholars of all classes flocked for instruction, especially in the medical sciences.[1]

Submission of Āmbhi. Āmbhi recognized Alexander as his lord, and received from him investiture as lawful successor of his deceased father the king of Taxila. In return for the favour shown to him by the invader, he provided the Macedonian army with liberal supplies, and presented Alexander with two

[1] The other great seat of learning, according to the Jātakas, was Benares, which seems to have derived its system of education from Taxila. Jīvaka, the court physician of Bimbisāra and Ajātasatru, took a seven-years' course at Taxila. The name is given by the Greek and Roman authors as Taxila (Τάξιλα), which is a close transcription of the Pāli or Prākrit Takkasilā. The Sanskrit form is Takshaśila. The remains, which have now been carefully surveyed and described by Sir John Marshall (*A Guide to Taxila*, Calcutta, 1918), include those of three distinct cities, namely, Bhir—Maurya and pre-Maurya; Sir Kap—Indo-Greek, Parthian, and Kadphises I; and Sir Sukh—of the time of Kanishka. The stratification proves conclusively both that Kanishka was later than the Parthian and Kadphises kings, and that he lived in the first or second century after Christ. There are also a large number of detached monuments which, with the exception of two stūpas that are probably Jain, are chiefly Buddhist stūpas and monasteries; but the vestiges of many pre-Buddhist edifices probably remain underground. The Buddhist establishments were in a state of decay when the Chinese traveller Hiuen Tsang visited them in the seventh century (Beal, i, 136–43; Watters, i, 240), and the kingdom was then tributary to Kashmīr. The Jātaka stories are full of references to the fame of Taxila as a university town, e.g. vol. ii (Rouse's transl.), 2, 32, 59, &c. The Susīma Jātaka places it in the kingdom of Gandhāra, i. e. of Peukelaotis and Peshāwar. Most of the Jātakas probably are anterior to Alexander's time. The romantic history of Apollonius of Tyana, by Philostratus, gives many details about Taxila in the first century of the Christian era, which would be extremely interesting if confidence could be felt in the truth of the alleged facts (Phillimore's transl., Oxford, 1912, Bk. II, chap. 20–42). Prof. Flinders Petrie believes in the reality of the Indian journey of Apollonius and dates it in A. D. 43–4 (*Personal Religion in Egypt*, 1909, p. 141). Sir. J. Marshall also holds this view, as he has found in his own discoveries remarkably strong corroboration of some of the details given by Philostratus (*Guide to Taxila*, 1918, pp. 15, 91). See also Conybeare's transl. of Philostratus, *Life of Apollonius*, New York, 1912.

hundred talents of coined silver,[1] 'three thousand oxen fatted for the shambles', ten thousand or more sheep, and thirty elephants.[2] Alexander, not to be outdone in generosity, bestowed on the donor a thousand talents from the spoils of war, along with many banqueting vessels of gold and silver, a vast quantity of Persian drapery, and thirty chargers caparisoned as when ridden by himself. This lavish generosity, although displeasing to Alexander's Macedonian officers, probably was prompted more by policy than by sentiment. It purchased a contingent of 5,000 men, and secured the fidelity of a most useful ally (Q. Curtius, viii, 12; Diodorus, xvii, 86; Arrian, v, 8).

Rāja of Abhisāra and Pōros.

While Alexander was at Taxila, the hill chieftain of Abhisāra, who really intended to join Pōros in repelling the invader (Diodorus, xvii, 87), sent envoys who professed to surrender to Alexander all that their master possessed. This mission was favourably received, and Alexander hoped that Pōros would display complaisance equal to that of his ally. But a summons sent requiring him to do homage and pay tribute was met with the proud answer that he would indeed come to his frontier to meet the invader, but at the head of an army ready for battle.

Advance to Hydaspes. April, 326 B.C.

Having stayed in his comfortable quarters at Taxila for sufficient time to rest his army (Diodorus, xvii, 87), Alexander led his forces, now strengthened by the Taxilan contingent and a small number of elephants, eastward to

[1] This 'coined' or 'stamped' silver (*signatum argentum*) probably consisted of the little flat ingots known to numismatists as 'punch-marked' pieces, because they are not struck with a die, but are marked irregularly by small punches of various patterns applied at different times. A hoard of these coins was found in the Bhiṛ mound at Taxila, deposited with a gold coin of Diodotus, gold jewellery and other relics (Marshall, *Guide to Taxila*, pp. 117, 118). For accounts of this curious coinage, which was used throughout India, see Rapson, *Indian Coins*, §§ 4–6; Cunningham, *Coins of Ancient India*, pp. 54–60, pl. I and II, 1, 2; and *Catal. of Coins in the Indian Museum*, vol. I, pp. 131–42. The punch-marked coins follow the monetary system of the Achaemenian dynasty of Persia (558–330 B.C.), as proved by Monsieur J. A. Decourdemanches (*J. As.*, Jan.-Fév. 1912, pp. 117–82). The early *copper* coinage of Taxila is described in the works cited.

[2] Arrian, chap. iii, p. 83. According to Curtius, the gifts consisted of 80 talents of coined silver and golden crowns for himself and all his friends, which Alexander returned.

meet Pōros, who was known to be awaiting him on the farther bank of the Hydaspes (Jihlam) river. The march from Taxila to Jihlam on the Hydaspes, in a south-easterly direction, a distance of about 100 or 110 miles, according to the route followed, brought the army over difficult ground and probably occupied a fortnight.[1] The hot season was at its height, but to Alexander all seasons were equally fit for campaigning, and he led his soldiers on and on from conquest to conquest, regardless of the snows of the mountains and the scorching heat of the plains. He arrived at Jihlam early in May, and found the river already flooded by the melting of the snow in the hills. The boats which had served for the passage of the Indus, having been cut into sections and transported on wagons to be rebuilt on the banks of the Hydaspes, were again utilized for the crossing of that river (Arrian, v, 8).

May, 326 B. C.

Preparation for passage of river.

In spite of the most elaborate preparations, the problem of the passage of the Hydaspes in the face of a superior force could not be solved without minute local knowledge; and Alexander was compelled to defer his decision as to the best feasible solution until he should have acquired the necessary acquaintance with all the local conditions. On his arrival he found the army of Pōros, fifty thousand strong, drawn up on the opposite bank. It was obvious that the horses of the cavalry, the arm upon which the Macedonian commander placed his reliance, could not be induced to clamber up the bank of a flooded river in the face of a host of elephants, and that some device for evading this difficulty must be sought.

Provision of boats.

Alexander, therefore, resolved, in the words of Arrian, to 'steal a passage'. The easiest plan would have been for the invader to wait patiently in his lines until October or November, when the waters would subside and the river might become fordable. Although such dilatory tactics did

[1] Alexander must have marched either by the northern road through the Bakrāla Pass, past Rohtās, to Jihlam; or by the road 20 miles farther south through the Bunhār Pass to Jalālpur. Possibly he may have utilized both roads. After his arrival at the river bank he was free to choose his battle-ground (Pearson, 'Alexander, Porus and the Panjab', *Ind. Ant.* 1905, p. 253, with map).

not commend themselves to the impetuous spirit of Alexander, he endeavoured to lull the vigilance of the enemy by the public announcement that he intended to await the change of season, and gave a colour of truth to the declaration by employing his troops in foraging expeditions and the collection of a great store of provisions. At the same time his flotilla of boats continually moved up and down the river, and frequent reconnaissances were made in search of a ford. 'All this,' as Arrian observes, 'prevented Pōros from resting and concentrating his preparations at any one point selected in preference to any other as the best for defending the passage' (v, 9). Rafts, galleys, and smaller boats were secretly prepared and hidden away among the woods and islands in the upper reaches of the river. These preliminaries occupied six or seven weeks, during which time the rains had broken, and the violence of the flood had increased. Careful study of the ground had convinced Alexander that the best chance of crossing in safety was to be found near a sharp bend in the river about 16 miles marching distance above his camp, at a point where his embarkation would be concealed by a bluff and an island covered with forest. Having arrived at this decision, Alexander acted upon it, not only, as Arrian justly remarks, with 'marvellous audacity', but with consummate prudence and precaution.

Beginning of July, 316 B.C. Reserve force. He left Krateros with a considerable force, including the Taxilan contingent of 5,000 men, to guard the camp near Jihlam, and supplied him with precise instructions as to the manner in which he should use this reserve force to support the main attack. Half-way between the standing camp and the chosen crossing-place three generals were stationed with the mercenary cavalry and infantry, and had orders to cross the river as soon as they should perceive the Indians to be fairly engaged in action. All sections of the army were kept in touch by a chain of sentries posted along the bank.

Night march. When all these precautionary arrangements had been completed, Alexander in person took command of a picked force of about 11,000 or 12,000 men, including the foot guards, hypaspist infantry, mounted archers, and 5,000 cavalry of various kinds, with which to effect the passage. In order to escape observation, he marched by night at some distance from the bank, and his movements were further concealed by a violent storm of rain and thunder which broke during the march. He arrived unperceived at the appointed place and found the fleet of galleys, boats, and rafts in readiness. The enemy had no suspicion of what was happening until the fleet appeared in the open river beyond the wooded island, and Alexander disembarked his force at daybreak without opposition. But when he had landed, he was disappointed to find that yet another deep channel lay in front, which must be crossed. With much difficulty a ford was found, and the infantry struggled through breast deep in the stream, while the horses swam with only their heads above water. The sole practicable road from the camp of Pōros involved a wide détour, which rendered prompt opposition impossible, and Alexander was able to deploy his dripping troops on the mainland before any attempt could be made to stop him.

The battle-field.

Then, when it was too late, the son of the Indian king came hurrying up with 2,000 horse and 120 chariots. This inadequate force was speedily routed with the loss of 400 killed, and of all the chariots. Fugitives carried the disastrous news to the camp of Pōros, who moved out with the bulk of his army to give battle, leaving a guard to protect his baggage against Krateros, who lay in wait on the opposite bank. The Indian army deployed on the only ground available, the plain now known as Karrī, girdled on the north and east by low hills, and about 5 miles in width at its broadest part. The surface was a firm sandy soil well adapted for military movements even in the rainy season.

The Indian army.

A stately force it was with which the Indian monarch moved forth to defend his country against the audacious invader from the west. Two hundred huge elephants, stationed at intervals of not less than a hundred feet from one another, and probably in eight ranks, formed the front in the centre.[1] The chief reliance of Pōros was on these monsters who would, it was calculated, terrify the foreign soldiers and render the dreaded cavalry unmanageable. Behind the elephants stood a compact force of 30,000 infantry with projections on the wings, and files of the infantry were pushed forward in the intervals between the elephants, so that the Indian army presented 'very much the appearance of a city—the elephants as they stood resembling its towers, and the men-at-arms placed between them resembling the lines of wall intervening between tower and tower' (Diodorus, xvii, 87). Both flanks were protected by cavalry with chariots in front. The cavalry numbered 4,000 and the chariots 300. Each chariot was drawn by four horses, and carried six men, of whom two were archers, stationed one on each side of the vehicle, two were shield-bearers, and two were charioteers, who in the stress of battle were wont to drop the reins and ply the enemy with darts (Q. Curtius, viii, 14).

Indian equipment. The infantry were all armed with a broad and heavy two-handed sword suspended from the left shoulder,[2] and a long buckler of undressed ox-hide. In addition to these arms each man carried either javelins or a bow. The bow is described as being

> 'made of equal length with the man who bears it. This they rest upon the ground, and pressing against it with their left foot thus discharge the arrow having drawn the string backwards: for the shaft they use is little short of being three yards long, and there is nothing which can resist an Indian archer's shot—neither shield nor breastplate, nor any stronger defence, if such there be' (Arrian, *Indika*, ch. xvi).

But great as was the power of the Indian bow, it was too cumbrous to meet the attack of the mobile Macedonian cavalry. The slippery state of the surface prevented the archers from resting the end of their weapons firmly on the

[1] See plan of the battle. The number of ranks is determined by the limitation of space. The plan shows exactly 200 elephants. I am indebted for it to my eldest son, who has plotted the details to scale.

[2] 'Many Rajputs carry the sword that way in our own time' (Hendley in *J.I.A.*, April, 1915, No. 130, p. 8).

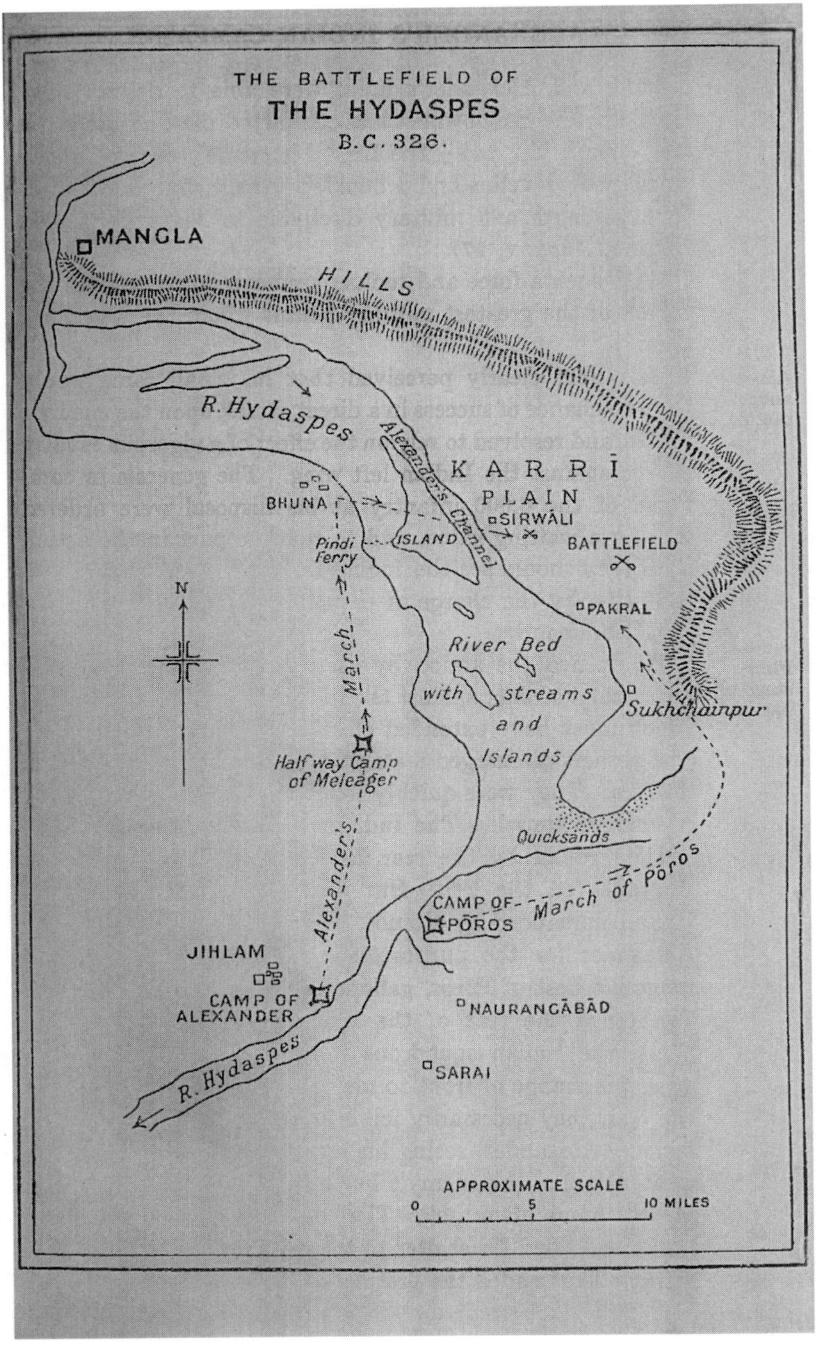
THE BATTLEFIELD OF
THE HYDASPES
B.C. 326.
MANGLA
HILLS
R. Hydaspes
Alexander's Channel
KARRĪ
PLAIN
BHUNA
SIRWĀLI
ISLAND
Pindi Ferry
BATTLEFIELD
PAKRAL
N
River Bed with streams and Islands
Sukhchainpur
Alexander's March
Halfway Camp of Meleager
Quicksands
CAMP OF PŌROS
March of Pōros
JIHLAM
CAMP OF ALEXANDER
NAURANGĀBĀD
SARAI
R. Hydaspes
APPROXIMATE SCALE
0
5
10 MILES

ground, and Alexander's horse were able to deliver their charge before the bowmen had completed their adjustments (Q. Curtius, viii, 14). The Indian horsemen, each of whom carried two javelins and a buckler, were far inferior in personal strength and military discipline to Alexander's men (Arrian, *Anab.* v, 17).

With such a force and such equipment Pōros awaited the attack of the greatest military genius whom the world has seen.

Alexander's tactics. Alexander clearly perceived that his small force would have no chance of success in a direct attack upon the enemy's centre, and resolved to rely on the effect of a vigorous cavalry charge against the Indian left wing. The generals in command of the 6,000 infantry at his disposal were ordered to play a waiting game, and to take no part in the action until they should see the Indian foot and horse thrown into confusion by the charge of cavalry under Alexander's personal command.

First stage of battle. He opened the action by sending his mounted archers, a thousand strong, against the left wing of the Indian army, which must have extended close to the bank of the river. The archers discharged a storm of arrows and made furious charges. They were quickly followed by the Guards led by Alexander himself. The Indian cavalry on the right wing hurried round by the rear to support their hard-pressed comrades on the left. But meantime two regiments of horse commanded by Koinos, which had been detached by Alexander for the purpose, swept past the front of the immobile host of Pōros, galloped round its right wing, and threatened the rear of the Indian cavalry and chariots. While the Indian squadrons were endeavouring to effect a partial change of front to meet the impending onset from the rear, they necessarily fell into a certain amount of confusion. Alexander, seeing his opportunity, seized the very moment when the enemy's horse were changing front, and pressed home his attack. The Indian ranks on both wings broke and 'fled for shelter to the elephants as to a friendly wall'. Thus ended the first act in the drama.

The elephant drivers tried to retrieve the disaster by urging their mounts against the Macedonian horse, but the phalanx, which had now advanced, began to take its deferred share in the conflict. The Macedonian soldiers hurled showers of darts at the elephants and their riders. The maddened beasts charged and crushed through the closed ranks of the phalanx, impenetrable to merely human attack. The Indian horsemen seized the critical moment, and, seeking to revenge the defeat which they had suffered in the first stage of the action, wheeled round and attacked Alexander's cavalry. But the Indians were not equal to the task which they attempted, and being repulsed, were again cooped up among the elephants. The second act of the drama was now finished.

Second stage of battle.

The third and last began with a charge by the Macedonian massed cavalry which crashed into the broken Indian ranks and effected an awful carnage. The battle ended at the eighth hour of the day (Plutarch, *Life*, ch. 60) in a scene of murderous confusion, which is best described in the words of Arrian, whose account is based on that of men who shared in the fight.

Third stage of battle.

'The elephants, he writes, 'being now cooped up within a narrow space, did no less damage to their friends than to their foes, trampling them under their feet as they wheeled and pushed about. There resulted in consequence a great slaughter of the cavalry, cooped up as it was within a narrow space around the elephants. Many of the elephant drivers, moreover, had been shot down, and of the elephants themselves some had been wounded, while others, both from exhaustion and the loss of their mahouts, no longer kept to their own side of the conflict, but, as if driven frantic by their sufferings, attacked friend and foe quite indiscriminately, pushed them, trampled them down, and killed them in all manner of ways. But the Macedonians, who had a wide and open field, and could therefore operate as they thought best, gave way when the elephants charged, and when they retreated followed at their heels and plied them with darts; whereas the Indians, who were in the midst of the animals, suffered far more from the effects of their rage.

Rout of Indians.

'When the elephants, however, became quite exhausted, and their attacks were no longer made with vigour, they fell back like ships backing water, and merely kept trumpeting as they retreated with their faces to the enemy. Then did Alexander surround with his cavalry the whole of the enemy's line, and signal that the infantry, with their shields linked together so as to give the utmost compactness to their ranks, should advance in phalanx. By this means the cavalry of the Indians was, with a few exceptions, cut to pieces in the action. Such also was the fate of the infantry, since the Macedonians were now pressing them from every side.

'Upon this all turned to flight wherever a gap could be found in the cordon of Alexander's cavalry.'

Capture of Pōros.

Meanwhile, Krateros and the other officers left on the opposite bank of the river had crossed over, and with their fresh troops fell upon the fugitives, and wrought terrible slaughter. The Indian army was annihilated; all the elephants being either killed or captured, and the chariots destroyed. Three thousand horsemen, and not less than twelve thousand foot soldiers were killed, and 9,000 taken prisoners. The Macedonian loss, according to the highest estimate, did not exceed a thousand.

Pōros himself, a magnificent giant, six and a half feet in height, fought to the last, but at last succumbed to nine wounds, and was taken prisoner in a fainting condition.

Alexander had the magnanimity to respect his gallant adversary, and willingly responded to his proud request to be 'treated as a king [1]'. The victor not only confirmed the vanquished prince in the government of his ancestral territory, but added to it other lands of still greater extent; and by this politic generosity secured for the brief period of his stay in the country a grateful and faithful friend.[2]

Boukephala.

The victory was commemorated by the foundation of two towns; one named Nikaia, situated on the battlefield; and

[1] Ὅτι βασιλικῶς μοι χρῆσαι, ὦ Ἀλέξανδρε.

[2] For disputed questions concerning the passage of the river, and the date and site of the battle see App. D, E. Opinions differ concerning the exact nature of the movements of Koinos; but to me the texts seem sufficiently plain. A mobile cavalry force had no difficulty in riding across the front of an army like that of Pōros; although, of course, such a feat would be impossible if that army had possessed rifles and guns. While Arrian's lucid description of the battle has been followed in the main, some details have been taken from other writers.

the other, named Boukephala, situated at the point whence Alexander had started to cross the Hydaspes. The latter was dedicated to the memory of Alexander's famous charger, which had carried him safely through so many perils, and had now at last succumbed to weariness and old age. Boukephala, by reason of its position at a ferry on the high road from the west to the Indian interior, became a place of such fame and importance as to be reckoned by Plutarch among the greatest of Alexander's foundations. It was practically identical with the modern town of Jihlam (Jhelum), and its position is more closely marked by the extensive elevated mound to the west of the existing town.

Nikaia.

The position of Nikaia, which never attained fame, is less certain; but probably should be sought at the village of Sukhchainpur to the south of the Karrī plain, the scene of the battle.[1]

Medal commemorating the battle.

An interesting numismatic memorial of the battle is the famous unique dekadrachm in the British Museum, 'showing on one side a Macedonian horseman driving before him a retreating elephant with its two riders, and on the other side a standing figure of Alexander holding a thunderbolt, and wearing the *Persian* helmet, and with ꓮ ('Αλεξάνδρου Βασιλέως ?) in the field. Mr. Barclay Head shows good reason for believing that this piece was struck in India as a medal for presentation to Macedonian officers who took part in the battle.[2]

The Glausai and Pōros II.

Alexander, having performed with fitting splendour the obsequies of the slain, offered the customary sacrifices, and celebrated games, left Krateros behind with a portion of the

[1] Arrian (v, 20) gives the true account of the death of Boukephalos. The site of Boukephala was determined, to my satisfaction, by Abbott ('On the Sites of Nikaia and Boukephala', *J. A. S. B.* 1852, p. 231). The mound referred to is known locally as 'Pindi', or 'the town', and yields large ancient bricks and numerous Graeco-Bactrian coins. Boukephala is mentioned in the Peutingerian Tables, by Pliny (vi, 20) and the author of the *Periplus* (ch. 47), as well as by Plutarch (*Fortune of Alexander*, Oration I, 9). Cunningham's identifications of the two towns are necessarily rejected as being based upon the theory that the passage of the river was effected at Jalālpur.

[2] See *ante*, plate 'Indian coins and medals', II, fig. 1, and *Num. Chron.*, 1906, p. 8, pl. I, 8.

CONTENTS OF PLATE OF INDIAN COINS AND MEDALS (2) IN THE BRITISH MUSEUM

No.	*King.*	*Obverse.*	*Reverse.*	*References and Remarks.*
1	Alexander.	A. standing, wearing Persian helmet, and holding thunderbolt. Mon. Ꭿ.	Horseman attacking elephant with riders.	Dekadrachm medal, probably struck to commemorate battle of Hydaspes. *Num. Chron.*, 1906, p. 8, Pl. i, 8.
2	Augustus.	Head of Augustus.	. . . . . .	Denarius; for comparison with No. 3.
3	Kozola Kadaphes (Kadphises I).	Head of king, with legend in Greek script.	. . . . . .	Bronze imitation of No. 2. As Gardner, *Catal.*, Pl. xxv, 5.
4	Huvishka.	Portrait bust of king; legend in modified Greek script.	. . . . . .	Gold. As Gardner, Pl. xxvii, 16.
5	Ditto.	Ditto.	. . . . . .	Gold. As Gardner, Pl. xxvii, 9.
6	Tiberius.	Head of Tiberius.	Emperor seated as Pontifex Maximus.	Denarius; for comparison with various Indian coins.
7	Nahapāna, Kshaharāta satrap.	Head of satrap, with modified Greek legend.	Thunderbolt and arrow. Kharoshṭhi version of Greek legend.	Rapson, *B. M. Catal.*, No. 243.
8	Chashṭana, Śaka satrap.	Head of satrap, with modified Greek legend.	Sun, or star, moon; *chaitya* symbol, river or snake. Brahmī legend of titles and name.	Rapson, *B. M. Catal.*, No. 260, &c. (=Pl. X, J. B.).
9	Rudrasiṁha, Śaka satrap.	Head of satrap, with traces of corrupt Greek legend.	*Chaitya* symbol. Brahmī legend of name and titles.	Rapson, *B. M. Catal.*, Pl. xvi, No. 911.
10	Kumāragupta I.	Head of king, with date, ?119.	Fantail peacock. Brahmī legend of name and titles.	As Cunningham, *A. S. Rep.*, vol. ix, Pl. v, 6, 7.
11	Toramaṇa Hūna.	Head of king to l., with date 52.	Fantail peacock. Brahmī legend of name and titles.	*Coins, Med. India*, Pl. ii. 11.
12	Aṃśuvarman of Nepāl.	Winged lion. Brahmī legend, *Śry-aṃśurvarma.*	Cow. Brahmī legend, *Kāmadēhi*, 'incarnation of Kāma'.	*Coins, Anc. India*, Pl. xiii, 6.
13	Mihiragula Hūna.	Barbarous bust of king, with name in Brahmī script.	Rude bull, walking l. Legend, *jayatu vṛishaḥ*, 'victory to the bull'.	As *I. M. Catal.*, vol. i, Pl. xxv, 5.
14	Bhoja or Mihira, Gurjara-Pratihāra, king of Kanauj.	Boar incarnation of Vishṇu, and solar symbol.	Traces of Sassanian type. Legend, imperfect, *Srīmad Ādi-varāha*, 'the fortunate primaeval boar', a title of both Vishṇu and the king.	As *I. M. Catal.*, vol. i, Pl. xxv, 18.

Indian Coins and Medals (2)

army, and orders to fortify posts and maintain communications. The king himself, taking a force of picked troops, largely composed of cavalry, invaded the country of a nation called Glausai or Glaukanikoi, adjacent to the dominions of Pōros. Thirty-seven considerable towns and a multitude of villages, having readily submitted, were added to the extensive territory administered by Pōros. The king of the lower hills, who is called Abisares by the Greek writers, finding resistance hopeless, again tendered his submission. Another Pōros, nephew of the defeated monarch, and ruler of a tract called Gandaris, sent envoys promising allegiance to the invincible invader, and sundry independent tribes (τῶν αὐτονόμων Ἰνδῶν) followed the example of these princes.

Middle of July, 326 B.C. Passage of Akesinēs.

Alexander, moving in a direction more easterly than before, crossed the Akesinēs (Chināb) at a point not specified, but certainly near the foot of the hills. The passage of the river, although unopposed, was difficult by reason of the rapid current of the flooded stream, which was 3,000 yards (15 *stadia*) in width, and of the large and jagged rocks with which the channel was bestrewn, and on which many of the boats were wrecked.[1]

Passage of Hydraōtes.

The king, having made adequate arrangements for supplies, reinforcements, and the maintenance of communications, continued his advance eastwards, probably passing close to the ancient fortress of Siālkōt. The Hydraōtes (Rāvī) river having been crossed without difficulty, Hephaistion was sent back in order to reduce to obedience the younger Pōros, who had revolted owing to feelings of resentment at the excessive favour shown to his uncle and enemy.

The independent tribes.

Alexander selected as the adversaries worthy of his steel the more important confederacy of independent tribes[2] which was headed by the Kathaioi, who dwelt upon the left or

[1] These particulars given by Arrian (v. 20) clearly prove that the Akesinēs was crossed near the foot of the hill, some 25 or 30 miles above Wazīrābād, where McCrindle places the crossing. The Chināb has changed its course very considerably, and lower down has wandered over a bed about 30 miles in breadth (Raverty, op. cit., 343).

[2] On the autonomous tribes see *post*, p. 302, and note on p. 98.

eastern side of the Hydraōtes, and enjoyed the highest reputation for skill in the art of war. Their neighbours, the Oxydrakai, who occupied the basin of the Hyphasis, and the Malloi, who were settled along the lower course of the Hydraōtes below Lahore, and were also famous as brave warriors, intended to join the tribal league, but had not actually done so at this time. The Kathaioi were now supported only by minor clans, their immediate neighbours, and the terrible fate which awaited the Malloi was postponed for a brief space.[1]

Pimprama and Sangala.

On the second day after the passage of the Hydraōtes, Alexander received the capitulation of a town named Pimprama, belonging to a clan called Adraïstai by Arrian; and, after a day's rest, proceeded to invest Sangala, which the Kathaioi and the allied tribes had selected as their main stronghold. The tribes protected their camp, lying under the shelter of a low hill, by a triple row of wagons, and offered a determined resistance.

Meanwhile, the elder Pōros arrived with a reinforcement for the besiegers of five thousand troops, elephants, and a siege train; but before any breach in the city wall had been effected, the Macedonians stormed the place by escalade, and routed the allies, who lost many thousands killed. Alexander's loss in killed was less than a hundred, but twelve hundred of his men were wounded—an unusually large proportion.

Sangala was razed to the ground, as a punishment for the stout resistance of its defenders.[2]

[1] For the correct location of the clans see the author's paper entitled 'The Position of the Autonomous Tribes of the Panjāb conquered by Alexander the Great' (*J. R. A. S.*, Oct., 1903). See the map, reprinted from that paper, with a slight alteration of the suggested position of the altars.

[2] Much nonsense has been written about the site of Sangala (Σάγγαλα), which was quite distinct from the Sākala of Hindu writers and of Hiuen Tsang. The assumption that the two towns were identical led Cunningham to identify Alexander's Sangala with a petty mound called 'Sangala Tibba' in the Jhang District. Mr. C. J. Rodgers conclusively proved this identification to be erroneous (*Report on Sangala Tibba*, News Press, Lahore, 1906; *Proc. A. S. B.* 1896, p. 81). The position of Sangala, which was razed to the ground, cannot be determined with precision, but it was in the Gurdāspur District. Sākala, the capital of Mihirakula, is represented by the modern Siālkōt, N.

Yet another river, the Hyphasis (Bias), lay in the path of the royal adventurer, who advanced to its bank, and prepared to cross, being determined to subdue the nations beyond. These were reputed to be clans of brave agriculturists, enjoying an admirable system of aristocratic government, and occupying a fertile territory well supplied with elephants of superior size and courage. Arrival at the Hyphasis.

Alexander, having noticed that his troops no longer followed him with their wonted alacrity, and were indisposed to proceed to more distant adventures, sought to rouse their enthusiasm by an eloquent address, in which he recited the glories of their wondrous conquests from the Hellespont to the Hyphasis, and promised them the dominion and riches of all Asia. But his glowing words fell on unwilling ears, and were received with painful silence, which remained unbroken for a long time. Alexander's address.

At last Koinos, the trusted cavalry general, who had led the charge in the battle with Pōros, summoned up courage to reply, and argued the expediency of fixing some limit to the toils and dangers of the army. He urged his sovereign to remember that out of the Greeks and Macedonians who had crossed the Hellespont eight years earlier, some had been invalided home, some were unwilling exiles in newly founded cities, some were disabled by wounds, and others, the most numerous, had perished by the sword or disease. Reply of Koinos.

Few indeed were those left to follow the standards ; and they were weary wretches, shattered in health, ragged, ill-armed, and despondent. He concluded his oration by saying : September, 326 B. C.

'Moderation in the midst of success, O king ! is the noblest of virtues, for, although, being at the head of so brave an army, you have naught to dread from mortal foes, yet the visitations of the Deity cannot be foreseen or guarded against by man.' [1]

lat. 32° 30′, E. long. 74° 32′ (Fleet, 'Sakala,' *Actes du xiv*[e] *Congrès des Orientalistes*, tome I).

[1] The address of Koinos, which is given in full by Arrian, seems to me to be in substance a genuine report of a real speech, and not merely an appropriate invention of the historian.

Orders for retreat.

The words of Koinos were greeted with loud applause, which left no doubt about the temper of the men. Alexander, deeply mortified, and unwilling to yield, retired within his tent; but emerged on the third day, convinced that further advance was impracticable. The soothsayers judiciously discovered that the omens were unfavourable for the passage of the river, and Alexander, with a heavy heart, gave orders for retreat, in September, 326 B.C.

The altars.

To mark the farthest point of his advance, he erected twelve huge altars, built of squared stone, and each fifty cubits in height, dedicated to the twelve great gods. Although the army had not passed the river, these massive memorials are alleged by Pliny to have been erected on the farther, i.e. northern, bank, where they long remained to excite the wonder and veneration of both natives and foreigners.[1] They probably stood at the point where the Biās flows from east to west between Indaura in the Kāngrā and Mīrthal in the Gurdāspur district, close to the foot of the hills. The cutting back of the northern bank, which has extended for about five miles, has swept away all traces of the buildings.[2]

The judicious Arrian simply records that:—

'Alexander divided the army into brigades, which he ordered to prepare twelve altars equal in height to the loftiest military towers, while exceeding them in breadth; to serve both as thank-offerings to the gods who had led him so far on the path of conquest, and as a memorial of his achievements. When the altars had been constructed, he

[1] 'Ad Hypasin . . . qui fuit Alexandri itinerum terminus, exsuperato tamen amne, arisque in adversa ripa dicatis' (Pliny, *Hist. Nat.*, Bk. vi, ch. 17).

[2] Vigne, *A Personal Narrative of a Visit to Ghazni, Kabul and Afghanistan* (1843), p. 11. Mr. H. L. Shuttleworth, I.C.S., informs me by letter dated Feb. 15, 1914, that he has examined the course of the Biās for 50 miles from the point where it leaves the hills to Mukerian ferry, and after considering all possible sites for the altars has come to the conclusion given in the text. He further states in a letter dated May 19, 1914, that no inscription or other material relic connects the Greeks with any of the three sites in Kāngrā and Mandī associated by tradition with Sikandar, who probably may be Sikandar Lodi as suggested by Moorcroft, and not Alexander the Great as supposed by Vigne. It is also to be remembered that Sultān Sikandar, the fierce iconoclastic king of Kashmīr, reigned from 1394–1420, and gave people good cause to remember him.

offered sacrifice upon them with the customary rites, and celebrated gymnastics and equestrian games.'

Worship at altars by Chandragupta.

The structures thus solemnly dedicated were well designed to serve their double purpose; and constituted a dignified and worthy monument of the piety and labours of the world's greatest general. Their significance was fully appreciated by the Indian powers which had been compelled to bend before the Macedonian storm. We are told that Chandragupta Maurya, the first emperor of India, who succeeded to the lordship of Alexander's conquests, and his successors for centuries afterwards, continued to venerate the altars, and were in the habit of crossing the river to offer sacrifice upon them.[1]

Travellers' tales.

But, if Curtius and Diodorus are to be believed, the noble simplicity of the monumental altars was marred by a ridiculous addition designed to gratify the king's childish vanity. The tale is given in its fullest form by Diodorus, who gravely informs us that after the completion of the altars, Alexander caused an encampment to be made thrice

[1] *Ἀλέξανδρος μὲν οὖν Ἡρακλέα τιμῶν καὶ πάλιν Ἀλέξανδρον Ἀνδρόκοττος, ἑαυτοὺς εἰς τὸ τιμᾶσθαι προῆγον ἀπὸ τῶν ὁμοίων.* 'Thus Alexander, honouring Hercules, and Androkottos [*scil.* Chandragupta] again honouring Alexander, got themselves honoured on the same ground' (Plutarch, *cir.* 90 A. D., 'How One can Praise oneself without exciting Envy', § 10, in *Morals*, ed. Teubner, and Shilleto's trans.). The same author, in his *Life of Alexander*, ch. lxii, states that 'he also erected altars for the gods which the kings of the Praisiai [*scil.* Magadha] even to the present day hold in veneration, crossing the river (i. e. from south to north) to offer sacrifices upon them in the Hellenic fashion'. Arrian, Curtius, and Diodorus agree that there were twelve altars. Curtius deposes to the 'squared stone', and Diodorus to the height of 50 cubits. Philostratus gives a different account, as follows:—

'And having crossed the Hydraötes and passed by several tribes (*ἔθνη*), they approached the Hyphasis; and 30 stades away from this river they came on altars bearing this inscription: "To Father Ammon and Heracles his brother, and to Athena Providence and to Zeus of Olympus and the Cabeiri of Samothrace and to the Indian Sun and to the Delphian Apollo".

'And they say there was also a brass column (*στήλην*) dedicated, and inscribed as follows: "Here Alexander stopped".

'The altars we may attribute to Alexander, who so honoured the boundaries of his empire; but I suppose the tablet was put up by the Indians dwelling on the other side of the Hyphasis, to their own glory for having stayed Alexander from any further advance' (*Apollonius of Tyana*, Bk. II, 43). Prof. Phillimore erroneously translates the plurals *βωμοῖς* and *βωμούς* as 'an altar', and renders *στήλην* as 'memorial tablet'.

the size of that actually occupied by his army, encircled by a trench 50 feet wide and 40 feet deep, as well as by a rampart of extraordinary dimensions. 'He further', the story continues, 'ordered quarters to be constructed as for foot-soldiers, each containing two beds 4 cubits in length for each man; and besides this, two stalls of twice the ordinary size for each horseman. Whatever else was to be left behind was directed to be likewise proportionately increased in size.' We are asked to believe that these silly proceedings were intended to convince the country people that the invaders had been men of more than ordinary strength and stature.[1]

It is incredible that Alexander could have been guilty of such senseless folly, and the legend may be rejected without hesitation as being probably based on distorted versions of tales told by travellers who had seen the altars.

APPENDIX D

Alexander's Camp; the Passage of the Hydaspes; and the Site of the Battle with Pōros

Problems are soluble.

The solution of the problems concerning the sites of Alexander's camp on the bank of the Hydaspes, the passage of that river, and the battle-field, may be attained, I believe, with sufficient accuracy by careful and impartial examination of the statements made by the ancient historians and of the actual topography.

Hydaspes river.

The Hydaspes (Vitastā, Bihat, or Jihlam, commonly called Jhelum) river has changed its course in a less degree than any of the other rivers of the Panjāb, and in the portion of its stream above Jalālpur, with which alone the present discussion is concerned, little material change has occurred. The solution of the three problems in question is consequently not complicated to any serious extent by doubts as to the ancient course of the river.[2]

[1] Diodorus, xvii, 95; Curtius, ix, 3.

[2] Greek, Ὑδάσπης or Βιδάσπης (Ptolemy); Sanskrit, *Vitastā*; Prākrit, *Vidastā*; Kashmīrī, *Vyath*; Panjābī, *Bihat* or *Wihat*. Muhammadan writers refer to the river as 'the river of Jihlam', that is to say, the river flowing past the town of Jihlam, where the royal ferry (*shāh guzar*) was situated. Modern usage has abbreviated the Muhammadan designation into 'the Jihlam', or, as it is commonly written, 'Jhelum'. Little deviation has occurred in the course of the stream, except near its junction with the Akesinēs or Chināb,

Nor is there any doubt as to the position of Taxila, the great city from which Alexander started on his march to the Hydaspes. Although Cunningham's description of the remains of the city is in many respects inadequate, his identification of the ruins at and near Shāhdhēri with the site of Taxila is certainly correct. The ruins, which are mere mounds scattered through the fields, are situated about 20 miles to the north-west of Rāwalpindi, and about 9 miles to the south-east of Hasan Abdāl village.[1] Taxila.

The distance from the site of Taxila to the town of Jihlam (Jhelum) in a direct line, as measured on the map, is about 90 miles, and the direct distance from Taxila to Jalālpur, some 30 miles lower down the river, is a few miles more. The northern or upper road from Shāhdhēri (Taxila) to the town of Jihlam via Rohtās and the Bakrāla Pass is 94 English miles. Roads or paths leading from Shāhdhēri to Jalālpur via Dudhiāl and the Bunhār Pass vary in length from 109 to 114 miles.[2] Taxila to Hydaspes.

Every one is agreed that Alexander must have reached the bank of the Hydaspes either at Jihlam or Jalālpur; no other place can be thought of. Both towns are situated on ancient lines of road commanding ancient ferries.

The invader's obvious goal unquestionably would have been Jihlam, which is appreciably nearer to Taxila, and has a ferry 'infinitely more convenient, and only one-third the width of the Jalālpur ferry'.[3] The road to either crossing-place is rugged and difficult, but a large force marching to Jalālpur would be more liable to entanglement in the intricate ravines of the Salt Range, and would encounter more formidable obstacles, than those met with on the road to Jihlam. The presumption, therefore, is that Alexander would have adopted the shorter and easier route and formed his camp near the town of Jihlam. The opinion that he followed this natural and obvious course of action has been advocated by Burnes, Court, and Abbott, who were all well qualified to express an authoritative opinion in virtue of their military experience and exact local knowledge. Route to Jihlam.

The rival theory that Alexander's camp was formed at Jalālpur, and that the passage of the river was effected a few miles above that town has been maintained by authorities of equal personal weight—Elphinstone, Cunningham, and Chesney —and these writers, being better known in Europe than their Jalālpur theory improbable.

which has been moved 'often and considerably' (Raverty, 'The Mihrān of Sind and its Tributaries', *J.A.S.B.*, part i, 1892, pp. 318, 329, 332; Stein, *transl. Rājat*, ii, 411).

[1] Shāhdēri is in N. lat. 33° 17′, E. long. 72° 49′ (*Imp. Gaz.* 1908, s. v.). The ruins extend over more than 12 square miles. Cunningham counted 55 *stūpas*, 28 monasteries, and 9 temples (*Reports*, ii, 151).

[2] Cunningham, *Archaeol. Survey Rep.*, ii, 112, 172.

[3] Abbott, in *J.A.S.B.*, 1852, p. 219.

opponents, have succeeded in winning general assent to the Jalālpur theory in spite of its inherent improbability.

Cunningham's view.

This theory has been defended at length by Cunningham, whose arguments would have gained additional force if they had been propounded after impartial examination of the site which Abbott, after careful survey, determined to be that of the battle-field. If the battle took place in the Karrī plain, as maintained by Abbott, Alexander's camp must have been at or close to Jihlam, and the passage of the river must have been effected above that town. But, unfortunately, Cunningham never attempted to meet Abbott's reasoning, nor did he examine the course of the river above Jihlam. Having formed in 1846 the opinion that Alexander's camp was at Jalālpur, Cunningham was content in 1863 to examine the Jalālpur position with a determination to make the topography fit in with his preconceived decision. He merely alludes to General Abbott's paper as 'an elaborate disquisition', and there is nothing to show that he ever studied it carefully.[1]

His river-distance argument.

Cunningham relies on three arguments in favour of the Jalālpur site for Alexander's camp. The third of these is that, according to Arrian (*Anab.* vi, 2, 4), the fleet when descending the Hydaspes from Nikaia, the town on the battle-field, reached the capital of Sophytes, king of the Salt Range, on the third day. The capital of Sophytes, according to Cunningham, was at Ahmadābād, 'which is just three days' distant for a laden boat from Jalālpur, but is six days from Jhelum',[2] and, consequently, Jalālpur suits the conditions better than Jhelum. This argument, on which Cunningham himself laid little stress, obviously depends on the correct identification of the capital of Sophytes. Inasmuch as the 'identification' proposed by Cunningham is a bare guess, quite unsupported by evidence, the argument based upon it does not demand further consideration.

Argument from Strabo.

The second and more important argument is based upon a passage of Strabo (xv, 32), which states that Alexander's 'route as far as the Hydaspes was for the most part towards the south, and thenceforward was more easterly as far as the Hypanis [=Hyphasis]; but throughout it kept closer to the foot of the mountains than to the plains'.[3]

Inasmuch as Jalālpur is nearly due south, while Jihlam is approximately south-south-east from Taxila, the Jalālpur position for the camp seems at first sight to suit the first clause of Strabo's statement better than the Jihlam position.

[1] *Reports*, ii, 174.

[2] *Reports*, ii, 37, 38, 180. On p. 38 Cunningham makes out that Bhera was the capital of Sophytes, while on p. 37 he makes the same assertion concerning Ahmadābād on the opposite bank.

[3] Ἡ μὲν οὖν μέχρι τοῦ Ὑδάσπου ὁδὸς τὸ πλέον ἦν ἐπὶ μεσημβρίαν· ἡ δ' ἐνθένδε πρὸς ἕω μᾶλλον μέχρι τοῦ Ὑπάνιος· ἅπασα δὲ τῆς ὑπωρείας μᾶλλον ἢ τῶν πεδίων ἐχομένη.

But in reality either position suits the text equally well. We do not know the points at which Alexander crossed the succeeding rivers, the Akesinēs and the Hydraōtes, nor the point at which he reached the most distant stream, Hyphasis [=Hypanis]. The assumption commonly made that Alexander crossed the Akesinēs (Chināb) at Wazīrābād does not rest on any evidence. Cunningham and the other authors who maintain the Jalālpur position forget the last clause of Strabo's statement to the effect that the whole route kept as close as possible to the foot of the hills. In another passage (xv, 26) Strabo explains that Alexander adopted this line of march because the rivers which traversed it could be crossed with greater facility near their sources than lower down. Refuted.

McCrindle, forgetting this most important general statement, which covers the whole route from Taxila to the Hyphasis, has constructed a map which represents Alexander as keeping away from the hills, and marching through the plains of the Panjāb past Jalālpur, Wazīrābād, Lahore, and Amritsar. The real line of march must have lain much farther to the north. The Hydaspes must have been crossed close to the spot where it emerges from the hills above Jihlam, and the army must subsequently have passed close to Siālkōt and Gurdāspur, keeping near the present frontier of the Kashmīr (Jamū) state. McCrindle.

The assumption that Alexander followed this line of march agrees accurately with every part of Strabo's statement. A line drawn from Jihlam to Siālkōt, or to the north of that place, is considerably more easterly in direction than a line drawn from Taxila to Jihlam.

Cunningham's second argument in favour of the Jalālpur position therefore fails, like the third.

The argument which Cunningham places first, and on which he lays most stress, is based on Pliny's figures for the distance from Peukolaitis (Chārsadda), via Taxila, to the Hydaspes (vi, 21). Pliny gives the distances as (1) from Peukolaitis to Taxila 60 Roman=55 English miles, and (2) from Taxila to the Hydaspes 120 Roman, or 110 English miles ; and Cunningham argues that these figures suit Jalālpur better than they suit Jihlam. But it is notorious that the figures in Pliny's text are often erroneous. For example, the very passage referred to gives the distance from the Hydaspes to the Hyphasis as 390 Roman miles, which is wildly wrong. It is rash, therefore, to rely on the figures in Pliny's text as we possess it. Cunningham himself was satisfied that the actual distance from Peukolaitis to Taxila, via Uhand, where Alexander crossed the Indus, is greater than that stated by Pliny, and proposed to correct the text (*Reports*, ii, 112). Argument from Pliny.

But, even if the figure of 120 Roman miles from Taxila to the Hydaspes be accepted as correct, it does not exclude the theory that Alexander's camp was at Jihlam. According to Cunningham Refuted.

(*Reports*, ii, 179) the distance by an old road is 94 miles. Pliny's distance is 110 English miles, and the difference is only 16 miles, which is insignificant, considering that we have no information concerning the route taken by Alexander in very difficult country, and no knowledge of the changes which have occurred in twenty-two centuries. The argument based on Pliny's figures is, consequently, worthless, whether the figures be right or wrong.

I have thus shown that all Cunningham's arguments for the Jalālpur theory fail, and that the Jihlam theory, so far from being opposed to Strabo's evidence, is actually supported by it.

Topography. The theory of Elphinstone and Cunningham is still more strongly opposed by the evidence of topographical facts than by that of Strabo.

The statements of Arrian, a critical writer, who had access to the best contemporary authorities and carefully weighed their testimony, are extremely clear.

The spot higher up the river to which Alexander marched by night in order to 'steal a passage' was situated at 'a remarkable bend' in the stream, which helped to conceal his movements.[1] There is no such bend at the spot above Jalālpur, between the villages of Mandiala and Kothera, where Cunningham locates the passage (*Reports*, ii, pl. LXVI). But there is such a bend at Bhūnā above Jihlam, where Abbott rightly locates it.

Night march. Arrian's excellent and vivid account (v, 11) clearly implies that Alexander made his night march parallel to the river. Having described the wooded bluff and island near the remarkable bend of the river, he goes on to say :—

> 'Now the bluff and the island were 150 stadia [=about 17 English miles] distant from the great camp. But along the whole of the bank he had posted running sentries at a proper distance for keeping each other in sight, and readily transmitting along the line any orders that might be received from any quarter.'

Half-way between the camp and the crossing-place Meleager and other officers were stationed with a considerable force, under orders to cross over in detachments as soon as they should see the Indians fairly engaged in action. The historian then goes on to state that Alexander marched 'at a considerable distance from the bank so that he might not be seen'. These statements prove that Alexander, when making his night march, kept an approximately straight course, parallel to the river bank, but sufficiently far from it to escape the enemy's observation.

Cunningham's theory erroneous. They are absolutely inconsistent with the theory of Cunningham, as expressed in his map (*Reports*, ii, pl. LXVI), which

[1] *Ἄκρα ἦν ἀνέχουσα τῆς ὄχθης τοῦ Ὑδάσπου, ἵνα ἐπέκαμπτεν ὁ ποταμὸς λόγου ἀξίως* (Arrian, *Anab.* v, 11).

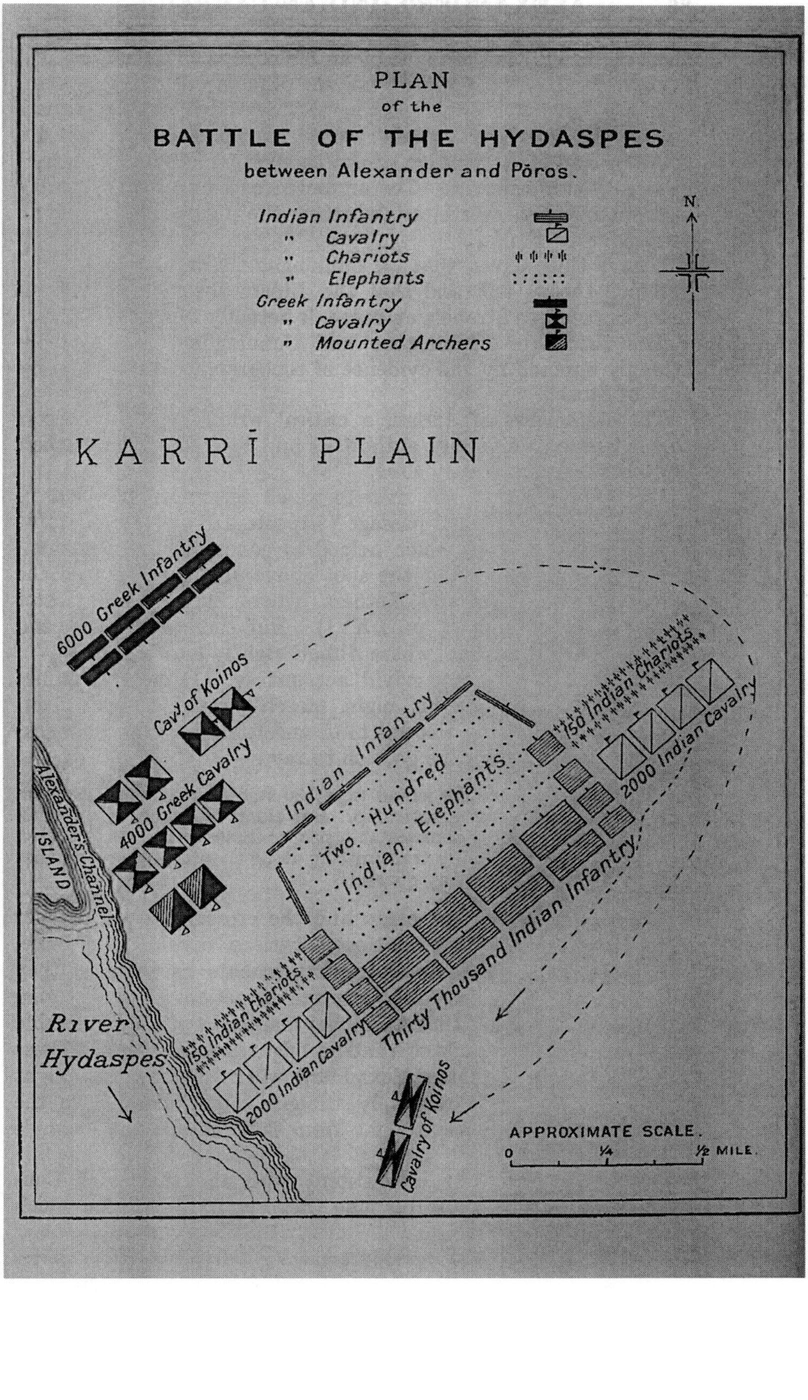
PLAN
of the
BATTLE OF THE HYDASPES
between Alexander and Pōros.
Indian Infantry
" Cavalry
" Chariots
" Elephants
Greek Infantry
" Cavalry
" Mounted Archers
N.
KARRĪ PLAIN
6000 Greek Infantry
Cavy. of Koinos
4000 Greek Cavalry
Alexander's Channel
ISLAND
Indian Infantry
Two Hundred
Indian Elephants
150 Indian Chariots
2000 Indian Cavalry
Thirty Thousand Indian Infantry
150 Indian Chariots
2000 Indian Cavalry
River
Hydaspes
Cavalry of Koinos
APPROXIMATE SCALE.
0
1/4
1/2 MILE.

represents Alexander as going round three sides of a rectangle among the ravines of the Salt Range, marching inland from Jalālpur nearly due north for seven or eight miles, then eastward for seven miles, and finally, two or three miles back to the river. The local facts at Jalālpur cannot be reconciled with the account of the night march as given by Arrian, and Cunningham's map is a desperate attempt to reconcile the irreconcilable, and to bolster up a preconceived theory based on fallacious premisses.

Description of river.

The descriptions of the river itself at the time when Alexander crossed it, as given by the ancient historians, are equally inconsistent with the Jalālpur theory. All authorities agree that the river was then in high flood owing to the melting of the snows in the mountains and incessant rain. But the width of the stream was only four stadia or 809 yards, whereas at Jalālpur at the same season, the end of June or the beginning of July, the river would have been more than double that width. The current was interrupted by numerous islands and sunken rocks. At Jalālpur there are neither rocks nor islands.[1]

The true theory.

If the Jalālpur theory be given up, and Alexander's camp be located at or near Jihlam, all topographical difficulties disappear. Alexander's march by night is then seen to have taken place at a moderate distance from the bank of the river, in a direction nearly parallel to the stream, and to have been directed to a point situated at a 'remarkable bend' of the river, distant from the supposed position of his camp about 13 or 14 miles in a direct line, which distance might well be estimated as 17 miles for marching purposes, if the route actually taken were slightly circuitous. It is, of course, impossible to define either the exact site of Alexander's camp or the precise spot where the army embarked on its perilous passage, and it is quite possible that 2 or 3 miles should be added to the approximate distance indicated by General Abbott's map.

Alexander on interior line.

By marching to the vicinity of Bhūnā near the 'remarkable bend' south-east of Manglā, Alexander gained the advantage of moving along an interior chord line, while his opponent on the opposite side of the river was compelled to go round the

[1] During the operations preceding the battle the soldiers of the opposing armies used to swim out to the islands and engage in combat. The river, confined by high banks, rushed in a seething torrent over sunken rocks (Curtius, viii, 13). The army during its progress to the Hyphasis was exposed for seventy days to violent storms of rain (Diodorus, xviii, 94; Strabo, xv, 27 ὕεσθαι συνεχῶς). In July Elphinstone found the river at Jalālpur to be 1 mile, 1 furlong, and 35 perches wide, and from 9 to 14 feet deep (Thornton, *Gazetteer*, s.v. 'Jhelum'). The ferry at Jihlam is only one-third of the width of that at Jalālpur, and there are 'no islands' at the latter place (Abbott, *J.A.S.B.*, 1852, p. 219). Mr. Pearson says that there are still wooded islands above Dārāpur, midway between Jihlam and Jalālpur (*Ind. Ant.*, 1905, p. 260).

outside of a curve. If the quicksands were in the same position in Alexander's time as they now are, the forces of Pōros must necessarily have covered a long circuit before they could approach the Macedonian landing-place. In any case, the distance which the Indians had to traverse was considerably longer than the chord traversed by Alexander.

Battle-field.

When the Macedonian army of about 11,000 men, after surmounting all the difficulties of the passage, ultimately found itself on the mainland, it entered a considerable plain of firm soil known as 'Karrī', girdled by low hills on the north and east. This plain at its widest part is about 5 miles broad, and afforded a sufficient, though not excessive, space for the battle. The river at the crossing-place runs over quartz boulders, and a still existing island, 'larger than the rest', corresponds closely with that described by the Greek historians as the place on which Alexander first landed, and may or may not have continued in existence since his time.

Alexander's channel.

The channel marked 'Alexander's channel', now considerably silted up, seems to be similar to that which the Macedonian army forded, and if not precisely identical, is certainly very close to the position of the channel crossed by Alexander. General Abbott is quite justified by his map in saying that 'the river is at this moment [1848] so exactly as described by Alexander's historians that the map might seem to be an ancient rather than a modern production'. General Abbott's 'elaborate disquisition' is based on a careful survey effected by two days' hard work from sunrise to evening each day, and his observations have never been contradicted or impugned. Cunningham simply took no notice of them.

Grote's opinion.

Grote, the historian of Greece, is the only author of repute who has shown due appreciation of Abbott's labours, and he has acknowledged that the general's memoir supplies 'highly plausible reasons in support of the hypothesis that the crossing took place near Jelum'. Mr. Grote's opinion would doubtless have become that of the learned world if General Abbott's essay had been published in an easily accessible form. Buried as it is in an old volume of the Asiatic Society's Journal, few people have read it; whereas the official publications of Sir Alexander Cunningham are widely known, and his opinions have been accepted too often without criticism.

Conclusion.

I have not the slightest doubt that Alexander marched to the Hydaspes by the shortest and easiest route open to him; that he struck the river at or near Jihlam, where he pitched his camp; that he crossed the stream where it was rocky and narrow, a little below the point where it emerges from the hills; and that the battle with Pōros was fought in the Karrī plain. The line of march between the Hydaspes and the Hyphasis cannot be precisely delineated, but it was certainly as close as possible to the foot of the hills, and must have passed near Siālkōt. Raverty was of the same opinion. He wrote to me in 1905: 'I quite agree with you as to Alexander's crossing-place over the Hydaspes . . . I well recollect when we crossed the river after the battle of Guzerāt, in pursuit of the Sikhs and Afghāns, that we crossed just at the place that you have mentioned, and the matter was discussed and Abbott's theory endorsed. We must give Alexander credit for some military knowledge at least, and that would naturally lead him to keep nearer the sources of the rivers in order to cross the more easily; and, at the same time, the hills on the north protected his flank.' [1]

APPENDIX E

The date of the Battle of the Hydaspes

Exact date doubtful.

The evidence of the ancient historians concerning the flooded state of the river, and the continued wet weather before, during, and after the battle, which has been cited in Appendix D, establishes beyond doubt that the battle was fought towards the end of June, or early in July. But certain positive statements which profess to define the date with greater precision have also been made, and must be briefly examined. Arrian makes two such statements, and a third is added by Diodorus.

Arrian's first statement.

Arrian's first statement (*Anab.* v, 9) that the battle was fought after the summer solstice, that is to say later than June 21, is undoubtedly correct, being in accordance with the evidence as to the state of the river and with the remark of Diodorus that when the army reached the Hyphasis it had endured violent showers of rain for seventy days. The MSS. all read *μετὰ τροπάς*, and the suggestion made by some editors to substitute *κατά* for *μετά* is unjustifiable.

Arrian's second statement.

But the second statement of Arrian (*Anab.* v, 19) that the battle was fought 'in the month of Mounychion of the year when Hēgemōn was Archon in Athens' seems to be partially inaccurate. The assertion of Diodorus (xvii, 87) that the entry into Taxila, in the spring preceding the battle, occurred during the year 'in which Chremēs was archon at Athens, and in which the Romans appointed Publius Cornelius and Aulus Postumius consuls', is apparently altogether erroneous. Neither the consuls nor the archon named can be accepted as correct.

Macedonian calendar.

The original authorities, the Macedonian officers of Alexander's army, probably expressed the date in terms of the Macedonian

[1] The name of the battle-field is more usually and correctly written Gujrāt. The battle took place on Feb. 21, 1849, and resulted in the annexation of the Panjāb.

calendar, and the divergent statements made by the historians may be due to errors in the conversion of Macedonian into Attic and Roman dates. As Mr. Hogarth has observed, it is impossible for a modern scholar to check such conversions, because our knowledge of the details of the Macedonian calendar is very imperfect, and little is known of the methods used for converting Macedonian dates into those expressed in terms of other calendars.[1]

Mounychion. The battle certainly was fought in the year 326 B.C., and the corresponding Attic year (=Ol. 113, 2) is supposed to have begun on June 25, 327, and ended on June 15, 326 B.C.[2] The close of Mounychion, the tenth month, even if the aid of an intercalary month be called in, cannot be brought down later than June 13. If there were no intercalary month, Mounychion should have ended on or about May 14. But, as we have seen, the battle occurred later than June 21, and it seems clear, therefore, that Arrian has wrongly named the Attic month. A rash proposal to substitute 'Metageitnion' for 'Mounychion', the reading of the MSS., is, as Grote observes, 'mere conjecture', and is, moreover, inconsistent with the statement that Hēgemōn was archon.

The archons. Chremēs certainly succeeded Hēgemōn as archon; and if Unger is right in assigning the end of the Attic year 327–6 B.C. to June 15, Diodorus, although wrong in ascribing the entry into Taxila to the archonship of Chremēs, would be right if he meant his readers to understand that the battle occurred after Chremēs had become archon. If, as other authorities suppose, the archonship of Chremēs did not begin until July 18, then Arrian will be right in stating that the battle was fought while Hēgemōn was still archon.

Explanation of error. Arrian's error in naming the month Mounychion may be explained plausibly by the supposition that Alexander reached the river bank in that month, and that by a slight carelessness the date of his arrival in camp was taken as the date of the great battle. The king's elaborate secret preparations for crossing the river must have occupied a long time, at least six or seven weeks, and if the camp was formed during Mounychion, early in May, the battle must have been fought at the very end of June, or, more probably, early in July.

Conclusion. Exact certitude is not attainable, and it is not possible to go much beyond the remark of Grote, that 'as far as an opinion can be formed, it would seem that the battle was fought about

[1] Hogarth, *Philip and Alexander of Macedon* (Murray, 1897), Appendix.

[2] Unger, 'Zeitrechnung der Griechen und Römer', in *Grundriss des klass. Allerth.*, pp. 742–4, 752, 755. But the exactness of the results of the inquiry appears to be doubtful. See also Cunningham, *Book of Indian Eras*, pp. 39, 44, 103; and note 1 in McCrindle, *Invasion of India by Alexander the Great*, 2nd ed., p. 274.

the end of June, or beginning of July 326 B. C., after the rainy season had commenced; towards the close of the archonship of Hēgemōn, and the beginning of that of Chremēs '.[1] I accept the archonship of Hēgemōn on the authority of Arrian, and believe that the battle took place early in July 326 B. C., in the last month, Skeirophorion, of the Attic year, a few days before Chremēs became archon.

[1] *History of Greece*, vol. xii, 51, note, ed. 1869. Mr. Pearson, however, basing his opinion on his personal knowledge of the rivers at all times of the year, and under all conditions, holds that 'the real date for the passage of the Hydaspes was, as stated by Arrian, the month of Mounychion in the archonship of Hēgemōn, and that Mounychion in that year occurred as early as April rather than as late as June. It was a matter of prime importance to cross the river before it was in high flood, and no sufficient explanation is given of the supposed delay' (*Ind. Ant.*, 1905, p. 257). Mr. Pearson, consequently, is obliged to disbelieve the positive statements of our authorities about the weather. The simple 'explanation of the supposed delay' is that Alexander was unable to 'steal a passage' earlier, and was obliged to make the best of unfavourable conditions, imposed on him through the delay caused by the vigilance of Pōros.

CHAPTER IV

ALEXANDER'S INDIAN CAMPAIGN: THE RETREAT

Retreat to Akesinēs.

THE retreating army retraced its steps, and arrived again without further adventure on the bank of the Akesinēs (Chināb), where Hephaistion had completed the building of a fortified town. Voluntary settlers from the neighbouring country and such of the mercenary troops as seemed unfit for active service were left to occupy and garrison this post, and Alexander began to prepare for his voyage down the rivers to the Great Sea.

Appointment of satrap.

Envoys bearing tribute from the kings of the lower hills, now known as the chieftainships of Rajauri and Bhimbhar and the British district of Hazāra, were received at this time. Alexander, who regarded his Indian conquests as permanent additions to the empire, and evidently cherished hopes of a return to the country, having accepted the tenders of submission, solemnly appointed the king of Abhisāra (Bhimbhar and Rajauri) to the office of satrap, and invested him with authority over the king of Urasā (Hazāra), who is called Arsakes by Arrian.[1]

Reinforcements.

About the same time a welcome reinforcement of 5,000 cavalry from Thrace, and 7,000 infantry, sent by the king's cousin, Harpalos, satrap of Babylon, arrived, bringing no less than 25,000 suits of armour inlaid with gold and silver. The new accoutrements were at once distributed to the ragged troops, and the old suits were burned.[2]

[1] The name Arsakes may be a corrupt form derived from Uraśā, its apparently Parthian guise being accidental. It is possible, however, that he may have been a Parthian.

[2] Curtius, ix, 3. Diodorus (xvii, 95) gives higher and less credible figures, namely, 30,000 infantry and 6,000 cavalry. Both authors agree as to the number of suits of armour, which must have required an enormous transport train. Diodorus adds that 100 talents of medicines were received at the same time.

Preparations for river voyage. Alexander then advanced to the Hydaspes (Jihlam), and encamped on the bank, probably on the site of the camp formerly occupied by Pōros. Several weeks were now devoted to the final preparations for the voyage down the rivers. All available country boats plying on the river were impressed for the service, and deficiencies were supplied by the construction of new vessels, for which the forests at the base of the hills afforded ample facilities. Crews were provided from the contingents of seafaring nations, Phoenicians, Cyprians, Karians, and Egyptians, who accompanied the army, and by the end of October, 326 B.C., all was ready. The fleet, which included eight galleys of thirty oars each, and a multitude of horse transports and small craft of all kinds, probably numbered nearly two thousand vessels.[1]

Promotion of Pōros. Before the voyage began Alexander convoked an assembly of his officers and the ambassadors of the Indian powers, and in their presence appointed Pōros to be king of all the conquered territories lying between the Hydaspes and the Hyphasis. These territories are said to have been occupied by seven nations, the Glausai, Kathaioi, and others, and to have comprised no less than two thousand towns. The opportunity was seized to effect a reconciliation between Pōros and his old enemy the king of Taxila, and the friendship between the two monarchs was cemented by a matrimonial alliance. The king of Taxila, who had vied with his rival in zealous service to the invader, was formally confirmed in his sovereignty of the country between the Indus and the Hydaspes.

Kingdom of Saubhūti. Alexander, who never neglected to make provision for the protection of his flank and rear, and for the uninterrupted

[1] Arrian (*Anab.* vi, 2), on the excellent authority of Ptolemy, son of Lagos, who became king of Egypt. The same author in *Indika*, ch. xix, probably on the authority of Nearchos, gives the total strength as 800 only (*νῆες δὲ αἱ σύμπασαι αὐτῷ ὀκτακόσιαι ἦσαν, αἵ τε μακραὶ καὶ ὅσα στρογγύλα πλοῖα, καὶ ἄλλα ἱππαγωγά, καὶ σιτία ἅμα τῇ στρατιῇ ἄγουσαι*). Curtius and Diodorus estimate the number of vessels as 1,000. Considering that 8,000 troops, several thousand horses, and vast quantities of supplies were carried, the higher estimate of Ptolemy must be admitted to be correct. Some editors arbitrarily change the 'eight hundred' of the *Indika* into '1,800', but the reading is 'eight hundred'.

maintenance of communications with the distant base in Europe, instructed Generals Hephaistion and Krateros to march with all possible speed to secure the capital of King Saubhūti (Sophytes, or Sopeithēs), lord of the fastnesses of the Salt Range stretching from Jihlam to the Indus, who submitted without resistance.[1]

The generals. The fleet was to be protected by an army of 120,000 men marching along the banks, under the generals above named; Krateros having the command on the right or western bank of the river, while the larger portion of the army, accompanied by two hundred elephants, was led by Hephaistion along the left or eastern bank. Philippos, satrap of the countries west of the Indus, had orders to follow three days later with the rear-guard.

Oct. 326 B.C. Voyage to first confluence. Thus escorted the vast fleet began its memorable voyage. At daybreak one morning towards the end of October, Alexander, having offered libations from a golden bowl to the river gods, his ancestor Herakles, Ammon, and any other god whom he was accustomed to reverence, gave the signal for starting by sound of trumpet. In stately procession, without confusion or disorder, the ships quitted their anchorage, and moved down stream to the astonishment of the crowds of natives lining the banks, who had never before seen horses on board ship. The plash of thousands of oars, the words of command, and the chants of the rowers wakened the echoes, which reverberated from bank to bank, and enhanced the amazement of the gaping throng of spectators. On the third day the fleet reached the place, perhaps Bhīra, where Hephaistion and Krateros had been ordered to pitch their camps facing each other

[1] The position of the kingdom of Sophytes is fixed by the remark of Strabo (xv, 30) that it included 'a mountain composed of fossil salt sufficient for the whole of India'. Curtius (ix, 1) misplaces Sophytes on the west of the Hyphasis, and is followed by McCrindle, whose map shows the kingdom as lying north of Amritsar, an impossible position. Cunningham (*Anc. Geog.*, p. 155) may or may not be right in placing the capital of Sophytes at Old Bhīra (properly 'Bahrah'), on the west side of the Jihlam. For the coins of Sophytes of Greek type see *ante*, Plate 'Indian Coins I', fig. 1; and Rapson, *Indian Coins*, §§ 9, 11; *Catal. of Coins in the Indian Museum*, vol. i, p. 7. The restoration of the name Saubhūti is due to M. Sylvain Lévi (*J.A.*, sér. viii, vol. xv, pp. 237–9).

on opposite sides of the river. Here a halt was made for two days to allow the rear-guard under the command of Philippos to come up, and that general, on his arrival, was directed to convert his force into an advance-guard and proceed along the bank of the river.

Rapids.

On the fifth day after leaving the halting-place, the fleet arrived at the first river confluence, where the Hydaspes met the greater stream of the Akesinēs. The channel where the waters of the two rivers then met was so very narrow that dangerous whirlpools were formed, and much disorder was occasioned in the fleet. Two of the warships were sunk with the greater part of their crews, and the vessel which carried Alexander was in imminent danger of sharing the same fate. By dint of great exertion on the part of the king and all concerned the bulk of the fleet was ultimately brought to a safe anchorage under the shelter of a headland, and the necessary steps were taken to repair the damage suffered.

Position of confluence.

It is impossible to determine the spot where these exciting incidents occurred. The confluence of the two rivers at Timmū (N. lat. 31° 10′) now takes place quietly, and presents none of the peculiarities to which Arrian and Curtius devote so much vivid description. All that can be said is that in Alexander's time the confluence must have been situated much farther to the north.

Courses of the rivers.

Our exact knowledge of the courses of the rivers in the Panjāb and Sind begins only from the date of the Arab invasion in 712 A.D., more than a thousand years subsequent to the expedition of Alexander. Concerning the changes which happened during that millennium absolutely nothing is known. But during the twelve hundred years that have elapsed since the Arab conquests changes on a stupendous scale are known to have occurred, and it is certain that similar effects must have been produced by the ever operating causes during the thousand years which intervened between Alexander and Muhammad bin Kāsim.[1] During the known

[1] Muhammad was the son of Kāsim. Elphinstone's blunder, 'Muhammad Kāsim', is repeated in most books on Indian history.

period, carthquakes, floods, changes of level, denudation, accretion, and alterations of climate all have contributed to transform the face of the country. The delta of the Indus has advanced more than 50 miles, and has thus lengthened the courses of the rivers, while necessarily diminishing their gradients and velocity. One huge river, the Hakrā or Wahindah, which formerly gave life and wealth to the desert wastes of Bikanīr, Bahāwalpur, and Sind, has ceased to exist; the Biās (Hyphasis) has forsaken its ancient independent bed, and become a tributary of the Sutlaj;[1] while the other rivers, the Indus, Jihlam (Hydaspes), Chināb (Akesinēs), and Rāvī (Hydraōtes) have all repeatedly changed their courses and points of junction.

Futility of 'identifications'.

These facts, although indisputably true, have been generally ignored in practice by the historians of Alexander, who have pretended to trace the line of his river voyage on modern maps, and to 'identify' town after town on the banks of the several rivers. All such identifications are vain. No man can tell in which of the ancient beds the Chināb or any of the other rivers named flowed in the time of Alexander, and, when the positions of the rivers are not ascertainable, it is clear that we cannot reasonably expect to identify places on their banks. The most that is possible is to give general indications of the course of the voyage and of the location of the principal nations encountered by Alexander. The sites of the towns and the precise positions

[1] Raverty gives as various correct spellings, Sutlaj, Sutlāj, and *Sh*uttlaj. This river, which was called Śatadra in Sanskrit, is rarely mentioned by the Greek or Roman authors under the name of Hesidrus. The Hypanis of Strabo is a variant for Hyphasis. A learned reviewer of the first edition says that 'exception may be taken to the strange remark that the Biās was in early days not a confluent of the Sutlej (p. 85); for the Rig Veda says that one flows into the other'. The only passage in the Rig Veda which mentions the Vipāśa is iii, 33, and that may be interpreted as referring to twin streams more or less parallel, but not necessarily confluent. Compare the reference to 'the Vipāś together with the Śatudrī' in the *Bṛihaddevatā* (Macdonell's ed., i, 114). The Sutlaj is the most erratic of the rivers of the Panjāb. The Biās or Biāh deserted its ancient channel about A. D. 1790, for the first time since it is heard of in history, and moved towards the east, combining with the Sutlaj, which shifted westwards simultaneously (Raverty, pp. 504, 505: see next note).

of the confluences and crossing-places mentioned by the ancient historians cannot be determined. Inasmuch as the courses of all the rivers were then much shorter than they now are, all the confluences must have been situated considerably farther north than at present, and this *a priori* inference appears to be fully supported by observation of the most ancient beds of the streams. The confluence of the Akesinēs and Hydaspes, the first of the four confluences described by Arrian, probably was situated not very far from the modern town of Jhang, and approximately in N. lat. 31°.[1]

The Siboi and Agalassoi.

Alexander here landed his troops in order to subjugate the adjoining tribes, called Siboi [2] and Agalassoi by Curtius, and to prevent them from joining the powerful nation of the Malloi (Sanskrit Mālavā), who dwelt lower down the river, and were known to be preparing for strenuous resistance. The Siboi, who are described as rude folk clad in the skins of wild beasts and armed with clubs, submitted, and were allowed to retain their freedom. Their neighbours, the Agalassoi, who were able to muster a force estimated at 40,000 foot and 3,000 horse, ventured to resist, and met with a terrible fate. Multitudes were put to the sword, and multitudes sold into slavery. Alexander advanced some

[1] The text is mainly based on Raverty's valuable work, 'The Mihrān of Sind and its Tributaries: a Geographical and Historical Study', in *J. A. S. B.*, 1892, Part I, with numerous maps, which has not attracted the attention that it deserves. The defects of form in that treatise, which is overloaded with 590 discursive notes, make it very difficult reading. The observations on Alexander's Indian campaign are scattered through the text and notes, and mixed up with remarks on the most diverse topics.

For general comments on the futility of current 'identifications' see pp. 155, 226, 250, 469, note 539, &c.; the Hydaspes (Jihlam), pp. 336–52; Akesinēs (Chināb), pp. 336–52; Hydraōtes (Rāvī), pp. 352–71; Hyphasis (Biās or Biāh), pp. 371–90; Sutlaj, pp. 391–418; Hakṛā, pp. 418–22, 454–66; general results, pp. 469–508; earthquakes and floods, pp. 392, 468, 470, &c.; changes of level, pp. 300, 470; alterations of climate, pp. 282, 354, 417; extension of coast-line, p. 272 (note 235), pp. 317, 469, 501, &c. The whole work is deserving of the most careful study. The author gives full references, so that his statements can be readily tested.

[2] Shorkot in the Jhang District was the capital of the Sibi country, its ancient name being Sibi—or Sivipura, as proved by an inscription dated 83 [G. E. = A. D. 402–3] on a huge copper cauldron from a Buddhist monastery, now in the Lahore Museum (Vogel in *J. P. H. Soc.*, vol. i, p. 174).

30 miles into their country, and captured their principal town. At a second town he met with an obstinate defence, which cost the lives of many Macedonians. The inhabitants, said to number 20,000, despairing of ultimate success, set fire to the town and cast themselves with their wives and children into the flames. The citadel escaped the fire, and was garrisoned by a detachment left behind for the purpose. The lives of 3,000 of its gallant defenders were spared.[1]

Voyage to second confluence.

These events probably took place to the north-east of Jhang, the operations having been undertaken in accordance with Alexander's invariable practice, in order to secure his flank and rear.

Information having been received that a confederacy of the Malloi, Oxydrakai, and other independent tribes occupying the river valleys was being formed with the intention of offering strenuous resistance to the invasion, Alexander hastened the movements of his fleet and army with the object of attacking the confederates severally in detail, before they could mature their plans and combine their forces. The fleet and the bulk of the army received orders to assemble at the next confluence, that of the Hydraōtes (Rāvī) with the Akesinēs (Chināb, including the Hydaspes or Jihlam).

The allied tribes.

Alexander in person landed with a picked force, largely composed, as usual, of mounted troops, to operate against the Malloi, the most formidable of the allied tribes, who occupied

[1] Arrian, *Anab.* vi, 5; Curtius, ix, 4; Diodorus, xvii, 96. The Agalassoi are distinguished by Diodorus only, who says that Alexander fired the town. The account in the text follows Curtius in respect of the voluntary immolation of the townspeople, an incident quite in keeping with Hindu character, and often repeated in later times. The Siboi were probably the ancestors of some of the half-wild tribes of pastoral Jāts, who now inhabit the same region. For discussion of the topography, see my paper, 'The Position of the Autonomous Tribes of the Panjāb conquered by Alexander the Great', in *J.R.A.S.*, Oct. 1903. These tribes are mentioned together in early Sanskrit literature. Weber pointed out that Āpiśali, one of the teachers cited by Pāṇini, speaks of the formation of the compound 'Kshaudraka-Mālavā (*scil.* senā)', 'the army of the Kshudrakas and Mālavās' (*J. A. S. B.*, pt. i, vol. lxi, 1892, p. 60).

The *Mahābhārata* couples them as forming part of the Kaurava host in the Great War (Pargiter, in *J. R. A. S.*, 1908, p. 329, citing, *Mbh.*, vi, 2106, 2584, 2646, 3852, 3853, 4808, 5484, 5648; vii, 183; and viii, 137).

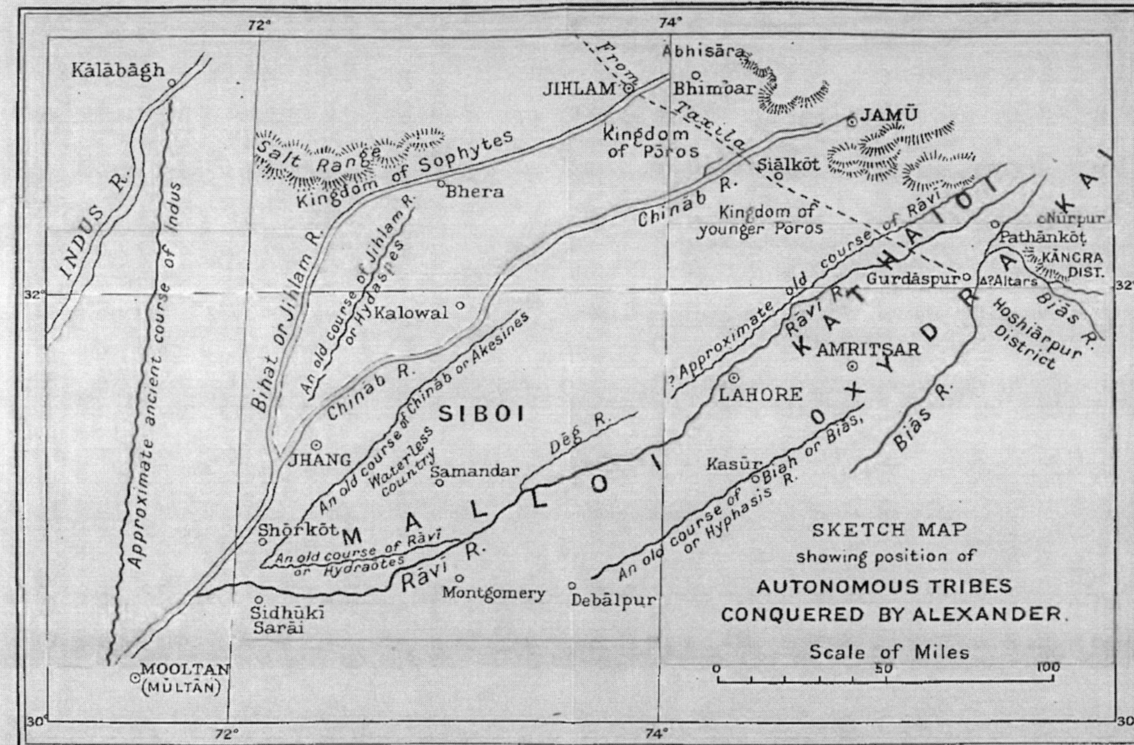
SKETCH MAP
showing position of
AUTONOMOUS TRIBES
CONQUERED BY ALEXANDER.
Scale of Miles
0 50 100
Kālābāgh
INDUS R.
Approximate ancient course of Indus
Salt Range
Kingdom of Sophytes
Bhera
JIHLAM
From Taxila
Abhisāra
Bhimbar
Kingdom of Pōros
JAMŪ
Siālkōt
Chinab R.
Kingdom of younger Poros
Bihat or Jihlam R.
An old course of Jihlam R. or Hydaspes
Kalowal
Chinab R.
An old course of Chinab or Akesines
Waterless country
SIBOI
JHANG
Samandar
Dēg R.
Shōrkōt
MALLOI
An old course of Rāvi or Hydraotes
Rāvi R.
Sidhūkī Sarāi
Montgomery
Debālpur
MOOLTAN (MULTĀN)
? Approximate old course of Rāvi
Rāvi R.
KATHAIOI
LAHORE
AMRITSAR
OXYDRAKAI
Kasūr
An old course of Biah or Biās, or Hyphasis R.
Biās R.
Gurdāspur
?Altars
Pathānkōt
Nūrpur
KĀNGRA DIST.
Hoshiārpur District
Biās R.
72°
74°
32°
30°

the fertile valley of the Hydraōtes, on both banks of the river. Their neighbours, the Oxydrakai (Sanskrit, Kshudrakā), who dwelt on the banks of the upper course of the Hyphasis, although ordinarily at war with the Malloi, had resolved to forget old enmities and to make common cause against the invader. The rival nations cemented the alliance by wholesale intermarriage, each giving and taking ten thousand young women for wives.[1] But personal jealousies, such as in all ages have reduced to futility political combinations in India, prevented the alliance from taking effect. While the allies were discussing the claims of rival generals to command, Alexander acted, and, with masterly strategy, sweeping down upon the Malloi, extinguished their military power before the Oxydrakai could come to their aid. The forces at the command of the confederacy should have sufficed, if properly handled, to annihilate the small flying column at Alexander's disposal; for they are said to have comprised 80,000 or 90,000 fully equipped infantry, 10,000 cavalry, and from 700 to 900 chariots.

Alexander's strategy.

The exact strength of the Macedonian field force is not stated, but it must have been very small, not exceeding a few thousands.[2] What it lacked in numbers was compensated for by its perfect mobility and the genius of its general. The Macedonians were alarmed at the magnitude of the opposing forces, and a repetition of the mutiny of the Hyphasis was with difficulty prevented by a stirring address delivered by the king. By two forced marches across the waterless uplands, now known as the *Bār*,[3] which separate the valleys of the Akesinēs and Hydraōtes, Alexander completely surprised the Malloi, most of whom were working unarmed in the fields. Many of the helpless wretches were ruthlessly cut down, 'without their even turning to offer

[1] Diodorus, xvii, 98.

[2] It consisted of the hypaspist infantry, the foot-archers, the Agrianian or Thracian light horse, the foot-guards under Peithōn, all the mounted archers, and half of the companion cavalry, or horse-guards. The force can hardly have exceeded 7,000 men in number.

[3] For the changes now effected in the *Bār*, see Sir James Douie, K.C.S.I., 'Canal Colonies in the Panjāb', 1915, reprinted from *The Monthly Bulletin* of Economics and Social Intelligence, year vi, No. 1, Jan. 1915.

resistance', and those who escaped the sword were shut up in the fortified towns.

Capture of towns.

One of these towns, with a citadel situated on a commanding height, was stormed under Alexander's personal direction, and 2,000 of the garrison were slain. Another town, against which Perdikkas had been sent, was found to be deserted. The inhabitants fled to the marshes in the river valley, but, even among the reeds and rushes, they could not escape the weapons of the Macedonian cavalry. Alexander then pushed on to the Hydraōtes, and caught up the retreating Malloi at the ford, inflicting severe loss upon them. He pursued them to the east of the river into the country now known as the Montgomery District, and took by mining and escalade a town inhabited by Brahmans. The king, with his customary disregard of danger, was the first man to scale the wall. The place was gallantly defended, but in vain; 'about 5,000 in all were killed, and as they were men of spirit, very few were taken prisoners'.

Retreat of the Malloi.

The Malloi, being hard pressed, recrossed the Hydraōtes, the passage of which they attempted to defend with 50,000 men; but they were no match for the Europeans, and fled 'with headlong speed' to the strongest fortified town in the neighbourhood. This small town, which cannot be identified precisely, and was situated somewhere near the boundary of the Jhang and Montgomery Districts, 80 or 90 miles to the north-east of Multan, was the scene of one of the most memorable incidents in Alexander's adventurous career, admirably described by Arrian from materials supplied by Ptolemy.[1]

Alexander's dangerous wound.

The Macedonians, already masters of the town, were endeavouring to scale the walls of the citadel, when Alex-

[1] The town was a small one (Strabo, xv, 33). The current assertion that it should be identified with Multān (=Mūlasthāna-pura, see Beal's *Hiuen Tsiang*, ii, 274) is absolutely baseless. The name Multān has no etymological connexion with the name Malloi, and Multān is much too far south. The campaign against the Malloi was fought in the valley of the Hydraōtes, where they occupied the fertile lowlands, corresponding to the Montgomery District and parts of Jhang. See Raverty, op. cit., p. 364, and my article in *J. R. A. S.*, Oct., 1903. Ptolemy himself did not take part in Alexander's defence, as some authors say that he did.

ander, thinking that the men bearing the ladders loitered too long, snatched one from the man carrying it, and mounted the wall, followed by only three companions, Peukestas, Leonnātos, and Abreas. Standing on the wall in his gleaming armour, the king was a mark for every missile, and, feeling that he could effect nothing where he was without support, boldly leaped down into the citadel followed by his three comrades. Abreas soon fell dead. Alexander, standing with his back to a tree that grew near the wall, slew the Indian governor and defended himself against all comers until his breast was pierced by an arrow and he fell. Peukestas bestrode him as he lay, covering him with the sacred shield brought from Ilion, while Leonnātos, although severely wounded like his surviving comrade, protected him from side attacks. The ladders having broken, the maddened Macedonians were for a time powerless to help their king, but at last a few managed to scramble up the earthen wall, while others broke in a gate, and so saved Alexander, who had fainted.

His recovery.

The barbed arrow was withdrawn by a bold operation which involved much bleeding and threatened immediate death, but Alexander's strong constitution eventually triumphed, and the dangerous wound was healed. The infuriated troops fell upon the unfortunate inhabitants, and slew them all—sparing neither man, woman, nor child.

When convalescent, Alexander was carried to the Hydraōtes, and conveyed by boat to the junction with the Akesinēs, where he met his fleet and army, under the command respectively of Nearchos and Hephaistion.

Submission of Malloi and Oxydrakai.

The survivors of the Malloi, whose nation had felt the full weight of Alexander's hand, now tendered their humble submission, and the Oxydrakai, whom fortunate procrastination had saved, feeling that resistance would be hopeless, purchased the conqueror's clemency by offers of tribute and the delivery of valuable gifts. Alexander, stern and even cruel to those who opposed him, but always courteous and generous to the submissive, readily accepted the proposals, presents, and excuses of the tribal envoys, a hundred in number, who are described as dignified men, of uncommon stature, clad in purple and gold, and riding in chariots. The presents are said to have included 1,030 four-horsed chariots, 1,000 bucklers of native manufacture, 100 talents of steel, great store of 'linen' goods, a quantity of tortoise-shells, the skins of large lizards, with tame lions and tigers, in addition to a contingent of 300 horsemen.[1]

Voyage to confluence with the Indus.

Philippos was then appointed satrap of the conquered nations; and the fleet, passing the third confluence, where the Hyphasis contributed its waters to the stream, continued

[1] These details are taken from Curtius, ix (chap. xxiii and xxiv of Delphin Edition). Arrian (vi, 14) mentions only 500 chariots, but Curtius probably had good authority for his statement. In the 10th impression of the annotated text by Dosson and Pichon (Paris, Hachette, 1916) the relevant chapters are numbered vii and viii. Chap. vii (p. 355) states that the two nations complied with a requisition for 2,500 horsemen, as in chap. xxiii of the Delphin Edition. The gifts in chap. viii (=xxiv of Delphin text) are as stated in my account, viz, 300 horsemen, 1,030 chariots, linen goods, lizard skins, &c. According to Delphin text (chap. xxiii) the envoys wore 'lineae vestes, intextae auro, purpuraque distinctae'. Prof. Jogeschandra Ray (*J.B.O.Res.Soc.*, vol. iii, June, 1917, 'Textile Industry in Ancient India') shows (pp. 187–97) that linen made of the fibre of the *atasi* (*alsi*) or flax plant was known in the time of the *Arthasāstra*, and for centuries before and after, but the manufacture was gradually superseded by cotton, and recently in Bengal by jute. The old general name for flax was *kshumā* (adj. *kshauma*). *Kshauma* was the name for linen, *dukūla* for the finest, and *aṭṭa* for the coarsest (p. 191). *Kshauma* was made from *atasi* fibre. It was used for bandages. *Dukūla* was woven of *atasi* thread. *Kshauma* was known in Vedic times, but after about the 12th century the correct meanings were forgotten and much confusion arose in the terminology, *kshauma* being taken to mean 'silk'. Coarse linen seems to have been made in Bengal as late as the eighteenth century (p. 196). The Bihār Planters' Association has proved that 'flax can be successfully grown and prepared at a profit in Bihār' [James Mackenna, *Agriculture in India*, 1915] (App., p. 236). Balfour (Cyclopaedia, 1885) observed that 'by proper treatment, however, good fibre can be got from plants raised in India'. Steel of peculiarly excellent quality has been produced in India from remote times. Curtius calls it *ferrum candidum*, which is assumed to mean 'steel', not 'tin', or more strictly, 'tin-plate' (*fer blanc*). Tortoise-shell (χελώνη) was still an article of Indian trade in the first century A. D. (*Periplus*, in *Ind. Ant.* viii, 111). The statement of Curtius (ix, 7) that Alexander imposed upon the Malloi and Oxydrakai 'the tribute which the two nations paid in instalments to the Arachosians' is unintelligible; and the name 'Arachosians' must be corrupt. Arachosia, the Kandahār country, cannot possibly have levied tribute from tribes in the Eastern Panjāb. Bacon makes a curious and inaccurate allusion to the Oxydrakai in his essay 'On the Vicissitudes of Things', apparently quoting loosely from Philostratos, *Life of Apollonios of Tyana*, ii, c. 33 (*Ind. Ant.*, 1906, p. 335).

its voyage to the fourth confluence, that of the Akesinēs (Chināb), including the Hydaspes (Jihlam), Hydraōtes (Rāvī), and Hyphasis (Biās), with the river which the ancient writers call the Indus. But it is probable that the 'lost river of Sind', the Hakrā or Wahindah, then existed, and that all the Panjāb rivers, including the Indus, joined it, and formed one great stream, afterwards known as the Mihrān of Sind.

Changes in rivers.

It is absolutely impossible to determine the position of any of the confluences in Alexander's time; but, long afterwards, in the days of the early Arab writers, all the rivers met at a place called Dosh-i-āb, or 'the Meeting of the Waters', in territory now belonging to the Bahāwalpur State.[1] Our complete uncertainty as to the courses of the rivers, which have ranged, as the old channels indicate, over a space of 110 miles wide in the region of the final confluence, deprives the remainder of Alexander's river voyage of much of its interest. His course in Upper Sind cannot be indicated even approximately, and it is impossible to fix accurately the position of either the towns or the nations mentioned by the historians.

Administrative arrangements.

The confluence of the combined Panjāb rivers with the 'Indus', wherever it may have been situated, was appointed to be the southern boundary of the satrapy of Philippos, to whom all the Thracians were made over along with an adequate force of infantry to form the garrison of his province. At about the same time the Bactrian nobleman, Oxyartes, father of Alexander's wife, Roxana, was deputed to the Paropanisadae, or the Kābul province, as satrap in succession to Tyriaspes, whose administration had been unsatisfactory. A city was founded at the confluence of the rivers with the 'Indus', which Alexander hoped would become prosperous and famous. Dockyards also were constructed.

[1] Raverty, op. cit., p. 473. The 'Meeting of the Waters' was near Bhagla or Baghlah, which is marked on the India Office map of 32 miles to the inch, in approximately N. lat. 28° 20′, E. long. 70° 30′. The four confluences are correctly enumerated by Arrian in *Anab.* vi, 14. The contradictory and unintelligible passage in the same author's *Indika*, ch. 4, is hopelessly corrupt.

Certain independent tribes, whom Arrian calls Abastanoi, Xathroi or Oxathroi, and Ossadioi, submitted or were subjugated, and it is noted that galleys of thirty oars and transport vessels were built and supplied by the Xathroi.[1] Although it is impossible to determine precisely either the correct names or the true positions of the tribes in Northern Sind mentioned by the various ancient authorities, the region occupied by the tribes referred to seems to be that lying to the north and south of N. lat. 28° and between E. long. 69° and 70° 30′. During this stage of the campaign, Krateros, who hitherto, from the beginning, had always marched on the right, or western, bank of each successive river, was transferred to the left, or eastern bank, which offered greater facilities for movement and was occupied by tribes less hostile than those on the other bank.[2]

Kingdom of Mousikanos. Alexander now hurried on in order to surprise the powerful monarch called Mousikanos by Arrian, who had proudly abstained from sending envoys or presents to the invader.

[1] Arrian, *Anab.* vi, 15. According to Curtius (ix, 8), Alexander came to a second nation called Malli (whom McCrindle confounds with the Malloi of the Rāvi), and then to the Sabarcae, a powerful tribe with a democratic form of government and no king. Their army was said to comprise 60,000 foot, 6,000 cavalry, and 500 chariots, under the command of three renowned generals. This nation submitted. The name Xathroi (v. l. Oxathroi) looks like a transcription of the Sanskrit Kshatriya. The Sabarcae are called Sambastai by Diodorus, who agrees with Curtius in his account of the government and military force of the tribe. Diodorus (xvii, 102) adds that two other tribes, the Sodrai and Massanoi, occupied both banks of the river, and that a city named Alexandria was founded within their borders, and occupied by a colony of 10,000 men. The attempts made by McCrindle and many other writers to localize these tribes are necessarily futile, inasmuch as we do not know where the river was. The mention in *Anab.* vi, 15, of Oxyartes as the colleague of Peithōn, satrap of the Lower Indus, is evidently, as Chinnock rightly observes, due to corruption of the text. The Thracians made over to Philippos seem to have been infantry; for the Agrianian light cavalry, who were Thracians, took part in subsequent operations.

[2] The words *διὰ τῆς Ἀραχωτῶν καὶ Δράγγων γῆς* in the passage (Arrian, *Anab.* vi, 15) describing the transfer of Krateros from the right to the left bank were evidently a blundering marginal note which has crept into the text. Krateros was sent from a point above the head of the Delta 'into Karmania by the route through the Arachotoi and Zarangoi' (*τὴν ἐπ' Ἀραχωτῶν καὶ Ζαράγγων*), as stated in ch. 17. McCrindle's theory that Krateros was sent, as stated in ch. 15, and subsequently recalled, seems to me very unsatisfactory. I have already noted another corruption in the text of the same chapter, due probably to the same cause, the absorption into the text of an erroneous gloss.

The capital of this stiff-necked king may be probably, although not certainly, identified with Alōr or Arōr, the ancient capital of Sind, now included in the Sukkur District, and situated in N. lat. 27° 39′, E. long. 68° 59′. The peculiarities of the people of this kingdom excited the surprise and admiration of the Macedonians. The inhabitants were believed to attain the age of a hundred and thirty years, their longevity being the result of good health secured by temperance in diet. Although their country possessed mines of both gold and silver, they refused to make use of either metal. Unlike the other Indians, they kept no slaves, employing in their stead 'young men in the flower of their age, as the Cretans employ the Aphamiōtai, and the Lacedaemonians the Helots'. They also resembled the Lacedaemonians in observing the custom of a public meal, at which the food served was the produce of the chase. They decline to study any science save that of medicine, and were reputed to have no system of civil law, the jurisdiction of the courts being confined to cases of murder and other violent crime.[1]

Submission and revolt of Mousikanos.

King Mousikanos, like the Malloi, being completely surprised by the rapidity of the movements of Alexander, who had reached the frontier before his departure from his last camp had been reported, hastened to meet the conqueror, bringing with him all his elephants and the choicest presents which India could offer. Alexander, with his habitual readiness to accept submission, received the king courteously, expressed much admiration of his capital and realm, and confirmed him in his sovereignty. But Mousikanos, acting under the advice of Brahman councillors, quickly repented of his ready submission, and revolted. Peithōn, the son of Agēnōr, who had been appointed satrap of the country to

[1] Strabo, xv, 34, 54. Strabo, on the authority of Onesikritos, points out that other authors do not seem to be justified in asserting that slavery was unknown everywhere in India. Megasthenes (Arrian, *Indikos*, ch. 10), affirmed it to be a great thing (μέγα) in India that all the Indians were free, and that no Indian slave existed (οὐδέ τινα δοῦλον εἶναι Ἰνδόν). In reality, mild praedial and domestic slavery seems to have been an institution in most parts of India from very remote times.

the south of the territory entrusted to Philippos, was sent in pursuit of the rebel;[1] while Alexander in person operated against the towns, some of which were destroyed, while others were occupied by garrisons. Mousikanos, having been captured by Peithōn, was executed along with the Brahmans who had instigated his defection.[2]

Oxykanos and Sambos.

Alexander next marched with a flying column against a chief named Oxykanos, who was taken prisoner. His two principal cities having been sacked, the other towns in the neighbourhood surrendered without attempting resistance; 'so much were the minds of all the Indians paralysed with abject terror by Alexander and the success of his arms.'[3] Another chieftain, named Sambos, whose capital was Sindimana,[4] and who had fled in terror, surrendered; and more Brahmans, who had instigated the revolt of an unnamed town, were executed. It is said that during this campaign on the Lower Indus 80,000 of the natives were killed, and multitudes sold as slaves.

After the execution of Mousikanos, the ruler of the Delta, which was known to the Greeks as Patalēnē, from its capital Patala, arrived in camp and proffered the submission of his kingdom, which was accepted. He was sent back to his country to prepare for the reception of the expedition.

Krateros sent home.

About the same time Krateros, one of Alexander's most trusted lieutenants, was detached with orders to conduct a large portion of the army into Karmania by the route leading through the territories of Arachosia (Kandahār)

[1] Peithōn was sole satrap of the Lower Indus, the mention of Oxyartes as his colleague being due to corruption of the text (*ante*, p. 104, note 1).

[2] *Κρεμάσαι Ἀλέξανδρος κελεύει.* McCrindle translates 'Alexander ordered the rebel to be hanged'; Gronovius renders 'Alexander crucifigi iubet'.

[3] *Οὕτω καὶ Ἰνδοὶ πάντες ἐδεδούλωντο ἤδη τῇ γνώμῃ πρὸς Ἀλεξάνδρου τε καὶ τῆς Ἀλεξάνδρου τύχης.* The translation is McCrindle's. Curtius speaks of 'the people known as the Musicani'; calls Oxykanos by the name of Porticanus; and states that his subjects were the Praesti. According to him, Porticanus was slain. The same author states that the troops of Sambos used poisoned swords (ix, 8).

[4] Sindimana may or may not have been Sihwān, with which it is commonly 'identified', for no better reason than that both names begin with S. The MSS. read Sindonalia. Readings of names in Strabo are open to much doubt. See Dübner's edition, Didot, Paris, 1853.

and Drangiana (Sistān).[1] The troops entrusted to Krateros comprised the brigades (τάξεις) of Attalos, Meleager, and Antigenes, besides some of the archers, the 'companions' or guards, and other Macedonians unfit for further active service. The elephants also accompanied this force.

Alexander's advance to Patala.

Alexander in person retained the command of the troops serving as marines, while Hephaistion was given supreme command of the rest of the army, which advanced on the right bank of the river. Krateros, who had been transferred to the left bank in Upper Sind, had, of course, been obliged to recross the stream in order to begin his homeward march. His place on the left bank was now taken by Peithōn, son of Agēnōr, who was given a mounted force of lancers and Agrianians, with instructions to place colonists in certain fortified towns, to suppress attempts at insurrection, maintain order, and ultimately rejoin Alexander at Patala. The prince (ὕπαρχος) and people of that city fled in terror, but were mostly reassured and induced to return to their homes (Arrian, *Anab.* vi, 17).

Patala.

The position of the city of Patala has been much disputed; but the best opinion is that it was at or near the very ancient site of Bahmanābād, situated in N. lat. 25° 52′ and E. long. 68° 52′, some 6 miles westward from the more modern city of Mansūriya. The apex of the Delta was probably near Kalari, about 40 miles north of Bahmanābād, in approximately N. lat. 26° 40′ and E. long. 68° 30′. For the discussion of Alexander's movements the identity of Patala and Bahmanābād may be assumed, although it cannot be fully proved.[2]

[1] All the experts are agreed that Krateros must have used the easy open route past Kalāt, through the Mulla (Mūla, Mulloh) Pass, along the modern caravan road. The Bolān and Quetta route did not come into use until recent times (Holdich, *The Gates of India*, 1910, p. 147; Sykes, *Ten Thousand Miles in Persia*, p. 49). The Mulla Pass is open all the year round (Masson, *Journeys*, ii, 120).

[2] Bahmanābād, Bahmannih, or Bahmannū, *not* Brahmanābād, as commonly and erroneously written. Under the name of Bahmanābād it was founded by Bahman, son of Isfandiyār, 'in the time of Gushtāsib, ruler of Irān-Zamīn'. Bahman is another name of Artaxerxes Longimanus, or Ahasuerus, who reigned from about 465 to 425 B.C. (Raverty, *Notes*, p. 510; Reinaud, *Ind. Ant.*, viii, 336). He was the grandson of Gushtāsib. But the site is much more ancient, and includes extensive prehistoric remains (*Progress Report, Arch. Survey W.I.* for 1896–7, par. 30–50; ibid., for

Exploration of Delta.

Alexander, considering Patala to be a position of high strategical importance, caused Hephaistion to construct a citadel there and to dig wells in the adjoining region. He proposed to make a great naval station at the point where the river divided, and remained sufficiently long on the spot to see some progress made in the construction of a roadstead and dockyard. He then resolved to explore personally both arms of the river down to the sea, and first sailed down the western or right branch, which probably debouched near or below Dēbal, the ancient port of Sind, distant about 15 miles from Thatha (Tatta). His sailors, accustomed to the tideless waters of the Mediterranean, were thrown into a state of great alarm and confusion by the ebb and flow of the tide, but ultimately Alexander succeeded in pushing on with some of the fastest vessels, and reaching the open sea. He sailed out a few miles into the deep, sacrificed bulls to Poseidon, and followed up the sacrifice by a libation, casting the golden vessels used in the ceremony into the ocean as a thank-offering.[1]

Preparations for leaving India.

He then returned to Patala, where he found the works of the new naval station well advanced, and proceeded to

1903–4, pp. 133–44). The site of Bahmanābād was discovered by Mr. Bellasis in 1854 (*Jo. Bo. Br. R. A. S.*, Jan., 1856). Mansūriya has been built from, and partly on, the ruins of the primitive city (Cousens, *Annual Rep. A. S. W., India*, 1903–4, pp. 132–44 ; 1908–9, pp. 79–87). Raverty's discursive note 105 (op. cit., pp. 196–205) gives much information. For the position of the apex of the Delta, and the city of Patala, see ibid., pp. 226, 461, 462. General Haig, who greatly underestimates the growth of the Delta, is certainly wrong in placing Patala below the latitude of Hyderābād (N. lat. 25° 23′, E. long. 68° 25′). The same writer was not aware of the evidence which led Raverty to place the most ancient known apex of the Delta 40 miles above Bahmanābād (*The Indus Delta Country*, pp. 1, 129, 135, 136, Kegan Paul & Co., 1894). Most books (e. g. Balfour's *Cyclopaedia*) erroneously identify Patala with Hyderābād.

[1] Curtius (ix, 9) gives a spirited and detailed account of the voyage from Patala to the sea. Thathah (Tatta) is in N. lat. 24° 45′, E. long. 67° 58′. In the seventeenth century (Sir Thomas Herbert, Thevernot, &c.) Dēbal or Dēwal was the southernmost town in Sind, and a much frequented seaport, distant about 15 miles from Thathah. The town has now utterly disappeared ; but it must have stood near to the shrine of Pīr Patho, or a little farther to the south-west, at the foot of the Makkahlī hills, and near the Bhāgar branch of the Indus, which was in those days a very great stream (Raverty, 'The Mihrān of Sind', pp. 317–31, note 315). Haig puts it at a ruin-covered site 20 miles SW. of Thathah (Holdich, *The Gates of India*, p. 310). That

explore the eastern, or left, branch of the river. Near its mouth he passed through a large lake, apparently that now known as the Samārāh lake, to the west of Umarkōt, and again reached the sea-shore in about latitude 25°.[1] Having spent three days in reconnoitring the coast and arranging for the construction of wells, he returned to Patala. Harbours and docks were built on the shores of the lake, and furnished with garrisons. Provisions to supply the forces for four months were collected, and all other necessary preparations were made for the two bold enterprises which he had planned: the voyage of the fleet along the coast to the Persian Gulf, and his own march with the army through Gedrosia in a direction, so far as might be practicable, parallel to the course of the fleet.

Alexander's plans.

His plans were conceived upon a comprehensive scale. Nearchos, the admiral who had successfully commanded the

identification seems to be correct. But Raverty (p. 321) makes a slip in saying that Herbert landed at 'Diul'. He landed at 'Swalley Road', off Sūrat (*Travels*, ed. 1677, p. 42). Diul is mentioned by him on p. 80 as a port.

[1] For an account of the Samārāh lake, see Raverty, op. cit., pp. 465, 477. It is marked as Samaro on the India Office map. In Alexander's time the Ran (Runn) of Cutch (Kachchh) must have been an estuary of the sea, extending northward to about parallel 25°, where the eastern arm of the great river fell into it. The lake was only a short distance from the mouth of the river (Arrian, *Anab.* vi, 20). The coast-line has extended enormously. The spot called Mughalbīn, where Akbar's officer, in Queen Elizabeth's time, stood to get a view of the ocean, is now quite 50 miles from the sea. Farther west, at Somniyāni, near the Purāli (Arabios) river, the coast has advanced at least 20 miles since Alexander's time. Most of the land to the south of Badīn, which stands in about N. lat. 24° 40′, has been formed since the reign of Akbar: the coast-line had a mean latitude of about 24° 30′ in the eighth century when the Arab conquest took place. In Alexander's time, a thousand years earlier, the coast-line was, of course, considerably farther north, but no man can delineate it with any approach to accuracy. The parallel of 25° may be taken as an approximate definition of the coast reconnoitred by Alexander. The land at the Kohrāī mouth (vulgo 'Khori Creek') now extends to about 23° 30′. (See Raverty, op. cit., pp. 468, 469, 470, 477, &c.; Haig, op. cit., pp. 136, 139; and a good paper by Mr. R. Sivewright 'Cutch and the Ran', *Geogr. Journal*, vol. xxix (1907), p. 518; also Sir Bartle Frere, 'Notes on the Runn of Cutch', ibid., 1871.) The first published account of the Runn is that by Alex. Burnes in his *Travels into Bokhara*, &c., 1835 (2nd ed., vol. i, chap. xvii). The sites of the old harbours were still pointed out, e. g. at Nerona, about 20 miles NNW. of Bhūj, at Charee, Puchum, &c. Anchor-stones were found, and at Wawania, the wreck of a large vessel 15 ft. below the surface (pp. 320–5). The same work gives details of the changes caused by the great earthquake of 1819.

flotilla during the ten months' voyage from Jihlam to the sea, was instructed to bring the fleet round the coast into the Persian Gulf as far as the mouth of the Euphrates, and to record careful observations of the strange lands and seas which he should visit. Alexander himself proposed to conduct the army back to Persia through the wilds of the country then called Gedrosia, and now known as Makrān, hitherto untrodden save by the legendary hosts of Semiramis and Cyrus, whom he desired to surpass. The king, who was independent of the winds, started on his march about the beginning of October, 325 B.C. Nearchos, being obliged to watch for the change of the monsoon, did not leave his anchorage in the river until two or three weeks later.[1]

Gedrosia. Although Gedrosia has usually remained outside the Indian political system, the province, or part of it, has been included from time to time within the dominions of the sovereigns of Hind, and its history cannot be regarded as altogether foreign to the history of India. But the satrapy of Gedrosia undoubtedly lay beyond the limits of India proper, and a summary narrative of the adventures met with by Nearchos on its coast and by his sovereign in its deserts will be sufficient to complete the story of Alexander's Indian campaign.

Alexander's Haven. Nearchos was detained for several days in the river, and, after much difficulty in making a passage for the ships round a bar, which obstructed the mouth of the western branch, ultimately got out to sea.[2] Contrary winds detained him for twenty-four days in a secure harbour, to which he gave the name of Alexander's Haven. The coast-line has been changed so much by both accretion and denudation that

[1] Nearchos is said to have started from his anchorage in the river on the twentieth day of the Athenian month Boëdromion (Sept.–Oct.), 325 B.C. This date seems to be correct. Alexander may have begun his march two or three weeks earlier. Aristoboulos (Strabo, xv, 17) is the authority for the descent of the rivers having lasted ten months. Patala was reached 'about the rising of the dog-star', July – August. The operations carried out at, or conducted from, Patala, must have occupied a considerable time.

[2] 'Bar', ἕρμα (*Indika*, 21). Some authors base 'identifications' on the translation of ἕρμα by 'rock'. Arrian goes on to say that Nearchos dug a channel through 'the softer part of the bar', ἵναπερ μαλθακὸν ἦν τοῦ ἕρματος.

attempts at detailed identifications of places near the mouth of the river are waste of time, but it is safe to affirm that the haven where Nearchos found shelter was not very far from the modern Karāchī (Kurrachee).[1] The admiral then crept cautiously along the inhospitable coast, his crews often suffering severely from lack of provisions and fresh water. After travelling 100 miles or so (850 *stadia*), the fleet reached the mouth of the river Arabis (the Habb), which formed the boundary between the Arabioi, the last people of Indian descent settled in this direction, and the Oreitai, who occupied an extensive territory to the west of the river.[2]

Having traversed an estimated distance of 800 *stadia* more, the fleet reached a place called Kokala, where the wearied crews were allowed to disembark and enjoy much needed rest. While the sailors were reposing here in a fortified camp (*Indika*, 23), Nearchos came into touch with Leonnātos, whom Alexander had detached with a field force to subdue the Oreitai (*Anab.* vi, 22). News arrived that a great battle had been fought in which Leonnātos had defeated the natives with terrible slaughter. The Oreitai are said to have lost 6,000 men and all their leaders out of a total force of 8,000 foot and 300 horse.[3] The Macedonian loss, although numerically small, was noteworthy because it included the colleague of Leonnātos, Apollophanes, who had recently been appointed satrap of the country.[4] Communications between Leonnātos and Nearchos having been established, the fleet was repaired and victualled, and sailors who had proved inefficient at sea were drafted into the army, their places being taken by

The Oreitai.

[1] Karāchī was founded in 1725 by some traders, migrating from another port which shoaled (Haig, 'Ibnu Batuta in Sindh', reprint, p. 410, from *Geogr. J.*).

[2] W. Tomaschek, 'Topographische Erläuterung der Küstenfahrt Nearchs vom Indus bis zum Euphrat' (*Sitzungs-Ber. d. Akad. d. Wissenschaften (philosoph-hist. Klasse)*, Wien, 1890, art. viii). The Habb is the Hab of *I.G.*

[3] Curtius, ix, 9.

[4] Arrian, *Indika*, 23. But the same author asserts in *Anabasis*, vi, 27, that Alexander, after his arrival at the Gedrosian capital, Poura (mod. Bāmpur), deposed Apollophanes from his satrapy, because he had utterly disregarded his instructions. Arrian then goes on to say that Thoas, who was appointed successor, soon died, and was succeeded by Sibyrtios. Curtius (ix, 10) asserts that the predecessor of Sibyrtios was Memnon, who was 'cut off by some malady'. I cannot reconcile these discrepancies.

men selected from the troops under the command of Leonnātos.

The savages.

Continuing their voyage westward, the ships passed along the coast near the mouth of the river Tomēros,[1] which was inhabited by a race of savages, ignorant of the use of iron, and armed only with wooden spears charred at the point to harden them. These wild men were covered with shaggy hair all over the body, and had claw-like nails strong enough to rip up fish and to split the softer kinds of wood. Their clothing was made of the skins of wild beasts or those of the larger fishes. After a skirmish with the savages, the fleet delayed for five days to effect repairs, and on the sixth day reached the rocky headland named Malana (now Rās Mālin) the western boundary of the Oreitai, who were not savages, but were dressed and armed like the inhabitants of India, although differing from them in language and customs.[2]

The Gedrosioi and Ichthyophagoi.

When the Malana cape had been passed, the inland people were known as Gedrosioi, and no longer as Oreitai.[3] The inhabitants of the coast continued to astonish the voyagers by their strange manners and customs. 'These poor wretches', we are told, 'had nothing but fish to live on', and so they were dubbed Ichthyophagoi, or 'Fish-eaters', by the Greeks. Whales, which were numerous along this coast, although very alarming to the sailors of the fleet, were extremely useful to the natives on shore, and supplied the materials for the better houses, which were built of whales' bones, the huge jaws serving as doorways, as they do still.[4]

[1] Now the Hingol.

[2] Diodorus agrees that the Oreitai in most respects closely resembled the Indians, but adds that they were in the habit of stripping the dead and exposing the bodies in the jungles to be devoured by the wild beasts.

[3] Arrian here uses the term Gedrosioi in a sense narrower than that of Strabo, who, when describing Ariāna (xv, ch. ii, 8, 9), seems to bring Gedrosia as far east as the Indus. No real discrepancy exists; the satrapy of Gedrosia doubtless included the country of the Oreitai and Arabioi as well as Gedrosia proper. The Oreitai are supposed to be now represented by the Lumri tribes of Las Bela, who claim Rājpūt descent. The Gadurs, one of the Lumri clans, may represent the Gedrosioi.

[4] The habits of the people on the coast are absolutely unchanged. Men, women, children, dogs, camels, cats, and cattle, all eat fish (*Geogr. J.*, 1896, p. 388). Philostratus was correctly informed when he wrote that 'the sheep of the country . . . are queer feeders—the shepherds pasture them on fish, as they do on figs in Caria' (*Apollonius*, iii, 55).

The seamen on board the ships of Nearchos, being superstitious like the sailors of all ages and countries, were much frightened at the weird tales told about an uninhabited island, which Arrian calls Nosala (*Indika*, 31), and which is now known as Astola, Astalu, Hashtalu, or Haftala—the Selēra of Philostratus. It lies nearly midway between Urmera and Pasni headlands, and is to this day as much an object of dread to the Med fishermen as it was long ago to the Greek sailors.[1] Enchanted isle.

Thus threading their way through all dangers, real or imaginary, the explorers made their way to a port called Badis, near Cape Jask at the entrance to the Straits of Ormuz, and so came into touch with the more civilized province of Karmania. Proceeding through the straits, the delighted mariners found themselves at Harmozeia (Ormuz), a charming place, producing everything that they wanted, except olives. Here the men came ashore and were gratefully enjoying their rest, when some of the more adventurous spirits strolled inland, and were astounded to meet a stranger wearing Greek clothes and speaking Greek. Tears came to their eyes as they heard the familiar sounds of home in that strange and distant land. Explanations having been exchanged, the stranger proved to be a straggler from Alexander's army, and gave the welcome information that the king was only five days' march distant. Arrival of fleet at Ormuz.

Nearchos and Archias at once arranged to go inland to meet their sovereign, and, after many difficulties, made their way to his presence, but so ragged and unkempt were they that Alexander at first could not recognize them. When at last he was convinced of his friends' identity, he assumed Meeting of Nearchos and Alexander.

[1] Holdich, *The Indian Borderland* (Methuen, 1901), p. 206; *The Gates of India*, p. 160. On the whole, according to this author, the coast-line of Makrān is not greatly changed, and most of the ports and landing-places visited by Nearchos can be identified, although many islands have been destroyed by erosion. The name of the province, which is generally spelt Makrān or Mekrān, is written Mukrān by Raverty. Holdich's lecture entitled 'A Retreat from India' (*J. United Service Inst. India*, 1894, p. 112, with map) is the best modern authority for the details of the Gedrosian march. The same author gives a map of Alexander's route in 'Notes on Ancient and Mediaeval Makran' (*Geogr. J.*, 1896).

hastily that they must be the sole miserable survivors from his lost fleet, and was in despair at the imagined disaster. But he was soon reassured by Nearchos, who told him that the ships were safe and sound, hauled up at the mouth of the Anamis river for repairs.

Voyage to the Tigris.

The admiral, having volunteered to conduct the fleet up the Gulf to Sūsa, returned to the coast, to which he was obliged to fight his way, and thence sailed on, with little adventure, to the mouth of the Euphrates. He then heard of Alexander's approach to Sūsa, and turning back, entered the Tigris to meet him, and 'it was thus that the expedition which had started from the mouth of the Indus was brought in safety to Alexander' (Arrian, *Indika*, 42).

Sufferings of Alexander's army.

The difficulties encountered by the army under the command of Alexander were even greater than those met and overcome by the fleet under Nearchos. The king seems to have been ignorant of the existence of the Hala range of mountains, which terminates in Cape Mālin. This great obstacle, which he was obliged to turn, deranged his plans, and compelled him to penetrate far into the interior, and for a time to lose touch with the fleet. The army suffered agonies from thirst, and the unfortunate followers perished by thousands. 'The blazing heat and want of water,' Arrian tells us, 'destroyed a great part of the army, and especially the beasts of burden, which perished from the great depth of the sand, and the heat which scorched like fire, while a great many died of thirst.' Ultimately, the remnant of the force worked its way back to the coast, emerging near the harbour of Pasni, almost on the line where the telegraph wire now runs, and its sufferings were at an end. But the soldiers had been obliged 'to burn the rich spoils taken from their enemies, for the sake of which they had marched to the utmost extremities of the East'. The success of the general was the ruin of the private.

Revolt in Panjāb.

While the army was still in Karmania, a report was received that Philippos, satrap of the Indian provinces north of the confluence of the Akesinēs with the Indus, had been treacherously murdered by his mercenary troops. Although

ALEXANDER THE GREAT: THE TIVOLI HERM

(See page xi)

this disquieting communication was accompanied by the information that the murderers had been slain by the satrap's Macedonian body-guard, Alexander was not then in a position to make permanent arrangements, and was obliged to content himself with sending a dispatch to India directing Āmbhi, king of Taxila, and Eudēmos, commandant of a Thracian contingent on the Upper Indus (Curtius, x, 1, 11), to assume the administration of the province until a satrap could be appointed in due course. The death of Alexander at Babylon in the following year (June, 323 B. C.) [1] effectually prevented any attempt being made to retain effective control over the conquered countries east of the Indus.

India abandoned by Macedonian government.

When the second partition of the empire was effected at Triparadeisos in 321 B. C., Antipater practically recognized the independence of India by appointing the native kings Pōros and Āmbhi as a matter of form to the charge of the Indus valley and Panjāb. Peithōn, whom Alexander had appointed satrap of the Indus Delta, was transferred to the provinces 'which bordered on the Paropanisadai', i. e. to Arachosia, &c., west of the Indus, and India was abandoned by the Macedonian government in reality, though not in name.[2] Eudēmos, alone of the Macedonian officers, retained some authority in the Indus valley until about 317.[3]

Duration of Alexander's campaign.

The Indian expedition of Alexander may be said to have lasted for three years, from May, 327 B. C., when he crossed the Hindū Kush, to May, 324 B. C., when he entered Sūsa. Out of this period about nineteen months were spent in India east of the Indus, from February or March, 326 B. C.,

[1] The attempts of German scholars to fix the precise day of the month are based on insufficient data (Hogarth, *Philip and Alexander of Macedon*, Appendix).

[2] Diodorus, xviii, 39: 'Antipater then divided the satrapies anew . . . and gave India, which bordered on the Paropanisadai, to Peithōn, the son of Agēnōr, and of the adjacent kingdoms he gave that which lay along the Indus to Pōros, and that along the Hydaspes to Taxiles, for it was impossible to remove their kings without royal troops under the command of some distinguished general.' In this passage the names of Pōros and Taxiles (i. e. Āmbhi, king of Taxila) evidently have been transposed. The Indus valley would naturally fall to the share of the Taxilan king, rather than to Pōros, whose dominions lay to the east of the Hydaspes.

[3] Arrian (*Anab.* vi, 27) writes Εὔδημος; Diodorus (xix, 14) writes Εὔδαμος.

when he crossed the bridge at Ohind, until September or October in the following year, when he entered the territory of the Arabioi.

The genius of Alexander.

Looked at merely from the soldier's point of view, the achievements wrought in that brief space of time are marvellous and incomparable. The strategy, tactics, and organization of the operations give the reader of the story the impression that in all these matters perfection was attained. The professional military critic may justly blame Alexander, as his own officers blamed him, for excessive display of personal heroism, and needless exposure to danger of the precious life upon which the safety of the whole army depended; but criticism is silenced by admiration, and by the reflection that the example set by the king's reckless daring was of incalculable value as a stimulus and encouragement to troops often ready to despair of success.

Three great enterprises.

The descent of the rivers to the ocean through the territories of civilized and well-armed nations, admittedly the best soldiers in the east, and the voyage of Nearchos from the Indus to the Tigris, may fairly be described as unqualified successes. The third great enterprise, the retirement of the army led by Alexander in person through Gedrosia,[1] would have been equally prosperous but for the occurrence of physical difficulties, which could not be foreseen owing to the imperfection of the information at the king's command. But even this operation was not a failure. Notwithstanding the terrible privations endured and the heavy losses suffered, the army emerged from the deserts as an organized and disciplined force, and its commander's purpose was attained.

Substantial success.

On the whole, Alexander's Indian campaign was a success. It was not really marred by the mutiny at the Hyphasis. If his soldiers had permitted him to plunge more deeply into the interior, he would probably have been unable to maintain the communication with his European base on which his safety depended, and his small, isolated force might have been overwhelmed by the mere numbers of his adversaries. Koinos and his fellow remonstrants may be credited with

[1] Gedrosia (Strabo and Pliny); Gadrosia (Γαδρωσία, Arrian).

having prevented the annihilation of the Macedonian army.

Asiatic weakness.

The triumphant progress of Alexander from the Himalaya to the sea demonstrated the inherent weakness of the greatest Asiatic armies when confronted with European skill and discipline. The dreaded elephants lost their terrors, and proved to be a poor defence against the Macedonian cavalry. The unopposed march of Krateros from Sind to Persia through Sīstān opened up an alternative land route and solved the problem of easy overland communication with Europe. The circumnavigation of the coast by Nearchos gave Alexander a third line of communication by sea, and, if he had lived, there is no reason to suppose that he would have experienced serious difficulty in retaining his hold upon the Panjāb and Sind.

Effects of Alexander's death.

All his proceedings prove conclusively that he intended the permanent annexation of those provinces to his empire, and the measures which he took for the purpose were apparently adequate to ensure success. But Alexander's premature death destroyed the fruits of his well-planned and successful enterprise. Within three years of his departure, his officers had been ousted, his garrisons destroyed, and almost all trace of his rule had disappeared. The colonies which he founded in India, unlike those established in the other Asiatic provinces, took no root. The campaign, although carefully designed to secure a permanent conquest, was in actual effect no more than a brilliantly successful raid on a gigantic scale, which left upon India no mark save the horrid scars of bloody war.[1]

India unchanged.

India remained unchanged. The wounds of battle were quickly healed; the ravaged fields smiled again as the patient oxen and no less patient husbandmen resumed their interrupted labours; and the places of the slain myriads

[1] A writer in the *Times Lit. Suppl.* of March 2, 1916, p. 101, speaks of Alexander's 'amazing insight in choosing sites for towns . . . Very little that he did was ever undone. And the greatest thing that he did was to give the whole (*sic*) civilized world for the first time a common language and culture, and to break down the barrier between East and West. In this way he may be called one of the chief forerunners of Christianity'.

were filled by the teeming swarms of a population, which knows no limit save those imposed by the cruelty of man, or the still more pitiless operations of nature. India was not hellenized. She continued to live her life of 'splendid isolation', and soon forgot the passing of the Macedonian storm.[1] No Indian author, Hindu, Buddhist, or Jain, makes even the faintest allusion to Alexander or his deeds.

[1] The paradox of Niese to the effect that the whole subsequent development of India was dependent upon Alexander's institutions is not, I think, true in any sense, or supported by a single fact. His words are: 'Man kann daher mit Recht behaupten, dass von den Einrichtungen Alexanders die ganze weitere Entwickclung Indiens abhängig gewesen ist' (*Geschichte der griechischen und makedonischen Staaten seit der Schlacht bei Chaeronea*, I. Teil, p. 508; Gotha, 1893). The often-quoted lines by Matthew Arnold (*Obermann*) are much more to the point:—

'The East bowed low before the blast
In patient, deep disdain;
She let the legions thunder past,
And plunged in thought again.

Mr. Edwyn Bevan has kindly drawn my attention to the following German publications on Alexander's Indian campaign, viz.:—

1. Max. Graf Yorck v. Wartenburg, *Kurze Uebersicht der Feldzüge Alexanders des Grossen*, Berlin, Mittler and Son, 1897. The author adopts the erroneous theory that the Hydaspes was crossed at Jalālpur, and, like the other writers cited in this note, shows no acquaintance with modern literature on the subject in English. His attempt to exhibit on a map the courses of the rivers in Alexander's time is purely imaginary, and unsupported by any evidence.

2. C. Schubert, 'Die Porusschlacht' (*Rheinisches Museum für Philologie*, Band lxvi (1901), pp. 543–62). Some of the author's views differ from mine. I do not believe that any serious advance of knowledge can be secured, until people agree as to the crossing-place and then test the historian's accounts by prolonged local investigation.

3. Hans Delbrück, *Geschichte der Kriegskunst u. a.*, erster Teil, 2te Auflage (Stilke, Berlin, 1908), pp. 214–25. I agree that Alexander probably did not bring 100,000 or 120,000 men across the Hindū Kush and that most of the statistics of armies in ancient authors are untrustworthy. See *supra*, p. 52, note 2.

I have looked through all the three publications and do not find reason to alter my text. The treatise by A. E. Anspach, *De Alexandri Magni Expeditione Indica* (Teubner, Leipzig, 1902, 1903) is useful for critical annotations on the Greek and Latin writers, but they are too minute for me to utilize.

CHRONOLOGY OF THE INDIAN CAMPAIGN OF ALEXANDER THE GREAT

FROM MAY, 327, TO MAY, 324 B. C.

DATE B. C.	EVENT.
327	**The Advance.**
Early in May .	Passage of Hindū Kush mountains over the Khāwak and Kaoshān passes.
June	From Nikaia (probably Jalālābād), Alexander with picked force proceeds to the subjugation of the mountains; Hephaistion with rest of army advancing to the Indus, probably through the valley of the Kābul river.
August . . .	Capture of stronghold of Astes (Hasti) by Hephaistion after thirty days' siege.
September . .	Alexander subdivides his force, advancing in person against the Aspasians; he crosses the Gouraios (Panjkora) river, captures Massaga of the Assakenians, and massacres 7,000 Indian mercenaries.
November . .	Siege of Aornos.
December . .	Capture of Aornos.
326	
January . . .	Arrival of Alexander at bridge-head at Ohind.
January to February	Halt of army for thirty days.
February or March	Passage of Indus 'in beginning of spring'; halt at Taxila.
April	Advance eastward.
May	Arrival at the Hydaspes (Jihlam) river.
Beginning of July	Battle of the Hydaspes; defeat of Pōros.
July	Foundation of Nikaia and Boukephala; passage of the Akesinēs (Chināb) river near the foot of the hills.
August . . .	Passage of the Hydraōtes (Rāvī) river, and conflict with the Kathaeans.
September . .	Arrival at the Hyphasis (Biās) river; refusal of army to proceed farther.
	The Retreat.
Sept.–October .	Retirement to the Hydaspes (Jihlam) river.
End of October .	Commencement of voyage down the rivers, and of march of army escorting the fleet.
325	
January . . .	Collapse of the Mallian power.
Till September .	Voyage continued, fighting with the Sogdoi, Sambos, Mousikanos, &c.
Beginning of October	Departure of Alexander to march through Gedrosia.
End of October .	Nearchos starts on voyage to the Persian Gulf.

DATE B. C.	EVENT.
324	
Early in January	Arrival of Alexander at Poura (Bāmpur), the Gedrosian capital, sixty days distant from Ora.
January . . .	Halt of army at Poura.
February . . .	March through Karmania, about 300 miles.
End of April or beginning of May	Arrival at Sūsa in Persia, after about 500 miles of marching from western frontier of Karmania.
323	
June	**Death of Alexander at Babylon.**

NOTE.—The time spent by Alexander in India proper, from his passage of the Indus in March, 326, until his departure for Gedrosia in the end of September or the beginning of October, 325, was about nineteen months. The voyage down the river occupied about ten months out of this period, and the march from India to Sūsa was effected in about seven months. The march from the Bactrian frontier, that is to say, the Hindū Kush, to the Indus, and the subjugation of the mountain tribes on the north-western frontier of India were completed in ten months.

I. May, 327, to February, 326, inclusive : march from Hindū Kush to Indus, about ten months.

II. March, 326, to September, 325, inclusive : in India proper, nearly nineteen months.

III. October, 325, to April, 324, inclusive : march to Sūsa, seven months.

TOTAL DURATION OF EXPEDITION, THREE YEARS.

CHAPTER V

CHANDRAGUPTA MAURYA AND BINDUSĀRA, FROM 322 B.C. TO 273 B.C.

Eudēmos.

WHEN Alexander quitted the Panjāb he posted no Macedonian garrisons in that province, making over the care of his interests to king Pōros, who must have been independent in practice. Āmbhi, king of Taxila, was also entrusted with authority as a colleague of Pōros. After the assassination of Philippos, Alexander had sent orders from Karmania to Eudēmos, commandant of a Thracian garrison on the Indus, to act as Resident pending the appointment of a satrap, and to supervise the native princes. But the officer had no adequate force at his command to enforce his authority, which must have been purely nominal. He managed, however, to remain in India, probably somewhere in the basin of the Indus, until about 317 B.C., when he departed to help Eumenes against Antigonos, taking with him a hundred and twenty elephants, and a small force of infantry and cavalry. He had obtained the elephants by treacherously slaying a native prince, perhaps Pōros, with whom he had been associated as a colleague.[1]

Peithōn, &c.

The province of Sind, on the Lower Indus, below the great confluence of the rivers, which had been entrusted by Alexander to Peithōn, son of Agēnōr, remained under Greek influence for a period still shorter. At the time of the second partition of the Macedonian empire in 321 B.C. at Triparadeisos, Antipater was avowedly unable to exercise any effective control over the Indian Rājas,[2] and Peithōn had been obliged already to retire to the west of the Indus.

[1] Ἐκ δὲ τῆς Ἰνδικῆς Εὔδαμος παρεγένετο μεθ' ἱππέων μὲν πεντακοσίων [v.l. τριακοσίων], πεζῶν δὲ τρισχιλίων [v.l. τριακοσίων], ἐλεφάντων δὲ ἑκατὸν εἴκοσι· τὰ δὲ θηρία ταῦτα παρέλαβε μετὰ τὴν Ἀλεξάνδρου τελευτήν, δολοφονήσας Πῶρον [v.l. πρῶτον] τὸν βασιλέα (Diodorus, xix, 14).

[2] Οὐ γὰρ ἦν τούτους τοὺς βασιλεῖς μετακινῆσαι χωρὶς βασιλικῆς δυνάμεως καὶ ἡγεμονίας ἐπιφανοῦς (Diodorus, xviii, 39).

The Indian provinces to the east of the river were consequently ignored in the partition, and Peithōn was content to accept the government of the regions bordering on the Paropanisadai, or Kābul country. That country probably continued to be administered by Roxana's father Oxyartes, whom Alexander had appointed satrap. Sibyrtios was confirmed in the government of Arachosia and Gedrosia; Stasandros, the Cyprian, was given Aria and Drangiana, and his countryman Stasanor was appointed governor of Bactria and Sogdiana.[1] These arrangements clearly prove that in 321 B. C., within two years of Alexander's death, the Greek power, to the east of the Indus, had been extinguished, with the slight exception of the small territory, wherever it may have been, which Eudēmos managed to hold for some four years longer.

Native revolt. The insecurity of the Macedonian authority in the newly annexed Indian provinces had been proved by the assassination of Philippos, the report of which was received while Alexander was in Karmania, and might be expected to return some day to the scene of his victories. His death in June, 323 B. C., dispelled all fears of his return, and the native princes undoubtedly took the earliest possible opportunity to assert their independence and exterminate the weak foreign garrisons. The news of Alexander's decease was known in India probably as early as August, but no serious fighting would have been undertaken by ordinary commanders until the beginning of the cold season in October; for Alexander's indifference to climatic conditions was not shared by Indian chiefs, who were accustomed to regulate their military movements strictly in accordance with precedent. We may feel assured that as soon as the news of the conqueror's death had been confirmed beyond doubt, and the season permitted the execution of military operations with facility, a general rising took place, and that Macedonian authority in India was at an end early in

[1] Ἀρίαν δὲ καὶ Δραγγιάνην Στασάνδρῳ τῷ Κυπρίῳ· τὴν δὲ Βακτριανὴν καὶ Σογδιανὴν Στασάνορι τῷ Σολίῳ, ἀπὸ τῆς αὐτῆς ὄντι νήσου (Diodorus, xviii, 9). McCrindle (*Invasion of India by Alexander the Great*, 2nd ed., p. 411) confounds these two officers.

322 B. C., except the small remnant to which Eudēmos continued to cling.

Early life of Chandragupta.

The leader of the revolt against the foreigners was an able adventurer, Chandragupta by name, at that time a young man, probably not more than twenty-five years of age. On the father's side he was a scion of the royal house of Magadha—the principal state in Northern India—and it has hitherto been supposed that his mother, or, according to another version, his grandmother, was of lowly origin, and that, in accordance with Hindu law, he belonged to her caste, and had to bear the reproach of inferior social rank. The family name Maurya, assumed by the members of the dynasty founded by Chandragupta, is said to be a derivative from Murā, his mother's or grandmother's name. There are, however, grounds for holding that Chandragupta, so far from being of low caste, was related to the respectable Early Nandas. Whatever be the truth, young Chandragupta in some way incurred the displeasure of his kinsman, Mahāpadma Nanda, the reigning king of Magadha, and was obliged to go into exile.[1] During his banishment he had the good fortune to see Alexander, and is said to have expressed the opinion that the Macedonian king, if he had advanced, would have made an easy conquest of the great kingdom on the Ganges, by reason of the extreme unpopularity of the reigning monarch.[2] Mahāpadma Nanda was reputed to be the son of a barber, who had secured the affections of the late queen. The guilty pair had then murdered the king, whose throne was seized by the barber-paramour. His son, the now reigning monarch, was avaricious and profligate, and naturally possessed few friends.

[1] 'He was born in humble life . . . when by his insolent behaviour he had offended Nandrus [=Nanda], and was ordered by that king to be put to death, he sought safety by a speedy flight' (Justin, xv, 4, with von Gutschmid's emendation of *Nandrum* for *Alexandrum*, McCrindle, pp. 327, 405). The *Mudrā Rākshasa* play lays great emphasis on the low-caste origin of Chandragupta, and on his relationship to the Nanda king. But see reference to Harit Krishna Deb's views in note 1, p. 44 *ante*. It is hardly safe to rely wholly for matter-of-fact history on a work of imagination composed several centuries after the events dramatized. The character of Mahāpadma Nanda himself may have suffered from tales spread by sectarian rancour.

[2] Plutarch, *Alexander*, ch. 62.

Usurpation of throne of Magadha. 322 B. C.

Chandragupta, having collected, during his exile, a formidable force of the warlike and predatory clans on the north-western frontier, attacked the Macedonian garrisons after Alexander's death, and conquered the Panjāb. It appears probable that before he undertook the expulsion of the foreign garrisons, he had already overthrown his unpopular relation, the Nanda king of Magadha, whom he deposed and slew. The dramatist who tells the story asserts, and no doubt with truth, that Nanda's race perished utterly and was exterminated. The adviser of the youthful and inexperienced Chandragupta in this revolution was a Brahman named Vishnugupta, better known by his patronymic Chānakya, or his surname Kautilya, by whose aid he succeeded in seizing the vacant throne. But the people did not gain much by the change of masters, because Chandragupta, 'after his victory, forfeited by his tyranny all title to the name of liberator, oppressing with servitude the very people whom he had emancipated from foreign thraldom'. He inherited from his Nanda predecessor a huge army, which he increased until it numbered 30,000 cavalry, 9,000 elephants, 600,000 infantry, and a multitude of chariots. With this irresistible force all the Northern States, probably as far as the Narbadā, or even farther, were overrun and subjugated; so that the dominions of Chandragupta, the first historical paramount sovereign or emperor in India, extended from the Bay of Bengal to the Arabian Sea.

Invasion of Seleukos Nikator.

While Chandragupta was engaged in the consolidation of his empire, a rival was laying the foundations of his power in Western and Central Asia, and preparing to attempt the recovery of Alexander's Indian conquests. In the course of the internecine struggle between the generals of Alexander, two had emerged as competitors for supreme power in Asia —Antigonos and Seleukos, who afterwards became known as Nikātor, or the Conqueror. Fortune at first favoured Antigonos, and drove his antagonist into exile; but, in

312 B. C. 312 B. C., Seleukos recovered possession of Babylon, and six years later felt himself justified in assuming the regal style

and title. He is conventionally described as king of Syria, but was in reality the lord of Western and Central Asia.[1] The eastern provinces of his realm extended to the borders of India; and he naturally desired to recover the Macedonian conquests in that country, which had been practically abandoned, although never formally relinquished. In pursuit of this object Seleukos crossed the Indus in or about 305 B. C., 305 B. C.
and attempted to imitate the victorious march of Alexander.[2] The details of the campaign are not known, and it is impossible to determine how far the invading army penetrated into the Gangetic valley, if at all, but the result of the war is certain.

Treaty between Seleukos and Chandragupta.

When the shock of battle came, the hosts of Chandragupta were too strong for the invader, and Seleukos was obliged to retire and conclude a humiliating peace. Not only was he compelled to abandon all thought of conquest in India, but he was constrained to surrender a large part of Ariāna to the west of the Indus. In exchange for the comparatively trifling equivalent of five hundred elephants, Chandragupta received the satrapies of the Paropanisadai, Aria, and Arachosia, the capitals of which were respectively the cities now known as Kābul, Herāt, and Kandahār. The satrapy of Gedrosia, or at least the eastern portion of it, seems also to have been included in the cession, and the high contracting powers ratified the peace by 'a matrimonial alliance', which phrase probably means that Seleukos gave a daughter to his Indian rival. This treaty may be dated in 303 B. C. 303 B. C.
As soon as it was concluded Seleukos started on his long march westward to confront Antigonos, whom he defeated and slew at Ipsos in Phrygia in 301 B. C.[3] Ipsos being 301 B. C.

[1] See Mr. Bevan's work, *The House of Seleucus*.

[2] 'Transitum deinde in Indiam fecit', &c. (Justin, xv, 4); *καὶ τὸν Ἰνδὸν περάσας ἐπολέμησεν Ἀνδροκόττῳ* [Chandragupta], *βασιλεῖ τῶν περὶ αὐτὸν Ἰνδῶν, μέχρι φιλίαν αὐτῷ καὶ κῆδος συνέθετο* (Appian, *Syr.* 55). Strabo (Bk. ii, ch. ii, 9) substitutes for the last two words, *συνθέμενος ἐπιγαμίαν*.

[3] Niese's notion that Chandragupta recognized the sovereignty of Seleukos (*die Oberhoheit des Seleukos anerkannte*) has no foundation, except the anecdote that Chandragupta paid honour to the altars set up by Alexander at the Hyphasis. The facts that Seleukos retired from India, giving up valuable provinces in exchange for only 500 elephants out of the 9,000 possessed by Chandragupta, that he entered into a matrimonial

distant at least 2,500 miles from the Indus, the march to it must have occupied a year or more.

North-western frontier. The range of the Hindū Kush mountains, known to the Greeks as the Paropanisos or Indian Caucasus, in this way became the frontier between Chandragupta's provinces of Herāt and Kābul on the south, and the Seleukidan province of Bactria on the north. The first Indian emperor, more than two thousand years ago, thus entered into possession of that 'scientific frontier' sighed for in vain by his English successors, and never held in its entirety even by the Moghal monarchs of the sixteenth and seventeenth centuries.

Achievements of Chandragupta. In the course of some eighteen years Chandragupta had expelled the Macedonian garrisons from the Panjāb and Sind, repulsed and humbled Seleukos the Conqueror, and established himself as undisputed supreme lord of at least all Northern India and a large part of Ariāna. These achievements fairly entitle him to rank among the greatest and most successful kings known to history. A realm so vast and various as that of Chandragupta was not to be governed by weakness. The strong hand which won the empire was needed to keep it, and the government was administered with stern severity.[1] About six years after the withdrawal of Seleukos, Chandragupta either abdicated or
298 B. C. died (298 B. C.), and handed on the imperial succession to his son Bindusāra, who is also known by the title of Amitraghāta, 'Slayer of Foes.'

Megasthenes, c. 302 B.C. Soon after the conclusion of peace in or about 303 B. C., Seleukos had sent as his envoy to the court of Chandragupta an officer named Megasthenes, who had been employed under Sibyrtios, satrap of Arachosia. The envoy resided for a con-

alliance, and sent an ambassador, clearly indicate the real nature of the relations between the sovereigns. Megasthenes exhibits the greatest respect for the Indian monarch, and never presumed to regard himself as the Resident at the court of a feudatory. Concerning the extent of the cession of Ariāna see Appendix F.

[1] Justin, xv, 4, and the details given by Megasthenes. The passage in Justin's compilation is one of the most important concerning Chandragupta. The testimonies of the various Greek and Roman authors are collected in McCrindle's books and in Wilson's preface to his translation of the *Mudrā Rākshasa*. That play, probably composed in the fifth century, very likely embodies a kernel of genuine historical tradition, of which I have made cautious use.

siderable time at Pātaliputra (now Patna), the capital of the Indian empire, and employed his leisure in compiling an excellent account of the geography, products, and institutions of India, which continued to be the principal authority on the subject until modern times. Although often misled by erroneous information received from others, Megasthenes is a veracious and trustworthy witness concerning matters which came under his personal observation, and his vivid account of Chandragupta's civil and military administration may be accepted without hesitation as true and accurate.[1] That account, although preserved in a fragmentary form, is so full and detailed that a modern reader is more minutely informed in many respects concerning the institutions of Chandragupta than he is about those of any Indian sovereign until the days of Akbar, the contemporary of Queen Elizabeth.

Pātaliputra, the imperial capital, which had been founded in the fifth century B. C., stood in the tongue of land formed by the confluence of the Sōn with the Ganges, on the northern bank of the former, and a few miles distant from the latter. The site is now occupied by the large native city of Patna and the English civil station of Bankipore, but the rivers changed their courses many centuries ago, and the confluence is at present near the cantonment of Dinapore, about 12 miles above Patna. The ancient city, which lies buried below its modern successor, was, like it, a long, narrow parallelogram, measuring about 9 miles in length and 1½ miles in breadth. It was defended by a massive

Pāṭaliputra, the capital.

[1] The fragments of Megasthenes have been collected and edited by Schwanbeck under the title of *Megasthenis Indika* (Bonn, 1846); and translated by McCrindle in *Ancient India as described by Megasthenes and Arrian* (Trübner, London, 1877). Arrian (*Indika*, 17) rightly brackets Nearchos and Megasthenes as trustworthy persons (δοκίμω ἄνδρε). Strabo, who was disgusted by some of the travellers' tales repeated by Megasthenes, unjustly stigmatizes him as a liar. The information collected by Megasthenes was supplemented by the works of other writers, of whose books fragments have been preserved by the authors to whom we are indebted for our knowledge of Megasthenes. For a list of these authors see Schwanbeck, op. cit., Index I. McCrindle's books, six in number, give a nearly complete collection of the passages in Greek and Roman authors treating of ancient India.

timber palisade, pierced by sixty-four gates, crowned by five hundred and seventy towers, and protected externally by a broad and deep moat, filled from the waters of the Sōn.[1]

Palace. The royal palace, although chiefly constructed of timber, was considered to excel in splendour and magnificence the palaces of Sūsa and Ekbatana, its gilded pillars being adorned with golden vines and silver birds. The buildings stood in an extensive park, studded with fish-ponds and furnished with a great variety of ornamental trees and shrubs.

Court. Here the imperial court was maintained with barbaric and luxurious ostentation. Basins and goblets of gold, some measuring six feet in width, richly carved tables and chairs of state, vessels of Indian copper set with precious stones, and gorgeous embroidered robes were to be seen in profusion, and contributed to the brilliancy of the public ceremonies. When the king condescended to show himself in public on state occasions he was carried in a golden palanquin, adorned with tassels of pearls, and was clothed in fine muslin embroidered with purple and gold. When making short journeys he rode on horseback, but when travelling longer distances he was mounted, like a modern

[1] See Lt.-Col. Waddell's treatise, *Discovery of the Exact Site of Asoka's Classic Capital of Pātaliputra* (Calcutta, 1892, and revised edition, 1903). Some fragments of the timber palisade have been found. The remains of one of the Maurya palaces are buried under the houses and fields of the village of Kumrāhār, on the south side of the railway between Bankipore and Patna. Excavations conducted at Kumrāhār by Dr. Spooner of the Archaeological Survey at the cost of the late Sir Ratan Tata, of Bombay, have revealed remains of a 'Hall of 100 Pillars', apparently copied from the prototype at Persepolis. The work, which is still in progress, has been partially described in *Ann. Rep. Arch. Survey of India, Eastern Circle*, 1912–13, pp. 55–61, and results of profound interest are expected. Sir J. Marshall has found a 'Mauryan *chaitya*-hall' at Sanchi. Another palace, that described by Hiuen Tsang, was in the city, probably in the neighbourhood of the Sadar Galī and Kallū Khan's Bāgh, where an Asoka pillar is hidden in a zenana (P. C. Mukharji, unpubl. report). The ruins at Kumrāhār represent the town of Ni-li, which Asoka built, as stated by Fa-hien. Cunningham was mistaken in believing that Pāṭaliputra had been mostly cut away by the rivers. Patna is in N. lat. 25° 37′, E. long. 85° 10′. Chāṇakya (*Arthaśāstra*, Bk. ii, ch. 3, revised English version by R. Shamasastry, Bangalore Government Press, 1915, pp. 56–60) lays down elaborate rules for the fortification of the capital.

Rāja, on an elephant with golden trappings.[1] Combats of animals were a favourite diversion, as they still are at the courts of native princes, and the king took delight in witnessing the fights of bulls, rams, elephants, rhinoceroses, and other animals. Gladiatorial contests between men were also exhibited. A curious entertainment, which seems not to be known in the present age, was afforded by ox-races, which were made the subject of keen betting, and were watched by the king with the closest interest. The course was one of 30 *stadia*, or 6,000 yards, and the race was run with cars, each of which was drawn by a mixed team of horses and oxen, the horses being in the centre with an ox on each side. Trotting oxen are still largely used for drawing travelling carriages in many parts of India, but the breed of racers seems to be extinct.[2]

Chase.

The principal royal amusement was the chase, which was conducted with great ceremony, the game in an enclosed preserve being driven up to a platform occupied by the king, who shot the animals with arrows; but, if the hunt took place in the open country, he used to ride an elephant. When hunting he was closely attended by armed female guards, who were obtained by purchase from foreign countries, and formed an indispensable element in the courts of the ancient Indian monarchs. The road for the sovereign's procession was marked off with ropes, which it was death to pass.[3] The institution of the Royal Hunt was abolished by Chandragupta's grandson, Asoka, in 259 B. C.

[1] Curtius, viii, 9; Strabo, xv, 69.

[2] Aelian, Περὶ ζῴων ἰδιότητος, Bk. xiii, ch. 18; Bk. xv, ch. 15. Compare the Burmese incident: 'Walking out one day, I met a waggon drawn by four stout oxen going at a hand-gallop, and driven by a country girl standing up in her vehicle, who seemed to manage the reins and a long whip with equal dexterity' (Symes, *Embassy to Ava*, vol. i, p. 294, Constable). That girl could have taken part in a race. Modern Burma presents many illustrations of ancient India. Dr. Coomaraswamy informs me that 'bull-racing' is a 'very common pastime in Ceylon and creates immense excitement. The bulls are harnessed to the light cars called "hackeries"'. In 1679, when Dr. Fryer was at Surat, ox-races were still in favour (Fryer, *A New Account*, &c., Hakluyt Soc., 1915, vol. iii, pp. 157, 158).

[3] Megasthenes, *Fragm.* xxvii. The Greek is τῷ δὲ παρελθόντι ἐντὸς μέχρι γυναικῶν θάνατος, which McCrindle renders 'it is death for man and woman alike to pass the

Habits of the king.

As a rule, the king remained within the precincts of the inner palace, under the protection of his Amazonian bodyguard, and appeared in public only to hear causes, offer sacrifice, and to go on military or hunting expeditions. Probably he was expected to show himself to his subjects at least once a day, and then to receive petitions and decide disputes in person. Like the modern Indians, Chandragupta took pleasure in massage or friction of the limbs, and custom required that he should indulge in this luxury while giving public audience; four attendants used to massage him with ebony rollers during the time that he was engaged in disposing of cases.[1] In accordance with Persian custom, which had much influence upon the Indian court and administration, the king ceremonially washed his hair on his birthday, which was celebrated by a splendid festival, at which the nobles were expected to make rich presents to their sovereign.[2]

Plots.

In the midst of all the gold and glitter, and in spite of the most elaborate precautions, uneasy lay the head that

ropes', but the Greek idiom will not bear this translation. Müller correctly renders 'quodsi quis interius ad mulieres [*scil.* to the female guards] usque accedit, interficitur'. This rendering, perhaps, would require the text to read τῶν γυναικῶν. The word τῶν may have dropped out. The female guards are mentioned in the Sanskrit plays. In the *Mudrā Rākshasa*, Act iii, Chandragupta is represented as attended by a girl named Sonottarā. The girls were bought from their parents (Strabo, xv, 55); and good-looking maidens for the royal harem (παρθένοι εὐειδεῖς πρὸς παλλακίαν) were still regularly imported in the first century A. D. at Barygaza (Broach), on the western coast (*Periplus*, ch. 49; see also chs. 8, 9, 31, 36; transl. Schoff; Longmans, 1912). Chāṇakya prescribes that 'On getting up from bed, the king should be received by troops of women armed with bows' (*Arthaśāstra*, Bk. i, ch. 21; revised English version by R. Shamasastry, Bangalore Government Press, 1915, p. 47).

[1] Such an attendant (*saṁvāhaka*) is a minor character in the *Toycart*, or *Little Clay-cart*, drama; transl. by Ryder, in *Harvard Oriental Series*, vol. iv (1905).

[2] Strabo, xv, 69; Herodotus, ix, 110. The fact is mentioned by Herodotus in connexion with the horrible story of the wife of Masistes. As the Persian hair-washing festival was celebrated on the king's birthday, the Indian imitation presumably was celebrated on the same occasion ('Persian Influence on Maurya India', *Ind. Ant.*, 1905, p. 201). The shaven heads, now favoured by most Hindus, were not fashionable in ancient India. The Indians, we are told, 'frequently comb, but seldom cut, the hair of their head. The beard of the chin they never cut at all, but they shave off the hair from the rest of the face, so that it looks polished' (Curtius, viii, 9).

wore the crown. The king's life was so constantly threatened by plots that he dared not incur the risk either of sleeping in the day-time or occupying the same bedroom two nights in succession.[1] The dramatist brings vividly before us the astuteness of the Brahman counsellor who detected the plots of both the poisoners and

'The brave men who were concealed
In the subtérrene avenue that led
To Chandragupta's sleeping chamber—thence
To steal by night, and kill him as he slept'.[2]

Military strength.

The army, to which Chandragupta owed his throne and empire, was maintained at enormous numerical strength, and so organized, equipped, and administered as to attain a high degree of efficiency, as measured by an Oriental standard. It was not a militia, but a standing army, drawing liberal and regular pay, and supplied by the government with horses, arms, equipment, and stores.[3] The force at the command of Mahāpadma Nanda is said to have numbered 80,000 horse, 200,000 foot, 8,000 chariots, and 6,000 fighting elephants. This huge force was greatly augmented by Chandragupta, who raised the numbers of the infantry to 600,000, and also had 30,000 horse, and 9,000 elephants, besides chariots, all permanently enrolled in a regularly paid establishment.[4] The elephants were esteemed the most valuable section of the imperial host, because, as Chānakya observes, 'it is on elephants that the destruction of an enemy's army depends'.[5]

Arms.

Each horseman carried two lances, resembling the kind called *saunia* by the Greeks, and a buckler. All the infantry carried the broadsword as their principal weapon, and as additional arms, either javelins, or bow and arrows. The arrow was discharged with the aid of pressure from the left

[1] Strabo, xv, 55. So, in Burma, king Badonsachen or Bodoahpra (A. D. 1782–1819), after his escape from a conspiracy, began the practice of changing daily his chamber and bed (Sangermano, *Burmese Empire*, ed. Jardine, p. 65).

[2] *Mudrā Rākshasa*, Act ii (Wilson, *Theatre*, ii, 184).

[3] Diodorus, ii, 41.

[4] Pliny, vi, 19; Plutarch, *Alex.* ch. 62.

[5] *Arthaśāstra*, Bk. vii, chap. 11 (*Ind. Ant.*, 1910, p. 68).

foot on the extremity of the bow resting upon the ground, and with such force that neither shield nor breastplate could withstand it.[1]

Chariots and elephants.

Each chariot, which might be drawn by either four or two horses, accommodated two fighting-men besides the driver; and an elephant, in addition to the mahout, or driver, carried three archers.[2] The 9,000 elephants therefore implied a force of 36,000 men, and the 8,000 chariots, supposing them to be no more numerous than those kept by Mahāpadma Nanda, required 24,000 men to work them. The total number of soldiers in the army would thus have been 600,000 infantry, 30,000 horsemen, 36,000 men with the elephants, and 24,000 with the chariots, or 690,000 in all, excluding followers and attendants.

Size of Indian armies.

These high figures, which may seem incredible at first sight, are justified by our knowledge of the unwieldy hosts used in war by Indian kings in later ages. For instance, Nuñez, the Portuguese chronicler, who was contemporary with Krishna Deva, the Rāja of Vijayanagar, in the sixteenth century (1509–29), affirms that that prince led against Raichūr an army consisting of 703,000 foot, 32,600 horse, and 551 elephants, besides camp followers.[3]

War Office.

The formidable force at the disposal of Chandragupta, by far the largest in India,[4] was controlled and administered under the direction of a War Office organized on an elaborate system. A commission of thirty members was divided into six Boards, each with five members, to which departments were severally assigned as follows: Board No. I, in

[1] Arrian, *Indika*, ch. 16.

[2] Strabo, xv, 52; Aelian, xiii, 10. The chariots of Pōros in the Panjāb were each 'drawn by four horses, and carried six men, of whom two were shield-bearers, two, archers posted on each side of the chariot, and the other two, charioteers, as well as men-at-arms, for when the fighting was at close quarters they dropped the reins and hurled dart after dart against the enemy' (Curtius, viii, 14; *ante*, p. 26).

[3] Sewell, *A Forgotten Empire*, p. 147. Many other proofs of the unwieldy size of Indian armies might be cited.

[4] 'The powerful Āndhra kingdom (*validior gens*) possessed only 100,000 infantry, 2,000 cavalry, and 1,000 elephants. 'Sed omnium in India prope, non modo in hoc tractu, potentiam claritatemque antecedunt Prasii, amplissima urbe ditissimaque Palibothra' [*scil.* Pāṭaliputra] (Pliny, vi, 19).

co-operation with the admiral—Admiralty; Board No. II—Transport, Commissariat, and Army service, including the provision of drummers, grooms, mechanics, and grass-cutters; Board No. III—Infantry; Board No. IV—Cavalry; Board No. V—War-chariots; Board No. VI—Elephants.

Efficient organization.

All Indian armies had been regarded from time immemorial as normally comprising the four arms, cavalry, infantry, elephants, and chariots; and each of these arms would naturally fall under the control of a distinct authority; but the addition of co-ordinate supply and admiralty departments appears to be an innovation due to the genius of Chandragupta. His organization must have been as efficient in practice as it was systematic on paper, for it enabled him not only, in the words of Plutarch, to 'overrun and subdue all India', but also to expel the Macedonian garrisons, and to repel the invasion of Seleukos.

Civil administration.

The details recorded concerning the civil administration of Chandragupta's empire, if not so copious as we might desire, are yet sufficient to enable us to realize the system of government; which, although, of course, based upon the personal autocracy of the sovereign, was something better than a merely arbitrary tyranny.

Municipal Commission.

The administration of the capital city, Pātaliputra, was provided for by the formation of a Municipal Commission, consisting of thirty members, divided, like the War Office Commission of equal numbers, into six Boards or Committees of five members each. These Boards may be regarded as an official development of the ordinary non-official *panchāyat*, or committee of five members, by which every caste and trade in India has been accustomed to regulate its internal affairs from time immemorial.

Industrial arts.

The first Municipal Board, which was entrusted with the superintendence of everything relating to the industrial arts, was doubtless responsible for fixing the rates of wages, and must have been prepared to enforce the use of pure and sound materials, as well as the performance of a fair day's work for fair wages, as determined by the authorities.

Artisans were regarded as being in a special manner devoted to the royal service, and capital punishment was inflicted on any person who impaired the efficiency of a craftsman by causing the loss of a hand or an eye.

Foreigners.

The second Board devoted its energies to the case of foreign residents and visitors, and performed duties which in modern Europe are entrusted to the consuls representing foreign powers. All foreigners were closely watched by officials, who provided suitable lodgings, escorts, and, in case of need, medical attendance. Deceased strangers were decently buried, and their estates were administered by the commissioners, who forwarded the assets to the persons entitled.[1] The existence of these elaborate regulations is conclusive proof that the Maurya empire in the fourth and third centuries B. C. was in constant intercourse with foreign states, and that large numbers of strangers visited the capital on business.

Vital statistics.

The third Board was responsible for the systematic registration of births and deaths, and we are expressly informed that the system of registration was enforced for the information of the government, as well as for facility in levying the taxes. The taxation referred to probably was a poll-tax, at the rate of so much a head annually. Nothing in the legislation of Chandragupta is more astonishing to the observer familiar with the lax methods of ordinary Oriental governments than this registration of births and deaths. The spontaneous adoption of such a measure by an Indian native state in modern times is unheard of, and it is impossible to imagine an old-fashioned Rāja feeling anxious 'that births and deaths among both high and low might not be concealed '. Even the Anglo-Indian administration, with its complex organization and European notions of the value of statistical information, did not attempt the collection

[1] These officials corresponded exactly with the Greek πρόξενοι, and it is possible that Chandragupta borrowed this institution from Greece. But his other arrangements show no trace of Greek influence. For a good account of προξενία, see Newton's *Essays on Art and Archaeology*, pp. 121–3 (' Consular Officers in India and Greece ', *Ind. Ant.*, 1905, p. 200).

of vital statistics until very recent times, and always has experienced great difficulty in securing reasonable accuracy in the figures.

Trade.

The important domain of trade and commerce was the province of the fourth Board, which regulated sales, and enforced the use of duly stamped weights and measures. Merchants paid a licence tax, and the trader who dealt in more than one class of commodity paid double.

Manufactures.

The fifth Board was responsible for the supervision of manufacturers on similar lines. A curious regulation prescribed the separation of new from old goods, and imposed a fine for violation of the rule. The reason for this prescription was that traffic in old goods, whether by sale or mortgage, was prohibited, unless official sanction had been obtained, which could be granted only on certain conditions.[1]

Tithe on sales.

The collection of a tithe of the value of the goods sold was the business of the sixth and last Board, and evasion of this tax was punishable with death. Similar taxation on sales always has been common in India, but rarely, if ever, has its collection been enforced by a penalty so formidable as that exacted by Chandragupta.

General municipal administration.

Our detailed information relates only to the municipal administration of Pātaliputra, the capital, but it is reasonable to infer that Taxila, Ujjain, and the other great cities of the empire were governed on the same principles and by similar methods. The 'Borderers' Edict' of Asoka is addressed to the officers in charge of the city of Tosali in Kalinga.[2]

In addition to the special departmental duties above detailed, the Municipal Commissioners in their collective capacity were required to control all the affairs of the city, and to keep in order the markets, temples, harbours, and generally speaking, all public works.[3]

[1] *Arthaśāstra*, Bk. iv, chaps. 2 and 7.

[2] V. A. Smith, *Asoka, the Buddhist Emperor of India*, 3rd ed., p. 193.

[3] Fragment xxxiv in Schwanbeck, from *Strabo*, xv, 1, 51; translated by McCrindle in *Ancient India as described by Megasthenes and Arrian*, p. 87, and again (re-

Viceroys. The administration of the distant provinces was entrusted to viceroys, probably, as a rule, members of the royal family. The information concerning the viceroyalties being more complete for Asoka's reign than for that of Chandragupta, the subject will be referred to again when Asoka's system of administration is discussed.

News-writers. In accordance with the usual practice of Oriental monarchies, the court kept watch over the more remote functionaries by means of special agents or 'news-writers', the *akhbār navīs* of modern times, who are called 'overseers' and 'inspectors' (ἔφοροι, ἐπίσκοποι) by the Greek authors, and are mentioned in the Asoka Edicts as the king's 'men', (*pulisāni*, Pillar Edict VI), or 'reporters' (*pativedakā*, Rock Edict VI). The duty of these officers was to superintend or oversee all that occurred in town or country and to make private reports to the government. Arrian notes that similar officers were employed by the authorities of the independent nations as well as by the monarchical governments of India. They did not disdain to utilize as coadjutors the courtesans of the camp and city, and must have transmitted at times to their masters strange packets of scandalous gossip.[1] Arrian's informants assured him that the reports sent in were always true, and that no Indian could be

vised) in *Ancient India as described in Classical Literature*, p. 54. The words ἀπὸ συσσήμου, twice mistranslated by McCrindle as 'by public notice', really mean 'with official stamp', the *abhijñāna-mudrā* of the *Arthaśāstra*, Bk. ii, chap. 21. Similar regulations continued in use until comparatively recent times. The French traveller Tavernier (1st ed., 1675) tells us that at Benares there were 'two galleries where they sell cottons, silken stuffs, and other kinds of merchandise. The majority of those who vend the goods are the workers who have made the pieces, and in this manner foreigners obtain them at first hand. These workers, before exposing anything for sale, have to go to him who holds the contract [*scil.* for collecting the tax on sales], in order to get the king's stamp impressed on the pieces of calico or silk, otherwise they are fined and flogged' (V. Ball, transl. Tavernier, *Travels in India*, I, 118).

It is interesting to note that the cotton fabrics of Benares were famous in Maurya times. The best kinds came from Madura in the south, the Konkan, Kalinga, Benares, Eastern Bengal (Vanga), Vatsa or Kauśāmbī, and Mahishmatī (Mandhāta on the Narbadā) (*Arthaśāstra*, Bk. ii, chap. 12). The harbours were those on the Sōn and Ganges rivers. The remains of the brick embankments along the old course of the Sōn can still be traced.

[1] The statement that the courtesans were utilized as informers is in Strabo, xv, 48.

accused of lying; but it is permissible to doubt the strict accuracy of this statement, although it is certainly the fact that the people of ancient India enjoyed a widespread and enviable reputation for straightforwardness and honesty.[1]

Penal code.

The general honesty of the people and the efficient administration of the criminal law are both attested by the observation recorded by Megasthenes, that while he resided in Chandragupta's camp, containing 400,000 persons, the total of the thefts reported in any one day did not exceed two hundred *drachmai*, or about eight pounds sterling. When crime did occur it was repressed with terrible severity. Ordinary wounding by mutilation was punished by the corresponding mutilation of the offender, in addition to the amputation of his hand. If the injured person happened to be an artisan devoted to the royal service, the penalty was death. The crime of giving false evidence was visited with mutilation of the extremities; and in certain unspecified cases, offences were punished by the shaving of the offender's hair, a penalty regarded as specially infamous.[2] Injury to a sacred tree,[3] evasion of the municipal tithe on goods sold, and intrusion on the royal procession going to the hunt were all alike capitally punishable. These recorded instances of severity are sufficient to prove that the code of criminal law, as a whole, must have been characterized by uncompromising sternness and slight regard for human life.

Land revenue.

The native law of India has ordinarily recognized agri-

[1] The evidence is summarized by Max Müller in *India, what can it teach us?* (8vo ed. 1883, p. 54).

[2] This was a Persian punishment. 'Lighter crimes are punished by cutting off the nose, or perhaps only the hair. Sometimes one-half of the scalp is shaved, and a tablet affixed to the neck, so inflicting disgrace on the offender' (Kingsmill, in *Athenaeum*, July 19, 1902, quoting a Chinese work of the sixth century, entitled *Wei-Shu*, with reference to the Sassanian period). The offences for which shaving of the head was one of the optional penalties are specified in the *Arthaśāstra*, Bk. iv. ch. 9. For petty thefts of articles worth ¼ to ½ a silver *paṇa* (say 3*d.* to 6*d.*) the penalties prescribed were (1) a fine of 6 *paṇas*, or (2) shaving the head, or (3) exile. If the value was between 1 *paṇa* and 2 *paṇas*, the penalties were (1) a fine of 24 *paṇas*, (2) shaving the head with a piece of brick, or (3) exile. The operation with the brick must have been extreme torture, a terrible punishment for a trivial theft. The value of the silver *paṇa* (146 grains of impure silver) may be taken as about a shilling.

[3] Curtius, viii, 9.

cultural land as being crown property, and has admitted the undoubted right of the ruling power to levy a crown rent, or 'land revenue', amounting to a considerable portion, either of the gross produce or of its cash value.[1] Even the English laws, which, contrary to general ancient custom, recognize private property in cultivable land, insist that the land revenue is the first charge on the soil, and permit the enforcement of the charge by sale of the land free of all incumbrances, in the event of default. The land revenue is still the mainstay of Indian finance. So it must have been in the days of Chandragupta. The details of his system of 'settlement', or valuation and assessment of the land, have not been preserved, and it is not known whether a fresh valuation was made annually, or at longer intervals. The normal share of the gross produce taken by the Crown is said to have been one-fourth; but in practice, no doubt, the proportion taken varied largely, as it does to this day, and all provinces could not be treated alike. Certain other unspecified dues were also levied. The army being a professional force, recruited from the fighting castes, the agricultural population was exempt from military service; and Megasthenes noted with surprise and admiration that the husbandmen could pursue their calling in peace, while the professional soldiers of hostile kings engaged in battle.[2]

Irrigation. The proper regulation of irrigation is a matter of prime

[1] 'Those who are well versed in the Śāstras admit that the king is the owner of both land and water, and that the people can exercise their right of ownership over all other things excepting these two' (Comment on *Arthaśāstra*, Bk. ii, chap. 24).

The Malabar coast offers an exception to the general rule. Dubois (*Hindu Manners*, &c., 3rd ed., Beauchamp (1906), p. 56) expounds the system of proprietary rights in land and of slavery as the special peculiarities of the Malabar coast, where the predial slaves went with the land, although they might be sold separately. He believed Malabar—i. e. the region occupied by 'the Nairs, the Coorgs, and the Tulus, the three aboriginal tribes of the Malabar coast', to be the only province in India where full private proprietary right 'has been preserved intact until the present day. . . . Here the lands may be alienated, sold, given away, or disposed of according to the will of the owners'.

[2] Strabo, xv, 40. In this passage the erroneous statement occurs that the cultivator received one-fourth of the produce. Diodorus correctly states that the land revenue was one-fourth of the gross produce.

importance in India; and it is much to the credit of Chandragupta that he maintained a special Irrigation Department charged with the duty of measuring the lands, and so regulating the sluices that every one should receive his fair share of the life-giving water. The allusion to the measurement of lands as part of the duty of the Irrigation Department indicates that a water-rate must have been levied, and the reference to sluices implies a regular system of canals.[1]

The Sudarśana lake.

The inscription of the Satrap Rudradāman, engraved soon after the year A. D. 150 on the famous rock at Girnār in Kāthiāwār, on which Asoka, four centuries earlier, had recorded a version of his immortal edicts, bears direct testimony to the care bestowed by the central government upon the question of irrigation, even in the most remote provinces. Although Girnār is situated close to the Arabian Sea, at a distance of at least 1,000 miles from the Maurya capital, the needs of the local farmers did not escape the imperial notice. Pushyagupta, the Vaisya, who was Chandragupta's governor of the western provinces, saw that by damming up a small stream a reservoir of great value for irrigation could be provided. He accordingly formed a lake called Sudarsana, 'the Beautiful', between the citadel on the east side of the hill and the 'inscription rock' farther to the east, but failed to complete the necessary supplemental channels. These were constructed in the reign of Chandragupta's grandson Asoka, under the superintendence of his representative, Rāja Tushāspha, who was then viceroy. These beneficent works constructed under the patronage of the Maurya emperors endured for four hundred years, but in the year A. D. 150 a storm of exceptional violence destroyed the embankment, and with it the lake.

Rebuilding of the dam.

The embankment was then rebuilt 'three times stronger' than before by order of the Saka Satrap Rudradāman, who has recorded the history of the work in an inscription which is the only known epigraphic record containing the names

[1] We know from the *Arthaśāstra* that heavy water-rates were actually levied, and that canals were maintained under strict regulations.

of Chandragupta and Asoka Maurya. Notwithstanding the triple strength of Rudradāman's masonry, it too failed to withstand the fury of the elements; the dam again burst, and was repaired once more in A. D. 458 by the local governor serving under Skandagupta. At some time unknown these ancient works fell to ruin, and the lake thus finally disappeared. Its site, buried in deep jungle, was so utterly forgotten that modern local inquirers have experienced difficulty in ascertaining its exact position.

Imperial care for irrigation.

The fact that so much pains and expense were lavished upon this irrigation work in a remote dependency of the empire is conclusive evidence that the provision of water for the fields was recognized as an imperative duty by the great Maurya emperors, and is a striking illustration of the accuracy of Megasthenes' remark that imperial officers were wont to 'measure the land, as in Egypt, and inspect the sluices by which water is distributed into the branch canals, so that every one may enjoy his fair share of the benefit'.[1]

Strict control.

The central government, by means of local officers, exercised strict control and maintained close supervision over all classes and castes of the population. Even the Brahman astrologers and soothsayers, and sacrificial priests, whom Megasthenes erroneously described as forming a separate class of 'philosophers' or 'sophists',[2] received

[1] Fragment xxxiv, in Strabo, xv, 1, 50. The antiquities of Girnār (Jūnāgaṛh) are described by Burgess in *Reports Archaeol. Survey W.I.*, vol. ii, and the position of the lake is defined by Cousens in the *Progress Report* of the same Survey for 1898–9, par. 49. For Rudradāman's inscription see the latest ed. by Prof. Kielhorn in *Ep. Ind.*, viii, 36, and the abstract version in Lüders's *List*, No. 965 (*Ep. Ind.*, x, App. p. 99). It is the earliest considerable inscription in the Sanskrit language. The earliest short inscription in pure Sanskrit known at present is that on the *yūpa* or sacrificial post at Isāpur near Mathurā, dated in the year 24 in the reign of Shāhi Vāsishka (*Ann. Rep. A. S., India*, for 1910–11, pp. 39–48, with plates. The inscription is only a few years earlier than that of Rudradāman). The term *rāshtriya* applied to Pushyagupta in that record should be rendered 'governor'. Tushāspha is called a 'Yāvana', but the form of the name shows that he must have been a Persian (*Ep. Ind.*, viii, 46, note).

See also note in *Ind. Ant.*, xlviii, Aug. 1919, pp. 145–6, by Hemchandra Raychauduri, who suggests that Tushāspha may have been a Greek (Yāvana) who had adopted an Iranian name, just as the Yāvana Dhammadeva, the Saka Ushavadāta, and the Kushān Vāsudeva adopted Hindu names.

[2] Megasthenes has a peculiar

their share of official attention, and were rewarded or punished according as their predictions and observations proved correct or mistaken. Among the artisans, shipbuilders and armour-makers were salaried public servants, and were not permitted, it is said, to work for any private person. The wood-cutters, carpenters, blacksmiths, and miners were subject to special supervision, of which the nature is not defined.

Riding regulations.

According to Strabo, no private person was permitted to keep either a horse or an elephant, the possession of either animal being a royal privilege. But this assertion is undoubtedly inaccurate, if taken as applicable to all parts of the country, and is corrected by the reasonable and detailed observations of Arrian (*Indika*, 17). That author tells us that the mounts used commonly were horses, camels, and asses, elephants being used only by the wealthy, and considered specially appropriate for the service of royalty. Except as regards asses, which are now looked upon with contempt, and restricted to the humblest services as beasts of burden for potters and washermen, the statement of Arrian applies accurately to modern India.[1] To ride an elephant

enumeration of the occupational classes (*γενεαί*), commonly mistranslated 'castes', which he reckoned as seven ('*ἐς ἑπτὰ μάλιστα γενεάς*' = to about 7): (1) the 'sophists' (*σοφισταί*); (2) agriculturists (*γεωργοί*); (3) herdsmen, shepherds, and graziers (*νομέες, ποιμένες, βουκόλοι*); (4) artisans and traders (*τὸ δημιουργικόν τε καὶ καπηλικὸν γένος*); (5) the military (*πολεμισταί*); (6) the overseers (*ἐπίσκοποι*); (7) the councillors (*οἱ ὑπὲρ τῶν κοινῶν βουλευόμενοι ὁμοῦ τῷ βασιλεῖ, ἢ κατὰ πόλιας ὅσαι αὐτόνομοι σὺν τῇσιν ἀρχῇσι*, Fragm. xxxii of Schwanbeck, from Arrian, *Indika*, 11, 12). Strabo calls No. 1, *τοὺς φιλοσόφους*; No. 3, *ποιμένων καὶ θηρευτῶν*; No. 4, *τοὺς ἐργαζομένους τὰς τέχνας καὶ τοὺς καπηλικοὺς καὶ οἷς ἀπὸ τοῦ σώματος ἡ ἐργασία*; No. 6, *ἔφοροι*; and No. 7, *οἱ σύμβουλοι καὶ σύνεδροι τοῦ βασιλέως*. His nomenclature of Nos. 2 and 5 agrees with Arrian's. The Brahman books, as is well known, reckon four classes or groups (*varṇa*) of castes (*jāti*), namely, Brahmans, Kshatriyas or Rājañyas, Vaiśyas, and Śūdras. It is a mistake to translate *varṇa* as 'caste'.

[1] Asses, however, were largely used in ancient India, that is to say, in the Panjāb, and on the mountain frontiers, as they were in Irān or Persia. They are mentioned in the *Rig Veda*; and many passages in the *Mahābhārata* mention asses, camels, and mules in association, as used by the Vāhīka and Madraka tribes in the Panjāb, of which Śākala (Siālkōt) was then the capital (Sylvain Lévi, *Ind. Ant.*, 1906, p. 17). See also *Arthaśāstra*, Bk. ii, ch. 29, Bk. vii, ch. 12, and Bk. ix, ch. 1. Mules were also employed for military purposes.

or camel, or in a four-horsed chariot was, he says, a mark of distinction, but anybody might ride or drive a single horse.[1] The *ekka*, or light carriage drawn by a single pony, still so much used in Northern India, is a very ancient conveyance.

Roads.

The roads were maintained in order by the officers of the proper department; and pillars, serving as milestones and sign-posts, were set up at intervals of 10 *stadia*, equivalent to a half *kos* according to the Indian reckoning, or 2,022½ English yards. The provision of these useful marks was made more liberally than it was afterwards by the Moghal emperors, who were content with one pillar to each *kos*. A royal, or grand trunk road, 10,000 *stadia* in length, connected the north western frontier with the capital.[2]

High degree of civilization.

The foregoing review of the civil and military system of government during the reign of Chandragupta proves clearly that Northern India in the time of Alexander the Great had attained to a high degree of civilization, which must have been the product of evolution continued through many centuries. Unfortunately no monuments have been discovered which can be referred with certainty to the period of Chandragupta or his son, and the archaeologist is unable to bring the tangible evidence afforded by excavation to support the statements of the Greek observers. The earliest known examples of Indian art and architecture, with very

[1] Chāṇakya prescribes capital punishment for the slayer of an elephant (Bk. ii, ch. 2). In Burma the king was sole proprietor of all elephants, and possessed 6,000. The privilege of riding on or keeping an elephant was an honour granted only to men of the first rank and consequence (Symes, *Embassy to Ava*, ii, 8: Constable).

[2] Strabo, xv, 11. The Moghal *kōs*, the interval between pillars still existing, averages 4,558 yards (Elliot, *Suppl. Glossary*, s.v. Kōs). Fleet takes *aḍhakosikya* in Pillar Edict VII to mean 'at distances of *eight* kos' instead of 'every half kos', as usually interpreted (*J. R. A. S.*, 1906, p. 417, 1912, p. 238); and maintains that in ancient India there was only one *kōs* measure, equal to about 1 mile 240 yards. But it is difficult to accept the form *aḍha* as equivalent to *ashṭa*, 'eight.' Three stadia were in use in the Roman world in the first century after Christ, namely, the Phileterian of 525 to the degree, or about 650 English feet, nearly a furlong; the Olympic of 600 to the degree, or about 600 feet; and that of Eratosthenes, of 700 to the degree, about 520 feet.

The stadium of the *Periplus* seems to be that of Eratosthenes, roughly speaking, the tenth of an English mile, and in all probability the same measure was used by Megasthenes (Schoff, *The Periplus of the Erythraean Sea*, 1912, p. 54).

slight exceptions, still date from the reign of Asoka, when indigenous art had not yet emerged from the primitive stage and when the Emperor himself was employing artists from Bactria or its neighbourhood for the erection of his famous memorials.[1] The exploration hitherto carried out at Taxila has resulted in the discovery of only one relic—an Aramaic inscription of the fourth century B. C.—which can be ascribed to a period anterior to Asoka. Further exploration at Taxila and of the sites of other cities of high antiquity, like Pātaliputra and Vaisāli, may possibly bring to light remains of the early Maurya period, as well as those of previous ages. It is not likely that the ruins of many recognizable buildings will be found, because the larger edifices of ancient India, like those of modern Burma, probably were constructed of timber for the most part, brick being used merely for foundations and plinths. Unless further exploration discloses an unexpected treasure of early Mauryan sculpture in stone or terra-cotta, materials for the history of art during the early Mauryan period must continue to be scanty. It would be unwise to assert that prior to the reign of Asoka the art of building in stone was absolutely unknown in India, or that all artistic work was executed in perishable material; but the ascertained facts indicate that before his day permanent materials were rarely and sparingly used either for architecture or for ornament.[2] Writing certainly was in common use by certain classes of the population long before the days of Chandragupta; when, according to the Greek authors, the bark of trees and cotton cloth served as writing material,[3] and it is

[1] Marshall, *Guide to Taxila*, 1918, p. 24.

[2] But, as stated in the footnote on page 34 *ante*, if R. P. Jayaswal's view is correct that the two highly polished 'Śaiśunāka' statues, now in the Indian Museum, Calcutta, are those of Udaya and Nandivardhana, and the Parkham statue likewise is that of Ajātaśatru, it is clear that India possessed a matured art of sculpture in stone several centuries before the Mauryan period, and that we have here specimens of statues of far greater antiquity than the statue of Kanishka, which has hitherto ranked as the oldest known statue in India.

[3] Nearchos is the original authority for the use of closely woven [cotton] cloth (Strabo, xv, 67). A century ago merchants and shopkeepers in Mysore universally employed long strips of cotton cloth, from 8 to 12 inches wide and 12 to

surprising that no inscriptions of his time on more permanent material have yet been found. But some records on either stone or metal probably exist, and may yet come to light.

Chāṇakya's *Art of Government.*

The description of the court and civil and military administration of Chandragupta Maurya, derived mainly from Greek authorities, as given in the preceding pages, was practically uncorroborated when the first edition of this book was published in 1904. But since that time an Indian scholar has made accessible by means of translation, the discourse on the Art of Government traditionally ascribed to Chānakya Vishnugupta, or Kautilya, the Brahman minister of Chandragupta. The researches of German scholars have established beyond doubt the fact that the treatise entitled *Arthaśāstra,* or the Science of Policy, is an authentic composition of the Maurya age. Whether or not it was actually written by Chānakya, as it professes to have been, is immaterial. The book certainly expounds the principles of statecraft current in his age, which must have guided his successful policy. It is of extraordinary value and interest, shedding 'more light upon the realities of ancient India, especially as concerns administration, law, trade, war, and peace, than any text which we possess'. The treatise may be read, from one point of view, as a commentary on and exposition of the notes recorded by the Greek observers. References to a few passages in illustration of certain details from that point of view, have been inserted above in the notes, but a fuller notice of some of

18 feet long, as writing material. In ancient times these strips (*kadettum*) were used for records and public documents. The Kanarese writing on them was done with a pencil of *balapum,* or *lapis ollaris,* and could be rubbed out and renewed. The strips were neatly folded and kept in cases (Wilson, *Mackenzie Collection,* p. 342 ; 2nd ed., Madras, 1882). The statement of Megasthenes (Strabo, xv, 53) that the Indians were 'ignorant of writing' is erroneous. The letter sent to Augustus by an Indian king was on parchment (Strabo, xv, 73). The bark referred to, that of the birch (*Betula utilis*), was used only in Northern India. 'The tender side of the barks of trees receives written characters like paper' (Curtius, viii, 9). Many of the apparent discrepancies in the Greek account of India are due to the fact that different authors refer to different parts of the country. General statements about India are always misleading.

the contents is indispensable, and will be found to add largely to the knowledge gained from the writings of the Greek authors.

Arthaśāstra describes pre-Maurya conditions.

It is not desirable to amalgamate the rules laid down in the *Arthaśāstra* with the descriptions recorded by the Greeks, because the latter present to us the impression made upon foreign observers of institutions actually existing at a particular date, 300 B. C. in round numbers, after the foundation of the Maurya empire; whereas the former express the arrangements favoured by Brahman ministers, as suitable for any independent kingdom at any time. The *Arthaśāstra* text-book cites the opinions of many earlier authors of unknown antiquity, and treats of the political state of India prior to the establishment of a paramount power by the Mauryas.[1] We may accept it as an authoritative account of political and social conditions in the Gangetic plain in the age of Alexander the Great, 325 B. C. The book does not concern itself with the Dravidian kingdoms of the South, which were organized in other fashions.

Autocracy tempered by reverence for Brahmans.

The only form of government described in detail by the author was an absolute autocracy. He makes merely passing allusions to the existence of tribal organizations among the Lichchhavis and other communities.[2] The free will of the

[1] 'This *Arthaśāstra* or Science of Polity has been made as a compendium of all those *Arthaśāstras* which, as a guidance to kings in acquiring and maintaining the earth, have been written by ancient teachers' (Bk. xv, ch. 1; Shamasastry, revised English version, 1915, pp. 515–16). 'Having seen innumerable discrepancies of commentators in their commentaries on *Śāstras*, Vishṇugupta composed the aphorisms and their commentary of his own' (ibid., p. 520).

[2] 'Sovereignty may be the property of a clan', *kulasya vā bhaved rājyam* (Bk. i, ch. 17, end). For names of tribal communities see Bk. xi, ch. 1 (Shamasastry, ibid., p. 455). The Mālavas, Kshudrakas, and other nations in the time of Alexander the Great, and the Lichchhavis and Yaudhēyas at a much later date, possessed tribal constitutions of a republican, or at any rate, oligarchical character. The Mālavas and Yaudhēyas were governed by *gaṇas*, according to Thomas, which represented a kind of senate or oligarchy (*J.R.A.S.*, 1915, p. 535). On this subject K. P. Jayaswal has a valuable article, 'Republics in the Mahābhārata', in *J.B. & O. Res. Soc.*, vol. i, pp. 173–8. He declares that the *gaṇa* refers to the whole body politic and not to the governing body or senate, and that the strength of the tribal constitution lay in united confederacy and obedience to leaders. The governing body consisted of *gaṇa-mukhyas* and a *pradhāna* or

autocrat, uncontrolled by any constitutional traditions or machinery, was restricted to a certain extent by the customary reverence for Brahmans, which was well established even at that early date. As a rule, Brahmans were exempt from capital punishment, the only exception being that a Brahman convicted of high treason might be executed by drowning, instead of being burnt alive as a member of another caste should be.[1] Brahmans convicted of certain other offences might be branded in the face, and then either banished or sent to the mines for life. Both Brahmans and ascetics were exempt from liability to judicial torture for the purpose of extracting a confession.[2]

The treatise applies only to a small kingdom.

The author assumes that the principles expounded by him are to be applied in the government of a small kingdom, surrounded by other similar kingdoms, all either actually or potentially hostile. The rules of the text-book do not provide for the needs of an extensive consolidated empire, and it is obvious that the work deals with the state of things as existing before the Mauryas had acquired paramount power.

Every kingdom actually or potentially hostile.

Permanent peace between neighbouring states was regarded as unattainable. We are instructed that

'whoever is superior in power shall wage war'; [3]

'whoever is rising in power may break the agreement of peace'; [4]

'the king who is situated anywhere on the circumference of the conqueror's territory is termed the enemy'; [5]

'when a king of equal power does not like peace, then the same amount of vexation as his opponent has received at his hands should be given to him in return; for it is power that brings about peace between any two kings; no piece

President. The subject is further discussed by Prof. D. R. Bhandarkar in the Carmichael lectures for 1918, 650–325 B. C., published by Calcutta University, 1919; and also by R. C. Majumdar in *Corporate Life in Ancient India* (Calcutta, Surendra Nath Sen, 1918); and by R. D. Mukharji in *Local Government in Ancient India* (Oxford Univ. Press, 1919). These tribal constitutions, which were a Mongolian institution, gradually disappeared together with many other non-Aryan institutions, as the Mongolian people and ideas were overborne by strangers who observed the Indo-Aryan or Brahmanical cult and customs.

[1] Bk. iv, ch. 11.

[2] Bk. iv, ch. 8.

[3] Bk. vii, ch. 1.

[4] Bk. vii, ch. 17.

[5] Bk. iv, ch. 2.

of iron that is not made red-hot will combine with another piece of iron '.[1]

No morality in statecraft.

The relations between the kingdoms prior to the consolidation of the Maurya empire consequently involved an unceasing struggle for existence. Might was right. No prince pretended to trust any other ruler for a moment, or to keep faith if he felt strong enough to break the pact. No considerations of morality were allowed to influence statecraft, which avowedly preferred the use of insidious and treacherous means, including every form of secret assassination. The maxim that the vices of ordinary people are virtues in kings was plainly enunciated, and, as history shows, was constantly acted on. Skill in intrigue was a better qualification for kingship than either power or enthusiasm.[2]

Universal suspicion and espionage.

The inveterate and universal suspicion which regulated the dealings between every Rāja and his fellow-rulers governed the conduct of the prince to his officials and subjects. Nobody was to be trusted. The government relied on a highly organized system of espionage, pervading every department of the administration and every class of the population. The formal rules concerning spies occupy a prominent place in the treatise, every chapter of which assumes that the working of the machinery of government depends mainly on the successful utilization of secret information.[3]

Employment of courtesans.

The statements of Strabo concerning the employment of courtesans as spies and informers are fully supported by regulations on the subject. The courtesans, indeed, were regarded to a large extent as court officials, women of that class, under the orders of a Superintendent and Deputy Superintendent, being appointed to hold the royal umbrella, golden pitcher, and fan, and to attend on the king when he was seated on his throne, or in his litter or chariot. A long chapter is devoted to the regulations concerning public women.[4] Cipher writing was used by the spies, and carrier

[1] Bk. vii, ch. 3.

[2] Bk. ix, ch. 1.

[3] The formal rules are mostly in Bk. i, ch. 11, 12.

[4] Bk. ii, ch. 27.

pigeons were employed to carry secret intelligence.[1] The Intelligence Department was controlled by five 'Institutes of Espionage', in which the reports were checked and verified.

Princes like crabs.

The king lived in continual terror of the members of his family, 'for on account of the kingdom the father hates his sons, and sons hate their father'.[2] Jahāngīr long afterwards expressed the same sentiment in the maxim that 'kingship regards neither son nor son-in-law. No one is a relation to a king'.[3] Another similar aphorism is that 'princes, like crabs, have a notorious tendency towards eating up their begetter'.[4]

The duty of a king.

The autocrat was expected to work hard. In language which recalls that of Asoka's edicts, the author directs that the king

> 'shall, therefore, attend personally to the business of gods, of heretics, of Brahmans learned in the Vedas, of cattle, of sacred places, of minors, the aged, the afflicted, and the helpless, and of women; all this in order of enumeration, or according to the urgency or pressure of those works.
>
> 'All urgent calls he shall hear at once, but never put off; for when postponed, they will prove too hard or impossible to accomplish'.[5]

Privy Council.

The king was assisted by a Privy Council, which should consist of either twelve or sixteen members, according to the opinion of certain authors, but should comprise as many councillors as the needs of the state demanded, according to the wiser judgement of Chānakya.[6]

Departments.

Eighteen departments of the administration are mentioned, and long lists of the chief officials are given. They include a Chamberlain, Collector-General, Accountant-General, Superintendent of Agriculture, Superintendent of Manufactures, and many others.[7]

No Boards.

The Boards described by Megasthenes as in charge of the business of the capital and the army are unknown to the

[1] Bk. ii, ch. 34.
[2] Bk. v, ch. 6.
[3] *Memoirs*, transl. Rogers and Beveridge, p. 52.
[4] Bk. i, ch. 17.
[5] Bk. i, ch. 19.
[6] Bk. i, ch. 15.
[7] Bk. i, ch. 12, 15.

author, who contemplated each such charge as the duty of a single officer. The creation of the Boards may have been an innovation effected by Chandragupta personally. The treatise confirms the Greek accounts in many particulars.

Salaries and coinage.

A curious table of rates of salary is given. The pay ranged from 48,000 silver *panas* a year for the heir apparent and certain high officers of state to 60 *panas* for a labourer.[1] No specimen of a silver *pana* is known, but it was presumably of the same weight as a copper *karsha*, namely, about 146 grains, or 9·46 grammes.[2] The ' punch-marked ' pieces of impure silver (*purāna* or *dharana*), which are known to have been in ordinary use in the author's time, are struck to a standard of about 56 grains, or 3·628 grammes. Possibly this silver *pana* may have been only a money of account. The value of a silver *pana*, which presumably was much alloyed like the ' punch-marked ' coins, may be taken as not far from a shilling.

Finance.

The sound doctrine is inculcated that ' all undertakings depend upon finance. Hence foremost attention shall be paid to the Treasury '.[3] It is impossible for me to go minutely into a description of the financial arrangements, and only a few points can be noted.

Land-revenue and water-rates.

The Superintendent of Agriculture, like a modern settlement officer, was required to assess land at rates varying according to the different methods of irrigation used. The normal share of the produce taken by the State as ' land-revenue ', or crown rent, being one-fourth, the amount taken as water-rate was approximately equal, varying from one-fifth to one-third. Various other dues also were exacted, so that the cultivator of irrigated land could not retain as much as half of the produce of his fields.[4]

Benevolences.

All subjects were further required to pay occasional ' benevolences ' on special occasions, levied at the king's discretion. The suggestions concerning the methods by which a necessitous monarch might extort money are of

[1] Bk. v, ch. 3.
[2] For coinage, see Bk. ii, ch. 12, 14.
[3] Bk. ii, ch. 8.
[4] Bk. ii, ch. 24.

more than Machiavellian wickedness. The history of Kashmīr supplies painful illustrations of the application of the author's prescriptions. One way or another the Crown took all it could get.

Sale of honours.

Modern financiers are not always averse from employing the 'policy of thinning the rich by exacting excessive revenue (*karśanam*), or causing them to vomit their accumulated wealth (*vamanam*)'.[1] Nor is the practice of selling honours strange to European politicians, though they do not usually care to express themselves in language so plain as that used by Chānakya, who says :—

> 'Wealthy persons may be requested to give as much of their gold as they can. Those who, of their own accord or with the intention of doing good, offer their wealth to the king shall be honoured with a rank in the court, an umbrella, or a turban, or some ornaments in return for their gold.'[2]

Taxes on sales.

In fortified towns the royal revenue was derived largely from taxes on sales, as stated by Megasthenes. In order to facilitate the collection of this important branch of the public income, the cardinal rule was laid down that commodities should not be sold at the place of growth or manufacture.[3] The law required that all articles for sale (excepting grain, cattle, and some others) should be brought to the toll-house near the town gate, there offered for sale, and if sold, taxed. Toll was paid only when actual sale took place. The rates of duty varied widely. Imports from abroad paid, as a rule, seven distinct taxes, aggregating about 20 per cent.; perishable goods, such as fruit and vegetables, were charged one-sixth of the value, or 16⅔ per cent.; while on many other classes of wares the rates of duty ranged from 4 to 10 per cent. Highly priced goods, such as precious stones, were assessed on special valuations made by experts. All goods brought for sale had to be marked with an official stamp. The Greek phrase, ἀπὸ συσσήμου, refers to that practice.[4]

[1] Bk. iv, ch. 3.
[2] Bk. v, ch. 2.
[3] Bk. ii, ch. 23.
[4] Bk. ii, ch. 21, 22. The ordinary practice in later times, and probably also in the Maurya

Statistics.

The Greek observations on the subject of vital statistics are illustrated by the regulations which require the Nāgaraka, or Town Prefect, to register every arrival in or departure from his jurisdiction. He was also bound to keep up a census statement giving in detail for each inhabitant the sex, caste, name, family name, occupation, income, expenditure, and possessions in cattle. Breaches of the fiscal regulations were punishable usually by fine or confiscation, but the penalty for wilful false statements was the same as that for theft, which might extend to death.[1]

Excise.

A regular system of excise licences was in force, special duties being levied on foreign liquors, including wines from Kapisa or Afghanistan. Modern temperance reformers may be scandalized by the regulations that

> 'liquor shops shall consist of many comfortable rooms, furnished with cots and seats. The drinking places shall possess such comforts as changing seasons require, always having garlands of flowers, scent, and perfume '.[2]

Penal code.

The Science of Government, we are told, may be defined as the science of punishment (*daṇḍa nīti*). The penal code, in consequence, was ferociously severe. The details in the treatise amply support the Greek references to the subject. As an illustration of the severity of punishment, it may suffice to note that theft by a government servant to the value of from 8 to 10 *panas* was punishable with death, as was theft of a value of from 40 to 50 *panas* by a non-official person.[3]

Judicial torture.

Judicial torture for the purpose of extorting a confession was recognized and freely used. Many gruesome regulations on the subject are recorded. The general principle laid down was that 'those whose guilt is believed to be true shall be subjected to torture', of which there were eighteen kinds, including seven varieties of whipping. In certain cases the victim might be 'subjected to one or all of the above kinds of torture'. The torture of women was sup-

age, was to do the stamping with red-lead (*sindūra*) (*Ep. Ind.*, vii, 230, with ref.).

[1] Bk. ii, ch. 35, 36.
[2] Bk. ii, ch. 25.
[3] Bk. iv, ch. 9.

posed to be limited to 'half the prescribed standard'.[1] All experienced magistrates know how deeply the tradition of torturing a prisoner in order to extort a confession is engrained in the mind of Indian policemen, and how difficult it is to check the practice even under modern conditions.

Chānakya's code not only authorized judicial torture and the capital penalty for petty offences, but also prescribed mutilation in numerous cases.

The *Artha-śāstra* a practical manual.

Many matters of interest and curiosity have been necessarily passed over, but the foregoing summary will, it is hoped, be sufficient to give the reader a fairly accurate notion of the principles on which the small kingdoms of Northern India were administered in the days of Alexander the Great. Although many of the rules in Chānakya's treatise are puerile, and some merely theoretical, the book on the whole was intended to be a practical manual of statecraft and administration, and as such it is well worth reading. Books like the so-called *Laws of Manu* and *Dharmaśāstras* set forth the Brahman ideal—the treatise of Chandragupta's minister openly discards ideals and presents a plain unvarnished statement of the immoral practice of kings and Brahman ministers in the fourth century before Christ, prior to the realization of the novel idea of a great empire extending over nearly all India.[2]

Success of Chandragupta.

Chandragupta ascended the throne at an early age, and inasmuch as he reigned only twenty-four years, must have abdicated or died before he was fifty years of age.[3] In this brief space of life he did much. The expulsion of the Macedonian garrisons, the decisive repulse of Seleukos the Conqueror, the subjugation of at least all Northern India

[1] Bk. iv, ch. 8.

[2] See App. F.

[3] He was but a youth when he saw Alexander in 326 or 325 B. C. (Plutarch, *Alex.* ch. 62).

'This Chandragupta! yet so young—so raised
To mighty empire, as the forest monarch,
Over subjected herds'
(*Mudrā Rākshasa*, Act vii; Wilson, ii, p. 249).

The statement in Turnour's and Wijesinha's versions of the *Mahāvaṁśa* that Chandragupta reigned for thirty-four years is due to a copyist's blunder (Rhys Davids, *Ancient Coins and Measures of Ceylon*, p. 41, note). Geiger's version (chap. v) correctly gives twenty-four years. Buddhist and Brahmanical authorities being agreed in the matter, the fact may be accepted as established.

from sea to sea, the formation of a gigantic army, and the thorough organization of the civil government of a vast empire were no mean achievements. The power of Chandragupta was so firmly established that it passed peacefully into the hands of his son and grandson, and his alliance was courted by the potentates of the Hellenistic world. The Greek princes made no attempt to renew the aggressions of Alexander and Seleukos upon secluded India, and were content to maintain friendly diplomatic and commercial relations with her rulers for three generations.[1]

Absence of Hellenic influence.

The Maurya empire was not, as some writers fancy that it was, in any way the result of Alexander's splendid but transitory raid. The nineteen months which he spent in India were consumed in devastating warfare, and his death rendered fruitless all his grand constructive plans. Chandragupta did not need Alexander's example to teach him what empire meant. He and his countrymen had had before their eyes for two centuries the stately fabric of the Persian Achaemenian monarchy, and it was that empire which impressed their imagination, and served as the model for their institutions, in so far as they were not indigenous. The little touches of foreign manners in the court and institutions of Chandragupta, which chance to have been noted by our fragmentary authorities, are Persian, not Greek; and the Persian title of satrap continued to be used by Indian provincial governors for ages, down to the close of the fourth century of the Christian era.[2]

Indian military organization.

The military organization of Chandragupta shows no trace of Hellenic influence. It is based upon the ancient Indian model, and his vast host was merely a development of the considerable army maintained by the kingdom of Magadha.

[1] For the curious anecdote about the powerful aphrodisiac drugs sent with other gifts by Chandragupta (Σανδρόκυττος) to Seleukos, see Phylarchos and Apollonios Dyskolos, in Müller, *Fragmenta Historicorum Graecorum*, i, 344.

[2] The Śaka satraps of Saurāshṭra, or Kāṭhiāwār, in Western India, were conquered by Chandragupta (II) Vikramāditya, of the Gupta dynasty, about A. D. 390. See 'Persian Influence on Maurya India', *Ind. Ant.* (1905), p. 201. A patriotic Hindu critic urges that Chandragupta needed to go no farther for his model than the story of Daśaratha in the Rāmāyaṇa.

The Indian kings relied chiefly upon their elephants, and in a lesser degree upon chariots and huge masses of infantry; the cavalry being few in comparison and inefficient. Alexander, on the contrary, made no use of elephants or chariots, and put his trust in small bodies of highly trained cavalry, handled with consummate skill and calculated audacity. In the art of war he had no successor. The Seleukidan kings were content to follow the Oriental system and put their trust in elephants.[1]

Alleged abdication of Chandragupta.

Jain tradition avers that Chandragupta Maurya was a Jain, and that, when a great twelve years' famine occurred, he abdicated,[2] accompanied Bhadrabāhu, the last of the saints called *śrutakevalins*, to the south, lived as an ascetic at Sravana Belgola in Mysore, and ultimately committed suicide by starvation at that place, where his name is still held in remembrance. In the second edition of this book I rejected that tradition and dismissed the tale as 'imaginary history'. But on reconsideration of the whole evidence and the objections urged against the credibility of the story, I am now disposed to believe that the tradition probably is true in its main outline, and that Chandragupta really abdicated and became a Jain ascetic. The traditional narratives, of course, like all such relations, are open to much criticism, and the epigraphical support is far from conclusive. Nevertheless, my present impression is that the tradition has a solid foundation on fact.[3]

298 B. C. Bindusāra.

When Chandragupta either abdicated or died, in the year 298 B. C., he was succeeded by his son Bindusāra. The Greek writers, however, do not know his name, and call the successor of Chandragupta by appellations which seem to be

[1] Bevan, *The House of Seleucus*, ii, 289.

[2] For abdication procedure, see *Rāsmālā* I, 72. The ex-king is treated as having died, cannot re-enter the capital, and takes a name in religion. See Tod's *Annals*, &c., ed. Crooke, Oxford Univ. Press, 1920, vol. i, 426; vol. iii, 1467, 1509.

[3] Mr. Lewis Rice has stoutly maintained the credibility of the tradition in many publications, the latest being *Mysore and Coorg from the Inscriptions*, 1909, pp. 3–9. Fleet was equally persistent on the other side, and has recorded his views in *Ind. Ant.*, xxi (1892), p. 287; *Ep. Ind.*, iii, 171 note; and several times in *J.R.A.S.* See also *Quart. Jour. Mythic Soc., Bangalore*, October, 1922, vol. xiii, pp. 430–47.

attempts to transcribe the Sanskrit epithet Amitraghāta, 'Slayer of foes,'[1]—a title which indicates that he was a conqueror. The friendly relations between India and the Hellenistic powers, which had been initiated by Chandragupta and Seleukos, continued unbroken throughout the reign of Bindusāra, at whose court Megasthenes was replaced by Deïmachos, as ambassador. The new envoy followed his predecessor's example by recording notes on the country to which he was accredited, but unfortunately very few of his observations have been preserved. When the aged founder of the Seleukidan monarchy was assassinated in 280 B.C., his place was taken by his son and colleague Antiochos Soter, who continued to follow his father's policy in regard to India.

Correspondence with Antiochos Soter.

The anecdote concerning the correspondence between Antiochos and Bindusāra, although trivial in itself, is worth quoting as a tangible proof of the familiar intercourse between the sovereign of India and his ally in Western Asia. Nothing, we are told, being sweeter than figs, Bindusāra begged Antiochos to send him some figs and raisin wine, and added that he would like him also to buy and send a professor. Antiochos replied that he had much pleasure in forwarding the figs and raisin wine, but regretted that he could not oblige his correspondent with the last-named article, because it was not lawful for Greeks to sell a professor.[2]

[1] For the Maurya chronology see *Asoka, the Buddhist Emperor of India* (Clarendon Press, 3rd ed., 1909), pp. 72, 73, 74. The name Bindusāra is attested by the Hindū *Vishṇu Purāṇa*, the Jain *Pariśishṭaparvan*, and the Buddhist *Mahāvaṁśa* and *Dīpavaṁśa*. The variants in other Purāṇas seem to be merely clerical errors. Ἐπέμφθησαν μὲν γὰρ εἰς τὰ Παλίμβοθρα, ὁ μὲν Μεγασθένης πρὸς Ἀνδρόκοττον, ὁ δὲ Δηΐμαχος πρὸς Ἀμιτροχάδην τὸν ἐκείνου υἱὸν κατὰ πρεσβείαν (Strabo, ii, 1, 9). The more corrupt form Allitrochades occurs in some texts, and evidently is due to confusion between ΑΛΛΙ and ΑΜΙ. Hegesandros, quoted by Athenaios (Müller, *Frag. Hist. Graec.*, vol. iv, p. 421), writes Ἀμιτροχάτης, which is an accurate transcription of the supposed Sanskrit original (see Schwanbeck, op. cit., p. 77). Indian kings are often known by one or other epithet, used as a secondary name.

[2] Οὕτω δὲ ἦσαν περισπούδασται πᾶσιν ἀνθρώποις αἱ ἰσχάδες (ὄντως γάρ, κατὰ τὸν Ἀριστοφάνην,

'Οὐδὲν γὰρ ὄντως γλυκύτερον τῶν ἰσχάδων'),

ὡς καὶ Ἀμιτροχάτην, τὸν τῶν Ἰνδῶν βασιλέα, γράψαι Ἀντιόχῳ, ἀξιοῦντα (φησὶν Ἡγήσανδρος) πέμψαι αὐτῷ γλυκὺν καὶ ἰσχάδας καὶ σοφιστὴν ἀγοράσαντα. Καὶ τὸν Ἀντίοχον ἀντιγράψαι—'Ἰσχάδας μὲν καὶ γλυκὺν ἀποστελοῦμέν σοι, σοφιστὴν δ' ἐν Ἕλλησιν οὐ νόμιμον πωλεῖσθαι' (Müller, loc. cit.).

Embassy of Dionysios.

Ptolemy Philadelphos, who ruled in Egypt from 285 to 247 B.C., also dispatched an envoy named Dionysios to the Indian Court, who, like his colleagues, wrote an account of his experiences, which was still available to Pliny in the first century of the Christian era.[1] It is uncertain whether Dionysios presented his credentials to Bindusāra or to his successor, Asoka.

Conquest of the Deccan.

Nothing is recorded concerning the internal policy of Bindusāra, whose reign lasted for twenty-five years, according to the Purāṇas, nor is any monument or inscription of his time known. But there is reason to believe that he continued his father's career of annexation and conquest within the borders of India, as indicated by his title or secondary name of Amitraghāta. The limits of the empire ruled by Asoka, son and successor of Bindusāra, are known with sufficient accuracy, and it is certain that his dominions, including semi-independent protectorates, extended southwards to about the latitude of Nellore (14° 27′ N.) and included the northern districts of Mysore.[2] The country south of the Narbadā cannot have been conquered by Asoka, whose only known annexation was that of the kingdom of Kalinga, on the coast of the Bay of Bengal, unless the conquest took place in the early years of his reign, about which we possess no information. The twenty-four years of the reign of Chandragupta seem to be fully occupied with the great events known to have been crowded into them. It is difficult to believe that he could have found time to do more than climb from obscurity to power, expel the Macedonian garrisons, repel the attack of Seleukos, effect a revolution and establish a dynasty at Pātaliputra, annex a large part of Ariāna, and extend his dominion from the Bay of Bengal to the Arabian Sea.

[1] Pliny, *Hist. Nat.* vi, 17. Pliny's work is believed to have been published in A.D. 77.

[2] According to Mr. Rice, 'an inscription of the twelfth century, at Bandanikke, Shikarpur taluk, Mysore, describes Kuntala as the province governed by the Mauryas. This, roughly speaking, would be the country between the rivers Bhima and Vedavati, bounded on the west by the Ghats, including Shimoga, Chitaldroog, Bellary, Dharwar, Bijapur, and adjacent parts to the north in Bombay and the Nizam's Dominions' (*Mysore Gaz.* (1897), i, 289).

Probably effected by Bindusāra.

The Deccan, or Peninsular India, down to approximately the latitude of Nellore, must therefore, apparently, have been subjugated by either Chandragupta or Bindusāra, because it was inherited from the latter by Asoka, whose only recorded war was the conquest of Kalinga; and it is more probable that the conquest of the south was the work of Bindusāra than that it was effected by his busy father. In fact, it may be affirmed with confidence that the conquest of the south actually was effected by Bindusāra. Tāranāth, using no doubt ancient authorities, asserts expressly that Bindusāra, who continued to be guided by the counsels of his father's minister, Kautilya or Chānakya, slew the kings and ministers of some sixteen capitals, and thus extended his empire from sea to sea. The sixteen states thus annexed cannot possibly have been in Northern India which was firmly held by Chandragupta. That testimony of the Tibetan historian is confirmed by the evidence of Māmulanār, an ancient Brahman Tamil poet and scholar, who refers frequently to invasions by the Mauryas in early times. The invaders advanced as far south as Madura and the neighbouring parts of the Tinnevelly District with 'a great army'. Those conquests in the extreme south were not held by the invaders. Asoka's inscriptions prove that in his time the Tamil states were independent neighbours of the northern empire, which included a southern Viceroyalty with its head-quarters at Suvarnagiri, or Golden Town, presumably situated in the ancient gold-field near Maski in the Raichūr District of the Nizam's Dominions, where an Asoka inscription exists. Faint memories of the Maurya conquest of the south lingered for centuries. The early Pallava inscriptions claim Asoka as one of the ancestors of the Pallava dynasty, and as late as the seventh century the Chalukya monarchs subdued Maurya chiefs in the Konkan.[1]

[1] Tāranāth (Schiefner, p. 89); S. Krishnaswami Aiyangar, *The Beginnings of South Indian History*, ch. ii, 'Mauryan Invasion of South India' (Madras, 1918); K. P. Jayaswal, 'The Empire of Bindusāra' (*J.B. & O. Res. Soc.*, ii, 79–83). For the Maurya survivals in Western India, see Fleet in *Bombay Gazetteer* (1896), vol. i, part II, pp. 202–4. The Maski inscription will be noticed further under the reign of Asoka.

A tradition recorded in an inscription of the twelfth century states that Kuntala, a province which included the western Deccan and the north of Mysore, was ruled by the Nandas, and the Kadamba kings claimed descent from Nanda.[1] The Nanda dynasty undoubtedly was extremely powerful, and it would be rash to maintain that the tradition must be baseless. If there be any truth in it, the northern attack on the south began long before the time of Bindusāra. With this brief glance the shadowy figure of Bindusāra passes from our view, and the next two chapters will be devoted to the history of Asoka, who rightfully claims a place in the front rank of the great monarchs, not only of India, but of the world.

APPENDIX F

The Extent of the Cession of Ariāna by Seleukos Nikator to Chandragupta Maurya

Extent of Cession. The statement in the text that the cession made in 303 B.C. by Seleukos Nikator to Chandragupta Maurya included the provinces of the Paropanisadae (Kābul), Aria (Herāt), Arachosia (Kandahār), and probably Gedrosia (Makrān), or a large part of that satrapy, is based upon the original authorities, which are five in number, namely, Strabo (two passages), Appian, Plutarch, Justin, and Pliny. The relevant extracts, being brief, may be quoted in full. All that has been written by modern authors on the subject is based upon these short extracts.

Strabo, I. (I) The two passages from Strabo are as follows: *μάλιστα ἐκ τῆς διαίτης ἐδόκει τῆς τότε πιστότατα εἶναι τὰ ὑπὸ τοῦ Ἐρατοσθένους ἐν τῷ τρίτῳ τῶν γεωγραφικῶν ἐκτεθέντα κεφαλαιωδῶς περὶ τῆς τότε νομιζομένης Ἰνδικῆς, ἡνίκα Ἀλέξανδρος ἐπῆλθε· καὶ ἦν ὁ Ἰνδὸς ὅριον ταύτης τε καὶ τῆς Ἀριανῆς, ἣν ἐφεξῆς πρὸς τῇ ἑσπέρᾳ κειμένην Πέρσαι κατεῖχον· ὕστερον γὰρ δὴ καὶ τῆς Ἀριανῆς πολλὴν ἔσχον οἱ Ἰνδοὶ λαβόντες παρὰ τῶν Μακεδόνων* (Bk. xv, ch. i (India), sec. 10 in Müller and Dübner's ed.).

Strabo, II. (II) *ἡ δὲ τάξις τῶν ἐθνῶν τοιαύτη· παρὰ μὲν τὸν Ἰνδὸν οἱ Παροπαμισάδαι, ὧν ὑπέρκειται ὁ Παροπάμισος ὄρος, εἶτ' Ἀραχωτοὶ πρὸς νότον, εἶτ' ἐφεξῆς πρὸς νότον Γεδρωσηνοὶ σὺν τοῖς ἄλλοις πρὸς τὴν παραλίαν ἔχουσιν· ἅπασι δὲ παρὰ τὰ πλάτη τῶν χωρίων παράκειται ὁ Ἰνδός. τούτων δ' [ἐκ μέρους] τῶν παρὰ τὸν Ἰνδὸν ἔχουσί τινα Ἰνδοί, πρότερον ὄντα Περσῶν. ἃ ἀφείλετο μὲν ὁ Ἀλέξανδρος τῶν Ἀριανῶν καὶ κατοικίας ἰδίας συνεστήσατο, ἔδωκε δὲ Σέλευκος ὁ*

[1] Rice, *Mysore and Coorg from the Inscriptions* (Constable, 1909), p. 3.

Νικάτωρ Σανδροκόττῳ, συνθέμενος ἐπιγαμίαν καὶ ἀντιλαβὼν ἐλέφαντας πεντακοσίους (ibid., Bk. xv, ch. ii, 9).

(III) Appian writes: καὶ τὸν Ἰνδὸν περάσας [Σέλευκος] ἐπολέμησεν Ἀνδροκόττῳ, βασιλεῖ τῶν περὶ αὐτὸν Ἰνδῶν, μέχρι φιλίαν αὐτῷ καὶ κῆδος συνέθετο (*Syr.* 55). Appian.

(IV) Plutarch, arguing that the accounts of the military force of the Prasii were not exaggerated, says: καὶ κόμπος οὐκ ἦν περὶ ταῦτα. Ἀνδρόκοττος γὰρ ὕστερον οὐ πολλῷ βασιλεύσας Σελεύκῳ πεντακοσίους ἐλέφαντας ἐδωρήσατο, καὶ στρατοῦ μυριάσιν ἑξήκοντα τὴν Ἰνδικὴν ἐπῆλθεν ἅπασαν καταστρεφόμενος' (*Alex.* ch. 62). Plutarch.

(V) Justin's testimony is: '[Seleucus] transitum deinde in Indiam fecit, quae post mortem Alexandri, veluti cervicibus iugo servitutis excusso, praefectos eius occiderat. Auctor libertatis Sandrocottus fuerat . . . cum quo facta pactione Seleucus, compositisque in oriente rebus, in bellum Antigoni descendit' (xv, 4). Justin.

(VI) Pliny, when treating of the Indus and the boundary of India, says: 'Etenim plerique ab occidente non Indo amne determinant, sed adiiciunt quatuor satrapias, Gedrosos, Arachotas, Arios, Paropamissadas' (Bk. vi, ch. 20, Basle ed., 1554 (*al.* ch. 23)). Pliny.

Interpretation of Strabo.

These texts comprise the whole of the direct evidence on the subject. It seems to me self-evident that the two passages of Strabo refer to the same event; and that when he says in the first that the Indians received from the Macedonians 'a large part of Arianē', which had been under the rule of the Persians up to the time of Alexander, he briefly alludes to the cession of the countries west of the Indus, formerly in the possession of the Persians, which Seleukos ceded to Chandragupta, as specifically stated in the second extract.

The other authorities.

The statements of Appian, Plutarch, and Justin do not deal in terms with the extent of the cession, but are of value as proving that Seleukos actually crossed the Indus, waged an unsuccessful war, and was obliged to make peace on conditions very favourable to his adversary, and very unfavourable to himself.

The four satrapies.

The observation of Pliny that numerous (*plerique*) authors include in India the four satrapies of Gedrosia, Arachosia, Aria, and the Paropanisadae must have been based on the fact that at some period previous to A. D. 77, when his book was published, those four provinces were actually reckoned as part of India. At what time other than the period of the Maurya dynasty is it possible that those provinces should have formed part of India? Pliny's information about the country was mainly drawn from the writings of Megasthenes and the other contemporaries of Alexander, Chandragupta and Seleukos; and the natural interpretation of his observation requires us to believe that the four satrapies in question were 'the large part of Arianē' ceded by Seleukos. Kābul and Kandahār frequently have been held by the sovereigns of India, and form part of the natural frontier of the country. Herāt (Aria) is undoubtedly more remote, but can be held with ease by the power in possession of Kābul and Kandahār.

Gedrosia. The satrapy of Gedrosia (or Gadrosia) extended far to the west, and probably only the eastern part of it was annexed by Chandragupta. The Mālin range of mountains, which Alexander experienced such difficulty in crossing, would have furnished a natural boundary. Whether Chandragupta undertook the administration of the whole of Gedrosia or not, I have no doubt that Seleukos abandoned to him all control over the province, and that it was included by numerous authors in India, along with Aria, Arachosia, and the Paropanisadae; because Seleukos, intent upon the urgent business of crushing Antigonos, was constrained to surrender the four outlying satrapies named by Pliny, and to concentrate his strength in Central and Western Asia.

APPENDIX G

The Arthaśāstra, or Kauṭilīya-Śāstra

Discovery of the text. It is more convenient to give the necessary information about the *Arthaśāstra* in an Appendix than in cumbrous footnotes.

A collection of maxims attributed to Chāṇakya, alias Kauṭilya, or Vishṇu-gupta, the Brahman minister of Chandragupta Maurya, has long been known (see Weber, *Hist. Indian Liter.* (Trübner), p. 210). But the *Arthaśāstra*, although mentioned and quoted by many ancient authors, had wholly disappeared from view until Mr. R. Shamasastry (Shama Sastri), the learned Librarian of the Oriental Library maintained by the Maharaja of Mysore, brought to notice a manuscript of the work belonging to a pundit in the Tanjore District.[1] The pundit was good enough to deposit the MS. in the library, along with an imperfect MS. of a commentary on the treatise by Bhaṭṭaswāmi. The translation of certain extracts published by Mr. Shamasastry in the *Indian Antiquary* for 1905 attracted attention, and enabled me to make valuable additions to the second edition of this history, published in 1908. Two other MSS. of the *Śāstra* were then found in the Münich Library, and another seems to exist in Calcutta.

Translation by Mr. R. Shamasastry. After the publication of the second edition of this history in 1908 several eminent German scholars devoted much attention to the study of Chāṇakya's treatise, and Mr. Shamasastry was encouraged to complete his rough translation, and also to print an edition of the text. This translation has now been superseded by Mr. Shamasastry's revised edition in one bound volume, Bangalore

[1] Mr. Shamasastry was later transferred to Bangalore, as Principal of the Chamarajendra Sanskrit College.

Government Press, 1915, with introductions by Fleet and the translator, and Index—pp. xxxii and 543.

Other scholars have not been slow to avail themselves of Mr. Shamasastry's valuable pioneer work, and a considerable literature is growing up around the text of the *Arthaśāstra*. Among the most important of these publications are (1) *Studies in Ancient Hindu Polity* (based on the Arthaśāstra of Kautilya) by Narendra Nath Law, M.A., B.L., vol. i, Longmans, Green & Co., 1914—a valuable analysis of parts of the treatise, especially civil law, from a lawyer's point of view; (2) *Public Administration in Ancient India* by Pramathnatha Banerjea (Macmillan, 1916)—a learned and accurate work; and (3) *The Positive Background of Hindu Sociology*, Book i, by Professor Benoy Kumār Sarkār (Pāṇini Office, Allahabad, 1914). Further discussion is bound to illuminate many parts of the text which still remain obscure. New Publications.

I have read and utilized the German publications named below, which supply additional references :— German discussions.

(1) A. Hillebrandt, 'Über das Kauṭilīyaśāstra und Verwandtes' (Sonderab. aus d. 86. *Jahresber. d. Schlesischen Gesellsch. f. vaterl. Cultur*, Breslau, 1908).

(2) Prof. Dr. Jolly, Vortrag (lecture), 'Ein altindisches Lehrbuch der Politik' (Sonderab. aus d. *Verhandlungen d. Intern. Vereinigung f. vergleich. Rechtswissenschaft u.s.w. in Berlin, zu Heidelberg*, 1911, Berlin).

(3) Same author, 'Arthaśāstra and Dharmaśāstra' (*Z.D.M.G.*, 1913, pp. 49–96).

(4) Hermann Jacobi, 'On the Authority of the Kautiliya,' translated in *Ind. Ant.*, 1918, from the German in *Sitzungsber. d. königl. preuss. Akademien d. Wissenschaften*, 1912, No. xxxviii. He finds that it is 'the work of the famous minister of Chandragupta, as established by both external and internal proofs'.

The researches of the German scholars have clearly established that the Arthaśāstra is a genuine ancient work (*echt und alt*) of Maurya age, and presumably attributed rightly to Chāṇakya or Kauṭilya. Professor Keith throws doubt on the authorship of Kauṭilya (*J. R. A. S.*, 1916, pp. 130–7), and refers to *Z. D. M. G.*, lxviii, 355–9 by Jolly. The German verdict, of course, does not exclude the possibility, or probability, that the existing text may contain minor interpolations of later date, but the bulk of the book certainly dates from the Maurya period. I have pointed out that its contents describe the state of things as existing immediately *before* the establishment of the Maurya empire, while Mr. Shamasastry suggests that it may refer back even to the pre-Buddhistic age (p. xviii). The book seems to be based on much more ancient treatises now lost, and a good deal of it must have been archaic in Maurya times. Maurya age of the work.

The treatise will continue to give occupation to scholars for a long time to come, from many points of view.

CHAPTER VI

ASOKA MAURYA

Asoka as Crown Prince.

ACCORDING to credible tradition, Asoka-vardhana,[1] or Asoka, as he is generally called, served his apprenticeship to the art of government during the lifetime of his father, Bindusāra, as viceroy successively of the North-western frontier province and of Western India. He was one of several sons, and was no doubt selected by his father, in accordance with the usual practice, as *Yuvarāja*, or Crown Prince, on account of his ability and fitness for the imperial succession.

Taxila.

Taxila, the capital of the north-western viceroyalty, which probably included Kashmīr, the Panjāb, and the provinces to the west of the Indus, was in those days one of the greatest and most splendid of the cities of the East, and enjoyed a special reputation as the head-quarters of Hindu learning. The sons of people of all the upper classes, chiefs, Brahmans, and merchants, flocked to Taxila, as to a university town, in order to study the circle of Indian arts and sciences, especially medicine. The territory surrounding the capital was rich and populous, and, two generations earlier, had formed a small independent state, weak enough to be in terror of its neighbours, and yet strong enough to render Alexander valuable assistance.

Taxilan customs.

The Greeks, who considered the little state to be well governed, noted with interest, and without disapprobation, the local customs, which included polygamy, the exposure of the dead to be devoured by vultures, and the sale in open markets of maidens who had failed to secure husbands in the ordinary course.[2]

[1] *Vishṇu-Purāṇa.* Aśoka is the correct Sanskrit form, but in Pāli and some Sanskrit MSS. the dental *s* is used.

[2] Strabo, Bk. xv, chs. 28, 62. For the marriage-mart, compare the Babylonian practice (Herod. i, 196). Exposure of the dead to be devoured by vultures was, and still is, a Persian (Pārsī) custom (Herod. i, 140). It is practised to this day in Tibet, and was in ancient times

The position of the city on the high road from Central Asia to the interior of India fitted it to be the capital of the north-west viceroy; and its strategical advantages are still recognized. Hasan Abdāl, close to its ruins, is a favourite ground for the manœuvres of the Indian army; and at Rāwalpindi, a few miles to the south-east, a huge cantonment guards the road to India against possible Alexanders advancing from the north-west.

Favourable position of the city.

Ujjain, the capital of Western India, was equally famous, and equally suitable as the seat of a viceregal government. Reckoned to be one of the seven sacred cities, viz. Benares (Kāsī), Hardwār (Māyā), Kānchī (Conjeeveram), Ayodhyā (Oudh), Dvāravatī (Dwarka), Mathurā, and Ujjain (Avantikā), and standing on the road leading from the busy ports of the western coast to the markets of the interior, it combined the advantages of a favourite place of pilgrimage with those of a great commercial dépôt. The city was recognized as the head-quarters of Indian astronomy, and longitudes were computed from its meridian.[1]

Ujjain.

The Ceylonese tradition that Asoka was residing at Ujjain when he was summoned to the capital by the news of his father's mortal illness may well be believed; although no credence can be given to the tales which relate that Asoka had a hundred brothers, ninety-nine of whom he slew, and so forth. These idle stories seem to have been invented by the monks chiefly in order to place a dark background of early wickedness behind the bright picture of his mature piety. Asoka certainly had brothers and sisters alive in the seventeenth or eighteenth year of his reign,[2] whose households were objects of his anxious care; and there is nothing to indicate that he regarded his relatives with jealousy. His grandfather, Chandragupta, 'a man of blood and iron', who had fought his way from poverty and exile to the imperial

Asoka's peaceful accession.

the usage of the Lichchhavis of Vaisāli, who appear to have been either Tibetans or a cognate people (*Ind. Ant.*, 1903, p. 233). See also S. C. Vidyabhusena, 'The Licchavi Race of Ancient India' (*J. A. S. B.*, vol. lxxx, part I (1902), No. 2).

[1] See the curious article 'Oojyne' in Yule and Burnell, *Glossary of Anglo-Indian Words*.

[2] 'Fourteenth year', according to the inscriptions, reckoning from the coronation.

throne, naturally was beset by jealousies and hatreds, and constrained to live a life of distrustful suspicion. But Asoka, who was born in the purple, and inherited an empire firmly established by half a century of masterful rule for two generations, presumably was free from the 'black care' which haunted his ancestor. His edicts display no sense of insecurity or weakness from first to last; and the probability is that he succeeded peaceably in accordance with his predecessor's nomination. It is, however, possible that the northern tradition which testifies to a contest for the succession between Asoka and Susīma, his eldest brother, may be founded on fact. It has more historical appearance than the stories told by the monks of Ceylon.[1]

273 or 272 B.C. Accession; 269 B.C. Coronation.

Inasmuch as the reign of Asoka lasted for fully forty years, he must have been a young man when, in or about the year 273 B.C., he undertook the government of the vast empire which had been won and kept by his grandfather and father. Nothing is recorded concerning the first eleven or twelve years of his rule, which presumably were spent in the current work of administration. His solemn coronation did not take place before the year 269 B.C., about four years after his accession, and this fact is almost the only circumstance which supports the notion that his succession was disputed. The anniversary of his coronation was always celebrated with ceremony, and specially marked by the pardon and release of prisoners.[2]

261 B.C. Kalinga war.

In the thirteenth year of his reign, or in the ninth, as reckoned from the coronation, Asoka embarked upon the one aggressive war of his life of which a record exists, and rounded off his dominions by the conquest of the kingdom of Kalinga, the strip of territory extending along the coast of the Bay of Bengal from the Mahānadī to the Godāvarī. The campaign was wholly successful, and Kalinga became an integral part of the Maurya dominions. Two special

[1] *Asoka*, 3rd ed., p. 249.

[2] For the chronology see *Asoka, the Buddhist Emperor of India* (Clarendon Press, 3rd ed., 1920); which also gives a summary of the legends, and a complete translation of the inscriptions.

edicts published a few years later show that the administration of the newly acquired territory caused much anxiety to the emperor, who, like all sovereigns, sometimes was not well served by his officers. The royal instructions, which enjoined just and paternal government, and specially insisted on sympathetic tactful treatment of the wilder tribes, were disregarded at times by officials, who had to be warned that disobedience of orders was not the way to win the favour of either heaven or their master.

Misery caused by the war.

The kingdom of Kalinga had maintained a considerable military force, which was estimated by Megasthenes as numbering 60,000 infantry, 1,000 cavalry, and 700 war elephants. The opposition offered to the invaders was so stubborn that the conquest involved immeasurable suffering. The victor records with sorrow that 150,000 persons were carried into captivity, 100,000 were slain, and that many times that number perished from famine, pestilence, and the other calamities which follow in the train of armies.

The remorse of Asoka.

The sight of all this misery and the knowledge that he alone had caused it smote the conscience of Asoka, and awakened in his breast feelings of 'remorse, profound sorrow, and regret'. These feelings crystallized into a steadfast resolve that never again should ambition lead him to inflict such grievous wrongs upon his fellow creatures; and four years after the conquest he was able to declare that 'the loss of even the hundredth or the thousandth part of the persons who were then slain, carried away captive, or done to death in Kalinga would now be a matter of deep regret to his Majesty'.

Asoka forswears war.

The king acted up to the principles which he professed, and abstained from aggressive war for the rest of his life. About this time he came under the influence of Buddhist teaching, his devotion to which increased more and more as the years rolled on. The 'chiefest conquest', he declares, is that won by the Law of Piety, and he begs his descendants to rid themselves of the popular notion that conquest by arms is the duty of kings; and, even if they should find themselves engaged in warfare, he reminds them that they might still find pleasure in patience and gentleness, and should regard as the only true conquest that which is effected through the Law of Piety, or Duty.[1]

Moral propaganda. Asoka from this time forth made it the business of his life to employ his unlimited autocratic power over a vast empire in the teaching, propagation, and enforcement of the ethical system, which he called the Law of Piety or Duty (*dhaṁma* or *dharma*), and had learned chiefly from his Buddhist instructors.

257, 256 B.C. In the seventeenth and eighteenth years of his reign he decided definitely upon his line of action, and proclaimed the principles of his government to his people in a series of edicts engraved upon the rocks, including Minor Rock Edict I and the Fourteen Rock Edicts, and laying down the general rules which must guide the conduct of the lieges.

These extraordinary documents were followed by others specially concerning the conquered province of Kalinga, the purport of which has been referred to above. The earliest of the whole series seems to be Minor Rock Edict I, a short document, known in seven slightly variant forms. From it, as read with the longer compositions, we learn that Asoka was a lay disciple (*upāsaka*) for more than two and a half years after his conversion to Buddhism, and that during that period he did not exert himself strenuously.[2] But more than a year before the issue of his proclamations he had joined the Monastic Order (*saṁgha*) and had begun to devote earnest effort to promoting the cause of religion. The peculiar edict, known as the Bhābrū or Second Bairāt Rock Edict, in which the king enumerates seven passages of the scriptures as specially meriting the attention of both the clergy and the laity, apparently belongs to the same time.[3]

[1] Rock Edict XIII.

[2] Compare the case of the king of Samataṭa (the delta of the Brahmaputra), in the seventh century:

'Le roi de cet état s'appelait *Holouo-ché-po-tch'a* (Rajabhaṭṭa [Watters, II, 188, and *J. & Proc. A.S.B.*, 1914, p. 87]); ce souverain se trouvait être un fervent adorateur des trois Joyaux (triratna) et il jouait le rôle de grand *ou-po-souo-kia* (oupâsaka)' (Chavannes, *Religieux éminents*, p. 128).

[3] Bhābrū, not Bhābrā, is correct. The inscription comes from one of the Bairāt hills, distant about 12 miles from the camping-ground at Bhābrū (*Prog. Rep. A. S. W. Circle*, 1909–10, para. 10).

In the year 249 B.C., when he had occupied the throne for about twenty-four years, Asoka made a solemn pilgrimage to the most sacred spots in the Buddhist Holy Land. Starting from Pātaliputra, the capital, he advanced northwards along the royal road to Nepāl, the course of which is marked by five great monolithic pillars,[1] through the districts now known as Muzaffarpur and Champāran, until he approached the base of the outer Himalayan range. About 249 B.C. Pilgrimage.

Probably he then turned westwards, without crossing the hills, and first visited the famous Lumbinī Garden—the Bethlehem of Buddhism—where, according to the legend, the pains of travail came upon Māyā, and she gave birth to Buddha as she stood under a tree. At this spot his guide and preceptor, Upagupta, addressed Asoka and said: 'Here, great king! was the Venerable One born.' A pillar inscribed with these words, still as legible as when they were incised, was set up by Asoka to preserve the memory of his visit, and stands to this day.[2] Birth-place of Buddha.

In due course Saint Upagupta led his royal disciple to Kapilavastu, the home of Buddha's childhood, now in the Tarāi;[3] to Sārnāth, near Benares, the scene of the Master's first success as a preacher; to Srāvastī, where he lived for many years;[4] to the Bodhi tree of Gayā, where he overcame the powers of darkness; and to Kusinagara, where he died.[5] Other holy places.

[1] Bakhirā; Lauṛiyā-Ararāj (Radhiah); Lauṛiyā-Nandangaṛh (Mathiah); Rāmpurwā (2).

[2] The latest revised translation is given in *Asoka*, 3rd ed., p. 221, with a facsimile of the text.

[3] Probably Piprāwā in the north of the Bastī district, on the frontier (Mukherji and V. A. Smith, *Explorations in the Nepalese Tarāi*, Arch. Survey, Imp. Ser., vol. xxvi, Calcutta, 1897). The Kapilavastu *of Hiuen Tsang* certainly is represented by Tilaura Kōṭ and neighbouring ruins, in the Nepalese Tarāi, about 10 miles to the NW. of Piprāwā.

[4] On upper course of the Rāptī, perhaps Sahēṭh-Mahēṭh on the boundary of the Goṇda and Bahraich Districts. Inscriptions discovered by the Archaeological Dept. seem to identify the site (*Annual Rep. A. S.*, 1908–9, p. 137). The difficulty is that the site does not suit the indications given by the Chinese pilgrims (see *J. R. A. S.*, 1900, pp. 1–24).

[5] In Nepāl, beyond the first range of hills (*J. R. A. S.*, Jan., 1902), as I still think. H. H. General Khadga Shamsher Jang Bahādur agrees with me in placing Kuśinagara in Nepāl, and believes the site to be at the junction of the Little, or Eastern, Rāptī (Achiravatī) with the Gandak (Hiraṇyavatī). His position is farther west than that which I had selected, but almost in the same latitude, and is very likely to be correct (*Pioneer Mail*, Allahābād, Feb. 26,

At all these holy places the king granted liberal endowments, and set up memorials, some of which have come to light in these latter days, after long ages of oblivion.

Asoka was monk and monarch.

Although a modern student may feel difficulty in believing that Asoka could have assumed monastic vows and robe while still exercising autocratic control over a vast empire, there is no doubt about the fact that he did so. Nine centuries later the Chinese pilgrim I-tsing noted that the image of Asoka was clothed in a monk's garment of a particular pattern.[1] The incongruity involved according to our notions in an emperor turning monk, without abdicating, did not strike I-tsing, who was familiar with the exactly similar case in his own country of the Emperor Wu-ti or Hsiao Yen, the first of the Liang dynasty, who was a devout Buddhist, and adopted the monastic garb on two occasions, in A. D. 527 and 529.[2] A less exact parallel is supplied by the story of a Jain king of Western India in the twelfth century, who assumed the title of 'Lord of the Order', and at various periods of his reign bound himself by vows of continence and abstinence.[3] A Buddhist monk is always at liberty to return to lay life, and it is probable that Asoka retired to a monastery from time to time for a short period, making suitable arrangements for carrying on the administration during his retreat. There is some reason to believe that Minor Rock Edict I and the Bhābrū Edict were issued while the emperor was thus in retreat at Bairāt. It is easy to understand that an all-powerful monarch could have arranged the apparent difficulty

1904). The discovery in the large *stūpa* behind the Nirvāṇa temple near Kasiā of an inscribed copper plate bearing the words [*parini*] *rvāṇa-chaitye tāmra-paṭṭa iti* has revived and supported the old theory that the remains near Kasiā in the east of the Gorakhpur District represent Kuśinagara (Pargiter, *J. R. A. S.*, 1913, p. 152).

But that theory is untenable, because Kuśinagara was, and long had been, deserted in the time of the Chinese pilgrims, whereas building was continuous at Kasiā all through the Gupta period and afterwards. In all probability the establishment near Kasiā, which appears to have been subordinate to the monastery of the Decease at Kuśinagara, was also known as a *parinivāṇa-chaitya*. See my article on Kuśinagara in Hastings, *Encycl. of Religion and Ethics*.

[1] Takakusu, transl. of I-tsing, *A Record of Buddhist Practices*, p. 73.

[2] Giles, *Hist. Chinese Liter.*, 1901, p. 133; *Ind. Ant.*, 1903, p. 236.

[3] Bühler, *Ind. Ant.*, vi, 154.

to his satisfaction in more ways than one. Asoka distinctly adopted the position of ruler of both church and state during the last twenty-five years of his life, just as Charlemagne did long afterwards in Europe.

Retrospect in the Seven Pillar Edicts.

In or about the year 243 B.C., when he had been on the throne for some thirty years, Asoka began the composition of a fresh series of documents, the Seven Pillar Edicts, which reiterated his earlier teaching and conclude with a formal retrospect of the measures adopted by him in furtherance of the ethical reforms which he had at heart. They also include a concise code of regulations concerning the slaughter and mutilation of animals, practices which he regarded with abhorrence.

The retrospect, strange to say, takes no notice of the foreign missions. Nor does it mention the Council of Buddhist elders, which was held at the capital at some time in his reign mainly for the purpose of suppressing schism in the church. It seems likely that the Council may have been convoked after the publication of the Pillar Edicts, but I cannot explain the failure to commemorate the foreign missions which occupy a prominent place in the Rock Edicts.

The Council of Pāṭaliputra.

The fact of the convocation of a Council is attested by such a large body of tradition that it may be accepted without hesitation, even though none of the alleged details can be regarded as historical. The Sārnāth Edict (with its variants), which was specially directed against the cardinal sin of schism, was issued, I think, as a result of the Council's proceedings. I do not accept the Ceylonese date for the Council, namely, 236 A.B., equivalent, according to my chronology, to 251 B.C., and am of opinion that the Council assembled at some time in the last ten years of the reign.[1]

Extent of empire.

The extent of the enormous empire governed by Asoka can be ascertained with approximate accuracy. On the north-west, it extended to the Hindū Kush mountains, and

[1] For the references concerning each class of the Edicts, see Bibliography at the end of this chapter. It is impossible for me to discuss the credibility of the dates in the Ceylonese chronology in footnotes. See my observations on the Buddhist Councils in *J. R. A. S.*, 1901, pp. 142–58.

included most of the territory now under the rule of the King of Afghānistān, as well as the whole, or a large part, of Balūchistān, and all Sind. The secluded valleys of Suwāt (Swat) and Bājaur probably were more or less thoroughly controlled by the imperial officers, and the valleys of Kashmīr and Nepāl certainly were integral parts of the empire. Asoka built a new capital in the vale of Kashmīr, named Srīnagar, at a short distance from the city which now bears that name.[1]

Asoka in Nepal.

In the Nepāl valley, he replaced the older capital Manju Pātan, by a city named Pātan, Lalita Pātan, or Lalitpur, which still exists, 2½ miles to the south-east of Kāthmandū, the modern capital. Lalita Pātan, which subsequently became the seat of a separate principality, retains the special Buddhist stamp impressed upon it by Asoka. His foundation of the city was undertaken as a memorial of the visit which he paid to Nepāl, in 250 or 249 B.C., when he undertook the tour of the holy places. He was accompanied by his daughter Chārumatī, who adopted a religious life, and remained in Nepāl when her imperial father returned to the plains. She founded a town called Devapatana, in memory of her husband Devapāla Kshatriya, and settled down to the life of a nun at a convent built by her to the north of Pasupatināth, which bears her name to this day. Asoka treated Lalita Pātan as a place of great sanctity, erecting in it five great *stūpas*; one in the centre of the town, and four others outside the walls at the cardinal points. All these monuments still exist, and differ conspicuously from more recent edifices. Some minor buildings are also attributed to Asoka or his daughter.[2]

[1] Stein, *Rājataraṅginī*, transl., Bk. I, v. 104; vol. ii, pp. 409, 411. The position of Asoka's capital is marked by the site known as Pāndrēthan, 'Old Town', situated about 3 miles above modern Srīnagar, to which the ancient name has been transferred.

[2] Oldfield, *Sketches from Nipal*, ii, 198, 246–52; *Ind. Ant.* xiii, 412. The northern *stūpa* at Pātan is called Ipi Tūda by Mr. Bendall (*A Journey in Nepāl*, p. 12). Oldfield writes the name Epi, or Zimpi Tandu, and the Residency Clerk writes it Impi. Zimpi Taudu appears to be correct (Lévi, *Le Népal*, vol. i, pp. 263, 331; ii, pp. 1–3, 344). This building, although now inside the town, is outside the old line of walls.

B. V. Darbishire, Oxford, 1907

Extent eastward.

Eastwards, the empire comprised the whole of Bengal (Vanga) as far as the mouths of the Ganges, where Tāmralipti,[1] the modern Tamlūk, was the principal port. The strip of coast to the north of the Godāvarī river, known as Kalinga, was annexed in 261 B.C. Farther south, the Āndhra kingdom, between the Godāvarī and the Krishnā (Kistna), appears to have been in some measure subordinate to the Emperor, though administered by its own Rājas. On the south-east, the N. Pennār river may be regarded as the limit of the imperial jurisdiction.

Extent southward.

The Tamil states extending to the extremity of the Peninsula, and known as the Chola and Pāndya kingdoms, certainly were independent, as were the Keralaputra and Satiyaputra states on the south-western, or Malabar coast.[2] The southern frontier of the empire may be described approximately as a line drawn from the mouth of the Pennār river near Nellore on the eastern coast through Cuddapah and to the south of Chitaldroog (N. lat. 14° 13′, E. long. 76° 24′) to the river Kalyānapuri on the western coast (about N. lat. 14°), which forms the northern boundary of the Tuluva country.[3]

Jungle tribes.

The wilder tribes on the north-western frontier and in the jungle tracts of the Vindhya mountains separating Northern from Southern India seem to have enjoyed a limited autonomy under the suzerainty of the paramount power. The

[1] Tāmralipti seems to be a Sanskritized form of Prākrit Tāmal-itti, which is equivalent to classical Tamil Tiramiḍa, i. e. Dramiḍa. The original forms would have been Tiramiḍatti and Dramīḍadatti (K. P. Jayaswal in *Ind. Ant.*, 1914, p. 64).

[2] Rock Edicts II, XIII.

[3] I cannot agree with Fleet (*J. R. A. S.*, 1909, p. 997 n.) that Minor Rock Edict II, of which three texts exist in N. Mysore, was addressed to a foreign power. Rock Edict II clearly states that the neighbouring or frontier states included the Cholas, Pāndyas, Keralaputra, and Satiyaputra. R. G. Bhandarkar (*Indian Review*, June, 1909) would place the Satiyaputra state near Poona, because families of several castes in the Poona district still bear the name *Sātpute*. But the edict groups the Satiyaputras with the Tamil powers, and I hold that their country may be identified with the Satyamangalam sub-division of the Coimbatore District and some adjoining territory (see note on p. 194, *post*). I still believe that the Maurya empire, including both territories directly administered and regions attached only by an ill-defined protectorate, extended to the south until it impinged on the frontiers of the ancient, well-established Tamil kingdoms.

empire comprised therefore, in modern terminology, Afghānistān south of the Hindū Kush, Balūchistān, Sind, the valley of Kashmīr, Nepāl, the lower Himalaya, and the whole of India Proper, except the southern extremity.

Viceroys. The central regions seem to have been governed directly from Pātaliputra under the king's personal supervision. The outlying provinces were administered by viceroys, of whom, apparently, there were at least four. The ruler of the north-west was stationed at Taxila, and his jurisdiction may be assumed to have included the Panjāb, Sind, the countries beyond the Indus, and Kashmīr. The eastern territories, including the conquered kingdom of Kalinga, were governed by a viceroy stationed at Tosali, the exact position of which has not been ascertained. The western provinces of Mālwa, Gujarāt, and Kāthiāwār were under the government of a prince, whose head-quarters were at the ancient city of Ujjain; and the southern provinces, beyond the Narbadā, were ruled by the fourth viceroy.[1]

Buildings. Asoka was a great builder; and so deep was the impression made on the popular imagination by the extent and magnificence of his architectural works that legend credited him with the erection of eighty-four thousand *stūpas*, or sacred cupolas, within the space of three years. When Fa-hien, the first Chinese pilgrim, visited Pātaliputra, the capital, at the beginning of the fifth century in the reign of Chandragupta

[1] The Mysore versions of Minor Rock Edict I convey the commands of Asoka to the officials of a town named Isila, probably represented by an ancient site near the places where the inscriptions exist, through the Prince and officials of Suvarṇagiri—that is to say, the commands received from Asoka were issued from Suvarṇagiri by the Prince and high officers residing there. I understand that Suvarṇagiri was somewhere in the south, and that the Prince was Asoka's Viceroy of the Deccan. Fleet guesses that Suvarṇagiri should be identified with Sōngir at Old Rājgir in Magadha, and on that basis elaborates a theory that Asoka was living in retirement at that place (*J.R.A.S.*, 1909, pp. 981–1016). I cannot find any evidence that Asoka abdicated, and I prefer to believe that Suvarṇagiri ('Golden Hill') was situated somewhere in one of the ancient goldfields. Maski, where the Asoka inscription was discovered in 1915, is situated in a country which 'abounds in numerous ancient gold workings' (*Hyderabad Archaeol. Series*, No. 1, 1915), and was an important settlement even in the late neolithic period (*Foote Coll. Indian Prehistoric*, vol. of notes, pp. 31, 125, 126).

Vikramāditya, the palace of Asoka was still standing, and was deemed to have been wrought by supernatural agency.

'The royal palace and halls in the midst of the city, which exist now as of old, were all made by the spirits which he employed, and which piled up the stones, reared the walls and gates, and executed the elegant carving and inlaid sculpture work, in a way which no human hands of this world could accomplish.'

These stately buildings have all vanished, and their remains lie buried for the most part beyond hope of recovery deep below the silt of the Ganges and Sōn rivers, overlaid by the East India Railway, the city of Patna, and the civil station of Bankipore. The excavations in progress have already revealed enough to attest the substantial truth of the pilgrim's enthusiastic description, and I myself have seen two huge and finely carved sandstone capitals—one with the acanthus-leaf ornament—dug up near Bankipore.

The numerous and magnificent monasteries founded by Asoka have shared the fate of his palaces, and are ruined beyond recognition.

Sāñchi *stūpas*.

The only buildings of the Asokan period which have escaped destruction, and remain in a state of tolerable preservation, are those forming the celebrated group of *stūpas*, or cupolas, at and near Sānchi, in Central India, not very far from Ujjain, where Asoka held court as viceroy of the west before his accession to the throne. The elaborately carved gateways of the railing round the principal monument, which have been so often described and figured, may have been constructed to the order of the great Maurya, and certainly are not much later than his time.

Monolithic pillars.

The massive monolithic sandstone pillars, inscribed and uninscribed, which Asoka erected in large numbers throughout the home provinces of the empire, some of which are 50 feet in height, and about 50 tons in weight, are not only worthy monuments of his magnificence, but also of the highest interest as the earliest known examples of the Indian stone-cutter's art in architectural forms. The design is a highly improved adaptation of a Persian model, and the mechanical execution is perfect.[1]

Cave-dwellings.

The caves with highly polished walls excavated in the intensely hard quartzose gneiss of the Barābar hills near Gayā by order of Asoka, for the use of the Ājīvika ascetics, an extremely ancient penitential order distinct from both the Jains and the Buddhists, recall Egyptian work by the mastery displayed over intractable material.[2]

Inscriptions.

The most interesting monuments of Asoka are his famous inscriptions, more than thirty in number, incised upon rocks, boulders, cave-walls, and pillars, which supply the only safe foundation for the history of his reign, and must be briefly described before I can enter upon the discussion of his doctrine and policy. The more important documents, which expound fully both his principles of government and his system of practical ethics, supply many interesting autobiographical details. The shorter documents include dedications, brief commemorative records, and other matter ; but all, even the most concise, have interest and value.[3]

Area covered by inscriptions.

The area covered by the inscriptions comprises nearly the whole of India (see map), extending from the Himalayas to Mysore, and from the Bay of Bengal to the Arabian Sea.

Language.

All the documents are written in various forms of Prākrit, that is to say, vernacular dialects closely allied to both literary Sanskrit and the Pāli of the Ceylonese Buddhist

[1] See *Asoka*, 3rd ed., pp. 117–24; *A History of Fine Art in India and Ceylon*, pp. 20, 59–62, Pls. II, XIII, and Figs. 28, 29 ; and 'The Monolithic Pillars or Columns of Asoka', *Z.D.M.G.*, 1911, pp. 221–40. Sir J. H. Marshall speaks of the 'extraordinary precision and accuracy which characterizes all Maurya work, and which has never, we venture to say, been surpassed even by the finest workmanship on Athenian buildings' (*Annual Rep. A. S.*, 1906–7, p. 89).

[2] The Ājīvikas were not Vaishnavas, as has been supposed (Bhandarkar, 'Epigraphic Notes and Questions', in *J. Bo. R. A. S.*, vol. xx, 1902 ; and *Ind. Ant.*, 1912, pp. 90, 286). See also the summary of the doctrines of the sect in the *Sāmaññaphala Sutta*, transl. by Rhys Davids, *Dialogues of the Buddha* (1899, p. 71), and Hoernle's exhaustive article, *s.v.* in *Encycl. Religion and Ethics*, vol. i (1908). The Ājīvikas were the forerunners of the Digambara Jains, and practically identical with them. See *J.R.A.S.*, 1913, pp. 669–74.

[3] All the documents describe the Emperor by his titles only, with the single exception of the Maski inscription which specifies his personal name, Asoka. Its opening words are *Devānampiyasa Asokasa*.

books, but not identical with either.[1] They were therefore obviously intended to be read and understood by the public generally, and their existence presupposes a widely diffused knowledge of the art of writing. The inscriptions designed for public instruction were placed either in suitable positions on high roads or at frequented places of pilgrimage where their contents were ensured the greatest possible publicity.

Script.

Two recensions of the Fourteen Rock Edicts, inscribed on rocks at places near the north-western frontier of India, were executed in the script locally current, now generally known to scholars as the Kharoshthī; which is a modified form of an ancient Aramaic alphabet, written from right to left, introduced into the Panjāb during the period of Persian domination in the fifth and fourth centuries B.C. All the other inscriptions are incised in one or other variety of the early Brāhmī alphabet, from which the Devanāgarī and other forms of the modern script in Northern and Western India have been evolved, and which is read from left to right.[2]

Eight classes.

The inscriptions readily fall into eight classes, which may be arranged in approximate chronological order as follows :—

I. The Minor Rock Edicts, of which No. I is found in seven recensions, all probably dating from 257 B.C., a little before the Fourteen Rock Edicts. No. II may be somewhat later.

II. The Bhābrū Edict, of about the same date as Minor Rock Edict I.

III. The Fourteen Rock Edicts, in seven recensions, dating from the thirteenth and fourteenth regnal years, as reckoned from the coronation, corresponding roughly to 257, 256 B.C.

IV. The two Kalinga Edicts, issued probably in 256 B.C., and concerned only with the newly conquered province.

V. The three dedicatory Cave Inscriptions at Barābar near Gayā, 257 and 250 B.C.

[1] Grierson holds that Pāli, the language of the Southern Buddhist scriptures, is a literary form of the ancient language spoken at Takshasilā. This accounts for its striking resemblance to Paisāchī Prākrit (*Ind. Ant.* 1915, p. 227 n.).

[2] Prof. Rapson is of opinion that 'the region in which both the Kharoṣṭhī and the Brāhmī scripts were at home may be fairly identified with the Jalandhar District of the Punjāb' (*J.R.A.S.*, 1905, p. 810).

VI. The two Tarāi Pillar Inscriptions, 249 B.C.

VII. The Seven Pillar Edicts, in six recensions, 243 and 242 B.C.

VIII. The Minor Pillar Edicts, about 240 B.C., or later.

Minor Rock Edicts.

The first Minor Rock Edict presents more difficulties in interpretation than any other Asoka document. These difficulties are being solved gradually, and it is now certain that the edict does not include a date.[1] Its high value for the personal history of Asoka has been referred to above. Edict No. II is merely a short summary of the Law or *Dharma*.

Bhābrū Edict.

The Bhābrū Edict is of the first importance in the history of the Buddhist Canon, because it enumerates seven passages in the scriptures which the emperor judged to merit the special attention of his people. All the passages have now been identified.[2] Asoka may have been residing at one of the Bairāt monasteries when he caused this unique document to be prepared.

The Fourteen Rock Edicts.

The Fourteen Rock Edicts contain an exposition of Asoka's principles of government and ethical system, each edict being devoted to a special subject. The different recensions vary considerably, and some do not include all the fourteen edicts. The whole series, in all its varieties, is confined to remote frontier provinces, which were under the government of viceroys. The emperor evidently was of opinion that in the home provinces, under his immediate control, it was not necessary to engrave his instructions on the rocks, other and more convenient methods of publication being available. But many years later he perpetuated his revised code in the home provinces also by incising it

[1] Three recensions of Minor Rock Edict I exist in Northern Mysore at localities near one another, namely, Śiddāpura, Jaṭinga-Rāmeśvara (14° 50′ N. lat., 76° 48′ E. long.) and Brahmagiri, and one in the Nizam's Dominions at Maski, 45 miles NW. from Śiddāpura. The other three are at Sahasrām (Sasseram) in the Shāhābād District, Bihār; Rūpnāth, in the Jabalpur (Jubbulpore) District, Central Provinces; and Bairāt in the Jaipur State, Rājputāna. Minor Rock Edict II is added to the Mysore texts only.

[2] The Bhābrū Edict is incised on a boulder, now in Calcutta, which was removed from the top of a hill at Bairāt. Minor Rock Edict I is incised on a rock at the foot of an adjoining hill.

upon several of the monolithic monumental pillars which it was his pleasure to erect in numerous localities.[1] The difficulty of obtaining the fine sandstone needed for the pillars may account for the fact that the area of their distribution is much smaller than that of the rock-inscriptions.

The Kaliṅga Edicts.

The two Kalinga Edicts are special supplements to the series of the Fourteen Rock Edicts intended to fix the principles on which the administration of the newly conquered province and the wild tribes dwelling on its borders should be conducted. They were substituted for certain edicts (Nos. XI, XII, XIII) of the regular series, which were omitted from the Kalinga recension, as being unsuitable for local promulgation.

Cave Inscriptions.

The three Cave Inscriptions at Barābar in the Gayā District, the Goratha-giri of the Mahābhārata,[2] are merely brief dedications of costly cave dwellings for the use of a monastic sect known as Ājīvika, the members of which went about naked, and were noted for ascetic practices of the most rigorous kind. These records are chiefly of interest as a decisive proof that Asoka was sincere in his solemn declaration that he honoured all sects; for the Ājīvikas were extreme fatalists, having little or nothing in common with the Buddhists.

Tarāi Pillar Inscriptions.

The two Tarāi Pillar Inscriptions, although extremely brief, are of much interest for many reasons, one of which is that they prove beyond question the truth of the literary tradition that Asoka performed a solemn pilgrimage to the sacred spots of the Buddhist Holy Land. The Rummindēī, or Padaria, inscription, which is in absolutely perfect pre-

[1] The positions of the Fourteen Rock Edicts are: (1) Shāhbāzgaṛhi, in the Yusufzī country, 40 miles north-east of Peshāwar; (2) Mānsahra or Mānsērā, in Hazārā District (Uraśā), Panjāb, the Kharoshṭhī script being used at both these places; (3) Kālsī, in the Lower Himalayas, 15 miles west from Mussoorie (Mansūrī); (4) Sopārā, in Thānā District, near Bombay; (5) the Girnār hill, near Jūnāgaṛh, in the Kāthiāwāṛ peninsula; (6) near Dhauli, to the south of Bhuvanēśvar in the Cuttack (Kaṭak) District, Orissa; and (7) at Jaugaḍa in the Ganjām District, Madras. The last two places were included in Kaliṅga; and the two Kaliṅga Edicts are added as appendices to the Dhauli and Jaugaḍa texts. See map.

[2] See *J. B. O. Res. Soc.* I, 159–71.

servation, has the great merit of determining, beyond the possibility of doubt, the exact position of the famous Lumbinī Garden, where, according to the legend, Gautama Buddha first saw the light. This determination either solves, or supplies the key to, a multitude of problems. The companion record at Niglīva, which is less perfectly preserved, gives the unexpected and interesting information that Asoka's devotion was not confined to Gautama Buddha, but included in its catholic embrace his predecessors, the 'former Buddhas'.[1]

The Pillar Edicts. The Seven Pillar Edicts, issued in their complete form in or about the year 242 B.C., when Asoka had reigned for some thirty years, and was nearing the close of his career of activity in worldly affairs, must be read along with the Fourteen Rock Edicts, to which they refer, and of which they may be considered an appendix. The principles enunciated in the earlier instructions are reiterated and emphasized in the later; the regulations enforcing the sanctity of animal life are amplified and codified; and the series closes with the most valuable of all the documents, Pillar Edict No. VII, preserved on one monument only, which recounts in orderly fashion the measures to promote 'the growth of piety' adopted by the emperor within his dominions during the course of his long reign.[2]

Minor Pillar Inscriptions. The historical interest of the Minor Pillar Inscriptions was not recognized until after the discovery of the Sārnāth Edict in 1905, when it appeared that the Sānchī and Kausāmbī Edicts, which had been known for many years, were merely variants of the better preserved Sārnāth text. Inasmuch as all the three documents deal with the penalties for schism

[1] The Rummindēī ruins lie 4 miles inside the Nepalese border, and a little to the west of the Tilār river, in approximately E. long. 85° 11′, N. lat. 25° 58′. Padariā is a neighbouring village. The Niglīva pillar, which apparently has been moved from its original position, now stands about 13 miles to the north-west from Rummindēī. For facsimile of Rummindēī inscription, see *Asoka, the Buddhist Emperor of India*, plate ii.

[2] The Pillar Edicts are found on six pillars: namely, on two at Delhi, of which one was brought from Topra near Umballa, and the other from Meerut (Mīraṭh); on one pillar at Allāhābād; and on one each at Lauṛiyā-Ararāj, Lauṛiyā-Nandangaṛh, and Rāmpurwā, all in the Champāran District of Tirhūt.

THE BIRTH-PLACE OF BUDDHA

(RUMMINDĒĪ PILLAR AND TEMPLE)

in the Church, it is reasonable to assume that they represent the decision of the Council convened to suppress schism. The Queen's Edict is concerned with the Almoner's Department.[1]

Relation of epigraphic and traditional evidence.

The foregoing summary exposition will perhaps suffice to enable the reader to form some notion of the extraordinary interest attaching to the unique series of inscriptions issued by Asoka between the years 257 and 232 B.C., which is the only safe foundation on which to build a history of his momentous reign. But tradition has its value as a secondary source of information, and a few words in explanation of the character of the traditional evidence for the Asokan history are indispensable.

The Asokan legend.

The rank growth of legend which has clustered round the name of Asoka bears eloquent testimony to the commanding influence of his personality. In the Buddhist world his fame is as great as that of Charlemagne in mediaeval Europe, and the tangle of mythological legend which obscures the genuine history of Asoka may be compared in mass with that which drapes the figures of Alexander, Arthur, and Charlemagne. The Asokan legend is not all either fiction or myth, and includes some genuine historical tradition; but is no better suited to serve as the foundation of sober history than the stories of the Morte d'Arthur or Pseudo-Kallisthenes are adapted to form the bases of chronicles of the doings of the British champion or the Macedonian conqueror. This obvious canon of criticism has been forgotten by most writers upon the Maurya period, who have begun at the wrong end with the late legends, instead of at the right end with the contemporary inscriptions.

Two streams of legend.

The legends have reached us in two main streams, the Ceylonese and the North-Indian. The accident that the Ceylonese varieties of the stories happen to be recorded in books which assume the form of chronicles with a detailed chronology, and have been known to European readers for many years, has given to the southern tales an illusory

[1] The Kauśāmbī and Queen's Edicts are incised upon the Allāhābād pillar in a way which shows that they must be later in date than the Pillar Edicts.

air of special authenticity. The earliest of the Ceylonese chronicles, the *Dīpavaṁśa*, which probably was compiled late in the fourth century after Christ, is some six centuries posterior to the death of Asoka, and has little claim to be regarded as a first-rate authority, although deserving respectful consideration.

Higher authority of the northern legends.

The North-Indian legends are at least as old; but being recorded in fragments scattered through many books, Indian, Nepalese, Chinese, and Tibetan, have received scant attention. All legendary material, of course, must be used with extreme caution, and only as a supplement to authentic data; but a moment's thought will show that legends preserved in Northern India, the seat of Asoka's imperial power, are more likely to transmit genuine tradition than those which reached the distant island of Ceylon in translations brought nobody knows how, when, or whence, and subsequently largely modified by local and sectarian influences. This presumption is verified when the two groups of legends are compared; and then it clearly appears that in certain matters of importance where they differ, the Northern version is distinctly the more credible.

APPENDIX II

The Inscriptions of Asoka; Bibliographical Note

(Based on that published in *Asoka*, 3rd ed., pp. 227–30, brought up to date.)

The older and obsolete publications of Prinsep, &c., are not cited. A full list of references up to 1902 will be found in R. OTTO FRANKE, *Pāli und Sanskrit*, Strassburg, 1902, pp. 1–5. The following list, recording publications up to and including 1919, is believed to be nearly complete, so far as important writings are concerned, but it is possible some articles may have been overlooked.

I. General

SENART, ÉMILE.—*Les Inscriptions de Piyadasi* (Paris, t. i, 1881; t. ii, 1886). This great work, although partially superseded by later discoveries and researches, is still indispensable for a thorough study of the inscriptions.

CUNNINGHAM, SIR A.—*Inscriptions of Asoka* (Calcutta, 1877). May be consulted for topographical details.

SMITH, V. A.—' Asoka Notes ' (12) in *Ind. Ant.* for 1903, 1905, 1908, 1909, 1910, and 1918 ; *Asoka, the Buddhist Emperor of India*, 3rd ed., 1920. The new edition of the inscriptions, with translation and commentary, by Prof. Hultzsch, has been suspended and indefinitely delayed by the War.

THOMAS, F. W.—'Notes on the Edicts of Asoka', in *J. R. A. S.*, 1914, 1915, 1919.

II. Minor Rock Edicts

These documents, studied in connexion with the Minor Pillar Edicts, have attracted special attention. The last word has not been said yet.

BÜHLER, G.—The three Siddāpura (Mysore) texts, ed. and transl. with facs., in *Ep. Ind.*, iii, 135–42 ; the three northern texts, Sahasrām, Bairāt, and Rūpnāth, ed. and transl. with facs. of Sahasrām and Rūpnāth in *Ind. Ant.*, vi (1877), pp. 149–60 ; and revised, ibid., vol. xxii (1893), pp. 299–306. See also ibid., vol. xxvi (1897), p. 334.

SENART and GRIERSON.—The three northern texts, in *Ind. Ant.*, vol. xx (1891), p. 154.

RICE, LEWIS.—Facs. of Siddāpura texts, all three, in *Ep. Carn.*, vol. xi (Bangalore, 1909) ; and of Brahmagiri text in *Mysore and Coorg from the Inscriptions* (London, 1909).

FLEET, J. F.—A series of papers in *J. R. A. S.*, for 1903, 1904, 1908, 1909, 1910, and 1911.

THOMAS, F. W.—*Ind. Ant.*, 1908, p. 21 ; ' Les Vivāsāh d'Asoka ', *J. Asiatique*, Mai–Juin 1910, important ; *J. R. A. S.*, 1913, p. 477.

HULTZSCH, PROF.—*J. R. A. S.*, 1910, pp. 142, 1308 ; 1911, p. 1114 ; 1913, p. 1053 (with Minor Pillar Edicts).

LÉVI, PROF. SYLVAIN.—' Vyuthena 256 ' in *J. Asiatique*, Jan.–Fév. 1911.

BHANDARKAR, D. R.—'Epigraphic Notes and Questions ', *Ind. Ant.*, 1912, pp. 170–3.

YAZDANI, G.—The Maski text. Ed. with plates in *Hyderabad Archaeol. Series*, No. i, Calcutta, 1915 ; commented on by Rice, *J. R. A. S.*, 1916, p. 838.

III. Bhābrū (Bhābrā) Edict

SENART and GRIERSON.—Revised ed. and transl. in *Ind. Ant.*, vol. xx (1891), p. 165.

BURGESS, J.—Facs. in *J. Asiatique*, 1887.

DAVIDS, T. W. RHYS.—*J. R. A. S.*, 1898, p. 639 ; *J. Pāli Text Soc.*, 1896.

HARDY, E.—*J. R. A. S.*, 1901, pp. 311, 577.

LÉVI, PROF. SYLVAIN.—'Notes sur diverses inscriptions de Piyadasi', Sec. ii, in *J. Asiatique*, Mai–Juin 1896. (Sec. i deals with the Minor Rock Edicts).

KOSAMBI, PROF. DH.—*Ind. Ant.*, vol. xli, 1912, p. 37.

HULTZSCH, PROF.—*J. R. A. S.*, 1909, p. 727; 1911, p. 1113–17.

EDMUNDS, A.—*J. R. A. S.*, 1913, p. 385.

BARNA, B. M.—*J. R. A. S.*, 1915, p. 805.

MITRA SAILENDRANATH.—*J. R. A. S.*, vol. xlviii (1919), p. 8.

IV. The Fourteen Rock Edicts

The standard edition is that by BÜHLER in *Ep. Ind.*, ii, pp. 447–72, with facs. of Girnār and Kālsī texts; transcripts of Girnār, Kālsī, Shāhbāzgaṛhi and Mānsahra texts, and version of Shāhbāzgaṛhi. Facs. of Edict XII, Shāhb., by same, in *Ep. Ind.*, i, 16; ed. and transl., by same, of Dhauli and Jaugaḍa texts in BURGESS, *Amarāvatī* (*A. S. S. I.*, 1887), pp. 114–25. Another facs. of Girnār text, with obsolete transl., in BURGESS, *Kāthiāwār and Kachh, A. S. W. I.*, pp. 93–127.

Edicts I, II, discussed in *J. Bo. Br. R. A. S.*, vol. xx (1902), and in *Ind. Ant.*, xlii (1913), pp. 253–8; vol. xlvii (1918), p. 48 and pp. 221–3; and *J. R. A. S.*, 1914, p. 393. For Edict III, see Fleet, *J. R. A. S.*, 1908, pp. 811–22; and *J. B. O. Res. Soc.*, iv, 37. Edict IV, discussed by HULTZSCH, *J. R. A. S.*, 1911, p. 785, and D. R. BHANDARKAR, *Ind. Ant.*, 1913, p. 25. See also *Ind. Ant.*, xliv (1915), p. 208. For Edict V, see *J. B. O. Res. Soc.*, iv, 144–6. For Edict VI, *Ind. Ant.*, xlvii (1918), p. 51. For Edict VIII, *Ind. Ant.*, vol. xlii (1913), p. 159; RHYS DAVIDS, *Dialogues*, 1st series, p. 190. For Edict IX, *J. R. A. S.*, 1913, p. 654. Edict XIII, *J. R. A. S.*, 1913, p. 655.

Many points connected with the series are examined by V. A. SMITH in 'Asoka Notes' (see *I. General*, above); and by R. O. FRANKE, 'Zu Açoka's Felsen-Edicten', in *Nachr. d. königl. Gesellsch. d. Wissenschaften zu Göttingen*, 1895.

The papers by MICHELSON, chiefly dealing with technicalities of etymology and phonetics, in *J. Amer. Or. Soc.*, 1911; *American J. Philology*, 1909, 1910; and *Indo-Germ. Forschungen*, 1910, 1911, are concerned to a considerable extent with the Fourteen Rock Edicts.

V. Kalinga Edicts

Revised, ed., and trans. by SENART and GRIERSON in *Ind. Ant.*, xix (1890), pp. 82–102; correcting the earlier transl. by BÜHLER, with facs. in BURGESS, *Amarāvati* (*A. S. S. I.*, 1887), pp. 125–31. See also Kern, *Manual of Indian Buddhism* (Strassburg, 1896), p. 61.

VI. The Seven Pillar Edicts

The standard ed. is BÜHLER'S, with transl. and facs. of some texts, in *Ep. Ind.*, ii (1894), pp. 245–74. Revised ed. and transl.

by SENART and GRIERSON in *Ind. Ant.*, xvii (1888), pp. 303–7 ; xviii (1889), pp. i, 73, 105, 300. Facs. of Delhi–Topra and Allāhābād texts, by BÜHLER and FLEET, in *Ind. Ant.*, xiii (1884), p. 306.

MONMOHAN CHAKRAVARTI.—' Animals in the Inscriptions of Piyadasi ' (*Memoirs A. S. B.*, Calc., 1906), for Ed. v.

T. MICHELSON in ' Notes on the Pillar Edicts of Asoka ' (*Indo-Germ. Forschungen* (Sonderabzug, Trübner, Strassburg, 1908)) gives valuable textual criticism with some interpretations. See ' Asokan Notes ' in *J. A. O. S.*, vol. xxxvi (1916), pp. 205–12.

For description of the Rāmpurwā pillars, see *J. R. A. S.*, 1908, p. 1085. Pillar Edict IV is discussed by Thomas, *J. R. A. S.*, 1916, pp. 120–3 ; for Pillar Edict VII, see D. R. Bhandarkar in *Ind. Ant.*, vol. xliii (1884), p. 310 ; THOMAS, *J. R. A. S.*, 1915, p. 97, and ibid., 1916, p. 122.

The Pillar Edicts present comparatively few difficulties.

VII. Minor Pillar Edicts

(1) Sārnāth.—VOGEL, discussion with facs. in *Ep. Ind.*, viii (1905–6), p. 168 ; SENART, *Comptes rendus de l'Acad. des Inscriptions*, 1907, p. 25 ; VENIS. *J. & Proc. A. S. B.*, vol. iii, N.S. (1907) ; NORMAN, ibid., vol. iv (1908) ; BOYER, *J. Asiatique*, t. x (1907), p. 119. See also THOMAS, *J. R. A. S.*, 1915, p. 112.

(2) Kauśāmbī.—SENART transcribed it in *Ind. Ant.*, xviii (1889), p. 309 ; facs. and transcript by BÜHLER, ibid., xix (1890), p. 126.

(3) Sāñchī.—BÜHLER ed. and transl. in *Ep. Ind.*, ii, 87, 367, 369 ; HULTZSCH, *J. R. A. S.*, 1911, p. 167.

(4) Queen's Edict.—BÜHLER ed. and transl. in *Ep. Ind.*, ii, 87, 367 ; and further revision in *Ind. Ant.*, xix (1890), p. 125. Emendation by HULTZSCH, *J. R. A. S.*, 1911, p. 1113. SENART, revised, ed., and transl. in *Ind. Ant.*, xviii (1889), p. 308.

The interpretation is connected with that of the Minor Rock Edicts, which see. For description of the pillar, see *Annual Rep. Arch. S.*, 1904–5, pp. 36, 68.

VIII. The Tarāi Commemorative Inscriptions

Both ed. and transl. by BÜHLER, with facs. in *Ep. Ind.*, v, 4. Discussion by V. A. SMITH, Introd. to MUKHURJI, *Report on Antiquities in the Tarāi, Nepāl*, Calcutta, 1901 ; and in *Ind. Ant.*, vol. xxxiv (1905), p. 10. PISCHEL in *Sitzungsb. d. kön. preuss. Akad. d. Wissenschaften*, 1903. FLEET, *J. R. A. S.*, 1908, pp. 471–98, 823. CHARPENTIÈR, *Ind. Ant.*, xliii (1914), pp. 17–20.

IX. Cave Dedications of Asoka and Daśaratha

All ed. and transl. by BÜHLER, with facs. in *Ind. Ant.*, xx (1891), p. 361. The Gorathagiri inscriptions are published by JACKSON in *J. B. O. Res. Soc.*, i (1915), pp. 159–71, with plates.

CHAPTER VII

ASOKA MAURYA (CONTINUED); AND HIS SUCCESSORS

Dhamma, or Law of Piety. THE edicts are devoted mainly to the exposition, inculcation, and enforcement of a scheme of practical ethics, or rule of conduct, which Asoka called *Dhaṁma*. No English word or phrase is exactly equivalent to the Prākrit *dhaṁma* (Sanskrit *dharma*), but the expression Law of Piety, or simply Piety, comes tolerably close to the meaning of the Indian term. The rendering Law of Duty may be used if preferred. The validity of this Law of Piety or Duty is assumed in the edicts, and no attempt is made to found it upon any theological or metaphysical basis. Theological ideas are simply ignored by Asoka, as they were by his master, Gautama; and the current Hindu philosophy of rebirth, inaccurately called metempsychosis, is taken for granted, and forms the background of the ethical teaching.

Sanctity of animal life. The leading tenet of Asoka's Buddhism, as of the cognate Jain system, and some varieties of Brahmanical Hinduism, was a passionate, uncompromising belief in the sanctity of animal life. The doctrine of the absolute, unconditional right of the meanest animal to retain the breath of life until the latest moment permitted by nature, is that of the edicts; and was based upon the belief that all living creatures, including men, animals, gods, and demons, form links in an endless chain of existence, or rather of 'becoming'.[1]

Doctrines of rebirth and *Karma*. The being that is now a god in heaven may be reborn in the course of aeons as an insect; and the insect, in its turn, may work up to the rank of a god. This belief, associated with the faith that the mode of rebirth is conditioned by

[1] The first of the three 'characteristic doctrines of Buddhism' is that 'all the constituents of being are transitory' (πάντα ῥεῖ); the second, that they are all misery; and the third, that they are lacking in an Ego (Warren, *Buddhism in Translations*, p. xiv).

the *karma*, the net ethical result, or balance of good or evil of the life of each creature at the moment of its termination, lies deep down at the roots of Indian thought, and is inseparably bound up with almost every form of Indian religion. Sometimes it is combined with theories which recognize the existence of a personal soul, but it is also firmly held by persons who utterly deny all forms of the soul theory.

Comparative disregard of human life.

It is easy to understand that believers in ideas of this kind may be led logically to regard the life of an insect as entitled to no less respect than that of a man. In practice, indeed, the sanctity of animal was placed above that of human life; and the absurd spectacle was sometimes witnessed of a man being put to death for killing an animal, or even for eating meat. The most pious Buddhist and Jain kings had no hesitation about inflicting capital punishment upon their subjects, and Asoka himself continued to sanction the death penalty throughout his reign. He was content to satisfy his humanitarian feelings by a slight mitigation of the sanguinary penal code inherited from his stern grandfather in conceding to condemned prisoners three days' grace to prepare for death.[1]

Early practice of Asoka.

In early life Asoka is believed to have been a Brahmanical Hindu, specially devoted to Siva, a god whose consort delights in bloody sacrifices; and he appears to have had no scruple about the shedding of blood. Thousands of living creatures used to be slain on the occasion of a banquet (*samāja*) to supply the kitchens of the overgrown royal household with curries for a single day. As he became gradually imbued with the spirit of Buddhist teaching, this wholesale daily slaughter became abominable in his eyes, and was stopped; only three living creatures at the most, namely, two peacocks and one deer, being killed each day; and in 257 B.C. even this limited butchery was put an end to.[2]

[1] Pillar Edict IV.

[2] Rock Edict I. D. R. Bhandarkar's comments in 'Epigraphic Notes and Questions' (*J. Bo. R. A. S.*, 1902) deserve attention. E. Thomas believed that Asoka was a Jain in early life, but without sufficient reason.

Abolition of the royal hunt.

Two years earlier, in 259 B. C., Asoka had abolished the royal hunt, which formed such an important element in the amusements of his grandfather's court. 'In times past,' he observes, 'their Majesties were wont to go out on pleasure tours, during which hunting and other similar amusements used to be practised.' But His Sacred and Gracious Majesty no longer cared for such frivolous outings, and had substituted for them solemn progresses devoted to inspection of the country and people, visits and largess to holy men, and preaching and discussion of the Law of Piety.[1]

Code of 243 B. C.

As time went on Asoka's passionate devotion to the doctrine of the sanctity of animal life grew in intensity ; and, in 243 B. C., resulted in the production of a stringent code of regulations applicable to all classes of the population throughout the empire, without distinction of creed. Many kinds of animals were absolutely protected from slaughter in any circumstances ; and the slaying of animals commonly used for food by the flesh-eating population, although not totally prohibited, was hedged round by severe restrictions. On fifty-six specified days in the year, killing under any pretext was categorically forbidden ; and in many ways the liberty of the subject was very seriously contracted.[2] While Asoka lived, these regulations were, no doubt, strictly enforced by the special officers appointed for the purpose ; and it is not unlikely that deliberate breach of the more important regulations was visited with the capital penalty, as it was later in the days of Harsha.

Reverence.

The second cardinal doctrine inculcated and insisted on by Asoka was that of the obligation of reverence to parents, elders, and preceptors. Conversely, superiors, while receiving

[1] Rock Edict VIII. The formula, 'His Sacred and Gracious Majesty', is a fair equivalent of *devānampiya piyadasi*, which words formed an official title, and cannot be rendered faithfully by etymological analysis. The words mean literally, 'Dear to the gods, of gracious mien.' According to G. Yazdani, *piyadasi* means 'well-wisher' (to all).

[2] Pillar Edict V. Compare Chāṇakya's rules in *Arthaśāstra*, Bk. ii, ch. 26. A notable difference is that Asoka's Edict does not give protection to the cow or other horned cattle, whereas the *Arthaśāstra* prohibits their slaughter under a penalty of a fine of 50 *paṇas*. See also Bk. xiii, ch. 5, transl. R. Shamasastry, Bangalore, 1915.

their due of reverence, were required to treat their inferiors, including servants, slaves, and all living creatures, with kindness and consideration.[1] As a corollary to these obligations, men were taught that the spirit which inspires reverence on the one side, and kindness on the other, should further induce them to behave with courteous decorum to relatives, ascetics, and Brahmans, and likewise to practise liberality to the same classes, as well as to friends and acquaintances.

Truthfulness. The third primary duty laid upon men was that of truthfulness. These three guiding principles are most concisely formulated in the Second Minor Rock Edict, which may be quoted in full :—

> 'Thus saith His Majesty :
> " Father and mother must be obeyed ; similarly, respect for living creatures must be enforced ; truth must be spoken. These are the virtues of the Law of Piety which must be practised. Similarly, the teacher must be reverenced by the pupil, and proper courtesy must be shown to relations.
> This is the ancient standard of piety—this leads to length of days, and according to this men must act ".'

Toleration. Among secondary duties, a high place was given to that of showing toleration for and sympathy with the beliefs and practices of others ; and a special edict, No. XII of the Rock series, was devoted to the exposition of this topic, The subjects of the imperial moralist were solemnly warned to abstain from speaking evil of their neighbours' faith ; remembering that all forms of religion alike aim at the attainment of self-control and purity of mind, and are thus in agreement about essentials, however much they may differ in externals.

Asoka's practice. Asoka openly avowed his readiness to act upon these latitudinarian principles by doing reverence to men of all sects, whether ascetics or householders, by means of donations and in other ways. The Cave Inscriptions, which

[1] For the law concerning slaves and servants see *Arthaśāstra*, Bk. iii, chs. 13, 14. The general rule was laid down that an Ārya could not be in the status of slavery (*Na tv-ev-āryasya dāsabhāvaḥ*), but it was subject to exceptions. When Megasthenes averred that slavery was unknown in India, he may have had some such rule in his mind.

record costly gifts bestowed upon the Ājīvikas, an independent sect of self-mortifying ascetics, testify that Asoka, like many other ancient kings of India, really adopted the policy of universal toleration and concurrent endowment.[1]

Limitations.

But his toleration, although perfectly genuine, must be understood with two limitations. In the first place, all Indian religions, with which alone Asoka was concerned, had much in common, and were all alike merely variant expressions of Hindu modes of thought and feeling. There was no such gap dividing them as that which yawns between Islam and Purānic Brahmanism. In the second place, the royal toleration, although perfect as regarding beliefs, did not necessarily extend to all overt practices. Sacrifices involving the death of a victim, which are absolutely indispensable for the correct worship of some of the gods, were categorically prohibited, at least at the capital, from an early period in the reign;[2] and were further restricted, in all parts of the empire, by the code promulgated later in the Pillar Edicts. The conscientious objector was not permitted to allege his conscience as a justification for acts disapproved on principle by the government. Men might believe what they liked, but must do as they were told.

True charity.

While almsgiving was commended, the higher doctrine was taught that 'there is no such charity as the charitable gift of the Law of Piety; no such distribution as the distribution of piety'.[3] The sentiment recurs in curiously similar language in Cromwell's earliest extant letter. He wrote from St. Ives: 'Building of hospitals provides for men's bodies; to build material temples is judged a work of piety; but they that procure spiritual food, they that build up spiritual temples, they are the men truly charitable, truly pious.'[4]

[1] The notion of toleration being a royal duty still survives. Bühler was 'told in Rājputāna, a rājā ought not to be exclusive in the point of worship, but favour all the various sects among his subjects' (*Ind. Ant.*, vi, 183). This principle has been acted on frequently. The *Arthaśāstra* goes so far as to prescribe that the king who has acquired a new territory 'should follow the people in their faith with which they celebrate their national, religious, and congregational festivals or amusements' (Bk. xiii, ch. 5).

[2] Rock Edict I.

[3] Rock Edict XI.

[4] Letter dated Jan. 11, 1635, in Carlyle's edition.

Asoka cared little for ritual, and was inclined to look with some scorn upon ordinary ceremonies, which, as he observes, 'bear little fruit, and are of doubtful efficacy'. Just as true charity consists in a man's efforts to diffuse a knowledge of the Law of Piety among his fellow creatures, so true ceremonial consists in the fulfilment of that law, which 'bears great fruit'; and includes kind treatment of slaves and servants, honour to teachers, respect for life, and liberality to ascetics and Brahmans. These things, with others of the same kind, are called 'the ceremonial of piety'.[1] **True ceremonial.**

The preacher looked to men's hearts rather than to their outward acts, and besought his congregation, the inhabitants of a vast empire, to cultivate the virtues of 'compassion, liberality, truth, purity, gentleness, and saintliness'. He hoped that the growth of piety would be promoted by the imperial regulations devised for that purpose; but, while enforcing those regulations with all the power of an autocrat, he relied more upon the meditations of individuals, stimulated by his teaching. 'Of these two means,' he says, 'pious regulations are of small account, whereas meditation is of greater value.'[2] **Virtues inculcated.**

Notwithstanding his avowal of the comparative powerlessness of regulations, the emperor did not neglect to provide official machinery for the promulgation of his doctrine, and the enforcement of his orders. All the officers of State, whom, in modern phraseology, we may call Lieutenant-Governors, Commissioners, and District Magistrates, were commanded to make use of opportunities during their periodical tours for convoking assemblies of the lieges, and instructing them in the whole duty of man. Certain days in the year were particularly set apart for this duty, and the officials were directed to perform it in addition to their ordinary work.[3] **Official propaganda.**

A special agency of Censors was also organized for the purpose of enforcing the regulations concerning the sanctity of animal life, and the observance of filial piety, in the **Censors.**

[1] Rock Edict IX. [2] Pillar Edict VII.
[3] Rock Edict III; the Kaliṅga Edicts.

most extended sense. These officers were expressly enjoined to concern themselves with all sects, and with every class of society, not excluding the royal family; while separate officials were charged with the delicate duty of supervising female morals.[1] In practice, this system must have led to much espionage and tyranny; and, if we may judge from the proceedings of kings in later ages, who undertook a similar task, the punishments inflicted for breach of the imperial regulations must have been terribly severe.

Similar action of Harsha,

It is recorded by contemporary testimony that in the seventh century King Harsha, who obviously aimed at copying closely the institutions of Asoka, did not shrink from inflicting capital punishment without hope of pardon on any person who dared to infringe his commands by slaying any living thing, or using flesh as food in any part of his dominions.[2]

and of Kumārapāla.

In the twelfth century, Kumārapāla, king of Gujarāt in Western India, after his conversion to Jainism in A. D. 1159, took up the doctrine of the sanctity of animal life with the most inordinate zeal, and imposed savage penalties upon violators of his rules. An unlucky merchant, who had committed the atrocious crime of cracking a louse, was brought before the special court at Anhilwāra and punished by the confiscation of his whole property, the proceeds of which were devoted to the building of a temple. Another wretch, who had outraged the sanctity of the capital by bringing in a dish of raw meat, was put to death. The special court constituted by Kumārapāla had functions similar to those of Asoka's Censors, and the working of the later institution sheds much light upon the unrecorded proceedings of the earlier one.[3]

Censors in Kashmir,

More modern parallels to Asoka's Censors are not lacking. In 1876, when a pious Mahārāja was in power in Kashmīr,

[1] Rock Edicts V, XII; Pillar Edict VII.

[2] Beal, Records, i, 214.

[3] Bühler, *Ueber das Leben des Jaina Mönches Hemachandra*, Wien, 1889, p. 39. For an account of Kumārapāla ('Koomâr Pâl) see A. K. Forbes, *Rās Mālā, Hindoo Annals of the Province of Goozerat in Western India*, 2 vols., Richardson, 1856, vol. i, ch. 11. The whole story of Kumārapāla's conversion (pp. 29–42) is instructive as a commentary on the Asoka edicts.

breaches of the commandments of the Hindu scriptures were treated by the State as offences, and investigated by a special court composed of five eminent pundits, belonging to families in which the office was hereditary, who determined appropriate penalties.[1]

and in the Deccan.

Up to the middle of the nineteenth century, and possibly until a later date, similar hereditary Brahman officers exercised jurisdiction over offenders charged with breaches of caste rules in Khandesh, the Deccan, and some parts of the Konkan, and imposed suitable expiations in the shape of fine, penance, or excommunication.[2]

These cases, ancient and modern, are sufficient to prove that when Asoka made an innovation by appointing Censors, officers who 'had never been appointed in all the long ages past', the new departure was in accordance with Hindu notions, and was consequently readily imitated in later times by rulers of various religions.

Almoner's department.

The practical piety of Asoka was exhibited in many works of benevolence, on which he dwells with evident pleasure and satisfaction. His theory of true charity did not hinder him from bestowing liberal alms. The distribution of the charitable grants made by the sovereign and members of the royal family was carefully supervised both by the Censors and other officials, who seem to have been organized in a Royal Almoner's Department.[3]

Provision for travellers.

Special attention was devoted to the needs of travellers, who have at all times evoked the sympathy of pious Indians. The provision made for wayfarers, including the dumb animals, which were never forgotten by Asoka, is best described in the monarch's own words: 'On the roads,' he says, 'I have had banyan-trees planted to give shade to man and beast; I have had groves of mango-trees planted; and at every half *kōs* I have had wells dug; rest-houses have been erected; and numerous watering-places have been prepared here and there for the enjoyment of man and

[1] Bühler, 'Report of a Tour', &c., in *J. Bo. Br. R. A. S.* (1876), vol. xii, Extra No., p. 21.

[2] *Calcutta Review* (1851), vol. xv, p. xxv; quoted in *Ind. Ant.* (1903), vol. xxxii, p. 365.

[3] Rock Edicts V, XII; Pillar Edict VII; Queen's Edict.

beast.'[1] Distances were carefully marked by pillars erected at convenient intervals, ever since Chandragupta's time.

Relief of sick.

The lively sympathy of Asoka with his suffering fellow creatures, human and animal, also found expression in the extensive provision of relief for the sick. Arrangements for the healing of man and beast were provided not only throughout all provinces of the empire, but also in the friendly independent kingdoms of Southern India and Hellenistic Asia; medicinal herbs and drugs, wherever lacking, being planted, imported, and supplied as needed.[2]

Animal hospital at Sūrat.

The animal hospitals, which still exist at Ahmadābād, Sūrat, and many other towns in Western India, may be regarded as either survivals or copies of the institutions founded by the Maurya monarch. The following account of the Sūrat hospital, as it was maintained late in the eighteenth century, probably would have been applicable with little change to the prototype at Pātaliputra :—

'The most remarkable institution in Sūrat is the Banyan Hospital, of which we have no description more recent than 1780. It then consisted of a large piece of ground enclosed by high walls, and subdivided into several courts or wards for the accommodation of animals. In sickness they were attended with the greatest care, and here found a peaceful asylum for the infirmities of old age.

'When an animal broke a limb, or was otherwise disabled, his owner brought him to the hospital, where he was received without regard to the caste or nation of his master. In 1772, this hospital contained horses, mules, oxen, sheep, goats, monkeys, poultry, pigeons, and a variety of birds; also an aged tortoise, which was known to have been there seventy-five years. The most extraordinary ward was that appropriated for rats, mice, bugs, and other noxious vermin, for whom suitable food was provided.' [3]

[1] Pillar Edict VII; Rock Edict II. Fleet translates *aḍhakosikya* as 'at distances of eight *kōs*' (*J. R. A. S.*, 1906, p. 417). See *ante*, p. 135.

[2] Rock Edict II.

[3] Hamilton, *Description of Hindostan* (1820), vol. i, p. 718, 4to ed.; Crooke, *Things Indian*, art. 'Pinjrapole' (Murray (1906)). The 'Banyan', or mercantile castes, who supported the hospital, are divided between the Jain and Vaishṇava religions, both of which go beyond Buddhism in an exaggerated regard for the sanctity of animal life.

These hospitals usually are so administered as to cause, perhaps, more suffering than they prevent.

Foreign propaganda.

The active official propaganda carried on by various agencies throughout the empire and dependent states did not satisfy the zeal of Asoka; who burned with a desire to diffuse the blessings of both his ethical system and distinctive Buddhist teaching in all the independent kingdoms with which he was in touch; and with this purpose organized an efficient system of foreign missions worked under his personal supervision, the results of which are visible to this day. His conception of the idea of foreign missions on a grand scale was absolutely original, and produced a well-considered and successful scheme, carried out with method and thoroughness in conjunction and harmony with his measures of domestic propaganda.

Extent of missions.

Before the year 256 B. C., when the Rock Edicts were published collectively, the royal missionaries had been dispatched to all the more or less dependent states and tribes on the frontiers of the empire, and in the wilder regions within its borders, to the independent kingdoms of Southern India, and to the Hellenistic monarchies of Syria, Egypt, Cyrene, Macedonia, and Epirus, then governed respectively by Antiochos Theos, Ptolemy Philadelphos, Magas, Antigonos Gonatas, and Alexander. The missionary organization thus embraced three continents, Asia, Africa, and Europe. The mission to Ceylon in the reign of Tissa was later in date by a few years.

Border states and tribes.

The Border states and tribes brought in this way within the circle of Buddhist influence included the Kāmbōjas,[1] who lived among the mountains either of Tibet or of the Hindū Kush; various Himalayan nations; the Gandhāras and Yavanas of the Kābul valley and regions still farther west; the Bhojas, Pulindas, and Pitēnikas dwelling among the hills of the Vindhya range and Western Ghāts;[2] and the

[1] Nepalese tradition applies the name *Kambōja-deśa* to Tibet (Foucher, *Iconographie bouddhique*, p. 134). But modern research indicates that the Kāmbōjas spoke an Iranian tongue, and probably should be located in the Hindū Kush mountains (Grierson, *J. R. A. S.*, 1911, p. 802).

[2] Bhojas, probably in Berār

Āndhra kingdom between the Krishnā and Godāvarī rivers.

Southern kingdoms.

The Dravidian peoples of the extreme south, below the fourteenth degree of latitude, being protected by their remoteness, had mostly escaped annexation to the northern empire. In Asoka's time their territories formed four independent kingdoms, the Chola, Pāndya, Keralaputra, and Satiyaputra. The capital of the Chola kingdom was Uraiyūr, or Old Trichinopoly, and that of the Pāndya realm was Korkai in the Tinnevelly District. The Keralaputra or Madura state comprised the Malabar coast south of the Tuluva country, and probably also the inland districts usually assigned to the Chera kingdom. The name Chera is a variant form of Kerala. The Satiyaputra country may be identified with the Satyamangalam subdivision of the Coimbatore District and some adjoining territory.[1] With all these kingdoms Asoka was on such friendly terms that he was at liberty to send his missionaries to preach to the people, and even to found monasteries in several places. One such institution was established by his younger brother Mahendra in the Tanjore District, probably then included in the Chola

(Ilichpur, see Collins on *Daśakumāracharita*, and *Bomb. Gaz.* (1896), vol. i, pt. ii, p. 27); Pulindas, among the Vindhya hills near the Narmadā (ibid., p. 138). But the term Pulinda was used vaguely, and sometimes meant Himalayan tribes (*J. R. A. S.*, 1908, p. 315). D. R. Bhandarkar, 'Dekkan of the Sātavāhana Period' (*Ind. Ant.*, xlviii, June, 1919), suggests that *pitēnikas* or *pitinikas*, which is associated with *Rāshtrikas* in Rock Edict V and with *Bhojas* in Rock Edict XIII, is really an adjective signifying 'one who enjoys property given by (his) father', and therefore that the Rashtrikas or Rathis and the Bhojas were feudatory chieftains who had obtained independence and become hereditary rulers. The word may, however, signify merely 'residents of Paithan' (on the Godāvari).

[1] I cannot agree with Prof. Bhandarkar that the Satiyaputra kingdom should be placed in the Ghāts near Poona. S. V. Venkatesvara suggests (*J. R. A. S.*, 1918, p. 54 and *Ind. Ant.*, xlviii, p. 24) that Kānchi may be meant, because (1) Patanjali enumerates Pāndya, Chola, Chera, and Kānchipura; (2) Kānchi is known to Brahmans as Satyavrata-kshetra; and (3) Satyavrata, the Manu, was considered lord of Dravida. This evidence is far from conclusive. In the seventeenth century there was a province called Satyamangalam in the Nāyak kingdom of Madura (*Ind. Ant.*, xlv, p. 200). It is possible that that may have been meant by Asoka. For the present I prefer my identification. A fortified pass of importance, leading from Mysore to Coimbatore, was known by the name of Satyamangalam [Satti mungalum] (Swartz, *Memoirs*, i, 367). See V. A. Smith, *Asoka*, 3rd ed., p. 161.

kingdom, where its ruins were still visible nine hundred years later.[1]

Princes as monks.

An ancient Chinese writer assures us that 'according to the laws of India, when a king dies, he is succeeded by his eldest son (*Kumārarāja*); the other sons leave the family and enter a religious life, and they are no longer allowed to reside in their native kingdom'.[2] This compulsory withdrawal from secular affairs did not necessarily imply the disappearance of the younger brother into obscurity. The church in India, especially Buddhist India, as in Roman Catholic Europe, offered a career to younger sons, and the able ecclesiastic sometimes attained higher fame than his royal relative. Mahendra's assumption of the yellow robe, in accordance with the rule above stated, was, in the first instance, probably due to political necessity rather than to free choice; but, whatever motive may have led him to adopt the monastic life, he became a devout and zealous monk and a most successful missionary.

Mahendra in Ceylon.

When Asoka determined some years later to extend his propaganda to Ceylon, he selected as head of the mission his monk brother, who presumably was already settled at his monastery in Southern India, and thence crossed over to Ceylon with his four colleagues. The teaching of the preachers, backed as it was by the influence of a monarch so powerful as Asoka, was speedily accepted by King Tissa (Devānampiya Tissa) of Ceylon with the members of his court, and the new religion soon gained a hold on the affections of the people at large.[3] Mahendra spent the rest of his life in Ceylon, and devoted himself to the establishment and organization of the Buddhist church in the island, where he is revered as a saint. His ashes are said to rest under a great cupola or *stūpa*, called Ambustāla, at Mihintalē, one of the

[1] Beal, *Records*, ii, 231; Watters, ii, 228.

[2] Ma-twan-lin, cited in *Ind. Ant.*, ix, 22.

[3] Don M. de Zilva Wickremasinghe assigns the reign of Devānaṁpiya Tissa to the period 253–213 B. C., and dates his successor Uttiya 213–203 B. C. (*Ep. Zeyl.*, vol. i, p. 81). Dates in the early history of Ceylon are only approximate. The dates indicate that the Ceylon mission took place late in Asoka's reign.

most remarkable among the many notable Buddhist monuments which are the glory of Ceylon.[1]

Sinhalese legend.

The Mahāvamsa chronicle, dating from the beginning of the sixth century after Christ, which gives a list of Asoka's missionaries and the countries to which they were deputed, makes no mention of the missions to the Tamil kingdoms of Southern India. This reticence may be plausibly explained by the fierce hostility between the Sinhalese and the Tamils of the mainland, which had begun long before the Christian era and lasted for many centuries. If Mahendra had migrated from his monastery near Tanjore to the island, the fact would have been most distasteful to the monks of the Great Vihāra, who would have been unwilling to feel indebted to a resident among the hated Tamils for instruction in the rudiments of the faith, and would have preferred that people should believe their religion to have come direct from the Holy Land of Buddhism. Some such motive seems to have originated the Sinhalese form of the legend of Mahendra, who is represented as an illegitimate son of Asoka, and is said to have been followed by a sister named Sanghamitrā ('Friend of the Order'), who did for the nuns of Ceylon all that her brother did for the monks. This legend, which is overlaid by many marvellous inventions, must be to a large extent fictitious.[2] The presumably true version, representing Mahendra as the younger brother of Asoka, was well remembered at the imperial capital Pātaliputra, where Fa-hien, at the beginning of the fifth century, was shown the hermitage of Asoka's saintly brother; and it was still the only version known to Hiuen Tsang in the seventh century. Even when the latter pilgrim took down the Sinhalese legends from the lips of the

[1] Mahendra is said to have died in the eighth year of king Uttiya, younger brother and successor of Tissa. Half of his relics were enshrined near the Thūpārāma, where the funeral took place, and half at Mihintalē, where he died.

[2] I used to reject absolutely the story of Sanghamitrā, but am now disposed to admit her real existence. If Mahendra was the brother of Asoka, she probably was the sister, not the daughter, of the latter. According to the *Mahāvaṁśa* her death occurred in the ninth year of the reign of king Uttiya. A ruined *stūpa* ENE. of the Thūpārāma is believed to have once contained her ashes (*Mahāvaṁśa*, ch. 20, transl. Geiger and Wijesinha; Smither, *Archit. Remains, Anurādhapura*, p. 9, Pl. III).

island monks whom he met at Kānchī, he applied the stories to the brother, not to the son, of Asoka.[1]

Alleged mission to Pegu.

The Mahāvamsa may be mistaken in attributing to Asoka the dispatch of missionaries to Pegu (*Sovanabhūmi*).[2] No such mission is mentioned in the inscriptions, and if it really occurred, it seems to have had little result. The Ceylon form of Buddhism appears to have been introduced effectively into Burma and Pegu at a very much later date ; and there is reason to believe that the earliest Burmese Buddhism was of the Tantric Mahāyāna type, imported direct from Northern India many centuries after Asoka's time.[3]

Missions to Hellenistic kingdoms.

Unfortunately no definite record has been preserved of the fortunes of the Buddhist missions in the Hellenistic kingdoms of Asia, Africa, and Europe ; nor are the names of the missionaries known. The influence of Buddhist doctrine on the heretical Gnostic sects appears to be undoubted ; and many writers have suspected that more orthodox forms of Christian teaching owe some debt to the lessons of Gautama ; but the subject is too obscure for discussion in these pages.[4]

Buddhism became a world religion.

It is, however, certain that Asoka, by his comprehensive and well-planned measures of evangelization, succeeded in transforming the doctrine of a local Indian sect into one of the great religions of the world. The personal ministry of Gautama Buddha was confined to a comparatively small area, comprising about four degrees of latitude and as many of longitude, between Gayā, Allāhābād, and the Himalaya. Within these limits he was born, lived, and died. When he died, about 543 B. C., Buddhism was merely a sect of Hinduism, unknown beyond very restricted limits, and with no better apparent chance of survival than that enjoyed by many other contemporary sects now long-forgotten.

[1] Beal, *Records*, ii, 246 ; Watters, ii, 230.

[2] Suvarṇabhūmi = Golden Coast of the Chinese. Schoff connects the name with the Gangetic port of Sunārgāon (*J. A. O. S.*, 37, 244).

[3] Temple, 'Notes on Antiquities in Rāmaññadesa' (*Ind. Ant.*, vol. xxii (1893), p. 359) : and my article (ibid., 1905, p. 180).

[4] See Edmunds, *Buddhist and Christian Gospels*, 4th ed., Philadelphia ; Richard Garbe, *Indien und das Christentum*, Tübingen (Mohr), 1914.

The effective organization of the monastic system by the Buddhists probably was the means of keeping their system alive and in possession of considerable influence in the Gangetic valley for the centuries which elapsed between the death of Gautama and the conversion of Asoka. His imperial patronage, gradually increasing as his faith grew in intensity, made the fortune of Buddhism, and raised it to the position which enables it still to dispute with Christianity the first place among the religions of the world, so far as the number of believers is concerned.

The work of Asoka. Asoka did not attempt to destroy either Brahmanical Hinduism or Jainism; but his prohibition of bloody sacrifices, the preference which he openly avowed for Buddhism, and his active propaganda, undoubtedly brought his favourite doctrine to the front, and established it as the dominant religion in both India and Ceylon. It still retains that position in the southern island, although it has vanished almost completely from the land of its birth, and has failed to retain its grasp upon many of its distant conquests.

Still, notwithstanding many failures, fluctuations, developments, and corruptions, Buddhism now commands, and will command for countless centuries to come, the devotion of hundreds of millions of men. This great result is the work of Asoka alone, and entitles him to rank for all time with that small body of men who may be said to have changed the faith of the world.

Comparison with Constantine. The obvious comparison of Asoka with Constantine, which has become a commonplace, is, like most historical parallels, far from exact. Christianity, when the emperor adopted it as the state creed, was already a power throughout the Roman Empire, and Constantine's adherence was an act of submission to an irresistible force rather than one of patronage to an obscure sect. Buddhism, on the contrary, when Asoka accorded to it his invaluable support, was but one of many sects struggling for existence and survival, and without any pretension to dictate imperial policy. His personal action, seemingly prompted and directed by his teacher Upagupta, was the direct cause of the spread of the doctrine beyond the limits of India ; and, if a Christian parallel must be sought, his work is comparable with that of Saint Paul, rather than with that of Constantine.

Upa-gupta.

Upagupta, to whom the conversion of Asoka is ascribed, is said to have been the son of Gupta, a perfumer, and to have been born at either Benares or Mathurā. Probably he was a native of the latter city, where the monastery built by him still existed in the seventh century. Tradition also associated his name with Sind, in which country he is said to have made frequent missionary journeys.[1]

Asoka's energy,

The vigorous and effective action taken by Asoka to propagate his creed and system of morals is conclusive proof of his absolute honesty of purpose, and justifies the modern reader in giving full credence to the devout professions made by him in the edicts. 'Work I must,' he observed, 'for the public benefit'; and work he did. The world still enjoys the fruit of his labours ; and his words, long lost, but now restored to utterance, ring with the sound of sincerity and truth.

and in-dustry.

Asoka was a hard-working king, as unwearied in business as Philip II of Spain, ready to receive reports 'at any hour and any place', and yet dissatisfied with the outcome of his industry. 'I am never,' he laments, 'fully satisfied with my exertions and dispatch of business.' Probably he worked too hard, and would have effected still more if he had done less. His ideal of duty was high, and, like the Stoic philosopher, he was bound to obey the law of his nature, and to toil on, be the result success or failure.

Character of Asoka.

The character of Asoka must be deduced from his words. The style is of the man, and I firmly believe that the edicts

[1] Beal, *Records*, i, 182 ; ii, 88, 273 ; Watters, Index, s.v., Upagupta ; Growse, *Mathurā*, 3rd ed., p. 142 ; Cunningham, *Reports*, xx, 32. The tradition may be true. 76 *stūpas* and 2 monasteries of about the sixth century A. D. have been found at Mīrpur Khās (*Ann. Rep. A. S. Western Circle*, 1916–17, p. 47) and 1 *stūpa* has been found at Tāndo Muhammad Khān (ibid., 1914–15, p. 66). The identity of Tissa, son of Moggali, the hero of the Ceylon tales, with the real personage Upagupta has been demonstrated by Waddell (*J. A. S. B.*, 1897, part i, p. 76 ; *Proc. A. S. B.*, 1899, p. 70). There is no sufficient reason to identify Tissa with the Mogaliputa of the Sāñchī relic caskets (*Bhīlsa Topes*, pp. 115, 120).

express his thoughts in his own words. They are written in a style far too peculiar and distinctive to be the work of a Secretary of State, and are alive with personal feeling. No secretary would have dared to put in his master's mouth the passionate expressions of remorse for the misery caused by the Kalinga war, leading up to the resolve to eschew aggressive warfare for the rest of his life, and the declaration that 'although a man do him an injury, His Majesty holds that it must be patiently borne, as far as it possibly can be borne'.[1]

The edicts reveal Asoka as a man who sought to combine the piety of the monk with the wisdom of the king, and to make India the kingdom of righteousness as he conceived it, a theocracy without a God; in which the government should act the part of Providence, and guide the people in the right way. Every man, he maintained, must work out his own salvation, and eat the fruit of his deeds. 'The fruit of exertion is not to be obtained by the great man only; because even the small man by exertion can win for himself much heavenly bliss; and for this purpose was given the precept—"Let small and great exert themselves".'[2] The government could only point out the road, which each man must travel for himself.

Reverence, compassion, truthfulness, and sympathy were the virtues which he inculcated; irreverence, cruelty, falsehood, and intolerance were the vices which he condemned. The preacher was no mere sermon-writer. He was a man of affairs, versed in the arts of peace and war, the capable ruler of an immense empire, a great man, and a great king.

Asoka's queens.

Asoka, like all Oriental monarchs, was a polygamist, and had at least two consorts, who ranked as queens. The name of the second of these ladies, Kāruvākī, is preserved in a brief edict signifying the royal pleasure that her charitable donations should be regarded by all officials concerned as her act and deed, redounding to her accumulation of merit.

[1] Rock Edict XIII. [2] Minor Rock Edict I (Rūpnāth).

She is described as the mother of Tīvara, who may be considered as a favourite child of the aged emperor at the time the edict was issued, late in his reign.

Legend of Kunāla.

Tradition avers that his faithful chief queen for many years was named Asandhimitrā, and that when she died, and Asoka was old, he married a dissolute young woman named Tishyarakshitā ; concerning whom and her step-son Kunāla, the old folk-lore tale, known to the Greeks as that of Phaedra and Hippolytus, is related with much imaginative embellishment. But folk-lore is not history, and the pathetic story of the blinded Kunāla must not be read or criticized as matter-of-fact narrative. The legend appears in diverse forms with various names.

Legend of Jalauka.

Another son of Asoka, named Jalauka, who plays a large part in Kashmīr tradition, although rather a shadowy personage, has more appearance of reality than Kunāla. He was reputed to have been an active and vigorous king of Kashmīr, who expelled certain intrusive foreigners, and conquered the plains as far as Kanauj. He was hostile to Buddhism and devoted to the worship of Siva and the Divine Mothers, in whose honour he and his queen, Isānadēvī, erected many temples at places which can be identified. The story of Jalauka, notwithstanding the topographical details, is essentially legendary, and no independent corroboration of the Kashmīr tradition has been discovered.[1]

Daśaratha.

Tīvara, the son mentioned in the Queen's Edict, is not heard of again, and may have predeceased his father. Dasaratha, a grandson of Asoka, certainly was a reality, being known from brief dedicatory inscriptions on the walls of cave-dwellings at the Nāgārjuni Hills, which he bestowed upon the Ājīvikas, as his grandfather had done in the neighbouring Barābar Hills. The script, language, and style of Dasaratha's records prove that his date was very close to that of Asoka, whom probably he directly succeeded, at least in the eastern provinces. Assuming this to be the fact, the

[1] Stein, transl. *Rājataranginī*, Bk. i, vv. 108–52. One of the confused Tibetan traditions assigns eleven sons to Asoka (Schiefner, *Tāranāth*, p. 48).

accession of Dasaratha may be dated in 232 B. C. His reign appears to have been short, and is allotted (under other names) eight years in two of the Purāṇas.

Samprati; Buddhist tradition.

The existence and succession of Samprati, another grandson of Asoka, although not verified by epigraphic record, are vouched for by a considerable body of tradition. The Buddhist prose romance, named *Asokāvadāna* (being part of the *Divyāvadāna*), tells a long story of Asoka's senile devotion to the church and consequent waste of the resources of the empire, which went so far that the ministers were compelled to remove him from power, and place Samprati, son of the blinded Kunāla, on the throne. We are not told what became of Asoka. According to this tale, the successors of Samprati were Vrihaspati, Vrishasena, Pushyadharman, and Pushyamitra, the last being described as of Maurya descent.[1]

Jain traditions.

The Jain literary tradition of Western India, which also recognizes Samprati as the immediate successor of Asoka, eulogizes him as an eminent patron of Jainism, who founded Jain monasteries even in non-Aryan countries. Almost all ancient Jain temples or monuments of unknown origin are ascribed by the popular voice to Samprati, who is, in fact, regarded as a Jain Asoka. One author describes him as being the sovereign of all India ('lord of Bharata with its three continents'), holding court at Pātaliputra; but other traditions place the seat of his government at Ujjain. It is

[1] Burnouf, *Introd.*, 2nd ed., p. 384; Schiefner, *Tāranāth*, p. 287. 'The name of Samprati is well known from Ajmēr to Saurāshtra, and his era is given in a valuable chronogrammatic catalogue in an ancient Jain manuscript from the temple of Nadol, at 202 of the Virat Saṃvat. He is mentioned both traditionally and by books as the great supporter of the Jain faith, and the remains of temples dedicated to Māhāvīra, erected by this prince, yet exist at Ajmēr, Kumbhalmēr, and Girnār' (Tod, *Annals*, &c., Oxford Univ. Press, 1920, vol. i, p. 290). The fortress of Jahāgpur, situated about 96 miles NE. of Udaipur and the same distance SSE. from Ajmēr, which guarded an important pass between Bundī and Mewār, is believed to have been founded by him. It was rebuilt by Rānā Kumbher in the fifteenth century. The tradition is supported by the existence of ancient Jain temples (*Rājputāna Gazetteer*, Simla, 1880, iii, 52). See also Forbes, *Rāsmālā*, 1856, i, p. 7. An inscription, dated 1686 V.E. = A.D. 1622, on a Jain temple at Nāḍlai in the Jodhpur State, Rājputāna, records the traditional belief that the original edifice had been built by Samprati (*Prog. Rep. A. S. W. I.*, 1909–10, p. 41).

obviously impossible to reconcile all these discrepant traditions, or to feel assured that a kernel of fact can be extracted from the husk of legend. The concurrence of Buddhist with Jain tradition may be accepted as good evidence that Samprati had a real existence in the flesh, although nothing certain is known about him. Perhaps the empire was divided immediately after Asoka's death, between his grandsons, Dasaratha taking the eastern, and Samprati the western provinces, but there is no clear evidence to support this hypothesis.[1]

Khotan legends.

The legends of Khotan assert a connexion between that kingdom and Asoka in more ways than one. According to one version of the story he banished certain nobles of Taxila to the north of the Himalaya as a punishment for their complicity in the wrongful blinding of his son Kunāla. These exiles elected one of their number to be king, who reigned in Khotan until he was defeated by a rival prince exiled from China. Another version of the tale asserts that the earliest ancestor of the royal family of Khotan was the prince Kunāla, Asoka's son, who was himself exiled from Taxila. These stories seem to be merely mythological explanations of the fact that the ancient civilization of Khotan was derived from both India and China. It is not likely, although it is not impossible, that Asoka's political jurisdiction should have extended into the basin of the Tārīm.[2]

Decline and fall of the Maurya dynasty.

The whole duration of the Maurya dynasty, according to Purānic authority, was 137 years, and if this period be accepted and reckoned from the accession of Chandragupta in 322 B. C., the dynasty must have come to an end in 185 B. C., which date certainly is approximately correct. Four princes who, according to the Purānic lists, succeeded Asoka's grandsons, and each reigned for a few years, are

[1] The Jain traditions (*Pariśihtaparvan*, ed. Jacobi; &c.) are summarized conveniently by Bhagwān Lāl Indraji and Mr. Jackson in *Bomb. Gaz.*, vol. i, part i (1896), p. 15. The lists of the successors of Asoka, as given in the *Purāṇas*, are hopelessly confused and discrepant.

[2] The stories, which will be found in the *Life* and *Travels* of Hiuen Tsang, in Rockhill's *Life of Buddha* and Sarat Chandra Das's articles on Tibetan history, are summarized and examined by Stein, in *Ancient Khotan*, pp. 156–66.

mere names [1]; and, if the real existence of Samprati and his successors be assumed, they are equally shadowy personages. The only certainty is that the great empire founded by Chandragupta, and gloriously maintained by his son and grandson, did not long survive the latter. The fall of the Maurya authority probably was due in large measure to a reaction promoted by the Brahmans, whose privileged position must have been seriously affected by the extreme favour which Asoka showed to the Buddhist monks. The prohibition of bloody sacrifices and the irritating proceedings of the Censors must have produced much unrecorded discontent, and we may fairly assume that when the strong hand of the old emperor dropped the sceptre, Brahman influence reasserted itself and produced a revolt against the inquisitorial tyranny of Asoka's system.[2] The descendants of Asoka whose names are recorded in the Purānas probably retained possession of only Magadha and the neighbouring home provinces. In or about 185 B. C. the last prince of the Maurya dynasty, named Brihadratha, was slain by his commander-in-chief, Pushyamitra (or Pushpamitra), who established a new dynasty known as that of the Sungas. The Āndhra state, between the Krishnā and Godāvarī rivers, was among the earliest defections, and rapidly grew into a powerful kingdom, stretching right across India, as will be narrated in the next chapter.

Local Maurya Rājas.

Descendants of the great Asoka continued as unrecorded local subordinate Rājas in Magadha for many centuries; the last of them, and the only one whose name has been preserved, being Pūrna-varman, who was nearly contemporary with the Chinese pilgrim, Hiuen Tsang, in the seventh century.[3]

[1] The names vary, probably because each king was known by more than one name. The existence of one of them, namely Sāliśūka, is confirmed by the astronomical work, the *Gārgī Samhitā*, which alludes to him in the well-known historical passage, quoted in App. I, *post.*

[2] See remarks of Maha. H. P. Sāstri in *J. & Proc. A. S. B.*, 1910, p. 259. He compares the case of king Pālaka of Ujjain in the ancient drama, the 'Toy-cart'. The Sunga, Kānwa, and Sātavāhana dynasties all were Brahman. So also was the Cheta dynasty of Orissa.

[3] Beal, *Records*, ii, 118, 174; Watters, ii, 115.

Petty Maurya dynasties, apparently connected in some unknown way with the imperial line, ruled in the Konkan, between the Western Ghāts and the sea, and some other parts of Western India, during the sixth, seventh, and eighth centuries, and are frequently mentioned in inscriptions.[1]

[1] Fleet, 'Dynasties of the Kanarese Districts', 2nd ed., in *Bombay Gazetteer*, vol. i, part ii (1896), pp. 282–4.

THE MAURYA DYNASTY

CHRONOLOGICAL TABLE

(Nearly exact dates.)

Year B. C.	Event.
326 or 325 . .	Chandragupta Maurya in his youth met Alexander the Great.
Sept. or Oct., 325	Alexander quitted India.
Feb., 324 . .	Alexander, while in Karmania, received news of the murder of his satrap Philippos, in India ; and placed Eudēmos and Āmbhi, king of Taxila, in charge of the Indian provinces.
June, 323 . .	Death of Alexander at Babylon.
323–322 (possibly a year or two years earlier)	Revolt of Panjāb under Chandragupta Maurya and destruction of Nanda dynasty of Magadha; **accession of Chandragupta Maurya as emperor of India.**
321	Second partition of Alexander's empire at Triparadeisos.
315	Seleukos Nikator compelled by Antigonos to retire to Egypt.
312	Recovery of Babylon by Seleukos.
Oct. 1, 212 . .	Establishment of Seleukidan era.
306	Assumption by Seleukos of title of king.
305 or 304 . .	Invasion of India by Seleukos.
303	Defeat of Seleukos by Chandragupta ; treaty of peace ; cession of a large part of Ariana by Seleukos.
303–301 . .	March of Seleukos against Antigonos.
302	Megasthenes ambassador of Seleukos at Pāṭaliputra.
301	Defeat and death of Antigonos at Ipsos in Phrygia.
298	**Accession of Bindusāra Amitraghāta as emperor of India.**
c. 296 . . .	Deïmachos ambassador of Seleukos at Pāṭaliputra.
285	Ptolemy Philadelphos, king of Egypt, acc.
280	Seleukos Nikator, king of Syria, d. ; Antiochos Soter, his son, acc.
278 or 277 . .	Antigonos Gonatas, king of Macedonia, grandson of Antiochos I, acc.
273	Alexander, king of Epirus, son of Pyrrhus, and opponent of Antigonos Gonatas, acc.
272	**Accession of Asoka-vardhana as emperor of India.**
269	Coronation (*abhisheka*) of Asoka.
264	Outbreak of First Punic War.
261	Conquest of Kaliṅga by Asoka ; Antiochos Theos, king of Syria, son of Antiochos Soter, acc.
259	Asoka abolished hunting, instituted tours devoted to works of piety, and dispatched missionaries.
258	Magas, king of Cyrēnē, half-brother of Ptolemy Philadelphos, died ; (?) Alexander, king of Epirus, died.
257	Minor Rock Edict I and Rock Edicts III and IV of Asoka, who instituted quinquennial official progresses for propagation of Law of Piety (*dharma*), and dedicated cave-dwellings at Barābar for the use of the Ājivikas.

YEAR B. C.	EVENTS.
256	Publication of complete series of Fourteen Rock Edicts, and of the Kalinga Borderers' Edict by Asoka, who appointed Censors of the Law of Piety (*dharmamahāmātrāḥ*).
255	Asoka enlarged for the second time the *stūpa* of Konākamana Buddha near Kapilavastu.
? 254 . . .	Publication by Asoka of the Kaliṅga Provincial's Edict.
250	Dedication by Asoka of a third cave-dwelling at Barābar for the use of the Ājīvikas.
249	Pilgrimage of Asoka to Buddhist holy places ; erection of pillars at Lumbinī Garden and near a *stūpa* of Konākamana ; (?) his visit to Nepāl, and foundation of Lalita Pātan ; his daughter Chārumatī becomes a nun.
? 248 . . .	Declaration of independence by Bactria and Parthia.
247	Ptolemy Philadelphos, king of Egypt, died.
247 or 246 . .	Antiochos Theos, king of Syria, grandson of Seleukos Nikator, died.
243	Composition by Asoka of Pillar Edict VI, confirming the Rock Edicts.
242	Publication by Asoka of complete series of Seven Pillar Edicts.
242 or 239 . .	Antigonos Gonatas, king of Macedonia, died.
241	Close of First Punic War ; rise of the kingdom of Pergamum.
? 240–232 . .	Minor Pillar Edicts of Asoka.
232	**Asoka died : Dasartha** (Kuśāla, *Vāyu P.*) acc., and dedicated Nāgārjuni caves to the Ājīvikas; **break-up of Maurya empire began.**
? 224 . . .	Sangata Maurya, king (Bandhupālita, *Vāyu P.*).
? 216 . . .	Sāliśūka Maurya, king (Indrapālita, *Vāyu P.*) ; ? defeated by Khāravēla of Orissa.
? 206 . . .	Somaśarman Maurya, king (Daśavarman, or Devavarman, *Vāyu P.*).
? 199 . . .	Śatadhanwan Maurya, king (Śatadhanus, *Vāyu P.*)
? 191 . . .	Bṛihadratha Maurya, king (Bṛijadaśva, *Vāyu P.*).[1]
185	**Pushyamitra Śunga, acc.**, having slain Bṛihadratha ; **final destruction of Maurya Empire.**

[1] The names of the successors of Asoka are taken from the *Vishnu Purāṇa*, omitting Suyaśas, for the reasons given in the text. Other names are given in Jain books and the Buddhist *Asokāvadāna*. The *Vāyu*, which is one of the oldest of the Purāṇas, gives only nine names for the dynasty, as in brackets, and also states the duration of each reign. The approximate dates given are assigned accordingly, on the assumption that the reign of Asoka lasted for about forty or forty-one years. Its duration, according to the *Vāyu Purāṇa*, was thirty-six, and according to the *Mahāvaṁśa*, thirty-seven years, both of which periods probably should be reckoned from the coronation. The Purāṇas agree in assigning 137 years to the Maurya dynasty, but the total of the lengths of reigns, according to the *Vāyu Purāṇa*, is only 133. The difference of four years may be accounted for by the interval between the accession and the coronation of Asoka. For further details see Pargiter, *Dynasties of the Kali Age*. The variant readings are numerous.

CHAPTER VIII

THE SUNGA, KANVA, AND ĀNDHRA DYNASTIES, 185 B.C. TO A.D. c. 225.

The Sunga Dynasty.

c. 185 B.C. Usurpation of Pushyamitra. Sunga.

PUSHYAMITRA, the commander-in-chief, having slain his master Brihadratha Maurya, usurped the vacant throne, and established himself as sovereign of the now contracted Maurya dominions;[1] thus founding a dynasty known to history as that of the Sungas.[2]

[1] The Puranic account of Pushyamitra's usurpation is confirmed by Bāṇa (seventh century), who evidently had access to documents now lost. His text is: *Pratijñā durbalaṁ cha baladarśanavyapadeśa-darśitāśesha-sainyaḥ senānīr anāryo Mauryaṁ Bṛihadrathaṁ pipesha Pushpamitraḥ svāminaṁ*, which may be translated: 'And reviewing the whole army, under the pretext of showing him his forces, the base-born (*anārya*) general Pushpamitra crushed his master, Bṛihadratha the Maurya, who, was weak in keeping his coronation oath (*pratijñā*).' The rendering combines the versions of Cowell and Thomas (*Harṣacarita*, transl. p. 193), of Bühler (*Ind. Ant.*, ii, 363), and of Jayaswal. The best text of the Purāṇas (Pargiter, pp. 31, 70) states simply that 'Pushyamitra, the commander-in-chief, will uproot Bṛihadratha and will rule the kingdom as king 36 years'.

[2] Manuscripts usually read Pushpamitra, but Pushyamitra is the correct form (Bühler, *Ind.Ant.*, ii, 362). Pushyamitra has been shown to be a synonym of Bahasatimitra or Bahaspati of the Khāravela inscription (K. P. Jayaswal, in *J. B. & O. Res. Soc.*, Part iv, Dec. 1917, pp. 473–80); and in view of the connexion between Brihaspati and the Pushya asterism, we must accept Pushya as correct. As the name of the founder of the dynasty and some of his descendants ended in *mitra*, M. M. Haraparshād Sāstri suggests, in my opinion wrongly, that the Sungas were Persians, worshippers of the sun (Mithra). The Sungas were followers of the *Sāma Veda* which is specially concerned with animal sacrifices, and they and the Kanvas appear to have led a Brahmanical reaction against Buddhism (*J. & Proc. A. S. B.*, 1912, p. 287). K. P. Jayaswal (*J. B. O. Res. Soc.*, iv, Sept. 1918) holds that the Sungas were Brahmans and occupied a high position in the theological world at that early date. Pushyamitra belonged to the family of the royal chaplain (*purohit*) of the Mauryas, who though heterodox since Asoka's reign probably retained the family nominally in its old position. According to the author, the later Mauryas were degenerate and politically weak, and Pushyamitra was forced to slay Bṛihadratha in the interests of the empire, which was threatened by the Yāvanas or Bactrian Greeks under Menander. The dynastic name Śunga is attested by the Purāṇas, Bāṇa (p. 193), and the Barhut (Bharhut)

The capital presumably continued to be, as of old, Pātaliputra, and probably all the central or home provinces of the empire recognized the usurper's authority, which perhaps extended to the south as far as the Narmadā river,[1] and may be assumed to have embraced the territories in the Gangetic basin, corresponding with the modern Bihār, Tirhūt, and the United Provinces of Agra and Oudh. It is unlikely that either the later Mauryas or the Sungas exercised any jurisdiction in the Panjāb. Wilson's belief that the arms of Pushyamitra reached the Indus was due to a misunderstanding.[2]

Extent of Sunga dominions.

Pushyamitra did not enjoy his dominions unchallenged. In or about 165 B. C. Khāravela, King of Kalinga, who was descended from the Cheta (Chaitra) family, invaded his territory and advanced to within a few miles of Pātaliputra. Pushyamitra made a strategic withdrawal to Mathurā, and Khāravela apparently considered it wise at the moment not to proceed farther than the Barābar Hills (Gorathagiri).

c. 165 B.C. First invasion of Khāravela.

The second invasion of Khāravela, four years later, was, however, more successful. Entering Northern India and marching at the foot of the Himalayas, he suddenly appeared before the capital of Magadha on the north side of the Ganges, which he crossed with the help of the famous elephants of Kalinga. Pushyamitra was forced to submit, and the treasures of his capital were seized by the victor, among them being a statue of the first Jina (Rishabhadeva), which had been carried away from Kalinga three centuries earlier by King Nanda I.[3]

c. 161 B.C. Second invasion of Khāravela.

inscription beginning with *Suganaṁ raje*, 'during the reign of the Sungas' (*Arch. S. W. I.* v, 73; *Ind. Ant.*, xiv, 138, with facsimile).

[1] 'The Queen [of Agnimitra, son of Pushyamitra] has a brother of inferior caste, Vīrasena by name; he has been placed by the king in command of a frontier fortress on the banks of the Mandākinī' (Introd. to *Mālavikāgnimitra*). Tawney (transl., p. 6) notes that 'the Mandākanī here probably means the Narmadā (Nerbudda). One of the Bombay manuscripts reads the Prākrit equivalent of Narmadā'. But Mr. Pargiter knows only two rivers named Mandākinī, namely, one in the Bānda District of Bundelkhaṇd, and the other, a southern tributary of the Godāvarī (*J. R. A. S.*, 1894, p. 260).

[2] Wilson, *Theatre of the Hindus*, ii, 353; Cunningham, *Num. Chron.*, 1870, p. 227.

[3] See K. P. Jayaswal, *J. B. O. Res. Soc.*, vol. iii, Dec. 1917, pp. 425–85; R. D. Banerji, ibid., pp.

c. 155–3 B. C. Invasion and repulse of Menander.

During the latter years of his reign, Pushyamitra was threatened by serious danger. Menander, a relative of the Bactrian monarch Eukratides, and king of Kābul and the Panjāb, having formed the design of emulating the exploits of Alexander, advanced with a formidable force into the interior of India. He annexed the Indus delta, the peninsula of Surāshtra (Kāthiāwār), and some other territories on the western coast; occupied Mathurā on the Jumna; besieged Madhyamikā (now Nagarī near Chitōr) in Rājputāna; invested Sākētam in Southern Oudh; and threatened Pātaliputra, the capital.

The invasion was repelled after a severe struggle, and the Greek king was obliged to retire to his own country, but he may have retained his conquests in Western India for a few years longer.[1]

India and Europe.

Thus ended the second and last attempt by a European general to conquer India by land. All subsequent invaders from the western continent have come in ships, trusting to their command of the sea, and using it as their base. From the repulse of Menander in or about 153 B. C. until the bombardment of Calicut by Vasco da Gama in A. D. 1502 India enjoyed immunity from attack under European leadership; and so long as the power in occupation of the country retains command of the sea, no attack made from the land side in the footsteps of the ancient invaders can have any prospect of permanent success.

Agnimitra's war with Vidarbha.

During the progress of the war with Menander, the outlying southern provinces extending to the Narmadā river were administered by the Crown Prince, Agnimitra, as viceroy, who had his capital at Vidisā, the modern Bhīlsā on the Betwā in Sindhia's territory. Agnimitra's youthful son, Vasumitra, was employed on active service under the orders of the king, his grandfather. Pushyamitra, who at this time must have been advanced in years, resolved to crown his military successes by substantiating and pro-

486–507. See also J. N. Sikdar, 'A Note on the Cheta Dynasty', *J. B. O. Res. Soc.*, vol. iv, Part i, March, 1918, pp. 99–100.

[1] See Appendix I at end of this chapter, 'The Invasion of Menander, and the Date of Patañjali'.

claiming a formal claim to the rank of Lord Paramount of Northern India. His pretensions received confirmation by the success of Agnimitra in a local war with his southern neighbour, the Rāja of Vidarbha (Berār), which resulted in the complete defeat of the Rāja, who was obliged to cede half of his dominions to a rival cousin; the river Varadā (Warda) being constituted the boundary between the two principalities.

Pushyamitra determined to revive and celebrate with appropriate magnificence the antique Vedic rite of the horse-sacrifice (*aśvamedha*), which, according to immemorial tradition, could only be performed by a paramount sovereign, and involved as a preliminary a formal and successful challenge to all rival claimants to supreme power, delivered after this fashion :—

Aśvamedha, or horse-sacrifice.

'A horse of a particular colour was consecrated by the performance of certain ceremonies, and was then turned loose to wander for a year. The king, or his representative, followed the horse with an army, and when the animal entered a foreign country, the ruler of that country was bound either to fight or to submit. If the liberator of the horse succeeded in obtaining or enforcing the submission of all the countries over which it passed, he returned in triumph with all the vanquished Rājas in his train; but, if he failed, he was disgraced, and his pretensions ridiculed. After his successful return, a great festival was held, at which the horse was sacrificed.' [1]

Yāvanas.

The command, at least nominally, of the guard attendant on the consecrated steed liberated by Pushyamitra was entrusted to his young grandson, Vasumitra, who is said to have encountered and routed a band of certain Yavanas, or western foreigners, who took up the challenge on the banks of the river Sindhu, which now forms the boundary between Bundēlkhand and the Rājputāna states.[2] These disputants may have been part of the division of Menander's army which had undertaken the siege of Madhyamikā in Rājputāna.

[1] Dowson, *Classical Dict.*, s. v. Aśvamedha. See also Barnett, *Antiquities of India* (1913), pp. 169–71. The rite was 'known to the Ṛigveda (2. 161, 162)': originally it was 'not improbably a sacrifice offered to the sun' (Macdonell in *J. R. A. S.*, 1916, p. 624).

[2] Not the Indus.

Celebration of the sacrifice.

The Yavanas and all other rivals having been disposed of in due course, Pushyamitra was justified in his claim to rank as the paramount power of Northern India, and straightway proceeded to announce his success by a magnificent celebration of the sacrifice at his capital. The dramatist, who has so well preserved the traditions of the time, professes to record the very words of the invitation addressed by the victorious king to his son the Crown Prince, as follows :—

'May it be well with thee ! From the sacrificial enclosure the commander-in-chief Pushpamitra sends this message to his son Agnimitra, who is in the territory of Vidisā, affectionately embracing him. Be it known unto thee that I, having been consecrated for the *Rājasūya* sacrifice,[1] let loose free from all check or curb a horse which was to be brought back after a year, appointing Vasumitra as its defender, girt with a guard of a hundred Rājpūts. This very horse wandering on the right [or " south "] bank of the Sindhu was claimed by a cavalry squadron of the Yavanas. Then there was a fierce struggle between the two forces. Then Vasumitra, the mighty bowman, having overcome his foes, rescued by force my excellent horse, which they were endeavouring to carry off. Accordingly, I will now sacrifice, having had my horse brought back to me by my grandson, even as Ansumat brought back the horse to Sagara. Therefore, you must dismiss anger from your mind, and without delay come with my daughters-in-law to behold the sacrifice.'[2]

Patañjali.

The performance of the solemn rite probably was witnessed by the celebrated grammarian Patañjali, who alludes

[1] The *rājasūya* was a ceremony of consecration of a king. The full ritual lasted for twelve months. It is explained in detail by R. L. Mitra in *J. A. S. B.*, part i, vol. xlv (1876), pp. 386–98 ; and by Barnett, *Antiquities of India* (1913), p. 167.

[2] *Mālavikāgnimitra*, 'The Story of Mālavikā and Agnimitra', Act v, transl. Tawney, p. 78, with the substitution of the word 'forces' for 'hosts', which is not suitable. Abstracts of the plot are given by Wilson (*Theatre of the Hindus*, vol. i, pp. 348–53, and Sylvain Lévi, *Théâtre Indien*, pp. 166–70). It has been edited by Tullberg (Bonn, 1840), and translated into English by Tawney (Calcutta, 1875), into German by Weber (Berlin, 1856), and twice into French, first by Foucaux, and later by Victor Henry (Paris, 1877, 1889). The historical tradition seems to be authentic. Kālidāsa, the author, probably lived during the Gupta period in the fifth century. H. C. Chakladar places him definitely in the early years of the fifth century during the reign of Chandragupta Vikramāditya ('Studies in the Kāmasutra of Vatsyayana', *J. B. & O. Res. Soc.*, 1919, vol. v, Part ii, p. 199). For the Sagara legend see Dowson, *Classical Dictionary*, s. v.

to the event in terms which imply that it occurred in his time.

Beginning of Brahmanical reaction.

The exaggerated regard for the sanctity of animal life, which was one of the most cherished features of Buddhism, and the motive of Asoka's most characteristic legislation, had necessarily involved the prohibition of bloody sacrifices, which are essential to certain forms of Brahmanical worship, and were believed by the orthodox to possess the highest saving efficacy. The memorable horse-sacrifice of Pushyamitra marked an early stage in the Brahmanical reaction, which was fully developed five centuries later in the time of Samudragupta and his successors.

Pushyamitra alleged to be a persecutor.

If credit may be given to the semi-mythological stories of Buddhist writers, Pushyamitra was not content with the peaceful revival of Hindu rites, but indulged in a savage persecution of Buddhism, burning monasteries and slaying monks from Magadha to Jālandhar, in the Panjāb. Many monks who escaped his sword are said to have fled into the territories of other rulers. It would be rash to reject this tale as wholely baseless, although it may be exaggerated.[1]

Persecutions in India.

Although the alleged proscription of Buddhism by Pushyamitra is supported by some evidence, it is true that the gradual extinction of that religion in India was due in the main to causes other than persecution ; while it is also true that from time to time fanatic kings indulged in savage outbursts of cruelty, and committed genuine acts of persecution directed against Jains or Buddhists as such. Well-established instances of such proceedings will be met with in the course of this history, and others, which do not come within its limits, are on record. That such outbreaks of wrath should have occurred is not wonderful, if we consider the extreme oppressiveness of the Jain and Buddhist prohibitions when ruthlessly enforced, as they certainly were by some Rājas, and presumably by Asoka. The wonder rather is that persecutions were so rare, and that as a rule the

[1] Tāranāth, Schiefner's transl., p. 81 ; *Divyāvadāna* in Burnouf, *Introduction*, 2nd ed., p. 384. Tāranāth, probably with truth, represents Pushyamitra as a Brahman, the domestic priest (*purohit*) of a certain king.

various sects managed to live together in harmony, and in the enjoyment of fairly impartial official favour.[1]

c. 149 B.C. The later Śungas.

When Pushyamitra, some five years subsequent to the retreat of Menander, died, after a long and eventful reign, he was succeeded by his son the Crown Prince, Agnimitra, who had governed the southern provinces during his father's lifetime. He reigned but a few years, and was succeeded by Vasujyeshtha, or Sujyeshtha, probably a brother, who was followed seven years later by Vasumitra, presumably that son of Agnimitra who as a youth had guarded the sacrificial horse on behalf of his aged grandfather. The next four reigns are said to have been abnormally short, amounting together to only seventeen years. The inference that the extreme brevity of these reigns indicates a period of confusion during which palace revolutions were frequent is confirmed by the one incident of the time which has survived in tradition. Sumitra, another son of Agnimitra, who was, we are told, inordinately devoted to the stage, was surprised when in the midst of his favourite actors by one Mitradeva, who 'severed his head with a scimitar, as a lotus is shorn from its stalk'.[2] The ninth king, Bhāgavata, is credited with a long reign of thirty-two years, but we know little about him.[3] The tenth king, Devabhūti or Devabhūmi,

[1] The reality of religious persecution of Buddhism in India, denied by Rhys Davids (*J. Pāli Text Soc.*, 1896, pp. 87–92), is affirmed by Hodgson, Sewell, and Watters (ibid., pp. 107–10). The instance of Śaśānka, described by the nearly contemporary Hiuen Tsang (Beal, *Records*, i, 212, ii, 42, 91, 118, 121), is fully proved. The case against Mihirakula is almost as strong. In ancient times Tibet and Khotan were closely connected with India. Tibetan history records a persecution of Buddhism by king Glang Darma (Langdarma), about A. D. 840 (Rockhill, *Life of the Buddha*, pp. 226, 243), and a similar event is recorded in Khotan annals, shortly before A. D. 741 (ibid., pp. 248–5; Sarat Chandra Dās, *J. A. S. B.*, pt. I, 1886, p. 200). A terrible persecution of the cognate religion Jainism occurred in Southern India in the seventh century (Elliot, *Coins of Southern India*, p. 126; *post*, ch. xvi, sec. 2). Ajayadeva, a 'Saiva king of Gujarāt (A. D. 1174–6), began his reign by a merciless persecution of the Jains, torturing their leader to death' (*Archaeol. S. W. I.*, vol. ix, p. 16). Several other well-established instances of severe persecution might be cited.

[2] Bāṇa, *Harṣa-carita*, ch. vi; Cowell and Thomas, transl., p. 192.

[3] There is an inscription of his on the stump of a Garuḍa pillar at Besnagar, 'when he had been crowned twelve years' (*A. S. Rep. I.*, 1913–14, pt. II, p. 190). See *I. M. Catalogue*, p. 146.

was, we are assured, a man of licentious habits, and lost his life while engaged in a discreditable intrigue. The dynasty thus came to an unhonoured end after having occupied the throne for a hundred and twelve years.[1]

The Kānva or Kānvāyana Dynasty.

The plot which cost the royal debauchee, Devabhūti, his throne and life was contrived by his Brahman minister Vasudeva, who seems to have controlled the state even during the lifetime of his nominal master.[2] Mitradeva, the slayer of Prince Sumitrà, probably belonged to the same powerful family, which is known to history as that of the Kānvas, or Kānvāyanas. The distinct testimony of both the Purānas and Bāna that Devabhūti, the tenth and last Sunga, was the person slain by Vasudeva, the first Kānva, forbids the acceptance of Professor Bhandarkar's theory that the Kānva dynasty should be regarded as contemporary with the Sunga.[3]

c. 73 B.C. Vasudeva Kāṇva.

[1] The 'Mitra' coins, of several kinds, found in Oudh, Rohilkhaṇḍ, Gōrakhpur, &c., probably belong to the Śungas, though only one name on the coins, that of Agnimitra, agrees with the Purānic lists. But this may be due to the fact that the Śungas apparently had alternative names (K. P. Jayaswal in *J. B. O. Res. Soc.*, iii). For detailed descriptions see Carlleyle and Rivett-Carnac, *J. A. S. B.*, 1880, pt. i, pp. 21–8, 87–90, with plates; Cunningham, *Coins of Ancient India*, pp. 69, 74, 79, 93; *Catal. of Coins in I. M.*, vol. i, p. 184.

The most authentic version of the Śunga history, according to the Purāṇas, as translated from the eclectic text, is as follows :—

'Puṣyamitra the commander-in-chief will uproot Bṛhadratha and will rule the kingdom as king 36 years. *His* son Agnimitra will be king 8 years. Vaṣujyeṣṭha will be king 7 years. *His* son Vasumitra will be king 10 years. Then his son Andhraka (Odraka) will reign 2 years. Pulindaka will then reign 3 years. *His* son Ghoṣa will be king 3 years. Next Vajramitra will be king 9 years. Bhāgavata will be king 32 years. His son Devabhūmi will reign 10 years. These ten Śunga kings will enjoy this earth full 112 years. From them the earth will pass to the Kāṇvas' (Pargiter, *Dynasties of the Kali Age*, pp. 30, 70. Variant readings are given in the notes). The details of the length of reigns do not agree with the total, 112.

[2] 'In a frenzy of passion the over-libidinous Çunga was at the instance of his minister Vasudeva reft of his life by a daughter of Devabhūti's slave-woman disguised as his queen' (Bāṇa, *Harṣa-carita*, ch. vi, transl. Cowell and Thomas, p. 193). 'The minister Vasudeva, forcibly overthrowing the dissolute king Devabhūmi because of his youth, will become king among the Śungas' (Pargiter, p. 71).

[3] *E. Hist. of Dekkan*, 2nd ed. in *Bomb. Gaz.*, vol. i, pt. ii, p. 163. I adopted this theory in my 'Āndhra Dynasty' (*Z. D. M. G.*, 1902, p. 658)—but now reject it.

c. 63–28 B. C. The later Kāṇvas.

Vasudeva seized the throne rendered vacant by his crime, and was succeeded by three of his descendants. The whole dynasty, comprising four reigns, covers a period of only forty-five years.[1] The figures indicate, as in the case of the Sungas, that the times were disturbed, and that succession to the throne was often effected by violent means. Nothing whatever is known about the reigns of any of the Kānva kings.[2] The last of them was slain about 28 or 27 B. C. by a king of the Āndhra or Sātavāhana dynasty, which at that time possessed wide dominions stretching across the table-land of the Deccan from sea to sea. Although no coins or monuments connecting the Āndhra kings with Pātaliputra, the ancient imperial capital, have yet been discovered, it is possible that they may have controlled the kingdom of Magadha for a time. The most ancient coins of the dynasty at present known are of northern type, and bear the name of Sāta, probably Sātakarni, the sixth king in the Purānic list, who was reigning about 150 B. C. The Āndhra coinage from first to last has many obvious affinities with the mint-ages of the north, which may be explained by the hypothesis that the dynasty really held Magadha as a dependency for a considerable period. But there is little evidence to support such a conjecture.[3]

Identity of the Āndhra king.

The Purānas treat the whole Āndhra dynasty as following the Kānva, and consequently identify the slayer of the last Kānva prince with Simuka or Sipraka, the first of the Āndhra line. But, as a matter of fact, the independent

[1] The Purānic text is :—

'He [*scil.* Vasudeva], the Kāṇvāyana, will be king 9 years. His son Bhūmimitra will reign 14 years. His son Nārāyaṇa will reign 12 years. His son Suśarman will reign 10 years.

These are remembered as the Śuṇgabhṛtya [*scil.* servants of the Śungas] Kāṇvāyaṇa kings. These 4 Kāṇva brahmans will enjoy the earth ; for 45 years they will enjoy this earth. They will have the neighbouring kings in subjection and will be righteous. In succession to them the earth will pass to the Āndhras' (Pargiter, p. 71; variants in the notes). The details of the length of reigns agree with the total, 45.

[2] The coins of Bhūmimitra seem to belong to the Kānva dynasty, and also probably the Deva coins (*I. M. Catalogue*).

[3] See the author's paper on the 'Āndhra Coinage' in *Z. D. M. G.*, 1903, pp. 605–27. An ancient Tamil poem, the *Chilappathikāram*, mentions the visit of a Chera prince to a Sātakarna king of Magadha (V. K. Pillai, *The Tamils Eighteen Hundred Years Ago*, p. 6).

Āndhra dynasty must have begun about 240 or 230 B. C.,[1] long before the suppression of the Kānvas about 28 B. C., and the Āndhra king who slew Susarman cannot possibly have been Simuka. It is impossible to affirm with certainty who he was, because the dates of accession of the several Āndhra princes are not known with accuracy. All that can be affirmed at present is that the slayer of Susarman, the last Kānva, apparently must have been one or other of three Āndhra kings, namely Nos. 11, 12, or 13. The year 28 B. C. may be accepted as the approximately true date of the extinction of the Kānva dynasty; because it depends, not on the duration assigned to each several Āndhra reign, but on the periods of 112 and 45 years respectively allotted to the Sunga and Kānva dynasties, which seem worthy of credence; and this date, 28 B. C., apparently must fall within the limits of one or other of the three Āndhra reigns named above.[2]

The Āndhra or Andhra Dynasty.

Earliest mention of the Āndhras.

Before proceeding to narrate the history of the Āndhra kings after the extinction of the Kānva dynasty we must cast back a glance to the more distant past, and trace the steps by which the Āndhra kingdom became one of the greatest powers in India.

300 B. C.

In the days of Chandragupta Maurya and Megasthenes, ths Āndhra nation, a Dravidian people, mentioned in the *Aitareya Brahmana* of very early date, and now represented by the large population speaking the Telugu language, occupied the deltas of the Godāvarī and Krishnā (Kistna) rivers on the eastern side of India, and was reputed to possess a military force second only to that at the command of the king of the Prasii, Chandragupta Maurya. The Andhra territory included thirty walled towns, besides

[1] The name of the Āndhra nation is extremely ancient, being mentioned in the *Aitareya Brāhmana* (vii, 18), 'a work which was certainly composed prior to 500 B. C.' (D. R. Bhandarkar, *Ind. Ant.* xlvii (1916), p. 70). The Āndhras are there represented as a Dasyu race, living on the fringes of the Aryan settlements and descended from Viśvāmitra.

[2] Close of Maurya dynasty, *c.* 185 B. C.; from which deduct 112+45=157, leaving 28.

numerous villages, and the army consisted of 100,000 infantry, 2,000 cavalry, and 1,000 elephants.[1] The capital of the state is believed to have been then Srī Kākulam, on the lower course of the Krishnā.[2] The nation thus described evidently was independent.

256 B. C. Āndhras tributary to Asoka.

When next mentioned in Asoka's edicts (256 B. C.) they were reckoned among the tribes and nations resident in or adjoining the outer circle of the empire, and perhaps subject to the imperial command, although doubtless enjoying a considerable degree of autonomy under their own Rāja.[3] The withdrawal of the strong arm of Asoka was the signal for the disruption of his vast empire. While the home provinces continued to obey his feeble successors upon the throne of Pātaliputra, the distant governments, including Kalinga, which he had taken so much trouble to annex, shook off the imperial yoke and reasserted their independence.

c. 240 or 230 B. C. Kings Simuka and Krishṇa.

The Āndhras were not slow to take advantage of the opportunity given by the death of the great emperor, and very soon after the close of his reign, or possibly even before its close, to assert their independent power under the government of a king named Simuka. The new dynasty extended its sway with such extraordinary rapidity that, in the reign of the second king, Krishna (Kanha), the town of Nāsik, near the source of the Godāvarī in the Western

[1] Pliny, *Hist. Nat.*, Book vi, 21, 22, 23, from information probably supplied by Megasthenes. The passage is fully discussed in the author's monograph, 'Āndhra History and Coinage' (*Z. D. M. G.*, 1902, 1903), to which reference may be made by readers desirous of examining in detail the sources of Āndhra history. See P. T. Srinivas Iyengar, 'Misconceptions about the Āndhras' (*Ind. Ant.*, (Nov., 1913), pp. 276–8). He argues that the Āndhras must have spoken Prākrit, not Telugu, and that their rule spread from west to east down the river valleys, and not as stated in the text.

[2] Burgess, 'The Stūpas of Amarāvatī and Jaggayapeta', *A.S.S.I.*, p. 3 (referring to Wilson, *Mackenzie MSS.*, vol. i, introd. p. cxvii, and Campbell, *Telugu Grammar*, introd. p. ii). The site of the ancient town (N. lat. 20° 28′, E. long. 85° 55′) has been cut away by the river (Rea, *Proc. Govt. Madras, Public*, No. 423, dated June 18, 1892).

[3] 'And likewise here, in the king's dominions, among the Yonas and Kambojas, in (?) Nābhaka of the Nābhitis, among the Bhojas and Pitinikas (? see p. 193, *note* 2, *ante*), among the Āndhras and Pulindas, everywhere men follow the Law of Piety as proclaimed by His Majesty' (Rock Edict XII).

Ghāts, was included in the Āndhra dominions, which thus stretched across India.

The third king, Srī Sātakarni, who is described as Lord of the West, was defied by Khāravela, king of Kalinga in the east, which kingdom also had recovered its independence after the death of Asoka.[1] *c.* 171 B.C. Khāravela.

Nothing more is heard of the Āndhra kings until one of them, as above related, in or about 28 B. C., slew the last of the Kānvas, and no doubt annexed the territory, whatever it may have been, which still recognized the authority of that dynasty. The Āndhra kings all claimed to belong to the Sātavāhana family, and many of them assumed the title or bore the name of Sātakarni. They are consequently often referred to by one or other of these designations, without mention of the personal name of the monarch, and it is thus sometimes impossible to ascertain which king is alluded to. As already observed, the real name of the slayer of Susarman Kānva is not known. *c.* 28 or 27 B. C. Extinction of Kāṇva dynasty.

[1] The Udayagiri or Hāthigumphā inscription of Khāravela, the Jain king of Kalinga, has now been edited by K. P. Jayaswal and R. D. Banerji in *J. B. O. Res. Soc.*, iii, pp. 425–507, with good facsimiles. The inscription is dated in the year $\frac{165}{164}$ of 'Rājā Muriya', *scil.* Chandragupta. We learn that Khāravela, surnamed Mahā Meghavāhana, the third of the Cheta or Chaitra dynasty of Kalinga, was anointed as Mahārāja when twenty-four years of age, having been already Crown Prince (*yuvarāja*) for nine years. In his second year he defied Sātakarni, by sending an army to the west. In his fifth year he repaired an aqueduct which had not been used for 300 years from the time of king Nanda, and in the same year, harassed the king of Rājagriha, i. e. of Magadha. In his twelfth year he watered his elephants in the Ganges, and compelled the king of Magadha to bow at his feet. In his thirteenth year he erected certain pillars.

The Nanda king mentioned in the inscription must be Nandivardhana or Nanda I, the date of whose accession as counted back from the fifth year of Khāravela approximates very closely to the date deduced by K. P. Jayaswal from the date in the dynastic lists of the Purāṇas (R. D. Banerji in *J. B. O. Res. Soc.*, iii, Dec. 1917), pp. 497–99). The Āndhra king alluded to can only be Śrī Sātakarni, No. 3 of the Purānic list, who is commemorated by a defaced, but happily inscribed, relief image at Nānāghāṭ, a pass leading from the Konkan to the ancient town of Junnār in the Poona District, Bombay (*A. S. W. I.*, vol. v, p. 59).

The synchronism of Sātakarṇi I with Khāravela proves conclusively that the Āndhra dynasty cannot have begun with the death of the last Kāṇva king. The date assigned to Sātakarṇi I is in full accord with the script of the Nānāghāṭ inscriptions, which include similar records of the first and second Āndhra kings, Simuka and Kṛishṇa (Lüders, *op. cit.*, Nos. 1113, 1114, 1144). The king of Magadha whom Khāravēla defeated was Pushyamitra of the Śunga dynasty.

King Hāla and Prākrit literature. The name of Hāla, the seventeenth king, by virtue of its association with literary tradition, possesses special interest. The anthology of erotic verses, written in the ancient dialect of Mahārāshtra, and entitled *Saptaśataka*, or 'Seven Centuries', professes to be the composition of Hāla, and is ascribed by tradition to Sālivāhana, another form of Sātavāhana. Prof. Sir R. G. Bhandarkar therefore has suggested that probably either king Hāla may have been the author of the work, or it may have been dedicated to him.[1] Other traditions also associate literature written in Prākrit with kings of the Āndhra dynasty. In their time and territory Sanskrit, apparently, was not in ordinary use as the language of polite literature.

Wars between Āndhras and foreigners. During the reigns of kings No. 23, Rāja Gautamīputra Srī Sātakarni, and No. 24, Rāja Vāsishtīputra Srī Pulumāyi, the Āndhras engaged in conflicts with the foreign tribes which had formed settlements and carved out kingdoms in Western India, subordinate apparently at first to the Indo-Parthian and subsequently to the Kushān sovereigns. Such conflicts between indigenous Rājas and alien chiefs frequently recur in the history of ancient India.

Satrap Bhūmaka Kshaharāta. The story of the foreign settlements in the regions now mostly included in the Bombay Presidency is fragmentary and obscure, but can be made out to some extent from study of coins and inscriptions. The earliest foreign ruler in the west whose name has been preserved was the Satrap Bhūmaka Kshaharāta, who struck coins with Parthian affinities, and may be presumed to have been subordinate to one or other of the Indo-Parthian kings, perhaps Gondophares. His exact date is not known, but he may be assigned approximately to the early years of the first century after Christ, and may have had predecessors. The Kshaharātas were connected with the Sakas, and may have immigrated from Sakastēnē, the modern Sīstān.

[1] *Early Hist. of the Dekkan*, 2nd ed., in *Bomb. Gaz.* (1896), vol. i, pt. ii, p. 171. M. M. Haraparshad Shastri (*Ep. Ind.*, xii, 320) notes that Hāla 'cannot be placed later than the first century A. D.', and that the *Saptaśatī* (as he calls it) mentions a king named Vikramāditya, who *may* be the founder of the era.

The next recorded Kshaharāta chief is Nahapāna, who may or may not have been the immediate successor of Bhūmaka, and may be assigned approximately to the middle of the first century after Christ, or possibly earlier. His name indicates Persian origin. At first he held the rank of Satrap, like Bhūmaka, but subsequently assumed the higher style of Great Satrap (*mahākshatrapa*), and was also known by the Indian title of Rāja. His dominions comprised a large area, extending from Southern Rājputāna as far northward as Ajmēr and Pushkar, to the Nāsik and Poona Districts in the Western Ghāts, and including the peninsula of Surāshtra or Kāthiāwār. His titles of Satrap and Great Satrap indicate subordination to a northern power, which can only have been that of the Kushāns.[1]

Great Satrap Nahapāna Kshaharāta.

The Āndhra king, No. 23, Rāja Gautamīputra Srī Sātakarni, who may be assumed to have come to the throne about the beginning of the second century A. D., succeeded in extirpating the Kshaharāta dynasty and annexing their dominions about A. D. 119. He signalized his victory by calling in the money issued by the vanquished princes during many years, restamping it in a crude fashion with his own insignia. At the height of his power he was master of the whole country watered by the Godāvarī, Berar, Mālwā, Kāthiāwār, Gujarāt, and the north Konkan.[2] He posed as the champion of the Hindu religions, including both Brahmanical Hinduism and Buddhism, as against the creeds of casteless foreigners, Sakas, Pahlavas, and others, and prided himself on having re-established the practice of caste rules. He thus 'restored the glory of the Sātavāhana race', and was in a position to gratify his Hindu sentiment

Extirpation of Kshaharātas by Gautāmīputra Sātakarṇi.

[1] D. R. Bhandarkar regards him as a viceroy of Kadphises II (*Ind. Ant.*, xlvii (1918), p. 76) and also of Kadphises I, who is called simply Kushāna in the Taxila scroll inscription of the year 136. The *Kuśana* of the Nāsik inscription 12 seems to mean the silver coinage of Nahapāna, who, like Kadphises I, imitated Roman coins. The varying heads on his coins appear to be merely imitations and not portraits at all. Minnagala, which according to the *Periplus* was the capital of Nahapāna, may be identified with Mandasor, in accordance with the latitude and longitude given by Ptolemy, nearly 2 degrees E. and 2 degrees N. of Barygaza.

[2] D. R. Bhandarkar in *Ind. Ant.*, xlvii, 1918, 'Dekkan of the Sātavāhana Period'.

by liberal donations to both Brahmans and Buddhists. It is a curious fact that, although the Āndhra kings clearly were officially Brahmanical Hindus, most of their recorded donations were made to Buddhist institutions.

Conquest of Pulumāyi by Rudradāman I.

About A. D. 128 Rāja Gautamīputra Srī Sātakarni was succeeded by his son, Rāja Vāsishthīputra Srī Pulumāyi, who had been his colleague,[1] and reigned for some thirty years. He was married to a daughter of Rudradāman I, the Saka Great Satrap of Ujjain, but the matrimonial connexion did not prevent the Great Satrap from twice defeating his son-in-law and taking from him most of the territory which Gautamīputra Sātakarni had won from the Kshaharātas. The relationship, however, so far influenced the victor that he did not proceed to extremities, as he would have done to a stranger. The aggrandizement of Rudradāman I must have been largely completed before A. D. 130, by which date he was in possession of Cutch, and certainly before A. D. 150, because we know that shortly after that date he placed on record a list of the numerous regions in Western India which owned his sway.

Careers of Rudradāman and Chashtana.

Rudradāman I, a learned and accomplished prince, who thus raised his house to the position of the leading power in the West, was the grandson of the great Satrap Chashtana, whose coins in silver and copper, inscribed with Greek, Brahmī, and Kharoshthī legends, are found in Gujarāt. The events of Chashtana's reign are not on record, but his approximate date is easily ascertained from the facts that his grandson is known to have been reigning in A. D. 130 and 150. Chashtana, therefore, may be placed in the period from about A. D. 80 to 110. These dates imply that Chashtana held his office as Great Satrap under the Kushān dynasty, that is to say, under Kadphises II, according to my chronology.[2] The Saka satraps of Surāshtra and Mālwā

[1] During his conjoint reign with Pulumāyi, Gautamīputra Śrī Sātakarṇi held sway over Āndhradesa, the hereditary Sātavāhana dominion, and Pulumāyi over Mahārāshtra (the Deccan) (D. R. Bhandarkar, ibid.).

[2] Bühler long ago recognized the true relation between Chashṭana and the Indo-Scythian kings. See transl. in *Ind. Ant.*, 1913, p. 189, of his old essay on Indian Inscriptions, &c. The Girnār inscription records the bursting

naturally followed the examples of their Kushān sovereigns by using the Saka era, then newly established. The abundance of dated coins and inscriptions permits of no doubt as to the outlines of the chronology of the dynasty founded by Chashtana, the history of which will be further noticed in connexion with the Gupta kings.

Yajña Śrī, c. A.D. 166 to 196.

After the death of Vāsishtīputra Pulumāyi about A. D. 156, the only notable Āndhra monarch was Gautamīputra Yajna Srī, who reigned for twenty-nine years, from about A. D. 166. His rare silver coins, imitating the satrap coinage, certainly prove a renewal of relations with the western satraps, and probably point to unrecorded conquests. It would seem that Yajna Srī must have renewed the struggle in which Pulumāyi II had been worsted, and that he recovered some of the provinces lost by that prince. The silver coins would then have been struck for circulation in the conquered western districts, just as similar coins were minted by Chandra-gupta Vikramāditya when he finally shattered the power of the Saka satraps. The numerous and varied, although rude, bronze and leaden coins of Yajna Srī, which formed the currency of the eastern provinces, confirm the testimony of inscriptions by which the prolonged duration of his reign is attested.[1] Some pieces bearing the figure of a ship probably should be referred to this reign, and suggest the inference that Yajna Srī's power was not confined to the land.

The last three kings.

His successors, apparently, in the eastern provinces, named Vijaya, Chandra Srī, and Pulumāyi IV, with whom

of the dam of the lake in A. D. 150, but the record itself must have been incised some years later (ibid., p. 190).

Benoytosh Bhattacharya in *J. B. O. Res. Soc.*, vi (1920), pp. 51–3, declares that the name on one of the two statues discovered with the statue of Kanishka at Mat, 9 miles north of Mathurā, is 'Chastana'. K. P. Jayaswal (ibid., v (1919), p. 511) accepts Bhattacharya's reading, and points out that the fact that this statue was found in the same *Devakula* as the statue of Kanishka justifies the view that Chastana was a relative of Kanishka and belonged to the same family.

[1] R. G. Bhandarkar's notion that the Āndhra dynasty comprised two distinct lines of kings, one western and one eastern, does not seem to be tenable. The evidence shows that most of the kings held both the western and eastern provinces.

the long series of Āndhra kings came to an end about A. D. 225, are mere names; but the real existence of Chandra Srī is attested by the discovery of a few leaden coins bearing his name.[1] Research probably will detect coins struck by both his next predecessor and immediate successor.

Duration of the dynasty.

The testimony of the Purānas that the dynasty endured for either 456 or 460 years, or, in round numbers, four centuries and a half, appears to be substantially accurate. The number of the kings also appears to be correctly stated as having been thirty. The following dynastic list has been constructed on the assumption that the best texts of the Purānas are right in fixing the number of kings as thirty, and therefore omits an extra king, No. 24 *a*, who appears only in a single manuscript of the *Vāyu Purāṇa*.[2]

Western India under the Āndhras.

Professor D. R. Bhandarkar has given a description, based upon the rock and cave inscriptions of Western India, of the social and economic features of the Deccan during the sway of the Āndhras.[3] Both Buddhism and Brahmanic Hinduism flourished at that period. Almost all the Buddhist caves in the Deccan were excavated under the rule of this dynasty, villages and lands being granted to defray the cost of their maintenance and to provide also for the sustenance of the *Bhikshus* who inhabited the caves during the rainy season. The provision of new robes for these mendicants was secured by the investment of funds in one of the craft-guilds (*sreni*), established in the neighbouring towns. The popularity of Brahmanism is apparent from the fact that Royalty performed many sacrifices, including the *Aśvamedha* and *Gavāmayana*, and paid heavy *dakshina* to Brahmans. The worship of Siva was popular,

[1] *Catal. Coins I. M.*, vol. i, p. 209; Rapson, *Catal. of Coins of the Āndhra Dynasty, &c.* (1908), pp. 30–3. Rapson is inclined to assign an earlier date to these coins. D. R. Bhandarkar ('Dekkan of the Sātavāhana Period', *Ind. Ant.*, xlvii (1918), p. 149 ff.) states that Vāsishtīputra Pulumāyi was succeeded by his brothers Śiva-Śrī-Sātakarṇi and Srī-Chandra-Sātī in turn, and that Gautamīputra Yajña Śrī was the last prince of the dynasty. He suggests that the latter was master of Āndhradesa and Mahārāshtra and that he probably seized Kāthiāwār and Eastern Mālwā from the Kshaharāta dynasty of Ujjain as his ancestor, the Āndhra king No. 23, had done before him.

[2] For the list see App. J.

[3] *Ind. Ant.*, xlviii (1919), pp. 77 ff.

and also the cult of Krishna under the names Samkarshana and Vāsudeva, while Indra and Dharma were widely revered. There seems to have been little or no antagonism between the two faiths, for the followers of Brahmanism excavated several caves for Buddhist monks, while foreigners like the Sakas and Ābhiras freely embraced either religion and assumed Hindu names.

Society was officially divided into at least four classes, the highest class being composed of the Mahārathis, the Mahābhojas, and the Mahāsenāpatīs, who were feudatory chieftains in charge of *rashtras* or districts, the Mahābhojas being located in the north Konkan, and the Mahārathis in the country above the Western Ghāts. The second class comprised both officials and non-officials, among the former being the Amātyas and Mahāmātras, and the Bhāndāgārikas, who were in charge of the treasuries; while the latter included the *Naigama* (merchant), the *Sārthavāha* (head of a caravan of traders), and the *Sresthin* (head of a trade-guild). In the third class were the *Lekhaka* (scribe), *Vaidya* (physician), *Hālakīya* (cultivator), *Suvarnakāra* (goldsmith) and *Gāndhika* (druggist). The fourth class included the *Vardhaki* (carpenter), *Mālākara* (gardener), *Lohavanija* (blacksmith), and *Dāsaka* (fisherman). The mercantile and cultivating classes were apparently subdivided into various *grihas* (homesteads) or *kutumbas* or *kulas* (families), the head of each of which was considered of sufficient importance to be designated respectively *Grihapati* or *Kutumbin*.

The currency of the country consisted of *kārshāpanas*, which were both silver and copper; *suvarnas*, the gold coins of the Kushān kings, one of which was equal in value to 35 silver *kārshāpanas*; and *kusanas*, a silver coinage probably introduced by Nahapāna or another Saka ruler, eight of which were equivalent to nine silver *kārshāpanas*.

Craft-guilds were a feature of the age. At Govardhan, near Nāsik, there were guilds of oil-pressers, hydraulic machine-artisans, potters, and weavers; while at Junnar there were similar guilds of corn-dealers, bamboo-workers, and braziers. These guilds acted as banks, in which money could be deposited at interest, such deposits being always made in the indigenous currency (*kārshāpanas*). Permanent endowments, such as those for religious purposes, were publicly proclaimed and registered in the records of a *nigama-sabha* or town-assembly.

The country profited from a flourishing foreign trade. Ships from the West sailed down the Red Sea to Broach and the Malabar coast, which supplied the two great inland marts of Paithan and Tagara, and probably visited the two harbours of Sopārā and Kalyān. The latter port was raised to the rank of a regular mart in the time of the elder Sarganes (probably Sātakarni, the third ruler of the dynasty); but its trade was subsequently restricted to narrow limits by Sandanes, who may have been a Saka official. The Saka Satraps certainly endeavoured to divert the trade from Broach direct through their own dominions in the northern Deccan. Other seaports supplying the Āndhra dominions were Semulla (Chaul), Mandagora (? Mandangad to the south of Bānkot), Palaipatmai, Melizeigara (? Jaygad or Janjira) and Buzantion.

The last of the Āndhras.

At present nothing is known concerning the causes which brought about the downfall of this dynasty, which had succeeded in retaining power for a period so unusually prolonged. It would seem that Yajna Srī was the last king to retain control of both the eastern and western provinces.[1] Scions of the Sātavāhana race appear to have established minor kingdoms in different parts of the Deccan. But the third century after Christ is one of the dark spaces in the spectrum of Indian history, and almost every event of that time is concealed from view by an impenetrable veil of oblivion. Vague speculation, unchecked by the salutary limitations of verified fact, is, at the best, unprofitable; and so we must be content to let the Āndhras pass away in the darkness. The Purānas present confused and corrupt

[1] D. R. Bhandarkar (ibid.) suggests that the Sātavāhanas lost Mahārāshtra owing to the irruption of the Ābhiras under Isvaradatta (A. D. 188–90), but continued to rule the eastern provinces until extinguished by a northern dynasty.

lists of numerous local dynasties, including Yavanas and Sakas, obviously foreigners, as having succeeded the Āndhras, which it is impossible to arrange in any intelligible fashion.[1]

APPENDIX I

The Invasion of Menander, and the Date of Patañjali

Authorities.

The authorities for the invasion of Menander are Strabo, who alone gives the Greek king's name (Bk. xi, sec. xi, 1 ; xv, sec. ii, 3) ; Patañjali, the contemporary Hindu grammarian ; the Sanskrit astronomical work, the *Gārgī Saṁhitā*, of uncertain date ; and Tāranāth, the Tibetan historian of Buddhism.

Strabo.

Strabo's informant, Apollodoros of Artemita, testifies that Menander crossed the Hypanis (Hyphasis, Biās) river, at which Alexander's advance had been arrested ; penetrated to the Isamus (τοῦ Ἰσάμου), which has not been identified ; and ultimately subjugated Patalēnē, or the Indus delta, the kingdom of Saraostos (Surāshtra, or Kāthiāwāṛ), and a territory on the western coast named Sigerdis. This statement is supported by the observation of the writer of the *Periplus*, who noticed, probably towards the close of the first century after Christ, that Greek coins of Apollodotos and Menander were still current at the port of Barygaza (Broach, Bharōch). This curious observation suggests the inference, that although Menander was compelled to retire quickly from the Gangetic valley, his rule must have continued for a considerable number of years in the territories on the western coast.

Madhyamikā.

The sieges of Sākētam and Madhyamikā by the Yavana, that is to say presumably Menander, are referred to by the grammarian Patañjali in terms which necessarily imply that those events occurred during the writer's lifetime. The proof that Madhyamikā is the correct reading and to be interpreted as the name of a city is due to Prof. Kielhorn (*Ind. Ant.* vii, 266). The identity of Madhyamikā with the ancient town of Nagarī, or Tambavatī Nagarī, one of the oldest sites in India, about 8 miles to the north of Chitōr in Rājputāna, is established by the coins found at Nagarī, and rarely elsewhere, with the legend *Majhimikāya śibijanapadasa*, '[Coin] of the Śibi people in Majhimikā (Madhyamikā) city' (D. R. Bhandarkar in *Prog. Rep. A. S. W. I.*, 1915–16, p. 52. See also Cunningham, *Reports*, vi, 201 ; xiv, 146, pl. xxxi). The Śibis of Madhyamikā probably emigrated from the Panjāb. Madhyamikā was a place of great importance which the Greek army could not neglect. Prof. D. R. Bhandarkar has

[1] For justification of the statements in the text, which differ from those made in earlier editions, see Appendix J.

found two inscriptions of the second century B.C. recording the performance of the *Aśvamedha* and *Vājapeya* sacrifices. The coins are rightly assigned to the middle of the second century B.C. The ruins at Nagarī include a square brick *stūpa* (converted into a Saiva temple) with remarkable tiles and terra cottas, and a *toraṇa* of Gupta date. Chitōr was largely built out of the ruins of Nagarī.

Sākētam. Sākētam (Sākēta) probably was a town in Southern Oudh, but not identical with Ajodhya, as it is often asserted to be. There seem to have been several places of the name (Weber, in *Ind. Ant.*, ii, 208). The identifications of the Shā-che of Fa-hien with the Viśākhā of Hiuen Tsang and with Sākētam, as made by Cunningham, are equally unsound (*J. R. A. S.*, 1898, p. 522; 1900, p. 3). At present the position of Sākētam cannot be determined precisely.

Date of Patañjali. The words of Patañjali in which he alludes to the horse-sacrifice of Pushyamitra (*iha Pushpamitram yājayāmaḥ*), when read with other relevant passages, permit of no doubt that the grammarian was the contemporary of that king as well as of the Greek invader presumed to be Menander. The question of Patañjali's date was the subject of prolonged controversy between Weber on one side and Goldstücker and Bhandarkar on the other. Ultimately Weber was constrained to admit the substantial validity of his opponents' arguments (*Hist. Ind. Lit.*, 2nd ed., Trübner, 1882, p. 224, note); and no doubt now remains that the date of Patañjali is fixed to 150–140 B.C. in round numbers. References are: Goldstücker, *Pāṇini, His Place in Sanskrit Literature*, pp. 228–38; *Ind. Ant.* i, 299–302; ii, 57, 69, 94, 206–10, 238, 362; xv, 80–4; xvi, 156, 172 (the Maurya passage).

The statement in the *Gārgī Saṁhitā*, a work ascribed by Max Müller to the second or third century after Christ, is to the following effect:—

Gārgī Samhitā. 'After speaking of the kings of Pāṭaliputra (mentioning Śāliśūka, the fourth successor of Asoka [*c.* 200 B.C.] by name), the author adds: "That when the viciously valiant Greeks, after reducing Sāketa (Oude), the Pañchāla country [probably the Doāb between the Jumna and Ganges], and Mathurā, will reach Kusumadhvaja, that is, the royal residence of Pāṭaliputra, and that then all provinces will be in disorder"' (Max Müller, *India, What can it Teach us?*, p. 298, ed. 1883; and Cunningham, *Num. Chron.*, 1890, p. 224).[1]

[1] Rapson (*Anc. Ind.*, 1914, p. 131) considers the book to be important, but does not discuss its date. It has never been edited, and the MS. of it which has been described is both fragmentary and corrupt. It is an astrological treatise, and almost the only example of its class, which was superseded in the fourth century by the Alexandrian science. Fleet (*J. R. A. G.*, 1912, p. 792) pointed out that the passage quoted is from a chapter of the *Gārgī-Saṁhitā* entitled the *Yuga-parāṇa*, and rightly observed that it cannot be as early as 50 B.C., as Kern long ago conjectured. The learned critic ignored Max Müller's view, and censured the author for using

The evidence of Tāranāth (A. D. 1608, resting on old works), as correctly translated by Schiefner, agrees with that of the *Divyāvadāna* (Burnouf, *Introd.*, 2nd ed., p. 384) in stating that Pushyamitra was the ally of unbelievers, and himself burnt monasteries and slew monks :— Tāranāth.

'Es erhob der Brahmanenkönig Puschjamitra sammt den übrigen Tirthja's Krieg, verbrannte von Madhyadeça bis Dschalamdhara eine Menge von Vihâra's,' &c. (p. 81).

The historian adds that, five years later, Pushyamitra died in the north.

Assuming that Pushyamitra died in 149 B. C., after a reign of thirty-six years, as stated in the best Purānic texts, the invasion of Menander may be assigned to the years 156–153 B. C., a date fully in accordance with the numismatic evidence.[1] Coins of Menander are common in India, both in the Panjāb and farther east and south. Forty of his coins were found in the Hamīrpur district to the south of the Jumna in 1877, and brought to the author, then on duty in that district. They were associated with coins of Eukratides, Apollodotos Soter, and Antimachos Nikēphoros, and were in good condition (*Ind. Ant.*, 1904, p. 217).

APPENDIX J

The Āndhras and connected Dynasties

The inscriptions and coins of both the Āndhras and the connected dynasties are fully discussed in Rapson, *Catalogue of the Coins of the Āndhra Dynasty*, &c., B. M., 1908, but the inscrip-

the book, which he denounced as 'quite late' and 'worthless'. But he gave no reason for discrediting Max Müller's guess that the work might date from the third century after Christ. No doubt some of the statements in the *Yugapurāṇa*, as in all Purāṇas, are absurd or erroneous, and the text probably is corrupt; e. g. *Kusumadhvaja* seems to be a mistake for *Kusumapura*. But such errors do not justify total rejection. The book correctly names Śāliśūka Maurya, who, according to the early *e* Vāyu MS. (Pargiter), reigned for thirteen years. I do not see any reason for refusing to believe that the *Yugapurāna* may date from the third century. Whatever the date of the existing text may be, it is most unlikely that the author should have invented the statement about the *dushṭa vikrāntāḥ* Yavanas. The name of the Yavana leader appears to have been lost owing to corruption of the text. As to Menander's date, I have followed Cunningham, in preference to Gardner, on whom Fleet relied. I still think that there is good reason for connecting the statement of the *Yugapurāṇa* with Menander, and for the chronology adopted. D. R. Bhandarkar, who at first supposed that the invader may have been Demetrios, now accepts the identification with Menander. The ruins of the town may date from Menander's siege.

[1] In the chronological table attached to his note on the Khāravela inscription (*J. B. O. Res. Soc.*, iii, 1917, pp. 506, 507), R. D. Banerji puts the death of Pushyamitra in 158 B. C., and Menander's invasion tentatively in 163 B. C. Pending the result of further research, I adhere to the dates given in the third edition of this work.

tions are most conveniently cited by the numbers in Prof. H. Lüders's excellent work, 'A List of Brahmī Inscriptions from the earliest times to about A. D. 400', published as an Appendix to *Epigraphia Indica*, vol. x, 1910. Mr. F. E. Pargiter's book, entitled *The Purāṇa Text of the Dynasties of the Kali Age*, Oxford, 1913, gives the Purānic lists in their most authentic form, with a full apparatus of variants. Mr. R. D. Banerji's essay, entitled 'The Scythian Period of Indian History', in *Indian Antiquary*, 1908, includes certain valuable hints on the history of Nahapāna, &c., which have helped to guide my judgement. The paper on the 'Nasik Hoard of Nahapāna's and Satakarni's Coins', with four plates, by the Rev. H. R. Scott, reprinted from the *J. Br. Br. R. A. S.*, 1907, supplies full details of the important Jogaltembhi hoard.

I have also considered Mr. V. Gopala Aiyar's paper, 'The Saka and Samvat Eras,' in the *Journal of the South Indian Association*, April 1911, vol. i, pp. 425–49.

With reference to those authorities I now proceed to give concisely in this Appendix, in lieu of footnotes, the reasons for the presentation of the history offered in this edition.

References to inscriptions apparently mentioning the Āndhra kings named in the Purānic list, as indicated by serial numbers, are :—

King No. 1—Lüders, No. 1113 ; No. 2—346, 1144 ; No. 3—1144, 1345 ; No. 23—1123, 1124, 1125 ; No. 24—1100, 1106, 1122, 1123, 1124, 1248 ; No. 25 ?—1279 ; No. 27—987, 1024, 1146, 1340 ; No. 29—1341. Doubtful identity—1112, 1120, 1202, 1203, 1204. Coins exist attributable, in some cases with doubt, to Nos. 6, 21, 22, 23, 24, 25, 27, 29, in the Āndhra list.

The Kshaharāta inscriptions are 1099, 1125, 1131, 1132, 1133, 1134, 1135, 1174. Coins exist of Bhūmaka and Nahapāna, and certain coins of Gautamīputra (Āndhra king, No. 23), are restruck on those of Nahapāna.

The list of Āndhra kings is taken from Pargiter, pp. 38–43, 71. The Purāṇas give the name of the first king as Śiśuka (*Mt.*), Sindhuka (*Vā, Bḍ*), or Śipraka (*Vṣ*), and state that 'the Āndhra S., with his fellow tribesmen, the servants of Suśarman, will assail the Kāṇvāyanas and him (Suśarman), and destroy the remains of the Śungas' power and will obtain this earth'. He is identified with Simuka of the Nānāghāṭ inscription, No. 1113, incised in script of about 200 B. C.

Krishṇa, king No. 2, clearly is Kaṇha of Nānāghāṭ record No. 1144 ; and king No. 3, Śrī Sātakarṇi or Mallakarṇi, must be the monarch mentioned in Khāravēla's inscription No. 346, and the Nānāghāṭ epigraph, No. 1114.

Hardly anything else being known about the first eighteen kings, it will suffice to enumerate their names, with the length of their reigns, as stated in Mr. Pargiter's list. They are (1) Śiśuka, &c., of MSS., Simuka of inscription, 23 years ;

(2) Krishṇa, his brother, 10 ; (3) Sātakarṇi or Mallakarṇi, son of (2), 10 ; (4) Pūrṇotsanga, 18 ; (5) Skandastambhi, 18 ; (6) Sātakarṇi, 56 ; (7) Lambodara, 18 ; (8) Āpīlaka, 12 ; (9) Meghasvāti, 18 ; (10) Svāti, 18 ; (11) Skandasvāti, 7 ; (12) Mṛigendra Svātikarṇa, 3 ; (13) Kuntala Svātikarṇa, 8 ; (14) Svātikarṇa, 1 ; (15) Pulomāvi [I], 36 ; (16) Arishṭakarṇa, 25 ; (17) Hāla, 5 ; (18) Mantalaka, 5.

The remaining twelve kings are exhibited in the annexed synchronistic table.

No doubt seems possible as to the identity of Gautamīputra, king No. 23, with *Śrī Sātakarṇi Gautamīputra*, or *Rāja Gautamīputra Sātakarṇi* of the inscriptions, who is known to have reigned at least twenty-four years, and was the father of No. 24, Pulomā[vi II]. That king, No. 24, seems to be the *Rāja Vāśishṭīputra Śrī Pulumāyi*, or *Śrī Pulumāyi Vā°*, or *Navanara-svāmī Vā° Śrī Pulumāyi*, or *Rāja Vā° Svāmī Śrī Pulumāyi*, or [*Rāja*] *Vā° Śrī Sātakarṇi* of various inscriptions.

But a difficulty arises as to the identity of three kings who issued coins of the 'bow and arrow' type, found, it is believed, only at Kolhāpur, in the Marāthā state of that name in the Western Ghāts. The coin legends, transcribed in Sanskrit form, are :—

I. *Rāja Vāśishṭhīputra Vilivāyakura* [I], sometimes restruck with

II. *Rāja Māṭharīputra Sivalakura*—sometimes restruck with

III. *Rāja Gautamīputra Vilivāyakura* [II]. The restrikings permit of no doubt about the serial order of these kings, but according to one view they were merely local governors and viceroys, and according to another, which I adopted definitely in earlier publications, they were members of the main dynasty. If the latter view be correct, the last named, Vilivāyakura II, must be king No. 23, the Gautamīputra of the Purāṇas. Professor D. R. Bhandarkar, however, rejects the identification of Vilivāyakura II with Gautamīputra, and regards him as belonging to a different line, which ruled separately in the country round Kolhāpur. According to the same authority, he or one of his predecessors was a contemporary of Pulumāyi II (*Ind. Ant.*, vol. xlix (1920), pp. 30–4). Another question is whether the strange word Vilivāyakura, which is probably either Telugu or Kanarese, should be regarded as a title or a proper name. In the previous edition of this work, the author inclined to the view that Vilivāyakura must be regarded as a name. The point is discussed by D. R. Bhandarkar in 'Dekkan of the Sātavāhana Period' (*Ind. Ant.* xlix (1920), pp. 31–4), and in my opinion still awaits a final solution.

Pulumāyi II, king No. 24, takes the name or title Sātakarṇi in the Kaṇheri inscription No. 11 = Lüders 994, and appears to have married the daughter of the Great Satrap Rudradāman I, who twice defeated him before A. D. 130. Pulumāyi, as stated in the

Purāṇas, was the son of Gautamīputra. It seems to me quite clear that this Pulumāyi II was the king defeated by Rudradāman I. If that view is correct, though it is not absolutely free from doubt, a firm chronological datum is obtained from which the dates of the dynasty can be reckoned approximately both backwards and forwards.

The identification of king No. 27 with the Yajña Śrī of numerous coins and inscriptions is obvious and certain.

Archaeologists have got into a bad habit of mixing up as 'Western Satraps' two distinct dynasties—namely, the Kshaharātas of Mahārāshṭra and the line of Chashṭana originally settled at Ujjain in Mālwā. No doubt both dynasties were satraps in the west, but they were entirely distinct, and it is better not to apply a common designation to both. Probably the capital of Nahapāna Kshaharāta was at or near Nāsik in the Western Ghāts; the original capital of Chashṭana certainly was Ujjain. Chashṭana's grandson Rudradāman annexed from Pulumāyi II Āndhra most of the territories which Pulumāyi's father had wrested from the Kshaharātas some years earlier. It is not necessary to believe that Gautamīputra Āndhra fought with Nahapāna personally. Study of the great Jogaltembhi hoard of more than 13,000 coins of Nahapāna proves that the coinage extended over many years, although always bearing the name of Nahapāna, who, I believe, was dead before Gautamīputra extirpated his family or clan. The arrow and thunderbolt of Nahapāna's coins connect him with the Parthians and the Northern Satraps Hagāna and Hagāmāsha.[1] The coinage of Chashṭana and his successors is quite different.

The Greek geographer Ptolemy, who died after A. D. 161, and lived at Alexandria for forty years, described Ujjain as the capital of Tiastanēs, who, no doubt, is rightly identified with Chashṭana. The date of composition of the *Geography* is not known, but if the book was written about A. D. 130 the information about Tiastanēs was not many years out of date.[2]

My view of the relations between the Āndhras and the two distinct dynasties of foreign satraps is concisely exhibited in the following tabular statement. It seems to me that all the data harmonize admirably. Almost all students are agreed that the inscriptions and coins of the Chashṭana line of satraps are dated in the Śaka era, and it is possible that the Kshaharāta records are dated in the same way.[3]

[1] *Catal. Coins in I. M.*, vol. i, p. 195. In that work Hagāna and Hagāmāsha seem to be dated too early.

[2] Baleokouros, mentioned by Ptolemy as ruling at Hippokoura, probably was the Āndhra king No. 23, who acquired the Kshaharāta dominions about A. D. 126. Hippokoura *may* mean Nāsik.

[3] This is denied by R. D. Banerji (*J. R. A. S.*, 1917, pp. 272–89), who takes the dates of the Kshaharāta inscriptions to refer to a different era, probably the regnal years of Nahapāna. The Parthian relations of his coinage indicate an early date.

THE LATER ĀNDHRA KINGS AND CONNECTED DYNASTIES

Āndhra Kings, Purāṇa List, Pargiter, pp. 35–43, 71.	Acc. c. A. D.	Inscriptions, Lüders's List, *Ep. Ind.*, vol. x, App.	Coins.	Kshaharāta Satraps of Mahārāshṭra.	Acc. c. A. D.	Śaka Satraps and Great Satraps of Ujjain.	Acc. c. A. D.	Remarks.
								(N.B. *Names given in Sanskrit form for the sake of uniformity of spelling.*)
YRS. 19. Purikasena . . 21	59							
20. Sundara Śātakarṇi 1	80	. . . . . .	The 'bow and arrow' coins of Vāśishṭhīputra Vilivāyakura [I] may belong to any one of these three kings (see Rapson, pp. 5, 6), but possibly belong to a different line (see *Ind. Ant.*, vol. xlix, 1920, pp. 30–4).	Bhūmaka, Satrap (coins only; no inscriptions or dates).	? 1–10 or B. C. ?	Chashṭana (son of Ghsamōtika), at first Satrap, later Great Satrap; also took Indian title of Rāja.	80	'Tiastanes' of Ptolemy = Chashṭana.
21. Chakora Śātakarṇi ½	81							
22. Śivasvāti . . . 28	81	? No. 1279, Amarāvatī, *Rāja Śrī Śivamaka Sata*; but it might belong to No. 25 or 26 below.	The 'bow and arrow' coins of *Māṭharīputra Śivalakura* have been assigned to this king (Rapson, p. 7). See also No. 25. They may be the coins of a separate line.	Bhūmaka's relation to Nahapāna is not known. Nahapāna, Satrap.	A.D. 40 or earlier?			
23. Gautamīputra . 21	102	Nos. 1123, 1125, 1126, Nāsik; to the 24th year.	Re-struck coins of Nahapāna with the legend *Rāja Gautamīputra Śrī Śātakarṇi* (Rapson, pp. lxxxix, 68–70).	Dakshamitrā, dau., m. to Ṛishabhadatta or Ushavadāta, governor of Nāsik, &c. Nahapāna may have died about A.D. 80. His dynasty was extirpated by Āndhra king No. 23, shortly before year 18 of that king, i.e. about A.D. 119. The Kshaharāta inscriptions are dated from 41 to 46 [Śaka], = A.D. 119–124; but Banerji takes these to represent a different era, perhaps the regnal years of Nahapāna.		Jayadāman, son of Chashṭana, Satrap only.	110	Āndhra king No. 23, has been considered as = Baleokouros of Ptolemy. But the latter may be a different king, contemporary of Gautamīputra (23) and Pulumāvi (24). Intelligible Greek legends occur on the coins of Nahapāna.
24. Pulomā[vi II], son of 23 28	123	Nos. 994, Kaṇhēri; 1122–4, 1147, Nāsik; 1100, 1106, Kārlē, and prob. 1248, Amarāvatī. *Rāja Vāśishṭhīputra Śrī Pulumāyi*; *svāmī* sometimes inserted before *Śrī*. *Vā- Śrī Śātakarṇi* in No. 994.	Eastern coins of *Rāja Vāśishṭhīputra Śrī Pulumāyi* (Rapson, p. 20).			Rudradāman [I], son of Jayadāman, Great Satrap (known dates A.D. 130 and 150; twice defeated Āndhra king No. 24, before A.D. 130).	128	
[24*a*. In *e* Vāyu only, 29 Śātakarṇi	—]	. . . . . .	. . . . . .			Dāmajadaśrī, Satrap and Great Satrap (no known dates), son of Rudradāman I.	155	
25. Śivaśrī Puloma[vi 7 III]	156	See Nos. 22, 26.	Prob. the eastern coins of *Rāja Vāśishṭhīputra Śiva Śrī Śātakarṇi*. But see Nos. 22 and 26.					
26 Śiva Skandha Śātakarṇi ? 3	163	? No. 1186, Banavāsi, mentioning prince *Śāta-* or *Śiva-Skandanāga Śrī*. See Nos. 22 and 25.	See Nos. 22 and 25 above.					
27. Yajñaśrī Śātakarṇika 29	166	Nos. 987, 1024, Kaṇhēri, and 1146, Nāsik, *Rāja Gautamīputra Svāmī Śrī Yajña Śātakarṇi*. No. 1340, China in Krishnā Dist., substituted *aryaka* for *svāmī*. To year 27.	Numerous types, with legend *Rāja Gautamīputra Śrī Yajña Śātakarṇi*, or parts of that legend (Rapson, pp. 34–45).			Jīvadāman, Great Satrap, son of Dāmajadaśrī.	178	Sundry complications in the succession of the Satraps and Great Satraps are omitted.
28. Vijaya . . . 6	195	. . . . . .	. . . . . .			Rudrasiṁha I, son of Rudradāman I, Satrap and Great Satrap.	180	
29. Chaṇḍaśrī (Chandra) Śātakarṇi 10	201	No. 1341, Kodavolu in Godāvarī Dist. *Rāja Vāśishṭhīputra Svāmī Śrī Chaṇḍa (Chandra) Śāta.*	Apparently eastern coins of *Rāja Vāśishṭhīputra Śrī Chandra Sāti*, or simply *Śrī Chandra Sāti* (Rapson, pp. 30, 33).			Rudrasena I, son of Rudrasiṁha I, Satrap and Great Satrap.	199	
30. Pulomāvi [IV] . 7	211	Probably *nil*.	? *nil*, but the attribution of some of the Pulomāvi coins is doubtful.			Sanghadāman, another son of Rudrasiṁha I, Great Satrap.	222	
End of Dynasty. 'These 30 Āndhra kings will enjoy the earth 460 years' (v. l. *Bḍ*, 456; *Vā*, 411; but ? corrupt).	225		Other coins exist which cannot be attributed definitely to any king in the list.			Dāmasena, another son of Rudrasiṁha I, Great Satrap.	223	

To face page 232.

CHAPTER IX

THE INDO-GREEK AND INDO-PARTHIAN DYNASTIES, FROM ABOUT 250 B. C. TO ABOUT A. D. 60

Hindū Kush the Maurya frontier.

THE story of the native dynasties in the interior must now be interrupted to admit a brief review of the fortunes of the various foreign rulers who established themselves in the Indian territories once conquered by Alexander, after the sun of the Maurya empire had set, and the north-western frontier was left exposed to foreign attack. The daring and destructive raid of the great Macedonian, as we have seen, had effected none of the permanent results intended. The Indian provinces which he had subjugated, and which Seleukos had failed to recover, passed into the iron grip of Chandragupta, who transmitted them to the keeping of his son and grandson. I see no reason to doubt that the territories west of the Indus ceded by Seleukos to his Indian opponent continued in possession of the successors of the latter, and that consequently the Hindū Kush range was the frontier of the Maurya empire up to the close of Asoka's reign.

Effects of Asoka's death.

But it is certain that the unity of the empire did not survive Asoka, and that when the influence of his dominating personality ceased to act, the outlying provinces shook off their allegiance and set up as independent states; of some of which the history has been told in the last preceding chapter. The regions of the north-western frontier, when no longer protected by the arm of a strong paramount native power in the interior, offered a tempting field to the ambition of the Hellenistic princes of Bactria and Parthia, as well as to the cupidity of the warlike races on the border, which was freely exploited by a succession of invaders. This chapter will be devoted, so far as the very imperfect materials available permit, to a sketch of the leading events in the annals of the Panjāb and trans-Indus provinces from the close of Asoka's reign to the establishment of the Indo-Scythian, or Kushān, power. Dates, it will be understood, are uncertain.

261 B. C. Antiochos Theos.

The spacious Asiatic dominion consolidated by the genius of Seleukos Nikator passed in the year 262 or 261 B. C. into the hands of his grandson Antiochos, a drunken sensualist, miscalled even in his lifetime Theos, or 'the god', and, strange to say, worshipped as such.[1] This worthless prince occupied the throne for fifteen or sixteen years; but towards the close of his reign his empire suffered two grievous losses, by the revolt of the Bactrians, under the leadership of Diodotos, and of the Parthians, under that of Arsakes.

Bactria.

The loss of Bactria was especially grievous. This province, the rich plain watered by the Oxus (Amū Daryā) after its issue from the mountains, had been occupied by civilized men from time immemorial. The country, which was said to contain a thousand towns,[2] always had been regarded, during the time of the Achaemenian kings, as the premier satrapy, and reserved as an appanage for a prince of the blood. When Alexander shattered the Persian power and seated himself upon the throne of the Great King, he continued to bestow his royal favour upon the Bactrians, who in return readily assimilated the elements of Hellenic civilization. Two years after his death, at the final partition of the empire in 321 B. C., Bactria fell to the share of Seleukos Nikator, and continued to be one of the most valuable possessions of his son and grandson.

The Parthians.

The Parthians, a race of rude and hardy horsemen, with habits similar to those of the modern Turkomans, dwelt beyond the Persian deserts in the comparatively infertile

[1] Antiochos Soter died between July 262 and July 261, at the age of sixty-four; and was succeeded by his son Antiochos Theos, then aged about twenty-four years, who put his brother Seleukos to death (Bevan, *House of Seleucus*, i, 168, 171, citing Eusebius, i, 249). The inscription found at Durdurkar proves that the second Antiochos was worshipped as a god during his life, and that priestesses were also appointed to conduct the worship of his queen Laodikē.

[2] 'Eukratides had a thousand cities which acknowledged his authority' (Strabo, Bk. xv, sec. ii, 3). 'Bactriana is the ornament of all Ariana' (ibid., Bk. xi, sec. xi, 1).

regions to the south-east of the Caspian Sea. Their country, along with the territories of the Chorasmioi, Sogdioi, and Arioi (Khwārizm, Samarkand, and Herāt), had been included in the sixteenth satrapy of Darius; and all the tribes named, armed like the Bactrians, with cane bows and short spears, supplied contingents to the host of Xerxes.[1] In the time of Alexander and the early Seleukidae, Parthia proper and Hyrkania, adjoining the Caspian, were combined to form a satrapy. The Parthians, unlike the Bactrians, had never adopted Greek culture; and, although submissive to their Persian and Macedonian masters, retained unchanged the habits of a horde of mounted shepherds, equally skilled in the management of their steeds and the use of the bow.[2]

These two nations, so widely different in history and manners—the Bactrians, with a thousand cities, and the Parthians, with myriads of moss-troopers—were moved at almost the same moment, about the middle of the third century B. C., to throw off their allegiance to their Seleukidan lord, and assert their independence. The exact dates of these rebellions cannot be determined, but the Bactrian revolt seems to have been the earlier; and there is reason to believe that the Parthian struggle continued for several years, not being ended until after the death of Antiochos Theos in 246 B. C., although the declaration of Parthian autonomy seems to have been made in 248 B. C.[3]

c. 250 B.C. Date of revolt of Bactrians and Parthians.

The Bactrian revolt was a rebellion of the ordinary

Diodotos I.

[1] Herod. iii, 93, 117; vii, 64–6.

[2] For a full account of Parthia see Canon Rawlinson's *Sixth Oriental Monarchy*, or his more popular work, *The Story of Parthia* in the *Story of the Nations* series.

[3] The leading ancient authority is Justin, Bk. xli, ch. 4; but the consuls whom he specifies to fix the date of the Parthian revolt are not correctly named. He calls the Bactrian leader Theodotus, and says that he revolted 'at the same period'. The details of the evidence for the dates of the two rebellions have been examined repeatedly by Cunningham, Rawlinson, Bevan, and other writers, with the result stated in the text. The date 248 is supposed by Prof. Terrien de Lacouperie to mark the beginning of the Arsakidan era. He agrees with Mr. Bevan in believing that the struggle for Parthian independence lasted for several years (*Sur deux ères inconnues*, reprint, p. 5). Mr. Bevan thinks that Justin intended to indicate the year 250–249 B. C. as that of the Parthian revolt (*House of Seleucus*, i, 286). Sir H. Howorth prefers the date 248–7 B. C. (*Num. Chron.*, 1905, p. 222).

Oriental type, headed by Diodotos, the governor of the province, who seized an opportunity to shake off the authority of his sovereign and assume the royal state. The Parthian movement was rather a national rising, led by a chief named Arsakes, who is described as being a man of uncertain origin but undoubted bravery, and inured to a life of rapine. Arsakes declared his independence, and so founded the famous Arsakidan dynasty of Persia, which endured for nearly five centuries (248 B. C. to A. D. 226). The success of both the Bactrian and Parthian rebels was facilitated by the war of succession which disturbed the Seleukidan monarchy after the death of Antiochos Theos.

c. 245 B.C. Diodotos II.

The line of Bactrian kings initiated by Diodotos was destined to a briefer and stormier existence than that enjoyed by the dynasty of the Arsakidae. Diodotos himself wore his newly won crown for a brief space only, and after a few years was succeeded (*c.* 245 B. C.) by his son of the same name, who entered into an alliance with the Parthian king.[1]

c. 230 B.C. Euthydēmos and Antiochos the Great.

Diodotos II was followed (*c.* 230 B. C.) by Euthydēmos, a native of Magnesia, who seems to have belonged to a different family, and to have gained the crown by successful rebellion. This monarch became involved in a long-contested war with Antiochos the Great of Syria (223–187 B. C.),
c. 208 B.C. which was terminated (*c.* 208 B. C.) by a treaty recognizing the independence of the Bactrian kingdom. Shortly after-
c. 206 B.C. wards (*c.* 206 B. C.) Antiochos crossed the Hindū Kush, and compelled an Indian king named Subhāgasena, who

[1] 'Arsaces . . . made himself master of Hyrcania, and thus, invested with authority over two nations, raised a large army, through fear of Seleucos and Theodotus, king of the Bactrians. But being soon relieved of his fears by the death of Theodotus, he made peace and alliance with his son; who was also named Theodotus; and not long after, engaging with king Seleucus [Kallinikos], who came to take vengeance on the revolters, he obtained a victory; and the Parthians observe the day on which it was gained with great solemnity, as the date of the commencement of their liberty' (Justin, Bk. xli, ch. 4). This explicit testimony outweighs the doubts expressed by numismatists concerning the existence of the second Diodotos. All the extant coins seem to belong to Diodotos II; his father probably did not issue coins in his own name. Sir H. Howorth, who thinks very little of Justin's authority, denies his statement that Arsakes killed Andragoras, the Seleukidan viceroy (*Num. Chron.*, 1905, pp. 217, 222).

probably ruled in the Kābul valley, to surrender a considerable number of elephants and large treasure. Leaving Androsthenes of Cyzicus to collect this war indemnity, Antiochos in person led his main force homeward through Arachosia and Drangiana to Karmania.[1]

c. 200–190 B. C. Demetrios king of the Indians.

Demetrios, son of Euthydēmos, and son-in-law of Antiochos, who had given him a daughter in marriage when the independence of Bactria was recognized, repeated his father-in-law's exploits with still greater success, and conquered a considerable portion of Northern India, presumably including Kābul, the Panjāb, and Sind (*c.* 190 B. C.).[2]

c. 175 B.C. Eukratides.

The distant Indian wars of Demetrios necessarily weakened his hold upon Bactria, and afforded the opportunity for successful rebellion to one Eukratides, who made himself master of Bactria about 175 B. C., and became involved in many wars with the surrounding states and tribes, which he carried on with varying fortune and unvarying spirit. Demetrios, although he had lost Bactria, long retained his hold upon his eastern conquests, and was known as 'King of the Indians'; but after a severe struggle the victory rested with Eukratides, who was an opponent not easily beaten and is credited with having 'reduced India under

c. 160–156 B. C. His Indian wars.

[1] Polybius, xi, 34. The name of the Indian king is given as Sophagasenas by the historian, which seems to represent the Sanskrit *Subhāgasena.*

[2] 'The Greeks who occasioned its [Bactria's] revolt, became so powerful by means of its fertility and [the] advantages of the country, that they became masters of Ariana and India, according to Apollodoros of Artemita. Their chiefs, particularly Menander (if he really crossed the Hypanis to the east and reached Isamus), conquered more nations than Alexander. These conquests were achieved partly by Menander, partly by Demetrios, son of Euthydēmos, king of the Bactrians. They got possession not only of Patalene but of the kingdoms of Saraostos and Sigerdis, which constitute the remainder of the coast. Apollodoros, in short, says that Bactriana is the ornament of all Ariana. They extended their empire even as far as the Seres and Phrynoi' (Strabo, Bk. xi, sec. xi, 1, in Falconer's version). The last clause may point to a temporary Greek occupation of the mountains as far to the east as the λίθινος πύργος of Ptolemy, the exact position of which cannot be determined at present (Stein, *Ancient Khotan*, p. 54, cancelling statement in *Sand-buried Ruins of Khotan*, p. 72). As regards Seres, see *J. A. O. S.*, vol. xxxvii, p. 240, for the identification of *Sera metropolis* with the old Chinese capital Singan-fu.

his power'. It is related that on one occasion, when shut up for five months in a fort with a garrison of only three hundred men, he succeeded in repelling the attack of a host of sixty thousand under the command of Demetrios.[1]

c. 156 B.C. But the hard-won triumph was short-lived. While Eukratides was on his homeward march from India attended by his son, probably Apollodotos, whom he had made his colleague in power, he was barbarously murdered by the unnatural youth, who is said to have gloried in his monstrous crime, driving his chariot wheels through the blood of his father, to whose corpse he refused even the poor honour of burial.[2]

Heliokles, &c. The murder of Eukratides shattered to fragments the kingdom for which he had fought so valiantly. Another son, named Heliokles, who assumed the title of 'the Just', perhaps as the avenger of his father's cruel death, enjoyed for a brief space a precarious tenure of power in Bactria. Strato I, who also seems to have belonged to the family of Eukratides, held a principality in the Panjāb for many years, and was perhaps the immediate successor of Apollodotos. Agathokles and Pantaleon (*c.* 190–180 B. C.), whose coins are specially Indian in character, were earlier in date, and contemporary with Euthydēmos and Demetrios. It is evident from the great variety of the royal names in the coin-legends, nearly forty in number, that both before and after the death of Eukratides, the Indian borderland was parcelled out among a crowd of Greek princelings, for the most part related either to the family of Euthydēmos and Demetrios or to that of their rival Eukratides. Some of these princelings, among whom was Antialkidas (*c.* 140–180 B. C.),[3] were subdued by Eukratides, who, if he had

[1] Justin, xli, 6.

[2] Ibid. All the leading numismatic authorities agree that Heliokles was a son of Eukratides. Cunningham (*Num. Chron.*, 1869, pp. 241–3) shows good reasons for believing that the parricide was Apollodotos, the eldest son of the murdered king. But (*contra*) the Kapiśa coins of Eukratides are sometimes restruck on those of Apollodotos (Rapson, *J. R. A. S.*, 1905, p. 784).

[3] Antialkidas is mentioned in an inscription, which may be dated between 140 and 130 B. C., found at Besnagar near Bhīlsā in Central India. The inscription was incised by direction of one Heliodorus of Taxila who was sent as an envoy

lived, might have consolidated a great border kingdom. But his death in the hour of victory increased the existing confusion, and it is quite impossible to make a satisfactory territorial and chronological arrangement of the Indo-Greek frontier kings contemporary with and posterior to Eukratides. Their names, which, with two exceptions, are known from coins only, will be found included in the list appended to this chapter (Appendix J).

c. 155 B.C. Menander's invasion of India.

One name, that of Menander, stands out conspicuously among the crowd of obscure princes. He seems to have belonged to the family of Eukratides, and to have had his capital at Kābul, whence he issued, in or about 155 B. C., to make the bold invasion of India described in the last chapter. About two years later he was obliged to retire and devote his energies to the encounter with dangers which menaced him at home, due to the never-ending quarrels with his neighbours on the frontier.

Menander's fame.

Menander was celebrated as a just ruler, and when he died was honoured with magnificent obsequies. He is supposed to have been a convert to Buddhism, and has been immortalized under the name of Milinda in a celebrated dialogue, entitled 'The Questions of Milinda', which is one of the most notable books in Buddhist literature.[1]

The last Greek king of Bactria.

Heliokles, the son of Eukratides, who had obtained Bactria as his share of his father's extensive dominion, was the last king of Greek race to rule the territories to the north of the Hindū Kush. While the Greek princes and princelings were struggling one with the other in obscure wars which history

to the ruler of Besnagar by Antialkidas, who ruled at Taxila. The inscription is valuable as fixing an early date for the *bhakti* cult of Vāsudeva, and as proving that people with Greek names and in the service of Greek kings had adopted the cult of Hindu gods (*Prog. Rep. A. S. W. Circle*, 1914–15, p. 59; *Ann. Rep. A. S. I.*, 1908–9 and 1913–14).

[1] The obsequies are described by Plutarch (*Reipubl. ger. praecepta*, quoted textually in *Num. Chron.*, 1869, p. 229). The 'Questions' have been translated by Rhys Davids in *S. B. E.*, vols. xxxv, xxxvi. For identification of Milinda with Menander, doubted by Waddell, see Garbe, *Beiträge zur indischen Kulturgeschichte*, Berlin, 1903, p. 109, note; Tarn, 'Notes on Hellenism in Bactria and India' (*J. Hell. Soc.*, 1902, p. 272); and Sarat Chandra Dās in *J. Buddhist Text and Research Soc.*, vol. vii (1904), pp. 1–6. The form *Milindra* occurs in Kshemendra's *Avadāna Kalpalata* and in the Tibetan Tangyur collection.

has not condescended to record, a deluge was preparing in the steppes of Central Asia, which was destined to sweep them all away into nothingness.

Expulsion of Sakas by Yüe-chi.

A horde of nomads, named the Yüe-chi, whose movements will be more particularly described in the next chapter, were driven out of North-western China about 170 B. C., and compelled to migrate westwards by the route to the north of the deserts.[1] Some years later, before 160 B. C., they encountered another horde, the Sakas or Se, who occupied the territories lying to the north of the Jaxartes (Syr Daryā) river, as already mentioned.[2]

Nomad invasion of Bactria and India.

The Sakas, accompanied by cognate tribes, were forced to move in a southerly direction, and in course of time entered India from the north, possibly by more roads than one. The flood of barbarian invasion spread also to the west, and burst upon the Parthian kingdom and Bactria in the period between 140 and 120 B. C. The Parthian king, Phraates II, the immediate successor of Mithradates I, was killed in battle with the nomads about 127 B. C.; and some four years later, Artabanus I, who followed him on the Parthian throne, met the same fate. The Hellenistic monarchy, which must have been weakened already by the growth of the Parthian or Persian power, was then finally extinguished. The last Graeco-Bactrian king was Heliokles, with whom Greek rule to the north of the Hindū Kush disappeared for ever.[3]

Śaka occupation of Sīstān, &c.

The valley of the Hīlmand (Erymandrus) river, the modern Sīstān, known as Sakastēnē, or the Saka country, probably had been occupied by Sakas at an earlier date, but it is possible that part of the influx in the second century B. C. may have reached that province.[4]

[1] 165 B. C. is the date commonly given by Chinese scholars. Franke dates the defeat of the Yüe-chi *about* 170 B. C. The southward migration of the Sakas, according to him, must be placed between 174 and 160, but nearer the latter date (*Beiträge zur Kenntniss der Türkvölker*, pp. 29, 55).

[2] *Ante*, p. 239.

[3] *Μάλιστα δὲ γνώριμοι γεγόνασι τῶν νομάδων οἱ τοὺς Ἕλληνας ἀφελόμενοι τὴν Βακτριανήν, Ἄσιοι, καὶ Πασιανοί, καὶ Τόχαροι, καὶ Σακάραυλοι, καὶ ὁρμηθέντες ἀπὸ τῆς περαίας τοῦ Ἰαξάρτου, τῆς κατὰ Σάκας καὶ Σογδιανοὺς ἣν κατεῖχον Σάκαι* (Strabo, xi, 8, 2). The attempts of various writers to identify the Asioi and other tribes named are unsuccessful.

[4] According to Sir H. McMahon

Branches of the barbarian stream which penetrated the Indian passes deposited settlements at Taxila in the Panjāb and Mathurā on the Jumna, where foreign princes, with the title of satrap, ruled for more than a century, seemingly in subordination to the Parthian power.

Yet another section of the horde, at a later date, perhaps about the middle of the first century after Christ, pushed on southwards and occupied the peninsula of Surāshtra or Kāthiāwār, founding a Saka dynasty which lasted until it was destroyed by Chandragupta II, Vikramāditya, about A. D. 390.

Satraps of Taxila and Mathurā.

Strato I, Sotēr, a Greek king of Kābul and the Panjāb, who was to some extent contemporary with Heliokles, was succeeded by Strato II, Philopator, his grandson; who again, apparently, was displaced at Taxila by certain foreign satraps, who may or may not have been Sakas. The satraps of Mathurā were closely connected with those of Taxila, and belong to the same period, about 50 B. C. or later.[1] Their names seem to be Persian.

Relations with Parthia.

The movements of the Sakas and allied nomad tribes were closely connected with the development of the Parthian or Persian power under the Arsakidan kings. Mithradates I, a very able monarch (*c.* 171 to 136 B. C.), who was for many years the contemporary of Eukratides, king of Bactria, succeeded in extending his dominions so widely that his power was felt as far as the Indus, and probably even to the

'the Scythians (Sakae) were turned out about 275 A. D.' (*Geogr. J.*, 1906, p. 209).

[1] The first known satrap of Taxila was Liaka, whose son was Patika. In the year 78 Liaka was directly subordinate to king Moga, who is generally supposed to be Maues or Mauas of the coins. Śodāsa, satrap of Mathurā in the year 72, was the son of satrap Rājuvula, whose later coins imitate those of Strato II. The era or eras to which those dates refer have not been determined. S. Konow holds that Śodāsa's inscription is dated in the Vikrama era (*Ep. Ind.*, xiv, 139). Rājuvula succeeded the satraps Hagāna and Hagāmāsha (? brothers), who displaced native Rājas named Gomitra, Rāmadatta, &c., of whom coins are extant. The coinage of the two Stratos, which covers a period of about seventy years, has been elucidated by Prof. Rapson (*Corolla Numismatica*, p. 245; Oxford, 1906). Vogel suggests that Rājuvula and his son may have been satraps subordinate to Huvishka, whose accession I place in A. D. 123 (*A. S. Prog. Rep.*, 1909–10, *N. Circle*, p. 9). If that be correct, the date 72 would be in the Saka era = A. D. 150. But there are difficulties.

east of that river. I see no good reason for doubting the truth of the explicit statement of Orosius that, subsequent to the defeat of the general of Demetrios and the occupation of Babylon, Mithradates I annexed to his dominions the territory of all the nations between the Indus and the Hydaspes, or Jihlam river. The chiefs of Taxila and Mathurā would not have assumed the purely Persian title of satrap, if they had not regarded themselves as subordinates of the Persian or Parthian sovereign; and the close relations between the Parthian monarchy and the Indian borderland at this period are demonstrated by the appearance of a long line of princes of Parthian origin, who now enter on the scene.[1]

Maues. The earliest of these Indo-Parthian kings apparently was Maues or Mauas, who attained power in the Western Panjāb perhaps about 95 B. C., and adopted the title of 'Great King of Kings' (βασιλέως βασιλέων μεγάλου), which had been used for the first time by either Mithradates I or Mithradates II. His coins are closely related to those of both those monarchs, as well as to those of the unmistakably Parthian border chief, who called himself Arsakes Theos. The king Moga, to whom the Taxilian satrap was immediately subordinate, is usually identified with the personage whose name appears on the coins as *Mauou* in the genitive case.[2]

[1] The exact limits of the reign of Mithradates I are not known. Justin (xli, 6) states that 'almost at the same time that Mithradates ascended the throne among the Parthians, Eukratides began to reign among the Bactrians; both of them being great men'. The text of the passage in Orosius is: 'Mithradates, tunc siquidem, rex Parthorum sextus ab Arsace, victo Demetrii praefecto Babylonam urbem finesque eius universos victor invasit. Omnes praeterea gentes quae inter Hydaspen fluvium et Indum iacent subegit' (Bk. v, ch. iv, sec. 16; ed. Zangemeister, Vienna, 1883). The event may be dated about 138 B. C., towards the close of the reign of Mithradates.

[2] For *Mauou* see Von Sallet, *Nachfolger*, p. 140. Von Gutschmid compares the name Maues or Mauas with that of Mauakēs (v. l. Mabakēs), who commanded the Śaka contingent of mounted archers in the army of Darius at Gaugamela or Arbela (Arrian. *Anab.*, iii, 8). The chronology is discussed in *J. R. A. S.*, 1903, p. 46, and in *Z. D. M. G.*, 1906, pp. 49–72. In the light of his discoveries at Taxila, Marshall varies the chronology hitherto accepted, discussing the subject in *Ann. Rep. A. S. India for* 1912–13 and very fully in *J. P. H. S.*, vol. iii. In this edition I have followed his view, particularly in regard to the date of Kanishka, which agrees with that of Sten Konow ('Indoskythische Beiträge' in *Sitzungs-*

The story of the Indo-Parthian dynasties really being that of certain outlying dependencies of the Parthian empire, we should be in a position to understand fully the relations of the Indo-Parthian rulers to the world of their day, if our knowledge of Parthian history were more complete than it is or is likely to be. The material actually available for the reconstruction in outline of Indo-Parthian history is so slight, consisting largely of inferences from numismatic details, that it is impossible to present an ordered narrative of indisputable facts, and the results of investigation necessarily must be in great part speculative. Subject to these cautions, the following sketch expresses my views of the facts—whether ascertained or merely probable—as obtained from special study of the question. The reader will understand that the dates suggested are open to correction.

Indo-Parthian kings.

Much obscurity has been caused by the failure of writers on the subject to recognize the plain truth that, besides some subordinate satraps, there were two main lines of Indo-Parthian princes, one of which ruled in Arachosia and Sīstān, while the other governed the Western Panjāb, or kingdom of Taxila. Maues, as has been seen, became king, perhaps, about 95 B. C., of the latter province, which, in or about 138 B. C., had been annexed to Parthia by Mithradates I. It is probable that the direct administration of the newly conquered province by the government of Ctesiphon lasted only for a few years. The struggle with the nomads, which cost Phraates II and Artabanus their lives, between 130 and 120 B. C., must have caused a relaxation in the grip of the central power on remote dependencies like the Indian borderlands; and it is highly probable that Maues, who may have been a Saka, availed himself of the opportunity thus offered to establish himself upon the Panjāb throne in the enjoyment of practical, if not theoretical, independence.

Two dynasties.

About the same time, or a few years later, Vonōnēs, a Parthian, became king of Arachosia and Sīstān, no doubt

Vonōnēs &c., in Arachosia.

ber. d. königl. preuss. Akad. der Wissenschaften, 1916). For the Indo-Parthian coins see *Catal. Coins I. M.*, vol. i, pp. 35–62.

as a feudatory of the Great King at Ctesiphon. Those territories were administered by him and his relatives for a brief period—some twenty-five years—the last of his line being his nephew Azes, who occupied the position of viceroy or subordinate colleague of his father Spalirises, brother of Vonōnēs.

Azes I, Azilises, Azes II.

The Parthian power, which had suffered severely from the shock of the nomad attacks, recovered under the vigorous government of Mithradates II, the Great (acc. *c.* 123 B. C.). Apparently, that strong ruler took over the direct government of the provinces which had been administered by Vonōnēs and his family, and also reasserted his suzerainty over the less accessible Panjāb. Azes, the viceroy of Arachosia and Sīstān, was then transferred to Taxila, where he succeeded Maues about 58 B. C., and governed the province as a subordinate king under Mithradates. Azes I was succeeded on the throne of the Panjāb, first by his son Azilises and then by his grandson Azes II. Azes I certainly was a powerful prince, and enjoyed a long reign, extending to nearly forty years. It is known that at the beginning of the Christian era no part of India was included in the Parthian empire, and it is not unlikely that during the course of his long reign Azes I succeeded in establishing his independence. The reigns of Azilises and Azes II seem to have occupied together about forty years. In the time of the latter, the *stratēgos*, or satrap, Aspavarma, and the satrap Zeiōnises assisted their sovereign in the administration of the Panjāb.

Reign of Gondopharēs.

About A. D. 20 Azes II is supposed to have been succeeded by Gondopharēs, who seems to have conquered Sind and Arachosia, making himself master of a wide dominion free from Parthian control. When he died, about A. D. 48, his kingdom was divided, the Western Panjāb falling to the share of his brother's son Abdagases, while Arachosia and Sind passed under the rule of Orthagnes, who was followed by Pakorēs. No successor of Abdagases is known. About the middle of the first century the Panjāb was annexed by the Kushān king, Kujula-Kara-Kadphises (Kadphises I).

Arachosia and Sind probably shared the fate of the Panjāb.[1]

Parthian chiefs in Indus delta.

But petty Parthian principalities may have continued to exist for some time longer in the delta of the Indus. The author of the *Periplus of the Erythraean Sea*, writing about A. D. 70, found the valley of the Lower Indus, which he called Scythia, under the rule of Parthian chiefs, engaged in unceasing internecine strife. The Indus at that time had seven mouths, of which only the central one was navigable. The commercial port, known to the traveller as Barbarikon, was situated upon this stream ; and the capital, Minnagar, lay inland. The extensive changes which have occurred in the rivers of Sind during the course of eighteen centuries preclude the possibility of satisfactory identifications of either of these towns.[2]

Gondopharēs and St. Thomas.

Special interest attaches to the Indo-Parthian king Gondopharēs because his name is associated in very ancient Christian tradition with that of St. Thomas, the apostle of the Parthians. The belief that the Parthians were allotted as the peculiar sphere of the missionary labours of St. Thomas goes back to the time of Origen, who died in the middle of the third century. The *Acts of St. Thomas*, nearly contem-

[1] According to Philostratus, Apollonius of Tyana twice visited Bardanes or Vardanes, king of Parthia, who reigned from *c.* A. D. 39 to 47, and resided at Babylon. Prof. Petrie seems to be right in holding that the travels of Apollonius in India should be dated in A. D. 43–44. At that time Philostratus represents the Western Panjāb as being under the government of King Phraōtes, evidently a Parthian. The Satrap on the eastern side of the Indus was subordinate to Phraōtes of Taxila and independent of Bardanes (*Apollonius*, Bk. I, ch. 28 ; Bk. II, ch. 17 ; Bk. III, ch. 58. For Phraōtes, see Bk. II, ch. 26–31). Although the details of the Indian travels are fictitious, Philostratus seems to have been right in placing the kingdom of Taxila under an independent Parthian ruler at or about the date named.

[2] *Periplus*, ch. 38. The work used to be ascribed erroneously to Arrian. It has been translated with notes by McCrindle (*Ind. Ant.*, viii, 1879, pp. 108–51), and by W. H. Schoff, 1912. The date A. D. 246 or 247 for the final redaction of the work proposed by Reinaud, is impossible. McCrindle dates it between A. D. 80 and 89. Mr. Schoff (p. 15) suggests A. D. 60, but in a subsequent letter to me he expresses his preference for A. D. 80. The best authenticated date is A. D. 70 or 71 (Kennedy in *J. R. A. S.*, 1918, p. 112). The 'Indus' should be understood to mean the Mihrān of Sind, including the Indus proper, as explained by Raverty. McCrindle's version was also published separately (Calcutta and London, 1879).

porary with Origen, as well as later tradition, generally associate the Indians, rather than the Parthians, with the name of the apostle, but the terms 'India' and 'Indians' had such vague signification in ancient times that the discrepancy is not great. The earliest form of the tradition clearly deserves the greater credit, and there is no apparent reason for discrediting the statement handed down by Origen that Thomas received Parthia as his allotted region.

The legend. The legend connecting St. Thomas with king Gondopharēs appears for the first time in the original Syrian text of the *Acts of St. Thomas*, which was composed at about the same date as the writings of Origen. The substance of the long story may be set forth briefly as follows :—

'When the twelve apostles divided the countries of the world among themselves by lot, India fell to the share of Judas, surnamed Thomas, or the Twin, who showed unwillingness to start on his mission. At that time an Indian merchant named Habbān [1] arrived in the country of the south, charged by his master, Gundaphar,[2] king of India, to bring back with him a cunning artificer able to build a palace meet for the king. In order to overcome the apostle's reluctance to start for the East, our Lord appeared to the merchant in a vision, sold the apostle to him for twenty pieces of silver, and commanded St. Thomas to serve king Gundaphar and build the palace for him.

'In obedience to his Lord's commands, the apostle sailed next day with Habbān the merchant, and during the voyage assured his companion concerning his skill in architecture and all manner of work in wood and stone. Wafted by favouring winds their ship quickly reached the harbour of Sandarūk.[3] Landing there, the voyagers shared in the marriage feast of the king's daughter, and used their time so well that bride and bridegroom were converted to the true faith. Thence the saint and the merchant proceeded on their voyage, and came to the court of Gundaphar, king of India. St. Thomas promised to build him the palace within the space of six months, but expended the monies given to him for that purpose in almsgiving; and, when

[1] Syriac—Habbān; Greek—Ἀββάνης; Latin—Abban or Abbanes.

[2] Syriac—Gundaphar, or Gūdnaphar; Greek—Γουνδαφόρος, Γουνδιαφόρος, or Γουντάφορος; Latin, Gundaforus, or Gundoforus.

[3] Syriac—Sandarūk, or Sanadrūk; Greek—Ἀνδράπολις; Latin—Andranopolis, Andranobolys, Andronopolis, or Adrianopolis.

called to account, explained that he was building for the king a palace in heaven, not made with hands. He preached with such zeal and grace that the king, his brother Gad,[1] and multitudes of the people embraced the faith. Many signs and wonders were wrought by the holy apostle.

Martyrdom of St. Thomas.

'After a time, Sifūr,[2] the general of king Mazdai,[3] arrived, and besought the apostle to come with him and heal his wife and daughter. St. Thomas hearkened to his prayer, and went with Sifūr to the city of king Mazdai, riding in a chariot. He left his converts in the country of king Gundaphar under the care of deacon Xanthippos.[4] King Mazdai waxed wroth when his queen Tertia [5] and a noble lady named Mygdonia [6] were converted by St. Thomas, who was accordingly sentenced to death and executed by four soldiers, who pierced him with spears on a mountain without the city. The apostle was buried in the sepulchre of the ancient kings; but the disciples secretly removed his bones, and carried them away to the West.' [7]

Criticism of the legend.

Writers of later date, subsequent to the seventh century, profess to know the name of the city where the apostle suffered martyrdom, and call it variously Kalamina, Kalamita, Kalamēna, or Karamēna, and much ingenuity has been expended in futile attempts to identify this city. But the scene of the martyrdom is anonymous in the earlier versions of the tale, and Kalamina should be regarded as a place in fairyland which it is vain to try and locate on a map. The same observation applies to the attempts at the identification of the port variously called Sandarūk, Andrapolis, and so

[1] Syriac and Latin—Gad; Greek—Γάδ. Other relatives of the king are also mentioned.

[2] Syriac—Sifūr; Greek—Σίφωρ, Σιφώρ, Σίφορος, Σιφώρας, or Σήμφορος; Latin—Saphor, Saphyr, Sapor, Siforus, Sephor, Siforatus, Sinforus, Sinfurus, or Symphoras.

[3] Syriac—Mazdai; Greek—Μισδαῖος, or Μισδέος,; Latin—Misdeus, Mesdeus, or Migdeus.

[4] Syriac—Xanthippos; Greek—Ξενοφῶν; Latin—omitted.

[5] Syriac—Tertia; Greek—Τερτία, Τερεντιανή, or Τερτιανή; Latin—Treptia, Tertia, Trepicia, or Triplicia.

[6] Syriac—Mygdonia; Greek—Μυγδονία; Latin—Mygdonia, or Migdonia.

[7] Sokrates Scholastikos (fifth century) and other writers testify that the relics were enshrined at Edessa in Mesopotamia, where a magnificent memorial church was erected. The story in the text and the references to early Christian writers are taken, without verification, from the almost exhaustive essay by W. R. Philipps, entitled 'The Connection of St. Thomas the Apostle with India' (*Ind. Ant.*, vol. xxxii, 1903, pp. 1–15, 145–60). Bishop Medlycott's book, *India and the Apostle Thomas*, 1905, supplies an invaluable collection of ecclesiastical texts.

forth. The whole story is pure mythology, and the geography is as mythical as the tale itself. Its interest in the eyes of the historian of India is confined to the fact that it proves that the real Indian king, Gondopharēs, was remembered after his death, and was associated in popular belief with the apostolic mission to the Indians, and so, according to Origen, with the Parthians. Inasmuch as Gondopharēs certainly was a Parthian prince, and was too little known to the world in general to be named in a legend unless he really had some connexion with the introduction of Christianity into his dominions, it is permissible to believe that a Christian mission actually visited the Indo-Parthians of the north-western frontier during his reign, whether or not that mission was conducted by St. Thomas in person. The traditional association of the name of the apostle with that of king Gondopharēs is in no way at variance with the generally received chronology of the reign of the latter as deduced from coins and an inscription.[1] On the other hand, it is to be observed that there is no trace of the subsequent existence of a Christian community in the dominions which had been ruled by Gondopharēs, and that if there be any truth in the tradition that the apostle was martyred at St. Thomas's Mount near Madras, he cannot possibly have suffered in the kingdom of Mazdai.[2] After much consideration, I am now

[1] The coins and inscription give the king's name in sundry variant forms (in the genitive case)—as Gondopharēs, Guduphara, Gudapharna, &c. The inscription, which was found at Takht-i-Bahai, NE. of Peshāwar, is dated in the 26th year of the Maharaya Guduphara, in the year 103 of an unspecified era. The archaeological evidence for the reign is discussed by Von Sallet (*Nachfolger Alexanders des Grossen*); Percy Gardner (*B. M. Catal. Coins of Greek and Scythic Kings of India*); Senart (*Notes d'épigraphie indienne*, No. iii, p. 11); V. A. Smith ('The Kushān period of Indian History', in *J. R. A. S.*, 1903, p. 40); and many other writers. Mr. R. D. Banerji believes the date 103 to refer to the Śaka era and so to be equivalent to A. D. 181, basing his opinion chiefly on characteristics of the Kharoshṭhī script in the inscriptions, and partly on an interpretation of Parthian history (*Ind. Ant.*, 1908, pp. 47, 62). But the history of Parthia is too imperfectly known to be of much help, and Kharoshṭhī palaeography needs further study. I am not convinced of the alleged late date for Gondopharēs which is not accepted by Sir J. H. Marshall. The stratification at Taxila shows that Gondopharēs preceded Kadphises I.

[2] Father Joseph Dahlmann, S.J., has devoted an ingenious treatise, entitled *Die Thomas-Legende und die ältesten historischen Beziehungen des Christentums zum*

of opinion that the story of the personal ministration and the martyrdom of St. Thomas in the realms of Gondopharēs and Mazdai should not be accepted. But unless a Christian mission connected by tradition with the rite of St. Thomas had visited the Indo-Parthian borderland it is difficult to imagine how the obscure name of Gondopharēs can have come into the story. If anybody chooses to believe that St. Thomas personally visited the Indo-Parthian kingdom his belief cannot be considered unreasonable. It is possible that, as Bishop Medlycott suggests, he may have first visited Gondopharēs, and then travelled to Southern India.

The alleged connexion of the apostle with Southern India and the Mailapur shrine near Madras, reverenced as San Thomé by the Portuguese, may be considered conveniently in this place. The traditions of the 'Christians of St. Thomas' on the western, or Malabar coast, assert that the apostle, coming from Socotra in A. D. 52, landed at Cranganore (Muziris of Pliny and the *Periplus*) on that coast, and laid the foundations of seven Christian centres in the province; that he passed over to the Malabar or Coromandel coast, where he suffered martyrdom near Mailapur; and that subsequent persecution extirpated the Christian churches of Coromandel. Bishop Medlycott, in a treatise full of abstruse learning, has endeavoured to prove the historical truth of this tradition, but, in my judgement, without complete success. Dr. J. H. Ogilvie, on the other hand, finds as 'the only safe verdict'—'that St. Thomas preached the Gospel of Christ in India is a certainty; that he laboured in the Punjāb, in the territories of King Gondopharēs, is extremely probable; that South India was a later field of his labours, and the scene of his martyrdom, is a tradition unverified,

Alleged mission of St. Thomas to S. India.

fernen Osten im Lichte der indischen Altertumskunde (Freiburg im Breisgau, 1912), to an attempt to establish the historical credibility of the Gondopharēs story. I have read his work carefully without being convinced. I have not read Heck, *Hat der heilige Apostel Thomas das Evangelium gepredigt?* Prof. Garbe, reviewing both works, comes to the conclusion that the Thomas legend in all its forms is undeserving of credit, and that the Christianity of Southern India probably came from Persia as a consequence of the persecution of Christians in that country in A. D. 343 and 414 (*Ostasiatische Zeitschrift*, I, 364).

and now in all likelihood unverifiable, though not beyond the bounds of possibility.'[1] The Mailapur legend of the martyrdom, like that of the *Acta*, may be purely mythical, and the Christians of Malabar may have applied the legend of the *Acta* to their own country. But, although the alleged martyrdom, whether in the kingdom of Mazdai or near Mailapur, may be confidently rejected as unhistorical, it must be admitted that a personal visit of the apostle to Southern India was easily feasible in the conditions of the time, and that there is nothing incredible in the traditional belief that he came by way of Socotra, where an ancient Christian settlement undoubtedly existed. The actual fact of such a personal visit cannot be either proved or disproved. I am now satisfied that the Christian Church of Southern India is extremely ancient, whether it was founded by St. Thomas in person or not, and that its existence may be traced back to the third century with a high degree of probability. Mr. Milne Rae carried his scepticism too far when he attributed the establishment of the Christian congregations to missionaries from the banks of the Tigris in the fifth or sixth century.[2]

The later Indo-Greek princes. For a period of nearly two centuries after the beginning of the nomad and Parthian invasions, the northern portions of the Indian borderland, comprising probably the valley of the Kābul river, the Suwāt valley, some neighbouring districts to the north and north-west of Peshāwar, and the Eastern Panjāb, remained under the government of local Greek princes; who, whether independent, or subject to the suzerainty of a Parthian overlord, certainly exercised the prerogative of coining silver and bronze money.

c. A. D. 20. Hermaios; Kadphises I. The last of these Indo-Greek rulers was Hermaios, who succumbed to the Yüe-chi, or Kushān, chief, Kadphises I, about A. D. 20, when that enterprising monarch added Kābul to the growing Yüe-chi empire.[3] The Yüe-chi chief at

[1] The Baird Lectures, *Apostles of India*, Hodder and Stoughton, 1915.

[2] See App. M.

[3] An outline of the approximate chronology will be found in the Synchronistic Table, Appendix L at the end of this chapter. Only the more important names are included in the table.

first struck coins jointly in the name of himself and the Greek prince, retaining on the obverse the portrait of Hermaios with his titles in Greek letters. After a time, while still preserving the familiar portrait, he substituted his own name and style in the legend. The next step taken was to replace the bust of Hermaios by the effigy of Augustus, as in his later years, and so to do homage to the expanding fame of that emperor, who, without striking a blow, and by the mere terror of the Roman name, had compelled the Parthians to restore the standards of Crassus (20 B. C.), which had been captured thirty-three years earlier.[1]

Still later probably are those coins of Kadphises I, which dispense altogether with the royal effigy, and present on the obverse an Indian bull, and on the reverse a Bactrian camel, devices fitly symbolizing the conquest of India by a horde of nomads.[2]

Meaning of numismatic record.

Thus the numismatic record offers a distinctly legible abstract of the political history of the times, and tells in outline the story of the gradual supersession of the last outposts of Greek authority by the irresistible advance of the hosts from the steppes of Central Asia.

Contact between Greece and India.

When the European historian, with his mind steeped in the conviction of the immeasurable debt owed to Hellas by modern civilization, stands by the side of the grave of Greek rule in India, it is inevitable that he should ask what was the result of the contact between Greece and India. Was Alexander to Indian eyes nothing more than the cavalry leader before whose onset the greatest armies were scattered like chaff, or was he recognized, consciously or unconsciously, as the pioneer of western civilization and the parent of model institutions? Did the long-continued government of Greek rulers in the Panjāb vanish before the assault of rude barbarians without leaving a trace of its existence save coins, or did it impress an Hellenic stamp upon the ancient fabric of Indian polity?

[1] Plate of coins, fig. 4, *ante*.

[2] In the twelfth century the Bactrian camel with two humps was still bred in Upper Sind (Al-Idrisi, quoted by Raverty, *J. A. S. B.*, vol. lxi, pt. i (1892), p. 224).

Niese's opinions.

Questions such as these have received widely divergent answers; but undoubtedly the general tendency of European scholars has been to exaggerate the hellenizing effects of Alexander's invasion and of the Indo-Greek rule on the north-western frontier. The most extreme 'Hellenist' view is that expressed by Herr Niese, who is convinced that all the later development of India depends indirectly upon the institutions of Alexander, and that Chandragupta Maurya recognized the suzerainty of Seleukos Nikator. Such notions are so plainly opposed to the evidence that they might be supposed to need no refutation, but they have been accepted to a certain extent by English writers of repute; who are, as already observed, inclined naturally to believe that India, like Europe and a large part of Asia, must have yielded to the subtle action of Hellenic ideas.

Slight influence of Alexander on India.

It is therefore worth while to consider impartially and without prejudice the extent of the Hellenic influence upon India from the invasion of Alexander to the Kushān or Indo-Scythian conquest at the end of the first century of the Christian era, a period of four centuries in round numbers.

The author's opinion that India was not hellenized by the operations of Alexander has been expressed in the chapter of this work dealing with his retreat from India,[1] but it is advisable to remind the reader of the leading facts in connexion with the more general question of hellenic influence upon Indian civilization during four hundred years. In order to form a correct judgement in the matter it is essential to bear dates in mind. Alexander stayed only nineteen months in India, and, however far-reaching his plans may have been, it is manifestly impossible that during those few months of incessant conflict he should have founded Hellenic institutions on a permanent basis, or materially affected the structure of Hindu polity and society. As a matter of fact, he did nothing of the sort, and within two years of his death, with the exception of some small garrisons under Eudēmos in the Indus valley, the whole apparatus of Macedonian rule had been swept away. After the year 316 B.C. not a trace of it

[1] *Ante*, p. 118.

remained. The only mark of Alexander's direct influence on India is the existence of a few coins modelled in imitation of Greek types which were struck by Saubhūti (Sophytes), the chief of the Salt Range, whom he subdued at the beginning of the voyage down the rivers.

Failure of Seleukos Nikator.

Twenty years after Alexander's death, Seleukos Nikator attempted to recover the Macedonian conquests east of the Indus, but failed, and more than failed, being obliged, not only to forgo all claims on the provinces temporarily occupied by Alexander, but to surrender a large part of Ariana, west of the Indus, to Chandragupta Maurya. The Indian administration and society so well described by Megasthenes, the ambassador of Seleukos, were Hindu in character, with some features borrowed from Persia, but none from Greece.[1] The assertion that the development of India depended in any way on the institutions of Alexander has no substantial basis of fact.

Maurya empire.

For eighty or ninety years after the death of Alexander the strong arm of the Maurya emperors held India for the Indians against all comers, and those monarchs treated with their Hellenistic neighbours on equal terms. Asoka was much more anxious to communicate the blessings of Buddhist teaching to Antiochos and Ptolemy than to borrow Greek notions from them. Although it certainly appears to be true that Indian plastic and pictorial art drew part of its inspiration from Hellenistic Alexandrian models during the Maurya period, the Greek influence merely touched the fringe of Hindu civilization, and was powerless to modify the structure of Indian institutions in any essential respect.

Invasion of Antiochos the Great.

For almost a hundred years after the failure of Seleukos Nikator no Greek sovereign presumed to attack India. Then Antiochos the Great (*c.* 206 B. C.) marched through the hills of the country now called Afghanistan, and went home by Kandahār and Sīstān, levying a war indemnity of treasure

[1] The duties of the officers maintained by Chandragupta to 'attend to the entertainment of foreigners' (Strabo, xv, 1, 50–2) were identical with those of the Greek *proxenoi* (πρόξενοι), and it is possible, though not proved, that the Indian institution may have been borrowed from the Greek (Newton, *Essays on Art and Archaeology*, p. 121; *Ind. Ant.*, 1905, p. 200).

and elephants from a local chief.[1] This brief campaign can have had no appreciable effect on the institutions of India, and its occurrence probably was unknown to many of the courts east of the Indus.

Subsequent Greek invasions.

The subsequent invasions of Demetrios, Eukratides, and Menander, which extended with intervals over a period of about half a century (*c.* 190–154 B. C.), penetrated more deeply into the interior of the country; but they too were transient raids, and cannot possibly have affected seriously the ancient and deeply rooted civilization of India. It is noticeable that the work attributed to the Hindu astronomer refers to Greeks as the 'viciously valiant Yavanas'. The Indians were impressed by both Alexander and Menander as mighty captains, not as missionaries of culture, and no doubt regarded both those sovereigns as impure barbarians, to be feared, not imitated.

The East has seldom shown much readiness to learn from the West; and when Indians have condescended, as in the cases of relief sculpture and the drama, to borrow ideas from European teachers, the thing borrowed has been so cleverly disguised in native trappings that the originality of the Indian imitators is stoutly maintained even by acute and learned critics.[2]

Greek occupation of Panjāb.

The Panjāb, or a considerable part of it, with some of the adjoining regions, remained more or less under Greek rule for more than two centuries, from the time of Demetrios (*c.* 190 B. C.) to the overthrow of Hermaios by the Kushāns (*c.* A. D. 20), and we might reasonably expect to find clear signs of hellenization in those countries. But the traces of Hellenic influence even there are surprisingly slight and trivial. Except the coins, which retain Greek legends on the obverse, and are throughout mainly Greek in type, although

[1] *Ante*, p. 236.

[2] The author is still firmly convinced that Weber and Windisch are right in tracing Greek influence on the form of the Sanskrit literary drama. See Weber, *Hist. Ind. Liter.* (Trübner, p. 217), and Windisch, *Der griechische Einfluss im indischen Drama*, Berlin, 1882. The contrary proposition is maintained by M. Sylvain Lévi (*Théâtre Indien*, pp. 343–66), with whom most scholars agree. The *origin* of Indian drama is quite another question. See Keith in *Z. D. M. G.*, 1910, pp. 535, 536.

they begin to be bilingual from the time of Demetrios and Eukratides, scarcely any indication of the prolonged foreign rule can be specified. The coinage undoubtedly goes far to prove that the Greek language was used to some extent in the courts of the frontier princes, but the introduction of native legends on the reverses demonstrates that it was not understood by the people at large. No inscriptions in that tongue have yet been discovered, and few Greek names have yet been found in Indian epigraphic records.[1]

Absence of Greek architecture.

Indications of the influence of Greek example and good taste are discernible in the domain of the fine arts, and a happy blend of Indian, Iranian, and Hellenic factors lent to Maurya sculpture its high quality; but if any buildings on a Greek plan were erected, they were apparently confined to Gandhāra. A temple with Ionic pillars, dating from about 80 B. C., has been discovered at Taxila, which was half-foreign and by no means an essentially Indian centre; but the plan of the building is not Greek, and the pillars, of foreign pattern, are merely borrowed ornaments.[2] The earliest known example of Indo-Greek sculpture belongs to the same period, the reign of Azes,[3] and not a single specimen

[1] See *J. Ind. Art.* Jan., 1900, p. 89; *J. R. A. S.*, 1903, p. 14, for the Theodore inscription in the Swat valley. A further inscription of Theodoros the 'meridarch' (μεριδάρχης) has been found on a relic casket, obtained from a Pathan village, now in the Lahore Museum. The title meridarch recurs on the inscribed copperplate from the Taxila (Shahdheri) stūpa No. 14, while the gold plate from stūpa No. 32 at the same place contains two other Greek names in corrupt forms (F. W. Thomas, *J. R. A. S.*, 1916, pp. 280, 285). The other Greek names include Heliodoros in the Besnagar inscription (*J. R. A. S.*, 1909, pp. 1053, 1087, 1093) and Agesilaos in the Kanishka casket record from Peshāwar (ibid., p. 1058). See also *Ann. Rep. A. S. W. C.*, 1914–15, pp. 59 ff. for further discoveries at the Besnagar site, including some sort of seal with the name Timitra, apparently = Demetrios, and a mould in steatite with a Graeco-Bactrian royal bust.

[2] Cunningham, *Arch. Rep.*, ii, 129; v, 69–72, 190, Pl. XVII, XVIII. The 'larger copper coins' of the foundation deposit must be those of Azes I (V. A. Smith, 'Graeco-Roman Influence on the Civilization of Ancient India', *J. A. S. B.*, 1889, vol. lviii, pt. i, pp. 115, 116). Growse found a fragment of sculpture in the Mathurā district, 'where a niche is supported by columns with Ionic capitals' (*Mathurā*, 3rd ed., p. 171). Cunningham published a plaster fragment of a *Roman* Ionic capital from the Ahinposh *stūpa* at Jalālābād (*Proc. A. S. B.*, 1879, p. 209, Pl. XI).

[3] The statuette in the pose of Pallas Athene (*J. A. S. B. ut supra*, p. 121, Pl. VII). The figure seems to have been intended to represent a Yāvanī doorkeeper.

can be referred to the times of Demetrios, Eukratides, and Menander, not to speak of Alexander. The well-known sculptures of Gandhāra, the region round Peshāwar, are much later in date, and are the offspring of cosmopolitan Graeco-Roman art.

Conclusion.

The conclusion of the matter is that the invasions of Alexander, Antiochos the Great, Demetrios, Eukratides, and Menander were in fact, whatever their authors may have intended, merely military incursions, which left no appreciable mark upon the institutions of India. The prolonged occupation of the Panjāb and neighbouring regions by Greek rulers had extremely little effect in hellenizing the country. Greek political institutions and architecture were ordinarily rejected, although to a small extent Hellenic example was accepted in the decorative arts, and the Greek language must have been more or less familiar to the officials at the king's courts. The literature of Greece probably was known slightly to some of the native officers, who were obliged to learn their masters' language for business purposes, but that language was not widely diffused, and the impression made by Greek authors upon Indian literature and science is hardly traceable until after the close of the period under discussion. The later and more important Graeco-Roman influence on the civilization of India will be noticed briefly in the next chapter.[1]

[1] The opinions expressed in the text agree generally with those held by Mr. Tarn, 'Notes on Hellenism in Bactria and India' (*J. Hellenic Studies*, 1902, pp. 268–93).

APPENDIX K

Alphabetical List of Bactrian and Indo-Greek Kings and Queens [1]

Serial No.	Name.	Greek title or epithet.	Remarks.
1	Agathokleia	Theotropos	Probably mother of Strato I, and regent during his minority.
2	Agathokles	Dikaios	Probably succeeded Pantaleon, No. 28, and was contemporary with Euthydēmos I or Demetrios.
3	Amyntas	Nikator	A little earlier than Hermaios.
4	Antialkidas	Nikēphoros	Contemporary with early years of Eukratides, *c.* 150 B.C.; apparently king of Taxila.
5	Antimachos I	Theos	Probably succeeded Diodotos II, No. 13, in Kābul.
6	Antimachos II	Nikēphoros	Later than Eukratides, No. 17, or possibly contemporary.
7	Apollodotos	Soter, Megas, Philopator [2]	Probably son of Eukratides, and king of entire Indian frontier.
8	Apollophanes	Soter	Probably contemporary with Strato I or II, in Eastern Panjāb.
9	Archebios	Dikaios, Nikēphoros	Probably connected with Heliokles.
10	Artemidoros	Anikētos	Later than Menander.
11	Demetrios	Anikētos	Son of Euthydēmos I, No. 18.
12	Diodotos I	——	No coins known; *c.* 250–245 B.C.
13	Diodotos II	Soter	Son of No. 12.
14	Diomedes	Soter	Apparently connected with Eukratides, No. 17.
15	Dionysios	Soter	Later than Apollodotos.
16	Epander	Nikēphoros	Probably later than Eukratides, No. 17.
17	Eukratides	Megas	Contemporary with Mithradates I; *c.* 175–156 B.C.
18	Euthydēmos I	——	Subsequent to Diodotos II, No. 13; *c.* 230–200 B.C.
19	Euthydēmos II	——	Probably son of No. 11.
20	Heliokles	Dikaios	Son of No. 17; last of Bactrian dynasty.
21	Hermaios	Soter	Last Indo-Greek king of Kābul; *c.* 10 B.C.–A.D. 20.

[1] Based on Von Sallet's lists, and brought up to date. The geographical and chronological position of many of the rulers named is so uncertain that an alphabetical list is the best.

[2] Cunningham (*Num. Chron.*, 1870, p. 81). Gardner (*B. M. Catal.*, p. 34) distinguishes A. Soter from A. Philopator, and Prof. Rapson is disposed to accept this view.

Serial No.	Name.	Greek title or epithet.	Remarks.
22	Hippostratos .	Soter, Megas.	Probably succeeded Apollodotos.
23	Kalliopē . .	——	Queen of Hermaios.
24	Laodikē . .	——	Mother of Eukratides.[1]
25	Lysias . . .	Anikētos . .	Predecessor of Antialkidas, No. 4.
26	Menander . .	Soter, Dikaios	Later than Eukratides ; invaded India about 155 B.C., but Gardner places him about 110 B.C.
27	Nikias . . .	Soter . . .	Later than Eukratides. His coins are found only in the Jhelum (Jihlam) District (*Panjāb Gaz.*, s.v. *Jhelum*).
28	Pantaleon . .	——	Contemporary with Euthydēmos I or Demetrios ; probably preceded Agathakles, No. 2 ; *c.* 190 B. C.
29	Peukelaos . .	Dikaios, Soter	Contemporary with Hippostratos (*J.A.S.B.*, 1898, part i, p. 131).
30	Philoxenos . .	Anikētos . .	Probably succeeded Antimachos II, No. 6.
31	Plato . . .	Epiphanes .	165 B.C., contemporary with Eukratides, No. 17 ; perhaps king of Sistān.[2]
32	(?) Polyxenos .	Epiphanes, Soter . .	*Num. Chron.*, 1896, p. 269 ; Prof. Rapson doubts the genuineness of the unique coin described.
33	Strato I . .	Soter, Epiphanes, Dikaios	Contemporary with Heliokles ; reigned long.
34	Strato II . .	Soter . . .	Grandson of No. 33.
35	Telephos . .	Euergetes . .	*J. A. S. B.*, 1898, part i, p. 130.
36	Theophilos . .	Dikaios . .	*J. A. S. B.*, 1897, part i, p. 1 ; connected with Lysias.
37	Zoilos . . .	Soter, Dikaios	Apparently later than Apollodotos, and nearly contemporary with Dionysios ; probably in Eastern Panjāb.

[1] Gardner (*B. M. Catal.*, p. 19). Heliokles seems to have been the name of the father, as well as of the son, of Eukratides.

[2] The letters on Plato's coin are interpreted as signifying the year 147 of the Seleukidan era, equivalent to 165 B. C. Sykes, *Ten Thousand Miles in Persia*, p. 363.

APPENDIX L. *Synchronistic Table, about* 280 B.C. *to about* A.D. 48

(The dates are uncertain, except for Syria and the Mauryas.)

B. C.	Syria.	Bactria.	Parthia (Persia).	N.W. Indian Frontier, Panjāb, and Kābul.	Interior India.	Remarks.
280	Antiochos Soter acc.			Maurya dynasty		
262 or 261	Antiochos Theos acc.					
c. 250		Diodotos I acc.				
c. 248			Arsakes I acc.			
c. 246	Seleukos Kallinikos acc. (Antiochos Hierax, rival)				Maurya dynasty	
c. 245		Diodotos II acc.				
c. 232–1						Death of Asoka.
c. 230		Euthydēmos acc.				
223	Antiochos III (the Great)					
c. 208						Recognition of Bactrian independence.
c. 206						Invasion of Kābul by Antiochos the Great.
c. 200–190				Demetrios; Antimachos		Indian conquests of Demetrios.
c.190–180				Euthydēmos II		
187	Seleukos Philopator acc.			Pantaleon, Agathokles		
185					Pushyamitra Śunga acc.	
c. 175		Eukratides acc.				
c. 174			Mithradates I acc.			
165		Plato (rival of Eukratides)				
c.160–140						
156		Heliokles		Apollodotos; Menander (Kābul)		
c. 155						
c. 149						Invasion of India by Menander.
c.140–130		*End of Bactrian dynasty*		Antialkidas	Agnimitra Śunga acc.	Śaka invasion of Bactria, &c.
c. 138						Conquest of Taxila by Mithradates I.
c. 136			Phraates II acc.			
124 or 123			Mithradates II acc.			
c. 120				Strato I		
c. 95				Strato II		
c. 90				Maues acc. (W. Panjāb)		
c. 65				Vonōnes acc.; Various Greek princes		
c. 73						
c. 58				Azes I acc. (Arachosia)	Vasudeva Kāṇva acc.	
c. 10				Satraps of Taxila and Mathurā		
c. A.D. 20				Hermaios acc.		
A. D. 20				Hermaios overthrown by Kushāns. Gondopharēs acc.		St. Thomas.
c. 48				Death of Gondopharēs		

APPENDIX M

The Christians of St. Thomas

Books cited.

In this Appendix I confine myself to the limited task of justifying the propositions in the text. It is out of the question to discuss fully the problems connected with the legend of St. Thomas and the origin of the ancient congregations of the 'Christians of St. Thomas' in Southern India. The following books are cited under the names of their respective authors :—

(1) MACKENZIE, G. T.—'History of Christianity in Travancore', 3rd ed., in *The Travancore State Manual*, 1906, vol. ii, pp. 114–219.

(2) RAE, G. MILNE.—*The Syrian Church in India.* (Blackwood, 1892.)

(3) MEDLYCOTT, BISHOP A. E.—*India and the Apostle Thomas.* (Nutt, 1905.)

(4) RICHARDS, W. J.—*The Indian Christians of St. Thomas.* (Bemrose, 1908.)

The Seven Churches.

The seven churches founded by St. Thomas are enumerated by Richards (p. 77) as (1) Kotta-kāyalil, (2) Gōkamangalam, (3) Niranam, (4) Chayil, (5) Kurakēni, (6) Quilon, (7) Palūr. Mackenzie gives the same list, with some variation of spelling, except that he substitutes Maliankara for Kurakēni. Rae (p. 361) gives the list as (1) Cranganore, (2) Quilon, (3) Palur, (4) Parur, (5) South Pallipuram [1] or Kokamungalum, (5) Neranum, (7) Nellakkul, called also Chael or Shail. Richards is responsible for the statement that

> 'One of the seven churches founded by St. Thomas was at a place named Chayal in the eastern hills of Travancore. It has long been abandoned, owing to wild animals, but the ruins remain, and would repay antiquarian research' (p. 91).

I cannot explain the discrepancies in the lists, or say anything more about the alleged ruins at Chayal (*alias* Nellakkul, Chael, or Shail).

Facts supporting the tradition.

St. Thomas is believed to have ordained priests from two families : namely, one at Shankarapuri, which died out, and the other at Pakalōnmattam, which survived into the nineteenth century, and supplied archdeacons in the Portuguese and bishops in the Dutch period (Mackenzie, p. 137 ; Richards, p. 76).

> 'There is no doubt,' Mr. V. Nagam Aiya observes, 'as to the tradition that St. Thomas came to Malabar and converted a few families of Nambudiris, some of whom were ordained by him as priests, such as

[1] 'Palli' in the name Pallipuram means 'church' or any non-Hindu place of worship.

those of Sankarapuri and Pakalomattam.[1] For in consonance with this long-standing traditional belief in the minds of the people of the Apostle's mission and labours among high-caste Hindus, we have [it] before us to-day the fact that certain Syrian Christian women, particularly of a Desom called Kunnamkolam, wear clothes as Nambudiri women do, move about screening themselves with huge umbrellas from the gaze of profane eyes as those women do, and will not marry, except perhaps in exceptional cases and that only recently, but from among dignified families of similar aristocratic descent. This is a valuable piece of evidence of the conduct of the community, corroborating the early tradition extant on the coast.' (*Manual*, II, 122.)

The martyrdoms.

Mr. Aiya goes on to notice the Malabar version of the Abbanes story of the *Acta*, which is given more fully from a Malayālam manuscript by Richards (p. 72).

The martyrdom of St. Thomas at any place may be doubted, because an early writer named Heracleon, cited by Clement of Alexandria (*c.* A. D. 200), states that Thomas was not martyred (Medlycott, p. 120). The Roman Catholic writers, of course, impugn the statement of Heracleon, but anybody is at liberty to believe it if he chooses to do so.

Christianity in Socotra.

The earliest testimony to the existence of a Christian Church in Socotra, derived from Persia, is that of Cosmas Indicopleustes, who wrote in A. D. 535. About a thousand years later (1542), St. Francis Xavier found nominally Christian congregations in the island, who claimed descent from the converts made by St. Thomas. The belief that Theophilus, the missionary sent out by Constantine about A. D. 354, visited Socotra appears to be erroneous (Medlycott, pp. 136, 138, 196–201).[2] Bishop Medlycott is, I think, right in holding that Theophilus visited Malabar and found Christians in that region.

A Ceylonese tradition.

Historical traditions of India and Ceylon when read together seem to carry the evidence for the existence of the Church in Malabar back to the third century. We learn from the Ceylonese chronicle, the *Mahāvaṁśa* (ch. xxxvi), composed about the beginning of the sixth century, that in the reign of king Gothakābhaya or Meghavarṇābhaya, whom Geiger places in A. D. 302–15, a learned Tamil heretic overcame an orthodox Buddhist theologian in controversy and gained the favour of the king, who placed his son under his tuition. The *Mahāvaṁśa* represents the victor in the disputation as being a monk named Sanghamitra, 'versed in the teachings concerning the exorcism of spirits and so forth'. Mr. K. G. Seshar Aiyar interprets this statement as meaning really that the successful controversialist was a Hindu, and identifies him with the famous Śaiva saint Māṇikka (or Māṇi)

[1] Richards spells 'Pakalōnmattam'. Aiya (*Manual*, II, 122) writes 'Pakalomattam', while Mackenzie (ibid., p. 137) writes 'Palomattam'. Probably the first form is correct.

[2] The statement at the top of p. 136 (Medlycott) that the story of the mission of Theophilus refers to Socotra, is a slip, contradicted on pp. 196, 201, and with good reason.

Vāśagar.[1] The Tamil lives of that personage affirm that the saint actually converted the king of Ceylon towards the end of his career. That king may be identified with Gothakābhaya, and it is possible that the author of the *Mahāvaṁśa* may have misrepresented the Śaiva Hindu Māṇikka Vāśagar as Sanghamitra, a Buddhist heretic.

Māṇikka Vāśagar in Malabar.

However little credit we may be disposed to give to the story about the conversion of the king of Ceylon, or to the identification of that king with Gothakābhaya of the *Mahāvamśa,* I see no reason for hesitating to believe the Indian tradition that Māṇikka Vāśagar visited Malabar and reconverted two families of Christians to Hinduism. The descendants of those families, who are still known as Manigrāmakars, are not admitted to full privileges as caste Hindus. Some traditions place the reconversion as having occurred about A.D. 270. If that date be at all nearly correct, the Malabar Church must be considerably older. So far as I can appreciate the value of the arguments from the history of Tamil literature, there seems to be good independent reason for believing that Māṇikka Vāśagar may have lived in the third century. Some authors even place him about the beginning of the second century.[2] If he really lived so early, his relation with the Church in Malabar would confirm the belief in its apostolic origin.

[1] *Tamilian Antiquary,* vol. i, no. 4, p. 54. The writer does not cite the statement in the *Mahāvaṁśa* correctly. The Tamil legend is given ibid., p. 66, and in Pope, *Tiruvāśagam,* p. xxxi.

There is a fine metal image of Māṇikka—a presumably idealistic portrait—shown as fig. 161, p. 263 of *South Indian Images* by H. K. Sastri (Madras Government Press, 1916).

[2] T. Ponnambalam Pillai, quoting various authorities, in *Tamilian Antiquary,* vol. i, No. 4, pp. 73–9; see also ibid., pp. 53–5; and Mackenzie, p. 138. The notion that the tradition about the origin of the Manigrāmakars has anything to do with Manicheans is untenable. Dr. Pope, shortly before his death, expressed his acceptance of the opinion that Māṇikka lived *not later* than the fourth century (*Tam. Ant., ut supra,* p. 54).

CHAPTER X

THE KUSHĀN OR INDO-SCYTHIAN DYNASTY FROM ABOUT A. D. 20 TO A. D. 225

THE migrations of the nomad nations of the Central Asian steppes, briefly noticed in the last preceding chapter, produced on the political fortunes of India effects so momentous that they deserve and demand fuller treatment. Yüe-chi migration.

A tribe of Turkī nomads, known to Chinese authors as the Hiung-nū, succeeded in inflicting upon a neighbouring and rival horde of the same stock a decisive defeat before the middle of the second century B. C. The date of this event is stated as 165 B. C. by most scholars, while Dr. Franke gives the limiting dates as 174 and 160 B. C. The Yüe-chi were compelled to quit the lands which they occupied in the province of Kan-suh in North-western China, and to migrate westwards in search of fresh pasture-grounds. The moving horde mustered a force of bowmen, estimated to number from one hundred to two hundred thousand; and the whole multitude must have comprised, at least, from half a million to a million persons of all ages and both sexes.[1]

In the course of their westward migration in search of grazing-grounds adequate for the sustenance of their vast numbers of horses, cattle, and sheep, the Yüe-chi, moving along the route past Kuchā (N. lat. 41° 38′, E. long. 83° 25′), to the north of the desert of Taklamakān, the Gobi of old maps, came into conflict with a smaller horde, named Wu-sun, which occupied the basin of the Ili river and its southern Defeat of the Wu-sun.

[1] The Yüe-chi were not snub-nosed Mongols, but big men with pink complexions and large noses, resembling the Hiung-nū in manners and customs (Kingsmill, *J. R. A. S.*, 1882, p. 7, of reprint of *Intercourse of China with Eastern Turkestan*). The Yüe-chi belonged to the Hu group of tribes, who seem to have been Iranians. The coins of Kanishka and Huvishka, as well as those of Kadphises II, present recognizable portraits. See Plates of Coins, *ante*.

tributaries, the Tékès and Kongès.[1] The Wu-sun, although numbering a force of only ten thousand bowmen, could not submit patiently to the devastation of their lands, and sought to defend them. But the superior numbers of the Yüe-chi assured the success of the invaders, who slew the Wu-sun chieftain, and then passed on westwards, beyond Lake Issyk-kūl, the Lake Tsing of Hiuen Tsang, in search of more spacious pastures. A small section of the immigrants, diverging to the south, settled on the Tibetan border, and became known as the Little Yüe-chi; while the main body, which continued the westward march, was designated the Great Yüe-chi.

Defeat of the Śakas.

The next foes encountered by the Yüe-chi were the Śakas, or Se, who doubtless included more than one horde; for, as Herodotus observes, the Persians were accustomed to use the term Sakai to denote all Scythian nomads.[2] The Śakas, who dwelt to the west of the Wu-sun, and to the north of the Jaxartes (Syr Daryā) also attempted to defend their lands; but met with even worse success than the Wu-sun, being compelled to vacate their pasture-grounds in favour of the victorious Yüe-chi, who occupied them. The Śakas were forced to migrate in search of new quarters, and, ultimately, as stated in the last preceding chapter, made their way into India through the northern passes.[3]

[1] Chavannes, *Turcs Occidentaux*, p. 263. According to Laufer, *The Language of the Yüe-chi*, p. 12, the Wu-sun as well as the Yüe-chi and the Ephthalites, were Scythic Iranians.

[2] In later times the Muhammadans were sometimes styled Śakas, as in the Baṭihāgaṛh inscription of Samvat 1385 from the Damoh District, Central Provinces (*Ep. Ind.*, xii, 45), and in several other instances.

[3] In the time of Darius, son of Hystaspes (500 B.C.), the Sakai, with the Caspii, formed the fifteenth satrapy; and, in the army of Xerxes, they were associated with the Bactrians under the command of Hystaspes, the son of Darius and Atossa (*Herod.* iii. 93; vii, 64). Now that the position of the Wu-sun has been determined, and the line of the Yüe-chi migration thus fixed, the approximate location of the Sakai must be as stated in the text. Strabo clearly states that the Sakai and allied tribes came from the neighbourhood of the Jaxartes. Canon Rawlinson's opinion that they occupied the Kāshgar and Yarkand territory in the days of Darius (*Herod.* transl., vol. ii, 403; v, 170) is no longer tenable. The Śaka migration is discussed fully in my paper, 'The Śakas in Northern India', *Z. D. M. G.*, 1907, pp. 403–21; and by Dr. F. W. Thomas in his valuable article 'Sakastana' (*J. R. A. S.*, 1906, pp. 181–216, 460–4). He shows

For some fifteen or twenty years the Yüe-chi remained undisturbed in their usurped territory. But meantime their ancient enemies, the Hiung-nū, had protected the infant son of the slain Wu-sun chieftain, who had grown to manhood under their care. This youth, with Hiung-nū help, attacked the Yüe-chi, and avenged his father's death by driving them from the lands which they had wrested from the Sakas. Being thus forced to resume their march, the Yüe-chi moved into the valley of the Oxus, and reduced to subjection its peaceful inhabitants, known to the Chinese as Ta-hia. The political domination of the Yüe-chi probably was extended at once over Bactria, to the south of the Oxus, but the head-quarters of the horde continued for many years to be on the north side of the river, and the pastures on that side sufficed for the wants of the new-comers. *c.* 140 B.C. Defeat of the Yüe-chi.

In the course of time, which may be estimated at one or two generations, the Yüe-chi lost their nomad habits; and became a settled, territorial nation, in actual occupation of the Bactrian lands south of the river, as well as of Sogdiana to the north, and were divided into five principalities. As a rough approximation to the truth, this political and social development, with its accompanying growth of population, may be assumed to have been completed about 10 B. C. The Yüe-chi settle down. 10 B. C.

For the next century nothing is known about Yüe-chi history; but more than a hundred years after the division of the nation into five territorial principalities, situated to the north of the Hindū Kush, the chief of the Kushān section of the horde, who is conventionally known to European writers as Kadphises I, succeeded in imposing his authority on his colleagues, and establishing himself as sole monarch of the Yüe-chi nation. His accession as such may be dated approximately in the year A. D. 40, which cannot be far wrong.[1] Unification of Yüe-chi kingdom. A. D. 40.

reasons for believing that Śakas had been settled in Sīstān from very early times, and for holding that an irruption of Śakas into that country in the second century B. C. is improbable. In my second edition I had assumed the reality of such an irruption, but now am disposed to agree with Dr. Thomas.

[1] Many books antedate the unification of the Kushān monarchy in consequence of a misunderstanding of a condensed version of the history given in Ma-twan-lin's Chinese encyclopaedia of the thirteenth century. The publica-

The Yüe-chi cross the Hindū Kush.

The pressure of population upon the means of subsistence, which had impelled the Yüe-chi horde to undertake the long and arduous march from the borders of China to the Hindū Kush, now drove it across the barrier, and stimulated Kadphises I to engage in the formidable task of subjugating the provinces to the south of the mountains.

Empire of Kadphises I.

He made himself master of Ki-pin, which may be interpreted as meaning Gandhāra, as well as of the Kābul territory,[1] and, in the course of a long reign, consolidated his

tion of translations of the original texts which the encyclopaedist abstracted has made the true meaning plain, although exact dates are not known. In a valuable paper 'Indoskythische Beiträge' in *Sitzungsber. d. königl. preuss. Akad. der Wissenschaften*, 1916, pp. 787–827, Sten Konow suggests (p. 814), and he may well be right, that the Śaka era was founded by Kadphises II, and that the Mālava or Vikrama era originated at Ujjain, and was established by a king named Vikrama, who defeated the Śakas, who preceded the Kushāns. The king called Kadphises I in the text is the Kieū-tsieū-k'io of the Chinese, and the Kozolakadaphes, Kozoulokadphises, and Kujulakarakadphises of various coins. The exact meaning of these names or titles is unknown. Full references will be found in my paper entitled 'The Kushān or Indo-Scythian Period of Indian History' (*J. R. A. S.*, 1903, pp. 1–64). I have given up the theory advocated in that essay that the Kushāns used the Laukika era. The name of the clan is spelled Kushana in the Kharoshṭhī script, which does not mark long vowels, but there is good Chinese and Sassanian evidence that the second vowel was long, e. g. the words *rabbā Kushān* on coins of Hormazd II (A. D. 302–9). See Drouin, 'Les Légendes des Monnaies Sassanides,' in *Revue Archéologique*, 1898, pp. 62 foll. I therefore follow Cunningham and Drouin in using the form 'Kushān' instead of the more fashionable 'Kushana'. Baron A. von Staël Holstein believes that Kusha (Kuṣa) 'was the correct name of the warlike race that gave Kaniṣka to the Buddhist world'. The forms transliterated as 'Kushān', &c., appear to be genitive plural of the name Kusha (Kuṣa). ('Was there a Kuṣana Race?' *J. R. A. S.*, Jan., 1914, pp. 79–88). Fleet and Allan disagree with the Baron (*J. A. R. S.*, 1914, pp. 369–81, 413). See also Fleet, ibid, 1915, p. 532 and Thomas, ibid, 1915, p. 532. Laufer (*Language of the Yüe-chi*, Chicago, 1917) denounces the speculations of A. v. S. Holstein as 'entirely inadmissible'. The names Yüe-chi and Kuṣana have no philological connexion, but are 'thoroughly independent'. Laufer agrees with F. W. Thomas (*J. R. A. S.*, 1906, p. 203) that Kuṣana was 'not a tribal name, but a family or dynastic title'. See also K. P. Jayaswal (*J. B. O. Res. Soc.*, vi, pp. 12–22), who suggests that Kushān was actually the personal name of Wema Kadphises' predecessor, Kadphises I.

[1] The Chinese texts, as Sylvain Lévi has proved conclusively, distinguish Ki-pin from Kao-fū, or Kābul. The signification of Ki-pin or Ka-pin has varied. In the seventh century, in the time of the Tang dynasty, it generally, although not invariably, meant Kapiśa, or North-eastern Afghanistan. Sten Konow in the paper mentioned in the preceding note (p. 811) holds that in Han times Ki-pin meant Gandhāra (the region including Taxila and Takht-i-Bahai). He seems to be right, and

power in Bactria, and found time to attack the Parthians. His empire thus extended from the frontiers of Persia to the Indus, or perhaps to the Jihlam, and included Sogdiana, now the Khanate of Bukhāra, with probably all the territories comprised in the existing kingdom of Afghanistan. The complete subjugation of the hardy mountaineers of the Afghan highlands, who have withstood so many invaders with success, must have occupied many years, and cannot be assigned to any particular year, but A. D. 50 may be taken as a mean date for the conquest of Kābul.

Extinction of Indo-Greek and Indo-Parthian power.

The Yüe-chi advance necessarily involved the suppression of the Indo-Greek and Indo-Parthian chiefs of principalities to the west of the Indus; and in the last preceding chapter proof has been given of the manner in which the coinage legibly records the outline of the story of the gradual supersession of Hermaios, the last Greek prince of Kābul, by the barbarian invaders.

The final extinction of the Indo-Parthian power in the Panjāb and the Indus valley probably was reserved for the reign of Kanishka.

c. A.D. 78. Kadphises II.

At the age of eighty Kadphises I closed his victorious reign, and was succeeded, in or about A. D. 77 or 78, by his son, who is most conveniently designated as Kadphises II.[1] This prince, no less ambitious and enterprising than his father, devoted himself to the further extension of the Yüe-chi dominion, and apparently completed the conquest of Northern India, commenced by his predecessor.

There is reason to believe that he conquered the Panjāb and a considerable part of the Gangetic plain, probably as far as Benares. It is probable that he extended his power

I relinquish my earlier view that the name signifies Kashmir, as suggested by Sylvain Lévi, in *J. A.*, tome vii, ser. ix, p. 161. See the learned observations of Watters (*On Yuan-chwang*, i, 259), who points out that 'in many Chinese treatises Ka-pin is a geographical term of vague and varying extension, and not the description of a particular country. It is applied in different works to Kapis, Nagar, Gandhāra, Udyāna, and Kashmir.' Sir M. A. Stein spells Ki-pin as Chi-pin. All Chinese names are spelt in a great variety of ways by different authors. Dates, also, are given with a certain amount of variation.

[1] Yen-kao-ching of the Chinese; Wima (Ooēmo) Kadphises, &c., of the coins.

to the mouths of the Indus and swept away, if they still existed, the petty Parthian princes who still ruled that region in the first century after Christ, but are heard of no more afterwards. The conquered Indian provinces were administered by military viceroys, to whom should be attributed the large issues of coins known to numismatists as those of the Nameless King, which are extremely common all over Northern India from the Kābul Valley to Ghāzīpur and Benares on the Ganges, as well as in Cutch (Kachchh) and Kāthiāwār.[1]

Relations with China. The embassy of Chang-kien[2] in 125–115 B. C. to the Yüe-chi, while they still resided in Sogdiana to the north of the Oxus, had brought the western barbarians into touch with the Middle Kingdom, and for a century and a quarter the emperors of China kept up intercourse with the Scythian powers. In the year A. D. 8 official relations ceased, and when the first Han dynasty came to an end in A. D. 23, Chinese influence in the western countries had been reduced to nothing. Fifty years later Chinese ambition reasserted itself, and for a period of thirty years, from A. D. 73 to 102, General Pan-chao led an army from victory to victory, nearly as far as the confines of the Roman empire,[3] and thus effected the greatest westward extension ever attained by the power of China. The king of Khotan, who had first made his submission in A. D. 73, was followed by several other princes,

A. D. 73–102.

[1] No inscriptions of Kadphises II being known, the evidence for the extent of his Indian dominions rests chiefly on the distribution of his coins. When the *Periplus* was written, about A. D. 80, Parthian chiefs still ruled the Indus delta. The proof that the Nameless King, Σωτὴρ μέγας, was contemporary with Kadphises II is given in detail by Cunningham (*Num. Chron.*, 1892, p. 71). His coins, mostly copper or bronze, include a few in base silver. Both Kadphises II and the Nameless King use the title *sōtēr-megas* ; but while the former calls himself *basileus basileōn*, 'king of kings', the latter describes himself as *basileus basileuōn*, 'reigning king'. The participle probably indicates subordinate rank. See *Catal. Coins in I. M.*, vol. I.

[2] See 'The Story of Chang K'ién, China's Pioneer in Western Asia', by Friedrich Hirth, in *J. Amer. Or. Soc.*, vol. xxxvii, pt. i, ii, cited in *J. R. A. S.*, 1918, p. 202.

[3] Prof. Douglas says that 'an army under General Pan-c'hao marched to Khoten, and even carried their country's flag to the shores of the Caspian Sea' (*China*, in Story of Nations Series, p. 18). M. Sylvain Lévi, referring to Mailla, *Histoire générale de la Chine*, says—' jusqu'aux confins du monde gréco-romain' (*Notes sur les Indo-Scythes*, p. 50).

including the king of Kāshgar, and the route to the west along the southern edge of the desert was thus opened to the arms and commerce of China. The reduction of Kuchā and Karashahr in A. D. 94 similarly threw open the northern road.

c. A.D. 90. War with China.

The steady advance of the victorious Chinese evidently alarmed the Kushān king, presumably Kadphises II, who regarded himself as the equal of the emperor, and had no intention of accepting the position of a vassal. Accordingly, in A. D. 90,[1] he boldly asserted his equality by demanding a Chinese princess in marriage. General Pan-chao, who considered the proposal an affront to his master, arrested the envoy and sent him home. Kadphises II, unable to brook this treatment, equipped a formidable force of 70,000 cavalry under the command of his viceroy Si, which was dispatched across the Tsung-ling range, or Tāghdumbāsh Pāmīr, to attack the Chinese. The army of Si probably advanced by the Tāshkurghān Pass, some fourteen thousand feet high,[2] and was so shattered by its sufferings during the passage of the mountains, that when it emerged into the plain below, either that of Kāshgar or Yārkand, it fell an easy prey to Pan-chao, and was totally defeated. Kadphises II was compelled to pay tribute to China, and the Chinese annals record the arrival of several missions bearing tribute at this period.[3]

Relations with Rome.

The Indian embassy which offered its congratulations to Trajan at some date after his return to Rome in A. D. 99 may have been dispatched by Kadphises II to announce his conquests.[4]

[1] According to Laufer (op. cit., p. 3), the demand was made in A. D. 87.

[2] For an account of Tāshkurghān in the Sarīkol tract of the mountains, see Stein, *Preliminary Report of Exploration in Chinese Turkestan*, pp. 11–13; *Sand-buried Ruins of Khotan*, ch. v; *Ancient Khotan*, p. 54, note 17.

[3] 'In the time of the Emperor Hwa [=Hiao-houo-ti, or Ho-ti] (89–105) they [the Indians] often sent messengers to China and presented something, as if it were their tribute. But afterwards those of the western regions rebelled (against the emperor of China), and interrupted their communication, until the second year of the period Yenhsi (159) in the reign of the Emperor Kwan [=Hwan-ti] (147–67)' (*Annals of Later Han Dynasty*, as translated by Prof. Legge in *India, What Can it Teach us?* p. 277).

[4] 'And to Trajan after he had arrived in Rome there came a great many embassies from barbarian courts, and especially from

Roman influence.

The Yüe-chi conquests opened up the overland path of commerce between the Roman empire and India. Kadphises I, who struck coins in bronze or copper only, imitated, after his conquest of Kābul, the coinage either of Augustus in his latter years, or the similar coinage of Tiberius (A. D. 14 to 38). When the Roman gold of the early emperors began to pour into India in payment for the silks, spices, gems, and dyestuffs of the East, Kadphises II perceived the advantage of a gold currency, and struck an abundant issue of orientalized *aurei*, agreeing in weight with their prototypes, and not much inferior in purity. In Southern India, which, during the same period, maintained an active maritime trade with the Roman empire, the local kings did not attempt to copy the imperial *aurei*, which were themselves imported in large quantities, and used for currency purposes, just as English sovereigns now are in many parts of the world.[1]

the Indians. . . . He (Trajan) having reached the ocean (at the mouth of the Tigris) saw a vessel setting sail for India' (Dion Cassius, *Hist. Rom.*, ix, 58; lxvii, 28; in McCrindle, *Anc. Ind.* (1901), p. 213).

[1] For weights and assays of Kushān coins, see Cunningham (*Coins Med. India*, p. 16). The opinions expressed by Von Sallet (*Nachfolger Alexanders*, pp. 56, 81) that the close resemblance between the heads of Kadphises I and Augustus is due to fortuitous coincidence, and that there is no reason to connect the weight of the Kushān coins with that of the imperial *aurei*, can only be regarded as strange aberrations of that distinguished numismatist. The one silver coin of Kadphises II which is known weighs 56½ grains, and thus agrees in weight, as Cunningham observed, with a Roman silver *denarius*. A silver coin of Huvishka, οκρο type, now in the museum of the Bombay Branch R. A. S., agrees in weight with the Indo-Parthian silver (*Prog. Rep. A. S. W. Circle*, 1915–16, p. 59). For an account of large finds of Roman coins in India, see Thurston, *Coin Catal. No.* 2 *of Madras Museum*; and, more fully, Sewell, 'Roman Coins found in India', *J. R. A. S.*, 1904, p. 591. The testimony of Pliny (*Hist. Nat.* xii, 18) to the drain of Roman gold in exchange for Indian, Arabian, and Chinese luxuries is well known:—'Minimaque computatione milies centena milia sestertiûm annis omnibus India et Seres peninsulaque illa imperio nostro adimunt. Tanto nobis deliciae et feminae constant. Quota enim portio ex illis ad deos quaeso iam uti ad inferos pertinet?'

The Roman coins in circulation in North-western India were not however all gold. 'As many as 69 Roman coins were found in Mrs. Howell's collection, most of which were silver and belonged to the various officers of the Roman Republic.' These coins were all collected from Kohat and the neighbouring regions and must have been in circulation there for the purposes of commerce. Seventeen of them belong to the Roman emperors, four to the 'coinage of Italy', and one to the 'coinage of Spain'. Forty-one pertain to the various officers of the Roman Republic, and one is unidentifiable. The remaining five, which are

The victorious reign of Kadphises II undoubtedly was prolonged, and may be supposed to have lasted for about thirty-two years, from A. D. 78 to 110.[1]

Duration of reign of Kadphises II.

c. A.D. 120. Kanishka acc.

Kadphises II was succeeded by Kanishka, who alone among the Kushān kings has left a name cherished by tradition, and famous far beyond the limits of India. His name, it is true, is unknown in Europe, save to a few students of unfamiliar lore, although it lives in the legends of Tibet, China, and Mongolia, and is scarcely less significant to the Buddhists of those lands than that of Asoka himself. Notwithstanding the widespread fame of Kanishka, his authentic history is scanty, and his chronological position strangely open to doubt. Unluckily no passage in the works of the accurate Chinese historians has yet been discovered which synchronizes him with any definite name or event in the well-ascertained history of the Middle Kingdom. The Chinese books which mention him are all, so far as is yet known, merely Buddhist works of edification, and not well

copper, belong to both republican and imperial times (*Prog. Rep. A. S. W. I.*, 1916–17, p. 51).

[1] No definite proof of the length of this reign can be given, but the extent of the conquests made by Kadphises II and the large volume of his coinage are certain indications that his reign was protracted. Cunningham assigned it a duration of forty years. My presentation of the history of Kanishka is largely based on the original and valuable essay by Mr. R. D. Banerji of the Indian Museum, entitled 'The Scythian Period of Indian History' (*Ind. Ant.*, 1908, pp. 25–75). Prof. Lüders's view that the Kanishka of the Ara record may have been the grandson of the Kanishka of the years 3 and 11 (*Sitzungsber. d. kön. preuss. Akad. d. Wissensch.*, 1912, p. 827) is accepted by Sten Konow (op. cit., p. 266 n., *ante*), who takes Vajheshka to be an alternative form of Vasishka (p. 819). He further explains his views in *Ep. Ind.*, xiv, pp. 130 ff. This view apparently is also accepted by K. P. Jayaswal in a paper on the 'Statue of Wema Kadphises and Kushān Chronology' (*J. B. O. Res. Soc.*, vi, pp. 12–22). The point requires further elucidation. I think that Prof. Lüders is right, and Sten Konow agrees (p. 805 n.), in reading *Kaïsarasa* 'Caesar', as a title of Kanishka in the Ara inscription, but the reading is not sufficiently clear to justify stress being laid upon it. The name of Kanishka is sometimes spelled Kāṇishka and the form Kanishtha (Kaniṣṭa), transliterated by the Chinese as Kanit'a, also occurs. In all probability the Śaka era was founded by Kadphises II; and possibly a new era, running from the accession or from the enthronement of Kanishka, came into use in Northern India, including Kābul, and continued in use in the reigns of his successors. Private inscriptions certainly so dated extend from the year 3 to the year 99. The evidence from Taxila makes it quite clear that the Kadphises kings preceded Kanishka.

adapted to serve as mines of historic fact. They are, in truth, as are the books of Tibet and Mongolia, translations or echoes of Indian tradition, and no student needs to be told how baffling are its vagaries. Kanishka and his proximate successors certainly are mentioned in an exceptionally large number of inscriptions, of which considerably more than a score are dated ; and it might be expected that this ample store of epigraphic material would set at rest all doubts, and establish beyond dispute the essential outlines of the Kushān chronology. But, unfortunately, the dates are recorded in such a fashion as to be open to various interpretations.[1]

Excavations at a small town called Māt in the Mathurā district have disclosed the remarkable life-size statue of Kanishka (see Plate) and two other headless statues of kings. The name and titles of Kanishka are inscribed on his skirt in plain script. The details of his dress and equipment are of interest, and differ from those shown on the coins.[2]

His date. I have no doubt whatever that the numismatic evidence alone—a class of evidence unduly depreciated by some historical students—proves conclusively that Kanishka lived at a time considerably later than the Christian era, subsequent to both Kadphises I and Kadphises II, and was exposed to the influence of the Roman empire. Many other lines of evidence, of great force when brought together, lead to the conclusion that Kanishka came to the throne early in the second century of the Christian era, and most probably in A. D. 120, directly succeeding Kadphises II.

Kanishka unquestionably belonged to the Kushān section

[1] The substantial controversy is between the scholars who place the accession of Kanishka in A. D. 78 and those who date it later in about A. D. 120. It is possible that the Kushān kings may have used a special era, distinct from the Śaka, but it is unlikely. If such an era was used, it began after, not before, A. D. 78. Sir J. H. Marshall, Director-General of the Archaeological Survey, has been convinced by the direct evidence of the stratification of the remains of Taxila that Kanishka reigned in the second rather than the first century of the Christian era. A nearly complete list of the dated inscriptions will be found in the author's paper on the Kushān period, cited *ante*, p. 266. For records of the third year of Kanishka at Sārnāth near Benares, see *Ep. Ind.*, viii, 173. Other additions also have been made to the list.

[2] For description of Māt, see Growse, *Mathurā*, 3rd ed., 1883, p. 391. See note 1 on next page.

of the Yüe-chi nation, as did the Kadphises kings, and there does not seem to be sufficient reason for believing that he was unconnected with them.[1] The coins of both Kadphises II and Kanishka, found together in many places, frequently display in the field the same four-pronged symbol, and agree accurately in weight and fineness, besides exhibiting a close relationship in the obverse devices.[2] If, as some scholars hold, the group of kings comprising Kanishka, Vāsishka, Huvishka, and Vāsudeva preceded Kadphises I, the coins of the two princes last named should be found together, as they are not, and those of Kadphises II and Kanishka should not be associated, as they are. We must accept the Chinese evidence that Kadphises II (Yen-kao-ching) 'conquered T'ien-chu (India), and then set up generals, who governed in the name of the Yüe-chi'. Nobody can dispute the fact that Kanishka, Vāsishka, and Huvishka were well established in power at Mathurā on the Jumna as well as in Kashmīr and in the intermediate Panjāb. It is not apparent how they could have attained that position prior to the 'conquest of India' by Kadphises II, as attested by the Chinese historian. Without further pursuing in detail a tedious archaeological argument, it will suffice to say here that ample and conclusive

[1] K. P. Jayaswal is of opinion that the statue of the seated king, discovered close to the statue of Kanishka near Mathurā, is that of Wema Kadphises (Kadphises II) and that Kanishka was the son of Kadphises II. This traverses the opinion put forward in the third edition of this work that Kanishka was not the son of Kadphises II, but of Vajheshka (*J. B. O. Res. Soc.*, v, p. 511 and vi, pp. 12–22). If the theories of K. P. Jayaswal in regard to the statue, and the views of Lüders and S. Konow in reference to the Kanishka of the Ara inscription are correct, it seems justifiable to infer that Kanishka was the son and immediate successor of Kadphises II. The difficulty in regard to the 'Nameless King' (*ante*, p. 268 n.) is explained by K. P. Jayaswal, by taking 'Kushān' to be the personal name of Kadphises I (*J. B. O. Res. Soc.*, vi, pp. 17–19). But this problem requires further elucidation.

[2] Examples of the association of the coins of Kadphises II and Kanishka are: (1) in Gopālpur *stūpa*, Gorakhpur District; coins of Kadphises II, Kanishka, Huvishka, and a much earlier prince, Ayu Mitra (*Proc. A. S. B.*, 1896, p. 100); (2) Benares hoard of 163 pieces, namely 12 of Kadphises II, and the rest (4 not read) of Kanishka and Huvishka (Thomas, Prinsep's *Essays*, I, 227 note); (3) Masson's collections from Beghrām, 25 miles from Kābul (ibid., pp. 344–51). See also *Ariana Antiqua*. The numerous coins found by Marshall at Taxila clearly establish the order of the dynasties as stated in the text.

reason can be shown for holding that the great majority of Indianists are right in placing the Kanishka group directly after that of the Kadphises kings. Our knowledge is so limited that difficulties remain, whatever theory be adopted, but the ordinary arrangement of the royal names appears to be strictly in accordance with the history of other nations, and with the phenomena of artistic, literary, and religious development.[1]

A. D. 120. Extent of his dominion.

Kanishka, then, may be assumed to have succeeded Kadphises II, to whom he was closely related, in or about A. D. 120. Tradition and the monuments and inscriptions of his time prove that his sway extended all over North-Western India, probably as far south as the Vindhyas, as well as over the remote regions beyond the Pāmīr passes.

Hiuen Tsang, who recorded the history or tradition which he learned in Kapisa, expressly states that 'when Kanishka reigned in Gandhāra his power reached the neighbouring states, and his influence extended to distant regions'. He kept order, we are told, over a wide territory reaching to the east of the Tsung-ling mountains, that is to say, 'the

[1] The chief supporters of the view that Kanishka and his immediate successors preceded the Kadphises kings, are Fleet (*J. R. A. S.*, 1903, 1905, 1906, 1913, various papers), Dr. O. Franke, of Berlin (*Beiträge aus chinesischen Quellen zur Kenntniss der Türkvölker und Skythen Zentralasiens*, Berlin, 1904), and Mr. James Kennedy. Franke lays stress on the fact that Chinese historians, as distinguished from Buddhist writers, never mention Kanishka. But he himself sufficiently answers this argument by the remark that 'with the year 124 A. D. the source was dried up from which the chronicler could draw information concerning the peoples of Turkestan' (p. 71 ; see also p. 80). The other argument on which he relies is based on the well-known story telling how, in 2 B. C., a Yüe-chi king communicated certain Buddhist books to a Chinese official. The inference drawn is that the king in question must have been Kanishka. I admit the premise, that is to say, the fact that in the year 2 B. C. the king of Yüe-chi knew and cared something about Buddhism ; but I deny the conclusion drawn by Franke and Sylvain Lévi. There is no difficulty in devising better explanations of the admitted fact. Franke (p. 96) greatly underrates the power and influence of Kanishka. This misunderstanding appears to be due to the learned author's avowed indifference to Indian archaeological evidence (p. 100). It seems to me that no historical problem can be solved satisfactorily without a careful review of the evidence of all kinds, and that reasoning which shrinks from grappling with certain classes of facts cannot claim to be decisive. The evidence now obtained from the excavations at Taxila and further research prove clearly that the order which I have adopted in the text is correct.

meridional range or ranges which buttress the Pāmīr region on the east and divide it from the Tārīm Basin.' [1] In India his coins are found constantly associated with those of Kadphises II from Kābul to Ghāzīpur on the Ganges, while their vast number and variety indicate a reign of considerable length.[2]

Relations with Rome.

The temporary annexation of Mesopotamia between the Euphrates and Tigris in A.D. 116 by Trajan brought the Roman frontier within 600 miles of the western limits of the Yüe-chi empire. Although the province to the east of the Euphrates was given up by Hadrian in the year after its annexation, there can be no doubt that at this period the rulers of Northern and Western India were well acquainted with the fame and power of the great empire in the west.[3]

Conquest of Kashmīr.

Kanishka may be credited with having completed in his earlier years the subjugation and annexation of the secluded vale of Kashmīr. He certainly showed a marked preference for that delightful country, where he erected numerous monuments, and founded a town, which, although now reduced to a petty village, still bears his honoured name.[4]

[1] Stein, *Ancient Khotan*, p. 27.

[2] Inscription at Suë Vihār, near Bahāwalpur, ed. Hoernle, *Ind. Ant.*, x, 324, dated in the year 11 in the reign of *mahārāja rājātirāja devaputra Kanishka*, on the 28th day of the month Daisios of the Macedonian calendar. That calendar might be used in connexion with any era, as it was used with the Pontic era of 297 B.C. by Pontic cities (*Num. Chron.*, 1905, p. 118). Similarly, Jahāngīr used the names of the Persian solar months with the Hijrī lunar year.

[3] The provinces abandoned by Hadrian were Armenia, Mesopotamia, and Assyria (Merivale, *Hist. of the Romans*, ch. lxvi).

[4] Stein, *Rājat.*, transl. bk. i, 168–72. Kanishkapura is now represented by the village of Kānispōr, 74° 28′ E. long., 34° 14′ N. lat., situated between the Vitastā (Bihat) river and the high road leading from Varāhamūla (Bārāmūla) to Srīnagar. The text of the Kashmīr chronicle is as follows: 'Then there were in this land three kings, called Hushka, Jushka, and Kanishka, who built three towns named after them. That wise king Jushka, who built Jushkapura with its Vihāra, was also the founder of Jayasvāmipura. These kings, who were given to acts of piety, though descended from the Turushka race, built at Śushkaletra and other places *mathas*, *chaityas*, and similar [structures]' (Stein, transl. *Rāja-tar.*, Bk. I, vv. 168–71). Kalhaṇa adds that during the rule of those powerful princes Kashmīr to a large extent was in the possession of the Buddhists. He dates them 150 years after the Nirvāṇa, which is, of course, absurd. Jushka suggests an alternative form of the name to be Juvishka. His reality is attested by the continued existence of his town, now the large village of Zukur, to the north of Srīnagar. There is no sufficient

Attack on Pāṭaliputra. Tradition affirms that he penetrated far into the interior of India, and attacked the king residing at the ancient imperial city of Pātaliputra. It is said that he carried off from that city a Buddhist saint named Aśvaghosha. Comparison of the different versions of this story gives reasons for accepting as true at least the bare fact that Kanishka and Aśvaghosha were contemporaries.[1] If the chronology adopted in this edition be correct, the Indo-Scythian or Kushān dynasty, during the reign of Kanishka, wielded authority over Western India, through the agency of the Śaka satraps of Ujjain, one of whom, Chastana, was probably related to the Kushān dynasty. There are grounds also for the belief that from the time of Kanishka to the reign of Vāsudeva, Kushān rule extended over Bihār.[2]

His capital. Kanishka's capital was Purushapura, the modern Peshāwar, the city which then guarded, as it now does, the main road from the Afghan hills to the Indian plains. There, in his latter days, when he had become a fervent Buddhist,

reason to identify him with Vāsudeva. He may have been merely a Viceroy in Kashmīr. Coins of Kanishka and Huvishka are abundant in that country. The word *Turushka* was often applied to Muhammadans, and meant, I think, simply 'foreigner from beyond the passes'. The term must not be interpreted as implying a belief that Kanishka, &c., belonged to the Turks, or any other distinct nomad people.

[1] Chinese translation, made in A. D. 472, of a lost Sanskrit work called the *Śrī Dharmapiṭaka-sampradāya-nidāna* (?), in Lévi, *Notes sur les Indo-Scythes*, p. 36. According to a Tibetan tradition, Kanishka dispatched a friendly invitation to Aśvaghosha, who, being unable to accept it on account of age and infirmities, sent his disciple Jñāna Yaśa in his stead (transl. of *Sumpāli Ch'oijūng* in *J. Buddhist Text Soc.*, 1893, pt. iii, p. 13). A variant version is given in Schiefner's *Tāranāth*, ch. xii; and another by Watters (ii, 104), who says that the saint was given to Ka-ni-t'a (Kanishka), king of the Yue-ti, as part of a war indemnity. The form Kanit'a, with aspirated *t*, used by the Chinese author, is explained by the tradition of the local Brahmans of Kanishkapura (Kānispōr), who ascribe the foundation of the place to Kanishṭha Rāja (Stein, transl. *Rājat.*, Bk. I, v. 168, note). This king, Kanit'a, treated the bhikshu with much kindness and esteem, and Aśvaghosha continued his labours in his new place of abode in Kashmīr. Watters adds that 'this great Buddhist, who apparently lived in the second century of our era, was a poet, musician, scholar, religious controversialist, and zealous Buddhist monk, orthodox in creed, and a strict observer of discipline'. Aśvaghosha was a pupil of Pārśva, who took a leading part in Kanishka's Council (Watters, i, 209); M. Foucher also holds independently, from 'le témoignage des bas-reliefs', that Aśvaghosha lived in the second century after Christ (*L'Art gréco-bouddhique*, i, 623).

[2] See *J. B. O. Res. Soc.*, vi (1920), p. 22.

INSCRIBED LIFE-SIZE STATUE OF KANISHKA, FROM MĀT IN MATHURĀ DISTRICT

(Photograph by Brajbāsi Friend & Co., Muttra)

he erected a great relic tower, which seems to have deserved to rank among the wonders of the world. The superstructure of carved wood rose in thirteen stories to a height of at least 400 feet, surmounted by a mighty iron pinnacle. When Song-yun, a Chinese pilgrim, visited the spot at the beginning of the sixth century, this structure had been thrice destroyed by fire, and as often rebuilt by pious kings. A monastery of exceptional magnificence which stood by its side,[1] was still flourishing as a place of Buddhist education as late as the ninth century when it was visited by Vīradeva, an eminent Buddhist scholar, who subsequently was appointed abbot of Nālandā in the reign of king Devapāla of Magadha (*c.* A. D. 844–92).[2]

The final demolition of this celebrated establishment undoubtedly must have been due to the Muhammadan invasions of Mahmūd of Ghaznī and his successors. Muslim zeal against idolatry was always excited to acts of destruction by the spectacle of the innumerable images with which Buddhist holy places were crowded.

Parthian war.

The ambition of Kanishka, as already observed, was not confined by the limits of India. He is alleged to have engaged in successful war with the Parthians, having been attacked by the king of that nation, who is described by the tradition as 'very stupid and with a violent temper'.[3]

[1] For the topography of Gandhāra, the region around Peshāwar, the only trustworthy authority is Foucher's admirable treatise, *Notes sur la géographie ancienne du Gandhāra* (Hanoi, 1902). Tāranāth (Schiefner, ch. xiii, p. 62) mentions the neighbouring town of Pushkalāvatī as a royal residence of Kanishka's son. The fullest description of the great relic tower is that by Song-yun (Beal, *Records*, vol. i, p. ciii, and in Chavannes's revised version, Hanoi, 1903). It is mentioned by Fa-hien (ch. xii) and Hiuen Tsang (Bk. ii, Beal, i, 99 ; Watters, i, 204). Even so late as A. D. 1030 Alberūnī alludes to the *Kanik-chaitya* (Sachau, transl. ii, 11). The monastery is described by Hiuen Tsang (Beal, i, 103). The identification of the site is due to Foucher (op. cit., pp. 9–13, with view and plan). The site indicated by Foucher has been excavated by the Archaeological Department with remarkable success, the most notable discovery being that of the now celebrated relic casket bearing an image and inscription of Kanishka whose Superintending Engineer had the Greek name of Agesilaos (*J. R. A. S.*, 1908, p. 1109 ; *Ann. Rep. Arch. S.*, India, 1908–9, pp. 38–60 ; *Hist. of Fine Art in India and Ceylon*, pp. 356–8, pl. lxxv).

[2] Ghosrāwa inscription, ed. and transl. by Kielhorn, *Ind. Ant.*, xvii (1888), pp. 307–12.

[3] Lévi, op. cit., p. 40.

The prince referred to may be either Chosroes (Khusrū), or one of the rival kings who disputed the possession of the Parthian throne between A. D. 108 and 130.[1]

Conquest of Kāshgar, Yarkand, and Khotan.

The most striking military exploit of Kanishka was his conquest of Kāshgar, Yarkand, and Khotan, extensive provinces of Chinese Turkestān lying to the north of Tibet and the east of the Pāmīrs, and at that time, as now, dependencies of China.[2] When Kadphises II had attempted the same arduous adventure in A. D. 90, he had failed ignominiously, as already related, and had been compelled to pay tribute to China; but, after the death of Pan-chao, Kanishka having secured the peaceful possession of India and Kashmīr, was in a better position to surmount the appalling difficulties of conveying an effective army across the passes of the Tāghdumbāsh Pāmīr, which no modern ruler of India would dare to face. Kanishka succeeded, where his predecessor had failed; and not only freed himself from the obligation of paying tribute to China, but exacted the surrender of hostages from a state tributary to the Chinese empire. The assertion made by one authority that the hostages included a son of the emperor of the Han dynasty does not appear to be worthy of belief. The territory of the ruler to whose family the hostages belonged seems to have been not very distant from Kāshgar.

The hostages.

The hostages were treated, as beseemed their princely rank, with the utmost consideration, and were assigned suitable residences at different Buddhist monasteries for each of the three seasons—the hot, the cold, and the rains. During the time of the summer heats, when the burning plains are not pleasant to live in, they enjoyed the cool breezes at a Hīnayānist monastery named Sha-lo-ka, perhaps meaning 'the Kāshgar monastery', situated in the hills of Kapisa, the modern Kāfiristān, beyond Kābul, which was erected specially for their accommodation. During the spring and autumn, including the rainy season, they resided in Gand-

[1] G. Rawlinson, *Parthia* (1893), p. 316.

[2] Yārkand represents the modern pronunciation. Yārkand often occurs in Muhammadan texts (Stein, *Anc. Khotan*, p. 87).

hāra, no doubt at the capital; while they spent the cold weather at an unidentified place in the Eastern Panjāb, to which the name of Chīnabhukti, or 'the Chinese allotment', was given in consequence. They were reputed to have introduced the pear and peach, previously unknown in that part of India, during their residence at Chīnabhukti. One of their number, before returning home, deposited a rich store of gold and jewels for the endowment of the Kapisa establishment, and they all continued to recognize the generosity with which they had been treated by remitting offerings for the benefit of the brethren. The grateful monks adorned their walls with paintings representing their guests, who are said to have been somewhat like Chinamen in appearance and dress. When Hiuen Tsang resided at the Kapisa monastery, during the rainy season of A. D. 630, he found that his hosts still cherished the memory of their benefactors, and celebrated services in their honour. He also stayed for fourteen months in A. D. 633–4 at the hostages' monastery in Chīnabhukti.

Story of the treasure.

The biographer of Hiuen Tsang tells a curious story about the treasure deposited by the hostage as an endowment for the Sha-lo-ka shrine at Kapisa; which was known to be buried under the feet of the image of Vaisravana, otherwise known as Kuvera, or Jambhala, the Great Spirit King, at the south side of the eastern gate of the hall of Buddha. An impious Rāja who had tried to appropriate the hoard was frightened away by portents which seemed to indicate the displeasure of its guardian spirit, and when the monks endeavoured to make use of it for the purpose of repairing the shrine, in accordance with the donor's intention, they, too, were terrified by similar manifestations.

While Hiuen Tsang was lodging at the shrine, the monks besought him to use his influence with the spirit to obtain permission to expend the treasure on urgently needed repairs of the steeple. The pilgrim complied, burned incense, and duly assured the guardian spirit that no waste or misappropriation would be permitted. The workmen who were set to dig up the spot then suffered no molestation, and at a depth of 7 or 8 feet found a great copper vessel containing several hundredweight of gold and a quantity of pearls. The balance of the treasure left after the repairs to the steeple has doubtless been appropriated long since by excavators less scrupulous than the pious Master of the Law.[1]

Echoes of Asoka legends.

The stories told about Kanishka's conversion and his subsequent zeal for Buddhism have so much resemblance to the Asoka legends that it is difficult to decide how far they are traditions of actual fact, and how far merely echoes of an older tradition. The Yüe-chi monarch did not record passages from his autobiography as Asoka did, and when we are informed in the pages of a pious tract that his conversion was due to remorse for the blood shed during his wars, it is impossible to check the statement.[2] Probably it is merely an echo of the story of Asoka, as told by himself.

[1] The grounds of the statements in the text are stated at length in App. L of the second edition, which need not be reprinted. It will suffice to note here a few points. The territory from which the hostages came was the Chinese dependency watered by the Sītā or Yārkand river and the so-called Chakshū, that is to say, the Oxus. The name Chakshū seems to have been obtained from the astronomer Bhāskara Achārya (Colebrooke, *Siddhānta Siromani*, &c., and Wilson, *Sanskrit Dict.*, s. v. *Meru*, quoted in Elliot, *Hist. of India*, I, 50). But Prof. Pāthak has shown (*Ind. Ant.*, 1912, p. 266) that the Sanskrit name for the Oxus should be Vakshū. I conclude, therefore, that 'Chakshū' is a clerical error for 'Vakshū', due to the confusion of the characters *ch* and *v*, which might easily occur in mediaeval script.

The hostages' monastery at Kapiśa was Hīnayānist, and therefore presumably connected with Hīnayānist Kāshgar rather than with Mahāyānist Yārkand. It is possible that the introduction of the Hīnayāna into Kāshgar may date from Asoka's time.

The treasure, according to Beal's version, consisted of 'several hundred *catties* of gold, and several scores [*scil.* of *catties*] of pearls'. The *catty* is a Chinese weight, said to be equal to about 1¼ lb. avoirdupois. The references for the hostages' story are :—

Hiuen Tsang (Yuan Chwang), *Records*, in Watters, I, 124, and Beal I, 57, for Kapiśa ; ibid., in Watters, I, 292, and Beal, I, 173 for Chīnabhukti ; and *Life*, p. 54, for Kapiśa. The story has been discussed by O. Franke, *Beiträge . . . zur Kenntnis der Türkvölker*, &c., Berlin (*Königl. Akad. d. Wissensch.*), 1904, pp. 80 foll. For identification of the Sītā river, see Stein, *Ancient Khotan* (1907), pp. 27, 35, 42. The correct transcription, *Chīnabhukti*, is due to Watters. The town lay to the SW. of Jālandhar, and must be sought in the Fīrōzpur District.

[2] 'Comme il avait en maintes occasions tué à la guerre plus de trois cent mille hommes, il sentit que sa faute devait être infailliblement punie dans l'avenir. Il fut pris au cœur d'angoisse ; aussitôt il confessa sa faute, se repentit, fit la charité, observa les défenses, fit élever un monastère et donner de la nourriture aux moines' (*Conte* 16, *Samyukta-ratnapitaka*, in Lévi, *Notes sur les Indo-Scythes*, p. 34).

The conversion of Kanishka.

Just as the writers of edifying books sought to enhance the glory of Asoka's conversion to the creed of the mild Sākya sage by blood-curdling tales of the king's fiendish cruelty during the days of his unbelief, so Kanishka was alleged to have had no faith either in right or wrong, and to have lightly esteemed the law of Buddha during his earlier life.[1] The most authentic evidence on the subject of his changes of faith is afforded by the long and varied series of his coins, which, like most ancient coinages, reflect the religious ideas both of the monarch in whose name they were struck, and of the peoples whom he subdued. The finest, and presumably the earliest, pieces bear legends, Greek in both script and language, with effigies of the sun and moon personified under their Greek names, Hēlios and Selēnē.[2] On later issues the Greek script is retained, but the language is Khotanese, a form of old Iranian, while the deities depicted are a strange medley of the gods worshipped by Greeks, Persians, and Indians.[3] The rare coins exhibiting images of Buddha Sākyamuni with his name in Greek letters are usually considered to be among the latest of the reign, but they are well executed, and may be earlier in date than is generally supposed.[4] Although it is impossible to fix the exact date of Kanishka's conversion, the event evidently did not occur until he had been for some years on the throne.

Buddha as a deity.

The appearance of the Buddha among a crowd of heterogeneous deities would have appeared strange, in fact would have been inconceivable to Asoka, while it seemed quite natural to Kanishka. The newer Buddhism of his day, which may be traced back to an earlier period and was

The *Notes*, revised by the author, have been translated by Philipps in *Ind. Ant.*, 1903, p. 381 ; 1904, p. 10.

[1] Beal, *Records*, i, 99.

[2] Spelt Salēnē on the coins.

[3] Besides the technical numismatic works, see Stein's remarkable paper on 'Zoroastrian Deities on Indo-Scythian Coins' (*Or. and Babyl. Record*, August, 1887, reprinted by Nutt in same year ; and, with additions, in *Ind. Ant.*, xvii (1888), p. 89). The theories of Sir M. Aurel Stein have been criticized adversely on philological grounds by Kirste, with the approval of Seiger, in *Vienna Or. J.*, II (1888), pp. 237–44. So far as I can understand the technical details, the critics are right. Dr. Kirste's paper was not known to me when my second edition was published.

[4] Von Sallet, *Nachfolger*, p. 195.

designated as the Mahāyāna, or Great Vehicle, must have been largely of foreign origin, and its development was the result of the complex interaction of Indian, Zoroastrian, Christian, Gnostic, and Hellenic elements, which had been made possible by the conquests of Alexander, the formation of the Maurya empire in India, and, above all, by the unification of the Roman world under the sway of the earlier emperors.[1] In this newer Buddhism the sage Gautama became in practice, if not in theory, a god, with his ears open to the prayers of the faithful, and served by a hierarchy of Bodhisattvas and other beings acting as mediators between him and sinful men.[2] Such a Buddha rightly took a place among the gods of the nations comprised in Kanishka's widespread empire,[3] and the monarch, even after his 'conversion', probably continued to honour both the old and the new gods, as, in a later age, Harsha did alternate reverence to Siva and Buddha.

Ghandhāra sculptures.

The celebrated Gandhāra sculptures, found abundantly in the Peshāwar district and neighbouring regions, the ancient Gandhāra, of which many excellent examples date from the time of Kanishka and his proximate successors, give vivid expression in classical forms of considerable artistic merit to this modified Buddhism, a religion with a complicated mythology and well-filled pantheon.[4] The florid Corinthian capitals and many other characteristic features of the style prove that the Gandhāra school was merely a branch of the cosmopolitan Graeco-Roman art of

[1] R. F. Johnston, *Buddhist China* (John Murray, 1913), who speaks with authority, gives a general survey of the Mahāyāna system and discredits the theory that its rise was directly due to Kanishka. On the contrary its growth may be traced from the earliest stages of the religion, back to the disputes and discussions of the Hīnayāna schools (review by W. P. Yetts, in *J. R. A. S.*, 1914, pp. 478–83).

[2] On Bodhisattvas, see Poussin's elaborate article in Hastings, *Encyclopaedia of Religion and Ethics.*

[3] It is noteworthy that the eminent Buddhist writer, Nāgārjuna, whose name is associated with that of Kanishka, was a native of Vidarbha.

[4] This fact, which was not recognized by the earlier writers on the subject, has been established by Grünwedel and Foucher. The sculptures include innumerable figures of Bodhisattvas. The leading authority is Foucher's masterly work, *L'Art gréco-bouddhique du Gandhāra* (vol. i, 1905; vol. ii, 1918). See also *A History of Fine Art in India and Ceylon*, ch. iv.

INSCRIBED BUDDHIST PEDESTAL FROM HASHTNAGAR, DATED 384

the early empire. The most competent critics are now generally agreed that the school reached its highest point of development early in the second century of the Christian era.[1]

Buddhist council.

In Buddhist ecclesiastical history the reign of Kanishka is specially celebrated for the convocation of a council, organized on the model of that summoned by Asoka. Kanishka's council, which is ignored by the Ceylonese chroniclers, who probably never heard of it, is known only from the traditions of Northern India, as preserved by Tibetan, Chinese, and Mongolian writers. The accounts of this assembly, like those of the earlier councils, are discrepant, and the details are obviously legendary.

Kanishka, we are told, studied the Buddhist scriptures in his leisure hours under the guidance of a monk, who attended daily at the palace to give him instruction. The king, becoming hopelessly puzzled by the conflicting doctrines of the various sects or schools, suggested to his adviser, the Venerable Pārsva, that it would be well to obtain an authoritative exposition of the truth. Pārsva gave his cordial approval to the suggestion, and arrangements were made accordingly for a general assembly of theologians. As a matter of fact, however, all the learned men assembled seem to have belonged to a single school, the Sarvāstivādins of the Hīnayāna, or Little Vehicle, whose practice, if we may judge from the contemporary sculptures, must have differed little from that of the Mahāyānists. The first question demanding settlement was that of the place of meeting. The king proposed his capital in Gandhāra, but objection was taken to the hot damp climate. Somebody then suggested Rājagriha, in Magadha, where the first council was reputed to have met. Ultimately it was decided to convoke the assembly in the pleasant climate of Kashmīr, at a monastery named Kundalavana, near the capital of that country. Vasumitra was elected president, and Aśvaghosha, the famous author, who, according to the story, had been carried

[1] The officers of the Archaeological Department are inclined to assign an earlier date.

off from Pātaliputra, was appointed vice-president. The members, 500 in number, devoted themselves to a thorough examination of theological literature from the most remote antiquity, and elaborated huge commentaries on the three main divisions of the Canon. The works so prepared included the *Mahāvibhāshā*, which still exists in Chinese, and is described as being an encyclopaedia of Buddhist philosophy. Dr. Takakusu, a highly competent authority, is of opinion that until this work shall have been made accessible to scholars it will be vain to argue about the Council of Kashmīr or its works. When the labours of the assembly were completed, the commentaries were copied on sheets of copper, which were deposited in a *stūpa* built for this purpose by order of king Kanishka. It is possible that these precious records may still exist buried under some mound near Srīnagar, and that a lucky chance may reveal them. After the conclusion of the business of the council, Kanishka renewed Asoka's donation of the kingdom of Kashmīr to the Church, and went home through the Bārāmūla Pass.[1]

[1] Hiuen Tsang, the leading authority (Beal, i, 117, 151; Watters, i, pp. 270–8; Takakusu's review of Watters, *J. R. A. S.*, 1905, p. 414), states that the council was convened in Kashmīr under the presidency of Vasumitra, by Kanishka, king of Gandhāra, acting on the advice of Pārśva or Pārśvika. Paramārtha (A. D. 499–569), in his biography of Vasubandhu (see App. N. of this edition) gives an independent account of the council as having been held in Kashmīr at some time in the fifth century ('in the five hundreds') after the Nirvāna. He does not name king Kanishka, and ascribes the summoning of the assembly to Kātyāyanīputra. According to him, Aśvaghosha was invited from Sāketa in the Śrāvastī province for the purpose of applying his well-known literary skill to the redaction of the commentaries drafted by the council (Takakusu, *J. R. A. S.*, 1905, p. 52).

Vasumitra's work, *Mahāvibhāshā Śāstra* (No. 1263 of Nanjio's Catal.), ascribed to the time of Kanishka, was an elaborate commentary on the *Jñānaprasthāna Śāstra*, the fundamental work of the Sarvāstivādin school (Takakusu; I-tsing, *Buddhist Practices*, p. xxi).

The Mongolians represent the council as engaged in the collection of the sayings of Buddha. It met at Jālandhar, which was in Kashmīr, according to the *Śāstra Chingola kereglegchi*, and in the kingdom of Gatchiin Kunasana, according to the history of Sanang Setsen (Klaproth, in Laidlay's *Fa-hian*, p. 249).

The Tibetan *Kah-gyur* represents the work of the council as being the third compilation of the doctrine of Buddha (Csoma Körösi, *As Res.*, vol. xx, quoted in *Eastern Monachism*, p. 188). Wassiljew (Schiefner, p. 298) observes that the *Bu-ston* refuses to acknowledge Kanishka's council; that the *Tangyur* describes the council in 400 *anno Buddhae* (one

No political importance should be attached to the assembly.

The legends published by M. Sylvain Lévi include a strange tale professing to relate the end of Kanishka, which possibly may be founded on fact.

Legend of Kanishka's death.

'The king', so runs the story, 'had a minister named Māthara, of unusual intelligence. He addressed Kanishka in these words: "Sire, if you wish to follow the advice of your servant, your power will assuredly bring the whole world into subjection. All will submit to you, and the eight regions will take refuge in your merit. Think over what your servant has said, but do not divulge it." The king replied: "Very well, it shall be as you say." Then the minister called together the able generals and equipped a force of the four arms. Wherever the king turned, all men bowed before him like herbage under hail. The peoples of three regions came in to make their submission; under the hoofs of the horse ridden by king Kanishka everything either bent or broke. The king said: "I have subjugated three regions; all men have taken refuge with me; the region of the north alone has not come in to make its submission. If I subjugate it, I shall never again take advantage of an opportunity against any one, be he who he may, but I do not yet know the best way to succeed in this undertaking." The king's people, having heard these words, took counsel together, and said: "The king is greedy, cruel, and un-

of the traditional dates of Kanishka), as having been led by Vatsiputra, and devoted to the doctrines of his school; while a Chinese account locates the assembly at Kandahār (? Gandhāra).

Tāranāth notes that some authors aver that the council met in the Kundalavana Vihāra in Kashmīr, while others locate it in the Kuvana monastery at Jālandhar; observing that the balance of authority favours the latter view. But the evidence, as it now stands, proves clearly that the council met in Kashmīr. Hiuen Tsang, when describing his visit to Jālandhar (Beal, i, 175; Watters, i, 296), makes no allusion to the council. The fact that in some books Kanishka is called the king of Jālandhar may have given rise to the belief that the council met at that city. The council, according to Tāranāth, settled the strife between the eighteen schools, which were all recognized as orthodox; and the three *piṭakas* were now either for the first time reduced to writing, or, so far as previously written, were purified from error. All kinds of Mahāyāna texts appeared about this time (Schiefner, p. 58).

For criticism of the legends of the earlier councils see the author's paper, 'The Identity of Piyadasi with Asoka Maurya, and some connected Problems' (*J. R. A. S.*, Oct., 1901). For the meaning of *Kundala* in Kashmīrī local names, see Stein, transl. *Rājatar.*, Bk. v, v. 106.

reasonable; his campaigns and continued conquests have wearied the mass of his servants. He knows not how to be content, but wants to reign over the four quarters. The garrisons are stationed on distant frontiers, and our relatives are far from us. Such being the situation, we must agree among ourselves, and get rid of him. After that we may be happy." As he was ill, they covered him with a quilt, a man sat on top of him, and the king died on the spot.' [1]

The reign of Kanishka appears to have lasted some forty-five years, and may be assumed to have terminated about A. D. 160.

Vāsishka. Very little is known about the successors of Kanishka. Inscriptions prove that Vāsishka was reigning at Mathurā in the year 24, and Huvishka between the years 33 and 60, while a prince of the name of Kanishka was reigning at Āra in the Panjāb [2] in the year 41. The best way to reconcile the apparent contradiction is to assume that Vāsishka and Huvishka were sons of Kanishka, who both acted in succession as Viceroys of Upper India while their father was warring beyond the mountains. Vāsishka, of whom no coins are known, seems to have predeceased his father, who was succeeded in his whole empire by Huvishka.[3] The extensive coinage of Huvishka may have been all issued after his succession to the imperial throne. Vāsishka, presumably, was not empowered to coin in his own name. If he had issued coins, it is hardly possible that some specimens should not have been discovered by this time.

Huvishka. The dominions of Huvishka certainly included Kābul,[4] Kashmīr, and Mathurā. At the last-named city, a splendid Buddhist monastery bore his name, and no doubt owed its

[1] *Śrī-Dharma-piṭaka*, &c., in *Notes*, p. 43; and an English version in *Ind. Ant.*, 1903, p. 388.

[2] The Āra inscription is in the Lahore Museum. As to the possibility of this being a record of a second Kanishka, see note on p. 271, *ante*.

[3] The name of Huvishka is written in several variant forms, including Hushka and Hoveshka, due to difficulties in transliterating a foreign name.

[4] Inscription of the year 51 on a brass vase obtained by Masson from one of the Khawāt *stūpas* in the Wardak District, about 30 miles marching distance SW. from Kābul. Edited and translated by Pargiter (*J. R. A. S.* 1912, pp. 1060–3, and *Ep. Ind.*, xi, pp. 202–19). See Sten Konow, 'Indoskythische Beiträge' in *Sitzungsber. d. Königl. Preuss. Akad. der Wissenschaften*, 1916, pp. 807–10.

existence to his munificence;[1] for, like Kanishka, he was a liberal patron of Buddhist ecclesiastical institutions. He also resembled his more famous predecessor in an eclectic taste for a strange medley of Greek, Indian, and Persian deities. The types on the coins of Huvishka include Herakles, Sarapis ('Sarapo'), Skanda with his son Visākha, Pharro, the fire-god, and many others, but the figure and name of Buddha are wanting. It would seem that the Buddhist convictions of these old Scythian kings were not very deeply seated, and it is probably justifiable to hold that the royal favour was granted to the powerful monastic organization of the Buddhists as much as to their creed. No prudent monarch in those days could afford to neglect the wealthy and influential order, which had spread its ramifications all over the empire.

Hushkapura. The town of Hushkapura, founded by Huvishka in Kashmīr, occupied a position of exceptional importance just inside the Bārāmūla Pass, then known as the 'western gate' of the valley, and continued for centuries to be a place of note. When Hiuen Tsang visited Kashmīr about A. D. 631, he enjoyed the liberal hospitality of the Hushkapura monastery for several days, and was escorted thence with all honour to the capital, where he found numerous religious institutions, attended by some five thousand monks. The town of Hushkapura is now represented by the small village of Ushkür, at which the ruins of an ancient *stūpa* are visible.[2]

Length of reign. The reign of Huvishka undoubtedly was prolonged, but all memory of its political events has perished. His abundant coinage is even more varied than that of Kanishka, with which it is constantly associated, and, like the contemporary sculpture, testifies to the continuance of Hellenistic influence. A few specimens of the gold coinage present well executed and characteristic portraits of the king, who was a determined-looking man, with strongly marked features, large, deep-set eyes, and aquiline nose.[3] So far as appears,

[1] Cunningham, *Arch. Rep.*, i, 238.

[2] Stein, *Rājatar.*, transl. Bk. i, v. 168; vol. ii, p. 438; Beal, *Life of Hiuen Tsiang*, p. 68.

[3] Gardner, *B. M. Catal.*, *Greek and Indo-Scythic Kings*, pl. xxvii, 9, xxviii, 9; V. A. Smith, *Catal.*

the Kushān power suffered no diminution during his reign, which may be assumed to have ended in or about A.D. 182.

Reign of Vāsudeva, ? A.D. 182–220.

Huvishka was succeeded by Vāsudeva, whose thoroughly Indian name, a synonym for Vishnu, is a proof of the rapidity with which the foreign invaders had succumbed to the influence of their environment. Testimony to the same fact is borne by his coins, almost all of which exhibit on the reverse the figure of the Indian god Siva, attended by his bull Nandi, and accompanied by the noose, trident, and other insignia of Hindu iconography. The inscriptions of Vāsudeva, mostly found at Mathurā, certainly range in date from the year 74 to the year 98 of the era used in the Kushān age, and indicate a reign of not less than twenty-five years. We may assume that his reign terminated in or about the year 220.[1]

Decay of Kushān power.

It is evident that the Kushān power must have been decadent during the latter part of the long reign of Vāsudeva, and apparently before its close, or immediately after that event, the vast empire of Kanishka obeyed the usual law governing Oriental monarchies, and broke up into fragments, having enjoyed a brief period of splendid unity. Coins bearing the name of Vāsudeva continued to be struck long after he had passed away, and ultimately present the royal figure clad in the garb of Persia, and manifestly imitated from the effigy of Sapor (Shāhpur) I, the Sassanian monarch who ruled Persia from A.D. 238 to 269.[2]

Plague.

It seems reasonable to believe that the decay of the Indo-Scythian monarchy must have been hastened by the terrible plague of A.D. 167, which started in Babylonia, and desolated the Roman and Parthian empires for several years. At Rome, as well as throughout Italy and the provinces, the

Coins I. M., vol. i, pl. xii; and *ante*, plate of Indian Coins and Medals II.

[1] K. P. Jayaswal holds that Vāsudeva was a contemporary of the western satrap Rudrasena (A.D. 199–222) (*J. B. O. Res. Soc.*, vi, p. 22).

[2] Von Sallet, *Nachfolger*, p. 63. *Catal. of Coins in I. M.* vol. i, pp. 63–92. Mr. R. D. Banerji holds that the successors of Vāsudeva were Kanishka II (Kaneshko), Vāsudeva II, and Vāsu[deva] III, basing his opinion on his interpretation of the obscure numismatic evidence ('Notes on Indo-Scythian Coinage', *J. & Proc. A. S. B.*, 1908, p. 81).

greater part of the inhabitants, and nearly all the troops, sank under the disease. Niebuhr expressed the opinion that 'the ancient world never recovered from the blow inflicted upon it by the plague which visited it in the reign of M. Aurelius'. It is not likely that India can have escaped.[1]

Absolutely nothing positive is known concerning the means by which the renewed Persian influence, as proved by numismatic facts, made itself felt in the interior of India. Bahrām (Varahrān) II is known to have conducted a campaign in Sīstān, at some time between 277 and 294; but there is no definite record of any Sassanian invasion of India in the third century, during which period all the ordinary sources of historical information dry up. No inscriptions certainly referable to that time have been discovered, and the coinage, issued by merely local rulers, gives hardly any help. The two great dynasties, the Kushān in Northern India, and the Āndhra in the tableland of the Deccan, disappear together almost at the moment (A.D. 226) when the Arsakidan dynasty of Persia was superseded by the Sassanian.[2] It is impossible to avoid hazarding the conjecture that the three events may have been in some way connected, and that the persianizing of the Kushān coinage of Northern India should be explained by the occurrence of a Persian invasion, such as that mentioned by Firishta as having occurred during the reign of the first Sassanian king.[3]

Sassanian influence on India.

[1] Eutropius, ch. xii. Merivale (*Hist. of the Romans under the Empire*, viii, pp. 332, 358, ch. lxviii) cites the authorities and gives a vivid description of the disaster.

[2] But the *Wei-lio* 'informs us that during the period of the Three Kingdoms (San-kuo, A.D. 221–277) Kashmīr (Ki-pin), Bactria (Ta-hia), Kābul (Kao-fu) and India (T'ien-ču) were all subject to the Great Yüe-či' (*San kuo ci, Wei ci*, ch. 30, p. 126; and Chavannes' translation, *T'oung Pao*, 1905, pp. 538, 539). Chavannes remarks 'Thus, in the middle of the third century, the power of the Kushān kings was at its climax. . . . the Chinese text shows that as late as A.D. 230 at least the Kushān dynasty was still in power (Laufer, *The Language of the Yüe-chi*, p. 13).

[3] Firishta in his Introduction (Elliot and Dowson, vi, 55) records that 'one year Ardeshīr Bābagān [A.D. 226-241] marched against India and reached as far as the neighbourhood of Sarhind. Jūnah was very much alarmed and hastened to do homage to him. He presented pearls and gold and jewels and elephants as tribute, and so induced Ardeshīr to retire'. The statement is confirmed by the existence of the coin from Jhelum District, described by V. A. Smith in *J. A. S. B.*, part i, vol. lxvi (1897), p. 5.

Foreign invasions.

So much, however, is clear, that Vāsudeva was the last Kushān king who continued to hold extensive territories in India. After his death there is no indication of the existence of a paramount power in Northern India. Probably numerous Rājas asserted their independence and formed a number of short-lived states, such as commonly arise from the ruins of a great oriental monarchy; but historical material for the third century is so completely lacking that it is impossible to say what or how many those states were. The period evidently was one of extreme confusion associated with foreign invasions from the north-west, which is reflected in the muddled statements of the *Purāṇas* concerning the Ābhīras,[1] Gardabbilas, Śakas, Yavanas, Bāhlīkas, and other outlandish dynasties named as the successors of the Āndhras. The dynasties thus enumerated clearly were to a large extent contemporary with one another, not consecutive, and none of them could claim paramount rank. It seems to be quite hopeless to attempt to reduce to order the Purānic accounts of this anarchical period, and nothing would be gained by quoting a long list of names, the very forms of which are uncertain.

Kushān kings of Kābul and Panjāb.

Coins indicate that the Kushāns held their own in the Panjāb and Kābul for a long time. It is certain that the Kushān kings of Kābul continued to be a considerable power until the fifth century, when they were overthrown by the White Huns. At the beginning of the fourth century one of them gave a daughter in marriage to Hormazd II, the Sassanian king of Persia; and when Sapor II besieged Amida in A.D. 360, his victory over the Roman garrison was won with the aid of Indian elephants and Kushān troops under the command of their aged king Grumbates, who occupied the place of honour, and was supported by the Śakas of Sīstān.[2]

[1] The settlements of the Ābhīras appear to have been very ancient; for their name is associated with that of the Sūdras in a dictum of Patañjali (second century B.C.); Kielhorn, *Mahābhāshya*, i, 252 (*Ind. Ant.*, xlvii (1918), p. 36).

[2] Cunningham, *Num. Chron.*, 1893, pp. 169–77, who seems to be right in identifying the Chionitai of Ammianus Marcellinus with the Kushāns; Drouin, 'Monnaies des Grands Kouchans', in *Rev. Num.*,

It is difficult to judge how far the foreign chiefs who ruled the Panjāb during the third century, and struck coins similar to those of Vāsudeva, yet with a difference, were Kushāns, and how far they belonged to other Asiatic tribes. The marginal legends of the coins of this class, which are written in a modified Greek script, preserve the name of either Kanishka or Vasu[deva] Kushān,[1] King of Kings, and so recognize the Kushān supremacy; but the name in Indian letters, placed by the side of the spear, is frequently monosyllabic, like a Chinese name, *Bha*, *Ga*, *Vi*, and so forth. These monosyllabic names seem to belong to chiefs of various Central Asian tribes who invaded India and acknowledged the supremacy of the Kushān or Shāhi kings of Kābul. One coin with the modified Kushān obverse, and the names *Pāsana*, *Nu*, *Shilada* in Indian Brāhmī characters in various parts of the field, has on the reverse a fire-altar of the type found on the coins of the earliest Sassanian kings. It is thus clear that in some way or other, during the third century, the Panjāb renewed its ancient connexion with Persia.[2] It is also certain that the later coinage of the Kushāns is clearly connected with that of the Sassanians, a fact which to my mind is fatal to theories which antedate Kanishka and his successors. **Subordinate chiefs.**

Nothing definite is recorded concerning the dynasties of Northern India, excluding the Panjāb, during the third century, and the early part of the fourth. The imperial city of Pātaliputra is known to have continued to be a place of importance as late as the fifth century, but there is little indication of the nature of the dynasty which ruled there during the third. Probably, for at any rate the greater portion of the period, the city was under Śaka rule. The **Blank in history of interior India.**

1896, p. 163. Gibbon (ch. xix) gives A. D. 360 as the date of the siege of Amida on the Tigris, the modern Diarbekir. Other authorities prefer 358 or 359.

[1] The coins usually have *Vasu*, not *Vāsu*.

[2] This is the coin referred to *ante*, p. 289 n. Drouin (*Rev. Num.*, 1898, p. 140) points out that the form of the altar is that found on the coins of Ardashīr, the first Sassanian king (225 or 226–41), as well as on those of some of his successors. See V. A. Smith, *Catal. of Coins in I. M.*, vol. i (1906), pp. 88, 89; and Banerji's corrections in 'Notes on Indo-Scythian Coinage' (*J. & Proc. A. S. B.*, 1908, p. 90).

high importance attached by the founder of the Gupta era in A.D. 320 to his alliance with a Lichchhavi princess suggests that during the third century the non-Aryan Lichchhavis of Vaisāli, who appear to have been closely related to the Tibetans, may have held Pātaliputra as tributaries or feudatories of the Kushān dynasty at Peshāwar. The only intelligible dynastic list for the period is that of the Śaka satraps of Western India, whose history will be more conveniently noticed in the next chapter in connexion with that of the Gupta emperors. The period between the extinction of the Kushān and Āndhra dynasties, about A.D. 220 or 230, and the rise of the imperial Gupta dynasty, nearly a century later, is one of the darkest in the whole range of Indian history.

APPROXIMATE KUSHĀN CHRONOLOGY[1]

DATE.	EVENT.
B. C.	
174	Death of Hiung-nū chief, Moduk.
c. 165	Expulsion of main body of Yüe-chi horde from Kan-suh by the Hiung-nū.
c. 163	Nan-tiu-mi, chief of the Wu-sun, killed by the Yüe-chi.
160	Death of Hiung-nū chief, Ki-yuk.
c. 160–50	Yüe-chi occupation of the Śaka territory; Śaka migration.
c. 150–140	Śaka invasion of India.
c. 140	Expulsion of Yüe-chi from Śaka territory by Koen-muo, the young Wu-sun chief, son of Nan-tiu-mi.
c. 138.	Reduction of the Ta-hia, both north and south of the Oxus, to vassalage by the Yüe-chi, who begin to settle down.
c. 135	Dispatch by Chinese emperor Wu-ti of Chang-k'ien as envoy to the Yüe-chi.
c. 125	Arrival of Chang-k'ien at Yüe-chi head-quarters, north of the Oxus.
c. 122–120	Return of Chang-k'ien to China.
c. 114	Death of Chang-k'ien.
c. 100	Extension of Yüe-chi settlements to the lands south of the Oxus; occupation of Ta-hia capital, Lan-sheu, south of the river, probably = Balkh.
c. 95	**Formation of five Yüe-chi principalities, including Kushān and Bāmiān.**
58–57	Epoch of the Mālava or Vikrama era.
c. 26	Indian embassy to Augustus.
2	A Chinese official instructed in Buddhist books by a Yüe-chi king. (*See* Franke, *Türkvölker*, p. 92 n.)
A. D.	
8	Temporary cessation of intercourse between China and the West.
14	Augustus, Roman emperor, died; Tiberius acc.
23	End of First, or Early Han dynasty of China.
38	Gaius (Caligula), Roman emperor, acc.
c. 40	Kadphises I (Kieū-tsieū-ki'o, Kozolakadaphes, &c.) acc.
c. 40–55	Consolidation of the five Yüe-chi principalities into one Kushān kingdom under Kadphises I; conquest by him of Kao-fū (Kābul), Ki-pin (Gandhāra), and Pota (? Bactria or more probably Arachosia).
41	Claudius, Roman emperor, acc.
c. 45–70	Destruction of Indo-Parthian power, and gradual conquest of Northern India by Kadphises I.
c. 48	Kadphises I succeeded Gondophernes at Taxila.
54	Nero, Roman emperor, acc.
c. 64	Buddhist books sent for by Chinese emperor, Ming-ti.
68, 69	Galba, Otho, and Vitellius, Roman emperors.
70	Vespasian, Roman emperor, (acc. Dec. 22, 69).
73–102	Victorious career of Pan-chao, the Chinese general, in Khotan, &c.
77	Publication of Pliny's *Natural History*.
78	Epoch of the Śaka or Sālivāhana era; Kadphises I died, aged 80; Kadphises II Kushān (Yen-kao-ching, Wema Kadphises, &c.), his son, acc.
79	Titus, Roman emperor, acc.

[1] Compare Appendix J, *ante*, p. 229.

DATE.	EVENT.
A. D.	
81	Domitian, Roman emperor, acc.
89–105	Ho-ti, Chinese emperor.
c. 90	Defeat of Kadphises II by Pan-chao.
94	Reduction of Kuchā and Kara-shahr by the Chinese under Pan-chao.
96	Nerva, Roman emperor, acc.
98	Trajan, Roman emperor, acc.
99	Arrival of Trajan in Rome.
c. 100	Indian embassy to Trajan ; Buddhist Council.
105	Overthrow by the Romans of the Nabataean kingdom of Petra in Arabia ; rise of Palmyra.
c. 110	Kadphises II died.
116	Conquest of Mesopotamia by Trajan.
117	Hadrian, Roman emperor, acc. ; retrocession of Mesopotamia.
c. 120	Kanishka Kushān, acc. ; year 1 of his regnal era.
c. 123	Sārnāth inscription of Kanishka (year 3).
123–6	Residence of Hadrian at Athens.
c. 130–52	Kanishka's conquests in Chinese Turkestan.[1]
131–6	War of Hadrian with the Jews.
138	Mānikyāla inscription of Kanishka (year 18) ; Antoninus Pius, Roman emperor, acc.
c. 150	Jūnāgaṛh inscription of Rudradāman, Western satrap.
c. 160	Death of Kanishka ; Huvishka Kushān, acc. as sovereign of whole empire.
161	Marcus Aurelius Antoninus, Roman emperor, acc.
162–5	Defeat of Parthian king, Vologeses III, by the Romans.
175	Eastern campaign of Marcus Aurelius.
180	Commodus, Roman emperor, acc.
c. 182	Vasudeva Kushān, acc.
192, 193	Pertinax and Julianus, Roman emperors.
193	Septimius Severus, Roman emperor, acc.
c. 200	Palmyra created a Roman colony.
211	Caracalla, Roman emperor, acc.
216	Parthian expedition of Caracalla.
217	Macrinus, Roman emperor, acc.
218	Elagabalus, Roman emperor, acc.
c. 220	Death of Vasudeva Kushān.
c. 220–60	Later Kushān kings.
222	Alexander Severus, Roman emperor, acc.
226	Foundation of Sassanian empire of Persia by Ardashīr or Artaxerxes I.
260	Defeat of Valerian, Roman emperor, by Sapor I.
273	Capture of Palmyra by Aurelian.
284–305	Diocletian, emperor.
360	Successful siege of Amida by Sapor II, with Kushān help.

[1] According to Franke, China lost Khotan in A. D. 152. Kanishka is not mentioned by name in the Chinese histories.

Franke (*Beiträge*, p. 99 n.) considers as doubtful the current identification of Po-ta (P'u-ta, Cantonese Pok-tiu) with Bactria, and suggests as the true equivalent the 'Paktyan land' (Πακτυικὴ γῆ), which he places to the north of Arachosia. See *ante*, p. 40, note 1.

CHAPTER XI

THE GUPTA EMPIRE, AND THE WESTERN SATRAPS; CHANDRA-GUPTA I TO KUMARAGUPTA I

FROM A.D. 320 TO 455.

Origin of the Gupta dynasty.

IN the fourth century light again dawns, the veil of oblivion is lifted, and the history of India regains unity and interest.

A. D. 308.

A local Rāja at or near Pātaliputra, bearing the famous name of Chandra-gupta,[1] wedded, in or about the year 308, a princess named Kumāra Devī, who belonged to the ancient Lichchhavi clan, celebrated ages before in the early annals of Buddhism. During the long period of about eight centuries which intervened between the reign of Ajātasatru and the marriage of Kumāra Devī the history of the Lichchhavis has been lost for the most part, although they are known to have established a dynasty in Nepāl, which used an era believed to run from A.D. 111.[2] They now come suddenly into notice again in connexion with this marriage, which proved to be an event of the highest political importance, as being the foundation of the fortunes of a dynasty destined to rival the glories of the Mauryas. Kumāra Devī evidently brought to her husband as her dowry valuable influence, which in the course of a few years secured to him a paramount position in Magadha and the neighbouring countries. It seems probable that at the time of this fateful union the Lichchhavis were masters or overlords of the ancient imperial city, and that Chandra-gupta, by means of his matrimonial alliance, succeeded to the power previously held by his wife's relatives. In the olden days the

[1] The names of the Chandra-guptas of the Gupta dynasty are spelt with a hyphen, to distinguish them from the Maurya.

[2] Lévi, *Le Népal*, i, 14; ii, 153.

Lichchhavis of Vaisāli had been the rivals of the kings of Pātaliputra, and apparently, during the disturbed times which followed the reign of Pushyamitra, they paid off old scores by taking possession of the city, which had been built and fortified many centuries earlier for the express purpose of curbing their restless spirit.

A. D. 320. Lichchhavi alliance; Chandragupta I. acc.

Certain it is that Chandra-gupta was raised by his Lichchhavi connexion from the rank of a local chief, as enjoyed by his father and grandfather,[1] to such dignity that he felt justified in assuming the lofty title of 'Sovereign of Mahārājas', usually associated with a claim to the rank of lord paramount. He struck coins in the joint names of himself, his queen, and the Lichchhavis; and his son and successor habitually described himself with pride as the son of the daughter of the Lichchhavis. Chandra-gupta, designated as the First, to distinguish him from his grandson of the same name, extended his dominion along the Gangetic valley as far as the junction of the Ganges and Jumna, where Allāhābād now stands; and ruled during his brief tenure of the throne a populous and fertile territory, which included Tirhūt, South Bihār, Oudh, and certain adjoining districts. His political importance was sufficient to warrant him in establishing, after the Oriental manner, a new era dating from his formal consecration or coronation, when he was proclaimed as heir to the imperial power associated by venerable tradition with the possession of Pātaliputra. The first year of the Gupta era, which continued in use for several centuries, and in countries widely separated, ran from February 26, A.D. 320, to March 13, 321; of which dates the former may be taken as that of the coronation of Chandra-gupta I.[2]

[1] His father was named Ghaṭotkacha, and his grandfather simply Gupta. A seal of Ghaṭotkacha, who, according to Allan, may be a different person, has been excavated at Basāṛh (Vaisāli) (*A.S. Ann. Rep.*, 1903–4, p. 107, Pl. xli, 14). Buddhist legend offers another instance of the participle Gupta alone serving as a proper name in the case of Upagupta (Gupta the Less), son of Gupta the perfumer.

[2] For the chronology of the dynasty see the author's paper, 'Revised Chronology of the Early or Imperial Gupta Dynasty' (*Ind. Ant.*, 1902, p. 257), which modifies the scheme as given in his numismatic works, but requires some

Before his death, which occurred perhaps about ten or fifteen years later, Chandra-gupta selected as his successor the Crown Prince, Samudragupta, his son by the Lichchhavi princess.[1] The paternal preference was abundantly justified by the young king, who displayed a degree of skill in the arts of both peace and war which entitles him to high rank among the most illustrious sovereigns of India.

A. D. 330 or 335. Samudragupta, acc.

From the moment of his accession, Samudragupta assumed the part of an aggressively ambitious monarch, resolved to increase his dominions at the expense of his neighbours. Wars of aggression never have been condemned by such public opinion as exists in the East, and no king who cared for his reputation could venture to rest contented within his own borders. Samudragupta had no hesitation in acting on

His aggressive spirit.

correction. Dates expressed in the Gupta era (G. E.) may be converted approximately into dates A. D. by the addition of 319 ; e. g. 82 G. E. = A. D. 401. For Gupta inscriptions as known in 1888, see Fleet, *Gupta Inscriptions* (*Corpus Inscr. Ind.*, vol. iii). The principal discoveries since the publication of that work are : (1) Bhitarī seal of Kumāragupta II, not dated (ed. V. A. Smith and Hoernle, *J. A. S. B.*, vol. lviii, part i, 1889) ; (2) Basāṛh seals of Ghaṭotkachagupta and queen of Chandra-gupta II (*Arch. S. Annual Rep.*, 1903–4, pp. 101–22, Pls. xl–xlii) ; (3) Bharadi Dih inscr. of Kumāragupta I, dated 117 G. E. (*A. S. Progr. Rep. of N. Circle*, 1907–8, p. 39 ; ed. in *J. A. S. B.*, vol. v, N. S. (1909), p. 457) ; (4) Dhanāidaha inscr. of same king, dated 113 G. E., the earliest known copper-plate grant (*J. A. S. B.*, *ut supra*, p. 459) ; (5) a valuable Gupta-Vākāṭaka grant, partially described by Mr. K. Pathak in *Ind. Ant.*, 1912, p. 214 ; (6) the Sārnāth inscriptions (*A. S. Progr. Rep. of N. Circle*, 1914–15, pp. 6, 14, 15 and App. E, p. vi, Nos. 1 and 4) ; (7) five copper-plates found at Damōdarpur in the Dinājpur district, which comprise inscriptions of Kumāragupta II and Budhagupta. Many other inscriptions dated in the Gupta era, but not giving the names of kings, have been discovered, including at least two in Burma (*A. S. Progr. Rep., Burma*, 1894, pp. 15, 20).

[1] Fleet, *J. R. A. S.*, 1909, p. 342. A few rare coins issued by Kācha or Kacha exist which closely resemble the issues of Samudragupta in certain respects. Some authors suppose Kācha or Kacha to be identical with Samudragupta, but the better opinion regards him as a rival brother of that king. His reign, if a reality, must have been very brief, probably not exceeding a few months. Nothing whatever being known about him except that he coined some gold pieces, Samudragupta may be regarded for all practical purposes as the immediate successor of his father. His selection is vividly described in the Allāhābād inscription : ' " Here is a noble man ! " With these words the father embraced him, with shivers of joy that spoke of his affection, and looked at him, with eyes heavy with tears and overcome with love—the courtiers breathing freely with joy and the kinsmen of equal grade looking up with sad faces—and said to him : " Protect then this whole earth " ' (Bühler, as transl. in *Ind. Ant.*, 1913, p. 176).

the principle that 'kingdom-taking' is the business of kings, and immediately after his succession to the throne plunged into war, which occupied many years of his unusually protracted reign.[1]

Epigraphic record.

When his fighting days were over he employed a learned poet, skilled in the technicalities of Sanskrit verse, to compose a panegyric of his achievements, which he caused to be engraved on one of the stone pillars set up six centuries before by Asoka and incised with his edicts.[2] Samudragupta, an orthodox Hindu, learned in all the wisdom of the Brahmans, and an ambitious soldier full of the joy of battle, although he had been interested as a young man, at his father's bidding, in the doctrine of Vasubandha, the Buddhist sage, made no scruple about setting his own ruthless boasts of sanguinary wars by the side of the quietest moralizings of him who deemed 'the chiefest conquest' to be the conquest of piety.

Samudragupta's anxiety to provide for the remembrance of his deeds was not in vain. The record composed by his poet-laureate survives to this day practically complete, and furnishes a detailed contemporary account of the events of the reign, probably superior to anything else of the kind in the multitude of Indian inscriptions. Although, unfortunately, the document is not dated, it may be assigned with approximate accuracy to the year A.D. 360, or a little later, and is thus, apart from its value as history, of great interest as an important Sanskrit composition, partly in verse and partly in prose, of ascertained age and origin.[3] The value as dated literature of the great historical inscriptions, although emphasized by Bühler many years ago, is still, perhaps, not fully recognized by scholars who occupy themselves primarily

[1] Authorities and details are fully discussed in the author's paper, 'The Conquests of Samudra Gupta' (*J. R. A. S.*, 1897, p. 859). A few corrections have been made necessary by subsequent research.

[2] The inscription is not posthumous (Bühler, in *J. R. A. S.*, 1898, p. 386). The pillar stands in the fort at Allāhābād, but not in its original position.

[3] Andrzej Gawrónski (Cracow) points out that the inscription does not mention the *aśvamedha*, as the coins and inscriptions do, and apparently it should be dated in the interval between the return from the south and the celebration of the sacrifice (*Festschrift*, Ernest Windisch, Leipzig, 1914, p. 170).

with the books preserved in libraries.[1] But our concern at present in the elaborate composition of Harishena is with its contents as an historical document, rather than with its place in the evolution of Sanskrit, and the exposition of its importance as a linguistic and literary landmark must be left to specialists.

His various campaigns.

The author of the panegyric classifies his lord's campaigns geographically under four heads: as those directed against eleven kings of the south; nine named kings of Āryāvarta, or the Gangetic plain,[2] besides many others not specified; the chiefs of the wild forest tribes; and the rulers of the frontier kingdoms and republics. He also explains Samudragupta's relation with certain foreign powers, too remote to come within the power of his arm. Although it is at present impossible to identify every one of the countries, kings, and peoples enumerated by the poet, and sundry matters of detail remain to be cleared up by future discovery and investigation, enough is known to enable the historian to form a clear idea of the extent of the dominions and the range of the alliances of the most brilliant of the Gupta emperors. The matter of the record being arranged on literary rather than historical principles, it is not possible to narrate the events of the reign in strict chronological order.

Conquest of Northern India.

But we may feel assured that this Indian Napoleon first turned his arms against the powers nearest him, and that he thoroughly subjugated the Rājas of the Gangetic plain, the wide region now known as Hindustan, before he embarked on his perilous adventures in the remote south. His treatment of the Rājas of the north was drastic; for we are told that they were 'forcibly rooted up', a process which necessarily involved the incorporation of their territories in the dominions of the victor. Among the nine names mentioned,

[1] Bühler's important essay, 'The Indian Inscriptions and the Antiquity of Indian Artificial Poetry,' published in a German periodical about 1889, has been rendered accessible by Prof. V. S. Ghate's English version in *Ind. Ant.*, 1913.

[2] Rājaśekhara (flor. A. D. 900) understood Āryāvarta to include all India, even the extreme south-east, north and west (Introd. to *Kavyamīmāmsa* (Gaikwad's Or. Series, No. 1) Baroda, 1916, p. xxiv).

only one can be recognized with absolute certainty, namely, that of Ganapati Nāga, whose capital was at Padmāvatī, now Padam Pawāyā, 25 miles north-east of the well-known city of Narwar, which is included in the Mahārāja Sindia's dominions.[1]

The greater part of these northern conquests must have been completed, and the subjugated territories absorbed, before Samudragupta ventured to undertake the invasion of the kingdoms of the south; a task which demanded uncommon boldness in design, and masterly powers of organization and execution.

Conquest of South Kosala and forest tribes.

The invader, marching due south from the capital, through Chutiā Nāgpur, directed his first attack against the kingdom of South Kosala in the valley of the Mahānadī, and overthrew its king, Mahendra.[2] Passing on, he subdued all the chiefs of the forest countries, which still retain their ancient wildness, and constitute the tributary states of Orissa and the more backward parts of the Central Provinces. The principal of those chiefs, who bore the appropriate name of Vyāghra Rāja, or the Tiger King, is not otherwise known to history. At this stage of the campaign, the main difficulties must have been those of transport and supply, for the ill-armed forest tribes could not have offered serious military resistance to a well-equipped army.

Conquests in extreme south.

Still advancing southwards, by the east coast road, Samudragupta vanquished the chieftain who held Pishtapura, the ancient capital of Kalinga, now Pithāpuram in the Godāvarī district, as well as the hill-forts of Mahendragiri and Kottūra in Ganjam; King Mantarāja, whose territory lay on the banks of the Kolleru (Colair) lake;[3] the neighbouring king

[1] Padam Pawāyā village lies in the apex of the confluence of the Sindhu and Pāra. The name seems to be derived from Padmāvatī, and local tradition asserts the identity. Nāga coins have been found there; also a palm-leaf capital with an inscription of the first or second century A. C. (*Ann. Rep. A. S. W. Circle*, 1914–15, p. 68; *A. S. R.*, 1915–16, pp. 101–10, Pl. lv–lviii).

[2] North Kosala corresponded roughly with Oudh, north of the Ghāgra river.

[3] For correct interpretation of *Kaurāḷaka* see Kielhorn in *Ep. Ind.*, vol. vi, p. 3. Koṭṭūra (Kothoor of *Indian Atlas*, sheet No. 108) lies twelve miles SSE. from Mahendragiri. The proper rendering of the passage was settled by Kielhorn and Fleet, in 1898. For Pishṭapura see Fleet, *Ind. Ant.*, xxx (1901), p. 26.

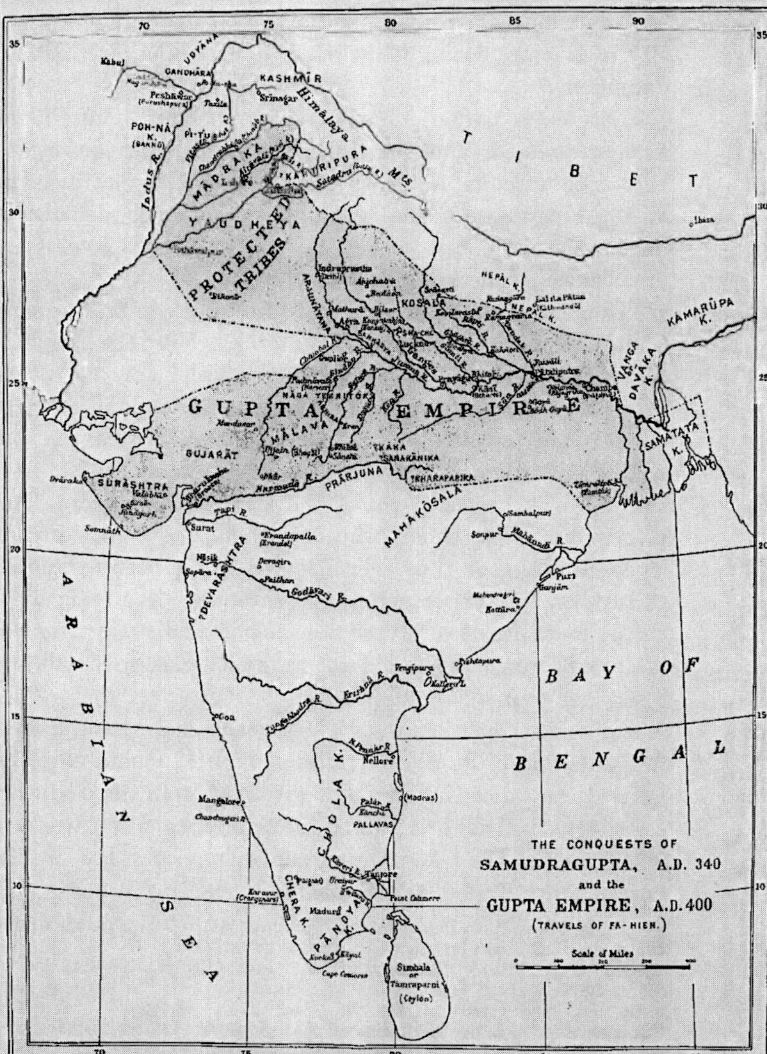

THE CONQUESTS OF SAMUDRAGUPTA, A.D. 340 and the GUPTA EMPIRE, A.D. 400 (TRAVELS OF FA-HIEN.)

of Vengī between the Krishnā and Godāvarī rivers, presumably a Pallava; and Vishnugōpa, the king of Kanchi, or Conjeeveram, to the south-west of Madras, almost certainly a Pallava. Then turning westwards, he subjugated a chieftain, named Ugrasēna, king of Pālakka, a place perhaps situated in the Nellore District.[1]

Return through Khāndēsh.

He returned homewards through the western parts of the Deccan, subduing on his way the kingdom of Devarāshtra, or the modern Mahratta country, and Erandapalla, or Khāndēsh.[2]

A. D. 350.

This wonderful campaign, which involved two or three thousand miles of marching through difficult country, must have occupied about two years at least, and its conclusion may be dated approximately in A.D. 350.

Rich spoils; parallel of Malik Kāfūr.

No attempt was made to effect the permanent annexation of these southern states; the triumphant victor admitting that he only exacted a temporary submission and then withdrew. But beyond doubt he despoiled the rich treasures of the south, and came back laden with golden booty, like the Muhammadan adventurer who performed the same military exploit nearly a thousand years later. Malik Kāfūr, the general of Alā-ud-dīn, Sultan of Delhi, during operations lasting from 1309 to 1311, repeated the performance of Samudragupta, and penetrated even farther south than his Hindu predecessor seems to have done. Malik Kāfūr occupied Madura in April, 1311, and from that base was able to reach Rāmesvarum, or Adam's Bridge, where he built a mosque, which was still standing when Firishta wrote his history in the sixteenth century.[3]

Tributary frontier states.

The enumeration by the courtly panegyrist of the frontier kingdoms and republics whose rulers did homage and paid tribute to the emperor, a title fairly earned by Samudragupta, enables the historian to define the boundaries of his

[1] *Ep. Ind.*, viii, 161.

[2] Fleet, in *J. R. A. S.*, 1898, p. 369.

[3] For conquest of Madura see Elliot, *Hist.* iii, 91. The mosque was repaired by Mujāhid Shah Bāhmani in A. D. 1376. The doubts expressed by Mr. Sewell (*A Forgotten Empire*, p. 42) are not well founded. Mr. Sewell apparently did not remember the occupation of Madura in 1311.

dominions with sufficient accuracy, and to realize the nature of the political divisions of India in the fourth century.

On the eastern side of the continent the tributary kingdoms were Samatata, or the delta of the Brahmaputra ; Kāmarūpa, or Assam ; and Davāka, which seems to have been practically synonymous with Vanga, lying between Karatoya on the west, the Ganges on the south, Meghna on the east, and the Khasi Hills on the north, and including both Dacca and Sunārgāon.[1] Farther west, the mountain kingdom of Nepāl, then, as now, retained its autonomy under the suzerainty of the paramount power, and the direct jurisdiction of the imperial government extended only to the foot of the mountains. The kingdom of Kartripura occupied the lower ranges of the Western Himalayas, including probably Kumāon, Almora, Garhwāl, and Kangra.[2]

Tribal republics.

The Panjāb, Eastern Rājputāna, and Mālwā for the most part were in possession of tribes or clans living under republican, or at any rate oligarchical, institutions.[3] The Yaudhēya tribe occupied both banks of the Sutlaj, while the Mādrakas held the central parts of the Panjāb. The reader may remember that in Alexander's time those regions were similarly occupied by autonomous tribes, then called the Malloi, Kathaioi, and so forth. The Jumna probably formed the north-western frontier of the Gupta empire. The Ārjunāyanas, Mālavas, and Ābhīras were settled in Eastern Rājputāna and Mālwā, and in this direction the river Chambal may be regarded as the imperial boundary. The line next turned in an easterly direction along the territories of minor nations whose position cannot be exactly deter-

[1] *J. & Proc. A. S. B.*, 1910, p. 144.

[2] Fleet suggests that the name may survive in Kartārpur in the Jālandhar district. C. F. Oldham refers to the Katuria Rāj of Kumāon, Garhwāl, and Rōhilkhand (*J. R. A. S.*, 1898, p. 198). See map of the Gupta Empire.

[3] On this subject see K. P. Jayaswal, 'Republics in the Mahābhārata' (*J. O. & B. Res. Soc.*, vol. i, pp. 173–8) ; R. C. Majumdar, *Corporate Life in Ancient India* (Calcutta, Surendra Nath Sen, 1918) ; R. D. Mukharji, *Local Government in Ancient India* (Oxford Univ. Press, 1919) ; and D. R. Bhandarkar's *Carmichael Lectures* for 1918, publ. by the Calcutta University, 1919.

mined, passing probably through Bhopāl, until it struck the Narmadā river, which formed the southern frontier.

Limits of empire.

The dominion under the direct government of Samudragupta in the middle of the fourth century thus comprised all the most populous and fertile countries of Northern India. It extended from the Brahmaputra on the east to the Jumna and Chambal on the west; and from the foot of the Himalayas on the north to the Narmadā on the south.

Beyond these wide limits, the frontier kingdoms of Assam and the Gangetic delta, as well as those on the southern slopes of the Himalayas, and the free tribes of Rājputāna and Mālwā, were attached to the empire by bonds of subordinate alliance; while almost all the kingdoms of the south had been overrun by the emperor's armies and compelled to acknowledge his irresistible might.

Relations with foreign powers.

The empire thus defined was by far the greatest that had been seen in India since the days of Asoka, six centuries before, and its possession naturally entitled Samudragupta to the respect of foreign powers. We are not, therefore, surprised to learn that he maintained diplomatic relations with the foreign Kushān princes of the north-west, whom he grouped together as 'Śaka chiefs', as well as with Ceylon and other distant islands.

Embassies from Ceylon.

Communication between the king of Ceylon and Samudragupta had been established accidentally about A.D. 360. Siri Meghavanna (Meghavarṇa), the Buddhist king of Ceylon, whose reign of twenty-seven years is assigned approximately to the period from A.D. 352 to 379, had sent two monks, one of whom is said to have been his brother, to do homage to the Diamond Throne and visit the monastery built by Asoka to the east of the sacred tree at Bōdh Gayā. The strangers, perhaps by reason of sectarian rancour, met with scant hospitality, and on their return to the island complained to the king that they could not find any place in India where they could stay in comfort. King Meghavarṇa recognized the justice of the complaint, and resolved to remedy the grievance by founding a monastery at which his subjects, when on pilgrimage to the holy places, should find adequate and suitable accommodation. He accordingly dispatched a mission to Samudragupta laden with the gems for which Ceylon has always been renowned, besides other valuable gifts, and requested permission to found a monastery on Indian soil. Samudragupta, flattered at receiving such attentions from a distant power, was pleased to consider the gifts as tribute, and gave the required permission. The envoy returned home, and, after due deliberation, King Meghavarṇa decided to build his monastery near the holy tree. His purpose, solemnly recorded on a copper plate, was carried out by the erection of a splendid convent to the north of the tree. This building, which was three stories in height, included six halls, was adorned with three towers, and surrounded by a strong wall 30 or 40 feet high. The decorations were executed in the richest colours with the highest artistic skill, and the statue of Buddha, cast in gold and silver, was studded with gems. The subsidiary *stūpas*, enshrining relics of Buddha himself, were worthy of the principal edifice. In the seventh century, when Hiuen Tsang visited it, this magnificent establishment was occupied by a thousand monks of the Sthavira school of the Mahāyāna, and afforded ample hospitality to pilgrims from Ceylon. The site is now marked by an extensive mound.[1]

Horse-sacrifice.

It was presumably after his return from the south that Samudragupta determined to celebrate his manifold victories and proclaim the universality of his dominion by reviving the ancient rite of the horse-sacrifice (*aśvamedha*), which had remained long in abeyance, and probably had not been performed in Northern India since the days of Pushyamitra. The ceremony was duly carried out with appropriate

[1] The synchronism of Meghavarṇa with Samudragupta, discovered by Sylvain Lévi from a Chinese work, has been discussed by the author in the paper on Gupta chronology already cited, and in 'The Inscriptions of Mahānāman at Bōdh-Gayā' (*Ind. Ant.*, 1902, p. 192). But Meghavarṇa reigned later than I supposed when those papers were written, A. D. 352 and 379 (transl. *Mahāvaṁśa* (1912), p. xxxix). His true dates may be slightly earlier.

splendour, and accompanied by lavish gifts to Brahmans, comprising, it is said, millions of coins and gold pieces. Specimens of the gold medals struck for this purpose, bearing a suitable legend and the effigy of the doomed horse standing before the altar, have been found in small numbers. Another memorial of the event seems to exist in the rudely carved stone figure of a horse which was found in Northern Oudh, and now stands in the Lucknow Museum with traces of a brief dedicatory inscription incised upon it, apparently referring to Samudragupta.[1]

Personal accomplishments of Samudragupta.

Although the courtly phrases of the official eulogist cannot be accepted without a certain amount of reservation, it is clear that Samudragupta was a ruler of exceptional capacity and unusually varied gifts. The laureate's commemoration of his hero's proficiency in song and music is curiously confirmed by the existence of a few rare gold coins depicting his majesty comfortably seated on a high-backed couch, engaged in playing the Indian lute.[2] The allied art of poetry was also reckoned among the accomplishments of this versatile monarch, who is said to have been reputed a king of poets, and to have composed numerous metrical works worthy of the reputation of a professional author. We are further informed that the king took much delight in the society of the learned, and loved to employ his acute and polished intellect in the study and defence of the sacred scriptures, as well as in the lighter arts of music and poetry. In his youth he extended his royal favour to Vasubandhu, the celebrated Buddhist author. The picture of Samudragupta as painted by his court poet reminds the reader of that of Akbar as depicted by his no less partial biographer, Abu-l Fazl.

Whatever may have been the exact degree of skill attained

[1] The fact that the mutilated inscription—*dda guttassa deyadhaṁma*—is in Prākrit suggests a shade of doubt. All other Gupta inscriptions are in Sanskrit (*J. R. A. S.*, 1893, p. 98, with plate). See Fig. 11 in plate of coins. The horse having been exposed to the weather outside the Lucknow Museum for years, the inscription has disappeared. The image is now inside the building. The inscription was legible when the first edition of this book was published.

[2] Plate of coins, Fig. 10.

by Samudragupta in the practice of the arts which graced his scanty leisure, it is clear that he was endowed with no ordinary powers; and that he was in fact a man of genius, who may fairly claim the title of the Indian Napoleon. Unfortunately, the portraits on his coins are not sufficiently good to give a clear notion of his personal appearance.

Recovery of his history. By a strange irony of fate this great king—warrior, poet, and musician—who conquered nearly all India, and whose alliances extended from the Oxus to Ceylon, was unknown even by name to the historians of India until the publication of this work. His lost fame has been slowly recovered by the minute and laborious study of inscriptions and coins during the last eighty years; and the fact that it is now possible to write a long narrative of the events of his memorable reign is perhaps the most conspicuous illustration of the success gained by patient archaeological research in piecing together the fragments from which alone the chart of the authentic early history of India can be constructed.

c. A. D. 375. The exact year of Samudragupta's death is not known, but he certainly lived to an advanced age, and enjoyed a reign of uninterrupted prosperity for nearly half a century. Before he passed away, he did his best to secure the peaceful transmission of the crown by nominating as his successor, from among many sons,[1] the offspring of his queen, Datta Devī, whom he rightly deemed worthy to inherit a magnificent empire.

Chandra-gupta II, &c. The son thus selected, who probably had been associated as Crown Prince (*yuvarāja*) with his father in the cares of government, assumed the name of his grandfather, in accordance with Hindu custom, and is therefore distinguished in the dynastic list as Chandra-gupta II. He also took the title of Vikramāditya ('Sun of Power'), and has a better claim than any other sovereign to be regarded as the original of the mythical king of that name who figures so largely in Indian legends. The precise date of his accession is not recorded, but it cannot be far removed from A. D. 375; and, pending the discovery of some coin or inscription to

[1] Eraṇ and Bhitarī inscriptions.

settle the matter, that date may be assumed as approximately correct. So far as appears, the succession to the throne was accomplished peacefully without contest, and the new emperor, who must have been a man of mature age at the time of his accession, found himself in a position to undertake the extension of the wide dominion bequeathed to him by his ever-victorious father. He did not renew Samudragupta's southern adventures, preferring to seek room for expansion towards the south-west.[1]

Conquest of Mālwā, Gujarāt, and Kāṭhiāwāṛ.

The greatest military achievement of Chandra-gupta Vikramāditya was his advance to the Arabian Sea through Mālwā and Gujarāt, and his subjugation of the peninsula of Surāshtra or Kāthiāwār, which had been ruled for centuries by the Śaka dynasty, of foreign origin, known to European scholars as the Western Satraps.[2] The campaigns which added those remote provinces to the empire must have occupied several years, and are known to have taken place between A. D. 388 and 401. The year 395 may be assumed as a mean date for the completion of the conquest, which involved the incorporation in the empire of the territory held by the Mālavas and other tribes, who had remained outside the limits of Samudragupta's dominion. The annexation of Surāshtra and Mālwā not only added to the empire provinces of exceptional wealth and fertility, but opened up to the paramount power free access to the ports of the western coast; and thus placed Chandra-gupta II in direct touch with the seaborne commerce with Europe

[1] M. M. Haraprasad Shastri seems to be right in identifying Chandra of the Iron Pillar with Chandravarman, king of Pushkaraṇa, Rājputāna, in the fourth century, who was contemporary with Samudragupta, and was brother of Naravarman (Mandasor inscr. of V. S. 461 = A. D. 404–5). The brothers were kings of Mālwā (*Ep. Ind.*, xii, 317). Pushkaraṇa (Pokharan or Pokurna), in 26° 55′ N. and 71° 55′ E. long., is a well-known town, and in Tod's time was still 'the most wealthy and powerful of the baronies of Mārwāṛ' (*Ind. Ant.*, 1913, pp. 217–19; *Annals of Rajasthan*, reprint (2nd ed., 1873), vol. i, p. 605). The Thākurs of Pokharan retain exceptional privileges reminiscent of their ancient royal rank.

[2] See *The History of Kathiawad from the Earliest Times*, by Capt. H. Wilberforce Bell, London, Heinemann, 1915. For the detailed history of the Western Satraps see the papers by Messrs. Rapson, Bhagwān Lāl Indrajī, and Biddulph, in *J. R. A. S.*, 1890, p. 639; 1899, p. 357.

through Egypt, and brought his court and subjects under the influence of the European ideas which travelled with the goods of the Alexandrian merchants. The foreign influence on the literature, art, and science of the Gupta age will be discussed briefly in the next chapter.

The Western Satraps. The so-called 'Western Satraps' comprise two distinct dynasties, ruling in widely separated territories. The Kshaharāta Satraps of Mahārāshtra, with their capital probably at Nāsik in the Western Ghāts, who had established their power at some time in the first century after Christ, were destroyed by Gautamīputra, an Āndhra king, in or about A. D. 119, their dominions being annexed to the Āndhra monarchy. The second satrapy of the west, founded by the Śaka Chashtana at Ujjain in Mālwā late in the first century after Christ, was immensely extended by Chashtana's grandson, Rudradāman I, who at some date between A. D. 128 and 150, and probably before A. D. 130, conquered from Gautamīputra's son, Pulumāyi II, all or nearly all the territory which Gautamīputra had taken from the Kshaharātas a few years earlier. The power of Rudradāman I was thus established not only over the peninsula of Surāshtra, but also over Mālwā, Cutch (Kachchh), Sind, the Konkan, and other districts—in short, over Western India. The capital of Chashtana and his successors was Ujjain, one of the most ancient cities of India, the principal dépôt for the commerce between the ports of the west and the interior, famous as a seat of learning and civilization, and also notable as the Indian Greenwich from which longitudes were reckoned. The place, which is still a considerable town with many relics of its past greatness, retains its ancient name, and was for a time the capital of Mahārāja Sindia.

Fall of the last satrap. Samudragupta, although not able to undertake the conquest of the west, had received an embassy from the son of another Rudradāman, the satrap Rudrasena, who must have been deeply impressed by the emperor's triumphant march through India. Chandra-gupta II, strong in the possession of the territory and treasure acquired by his father, resolved to crush his western rival, and to annex the valuable provinces which owned the satrap's sway. The motives of an ambitious king in undertaking an aggressive war against a rich neighbour are not far to seek; but we may feel assured that differences of race, creed, and manners supplied the Gupta monarch with special reasons for desiring to suppress the impure foreign rulers of the west. Chandragupta Vikramāditya, although tolerant of Buddhism and Jainism, was himself an orthodox Hindu, specially devoted to the cult of Vishnu, and as such cannot but have experienced peculiar satisfaction in 'violently uprooting' foreign chieftains who probably cared little for caste rules. Whatever his motives may have been, he attacked, dethroned, and slew the satrap Rudrasinha, son of Satyasinha, and annexed his dominions. Scandalous tradition affirmed that 'in his enemy's city the king of the Śakas, while courting another man's wife, was butchered by Chandra-gupta, concealed in his mistress's dress'; [1] but the tale does not look like genuine history. The last notice of the satraps refers to the year A. D. 388, and the incorporation of their dominions in the Gupta empire must have been effected soon after that date.

Character of Chandra-gupta II.

The Gupta kings, excepting the founder of the dynasty, all enjoyed long reigns, like the Moghals in later times. Chandra-gupta Vikramāditya occupied the throne for nearly forty years, and survived until A. D. 413. Little is known concerning his personal character; but the ascertained facts of his career suffice to prove that he was a strong and vigorous ruler, well qualified to govern and augment an extensive empire. He loved sounding titles which proclaimed his martial prowess, and was fond of depicting himself on his coins as engaged in successful personal combat with a lion, after the old Persian fashion.

The capital.

There are indications that Pātaliputra, although it may have been still regarded as the official capital, ceased to be the ordinary residence of the Gupta sovereigns after the completion of the extensive conquests effected by Samudragupta. The Maurya emperors, it is true, had managed to

[1] *Harṣa-carita*, transl. Cowell and Thomas, p. 194.

control a dominion very much larger than that of the Guptas from the ancient imperial city, but, even in their time, its remoteness in the extreme east must have caused inconvenience, and a more central position for the court had obvious advantages. Ajodhya, the legendary abode of the hero Rāma, the ruins of which have supplied materials for the building of the modern city of Fyzabād in Southern Oudh, enjoyed a more favourable situation, and appears to have been at times the head-quarters of the government of both Samudragupta and his son, the latter of whom probably had a mint for copper coins there. There is reason to believe that during the fifth century Ajodhya, rather than Pātaliputra, was the premier city of the Gupta empire.

Kauśāmbī. The Asoka pillar on which Samudragupta recorded the history of his reign is supposed to have been erected originally at the celebrated city of Kausāmbī, which stood on the high road between Ujjain and Northern India, and was no doubt honoured at times by the residence of the monarch.[1] The real capital of an Oriental despotism is the seat of the despot's court for the time being.

Pāṭaliputra. Pātaliputra, however, although necessarily considerably neglected by warrior kings like Samudragupta and Vikramāditya, continued to be a magnificent and populous city throughout the reign of the latter, and apparently was not ruined until the time of the Hun invasion in the sixth century. When the Chinese pilgrim, Hiuen Tsang, lived in the neighbourhood (640), he found the greater part of the ancient site covered by hundreds of ruins. 'The city', he tells us, 'had long been a wilderness', save for a small walled town near the Ganges, with about 1,000 inhabitants. Harsha, when he ruled Northern India as paramount sovereign (612–47), made no attempt to restore the old imperial capital, preferring to make Kanauj, situated between the Ganges and Jumna, the seat of his government. Dharmapāla, the second and, perhaps, the most powerful of the Pāla

[1] For discussion of the site of Kauśāmbī see the author's papers, 'Kauśāmbī and Śrāvasti', in *J. R. A. S.*, 1898, p. 503; and 'Śrāvastī', ibid., 1900, p. 1.

kings of Bengal and Bihar, evidently took some steps to renew the glory of Pātaliputra, because we know that in the thirty-second year of his reign (about A. D. 811) he held his court there. After that glimpse of the old city, we lose sight of it again until 1541, when it had sunk to the rank of 'a small town, dependent on Bihār, which was the seat of government'. Shēr Shah, being impressed by the strategical advantages of the position, then built a fort at the cost of half a million of rupees. 'Bihār from that date was deserted and fell to ruin, while Patna became one of the largest cities of the province.' The prosperity thus restored by the action of Shēr Shah has never been lost.

In 1912, Patna once more became a capital, as the headquarters of the newly constituted Province of Bihār and Orissa. The civil station of Bankipore, which forms a suburb of Patna, stands on part of the site of Pātaliputra.[1]

A. D. 405–11. Fa-hien.

We are fortunate enough to possess in the work of Fa-hien, the earliest Chinese pilgrim, a contemporary account of the administration of Chandra-gupta Vikramāditya, as it appeared to an intelligent foreigner at the beginning of the fifth century. The worthy pilgrim, it is true, was so absorbed in his search for Buddhist books, legends, and miracles that he had little care for the things of this world, and did not trouble even to mention the name of the mighty monarch in whose territories he spent six studious years. But now and then he allowed his pen to note some of the facts of ordinary life, and in more than one passage he has recorded particulars, which, although insufficient to gratify the curiosity of the twentieth century, yet suffice to give a tolerably vivid picture of the state of the country. The picture is a pleasing one on the whole, and proves that Vikramāditya was capable of bestowing on his people the benefits of orderly government in sufficient measure to allow them to grow rich in peace and prosper abundantly.

[1] Watters, *On Yuan Chwang's Travels in India*, ii, 87. Dharmapāla's Khālimpur grant in *Ep. Ind.*, iv, 252. *Tārīkh-i-Dāūdī* in Elliot, *History*, iv, 477.

Splendours of Pāṭaliputra.

On the occasion of his first visit to Pātaliputra the traveller was deeply impressed by the sight of Asoka's palace, which was at that time still in existence, and so cunningly constructed of stone that the work clearly appeared to be beyond the skill of mortal hands, and was believed to have been executed by spirits in the service of the emperor. Near a great *stūpa*, also ascribed to Asoka, stood two monasteries, one occupied by followers of the Mahāyāna, and the other by those of the Hīnayāna sect. The monks resident in both establishments together numbered six or seven hundred, and were so famous for learning that their lectures were frequented by students and inquirers from all quarters. Fa-hien spent three years here studying Sanskrit, and was made happy by obtaining certain works on monastic discipline as taught by various schools, for which he had sought elsewhere in vain. He describes with great admiration the splendid procession of images, carried on some twenty huge cars richly decorated, which annually paraded through the city on the eighth day of the second month, attended by singers and musicians; and notes that similar processions were common in other parts of the country.[1]

Free hospital.

The towns of Magadha were the largest in the Gangetic plain, which Fa-hien calls by the name of Central India or the Middle Kingdom; the people were rich and prosperous, and seemed to him to emulate each other in the practice of virtue. Charitable institutions were numerous; rest-houses for travellers were provided on the highways, and the capital possessed an excellent free hospital endowed by benevolent and educated citizens.

'Hither come', we are told, 'all poor or helpless patients suffering from all kinds of infirmities. They are well taken care of, and a doctor attends them; food and medicine being supplied according to their wants. Thus they are made quite comfortable, and when they are well, they may go away.'[2]

It may be doubted if any equally efficient foundation was

[1] *Travels*, ch. xxvii, in any of the versions.

[2] Ibid., Giles's version.

to be seen elsewhere in the world at that date; and its existence, anticipating the deeds of modern Christian charity, speaks well both for the character of the citizens who endowed it, and for the genius of the great Asoka, whose teaching still bore such wholesome fruit many centuries after his decease.[1]

Buddhism. In the course of a journey of some 500 miles from the Indus to Mathurā on the Jumna, Fa-hien passed a succession of Buddhist monasteries tenanted by thousands of monks; and in the neighbourhood of Mathurā found twenty of these buildings occupied by three thousand residents. Buddhism was growing in favour in this part of the country.[2]

Prosperity of Mālwā. The region to the south of Mathurā, that is to say, Mālwā, specially excited the admiration of the traveller; who was delighted alike with the natural advantages of the country, the disposition of the people, and the moderation of the government. The climate seemed to him very agreeable, being temperate, and free from the discomforts of frost and snow with which he was familiar at home and in the course of his journey. The large population lived happily under a sensible government which did not worry. With a glance at Chinese institutions, Fa-hien congratulates the Indians that 'they have not to register their households, or attend to any magistrates and rules'. They were not troubled with passport regulations, or, as the pilgrim bluntly puts it: 'Those who want to go away, may go; those who want to stop, may stop.' The administration of the criminal law seemed to him mild in comparison with the Chinese system. Most crimes were punished only by fines, varying

[1] Sir H. Burdett (*Encycl. Brit.*, 11th ed., s.v. Hospitals) states that in Christian days no establishments for the relief of the sick were founded until the reign of Constantine (A. D. 306–37). Late in the fourth century Basil founded a leper hospital at Caesarea, and St. Chrysostom established a hospital at Constantinople. A law of Justinian (A. D. 527–62) recognized *nosocomia* or hospitals among ecclesiastical institutions. The Maison Dieu or Hôtel Dieu of Paris is sometimes alleged to be the oldest European hospital. It dates from the seventh century (Florence Nightingale in *Chambers's Encycl.*, 1904).

[2] *Travels*, ch. xvi. The 'temples' and 'priests' apparently were Buddhist. The versions of this chapter differ considerably: those of Legge and Giles have been used in the text.

in amount according to the gravity of the offence, and capital punishment would seem to have been unknown. Persons guilty of repeated rebellion, an expression which probably includes brigandage, suffered amputation of the right hand; but such a penalty was exceptional, and judicial torture was not practised. The revenue was mainly derived from the rents of the crown lands, and the royal officers, being provided with fixed salaries, had no occasion to live on the people.

Buddhist rule of life.

The Buddhist rule of life was generally observed. 'Throughout the country', we are told, 'no one kills any living thing, or drinks wine, or eats onions or garlic[1] . . . they do not keep pigs or fowls, there are no dealings in cattle, no butchers' shops or distilleries in their market-places.' The Chandāla, or outcaste tribes, who dwelt apart like lepers, and were required when entering a city or bazaar to strike a piece of wood as a warning of their approach, in order that other folk might not be polluted by contact with them,[2] were the only offenders against the laws of piety (*dharma*), and the only hunters, fishermen, and butchers. Cowrie shells formed the ordinary currency.[3] The Buddhist monasteries were liberally endowed by royal grants, and the monks received alms without stint—houses, beds, mattresses, food, and clothes were never lacking to them wherever they might go.

Good government.

These particulars, as collected and narrated by the earliest Chinese traveller in India, permit of no doubt that the

[1] Onions and garlic are regarded as impure by many castes. Onions, it is alleged, are supposed when cut to resemble flesh. Garlic, perhaps, was originally condemned as being a foreign innovation. Gopāditya, an ancient king of Kashmīr, punished Brahmans who ate garlic (Stein, transl. *Rājat.*, Bk. i, 342). Possibly the prohibition rests on deeper reasons, as expressed in Jain philosophy. 'Of course, onions, potatoes and all roots, being inhabited by more than one *jīva*, must never be eaten' (Stevenson, *The Heart of Jainism*, 1915, p. 213).

[2] 'Beyond the walls the outcastes dwell,
'Tis worse than death to touch such men.' (Gover, *Folk-Songs of Southern India*, p. 58).

[3] This statement must not be pressed to mean that coins did not exist. Chandra-gupta Vikramāditya coined freely in gold, as well as sparingly in silver and bronze or copper. His archer type gold coins may be described as being common.

dominions of Chandra-gupta Vikramâditya were well governed; the authorities interfering as little as possible with the subject, and leaving him free to prosper and grow rich in his own way. The devout pilgrim pursued his Sanskrit studies for three years at Pātaliputra, and for two years at the port of Tāmralipti (Tamlūk), without let or hindrance, and it is clear that the roads were safe for travellers.[1] Fa-hien never has occasion to complain of being stripped by brigands, a misfortune which befell his successor Hiuen Tsang in the seventh century more than once. Probably India has never been governed better, after the Oriental manner, than it was during the reign of Vikramāditya. The government did not attempt to do too much; but let the people alone, and was accordingly popular. The merciful teachings of Buddhism influenced the lives of all classes, except the most degraded; while, inasmuch as the sovereign was a Brahmanical Hindu, the tendency to the harassing kind of persecution, which a Buddhist or Jain government is apt to display, was kept in check, and liberty of conscience was assured. Fa-hien, as a pious devotee, necessarily saw everything through Buddhist spectacles, but it is evident that, with a Brahmanical supreme government, Hinduism of the orthodox kind must have been far more prominent than his account would lead the reader to suppose, and sacrifices must have been permitted. In fact, the Brahmanical reaction against Buddhism had begun at a time considerably earlier than that of Fa-hien's travels; and Indian Buddhism was already upon the downward path, although the pilgrim could not discern the signs of decadence.

Certain localities unprosperous.

While the general prosperity and tranquillity of the empire under the rule of Chandra-gupta Vikramāditya are abundantly proved by the express testimony of Fa-hien, and by his unobstructed movements in all directions during many years, certain districts did not share in the general well-being, and had retrograded in population and wealth.

[1] *Travels*, chh. xxxvi, xxxvii, Tamlūk, in the Midnapur District of Bengal, is now some 60 miles from the sea.

The city of Gayā, we are informed, was empty and desolate; the holy places of Bōdh-Gayā, 6 miles to the south, were surrounded by jungle; and an extensive tract of country near the foot of the mountains, which had been the seat of a large population in the fifth century B. C., was now sparsely inhabited. The great city of Srāvastī, on the upper course of the Rāptī, was occupied by only two hundred families; and the holy towns of Kapilavastu and Kusinagara were waste and deserted, save for a scanty remnant of monks and their lay attendants, who clung to the sacred spots, and derived a meagre subsistence from the alms of rare pilgrims. The causes of this decay are unknown.[1]

A. D. 413. Kumāragupta I, acc.

A son of Vikramāditya by one of his queens named Dhruva Devī ascended the throne as a young man in A. D. 413, and reigned for more than forty years. He is known to history as Kumāragupta I, in order to distinguish him from his great-grandson of the same name. The events of this king's reign are not known in detail, but the distribution of the numerous contemporary inscriptions and coins permits of no doubt that during the greater part of his unusually prolonged rule the empire suffered no diminution.[2] On the contrary, it probably gained certain additions, for Kumāra, like his grandfather, celebrated the horse-sacrifice as an assertion of his paramount sovereignty; and it is not likely that he would have indulged in this vaunt unless to some extent justified by successful warfare. But the extant records furnish no information concerning specific events, beyond the fact that at the close of his reign, that is to say, in the middle of the fifth century, Kumāra's dominions suffered severely from the irruption of the Hun

[1] *Travels*, chh. xx, xxii, xxiv, xxxi.

[2] The only definitely dated political event of Kumāragupta's reign which I can specify is the arrival in China in the year A. D. 428, of an embassy sent by a Rāja named Yue-ai, 'Moon-loved' (? Chandrapriya), who was lord of the Ka-p'i-li country, which may be identified, as proposed by Lieut.-Col. A. Wilson, with the Khasia Hills region to the west of the Kapili river in Assam. If this be correct, Yue-ai is to be interpreted as a phonetic transcript of the common Khasia name U-Ai, to which the Chinese author assigned a meaning in his own language. See Watters, *J. R. A. S.*, 1898, p. 540.

hordes, who had burst through the north-western passes, and spread in a destructive flood all over Northern India. Before entering upon the discussion of the Hun invasion and the consequent break-up of the Gupta empire, it is desirable to pause, in order to record a few brief observations on the significance of the rule of the great Gupta sovereigns in the evolution of Indian language, literature, art, science, and religion.[1]

[1] See R. G. Bhandarkar's brilliant essay, *A Peep into the Early History of India from the Foundation of the Maurya Dynasty to the Downfall of the Imperial Gupta Dynasty* (322 B. C.–*c.* A. D. 500), Bombay, 1900; reprinted from the *J. Bo. R. A. S.* In spite of an untenable theory of the Kushān chronology, that paper is the best short account of the early history of India which has yet appeared.

CHAPTER XII

THE GUPTA EMPIRE (CONTINUED); AND THE WHITE HUNS

FROM A. D. 455 TO 606

Prevalence of Buddhism from 200 B.C. to A. D. 200.

THE general prevalence of Buddhism in Northern India, including Kashmīr, Afghanistan, and Suwāt, during the two centuries immediately preceding and the two next following the Christian era, is simply attested by the numerous remains of Buddhist monuments erected during that period, and a multitude of inscriptions, which are almost all either Buddhist or Jain. The Jain cult, which was closely related to the Buddhist, does not appear to have gained very wide popularity, although it was practised with great devotion at certain localities, of which Mathurā was one.

Hinduism not extinct.

But the orthodox Hindu worship, conducted under the guidance of Brahmans, and associated with sacrificial rites abhorrent to Jain and Buddhist sentiment, had never become extinct, and had at all times retained a large share of both popular and royal favour. Kadphises II, the Kushān conqueror, was himself conquered by captive India, and adopted with such zeal the worship of Siva as practised by his new subjects that he constantly placed the image of that Indian god upon his coins, and described himself as his devotee. Many other facts concur to prove the continued worship of the old Hindu gods during the period in which Buddhism unquestionably was the most popular and generally received creed.

Religion of the foreign kings.

In some respects, Buddhism in its Mahāyāna form was better fitted than the Brahmanical system to attract the reverence of casteless foreign chieftains; and it would not be unreasonable to expect that they should have shown a decided tendency to favour Buddhism rather than Brahmanism ; but the facts do not indicate any clearly marked general preference for the Buddhist creed on the part of the foreigners. The only distinctively Buddhist coins are the few rare pieces of that kind struck by Kanishka, who undoubtedly, in his later years, liberally patronized the ecclesiastics of the Buddhist church, as did his successor Huvishka ; but the next king, Vāsudeva, reverted to the devotion for Siva, as displayed by Kadphises II. So the later Śaka satraps of Surāshtra seem to have inclined personally much more to the Brahmanical than to the Buddhist cult, and they certainly bestowed their patronage upon the Sanskrit of the Brahmans rather than upon the vernacular literature.

Connexion between Mahāyāna and Hinduism.

The development of the Mahāyāna school of Buddhism, which became prominent and fashionable from the time of Kanishka, about the beginning of the second century, was in itself a testimony to the reviving power of Brahmanical Hinduism. The newer form of Buddhism had much in common with the older Hinduism, and the relation is so close that even an expert often feels a difficulty in deciding to which system a particular image should be assigned.

Revival of Sanskrit.

Brahmanical Hinduism was the religion of the pundits, whose sacred language was Sanskrit, a highly artificial literary modification of a vernacular speech of the Panjāb. As the influence of the pundits upon prince and peasant waxed greater in matters of religion and social observance, the use of their special vehicle of expression became more widely diffused, and gradually superseded the vernacular in all documents of a formal or official character. In the third century B. C. Asoka had been content to address his commands to his people in language easy to be understood by the vulgar ; but, in the middle of the second century after Christ, the satrap Rudradāman felt that his achievements could be adequately commemorated only in elaborate Sanskrit. It is impossible to go more deeply into the subject in these pages, and it must suffice to observe that the revival of the Brahmanical religion was accompanied by the diffusion and extension of Sanskrit, the sacred language of the Brahmans.[1]

The Hindu reaction in Gupta period.

Whatever may have been the causes, the fact is abundantly established that the restoration of the Brahmanical religion to popular favour, and the associated revival of the Sanskrit language, became noticeable in the second century, were fostered by the satraps of Gujarāt and Surāshtra during the third, and made a success by the Gupta emperors in the fourth and fifth centuries. These princes, although perfectly tolerant of both Buddhism and Jainism, and in at least three cases personally interested in the former, were themselves beyond question officially orthodox Hindus, usually guided by Brahman advisers, and skilled in Sanskrit, the language of the pundits.[2] An early stage in the reaction against Buddhist condemnation of sacrifice had been marked by Pushyamitra's celebration of the horse-sacrifice towards the close of the second century. In the fourth, Samudragupta revived the same ancient rite with added splendour; and in the fifth, his grandson repeated the solemnity. Without going further into detail, the matter may be summed up in the remark that coins, inscriptions, and monuments agree in furnishing abundant evidence of the recrudescence during the Gupta period of Brahmanical Hinduism at the expense of Buddhism, and of the favour shown by the ruling powers to 'classical' Sanskrit at the expense of the more popular literary dialects, which had enjoyed the patronage of the Āndhra kings.

Vikramāditya and Kālidāsa.

It is probable that the popular legend of Rāja Bikram of Ujjain, the supposed founder of the Vikrama era dating

[1] The reader who desires to pursue the subject should consult Professor Otto Franke's book, *Pāli und Sanskrit, in ihrem historischen und geographischen Verhältniss auf Grund der Inschriften und Münzen*, Strassburg, 1903.

[2] The three cases referred to are those of Chandra-gupta I and Samudragupta, the patrons of Vasubandhu, and Naragupta Bālāditya, who erected buildings at Nālandā and was regarded by Hiuen Tsang as an earnest Buddhist. Chandra-gupta II must have been specially religious. His minister in the Vdayagiri inscription (Fleet, *G. I.*, No. 6, p. 35) describes him as *rājādhirājarshi*, a combination of King and Rishi. So Rājā Bhīmasena in A. D. 601 describes himself as belonging to a family like, or equal to (*tulya*) the royal sages—*rājādhirājarshi*—*scil.* the Guptas (Hīra Lāl, *Descr. List*, p. 83).

from 58 B. C., has been coloured by indistinct memories of the glories of Chandra-gupta II Vikramāditya, who certainly conquered Ujjain towards the close of the fourth century of the Christian era. Tradition associates nine gems of Sanskrit literature with Rāja Bikram, the most resplendent of the nine being Kālidāsa, who is admitted by all critics to be the prince of Sanskrit poets and dramatists. In my judgement it is now established that Kālidāsa lived and wrote in the fifth century, his literary activity extending over a long period, probably not less than thirty years. Although it is difficult to fix the dates of the great poet's career with precision, it appears to be probable that he began to write either late in the reign of Chandra-gupta II or early in the reign of Kumāragupta I. The traditional association of his name with Rāja Bikram of Ujjain is thus justified by sober criticism.[1]

[1] Kālidāsa shows such intimate knowledge of small rivers and other details in Western Mālwā that in all probability he must have been a native of Mandasor (Dāsapura) or of some place in the immediate neighbourhood, and would thus have been brought into close touch with the court of Ujjain and the active life which centred in that capital (M. M. Haraparshad Shastri in *J. B. & O. R. Soc.*, vol. i, pp. 197–212).

The date of Kālidāsa has been the subject during recent years of much discussion, summed up, until November, 1911, by B. Liebich in his paper entitled 'Das Datum des Kālidāsa' (*Indogerm. Forschungen*, Strassburg, Band xxxi (1912), pp. 198–203). Among earlier references are: Macdonell, *Hist. of Sanskrit Liter.* (1900), p. 324, where Kālidāsa is assigned to the beginning of the fifth century; Keith (*J. R. A. S.*, 1909, pp. 433–9) who places the poet in the reign of Chandra-gupta II, though the mention of the Hūnas in *Raghuvaṁśa* iv makes it difficult to assign that work to a date so early. See *J. R. A. S.*, 1909, pp. 731–9; and *Ind. Ant.*, 1912, p. 265. The theory of Hoernle (*J. R. A. S.*, 1909, p. 112), which places Kālidāsa's activity in the first half of the sixth century, has no defenders, and seems to me to rest upon erroneous premises. It is not unlikely that the early descriptive poems of Kālidāsa, namely, the *Ṛitusamhāra* and the *Meghadūta*, may have been composed before A. D. 413, that is to say, while Chandra-gupta II was on the throne, but I am inclined to regard the reign of Kumāragupta I (413–55) as the time during which the poet's later works were composed, and it seems possible, or even probable, that the whole of his literary career fell within the limits of that reign. It is also possible that he may have continued writing after the accession of Skandagupta. But I have no doubt that he flourished in the fifth century during the time when the Gupta power was at its height. For the order of composition of Kālidāsa's works, see M. M. Haraparshad Shastri in *J. B. O. Res. Soc.*, vol. ii, pp. 179–89.

Intellectual activity of the Gupta period.

The Gupta period, taken in a wide sense as extending from about A. D. 300 to 650, and meaning more particularly the fourth and fifth centuries, was a time of exceptional intellectual activity in many fields—a time not unworthy of comparison with the Elizabethan and Stuart period in England.[1] In India all the lesser lights are outshone by the brilliancy of Kālidāsa, as in England all the smaller authors are overshadowed by Shakespeare. But, as the Elizabethan literature would still be rich even if Shakespeare had not written, so, in India, if Kālidāsa's works had not survived, enough of other men's writings would remain to distinguish his age as extraordinarily fertile in literary achievement.

Literature.

The remarkable drama, entitled *The Little Clay Cart*, one of the most interesting of Indian plays, is now believed to date from the fifth or sixth century, if not from an earlier time. Another equally remarkable play, the *Mudrā-Rākshasa*, which tells the story of the usurpation of the crown by Chandragupta Maurya, probably is at least quite as old. Professor Hillebrandt is inclined to assign its composition to the reign of Chandra-gupta II (*c.* A. D. 400).

The *Vāyu Purāna*, one of the oldest of the eighteen Purānas, clearly should be attributed in its existing form to the first half of the fourth century, and the Laws of Manu, as we now know the book, may be dated from about the beginning of the Gupta period. Without going further into detail, and so trespassing on the domain of the historian of Sanskrit literature, it may suffice to cite Professor R. G. Bhandarkar's observation that the period was distinguished by 'a general literary impulse', the effects of which were visible in poetry, as well as in law books and many other forms of literature.

Science.

In the field of mathematical and astronomical science the Gupta age is adorned by the illustrious names of Āryabhata (born A. D. 476) and Varāhamihira (died A. D. 587). Mr. Kaye, a competent authority, holds that 'the period when

[1] 'The Gupta period is in the annals of classical India almost what the Periclean age is in the history of Greece' (Barnett, *J. R. A. S.*, 1917, p. 417).

mathematics flourished in India commenced about A. D. 400 and ended about A. D. 650, after which deterioration set in.' [1]

Art; architecture.

We have seen how Samudragupta practised and encouraged music. The other arts, too, shared the favour of the Gupta kings and prospered under their intelligent patronage. The accident that nearly the whole of the Gupta empire was repeatedly overrun and permanently occupied by Muslim armies, which rarely spared a Hindu building, accounts for the destruction of almost all large edifices of the Gupta age. But the researches of recent years have disclosed abundant evidence of the former existence of numerous magnificent buildings, both Buddhist and Brahmanical, which had been erected in the fifth and sixth centuries. A few specimens of architectural compositions on a considerable scale may still be seen in out-of-the-way places, which lay apart from the track of the hosts of Islam, and the surviving miniature shrines of the period are fairly numerous. Enough is known to justify the assertion that the art of architecture was practised on a large scale with eminent success.

Sculpture, painting, and die-cutting.

The allied art of sculpture, usually cultivated in India as an accessory to architecture, attained a degree of perfection not recognized until recently. The best examples, indeed, are so good that they may fairly claim the highest rank among the efforts of Indian sculptors. Painting, as exemplified by some of the best frescoes at Ajantā and the cognate works at Sīgiriya in Ceylon (A. D. 479–97), was practised with equal, or, perhaps, greater success. Certain gold Gupta coins are the only pieces issued by Hindu kings entitled to rank as works of art.

Causes of the activity of the Gupta period.

It is apparent, therefore, that the rule of the able and long-lived monarchs of the Gupta dynasty coincided with an extraordinary outburst of intellectual activity of all

[1] For further information see G. R. Kaye, *Indian Mathematics*, Thacker, Spink & Co., Calcutta, 1915. H. P. Sāstri points out that Indian astronomers were in the habit of recording the date of their birth, and he shows good reason for believing that Varāhamihira indicates, without expressly affirming, A. D. 505 to be the date of his birth (*J. & Proc. A. S. B.*, 1912, pp. 275–8).

kinds. The personal patronage of the kings no doubt had much effect, but deeper causes must have been at work to produce such results. Experience proves that the contact or collision of diverse modes of civilization is the most potent stimulus to intellectual and artistic progress, and, in my opinion, the eminent achievements of the Gupta period are mainly due to such contact with foreign civilizations, both on the east and on the west. The evidence as to the constant interchange of communications with China is abundant, and although the external testimony to intercourse with the Roman empire is less copious, the fact of such intercourse is indisputable. The conquest of Mālwā and Surāshtra or Kāthiāwār by Chandra-gupta II Vikramāditya, towards the close of the fourth century, opened up ways of communication between Upper India and western lands which gave facilities for the reception of European ideas. The influence of the Alexandrian schools on the astronomy of Āryabhata is undoubted, and the imitation of Roman coins by Gupta kings is equally obvious. In art and literature the proof of the action of foreign influence is necessarily more difficult, but in my judgement the reality of that action is well established. It is difficult, for instance, to deny the relationship between the sculpture of the Sleeping Vishnu at Deogarh and the class of Graeco-Roman works represented by the Endymion at Stockholm. It is impossible to pursue the subject further in this place, but the references in the note will enable any inquirer interested to follow up the cumulative proofs that the remarkable intellectual and artistic output of the Gupta period was produced in large measure by reason of the contact between the civilization of India and that of the Roman empire. Some critics have thought that Chinese ideas may be traced in the Ajantā frescoes, and they may be right.[1]

[1] The date of the *Little Clay Cart* (*Mṛich-chhakaṭikā*) is unknown. Prof. S. Lévi guesses that it may be posterior to Kālidāsa (*Théâtre Indien*, p. 208). I am disposed to follow older authors in assigning an earlier date. See transl. by Ryder in Harvard Or. Ser. Concerning the date of the *Mudrā-Rākshasa*, see Haas, ed. and transl., p. 39 (Columbia Univ. Press, N.Y., 1912); Hillebrandt, 'Ueber das *Kauṭilīya-śāstra* und Verwandtes' (*86. Jahresber. der*

Comparison of the notes recorded by Fa-hien, the first Chinese pilgrim, at the beginning of the fifth, and by his great successor, Hiuen Tsang, in the first half of the seventh century, proves beyond question that Buddhism suffered a gradual decay during the Gupta period. But that decay was hardly discernible by people living in those ages, who saw a powerful and wealthy monastic order continuously wielding immense influence and housed in splendid convents. The discovery of the numerous remains of magnificent Buddhist monasteries of Gupta age has been one of the surprises of archaeological research. The Gupta kings, although officially Brahmanical Hindus with a special devotion to Vishnu, followed the usual practice of ancient India in looking with a favourable eye on all varieties of Indian religion. The first Chandra-gupta, who had been a follower of the Sānkhya philosophy, afterwards listened with conviction to the arguments of Vasubandhu, the Buddhist sage, to whose instruction he commended his son and heir, Samudragupta. At a later time, Naragupta Bālāditya, who erected handsome buildings at Nālandā, the Religion.

Schlesischen Gesellschaft für vaterl. Cultur, July, 1908, p. 29; Tawney in *J. R. A. S.*, 1908, p. 910; 1909, p. 147. For the age of the Purāṇas see detailed discussion in Mr. Pargiter's book, *The Dynasties of the Kali Age*, and App. A, *ante*, p. 22.

Mr. Kaye's observations on the relations between Indian and Greek mathematical science will be found in *J. R. A. S.*, 1910, p. 759; *J. & Proc. A. S. B.*, 1911, p. 813; and in 'Influence Grecque dans le Développement des Mathématiques Hindoues' (*Scientia*, vol. xxv, 1919, Bologna).

For questions concerning art and architecture, see *A History of Fine Art in India and Ceylon*, and the references given in that work; and in the author's paper, 'Indian Sculpture in the Gupta Period' (*Ostas. Zeitschr.*, April-Juni, 1914).

The references to communications between India and China are collected in Duff, *The Chronology of India*, 1899. The Rāja of the Ka-p'i-li country sent an embassy in A. D. 428 (Watters, *J. R. A. S.*, 1898, p. 540). Embassies, some probably only commercial ventures, number six from 502 to 515. There were also many journeys of pilgrims and missionaries.

For communications with the Roman empire, see Priaulx, *Indian Embassies to Rome* (bound with Apollonius of Tyana), Quaritch, 1873; Reinaud, *Relations politiques et commerciales de l'Empire Romain avec l'Asie orientale*; and Duff, op. cit.

The Roman influence on the Gupta coinage is discussed in my 'Coinage of the Early or Imperial Gupta dynasty', *J. R. A. S.*, 1889. See also Sewell, 'Roman Coins found in India', ibid., 1904, pp. 591–637. The Gupta Buddhist monasteries at Sārnāth, Kasiā, &c., are described in the *Annual Reports* of the Archaeol. Survey since 1902–3.

ecclesiastical capital of the church, was regarded by Hiuen Tsang as having been a fervent Buddhist.[1]

The Pushyamitra war.

The golden age of the Guptas comprised a period of a century and a quarter (A. D. 330–455), covered by three reigns of exceptional length. The death of Kumāragupta I, which can be fixed definitely as having occurred early in 455, marks the beginning of the decline and fall of the empire. Even before his death, his kingdom had become involved, about the year 450, in serious distress by a war with a rich and powerful nation named Pushyamitra, otherwise almost unknown to history.[2] The imperial armies were defeated, and the shock of military disaster had endangered the stability of the dynasty, which was 'tottering' to its fall, when the energy and ability of Skandagupta, the Crown Prince, restored the fortunes of his family by effecting the overthrow of the enemy. A small detail recorded by the contemporary document indicates the severity of the struggle; for we are told that the heir-apparent, while preparing to retrieve the calamities of his house, was obliged to spend a night sleeping on the bare ground.

Defeat of the Huns.

When Skandagupta came to the throne, in the spring of 455, he encountered a sea of troubles. The Pushyamitra danger had been averted, but one more formidable closely followed it, an irruption of the savage Huns, who had poured down from the steppes of Central Asia through the north-western passes, and carried devastation over the smiling plains and crowded cities of India. Skandagupta, who probably was a man of mature years and ripe experience, proved equal to the need, and inflicted upon the barbarians a defeat so decisive that India was saved for a time. His mother still lived, and to her the hero hastened

[1] See Appendix N, 'Vasubandhu and the Guptas.'

[2] Conjectured by Fleet (*Ind. Ant.* xviii, 228) to belong to the region of the Narmadā; but, more probably, in the north. Hoernle (*J. R. A. S.*, 1909, p. 126) plausibly identifies the Pushyamitras with the Maitrakas under Bhatārka, who founded the Valabhī dynasty. The Purāṇas mention Pushyamitras and Paṭumitras among the miscellaneous dynasties, apparently foreign, who are enumerated just before the passage relating to the Guptas (Pargiter, *Dynasties of the Kali Age*, p. 73).

with the news of his victory, 'just as Krishna, when he had slain his enemies, betook himself to his mother Dēvakī.' Having thus paid his duty to his living parent, the king sought to enhance the religious merit of his deceased father by the erection of a pillar of victory, surmounted by a statue of the god Vishnu, and inscribed with an account of the delivery of his country from barbarian tyranny through the protection of the gods.[1]

The western provinces.

It is evident that this great victory over the Huns must have been gained at the very beginning of the new reign; because another inscription, executed in the year 458, recites Skandagupta's defeat of the barbarians, and recognizes his undisputed possession of the peninsula of Surāshtra (Kāthiāwār), at the western extremity of the empire. The king had appointed as viceroy of the west an officer named Parnadatta, the possessor of all the virtues, according to the official poet; and the viceroy gave the responsible post of governor of the capital city, Jūnāgarh, to his own son, who distinguished his tenure of office by rebuilding the ancient embankment of the lake under the Girnār hill, which had again burst with disastrous results in the year of Skandagupta's accession. The benevolent work was completed in the following year, and consecrated a year later by the erection of a costly temple of Vishnu.[2]

The eastern provinces.

The dedication three years afterwards by a private Jain donor of a sculptured column at a village in the east of the Gorakhpur district, distant about 90 miles from Patna, testifies to the fact that Skandagupta's rule at this early period of his reign included the eastern as well as the western provinces.[3]

The central provinces.

Five years later, in the year 465, the dedication of a temple to the Sun, in the country between the Ganges and Jumna

[1] The column still stands at Bhitarī, in the Ghāzīpur District, to the east of Benares, but the statue has disappeared (Cunningham, *Archaeol. Rep.*, vol. i, pl. xxix). The inscription on the column, which records the events related in the text, has been edited and translated by Fleet (*Gupta Inscriptions*, No. 13). The allusion to the Kṛishna legend is interesting. See *J. R. A. S.*, 1907, p. 976.

[2] Ibid., No. 14; *ante*, p. 140.

[3] Ibid., No. 15, the Kahāon inscription.

now known as the Bulandshahr District, made by a pious Brahman in the reign of Skandagupta, described in the customary language as 'augmenting and victorious', indicates that the central portion of the empire also enjoyed a settled government.[1] The conclusion therefore is legitimate that the victory over the barbarian invaders was gained at the beginning of the reign, and was sufficiently decisive to secure the general tranquillity of all parts of the empire for a considerable number of years.

c. A. D. 465–70. Renewed Hun invasion.

But, about A. D. 465, a fresh swarm of nomads poured across the frontier, and occupied Gandhāra, or the north-western Panjāb, where a 'cruel and vindictive' chieftain usurped the throne of the Kushāns, and 'practised the most barbarous atrocities'.[2] A little later, about 470, the Huns advanced into the interior, and again attacked Skandagupta in the heart of his dominions. He was unable to continue the successful resistance which he had offered in the earlier days of his rule, and was forced at last to succumb to the repeated attacks of the foreigners; who were, no doubt, constantly recruited by fresh hordes eager for the plunder of India.

Debasement of the currency.

The financial distress of Skandagupta's administration is plainly indicated by the abrupt debasement of the coinage in his latter years. The gold coins of his early and prosperous days agree in both weight and fineness with those of his ancestors, but the later issues, while increased in gross weight, so as to suit the ancient Hindu standard of the *suvarṇa*, exhibit a decline in the amount of pure gold in each piece from 108 to 73 grains.[3] This marked lowering of the purity of the currency, which was accompanied by a corresponding degradation in the design and execution of

[1] Ibid., No. 16.

[2] Sung-yun or Song Yun, Chinese pilgrim, A. D. 520, in Beal, *Records*, vol. i, p. c, and Chavannes's revised version (Hanoi, 1903). But the name 'Laelih', given to this chieftain by Beal, who has been copied by Cunningham and many other writers, is purely fictitious, and due to a misreading of the Turkish title *tégin* (Chavannes, *Les Turcs Occidentaux*, p. 225 note).

[3] The earlier Gupta coins, like the Kushān, are Roman *aurei* in weight and to some extent in design. The later pieces are Hindu *suvarṇas*, intended to weigh about 146 grains (9½ grammes) each, and are coarse in device and execution.

the dies, evidently was caused by the difficulty which the treasury experienced in meeting the cost of the Hun war.

The death of Skandagupta, who assumed the title Vikramāditya like so many Indian kings, may be assumed to have occurred about the year 467. When he passed away, the empire perished, but the dynasty remained, and was continued in the eastern provinces for several generations. Skanda left no heir male capable of undertaking the cares of government in a time of such stress, and was accordingly succeeded on the throne of Magadha and the adjacent districts by his brother, Puragupta, the son of Kumāragupta I by Queen Ānanda.[1]

c. A. D. 467. Puragupta, acc.

This prince, whose reign in Magadha possibly synchronized with that of Skandagupta, survived his brother for a very brief period. The only event which can be assigned to his reign is a bold attempt to restore the purity of the coinage. The rare gold coins, bearing on the reverse the title Prakāsāditya, which are generally ascribed to Puragupta, although retaining the gross weight of the heavy *suvarṇa*, contain each 121 grains of pure gold, and are thus equal in value to the *aurei* of Augustus, and superior in intrinsic value to the best Kushān or early Gupta coins.[2]

Reform of currency.

Puragupta was succeeded, about A. D. 467, by his son Narasimhagupta, who gave public proof of his partiality for Buddhism by building at Nālandā, in Magadha, the principal seat of Buddhist learning in Northern India, a brick temple more than 300 feet high, according to Hiuen Tsang, which was remarkable for the delicacy of its decorations and the lavish use of gold and gems in its furniture.[3]

c. A. D. 467 to 473. Narasiṁhagupta Bālāditya.

[1] R. D. Banerji ('The Chronology of the late Imperial Guptas', *Annals of Bhandarkar Institute*, vol. i, pt. i, 1919) believes that Puragupta set himself up as a rival in Magadha, the home province of the Guptas, during Skandagupta's absence at the time of the Hun invasion, and that Puragupta died about the same date, or very shortly after, Skandagupta.

[2] An admitted difficulty in reconciling the testimony of the inscription on the Bhitarī seal (*J. A. S. B.*, vol. lviii, part i, pp. 84–105) with that of other records is best solved in the manner stated in the text. The absence of Skandagupta's name on the seal is accepted by R. D. Banerji (ibid.) as proof that he and his brother Puragupta were at enmity. For assays of the gold coins see Cunningham, *Coins of Med. India*, p. 16.

[3] Chavannes, *Religieux émin-*

The vigorous and successful action taken by Bālāditya to resist the tyranny of the Huns will be described presently.

C. A. D. 473. Kumāragupta II.

Narasimhagupta was succeeded by his son, Kumāragupta II, to whose time the fine seal of alloyed silver found at Bhitarī in the Ghāzīpur District belongs.[1] According to the chronology here followed, Kumāragupta II must have been very young when he came to the throne, and cannot have reigned for more than a year or two, in view of the fact that a prince named Budhagupta is acknowledged in a Sārnāth image inscription as the reigning sovereign in A. D. 476. The dominions of Kumāragupta II, like those of his father and grandfather, were evidently restricted to the eastern provinces of the empire of his earlier ancestors.

C. A. D. 473–500. Budhagupta.

The precise identity of Budhagupta is as yet undetermined. He may possibly have been governor of Mālwā under Skandagupta, and after disowning allegiance to Narasimhagupta and Kumāragupta II, whose hold on Mālwā was doubtless precarious, have finally overthrown Kumāragupta II. It seems tolerably certain that his stronghold was in Mālwā, that his sway there lasted till A. D. 494, if not later, and that by A. D. 476 he was in possession of Benares.[2]

The Later Guptas of Magadha; the Maukharis.

The imperial line passes by an obscure transition into a dynasty comprising eleven Gupta princes, who appear to have been for the most part merely local rulers in Magadha. These 'Later Guptas of Magadha', as they are called by archaeologists, shared the rule of that province with another dynasty of Rājas, who had names ending in *-varman*, and

ents, p. 94; Watters, ii, 170; Beal, ii, 173. For Tibetan account of Nālandā, see citation in Keay, *Ancient Indian Education* (Oxford Univ. Press, 1918, p. 105).

Nālandā is now known as Bargāon (not Baṛāgāon), which is simply a modern name, meaning 'village with a conspicuous banyan tree', which stands there. Such names are extremely common in N. India (Bloch in *J. R. A. S.*, 1909, p. 440).

[1] *J. A. S. B.*, part i, vol. lviii (1889), pl. vi.

[2] R. D. Banerji, 'The Chronology of the Late Imperial Guptas' (*Annals of Bhandarkar Institute*, vol. i, part i, 1919). See also Parma Lal, 'The Dates of Skandagupta and his Successors' (*Hindustan Review*, January, 1918); and Romesh. C. Majumdar, 'Revised Chronology of the Later Gupta Emperors' (*Ind. Ant.*, 1918, p. 166).

belonged to a clan called Maukhari. The territorial division between the two dynasties cannot be defined precisely, but the Maukhari dominion in the middle of the sixth century included Oudh. Their relations with one another were sometimes friendly and sometimes hostile, but the few details known are of little importance.[1]

Chinese Buddhist mission.

The political decadence of Magadha never affected the reputation of the kingdom as the centre and head-quarters of Buddhist learning, which continued to be cultivated sedulously at Nālandā and other places under the Pāla kings up to the time of the Muhammadan conquest at the close of the twelfth century, when the monasteries with their well-stocked libraries were reduced to ashes. A good illustration of the reverence with which the Buddhist Holy Land continued to be regarded in the later Gupta age by foreign students of the doctrine of Gautama is afforded by the fact that, in the year A. D. 539, Wu-ti, or Hsiao Yen, the first Liang emperor of China and an ardent Buddhist, sent a mission to Magadha for the purpose of collecting original Mahāyānist texts and obtaining the services of a scholar competent to translate them. The local king, probably either Jīvitagupta I or Kumāragupta, gladly complied with the wishes of his imperial correspondent, and placed the learned Paramārtha at the disposal of the mission, which seems to have spent several years in India. Paramārtha then went to China, taking with him a large collection of manuscripts, many of which he translated. He arrived in the neighbourhood of Canton in A. D. 546, was presented to the emperor in 548, and died in China in 569, at the age of seventy. It was in the reign of the same emperor (502–49) that Bodhidharma, the son of a king in Southern India, and reckoned as the twenty-eighth Indian and first Chinese patriarch, came to China in A. D. 520, and after a short stay at Canton, settled at Lo Yang. His miracles are a favourite subject of Chinese artists.[2]

[1] For these dynasties see Fleet, *Gupta Inscriptions*, and Dr. Hoernle's observations on the Bhitarī seal. For Maukhari coins, see Burn, *J. R. A. S.*, 1906, p. 843; *Ep. Ind.*, xiv, 114.

[2] Bushell, *Chinese Art*, i, 24.

Āditya-sena; Jīvita-gupta II. The most notable member of the Later Gupta dynasty [1] was Ādityasena, who asserted his independence after the death of the paramount sovereign, Harsha, in A. D. 647, and even presumed to celebrate the horse-sacrifice in token of his claim to supreme rank. The last known Rāja of the dynasty was Jīvitagupta II, who reigned early in the eighth century. About the end of that century, or at the beginning of the ninth, Magadha passed under the sway of the Pāla kings of Bengal, whose history will be noticed in a subsequent chapter.

A. D. 510. Bhānu-gupta. In addition to the records of Budhagupta, who seems to have belonged to the imperial line and to have acquired the sovereignty of the northern provinces, we find in the western province of Mālwā records of a Rāja named Bhānugupta, who at the beginning of the sixth century occupied a dependent position and presumably was subordinate to the Hun chieftains.

Dynasty of Va-labhī. c. A. D. 490–770. Towards the close of the fifth century, a chief named Bhatārka, who belonged to a clan called Maitraka,[2] probably of foreign origin, established himself at Valabhī in the east of the peninsula of Surāshtra (Kāthiāwār), and founded a dynasty which lasted until about A. D. 770, when it is supposed to have been overthrown by Arab invaders from Sind. The earlier kings of Valabhī do not appear to have been independent, and were doubtless obliged to pay tribute to the Huns; but, after the destruction of the Hun domination, the lords of Valabhī asserted their independence, and made themselves a considerable power in the west of India, both on the mainland and in the peninsula of Surāshtra. The city was a place of great wealth when visited by Hiuen Tsang in the seventh century, and was famous in Buddhist church history as having been the residence of two distinguished teachers, Gunamati and Sthiramati, in the sixth

[1] R. D. Banerji in his history in Bengali, *Bangālāi Itihās*, traces the descent of the Later Guptas from Govindagupta, second son of Chandra-gupta II (Thomas, in *J. R. A. S.*, 1917, p. 855).

[2] Hultzsch, *Ep. Ind.*, iii, 320; correcting earlier interpretations. The original and more authentic form of the name is Bhaṭakka. Bhatārka is a Sanskritized spelling (*Ep. Ind.*, xi (1913), p. 105). See N. G. Majumdar in *Ind. Ant.*, vol. xlviii (1919), pp. 207–8 for reference to composition of Bhaṭakka's army.

century. I-tsing, a junior contemporary of Hiuen Tsang, tells us that in his time Nālandā in South Bihār and Valabhī were the two places in India which deserved comparison with the most famous centres of learning in China, and were frequented by crowds of eager students, who commonly devoted two or three years to attendance at lectures on Buddhist philosophy. This statement explains the assertion of Hiuen Tsang that Mo-la-p'o, or Western Mālava, and Magadha were the two countries of India in which learning was prized, because Valabhī and Mo-la-p'o were then politically one, both territories apparently being under the government of Dhruvabhata, the son-in-law of King Harsha, paramount sovereign of Northern India. After the overthrow of Valabhī, its place as the chief city of Western India was taken by Anhilwāra (Nahrwālah, or Pātan), which retained that honour until the fifteenth century, when it was superseded by Ahmadābād.[1] The above observations will, perhaps, be sufficient to give the reader a notion of the way in which some of the fragments of the Gupta empire were apportioned among various native dynasties.

Two streams of Hun migration.

But the Huns, the foreign savages who shattered that empire, and dominated a large part of it for a short period, merit more explicit notice. The nomad tribes known as Huns, when they moved westwards from the steppes of Asia to seek subsistence for their hungry multitudes in other climes, divided into two main streams, one directed towards the valley of the Oxus, and the other to that of the Volga.

The Huns in Europe; Attila.

The latter poured into Eastern Europe in A. D. 375, forcing the Goths to the south of the Danube, and thus

[1] The ruins of Valabhī at Walā, 18 or 20 miles north-west of Bhāonagar, are mostly underground. The history is given by Burgess in *A. S. W. I.*, vol. ii, (1876), pp. 80–6, though his account is partly obsolete; and by Bhagwān Lal Indraji and Jackson in *Bomb. Gaz.* (1896), vol. i, part i, pp. 78–106. The latest dynastic list is that in Kielhorn's 'Supplement to List of Northern Inscriptions', App. B, p. 11 (*Ep. Ind.*, vol. viii, April, 1905). For approximate date of destruction of Valabhī as a capital see Burgess, *A. S. W. I.*, vol. vi, p. 3; vol. ix, p. 4. But certain traditions assert that the city was destroyed by Gūjars from Sind (*J. A. S. B.*, part i, vol. lv (1886), p. 181). Valabhī even now exists as a country town (*Bomb. Gaz.*, *ut supra*, p. 95, note 1).

indirectly causing the sanguinary Gothic war, which cost the Emperor Valens his life in A. D. 378. The Huns quickly spread over the lands between the Volga and the Danube; but, owing to chronic disunion and the lack of a great leader, failed to make full use of their advantageous position until Attila appeared, and for a few years welded the savage mass into an instrument of such power that he was 'able to send equal defiance to the courts of Ravenna and Constantinople'.[1]

c. A. D. 470.

His death, in A. D. 453, severed the only bond which held together the jealous factions of the horde, and within a space of twenty years after that event the Hunnic empire in Europe was extinguished by a fresh torrent of barbarians from Northern Asia.

A. D. 455–84. White Huns of Oxus valley.

The Asiatic domination of the Huns lasted longer. The section of the horde settled in the Oxus valley, and probably different in race, became known as the Ephthalites or White Huns, and gradually overcame the resistance of Persia, which ceased when King Fīrōz was killed in A. D. 484. Swarms of these White Huns also assailed the Kushān kingdom of Kābul, and thence poured into India. The attack repelled by Skandagupta in A. D. 455 must have been delivered by a comparatively weak body, which arrived early, and failed to effect a lodgement in the interior.[2]

A. D. 500. Toramāṇa.

About ten years later the nomads, having appeared in greater force, overwhelmed the kingdom of Gandhāra, or Peshāwar; and starting from that base, as already related, penetrated into the heart of the Gangetic provinces, and overthrew the Gupta empire.[3] The collapse of Persian opposition in 484 must have greatly facilitated the eastern movement of the horde, and allowed immense multitudes to cross the Indian frontier. The leader in this invasion of India, which, no doubt, continued for years, was a chief-

[1] Gibbon, ch. xxxv.

[2] Hoernle (*J. R. A. S.*, 1909, p. 128) denies the reality of the Hun invasion at the beginning of Skandagupta's reign, and dates the Bhitarī inscription as late as 468. But for the reasons stated (*ante*, p. 327) that inscription must have been recorded quite early in the reign. It mentions defeats of both the Pushyamitras and the Huns.

[3] *Ante*, p. 328.

tain named Toramāna, who is known to have been established as ruler of Mālwā in Central India prior to A. D. 500. He assumed the style and titles of an Indian 'sovereign of *māhārājas*'; and Bhānugupta, as well as the king of Valabhī and many other local princes, must have been his tributaries.[1]

c. A. D. 502. Mihiragula, acc.

When Toramāna died, about A. D. 502, the Indian dominion which he had acquired was consolidated sufficiently to pass to his son Mihiragula, whose capital in India was Sākala, the modern Siālkot, in the Panjāb.[2]

Extent of Hun empire in Asia.

India at this time was only one province of the Hun empire. The head-quarters of the horde were at Bāmyin in Bādhaghīs near Herāt, and the ancient city of Balkh served as a secondary capital.[3] The Hun king, to whose court, whether at Bāmyin or Herāt cannot be determined, Song-Yun, the Chinese pilgrim-envoy, paid a visit in A. D. 519, was a powerful monarch levying tribute from forty countries, extending from the frontier of Persia, on the west, to Khotan on the borders of China in the east. This king was either Mihiragula himself, or his contemporary overlord, more probably the latter. The local Hun king of Gandhāra, to whom Song-Yun paid his respects in the following year, A. D. 520, must be identified with Mihiragula. He was then engaged in a war with the king of Kashmīr (Ki-pin), which had already lasted for three years.[4]

[1] Three inscriptions naming Toramāṇa are known: namely, (1) at Ēraṇ, in Sāgar district, Central Provinces, dated in the first year of his reign (Fleet, *Gupta Inscr.*, No. 36); (2) at Kura in the Salt Range, of which the date is lost (*Ep. Ind.*, i, 238); and (3) at Gwālior, Central India, dated in the fifteenth year of Mihiragula, son of Toramāṇa (Fleet, No. 37). The silver coins of Toramāṇa, which imitate the Surāshtran coins of the Western Satraps and Guptas, are dated in the year 52, apparently reckoned from a special Hun era, probably beginning in A. D. 448 (*J. A. S. B.*, vol. lxiii, part i (1894), p. 195).

[2] The name of Mihiragula ('Sunflower') also appears in the Sanskritized form of Mihirakula. His coins are numerous at Chiniōt and Shāhkōt, situated respectively in the Jhang and Gujrānwāla Districts of the Panjāb. The coins of Toramāṇa and Mihiragula are fully described in *J. A. S. B.*, 1894, part i.

[3] Chavannes, *Turcs Occidentaux*, pp. 224, 226. Gurgān (Gorgō), often asserted to be the Ephthalite capital, really was a frontier town belonging to Persia (Chavannes, op. cit., pp. 223, 235 note).

[4] Beal, *Records*, vol. i, pp. xci, c. The name Lae-lih, given by Beal,

Gollas.

With reference apparently to the same date approximately, the monk Cosmas Indicopleustes, who wrote a curious book in A. D. 547, describes a White Hun king, whom he calls Gollas, as being lord of India, from which he exacted tribute by oppression, enforcing his demands with the aid of two thousand war elephants and a great host of cavalry. This king, Gollas, certainly must have been Mihiragula.[1]

Tyranny of Mihiragula.

All Indian traditions agree in representing Mihiragula as a bloodthirsty tyrant, 'the Attila of India,' stained to a more than ordinary degree with the 'implacable cruelty' noted by historians as characteristic of the Hun temperament.[2] Indian authors having omitted to give any detailed description of the savage invaders who ruthlessly oppressed their country for three-quarters of a century, recourse must be had to European writers to obtain a picture of the devastation wrought and the terror caused to settled communities by the fierce barbarians.

Description of the Huns.

The original accounts are well summarized by Gibbon :—

'The numbers, the strength, the rapid motions, and the implacable cruelty of the Huns were felt, and dreaded, and magnified by the astonished Goths; who beheld their fields and villages consumed with flames, and deluged with indiscriminate slaughter. To these real terrors, they added the surprise and abhorrence which were excited by the shrill voice, the uncouth gestures, and the strange deformity of the Huns. . . . They were distinguished from the rest of the human species by their broad shoulders, flat noses, and small black eyes deeply buried in the head; and, as they were

is, as already noted, fictitious (*ante*, p. 328 note). In the time of Song-Yun Ki-pin usually signified Kashmīr, though at times it seems to have meant, or included, Gandhāra also. In the seventh century Ki-pin ordinarily, though not invariably, meant Kapiśa, or North-eastern Afghanistan (Chavannes, *Song Yun*, pp. 37, 39).

[1] McCrindle's translation (Hakluyt Society, 1897), p. 597.

[2] Hiuen Tsang; *Rājataraṅgini*. The Turushka king of Tāranāth (Schiefner, p. 94) may mean Mihiragula. There are some grounds for the belief that the horrible tales told about Mihiragula are to some extent Brahman inventions, due to the fact that he was a sun-worshipper, who favoured Zoroastrian priests. The 'Gandhāra Brahmans' of *Rājatarangini*, Bk. i, v. 307, apparently were 'Zoroastrian Mobeds' (J. J. Modi in *Anthrop. Papers*, vol. ii (1918), p. 340). Zoroastrianism seems to have had a great hold on the Panjāb and part of Rājputāna in the sixth century.

almost destitute of beards, they never enjoyed the manly graces of youth or the venerable aspect of age.'[1]

The Indians, like the Goths, experienced to the full the miseries of savage warfare, and suffered an added horror by reason of the special disgust felt by fastidious, caste-bound Hindus at the repulsive habits of barbarians to whom nothing was sacred.

c. A. D. 528. Defeat of Mihiragula.

The cruelty practised by Mihiragula became so unbearable that the native princes, under the leadership of Yasodharman, a Rāja of Central India, appear to have formed a confederacy against the foreign tyrant.[2] About the year A. D. 528, they accomplished the delivery of their country from oppression by inflicting a decisive defeat on Mihiragula.

Mihiragula in Kashmīr.

Meanwhile, according to the testimony of Hiuen Tsang, Mihiragula's younger brother had taken advantage of the misfortunes of the head of the family to usurp the throne of Sākala, which he was unwilling to surrender. Mihiragula, after spending some time in concealment, took refuge in Kashmīr, where he was kindly received by the king, who placed him in charge of a small territory. The exile submitted to this enforced retirement for a few years, and then took an opportunity to rebel and seize the throne of his benefactor. Having succeeded in this enterprise, he attacked the neighbouring kingdom of Gandhāra. The king, perhaps himself a Hun, was treacherously surprised and slain, the royal family was exterminated, and multitudes of people were slaughtered on the banks of the Indus. The savage invader, who worshipped as his patron deity Siva, the god of destruction, exhibited ferocious hostility against the peaceful Buddhist cult, and remorselessly overthrew the *stūpas* and monasteries, which he plundered of their treasures.

Death of Mihiragula.

But he did not long enjoy his ill-gotten gains. Before the year was out he died; and 'at the time of his death there were thunder and hail and a thick darkness, and the earth shook and a mighty tempest raged. And the holy

[1] Gibbon, ch. xxvi.

[2] See J. J. Modi, 'The Early History of the Huns' (*J. B. B. R. A. S.*, vol. xxiv (1916–17), pp. 589–95). Panna Lall also rejects the legend recorded by Hiuen Tsang.

saints said in pity: "For having killed countless victims and overthrown the law of Buddha, he has now fallen into the lowest hell, where he shall pass endless ages of revolution"'. Thus the tyrant met the just reward of his evil deeds in another world, if not in this. The date of his death is not known exactly, but the event must have occurred in or about the year 542, just a century before Hiuen Tsang was on his travels. The rapidity of the growth of the legend concerning the portents attending the tyrant's death, though perhaps in a measure due to *odium theologicum*, emphasizes the depth of the impression made by his outlandish cruelty; which is further attested by the Kashmīr tale of the fiendish pleasure which he is believed to have taken in rolling elephants down a precipice.[1]

Yaśodharman.

Yasodharman, the Central Indian Rāja, who has been mentioned as having taken an active part in the supposed confederacy formed to obtain deliverance from the tyranny of Mihiragula, is known from three inscriptions only, and is not mentioned by Hiuen Tsang, who wrongly gives the sole credit for the victory over the Huns to Bālāditya, king of Magadha.[2] Yasodharman erected two columns of victory inscribed with words commemorating the defeat of the foreign invaders. In these records he claims to have brought under his sway lands which even the Guptas and Huns

[1] Hiuen Tsang, in Beal, *Records*, vol. i, pp. 165–72; Watters, I, i, 288. It is not easy to explain why the pilgrim alleges (p. 167) that Mihiragula lived 'some centuries' before his time. The Chinese words, *sho-pih-nien-tsin*, are said not to be capable of any other interpretation (Beal, *Ind. Ant.*, xv, 345). Watters is inclined to think that the tale told by Hiuen Tsang refers to a Mihiragula of much earlier date. Fleet suggests that there may be an error in the Chinese text. K. B. Pathak in 'New Light on Gupta Era and Mihirakula' (*Ind. Ant.*, xlvii, 1918) shows good reasons for discarding the pilgrim's statement as baseless, basing his view upon the evidence of Jain chronicles, supported by certain inscriptions and coins. He appears to me to be correct. Hiuen Tsang's travels extended from 629 to 645. For the Kashmīr legends see Stein, transl. *Rājat.*, Bk. i, pp. 289–325.

[2] The weight of evidence is now decidedly in favour of the rejection of Hiuen Tsang's story. The evidence in favour of the view that Yasodharman, king of Mālwā, was responsible for the final defeat of Mihiragula is summed up by J. J. Modi in 'The Early History of the Huns' (*J. B. B. R. A. S.*, vol. xxiv (1916–17), pp. 594–5); and this view is accepted by other scholars, e. g. K. B. Pathak in *J. B. B. R. A. S.*, vol. xix, p. 39.

could not subdue, and to have been master of Northern India from the Brahmaputra to the Western Ocean, and from the Himalaya to Mount Mahendra, which probably should be understood to mean the southernmost peak (Mahendragiri) of the Travancore Ghāts. But the indefinite, conventional expression of the boasts suggests that Yasodharman made the most of his achievements, and that his court poet was no stranger to Oriental hyperbole. Nothing whatever is known about either his ancestry, or his successors; his name stands alone and unrelated. His reign may have covered roughly the first half of the sixth century, but its precise duration is unknown; and his claim to fame rests solely upon his magniloquent inscriptions.[1]

c. A. D. 565. Fall of the Hun empire in Asia.

The dominion of the White Huns in the Oxus valley did not long survive the defeat and death of Mihiragula in India. The arrival of the Turks in the middle of the sixth century changed the situation completely. The Turkish tribes, having vanquished a rival horde called Joan-joan, made an alliance with Khusrū Anūshīrvān, king of Persia, grandson of Fīrōz, who had been killed by the Huns in A. D. 484, and the allies at some date between 563 and 567 destroyed the White Huns. For a short time the Persians held Balkh and other portions of the Hun territory; but the gradual weakening of the Sassanian power soon enabled the Turks to extend their authority towards the south as far as Kapisa, and annex the whole of the countries which had been included in the Hun empire.[2]

Connotation of Hūna.

In later Sanskrit literature the term 'Hun' (*Hūna*) is employed in a very indeterminate sense to denote a foreigner from the north-west, in the same way as the word *Yavana* had been employed in ancient times, and as *Wilāyatī* is now understood. One of the thirty-six so-called 'royal' Rājpūt clans actually was given the name of Hūna.[3] This

[1] Inscriptions Nos. 33, 34, 35 in Fleet, *Gupta Inscriptions*.

[2] Chavannes, op. cit., pp. 226–9,

[3] Bühler, *Ep. Ind.*, i, 225: Sylvain Lévi, *Notes chinoises sur l'Inde*, No. iii, 'La Date de Candragomin' (Hanoi, 1903), p. 25. See also Tod's *Annals and Antiquities of Rājasthān* (ed. Crooke, 1920, vol. i, pp. 131–3, and list facing p. 98). A Brahman poet of Southern India, writing about A. D. 1600, applied the term Hūna to the Portuguese, whom he de-

vagueness of connotation raises some doubt as to the exact meaning of the term Hūna as applied to the clans on the north-western frontier against whom Harsha of Thānēsar and his father waged incessant war at the close of the sixth and the beginning of the seventh century. But it is unlikely that within fifty years of Mihiragula's defeat the true meaning of Hūna should have been forgotten ; and the opponents of Harsha may be regarded as having been outlying colonies of real Huns, who had settled among the hills on the frontier.

The Gurjaras.

The Hūnas are often mentioned in books and inscriptions in connexion with the Gurjaras, whose name survives in the modern Gūjars, a caste widely distributed in North-western India. The early Gurjaras seem to have been foreign immigrants, closely associated with, and possibly allied in blood to the White Huns. They founded a considerable kingdom in Rājputāna, the capital of which was Bhilmāl or Srīmāl, about 50 miles to the north-west of Mount Ābū. In course of time the Gurjara-Pratihāra kings of Bhilmāl conquered Kanauj and became the paramount power in Northern India, as will be related in the fourteenth chapter. The minor Gurjara kingdom of Bharōch (Broach) was an offshoot of the Bhilmāl monarchy.

Origin of the Rājpūt clans.

In this place I desire to draw attention to the fact, long suspected and now established by good evidence, that the foreign immigrants into Rājputāna and the upper Gangetic provinces were not utterly destroyed in the course of their wars with the native powers. Many, of course, perished, but many more survived, and were merged in the general population, of which no inconsiderable part is now formed by their descendants. The foreigners, like their forerunners the Śakas and Yüe-chi, universally yielded to the wonderful assimilative power of Hinduism, and rapidly became Hinduized. Clans or families which succeeded in winning chieftainship were admitted readily into the frame of Hindu polity as Kshatriyas or Rājpūts, and there is no doubt that the Parihārs and many other famous Rājpūt clans of the

scribed as 'very despicable, devoid of tenderness, regardless of Brahmans, and careless of ceremonial purity' (Burnell, cited by Morse Stephens, *Albuquerque*, p. 206).

north were developed out of the barbarian hordes which poured into India during the fifth and sixth centuries. The rank and file of the strangers became Gūjars and other castes, ranking lower than the Rājpūts in the scale of precedence. Farther to the south, various indigenous, or 'aboriginal', tribes and clans underwent the same process of Hinduized social promotion, in virtue of which Gonds, Bhars, Kharwārs, and so forth emerged as Chandēls, Rāthōrs, Gaharwārs, and other well-known Rājpūt clans, duly equipped with pedigrees reaching back to the sun and moon. The process will be discussed further and illustrated in some detail when I come to deal with the mediaeval dynasties of the north.

Exemption of India from foreign attack.

The extinction of the Ephthalite power on the Oxus necessarily dried up, or at least greatly contracted, the stream of barbarian immigration into India, which enjoyed, so far as is known, almost complete immunity from foreign attack for nearly five centuries after the defeat of Mihiragula.[1] The following chapters will tell how she made use, or failed to make use, of the opportunity thus afforded for internal development unchecked by foreign aggression.

Second half of sixth century almost a blank.

Very little is known about the history of India during the second half of the sixth century. It is certain that no paramount power existed, and that all the states of the Gangetic plain had suffered severely from the ravages of the Huns and connected tribes; but, excepting bare catalogues of names in certain local dynastic lists, few facts of general interest have been recorded.

Mo-la-p'o.

One of the many states into which India was divided during those troublous times deserves special notice, because the brief reference to its affairs by Hiuen Tsang has given occasion for much discussion and some misunderstanding. In A. D. 641, or early in 642, the pilgrim, after leaving

[1] Defeat of Mihiragula about A. D. 528; permanent occupation of the Panjāb by Mahmūd of Ghaznī, about A. D. 1023. The Arab conquest of Sind, in the eighth century, was an isolated operation, producing little impression on the rest of India. If any incursions by nomads occurred during the seventh, eighth, ninth, and tenth centuries, they have not been recorded.

Barōch (Broach), travelled in a north-westerly direction for a considerable distance, apparently overstated in the Chinese text, until he arrived in a country called Mo-la-p'o, a name phonetically equivalent to Mālava. The unnamed capital, which was situated to the south-east of a great river, or, according to another reading, of the Mahi, has not been identified. If the 'great river' means the Sābarmatī, the capital may have stood at or near the site of Ahmadābād.[1] Although it is impossible to reconcile all the data given in the pilgrim's text, and several details are open to controversy, it is clear that the kingdom or country of Mo-la-p'o essentially comprised the basin of the Mahi river, with the region to the east of the Sābarmatī and a portion of the hilly tract of Southern Rājputāna, perhaps extending as far east as Rutlam. Mo-la-p'o was bounded on the north by the Gurjara kingdom of Bhinmāl, on the north-west by the subordinate principality or province of Ānandapura (Varnagar), lying to the west of the Sābarmatī, and on the east by the kingdom (Avanti or Eastern Mālwā), of which Ujjain was the capital. Besides Ānandapura, two other countries, Ki-t'a or Ki-ch'a, and Su-la-ch'a or Su-la-tha were dependencies of Mo-la-p'o. The latter dependency certainly is to be identified with Soratha (Surāshtra), or Southern Kāthiāwār. The identity of the former is disputed—some good authorities holding the Chinese name to mean the Kaira (Kheda, Khetaka) District, while others believe it to mean Kachchh (Cutch).

Dhruvabhaṭa.

The territory of Valabhī (Walā) in Eastern Kāthiāwār, which intervened between Mo-la-p'o and Surāshtra, had a king of its own, Dhruvabhata by name (Dhruvasena Bālāditya of inscriptions), who was the son-in-law of Harsha (Sīlāditya), paramount sovereign of Northern India. Some years before the pilgrim's visit, Dhruvabhata had been defeated by Harsha, and the matrimonial alliance seems to have been one of the arrangements made when peace was declared. In 643, when Harsha held the solemn assemblies at Kanauj and Prayāga (Allahābād), in which Hiuen Tsang

[1] The old Hindu name of the city represented by Ahmadābād was Asāwal.

took part, the Rāja of Valabhī attended as a vassal prince in the train of his father-in-law. The pilgrim does not say a word about the nature of the government of Mo-la-p'o and its three dependencies, Ānandapura, Surāshtra, and (?) Cutch, the reason apparently being that all these countries were administered on behalf of Harsha, whose father had fought the king of Mālava, perhaps Mo-la-p'o, at the close of the sixth century. The fact that Dhruvabhata is named as the Rāja or king of the Valabhī territory interposed between Mo-la-p o and its dependency, Surāshtra, can be explained by assuming that Harsha (Sīlāditya) purposely allowed his son-in-law to occupy a semi-independent position, governing not only Valabhī, but also Mo-la-p'o and its dependencies.

Śīlāditya, king of Mo-la-p'o.

Study of the local records drew the attention of Hiuen Tsang to the history of Dhruvabhata's uncle, Sīlāditya, who had been king of Mo-la-p'o sixty years before. This prince was famed as having been a man of eminent wisdom and great learning, a zealous Buddhist, and so careful to preserve animal life that he caused the drinking water for his horses and elephants to be strained, lest perchance any creature living in the water should be injured. By the side of his palace he had built a Buddhist temple, remarkable for its artistic design and rich ornament, in which the images of the Seven Buddhas were enshrined. It was his custom to hold a grand assembly every year, at which the canonical dues and gifts were presented to the monks with liberality. This pious practice had been continued for successive generations to the time of Hiuen Tsang's visit.

Śīlāditya Dharmāditya of Mo-la-p'o.

M. Sylvain Lévi seems to be right in identifying this religious monarch with the Buddhist Sīlāditya I, surnamed Dharmāditya, 'the Sun of Piety', of the Valabhī dynasty, who reigned from about A. D. 595 to 610 or 615;[1] for, although those dates do not agree with all the indications given by Hiuen Tsang, it is certain that Dhruvabhata, the reigning Rāja of Valabhī, was a nephew of Sīlāditya Dharmāditya,

[1] A new copper-plate grant of Śīlāditya I, dated A. D. 608–9, has recently been deciphered by Mr. R.D. Banerji (*Prog. Rep. A.S.W.I.*, 1920, p. 54). It records a grant of land for the maintenance of a temple of the Sun-god.

while Hiuen Tsang states that he was the nephew of the pious Sīlāditya, the former king of Mo-la-p'o. The apparently necessary inference is that Sīlāditya Dharmāditya must have been king of Mo-la-p'o by conquest in addition to his ancestral realm of Valabhī.[1] Both territories subsequently were conquered by Harsha, and became subject to him as their suzerain.

Mo-la-p'o distinct from Ujjain. The serious misunderstanding of the story above alluded to consisted in the erroneous belief held by Beal and several other writers that Mo-la-p'o, or Western Mālava, was identical with the kingdom of Ujjain, otherwise known as Avanti or Eastern Mālava. Beal actually designated Sīlāditya of Mo-la-p'o as ' Sīlāditya of Ujjain ', forgetting that Hiuen Tsang described the territory of Ujjain as a separate kingdom equal in size to Mo-la-p'o, and in his time ruled by a Brahman Rāja. Sīlāditya, the former Rāja of Valabhī and Mo-la-p'o, was considered to be a Kshatriya, and there is no reason to suppose that he had anything to do with Ujjain.

Harsha (Sīlāditya), of Kanauj, is described by his friend Hiuen Tsang as being of the Vaisya caste, although he seems to have taken rank as a Kshatriya. The erroneous identification of Mo-la-p'o with the kingdom of Ujjain has given rise to much confusion in the treatment of the history of Harsha's period, and the main purpose of the observations made in the first edition of this work was the rectification of that embarrassing error. Those observations, which were themselves erroneous in certain respects, have now been corrected in the light of subsequent criticism and discussion.[2]

[1] Hoernle seeks to prove that the elder Śīlāditya should be identified with Yaśodharman, the conqueror of the Huns, but without success, in my judgement (*J. R. A. S.*, 1909, p. 122).

[2] It is impossible to discuss the Mo-la-p'o problem fully within the limits of a note. References are: Hiuen Tsang (Beal, ii, pp. 260–70; Watters, ii, pp. 242–8); Cunningham, *Anc. Geogr.*, pp. 489–94; Stein, transl. *Rājatar.*, vol. i, p. 66; Max Müller, *India, What can it Teach us?* p. 288; Hoernle (*J. R. A. S.*, 1903, p. 553); Vincent Smith (*Z. D. M. G.*, 1904, pp. 787–96); Burn (*J. R. A. S.*, 1905, p. 837); Grierson (*J.R.A.S.*, 1906, p. 95); Burgess (ibid., p. 220; *Ind. Ant.*, 1905, p. 195); Sylvain Lévi (*Journal des Savants*, Oct., 1905, pp. 544–8). The text, which differs from that in the first edition, is based on consideration of all the above-mentioned publications. Some special points may be noted. Mo-la-p'o did not include Bhinmāl (Bhilmāl, Bhinnamāla, Bhillamāla, also called Śrīmāl), repre-

DATE A. D.	EVENT.	REMARKS.
c. 271 . .	Gupta	Jain date for commencement of Gupta dynasty.
c. 290 . .	Ghatoṭkacha	
c. 308 . .	Lichchhavi marriage of Chandra-gupta I	
320 . .	**Chandra-gupta I acc.** to independent power	Foundation of Gupta Era, of which year 1 began February 26, 320
c. 330 . .	**Samudragupta acc.**	
c. 330–6 . .	Campaigns in Northern India	
c. 347–50 .	Campaign in Southern India	
c. 351 . .	Horse-sacrifice	
c. 360 . .	Embassy from King Meghavarṇa of Ceylon	
c. 380 . .	**Chandra-gupta II acc.**	
c. 395 . .	Conquest of Western India	
401 . . .	Udayagiri inscription	G. E. 82
405–11 . .	Travels of Fa-hien in Gupta empire	,, 86–92
407 . . .	Gaṛhwā inscription	,, 88
409 . . .	Silver coins of western type	,, 90
412 . . .	Sāñchī inscription	,, 93
415 . . .	**Kumāragupta I acc.**	,, 94
415 . . .	Bilsaṛ inscription	,, 96
417 . . .	Gaṛhwā inscription	,, 98
432 . . .	Mathurā and Natore in N. Bengal inscriptions [1]	,, 113
436 . . .	Mandasōr inscription	V.S. 493 (= G.E. 117)
,, . . .	Bharadi inscription	G. E. 117
440 . . .	Silver coins	,, 121
443 . . .	Silver coins	,, 124
447 . . .	Silver coins	,, 128

senting P'i-lo-mo-lo, the capital of Kū-che-lo (Gūjara), the Gurjara kingdom of Rājputāna ; nor did it include Ujjain, N. lat. 23° 11′, E. long. 75° 47′, which was the capital of a separate kingdom (Avanti). Three texts of Hiuen Tsang give the name or epithet of the river as *Mo-ha*, =*mahā*, 'great' ; only the D text, which Lévi follows, reads *Mo-hi*, = *Mahī* (Watters). The bearings indicate that the river meant was the Sābarmatī rather than the Mahi. The identification of Ānandapura with Vaṛnagar is fully proved. Ki-t'a or Ki-ch'a is a good phonetic equivalent for Kheṭa (Kheṭaka, Kheḍa), the modern 'Kaira' District, but St. Martin, Julien, and Watters prefer to identify it with Kachchh (Cutch), and I am disposed to agree with them. The identity of Su-la-ch'a or Su-la-tha with Soraṭha or Surāshṭra, Southern Kāṭhiāwār, is established by the mention of the hill Yüh-shan-to, or Yhu-shen-to, = Ujjanta (Ujjayanta, Ujjinta), = Girnār. Dhruvabhaṭa was the son-in-law of Harsha (Śīlāditya), not of his son (Watters, ii, 247). P'i-lo-mo-lo = Bhilmala (Watters, ii, 250). For dates of Hiuen Tsang's visits to Mo-la-p'o, &c., see 'Itinerary' in Watters, ii, 335.

[1] The Natore inscription of A. D. 432 is the earliest copper-plate known (*J. & Proc. A. S. B.*, 1911, Feb., *Ann. Rep.*, p. xviii).

DATE A.D.	EVENT.	REMARKS.
448 . . .	Silver coins and Mankuwār inscription. Establishment of Huns in Oxus basin, and epoch of Hun era	G. E. 129
449 . . .	Silver coins	„ 130
c. 450 . .	Pushyamitra war	„ 131
454 . . .	Silver coins	„ 135
455 . . .	Silver coins	„ 136
455 . . .	**Skandagupta acc.**; first Hun war	„ 136
456 . . .	Embankment of lake at Girnār rebuilt	„ 137
457 . . .	Temple erected there	„ 138
460 . . .	Kahāon inscription (Gōrakhpur District)	„ 141
463 . . .	Silver coins	„ 144
464 . . .	Silver coins	„ 145
465 . . .	Indōr inscription (Bulandshahr District)	„ 146
467 . . .	Silver coins	„ 148
	Puragupta (?)	
	Narasiṁhagupta acc.	
c. 470–80 .	Second Hun war	„ 151–61
473 . . .	Mandasor inscription	529 Mālava era expired
473 . . .	**Kumāragupta II acc.**	G. E. 154
476 . . .	Budhagupta	„ 157
	Āryabhata, astronomer, born	
477 . . .	Pāli inscription (*Ep. Ind.*, ii, 363)	„ 158
c. 480–90 .	Partial break up of Gupta empire	
484 . . .	Fīrōz, king of Persia, killed by the Huns	
c. 490 to 770	**Dynasty of Valabhī**	
500–2 . .	Toramāṇa in Mālwā	
502–42 . .	**Mihiragula**	
520 . . .	Song-Yun visited White Hun king of Gandhāra	
c. 528 . .	Defeat of Mihiragula by Yaśodharman	
c. 535 to 720	**Later Gupta dynasty of Magadha**	
c. 595 to 615	**Śīlāditya of Mo-la-p'o and Valabhī**	

APPENDIX N

Vasubandhu and the Guptas

Biblio-graphy.

The difficult problem of the date of Vasubandhu, the famous Buddhist author, and the connected question of the identity of the Gupta sovereigns with whom he had intimate relations, have given occasion for voluminous discussion and wide divergence of opinion.[1]

[1] *Ind. Ant.*, 1911, p. 170 (Pathak); 264 (Hoernle); 312 (Narasiṁhachar); ibid., 1912, p. 1 (D. R. Bhandarkar); 15 (H. P. Śāstrī); 244 (Pathak); *J. & Proc. A. S. B.*, 1905, p. 227 (Vidyābhūshana); and, the most important, Noël Peri, 'A propos de la Date de Vasubandhu' (*Bull. de l'École fr. d'Extrême-Orient*, t. xi (1911), pp. 339–90). Those publications, especially the last named, give many earlier references, among which the most significant are Hiuen Tsang (Yuan Chwang), in Watters, i, 210–12, and Takakusu on Paramārtha's Life of Vasubandhu in *J. R. A. S.*, 1905, pp. 44–53.

M. Noël Peri, whose arguments are based upon innumerable Chinese texts, upon the date of Harivarman's great work, translated by Kumārajīva (383–412 in China),[1] upon the date of the partial translation by Dharmaraksha between A. D. 414 and 421 of the *Yogāchārya bhūmi Śāstra* by Asanga, elder brother of Vasubandhu,[2] and upon other data, points out that Vasubandhu, who is said to have attained the age of eighty, lived in the fourth century and must have died soon after the middle of that century.[3] M. Peri is unquestionably correct.

As to Vasubandhu's connexion with the Guptas, we have the testimony of Vāmana (*c.* A. D. 800), Pramārtha, who wrote between A. D. 546 and 569, and of Hiuen Tsang (Yuan Chwang) who took his notes at Peshāwar, the birthplace of Vasubandhu, probably in A. D. 631, and certainly finished his book in 648 (Watters, i, 12). I discussed their testimony fully in the third edition of this work.

This evidence points to the fact that the Gupta king who patronized him was the learned and accomplished Samudragupta, son and successor of Chandra-gupta I, who may have been actually known as Vikramāditya. That title, even if not actually assumed by Chandra-gupta I, may have been traditionally assigned to him, as being a recognized title applicable to any Gupta king. Without doubt Samudragupta was actually in possession of both Ayodhyā and Sravastī, and probably his father was so likewise : and if the recorded traditions connecting Vasubandhu with a Gupta king are well founded, it follows that Samudragupta in his youth must have borne the titles of both Chandraprakāśa (-prabhāva) and Bālāditya or Parāditya.

In brief, one must conclude that Samudragupta received Vasubandhu, the Buddhist author and patriarch, at court, either as a minister or as an intimate counsellor, with the sanction and approval of his father Chandra-gupta I, and, further, that Samudragupta, although officially a Brahmanical Hindu, studied Buddhism in his youth with interest and partiality.

[1] Takakusu denies that a Life of Vasubandhu by Kumārajīva ever existed (*J. R. A. S.*, 1905, p. 39).

[2] If this alleged fact is correctly stated it alone is conclusive. Takakusu gives the works of Asanga as three, namely (1) *Saptadaśa-bhūmi sūtra* ; (2) *Mahāyāna-sūtra upadeśas* ; (3) *Mahāyāna-samparigraha-śāstra* (*J. R. A. S.*, 1905, p. 35).

[3] Prof. Macdonell adopted this view long ago, on the ground that works of Vasubandhu were translated into Chinese in A. D. 404 (*Hist. Sansk. Literature*, 1900, p. 325). Mr. S. C. Vidyābhūshana, relying on Tibetan authorities, also places Vasubandhu in the fourth century, and makes him contemporary with the Tibetan king, Lha-tho-ri, who is supposed to have died in A. D. 371 (*J. & Proc. A. S. B.*, 1905, p. 227).

CHAPTER XIII

THE REIGN OF HARSHA FROM A.D. 606 TO 647

Seventh century: sources of history.

THE deficiency of material which embarrasses the historian when dealing with the latter half of the sixth century is no longer experienced when he enters upon the seventh. For this period he is fortunate enough to possess, in addition to the ordinary epigraphic and numismatic sources, two contemporary literary works, which shed much light upon the political condition of India generally, and supply, in particular, abundant and trustworthy information concerning the reign of Harsha, who ruled the North as paramount sovereign for more than forty years. The first of these works is the invaluable book of travels compiled by the Chinese pilgrim, Hiuen Tsang, who visited almost every part of India between A. D. 630 and 644, and recorded observations more or less minute about each state and province. The narrative in the *Travels* is supplemented by the pilgrim's biography, written by his friend Hwui-li, which supplies many additional details. The second work alluded to is the historical romance entitled 'The Deeds of Harsha' (*Harsha-charita*), composed by Bāna, a Brahman author, who lived at the court and enjoyed the patronage of the hero of his tale. Further information of much interest and importance is given by the official Chinese histories; and when all sources are utilized, our knowledge of the events of the reign of Harsha far surpasses in precision that which we possess respecting any other early Indian king, except Chandragupta Maurya and Asoka.

Rāja Prabhākara-vardhana of Thānēsar.

From remote ages the country surrounding the city of Thānēsar (Sthānvisvara)[1] has been holy ground, known as

[1] *Sthāṇvīsvara*, from *Sthāṇu*, a name of Śiva, locally used, and *īśvara*, 'lord' (Bāṇa). The name is also spelt *Sthāneśvara*, from *sthāna*, 'shrine', and *īśvara*.

the 'Land of Kuru', and famous as the battle-field of legendary heroes. In the latter part of the sixth century, the Rāja of Thānēsar, Prabhākara-vardhana by name, had raised himself to considerable eminence by successful wars against his neighbours, including the Mālavas, the Hun settlements in the North-western Panjāb, and the Gurjaras, probably those of Rājputāna, but possibly those of the Gurjara kingdom in the Panjāb, now represented by the Gujarāt and Gujrānwāla Districts. The fact that his mother was a princess of Gupta lineage no doubt both stimulated his ambition and aided its realization.[1]

His war with the Huns.

In the year 604, this energetic Rāja had dispatched his elder son Rājya-vardhana, a youth just entering upon manhood, with a large army to attack the Huns on the north-western frontier; while his younger and favourite son, Harsha, four years junior to the Crown Prince, followed his brother with a cavalry force at a considerable interval. The elder prince having advanced into the hills to seek the enemy, the younger lingered in the forests at the foot of the mountains to enjoy the sport of all kinds which they offered in abundance.

A. D. 605. Rājya-vardhana acc.

While thus pleasantly employed, Harsha, who was then a lad fifteen years of age, received news that his father lay dangerously ill with a violent fever. He returned to the capital with all speed, where he found the king in a hopeless condition. The disease quickly ran its course, and all was over long before the elder son, who had been victorious in his campaign, could return to claim his birthright. There are indications that a party at court inclined to favour the succession of the younger prince; but all intrigues were frustrated by the return of Rājya-vardhana, who ascended

[1] The family genealogy is given in the inscriptions, viz. (1) Sonpat seal (*Gupta Inscr.*, No. 52); (2) Banskhera copper-plate (*Ep. Ind.*, iv, 208); (3) Madhuban copper-plate (ibid., i, 67). Mahāsenaguptā was the mother of Prabhākara-vardhana, who was also called Pratāpaśīla. His queen was Yaśomatī. Harsha's full name was Harsha-vardhana. The coins found in the Fyzabad District, Oudh, bearing the names or titles Pratāpaśīla and Śīlāditya, appear to have been issued respectively by Prabhākara-vardhana and Harsha (Burn, *J. R. A. S.*, 1906, p. 845). Hoernle has another theory (ibid., 1909, p. 446).

the throne in due course. He had hardly seated himself when news arrived which compelled him again to take the field.

War with Mālwā. A courier brought the distressing intelligence that king Grahavarman Maukhari, husband of Rājyasrī, sister of the princes, had been slain by the king of Mālwā,[1] who cruelly misused the princess, 'confining her like a brigand's wife, with a pair of iron fetters kissing her feet', at Kanauj. Rājya-vardhana, resolute to avenge his sister's wrongs, started at once with a mobile force of 10,000 cavalry; leaving the elephants and heavy troops behind in his brother's charge. The king of Mālwā was defeated with little effort, but the joy of victory was turned into sorrow by the receipt of intelligence that the victor had been treacherously slain by the vanquished king's ally, Sasānka, king of Central Bengal,[2] who had inveigled Rājya-vardhana by fair promises to a conference, and had assassinated him when off his guard. Harsha was further informed that his widowed sister had escaped from confinement, and fled to the Vindhyan forests for refuge; but no certain news of her hiding-place could be obtained.

A. D. 606. Harsha acc. The murdered king was too young to leave a son capable of assuming the cares of government, and the nobles seem to have hesitated before offering the crown to his youthful brother. But the disorder and anarchy from which the country suffered during the interregnum forced the councillors of state to come to a decision concerning the succession. The ministers, acting on the advice of Bhandi, a slightly senior cousin, who had been educated with the young princes, ultimately resolved to invite Harsha to

[1] Doubts have been expressed as to the situation of the Mālwā (Mālava) referred to, which is quite uncertain. Tāranāth (Schiefner, p. 251) mentions a 'Mālava in Prayāga'. Grahavarman may or may not have been lord of Kanauj. He was the son of Avantivarman, mentioned in an inscription from the Shāhābād District in South Bihār (Fleet, *Gupta Inscr.*, p. 215).

[2] Gauḍa (Bāṇa); probably identical with Karṇa-suvarṇa (Hiuen Tsang). The capital is supposed by Beveridge to have been at Rangāmāṭi, 12 miles south of Murshidābād (*J.A.S.B.*, lxii, pt. i (1893), pp. 315–28). But Monmohan Chakravarti argues that more probably it was Lakshmaṇāvati (Lakhnauti or Gauṛ) (ibid., vol. iv, N.S. (1908), p. 281).

undertake the responsibilities of the royal office. For some reason, which is not apparent on the face of the story, he scrupled to express his consent, and it is said that he consulted a Buddhist oracle before accepting the invitation. Even when his reluctance, whether sincere or pretended, had been overcome by the favourable response of the oracle, he still sought to propitiate Nemesis by abstaining at first from the assumption of the kingly style, modestly designating himself as Prince (*Rājaputra*) Sīlāditya.

Era of Harsha. These curious details indicate clearly that some unknown obstacle stood in the way of Harsha's accession, and compelled him to rely for his title to the crown upon election by the nobles rather than upon his hereditary claims. The Chinese work entitled *Fang-chih* represents Harsha as 'administering the government in conjunction with his widowed sister', a statement which suggests that he at first considered himself to be Regent on behalf of his sister, or possibly, an infant child of his late brother.[1] There is reason to suppose that Harsha did not boldly stand forth as avowed king until A. D. 612, when he had been five and a half or six years on the throne, and that his formal coronation or consecration took place in that year. The era called after his name, of which the year 1 was A. D. 606–7, dated from the time of his accession in October, 606.[2]

Whatever may have been the motives which influenced the nobles of Thānēsar in their hesitation to offer their allegiance to young Harsha, the advice of Bhandi was justified abundantly by the ability of his nominee, who quickly proved his right to rule.

Recovery of Rājyaśrī. The immediate duties incumbent upon him obviously were the pursuit of his brother's murderer, and the recovery

[1] Watters, i, 345.

[2] Kielhorn (*Ind. Ant.*, xxvi, 32). Twenty inscriptions dated in the Harsha era are known (*Ep. Ind.*, vol. v, App. Nos. 528–47). When Hiuen Tsang was with Harsha, in A. D. 643, the king's reign was reckoned as having lasted for more than thirty years (*Records*, i, 213; 'lord of India for thirty years and more', *Life of Hiuen Tsang*, p. 183). The quinquennial assembly in the spring of A. D. 643 was the sixth held in the reign (Beal, *Life of Hiuen Tsang*, p. 184). The period of five and a half years (Julien), or six years (Watters), spent in the preliminary subjugation of the north, is not included in this computation.

of his widowed sister. The latter task, being the more urgent, was undertaken in all haste, even at the cost of permitting the assassin's escape. The haste shown was none too great; for the princess, despairing of rescue, was on the point of burning herself alive with her attendants, when her brother, guided by aboriginal chiefs, succeeded in tracing her in the depths of the Vindhyan jungles. The details of the campaign against Sasānka have not been recorded, and it seems clear that he escaped with little loss. He is known to have been still in power as late as the year 619; but his kingdom probably became subject to Harsha at a later date.[1]

Harsha's scheme of conquest. Harsha, having recovered his sister—a young lady of exceptional attainments, learned in the doctrines of the Sammitīya school of Buddhism—devoted his signal ability and energy to the prosecution of a methodical scheme of conquest, with the deliberate purpose of bringing all India 'under one umbrella'. He possessed at this stage of his career a force of 5,000 elephants, 20,000 cavalry, and 50,000 infantry. Apparently he discarded as useless the chariots which constituted, according to ancient tradition, the fourth arm of a regularly organized Indian host; although they were still used in some parts of the country.[2]

Five years' war. With this mobile and formidable force Harsha overran Northern India; and, in the picturesque language of his contemporary the Chinese pilgrim, 'he went from east to west subduing all who were not obedient; the elephants were not unharnessed, nor the soldiers unhelmeted.' By the end of five and a half years the conquest of the north-western regions, and probably also of a large portion of Bengal, was completed; and his military resources were so increased that he was able to put in the field 60,000 war elephants and 100,000 cavalry. He then reigned happily for thirty-five years longer, and during that period devoted

[1] Ganjām copper-plate inscription, dated G. E. 300, A. D. 619–20 (*Ep. Ind.*, vi, 143). Hiuen Tsang refers to Śaśānka as a recent king, and mentions no successor.

[2] In his general description of India, Hiuen Tsang tells how the general of an Indian army rode in a four-horsed chariot, protected by a body-guard (Beal, *Records*, i, 82).

most of his immense energy to the government of his extensive dominions.[1] His last recorded campaign, an attack on the sturdy inhabitants of Ganjām, on the coast of the Bay of Bengal, took place in A. D. 643.

Defeat by Pulakēśin II, Chalukya. A.D. 620.

His long career of victory was broken by one failure. Pulakēsin II, the greatest of the Chalukya dynasty, whose achievements will be noticed more fully in a later chapter, vied with Harsha in the extent of his conquests, and had raised himself to the rank of lord paramount of the South, as Harsha was of the North. The northern king, who could not willingly endure the existence of so powerful a rival, essayed to overthrow him, advancing in person to the attack, with 'troops from the five Indies[2] and the best generals from all countries'. But the effort failed. The king of the Deccan guarded the passes on the Narmadā so effectually that Harsha was constrained to retire discomfited, and to accept that river as his frontier. This campaign may be dated about the year A. D. 620.[3]

[1] The pilgrim's statement that the king, after the subjugation of Northern India, completed in 612, 'reigned in peace for thirty years without raising a weapon', must not be interpreted literally, for as a matter of fact, the wars with Pulakēśin II and Valabhī occurred. 'The text is *Ch'ui-san-shih-nien-ping-ko-pu-ch'i*. Here the word *ch'ui* is employed, as frequently, to denote "don the imperial robe", that is "to reign gently and happily"' (Watters, i, 343, 346). Similar phrases are used as commonplaces in Sanskrit inscriptions.

[2] 'The five Gaudas or "five Indies", viz. Svārasvata (the Panjāb), Kānyakuvja (Kānoja), Gauda (Bengal), Mithilā (Darbhāngā), and Utkala (Orissa) were formerly more allied to one another than they are now. We find the Bengalis to have been in close touch with the people of other parts of Āryāvarta.

'The old Bengali poems were known by the common name of Panchāli. This word shows that we owe at least some forms of the old Bengali metres to Panchāla or Kānoja.

'Svārasvata or the Panjāb gave us its Caka era, which was adopted by the Bengalis as it was by the people of other parts of India.

'The civilization of Bengal—the new learning, especially that of logic, which made the *tols* of Nadia famous throughout India, came from Mithilā, when Magadha, its glorious days over, had ceased to give light to Eastern India.

'With Kalinga or Orissa, Bengal in the past was inseparably associated. Our prophet Chaitanya Deva counts more votaries among the Uriyā people than in Bengal itself. So we find that the five Gaudas, as the five influential provinces of Āryāvarta were called, had in the past ages a greater touch with one another, and exchanged their thoughts and ideals more freely than now' (Dinesh Chandra Sen, *History of Bengali Language and Literature*, Calcutta Univ., 1911).

[3] Ma-twan-lin, the Chinese encyclopaedist (Max Müller, *India*,

War with Valabhī. The war with Valabhī, which resulted in the complete defeat of Dhruvasena (Dhruvabhata) II, and the flight of that prince into the dominions of the Rāja of Bharōch (Broach), who relied probably on the powerful support of the Chalukya monarch, seems to have occurred later than A.D. 633 and before Hiuen Tsang's visit to Western India in 641 or 642. Dhruvabhata, as already related, was compelled to sue for peace, to accept the hand of the victor's daughter, and to be content with the position of a feudatory vassal. The same campaign may be presumed to have involved the submission of the kingdoms or countries of Ānandapura, Ki-c'ha, or (?) Cutch, and Soratha, or Southern Kāthiāwār, all of which in A.D. 641 were still reckoned to be dependencies of Mo-la-p'o, or Western Mālava, formerly subject to Valabhī.[1]

Extent of Harsha's empire. In the latter years of his reign the sway of Harsha over the whole of the basin of the Ganges (including Nepāl),[2] from the Himalaya to the Narmadā, besides Mālwā, Gujarāt, and Surāshtra, was undisputed. Detailed administration of course remained in the hands of the local Rājas, but even the king of distant Assam (Kāmarūpa) in the east obeyed the orders of the suzerain, whose son-in-law, the king of Valabhī in the extreme west, attended in the imperial train.

His progresses. For the control of his extensive empire, Harsha relied upon his personal supervision, exercised with untiring energy, rather than upon the services of a trained bureaucracy. Except during the rainy season, when travelling with a huge camp was impracticable and opposed to Buddhist rule, he was incessantly on the move, punishing evil-doers, and rewarding the meritorious. Luxurious tents, such as were used by the Moghal emperors, and still form the

p. 287). Fleet's date, 609 or 610, is impossible, Harsha being then engaged in the subjugation of Northern India.

[1] Grant of Dadda of Bharōch (*Ind. Ant.*, xiii, 70). The event is discussed by M. Ettinghausen in pp. 47–9 of his interesting monograph, *Harsa Vardhana, empereur et poète de l'Inde septentrionale,* A.D. 606–48; Louvain, 1906.

[2] Sylvain Lévi and Ettinghausen (pp. 47, 184) deny the conquest of Nepāl by Harsha and the use of his era in that country; but, I think, without adequate reason. See *Ind. Ant.*, xiii, 421; Kielhorn, *List of Northern Inscriptions, Ep. Ind.*, vol. v, App. p. 75.

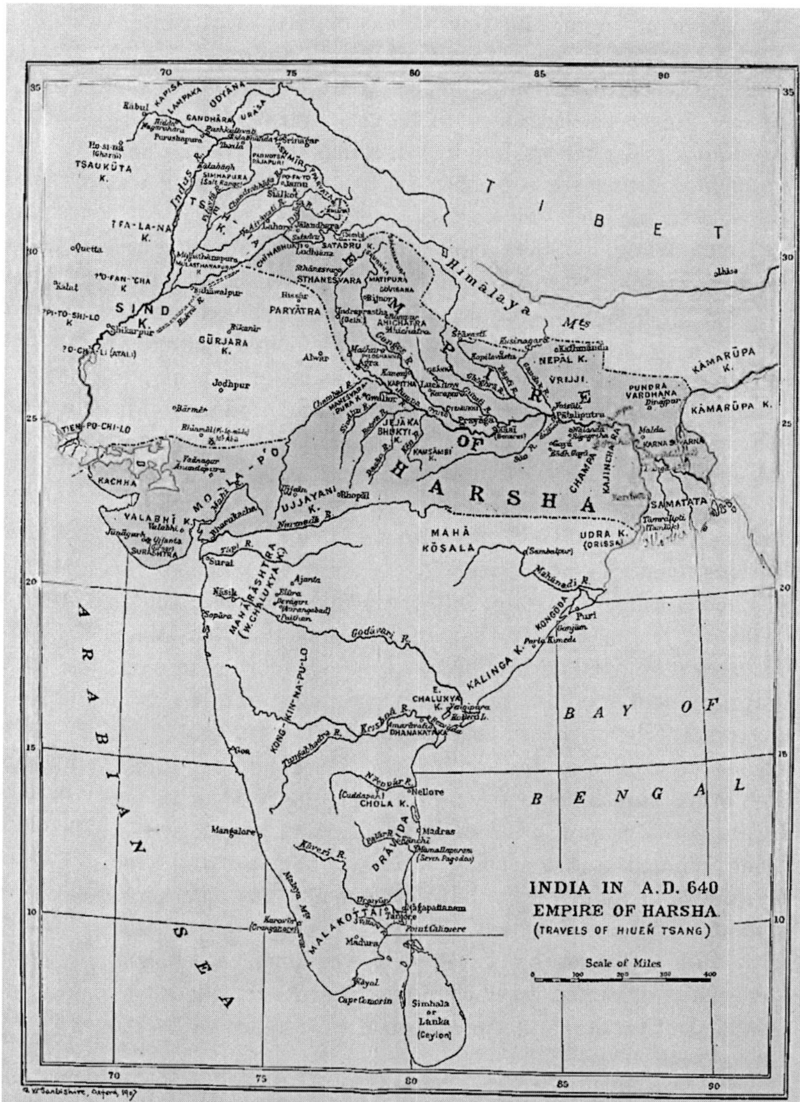
INDIA IN A.D. 640
EMPIRE OF HARSHA
(TRAVELS OF HIUEN TSANG)
Scale of Miles
0 100 200 300 400
TIBET
Himālaya Mts
EMPIRE OF HARSHA
ARABIAN SEA
BAY OF BENGAL
SIND K.
GŪRJARA K.
PARYĀTRA
STHANESVARA
NEPĀL K.
VRIJJI
KĀMARŪPA K.
PUNDRA VARDHANA
SAMATATA
UDRA K. (ORISSA)
MAHĀ KŌSALA
UJJAYANI K.
VALABHĪ K.
KACHHA
MAHĀRĀSHTRA (W. CHALUKYA K.)
KALINGA K.
E. CHALUKYA K.
CHOLA K.
DRĀVIDA
MALAKOTTA
Simhala or Lanka (Ceylon)
Kābul
Quetta
Jodhpur
Bhopāl
Ajanta
Ellūra
Surat
Goa
Mangalore
Nellore
Madras
Madura
Cape Comorin
Puri
Pātaliputra
Malda
Kalat
Shikārpur
Alwar
Agra
Kanauj
Prayāga
Kausāmbī
Srinagar
Lahore
Jalandhara
Bikanir
Godāvarī R.
Mahānadī R.
Krishnā R.
Narmadā R.
Tāpti R.
Chambal R.
Kāverī R.
Tungabhadra R.
Indus R.
Point Calimere
Kāyal
70 75 80 85 90
35 30 25 20 15 10

movable habitations of high Anglo-Indian officials, had not then been invented, and Harsha was obliged to be content with a 'travelling palace' made of boughs and reeds, which was erected at each halting-place, and burnt at his departure.[1] He was accustomed to move in great state, being accompanied by several hundred drummers, who beat a note on golden drums for each step taken. No other king was allowed to use such 'music-pace drums'.[2]

Civil administration.

Hiuen Tsang, like his predecessor Fa-hien, more than two centuries earlier, was favourably impressed by the character of the civil administration, which he considered to be founded on benign principles. The principal source of revenue was the rent of the crown lands, amounting, in theory at all events, to one-sixth of the produce. The officials were remunerated by grants of land; compulsory labour upon public works was paid for; taxes were light; the personal services exacted from the subject were moderate in amount; and liberal provision was made for charity to various religious communities.

Police and crime.

Violent crime was rare, but the roads and river routes evidently were less safe than in Fa-hien's time, as Hiuen Tsang was stopped and robbed by brigands more than once. Imprisonment was now the ordinary penalty, and it was of the cruel Tibetan type; the prisoners, we are told, 'are simply left to live or die, and are not counted among men'. The other punishments were more sanguinary than in the Gupta period: mutilation of the nose, ears, hands, or feet being inflicted as the penalty of serious offences, and even for failure in filial piety; but this penalty was sometimes commuted for banishment. Minor offences were visited with fines. Ordeals by water, fire, weighment, or poison were much esteemed as efficient instruments for the ascertainment of truth; and are described with approval by the Chinese pilgrim.

[1] Beal, *Records*, ii, 193; Watters, ii, 183. The kings of Burma in the eighteenth century followed the same practice. A spacious and by no means uncomfortable dwelling of the royal order of architecture was erected in a day (Symes, *Embassy to Ava*, i, 283, Constable).

[2] Beal, *Life of Hiuen Tsiang*, p. 173.

Official records. Official records of public events were kept in every province by special officers, whose duty it was to register 'good and evil events, with calamities and fortunate occurrences'. Such records were, no doubt, consulted by the writers of the great historical inscriptions, but no specimen of them has survived.

Education and literature. Education evidently was diffused widely, especially among the Brahmans and numerous Buddhist monks; and learning was honoured by the government. King Harsha was not only a liberal patron of literary merit, but was himself an accomplished calligraphist and an author of reputation. Besides a grammatical work, three extant Sanskrit plays

AUTOGRAPH OF KING HARSHA.

and sundry compositions in verse are ascribed to his pen; and there is no reason for hesitating to believe that he had at least a large share in their composition, for royal authors were not uncommon in ancient India. One of these plays, the *Nāgānanda*, which has an edifying Buddhist legend for its subject, is considered to rank among the best works of the Indian theatre; and the other dramas, the *Ratnāvalī*, or 'Necklace', and the *Priyadarsikā*, or 'Gracious Lady', although lacking in originality, are praised highly for their simplicity of both thought and expression.[1]

Bāṇa. The greatest ornament of the literary circle at Harsha's court was the Brahman Bāna, author of the historical romance devoted to a panegyrical account of the deeds of

[1] The facsimile of Harsha's autograph is from the Banskhera inscription. Presumably it was engraved from a tracing of the original. Similar facsimile royal signatures frequently occur in Mysore inscriptions (*A. S. Prog. Rep.*, 1911–12, para. 109, &c.). For the plays see Wilson, *Hindu Theatre*; Sylvain Lévi, *Théâtre Indien*; and Boyd's translation of the *Nāgānanda*. For royal authors see *Ind. Ant.*, xx, 201. Ettinghausen discusses the literary history of Harsha's reign in chapter iii of his work.

his patron, which is an amazingly clever, though irritating, performance ; executed in the worst possible taste, and yet containing passages of admirable and vivid description. The man who attributes to the commander-in-chief, Skandagupta, 'a nose as long as his sovereign's pedigree,' may be fairly accused of having perpetrated the most grotesque simile in all literature. But the same man could do better, and shows no lack of power when depicting the death-agony of the king. 'Helplessness had taken him in hand : pain had made him its province, wasting its domain, lassitude its lair. . . . He was on the confines of doom, on the verge of the last gasp, at the outset of the Great Undertaking, at the portal of the Long Sleep, on the tip of death's tongue ; broken in utterance, unhinged in mind, tortured in body, waning in life, babbling in speech, ceaseless in sighs ; vanquished by yawning, swayed by suffering, in the bondage of wracking pains.' Such writing, although not in perfect good taste, unmistakably bears the stamp of power.[1]

Harsha's latter days. One campaign had sated Asoka's thirst for blood ; thirty-seven years of warfare, continuous for six years, and intermittent for the rest of the time, were needed by Harsha before he could be content to sheathe the sword. His last campaign was fought against the people of Ganjām (Kongōda) in A. D. 643, and then at last this king of many wars doffed his armour, and devoted himself for his few remaining years to the arts of peace and the practice of piety, as understood by an Indian despot. He obviously set himself to imitate Asoka, so that the narrative of the doings in the latter years of Harsha's reign reads like a copy of the history of the great Maurya.

His devotion. At this period the king began to show marked favour to the quietist teachings of Buddhism, first in its Hīnayāna, and afterwards in its Mahāyāna form. He led the life of a devotee, enforcing the Buddhist prohibitions against the destruction of animal life with the utmost strictness and

[1] The translation of Bāṇa's work by Dr. F. W. Thomas and the late Professor Cowell, published by the Royal Asiatic Society in 1897, is a triumph of skill.

scant regard for the sanctity of human life. 'He sought', we are told, 'to plant the tree of religious merit to such an extent that he forgot to sleep and eat'; and forbade the slaughter of any living thing, or the use of flesh as food throughout the 'Five Indies' under pain of death without hope of pardon.

Benevolent and religious institutions. Benevolent institutions on the Asokan model, for the benefit of travellers, the poor, and sick, were established throughout the empire. Rest-houses (*dharmsālā*) were built in both the towns and rural parts, and provided with food and drink, physicians being stationed at them to supply medicines to the necessitous without stint. The king also imitated his prototype in the foundation of numerous religious establishments, devoted to the service of both the Hindu gods and the Buddhist ritual. In his closing years the latter received the chief share of the royal favour; and numerous monasteries were erected, as well as several thousand *stūpas*, each about 100 feet high, built along the banks of the sacred Ganges. These latter structures doubtless were of a flimsy character, built chiefly of timber and bamboos, and so have left no trace; but the mere multiplication of *stūpas*, however perishable the materials might be, was always a work of merit. Although Buddhism was visibly waning in the days of Harsha and Hiuen Tsang, the monks of the order were still numerous, and the occupants of the monasteries enumerated by the pilgrim numbered nearly two hundred thousand.[1] A monastic population of such magnitude offered abundant opportunities for the exercise of princely liberality.

State of religion. The picture of the state of religious belief and practice in India during the seventh century, as drawn by the contemporary authors, is filled with curious and interesting details. The members of the royal family to which Harsha belonged freely acted on their individual preferences in the matter of religion. His remote ancestor, Pushyabhūti, is recorded to have entertained from boyhood an ardent devotion towards Siva, and to have turned away from all

[1] *J.R.A.S.*, 1891, pp. 418–21.

other gods. Harsha's father was equally devoted to the worship of the Sun, and daily offered to that luminary 'a bunch of red lotuses set in a pure vessel of ruby, and tinged, like his own heart, with the same hue'. The elder brother and sister of Harsha were convinced Buddhists, while Harsha himself distributed his devotions among the three deities of the family, Siva, the Sun, and Buddha;[1] and erected costly temples for the service of all three. But, in his latter years, the Buddhist doctrines held the chief place in his affections; and the eloquence of the Chinese Master of the Law induced him to prefer the advanced teaching of the Mahāyāna sect to the more primitive Hīnayāna doctrine of the Sammitīya school with which he had been familiar previously.

Royal eclecticism.

The religious eclecticism of the royal family was the reflection and result of the state of popular religion at the time. Buddhism, although it had certainly lost the dominant position in the Gangetic plain which it had once held, was still a powerful force, and largely influenced the public mind. The Jain system, which had never been very widely spread or aggressive in the North, while retaining its hold on certain localities, especially at Vaisāli and in Eastern Bengal, could not pretend to rival the general popularity of either Buddhism or Purānic Hinduism. The last-named modification of the Hindu system was now firmly established, and the earlier Purānas were already revered as ancient and sacred writings. The bulk of the population in most provinces was then, as now, devoted to the service of the Purānic gods; each man and woman being, of course, free to select a particular deity, Siva, the Sun, Vishnu, or another, for special adoration according to personal predilection. As a rule, the followers of the various religions lived peaceably together; and no doubt many people besides the king sought to make certain of some divine support by doing honour to all the principal objects of popular worship in turn.

[1] It is, of course, not strictly accurate to describe Buddha as a deity; but, when the Buddhism of the seventh century is in question, the inaccuracy is little more than formal.

Persecution by Śaśāṅka.

But, while toleration and concord were the rule, exceptions occurred. The king of Central Bengal, Sasānka, who has been mentioned as the treacherous murderer of Harsha's brother, and probably was a scion of the Gupta dynasty, was a worshipper of Siva, hating Buddhism, which he did his best to extirpate. He dug up and burnt the holy Bodhi tree at Bōdh Gayā, on which, according to legend, Asoka had lavished inordinate devotion; broke the stone marked with the footprints of Buddha at Pātaliputra; destroyed the convents, and scattered the monks, carrying his persecutions to the foot of the Nepalese hills. These events, which are amply attested by the evidence of Hiuen Tsang, who visited the localities thirty or forty years later, must have happened about A.D. 600. The Bodhi tree was replanted after a short time by Pūrna-varman, the local Rāja of Magadha, who is described as being the last descendant of Asoka, and as such was specially bound to honour the object venerated by his great ancestor.

Sectarian animosity.

The details given by Hiuen Tsang and his biographer prove that at times bitter animosity marked the relations of the two great sections of the Buddhist church with one another; and that equal ill-feeling was evoked in the breasts of Purānic Hindus, when they beheld the royal favours lavished upon their Buddhist rivals. It is clear, therefore, that general statements concerning the perfect religious toleration enjoyed in ancient India can be accepted only with a certain amount of reservation. Official persecutions and popular ebullitions of sectarian rancour undoubtedly occurred from time to time, although they were not frequent.

Disputations.

Harsha himself sometimes offended against the principle of perfect religious toleration and equality. Like Akbar, and many other Indian sovereigns, he was fond of listening to the expositions of rival doctors, and heard with pleasure the arguments adduced by the learned Chinese traveller in favour of the Mahāyāna form of Buddhism, with the doctrines of which he does not seem to have been familiar. An interesting illustration of the comparative freedom of ancient Hindu society from the trammels of the system of female seclusion favoured by the Muhammadans, is afforded by the fact that his widowed sister sat by the king's side to hear the lecture by the Master of the Law, and frankly expressed the delight which she received from the discourse. One Chinese authority even asserts that Harsha administered the government in conjunction with her, as already noted.[1]

Harsha's proclamation.

The king was determined that his favourite should not be defeated in controversy; and when opponents were invited to dispute the propositions of the Chinese scholar, the terms of the contest were not quite fair. Harsha, having heard a report that Hiuen Tsang's life was in danger at the hands of his theological rivals, issued a proclamation concluding with the announcement that

> 'if any one should touch or hurt the Master of the Law, he shall be forthwith executed; and whoever speaks against him, his tongue shall be cut out; but all those who desire to profit by his instructions, relying on my goodwill, need not fear this manifesto'.

The pilgrim's biographer naïvely adds that

> 'from this time the followers of error withdrew and disappeared, so that when eighteen days had passed, there had been no one to enter on the discussion'.[2]

[1] The *Fang-chih* (Watters, i, 345).

[2] Beal, *Life of Hiuen Tsiang*, p. 180. In the second edition, a legend related by Tāranāth (Schiefner, p. 128) concerning a certain king named Śrī Harsha, was erroneously applied to Harsha of Kanauj. The historian states that Śrī Harsha enticed 12,000 followers of outlandish religions to assemble in a wooden building, where he burnt them all alive with their books, and so reduced the religion of the Persians and Śakas to very narrow limits for nearly a century. This atrocity is said to have taken place near Multān. Tāranāth adds that Śrī Harsha, in order to atone for his sins, built four great monasteries severally situated in Maru (Mārwāṛ), Mālava, Mewāṛ, Pituva, and Chitavara, in each of which 1,000 monks were maintained. I cannot identify Pituva or Chitavara, nor can I determine the date; but it is clear that Śrī Harsha must have been a chief in Rājputāna, probably of Mārwāṛ, the first country named. The sixth century seems to be indicated as the time. Harsha was born in Mārwāṛ, and ruled all the kingdoms of the west (ibid., p. 126). Ettinghausen (*Harśa Vardhana*, p. 84), who also erroneously identified the Śrī Harsha of Mārwāṛ with Harsha of Kanauj, cites Ceylonese versions of the story of the burning. I have not yet found a Rāja Harsha in the Rājputāna lists, but there was a town called Harshapura in Mewāṛ (*Ind. Ant.*, 1910, p. 187), which may have been named after the hero of Tāranāth's story.

Assembly at Kanauj.

King Harsha was so delighted with the discourse of Hiuen Tsang, whom he had met while in camp in Bengal, that he resolved to hold a special assembly at Kanauj, then his capital, for the purpose of giving the utmost publicity to the Master's teaching. The king marched along the southern bank of the Ganges, attended by an enormous multitude; his ally Kumāra, King of Kāmarūpa, with a large but less numerous following, keeping pace with him on the opposite bank. Advancing slowly in this way, Harsha, Kumāra, and the attendant host reached Kanauj in the course of ninety days, and there encamped, in February or March, A.D. 643.[1] The sovereign was received by Kumāra, the Rāja of Kāmarūpa, who had accompanied him on the march, the Rāja of Valabhī in Western India, who was connected with him by marriage, and eighteen other tributary rājas; as well as by four thousand learned Buddhist monks, including a thousand from the Nālandā monastery in Bihār, and some three thousand Jains and orthodox Brahmans.

Ceremonies.

The centre of attraction was a great monastery and shrine specially erected upon the bank of the Ganges, where a golden image of Buddha, equal to the king in stature, was kept in a tower, 100 feet high. A similar but smaller image, 3 feet in height, was carried daily in solemn procession, escorted by the twenty rājas and a train of three hundred elephants. The canopy was borne by Harsha in person, attired as the god Sakra, while his ally, Rāja Kumāra, the most important of the princes in attendance, was clad as the god Brahmā, and had the honour of waving a white fly-whisk. The sovereign, as he moved along, scattered on every side pearls, golden flowers, and other precious substances, in honour of the 'Three Jewels'—Buddha, the Religion, and the Order; and, having with his own hands washed the image at the altar prepared for the purpose, bore it on his shoulder to the western tower, and there offered to it thousands of silken robes, embroidered with gems. Dinner was succeeded by a public disputation of the one-sided kind already described; and in the evening

[1] 'It was now the second month of springtime' (Beal, *Records*, i, 218).

the monarch returned to his 'travelling palace', a mile distant.

These ceremonies, which lasted for many days, were terminated by startling incidents. The temporary monastery, which had been erected at vast cost, suddenly took fire, and was in great part destroyed; but when the king intervened in person, the flames were stayed, and pious hearts recognized a miracle.

Attempt on Harsha's life.

Harsha, attended by his princely train, had ascended the great *stūpa* to survey the scene, and was coming down the steps, when a fanatic, armed with a dagger, rushed upon him and attempted to stab him. The assassin, having been captured instantly, was closely interrogated by the king in person, and confessed that he had been instigated to commit the crime by certain 'heretics', who resented the excessive royal favour shown to the Buddhists. Five hundred Brahmans of note were then arrested, and being 'straitly questioned', were induced to confess that, in order to gratify their jealousy, they had fired the tower by means of burning arrows, and had hoped to slay the king during the resulting confusion. This confession, no doubt extorted by torture, probably was wholly false; but, whether true or not, it was accepted, and on the strength of it the alleged principals in the plot were executed, and some five hundred Brahmans were sent into exile.

A. D. 643. Charitable distribution at Prayāga.

After the close of the proceedings at Kanauj, Harsha invited his Chinese guest to accompany him to Prayāga (Allāhābād), at the confluence of the Ganges and Jumna, to witness another imposing ceremonial. The Master of the Law, although anxious to start on his toilsome homeward journey, could not refuse the invitation, and accompanied his royal host to the scene of the intended display. Harsha explained that it had been his practice for thirty years past, in accordance with the custom of his ancestors, to hold a great quinquennial assembly on the sands where the rivers meet, and there to distribute his accumulated treasures to the poor and needy, as well as to the religious of all denominations. The present occasion (A. D. 643) was the sixth of the series, which evidently had not been begun until Harsha had consolidated his power in the north.

Proceedings. The assembly was attended by all the vassal kings and a vast concourse of humbler folk estimated to number half a million, including poor, orphans, and destitute persons, besides specially invited Brahmans and ascetics of every sect from all parts of Northern India. The proceedings lasted for seventy-five days, terminating apparently about the end of April, and were opened by an imposing procession of all the rājas with their retinues. The religious services were of the curiously eclectic kind characteristic of the times. On the first day, an image of Buddha was set up in one of the temporary thatched buildings upon the sands, and vast quantities of costly clothing and other articles of value were distributed. On the second and third days respectively the images of the Sun and Siva were similarly honoured, but the accompanying distribution in each case was only half the amount of that consecrated to Buddha. The fourth day was devoted to the bestowal of gifts on ten thousand selected religious persons of the Buddhist order, who each received one hundred gold coins, a pearl, and a cotton garment, besides choice food, drink, flowers, and perfumes. During the next following twenty days, the great multitude of Brahmans were the recipients of the royal bounty. They were succeeded by the people whom the Chinese author calls 'heretics', that is to say, Jains and members of sundry sects, who received gifts for the space of ten days. A like period was allotted for the bestowal of alms upon mendicants from distant regions; and a month was occupied in the distribution of charitable aid to poor, orphaned, and destitute persons.

Extent of gifts. 'By this time the accumulation of five years was exhausted. Except the horses, elephants, and military accoutrements, which were necessary for maintaining order and protecting the royal estate, nothing remained. Besides these the king freely gave away his gems and goods, his clothing and necklaces, ear-rings, bracelets, chaplets, neck-jewel and bright head-jewel, all these he freely gave without stint. All being given away, he begged from his sister [Rājyaśri] an ordinary second-hand garment, and having put it on, he paid worship to the "Buddhas of the ten regions", and rejoiced that his treasure had been bestowed in the field of religious merit.'

Departure of Hiuen Tsang.

The strange assembly, which in general appearance must have much resembled the crowded fair still held annually on the same ground, then broke up; and, after a further detention of ten days, Hiuen Tsang was permitted to depart. The king and Kumāra Rāja offered him abundance of gold pieces and other precious things, none of which would he accept save a fur-lined cape, the gift of Kumāra. But although the Master of the Law uniformly declined gifts intended to serve his personal use, he did not disdain to accept money for the necessary expenses of his arduous journey overland to China. These were provided on a liberal scale by the grant of three thousand gold and ten thousand silver pieces carried on an elephant. A rāja named Udhita was placed in command of a mounted escort, and charged to conduct the pilgrim in safety to the frontier. In the course of about six months of leisurely progress interrupted by frequent halts, the rāja completed his task, and brought his sovereign's guest in safety to Jālandhar in the east of the Panjāb, where Hiuen Tsang stayed for a month. He then started with a fresh escort, and, penetrating with difficulty the defiles of the Salt Range, crossed the Indus, and ultimately reached his home in distant China by the route over the Pāmīrs and through Khotan, in the spring of A.D. 645.[1]

His death.

The pilgrim did not come home empty-handed. Notwithstanding losses on more than one occasion, due to accident or robbery, he succeeded in bringing safely a hundred and fifty particles of Buddha's bodily relics; sundry images of the Teacher in gold, silver, and sandal-wood; and no less than 657 distinct volumes of manuscripts, carried upon twenty horses. The rest of his life was mainly devoted to the work of translation, and he had completed the Chinese

[1] 'Yuan-chuang returned to China, and arrived at Ch'ang-an in the beginning of 645, the nineteenth year of T'ang T'ai Tsung' (Watters, i, 11). See map and itinerary appended to vol. ii of Watters's work.

versions of seventy-four separate works when he brought his literary labours to a close in the year A.D. 661. He lived in peace and honour for three years longer, and then calmly passed away, leaving behind him a reputation for learning and piety surpassing that of any other Buddhist doctor.

A.D. 647. Death of Harsha.

The pages of Hiuen Tsang and his biographer give the latest information about King Harsha, who died either at the end of 646 or the beginning of 647, not long after his distinguished guest's departure.

Inter-course with China.

During his lifetime he maintained diplomatic intercourse with the Chinese empire. A Brahman envoy, whom he had sent to the emperor of China in 641, returned in A.D. 643, accompanied by a Chinese mission bearing a reply to Harsha's dispatch. The mission remained for a considerable time in India, and did not go back to China until A.D. 645. The next year, Wang-hiuen-tse, who had been the second in command of the earlier embassy, was sent by his sovereign as head of a new Indian mission, with an escort of thirty horsemen. Early in A.D. 647, or possibly at the close of 646, King Harsha died, leaving no heir, and the withdrawal of his strong arm plunged the country into disorder, which was aggravated by famine.

Arjuna, or Arunāsva, a minister of the late king, usurped the throne, and took the field with 'barbarian' troops against the Chinese mission. The members of the escort were massacred, or taken prisoners, and the property of the mission, including the articles presented by Indian kings, was plundered; but the envoys, Wang-hiuen-tse and his colleague, were fortunate enough to escape into Nepāl by night.

Defeat of the usurper by the Chinese envoy.

The reigning king of Tibet, the famous Srong-tsan Gampo, who was married to a Chinese princess, succoured the fugitives, and supplied them with a force of twelve hundred picked soldiers supported by a Nepalese contingent of seven thousand horsemen, Nepāl at that time being subject to Tibet. With this small army Wang-hiuen-tse descended into the plains, and, after a three days' siege, succeeded in storming the chief city of Tirhūt. Three thousand of the garrison were beheaded, and ten thousand persons were drowned in the neighbouring river, perhaps the Bāgmatī. (?) Arjuna fled, and having collected a fresh force, offered battle. He was again disastrously defeated and taken prisoner. The victor promptly beheaded a thousand prisoners, and in a later action captured the entire royal family, took twelve thousand prisoners, and obtained more than thirty thousand head of horses and cattle. Five hundred and eighty walled towns made their submission during the course of the campaign, and Kumāra, the king of Eastern India, who had attended Harsha's assemblies a few years earlier, sent in abundant supplies of cattle and accoutrements for the victorious army. Wang-hiuen-tse brought the usurper as a prisoner to China, and was promoted for his services. Afterwards, in A.D. 650, when the emperor T'ai Tsung died and his mausoleum was erected, the approach to the building was adorned by statues, which included the effigies of the Tibetan king, Srong-tsan Gampo, and of the usurper, (?) Arjuna. Tirhūt apparently remained subject for some time to Tibet, which was then a powerful state, strong enough to defy the Chinese empire. Thus ended this strange episode, which, although known to antiquaries for many years, has hitherto escaped the notice of the historians of India.

Third visit of Wang-hiuen-tse.

Wang-hiuen-tse once more visited the scene of his adventures, being sent by imperial order in A.D. 657 to offer robes at the Buddhist holy places. He entered India through Nepāl, by the Lhāsa road, which was then open and used by many Buddhist pilgrims; and, after paying his respects at Vaisāli, Bōdh-Gayā, and other sacred spots, returned home through Kapisa, or Northern Afghanistan, by the Hindū Kush and Pāmīr route.[1]

[1] The story of Wang-hiuen-t'se is fully related in Sylvain Lévi's article, 'Les Missions de Wang-Hiuen-T'se dans l'Inde' (*J. As.*, 1900), which has been translated in *Ind. Ant.*, 1911, pp. 111 *seqq.* The name of the usurper appears in the Chinese text as Na-fū-ti O-lo-na-shuen, which may represent either Arjuna or Aruṇāśva. Lt.-Col. Waddell's valuable article 'Tibetan Invasion of India in A.D. 647 and its Results' (*As. Qu. Rev.*, Jan., 1911), emphasizes the

Kashmīr in the seventh century.

The observations of Hiuen Tsang throw considerable light upon the political arrangements of India in the regions beyond the limits of Harsha's empire during the seventh century. In the north, Kashmīr had become the predominant power, and had reduced the kingdoms of Taxila and the Salt Range (Simhapura), as well as the minor principalities of the lower hills,[1] to the rank of dependencies.

The Panjāb.

The greater part of the Panjāb between the Indus and the Biās rivers was comprised in the kingdom called Tseh-kia, or Chēh-ka, by the pilgrim, the capital of which was an unnamed city situated close to Sākala (Siālkot), where the tyrant Mihiragula had held his court. The province of Multān, where the Sun-god was held in special honour, and a country called Po-fa-to, probably Jamū, to the north-east of Multān, were dependencies of this kingdom.

Sind.

Sind was remarkable for being under the government of a Buddhist king belonging to the Sūdra caste, and for the large number of Buddhist monks which the country supported, estimated at ten thousand. But the quality was not in proportion to the quantity; most of the ten thousand being denounced as idle fellows given over to self-indulgence and debauchery. The Indus delta, to which the pilgrim gives the name of 'O-tien-p'o-chi-lo, was a province of the kingdom of Sind.[2]

Alōr, the capital.

From other sources of information we learn that the kingdom of Sind, of which Balūchistan was a dependency, in those days was rich and powerful, far more populous and fertile than it is now. It occupied the whole valley of the Indus from the neighbourhood of the Salt Range to the sea, and was separated from India proper by the 'lost river', the Hakrā or Wahindah, the Sin-tu of Hiuen Tsang. The capital, to which the pilgrim gives the name of P'i-shan-p'o-

true position of Tibet at that time, and corrects the date of Harsha's death.

[1] Uraśā, or Hazāra; Parnōtsa, or Punach; Rājapuri, or Rajauri, the ancient Abhisāra.

[2] The proper Indian equivalents of Tseh-kia, Po-fa-to, and 'O-tien-p'o-chi-lo are not known with any approach to certainty. See map. Many *stūpas* and other Buddhist remains in Sind, hitherto overlooked, are now coming to light (*A. S. W. I., Prog. Rep.*, 1909–10, p. 40).

pu-lo, was Arōr or Alōr, on the west bank of the Hakrā, a large fortified city, the ruins of which are still traceable 5 miles to the south-east of Rohri (Rūrhī) in the Sukkur (Sakhar) District, N. lat. 27° 39′, E. long. 68° 59′. According to a romantic legend, the ruin of the city was effected, about A.D. 800, by a merchant named Saif-ul-Mulūk, who diverted the waters of the river in order to save a beautiful girl from the clutches of a licentious rāja.

Kings of Sind.

The Buddhist king of the Sūdra caste mentioned by the pilgrim must be Sihras Rāi, son of Dīwajī, who was succeeded by his son Sāhasī. During the reign of Sihras Rāi, the ever-victorious Arabs, then in the first flush of enthusiasm, entered Makrān (Balūchistan), and were met by Sihras Rāi, who was defeated and slain. Makrān was permanently occupied by the invaders late in A.D. 644, and about two years later, Sāhasī, who continued to oppose the foreign enemy, shared his father's fate. The sceptre then passed into the hands of a Brahman minister named Chach, who ruled for about forty years. Sind was invaded by the Arabs in A.D. 710–11 (A.H. 92), under the command of Muhammad, the son of Kāsim, who defeated and killed Dāhir, the son of Chach, in June, A.D. 712. From that date the ancient Hindu kingdom was extinguished, and the province passed permanently into Muslim hands.[1]

Central India.

The kings of Ujjain and other kingdoms in Central India, which must have been more or less subject to Harsha's control, belonged to the Brahman caste. The Ujjain country supported a dense population, comprising few Buddhists. Most of the monasteries were in ruins, and only three or four, occupied by some three hundred monks, were in use. The early decay of Buddhism in this region, which was sanctified by the traditions of Asoka, and included the magnificent buildings at Sānchī, is a curious fact, at present unexplained.

[1] Raverty, *Notes on Afghanistan*, pp. 566–70, 663; *J. A. S. B.*, part i (1902), pp. 233, 239, 251; Elliot, *Hist. of India*, vol. i, Note B, p. 405. Raverty's statements are more accurate than those of Elliot, which contain many errors. The name which Elliot (p. 405) reads as 'Kanauj' really is Kinnauj, a dependency of Multān,

Kāmarūpa.

Bhāskara-varman, or Kumāra Rāja, the King of Kāmarūpa, or Assam, who played such a prominent part in Harsha's ceremonials, also was described as being by caste a Brahman, and without faith in Buddha; although well disposed towards learned men of all religions. He was so far subject to the sovereign of Northern India, that he could not afford to disobey Harsha's commands.[1]

Kaliṅga.

Kalinga, the conquest of which had cost Asoka such bitter remorse nine hundred years earlier, was depopulated, and mostly covered with jungle. The pilgrim observes in picturesque language that 'in old days the kingdom of Kalinga had a very dense population. Their shoulders rubbed one with the other, and the axles of their chariot wheels grided together, and when they raised their arm-sleeves a perfect tent was formed'. Legend sought to explain the change by the curse of an angry saint.

Other kingdoms.

Hiuen Tsang's account of Kashmīr, Nepāl, and the kingdoms of the South and West will be noticed in due course in subsequent chapters.

Effect of Harsha's death.

Harsha's death loosened the bonds which restrained the disruptive forces always ready to operate in India, and allowed them to produce their natural result, a medley of petty states, with ever-varying boundaries, and engaged in unceasing internecine war. Such was India when first disclosed to European observation in the fourth century B.C., and such it always has been, except during the comparatively brief periods in which a vigorous central government has compelled the mutually repellent molecules of the body politic to check their gyrations and submit to the grasp of a superior controlling force.

India's normal condition.

The visitation of the Hun invasions had caused such suffering that the wholesome despotism of Harsha was recognized as a necessary remedy. When he died, the

[1] An undated copperplate inscription of Bhāskara-varman has been described in *Ind. Ant.*, 1914, p. 25, and edited with facsimiles by Radha Govinda Basak in *Ep. Ind.*, xii, 65–79. He believes that at first Bhāskara was in terror of Śaśāṅka, but when Śaśāṅka died later than 619, his kingdom passed into the hands of Harsha. Bhāskaravarman may have obtained Karṇa-suvarṇa in Bengal, whence the copperplate was issued, after the defeat of the usurper.

wounds inflicted by the fierce foreign savages had long been healed, while the freedom of the country from external attack relieved men's minds from feeling the necessity for a deliverer; and so India instantly reverted to her normal condition of anarchical autonomy.

Freedom from foreign aggression for five centuries.

Excepting the purely local incursions of the Arabs in Sind and Gujarāt during the eighth century, interior India was exempt from serious foreign aggression for nearly five hundred years, from the defeat of Mihiragula in A.D. 528 until the raids of Mahmūd of Ghazni at the beginning of the eleventh century, and was left free to work out her destiny in her own fashion.

Polity, literature, and religion.

In political institutions no evolution took place. No sovereign arose endowed with commanding abilities and capable of welding together the jarring members of the body politic, as Chandragupta Maurya, Asoka, and in a lesser degree the Gupta kings and Harsha of Kanauj had done. The nearest approach to the position of universal lord of Northern India was made by Mihira Bhoja of Kanauj (*c.* A.D. 840–90), but unluckily we know next to nothing about his character or administration. Even the heavy pressure of Muslim invasion failed to produce effective cohesion of the numberless Hindu States, which, one by one, fell an easy prey to fierce hordes of Arabs, Turks, and Afghans, bound together by stern fanaticism. Literature, although actively cultivated and liberally patronized at many local courts, sank far below the level attained by Kālidāsa. In mathematics, astronomy, or any other branch of science, little or no advance was made. Religion suffered a grave loss by the gradual extinction of Buddhism, which, in virtue of imperceptible changes, became merged in various Hindu sects. Only in Magadha and the neighbouring countries the religion of Gautama, under new forms, preserved a vigorous existence for four centuries (*c.* A.D. 780–1193), sustained by the support of Dharmapāla and his successors of the Pāla dynasty.

Fine art.

The art of sculpture, devoted in most places to the service of the Hindu gods, and in the Pāla dominions to that of modified Buddhism, was developed in diverse styles by many schools of artists. The aesthetic value of that abundant mediaeval sculpture is the subject of keen controversy, admirers seeing in it the highest achievement of Hindu genius, while other critics are repelled by its lack of restraint and its tendency to lapse into ugly grotesqueness. The paintings of mediaeval times, unfortunately, have disappeared utterly, so that it is impossible to judge whether pictorial skill advanced or declined. The art of coinage certainly decayed so decisively that not even one mediaeval coin deserves notice for its aesthetic merits.

Architecture. But architecture was practised on a magnificent scale. Although most of the innumerable buildings erected were destroyed during the centuries of Muhammadan rule, even the small fraction surviving is enough to prove that the Hindu architects were able to plan with grandeur and to execute with a lavishness of detail which compels admiration while inviting hostile criticism by its excess of cloying ornament.

Petty states. The three following chapters, which attempt to give an outline of the salient features in the bewildering annals of Indian petty states when left to their own devices for several centuries, may perhaps serve to give the reader a notion of what India always has been when released from the control of a supreme authority, and what she would be again, if the hand of the benevolent power which now safeguards her boundaries should be withdrawn.

CHRONOLOGY OF THE SEVENTH CENTURY

A.D.	EVENT.
600	Hiuen Tsang, Chinese pilgrim, born.
c. 600	Persecution of Buddhism by Śaśāṅka.
605	Rājya-vardhana, Rāja of Thānēsar, *acc.*
606	Harsha-vardhana, Rāja of Thānēsar, *acc.*
606–12	Conquest of Northern India by Harsha.
608	Pulakeśin II Chalukya, *acc.*
609	Pulakeśin II Chalukya, crowned.
Oct. 612	Harsha crowned ; his era established, as from 606.
615	Kubja Vishṇu-vardhana (Vishamasiddhi), viceroy of Vengī.
618	Kao-tsu, first T'ang emperor of China, *acc.*
619–20	Ganjām inscription of Śaśāṅka.
c. 620	Defeat of Harsha by Pulakeśin II Chalukya.
622	Muhammadan era of the Hijra or 'flight'.
627	T'ai Tsung, emperor of China, *acc.*
628–9	Banskhera inscription of Harsha.
629	Hiuen Tsang began his travels.
629	Accession of Srong-tsan-Gampo, king of Tibet.
630–1	Madhuban inscription of Harsha.
c. 635	Conquest of Valabhī by Harsha.
636	Nestorian Christianity introduced into China by Alopen.
641	Harsha sent embassy to China ; king Srong-tsan-Gampo of Tibet married Chinese princess Wen-cheng ;[1] Sassanian king Yezdegird defeated by the Arabs at Nahavend ; Arab conquest of Egypt.
642	Death of Pulakeśin II Chalukya.
643	Harsha's expedition to Ganjām ; his meeting with Hiuen Tsang ; Chinese mission of Li-I-piao and Wang-hiuen-t'se ; Harsha's assemblies at Kanauj and Prayāga ; Hiuen Tsang started on return journey.
645	Arrival of Hiuen Tsang in China.
646	Dispatch of second mission of Wang-hiuen-t'se.
647	Death of Harsha.
647–8	Usurpation of (?) Arjuna and his defeat by Chinese, Nepalese, and Tibetans ; publication of Hiuen Tsang's *Travels*.
649	Death of T'ai Tsung, emperor of China ; Kao-tsung, *acc.*
657	Third mission of Wang-hiuen-t'se.
661–5	Greatest extension of Chinese dominions.
664	Death of Hiuen Tsang.
670	Defeat of Chinese by Tibetans.
671	I-tsing, Chinese pilgrim, began his travels.
675–85	I-tsing resided at Nālandā.
691	I-tsing composed his *Record*.
695	I-tsing returned to China.
c. 698	Death of Srong-tsan-Gampo, king of Tibet.

[1] Date of marriage according to Waddell and Sarat Chandra Dās.

CHAPTER XIV

THE MEDIAEVAL KINGDOMS OF THE NORTH

FROM A.D. 647 TO 1200

I

Relations with China and Tibet

Chinese influence on northern frontier of India.

THE tenacity of the Chinese government in holding on to the most distant possessions of the empire has been exemplified in recent times by the recovery of Kāshgaria and Yunnan from Muhammadan powers, and of Kulja from the Russians. The history of the seventh and eighth centuries offers many illustrations of the same characteristic, and exhibits China as making the most determined efforts to exercise influence in, and assert suzerainty over, the countries on the northern frontier of India.

A. D. 502–56. Ephthalite empire.

In the first half of the sixth century the power of China in the 'Western countries' had vanished, and the Ephthalites, or White Huns, ruled a vast empire, which included Kāshgaria—the 'Four Garrisons' of Chinese writers—Kashmīr,[1] and Gandhāra, the region near Peshāwar.

A. D. 565. Empire of Western Turks.

About the year 565 ('between 563 and 567') the Ephthalite dominion passed into the hands of the Western Turks and Persians; but the grasp of the latter power on the provinces south of the Oxus soon relaxed, and the Turks became the heirs of the Ephthalites in the whole of their territory as far as the Indus. Accordingly, in A. D. 630, when Hiuen Tsang was on his way to India, his safety was assured by passports granted by Tong-she-hū, the 'Kazan', or supreme chief of the Western Turks, which guaranteed him protection as far as Kapisa.[2]

[1] Ki-pin, which term was usually understood to mean Kashmīr by Chinese writers of the sixth century, in the time of the Wei dynasty (Chavannes, *Song Yun*, p. 37).

[2] Ki-pin, which ordinarily meant Kapiśa, the country to the north of the Kābul river, for Chinese writers of the seventh century, in the time of the T'ang dynasty.

In the same year the pilgrim's powerful protector was assassinated, and the Chinese, under the guidance of the emperor T'ai-tsung, the second prince of the Tang dynasty, inflicted upon the Northern or Eastern Turks a defeat so decisive that the vanquished became slaves to the Chinese for fifty years.

A. D. 630. Chinese defeat of Northern Turks.

When relieved from fear of the Northern Turks, the Chinese were able to turn their arms against the western tribes, and in the years 640–8 succeeded in occupying Turfān, Kara-shahr, and Kuchā, thus securing the northern road of communication between the East and West.

A. D. 640–8. Chinese conquest of Kuchā, &c.

At this time Tibet was under the rule of the famous king, Srong-tsan-Gampo (acc. A.D. 629), who founded Lhāsa in A.D. 639, introduced Buddhism into his country, and, with the help of Indian scholars, devised the Tibetan alphabet.[1] While still very young he married Bhrikuti, a daughter of the king of Nepāl, and two years later, in A.D. 641, he succeeded with much difficulty in winning by his victories the hand of the princess Wen-cheng, daughter of the Chinese emperor, T'ai-tsung. Both these ladies being zealous Buddhists, converted their young husband, and so determined the whole course of Tibetan history. The Church has not been slow to recognize the merit of its patrons. The king has been deified as an incarnation of Buddha, Avalokitesvara, the Saviour, while his Nepalese consort is revered as the 'Green Tārā' and the Chinese princess as the 'White Tārā'. The Chinese marriage secured the maintenance of friendly relations between Tibet and China during the life of Srong-tsan-Gampo, which ended, according to most authorities, in or about A.D. 698, but may possibly have come to a close several years earlier. In consequence, the Chinese envoys, in the years 643–5, when on their way to the court of Harsha, were able to pass through Tibet and its dependency Nepāl as allied countries, and both those kingdoms willingly sent

Friendly relations with Tibet.

[1] The Tibetan alphabet really is that of Khotan, learned by Thon-mi Sambhota in Kashmīr from a learned Brahman of Khotan (*Ep. Ind.*, xi, 266; Hoernle, *Manuscript Remains of Buddhist Literature from E. Turkestan*, Clarendon Press, 1916, p. xvii). According to tradition, Khotan came under Tibetan rule in the seventh century.

troops to rescue Wang-Hiuen-tse from the troubles into which he fell after Harsha's death.[1]

A. D. 659–61. China in possession of empire of Western Turks.

The work of subduing the Turks, begun by the emperor T'ai-tsung, was continued by his successor Kao-tsung (649–83), and, by the year 659, China was nominally mistress of the entire territory of the Western Turks, which was then formally annexed. In 661–5 China enjoyed unparalleled prestige, and had reached a height of glory never again attained. Kapisa (Ki-pin) was a province of the empire, and the imperial retinue included ambassadors from Udyāna, or the Suwāt valley, and from all the countries extending from Persia to Korea.

A. D. 670. Occupation of Kāshgaria by the Tibetans.

But this magnificent extension of the empire did not last long. A terrible defeat inflicted by the Tibetans in 670 deprived China of Kāshgaria, or the 'Four Garrisons', which remained in the hands of the victors until A. D. 692, when the province was recovered by the Chinese.

A. D. 744. Final overthrow of the Northern Turks.

Between 682 and 691 the Northern Turks had regained a good deal of the power which had been shattered by the defeat of 630, and even exercised a certain amount of control over the western tribes. But internal dissension was at all times the bane of the Central Asian nations, and the Chinese well knew how to take advantage of the national failing. They intervened in the tribal quarrels, with the support of the Uigurs and Karluks, with such effect that in 744 the Uigurs established themselves on the Orkhon in the eastern part of the Turkish territory; while, on the west, the Karluks gradually occupied the country of the Ten Tribes, and took

[1] Sarat Chandra Dās (*J.A.S.B.*, vol. i, pt. i (1881), pp. 217–22); Waddell, *The Buddhism of Tibet, or Lamaism* (1895), pp. 20–4. The dates of the Tibetan historians for the birth of Srong-tsan Gampo range from A. D. 600 to 617, but the latter date seems to be correct, and is accepted by M. L. de Milloué. That author states that Srong-tsan Gampo married both the Nepalese and Chinese princesses between A. D. 628 and 631. Waddell and Sarat Chandra Dās agree on the date 641 (L. de Milloué, *Bod-Youl ou Tibet*, Paris, 1906, pp. 139, 164–6). The Chinese pretend that they defeated the Tibetans, but the emperor would never have given the princess in marriage to a defeated enemy. Chinese authors habitually represent defeats as victories.

There is a good sketch of Tibetan history by Sir R. Temple in *Ind. Ant.*, 1916, pp. 38–41, 47, being part of an article 'Outlines of Indo-Chinese History', which is important.

possession of Tokmak and Talas, the former residences of the Turkish chiefs, to the west of Lake Issyk-kūl.

Between 665 and 715 the government of China was unable to interfere effectually in the affairs of the countries between the Jaxartes (Syr Daryā) and the Indus ; the southern route to the west through Kāshgaria having been closed by the Tibetans, and the roads over the Hindū Kush blocked by the conquests of Kotaiba, the Arab general, who was busily engaged in spreading the religion of the Prophet throughout Central Asia.

A. D. 665–715. Routes between China and the west closed.

The accession of the emperor Hiuen-tsung, in 713, marks a revival of Chinese activity ; and determined efforts were made by means of both diplomacy and arms to keep open the Pāmīr passes, and to check the ambition of the Arabs and Tibetans, who sometimes combined. In 719, Samarkand and other kingdoms invoked the aid of China against the armies of Islam ; while the Arab leaders sought to obtain the co-operation of the minor states on the Indian borderland. The chiefs of Udyāna (Suwāt), Khottal (west of Badakshān), and Chitrāl, having refused to listen to Muslim blandishments, were rewarded by the emperor of China with letters patent conferring on each the title of king ; and a similar honour was bestowed upon the rulers of Yasin (Little Po-lu), Zabulistan (Ghaznī), Kapisa, and Kashmīr. China made every effort to organize these frontier kingdoms, so as to form an effective barrier against both Arabs and Tibetans. Chandrāpīda, king of Kashmīr, received investiture as king from the emperor in 720, and his brother Muktāpīda-Lalitāditya was similarly honoured in 733.

A. D. 715–47. Revival of Chinese influence on borders of India.

A few years later—in 744 and 747—Chinese influence had been so far extended that the emperor granted titles to the king of Tabaristān, south of the Caspian. In the latter year a Chinese army crossed the Pāmīrs, in spite of all difficulties, and reduced the king of Yasin to subjection.

But, as in the seventh century, so in the eighth, the Chinese dominion over the western countries was short-lived, and was shattered by a disastrous defeat inflicted in 751 on the Chinese general Sien-chi by the Arabs, who were aided by

A. D. 751. Rout of Chinese by Arabs and Karluks.

the Karluk tribes. Indirectly this disaster had an important consequence for European civilization. The art of making paper, up to that time a monopoly of remote China, was introduced into Samarkand by Chinese prisoners, and so became known to Europe, with results familiar to all.[1]

Buddhism in Tibet. During the long reign of Thi-(or Khri-)srong-de-tsan (A.D. 743–789)[2] the development of Buddhism in Tibet was encouraged with a zeal which did not shrink from persecution of the adherents of the rival indigenous Bon (or Pon) religion. The Indian sages, Sânta-rakshita and Padma-sambhava, were invited to court, and with their aid a system of clerical government was instituted, which survives to this day as Lamaism. The work of Thi-srong-de-tsan was continued and carried further by King Ralpachan (A.D. 816–38), but his successor, Langdarma, hated Buddhism, and did his best to extirpate it. A Lama avenged the wrongs of his co-religionists by assassinating the king, A.D. 842. During the eleventh century (A.D. 1013 and 1038), Buddhist missionaries from Magadha securely re-established Buddhism as the official and predominant religion of Tibet.[3]

Contact with China. In the reign of Ralpachan a severe struggle with China took place, which was terminated by a peace recorded (822) in bilingual inscriptions at Lhâsa. In subsequent ages Tibetan relations with the Chinese empire varied much from time to time, but whatever they might be, they did not concern India. The final attainment of supremacy by China over Tibet was deferred until 1751. Since that date the

[1] The foregoing account of the relations of China with the states on the northern frontier of India is chiefly derived from the learned and valuable work by Professor Chavannes, *Documents sur les Toukiue (Turcs) Occidentaux*, St. Pétersbourg, 1903. For the geography, see the map in that work, or Stanford's map appended to vol. ii of Watters, *On Yuan Chwang*. Sir M. A. Stein also treats of the relations of China with the frontier countries of India in the early chapters of *Ancient Khotan*, 1907.

[2] The dates in the text are those given by Sarat Chandra Dās and Waddell (*Encycl. Brit.*, 11th ed.). M. de Milloué (pp. 165, 166) gives 740–86.

[3] Sarat Chandra Dās (*J.A.S.B.*, vol. l, part i (1881), pp. 224–38); Waddell, *The Buddhism of Tibet, or Lamaism*, p. 24; Lévi, *Le Népal*, II, 177, 178. The dates in the text are those of Lévi. M. de Milloué differs widely, assigning the reign of Langdarma to the years 899–902 (*op. cit.*, pp. 170, 171).

Chinese government has always endeavoured to keep Europeans out of Tibet, and has generally succeeded in doing so. Tibetan affairs, consequently, long remained completely apart from Indian history. Contact between the politics of India and those of China had ceased in the eighth century,[1] owing to the growth of Tibetan power at that time. It was not renewed until the conquest of Upper Burma in 1885, which made the Indian and Chinese empires conterminous. In these latter days, Tibet, which had been a dependency of China in greater or less degree for several centuries, has again come within the purview of the Indian government, and its affairs have been the subject of Anglo-Chinese diplomacy.[2]

II

Nepāl

Extent of Nepāl.

The kingdom of Nepāl, as at present constituted, is a considerable self-governed state extending from Sikkim on the east to Kumāon on the west, for a distance of about 500 miles along the northern frontier of Tirhūt, Oudh, and the Agra Province. Except for a narrow strip of lowlands known as the Tarāi, the whole country is a maze of mountains and valleys. Strictly speaking, the name Nepāl should be restricted, and was confined in ancient times to the enclosed valley, about 20 miles in length by 15 in breadth, within which Kāthmandū, the capital, and many other towns and villages are situated. The policy of the existing government rigorously excludes Europeans from almost every part of the state except that valley, and consequently very little is known about the rest.

In Samudragupta's time.

The earliest definite historical information concerning Nepāl, meaning the valley, is the statement in Samudragupta's great Allāhābād inscription of the fourth century

[1] 'Vers 760, la perte du pays de Ko-long sépare définitivement les Chinois de l'Inde' (Lévi, *Le Népal*, ii, 175).

[2] 'The strange story of our dealings with Tibet and its ruler ends with the offer of the Dalai Lama to send us assistance in the Great War of 1914' (*A Historical Geography of the British Dependencies*, vol. vii, India, pt. ii, by P. E. Roberts, Clarendon Press, 1920, p. 575).

after Christ, that, like Kāmarūpa or Assam, it was an autonomous frontier state, paying tribute and yielding obedience to the paramount Gupta power. The tribute probably was little more than nominal and the obedience intermittent. At the present day the Nepālese Government, although practically independent, sends presents or tribute to the Emperor of China, and recognizes in a vague way the suzerainty of that potentate, while receiving a British Resident and subordinating its foreign policy to the direction of the Government of India.

In Asoka's time. Local tradition affirms that long before the time of Samudragupta, in the days of Asoka, in the third century B.C., the valley was under his control, and this tradition is confirmed by the existence at the town of Pātan of monuments attributed to him and his daughter, and by inscriptions which prove that the lowlands at the foot of the hills were an integral part of his empire.[1] The distance from Pātaliputra to the valley of Nepāl not being great, it is probable that that territory formed part of the home provinces and was administered directly from the Maurya capital.

Local annals. It is impossible to say exactly what happened between the time of Asoka and that of Samudragupta. The local annals, which exist in abundance, do not bear strict criticism, and give little information of value. The ruling dynasty during the sixth and the early part of the seventh century was a Lichchhavi family, but its exact connexion with the Lichchhavis of Vaisāli is not ascertainable. The Nepālese Lichchhavis are described by Hiuen Tsang as being eminent scholars and believing Buddhists, ranking as Kshatriyas.[2]

Seventh century and later. During the seventh century Nepāl occupied the position of a buffer state between Tibet on the north, then a great power in Asia, and the empire of Harsha of Kanauj on the south. King Amsuvarman, founder of the Thākuri dynasty, who died about A.D. 642, was in close touch with Tibet by reason

[1] Pātan, 3 miles south of Khātmandū, and Bhatgaon, 9 miles east of it, were each the capital of a separate principality for a long time before 1768, the date of the Gurkha conquest of Nepāl.

[2] Watters, ii, 84. Probably the pilgrim did not visit Nepāl.

of his daughter's marriage to Srong-tsan-Gampo, the monarch of that country, who was strong enough to compel the emperor of China to give him the princess Wen-cheng as second consort in 641.[1] After Harsha's death Tibetan and Nepālese troops acted together in support of Wang-hiuen-tse, the Chinese envoy, and against the usurper of Harsha's throne (*ante*, p. 366). It is also certain that at the beginning of the eighth century Nepāl was still dependent on Tibet, and continued in that position until A.D. 703, when it, together with Tirhūt, shook off dependence on Tibet. The Tibetan king was killed in the course of the war.[2] The reason for the introduction of a new Nepālese era dating from October, A.D. 879, is not known. Chinese relations with Nepāl and India had come to an end soon after the middle of the eighth century. In recent times wars between China and Nepāl have resulted in a complimentary recognition by the smaller state of the suzerainty of the greater.

Gurkha conquest.

The confused and bloodstained story of the various petty dynasties which ruled in Nepāl up to A.D. 1768 possesses no general interest. In that year the Gurkhas conquered the country, and established the dynasty which now rules Nepāl through the agency of powerful ministers who have taken over all the substantial functions of sovereignty, reducing the nominal monarchs to a position of absolute insignificance.

Nepālese Buddhism.

Buddhism, in its early pure form, was introduced into the valley by Asoka, whose daughter is believed to have erected sacred edifices near the capital, which are still pointed out. Little or nothing is known concerning the religious history of the country for many hundred years afterwards. In the seventh century the prevailing religion appears to have been a much modified Tantric variety of the 'Great Vehicle' Buddhist doctrine, allied so closely to the orthodox Hindu cult of Siva as to be distinguishable from it with difficulty.

[1] Between A.D. 628 and 631, according to M. de Milloué (*op. cit.*, p. 164).

[2] See E. H. Parker, 'China, Nepaul, Bhutan, and Sikkim', in *J. Manchester Oriental Soc.*, 1911, pp. 129–52.

In the course of ages the corruption of the church increased, and Nepāl now presents the strange spectacle of so-called monasteries swarming with the families of married 'monks' engaged in all sorts of secular occupations.[1] The spontaneous progress of the decay of Buddhism, which had been operating in Nepāl for centuries, has been much hastened by the action of the Gurkha Government, to which Buddhist rites are obnoxious ; and there is good reason to believe that in the course of a few generations Nepālese Buddhism will be almost extinct.

Decay of Buddhism in India.

The total disappearance of the Buddhist worship from India, the land of its birth, has been the subject of much discussion and some misconception. Until lately the assumption commonly was made that Buddhism had been extinguished by a storm of Brahman persecution. That is not the true explanation. Occasional active persecutions by Hindu kings, like Sasānka, which no doubt occurred, though rarely, formed a factor of minor importance in the movement which slowly restored India to the Brahmanical fold. The furious massacres perpetrated in many places by Musalman invaders were more efficacious than orthodox Hindu persecutions, and had a great deal to do with the disappearance of Buddhism in several provinces. But the main cause was the gradual, almost insensible, assimilation of Buddhism to Hinduism, which attained to such a point that often it is nearly impossible to draw a line between the mythology and images of the Buddhists and those of the Hindus. This process of assimilation is going on now before our eyes in Nepāl, and the chief interest which that country offers to some students is the opportunity presented by it for watching the manner in which the octopus of Hinduism is slowly strangling its Buddhist victim. The automatic compression of the dying cult by its elastic rival is aided by the action of the Government, which throws its influence and favour on

[1] Married monks are allowed by certain Tibetan sects (de Milloué, p. 176), and used to be recognized by the Vajrayāna sect in Bengal and Eastern India (N. N. Vasu, *Modern Buddhism and its Followers in Orissa*, Calcutta, 1911, pp. 4, 13, 17).

the side of the Hindus, while abstaining from violent persecution of the Buddhists.[1]

III

Kāmarūpa or Assam

Extent of kingdom.

The ancient kingdom of Kāmarūpa, although roughly equivalent to Assam, generally occupied an area larger than that of the modern province, and extended westward to the Karatōya river,[2] thus including the Kūch Bihār State and the Rangpur District. The earliest notice of the kingdom which is of any use for the purposes of the historian is the statement in Samudragupta's inscription on the Allāhābād pillar, recorded about A.D. 360 or 370, that Kāmarūpa was then one of the frontier states outside the limits of the Gupta empire, but paying tribute and owing a certain amount of obedience to the paramount power.[3]

Hiuen Tsang.

The next glimpse of this remote region is afforded by the Chinese pilgrim Hiuen Tsang. When he was staying for the second time at the Nālandā monastery, early in A.D. 643, he was compelled, much against his will, to pay a visit to the king of Kāmarūpa, who insisted on making the acquaintance of the renowned scholar, and would not take a refusal. After a short stay at the capital of Kāmarūpa, Harsha Sīlāditya, the Kanauj sovereign, sent a message commanding that Hiuen Tsang should be sent to him. The king replied that Harsha might take his head if he could, but should not get his Chinese visitor. However, when Harsha sent a peremptory order to the effect that he would trouble the king to send back his head by the messenger, that potentate,

[1] Most books concerning Nepāl are superseded to a large extent by Sylvain Lévi's comprehensive treatise entitled *Le Népal*, t. i and ii, 1905; t. iii, 1908. Wright's *History of Nepāl* (Cambridge, 1877) gives a translation of one recension of the traditional annals. The coinage is described in *Catal. Coins I. M.*, vol. i, pp. 280–93, and more fully by E. H. Walsh, 'The Coinage of Nepal' (*J.R.A.S.*, 1908, pp. 669–760), with seven plates. Oldfield's *Sketches from Nipāl* is a good descriptive work.

[2] Mr. Blochmann spells the name as Karataya; others write Karatōya, which seems to be correct.

[3] *J.R.A.S.*, 1890, p. 879.

on second thoughts, deemed it advisable to comply with the request of his suzerain, and hastened to meet Harsha, bringing the pilgrim with him.

Bhāskaravarman or Kumāra. This king was named Bhāskaravarman, and was also known as Kumāra. He belonged to a very ancient dynasty, which claimed to have existed for a thousand generations. Hiuen Tsang describes him as being a Brahman by caste, but the form of his name indicates that he considered himself to be a Kshatriya or Rājpūt, and it would seem that the pilgrim really meant that Bhāskaravarman was a Brahmanical Hindu in religion. He may have been a 'Brahmakshatrī', as the Sena kings were in later times. Buddhism was scarcely known in his country, which did not contain a single monastery.[1]

The Pāla dynasty. Practically nothing more is on record concerning the political history of Kāmarūpa for several centuries. The kingdom was included in the dominions of some of the Pāla kings of Bengal, and Kumārapāla, a member of that dynasty, in the twelfth century appointed his minister Vaidyadeva as ruler of the province with royal powers.[2]

The Āhōms. Early in the thirteenth century, about A.D. 1228, the invasions of the Shān tribe named Āhōm began. Gradually the Āhōm chiefs made themselves masters of the country, and established a dynasty which lasted until the British occupation in 1825.[3] The dynastic history of Kāmarūpa, being only of local interest, need not be considered further.

Religion. The claims which the province can fairly make on the respectful attention of the outer world rest on other grounds. It is a gate through which successive hordes of immigrants from the great hive of the Mongolian race in Western China have poured into the plains of India, and many of the resident tribes still are almost pure Mongolians. The religion of such tribes is of more than local concern, because it supplies the clue to the strange Tantric developments of both Buddhism and Hinduism which are so characteristic of

[1] Beal, i, 215–17; ii, 195–8; Watters, i, 349; ii, 195–7; *Life of Hiuen Tsiang*, p. 172.

[2] *Ep. Ind.*, ii, 355.

[3] *Catal. Coins I. M.*, vol. i, p. 294; J. Allan, 'The Coinage of Assam' (*Num. Chron.*, 1909, pp. 300–31, with three plates).

mediaeval and modern Bengal. The temple of Kāmākhyā near Gauhāti is one of the most sacred shrines of the Sākta Hindus, the worshippers of the female forms of deity, while the whole country is renowned in Hindu legend as a land of magic and witchcraft. The old tribal beliefs are being abandoned gradually in favour of extreme, or even fanatical, Hindu orthodoxy, and the history of Assam offers many examples of the process by which Brahman priests have established their influence over non-Aryan chiefs step by step, and drawn them within the roomy fold of Hinduism. All the various methods of conversion and absorption enumerated by Sir Alfred Lyall and Sir H. Risley have been adopted from time to time.[1]

Another good claim to notice is based upon the fact that Assam is one of the few Indian provinces the inhabitants of which successfully beat back the flowing tide of Muhammadan conquest, and maintained their independence in spite of repeated attempts to subvert it. The only Musalman invasion of Kāmarūpa which comes within the limits of the period treated in this volume is the expedition rashly undertaken in A.D. 1204–5 (A.H. 601) by the son of Bakhtyār, Muhammad, the conqueror of Bengal and Bihār. He advanced northwards along the bank of the Karatōya river, which then formed the western frontier of Kāmarūpa, and succeeded in penetrating into the mountains to the north of Darjeeling, but being unable to obtain any secure foothold, was obliged to retreat. His retirement was disastrous. The people of Kāmarūpa having broken down the great stone bridge of many arches, which was the only means by which he could cross the river in safety, nearly all his men were drowned. The leader of the expedition managed to swim across with about a hundred horsemen, and then fell ill from distress at his failure. Next year, A.D. 1205–6 (A.H. 602), he was assassinated.[2] Subsequent Muhammadan incursions

Muhammadan attacks.

[1] Gait, *History of Assam*, Calcutta, 1906; Sir Alfred Lyall, *Asiatic Studies*, First Series, ch. v; Risley, *Census of India*, 1901, Report, pt. i, pp. 519–21, 531.

[2] Raverty, transl. *Ṭabaḳāt-i-Nāṣirī*, pp. 560–73; *J. A. S. B.*, vol. xlv, pt. i (1876), pp. 330–3; Blochmann, ibid., vol. xliv, pt. i (1875), pp. 276–85. I accept Raverty's chronology.

were equally unsuccessful. The Muslim historian, who accompanied Mīr Jumla on his invasion of the country in 1662, expresses in striking phrases the horror with which the country and its people were regarded by strangers.[1] The kingdom retained its autonomy until 1816, when the Burmese appeared and occupied the country until 1824. They were expelled by British troops, and early in 1826 Assam became a province of the Indian empire.

IV

Kashmīr

Kashmīr: early history.

A detailed account of the history of Kashmīr would fill a volume; in this place a brief notice of some of the leading passages will suffice. The valley had been included in the Maurya empire in the time of Asoka, and again in the Kushān dominion in the days of Kanishka and Huvishka. Harsha, although not strong enough to annex Kashmīr, was yet able to compel the king to surrender a cherished relic, an alleged tooth of Buddha, which was carried off to Kanauj. The authentic chronicles of the kingdom begin with the Karkota dynasty, which was founded by Durlabhavardhana during Harsha's lifetime. Hiuen Tsang spent two years in Kashmīr, from about May 631 to April 633, and was received with distinguished honour by the unnamed reigning king, presumably Durlabhavardhana. That prince and his son Durlabhaka are credited with long reigns.

A. D. 720. Chandrāpīḍa; A. D. 733–69. Muktāpīḍa.

The latter was succeeded by his three sons in order; the eldest of whom, Chandrāpīda, received investiture as king from the Emperor of China in 720; by whom the third son Muktāpīda, also known as Lalitāditya, was similarly honoured in 733. This prince, who is said to have reigned for thirty-six years, extended the power of Kashmīr far beyond its normal mountain limits, and about the year 740 inflicted a crushing defeat upon Yasovarman, king of Kanauj.[2] He also vanquished the Tibetans, Bhūtias, and

[1] See Jadunath Sarkar, 'Assam and the Ahoms in A. D. 1660' (*J. B. & O. Res. Soc.*, vol. i, pp. 179–95).

[2] Between 736 and 747 (Lévi and Chavannes, 'Itinéraire d'Ou-

THE MĀRTĀNDA TEMPLE OF THE SUN, KASHMĪR

the Turks on the Indus. His memory has been perpetuated by the famous Mārtānda temple of the Sun, built by him, and still existing. The acts of this king, and all that he did, with something more, are set forth at large in Kalhana's chronicle.

Jayāpīda, or Vinayāditya, the grandson of Muktāpīda, is credited with even more adventures than those ascribed to his grandfather. Probably it is true that he defeated and dethroned the king of Kanauj, apparently Vajrāyudha. But the romantic tale of his visit *incognito* to the capital of Paundravardhana in Bengal, the modern Rājshāhi District, then the seat of government of a king named Jayanta, unknown to sober history, seems to be purely imaginary. The legend of his expedition against a king of Nepāl, with the strange name Aramudi, of his capture and imprisonment in a stone castle, and of his marvellous escape, equally belongs to the domain of romance. The details of the acts of cruelty and oppression, due to avarice, which disgraced the later years of his reign, read like matters of fact, and unhappily are quite in accordance with the low moral standard of most of the rulers of Kashmīr. The chronicler closes his narrative with the following quaint comment: **Jayāpīda; close of the eighth century.**

'Such was for thirty-one years the reign of this famous king, who could not restrain his will. Princes and fishes, when their thirst is excited by riches and impure water respectively, leave their place and follow evil ways, with such result that they are brought into the strong net of death—the former by changes which fate dictates, and the latter by troops of fishermen.'

The substantial existence of Jayāpīda is testified by the survival of multitudes of exceedingly barbarous coins inscribed with his title Vinayāditya.[1]

The reign of Avantivarman, in the latter part of the ninth century, was notable for his enlightened patronage of literature, and for the beneficent schemes of drainage and **A. D. 855–83. Avantivarman.**

kong,' in *J. A.*, 1895, p. 353). See V. A. Smith, 'The History of the City of Kanauj and of King Yaśovarman' (*J. R. A. S.*, 1908, pp. 765–93).

[1] Stein, *transl. Rājatar.*, Bk. iv; *Catal. Coins I. M.*, vol. i, pp. 266, 269.

irrigation carried out by Suyya, his minister of public works.[1]

A. D. 883–902. Śankaravarman. The next king, Sankaravarman, distinguished himself in war; but is chiefly remembered as the author of an ingenious system of fiscal oppression, and the plunderer of temple treasures. The details of his exactions are worth reading as proving the capacity for unlimited and ruthless extortion of an Oriental despot without a conscience.[2]

End of the Shāhiya dynasty. During his reign the last of the Turki Shāhiya kings, the descendants of Kanishka, was overthrown by the Brahman Lalliya. The Turkī Shāhiya kingṣ had ruled in Kābul until the capture of that city by the Arab general Yakūb-i-Lāis in A. D. 870 (A. H. 256).[3] After that date the capital was shifted to Ohind, on the Indus. The dynasty founded by Lalliya, known as that of the Hindu Shāhiyas, lasted until A. D. 1021, when it was extirpated by the Muhammadans.[4]

Famine in A. D. 917–18. In the reign of the child-king Pārtha and his father Pangu, the regent, an awful famine occurred in the year A. D. 917–18, thus described by the Brahman historian of a Hindu government:—

'One could scarcely see the water in the Vitastā (Jihlam), entirely covered as the river was with corpses soaked and swollen by the water in which they had long been lying. The land became densely covered with bones in all directions, until it was like one great burial-ground, causing terror to all beings. The king's ministers and the Tantrins (Praetorian guards) became wealthy, as they amassed riches by selling stores of rice at high prices. The king would take that person as minister who raised the sums due on the Tantrins' bills, by selling the subjects in such a condition. As one might look from his hot bath-room upon all the people outside distressed by the wind and rain of a downpour in the forest, thus for a long time the wretched Pangu, keeping in his palace, praised his own comfort while he saw the people in misery.'[5]

This gruesome picture may give cause for reflection to some critics of modern methods of famine relief.

[1] Stein, *transl. Rājatar.*, Bk. v, vv. 2–126.

[2] Ibid., 128–227.

[3] Raverty, *Notes on Afghanistan*, pp. 63, 64.

[4] Stein, *Zur Geschichte der Çahis von Kābul* (Stuttgart, 1893).

[5] Stein, *transl. Rājatar.*, Bk. v, vv. 271–7.

Pārtha chastised his people with whips, but his son Unmattāvanti, 'who was worse than wicked,' chastised them with scorpions. 'With difficulty', sighs the chronicler, 'I get my song to proceed, since from fear of touching the evil of this king's story it keeps back like a frightened mare.' Parricide was one of his many crimes. The details of his brutalities are too disgusting for quotation. Happily his reign was short, and he died the victim of a painful disease in A. D. 939.[1] *Unmattāvanti, A. D. 937–9.*

During the latter half of the tenth century, power was in the hands of an unscrupulous queen, named Diddā, the granddaughter of a Shāhiya king, who, first as a queen-consort, then as regent, and ultimately as sovereign for twenty-three years, misgoverned the unhappy state for half a century. *A. D. 950–1003. Queen Diddā.*

In the reign of her nephew, Sangrāma, the kingdom suffered an attack from Mahmūd of Ghaznī; and, although its troops were defeated by the invader, preserved its independence, which was protected by the inaccessibility of the mountain barriers. *A. D. 1003–28. Saṅgrāma.*

During the second half of the eleventh century, Kashmīr, which has been generally unfortunate in its rulers, endured unspeakable miseries at the hands of the tyrants Kalasa and Harsha. The latter, who was evidently insane, imitated Sankaravarman in the practice of plundering temples, and rightly came to a miserable end. Few countries can rival the long Kashmīr list of kings and queens who gloried in shameless lust, fiendish cruelty, and pitiless misrule. *A. D. 1063–89. Kalasa. A. D. 1089–1101. Harsha.*

A local Muhammadan dynasty obtained power in 1339, and the religion of Islam gradually spread in the valley during the fourteenth century; but the natural defences of the kingdom effectually guarded it against the ambition of the sovereigns of India, until Akbar conquered it in 1587, and incorporated it in the Moghal empire.[2] *A. D. 1339. Muhammadan local dynasty.*

[1] Stein, *transl. Rājatar.*, Bk. v, vv. 414–48.

[2] Full details of Kashmīr history will be found in the text and commentary of Stein's translation of the *Rājataraṅginī*.

V

The kingdoms of Kanauj (Pañchāla), the Panjāb, Ajmēr, Delhi, and Gwālior; Muhammadan conquest of Hindustan.

Kanauj city. Before proceeding to discuss the history of the kingdom of Kanauj, it will be well to give some account of the famous capital city, which is now represented by a petty Muhammadan country town (N. lat. 27° 3′, E. long. 79° 56′) in the Farrukhābād District of the United Provinces. Kanauj was of high antiquity. It is mentioned in several passages of the *Mahābhārata*, and alluded to by Patanjali in the second century B.C. as a well-known place. It has been so completely destroyed that nothing beyond rubbish heaps remains to testify to the former existence of its gorgeous temples, monasteries, and palaces. Commentators usually take it for granted that Kanauj is mentioned twice, under the variant names of Kanagora and Kanogiza,[1] in Ptolemy's *Geography*, written about A.D. 140, but there is little reason to warrant the belief. The first certain mention of the city with any descriptive details is in the *Travels* of the Chinese pilgrim Fa-hien, who visited Kanauj about A.D. 405, during the reign of Chandra-gupta II, Vikramāditya. His remark that the city possessed only two Buddhist monasteries of the Hīnayāna school and one *stūpa* suggests that it was not of much importance at the beginning of the fifth century.[2] Probably it grew under the patronage of the Gupta kings, but the great development of the city clearly was due to its selection by Harsha for his capital. When Hiuen Tsang stayed there, in 636 and 643, a marked change had occurred since Fa-hien's time. The later pilgrim, instead of two monasteries, found upwards of a hundred such institutions, crowded by more than 10,000 brethren of both the great schools. Hinduism flourished as well as Buddhism, and could show more than two hundred temples, with thousands

[1] Bk. vii, ch. 1, sec. 52; ch. 2, sec. 22; transl. McCrindle, *Ind. Ant.*, xiii, 352, 380.

[2] *Travels*, ch. xviii.

of worshippers. The city, which was strongly fortified, then extended along the east bank of the Ganges for about 4 miles, and was adorned with lovely gardens and clear tanks. The inhabitants were well-to-do, including some families of great wealth; they dressed in silk, and were skilled in learning and the arts.[1]

Captured and destroyed.

Although Kanauj had been captured several times by hostile armies during the ninth and tenth centuries, it recovered quickly from its wounds, and when Mahmūd appeared before its walls, at the end of A.D. 1018, was still a great and stately city, defended by seven distinct forts or fortifications and reputed to contain 10,000 temples. The Sultan destroyed the temples, but seems to have spared the city. The removal of the capital of Panchāla to Bārī must have greatly reduced the population and importance of Kanauj, although it revived to some extent under the rule of the Gaharwār Rājas in the twelfth century. The subjugation of Rāja Jaichand's territory, including the city, in A.D. 1194 (A.H. 590), by Shihāb-ud-dīn, reduced it to insignificance for ever. Its final destruction was the work of Shēr Shah, who built a new town close by, called Shēr Sūr, to commemorate his victory over Humāyūn in 1540. The Muhammadan historian who chronicles the event observes that he could not find any satisfactory reason for the destruction of the old city, and that the act was very unpopular.[2]

Kingdom of Pañchāla.

Kanauj, although it twice attained the dignity of being the capital of Northern India, for the first time under Harsha in the seventh century, and for the second time under Mihira Bhoja and Mahendrapāla in the ninth and tenth centuries, was primarily the capital of the kingdom of Panchāla. According to the story told in the *Mahābhārata*, Northern Panchāla, with its capital Ahichchhatra, fell to the share of Drona, while Southern Panchāla, with its capital Kāmpilya, became the kingdom of Drupada. Ahichchhatra, the modern

[1] Watters, i, 340; Beal, i, 206.

[2] Elliot, *Hist. of India*, iv, 419. The author, Abbās, wrote in the reign of Akbar, about 1580. For other particulars, see V. A. Smith, 'A History of the City of Kanauj' (*J. R. A. S.*, 1908, pp. 765–93). I was mistaken in asserting that the city was sacked by Shihāb-ud-dīn.

Rāmnagar in the Barēli (Bareilly) District, was still a considerable town when visited by Hiuen Tsang in the seventh century. Little is known about the history of Kāmpilya, apparently the modern Kampil in the Farrukhābād District.[1] Both the ancient capitals were thrown into obscurity by the rapid development of Kanauj under Harsha's rule, and after his time that city was the undisputed capital of Panchāla.

Anarchy after Harsha's death. Harsha's death, in A.D. 647, was followed by a period of disturbance and anarchy throughout his wide dominions. We do not know what happened to the kingdom of Panchāla immediately after the suppression of the usurper, about A. D. 650, by the Chinese ambassador with the help of his Nepalese and Tibetan allies, as related in the thirteenth chapter.

Rājas of Kanauj in the eighth century. After Harsha's death the earliest known king of Kanauj was Yasovarman, who sent an embassy to China in A.D. 731,[2] and nine or ten years later was dethroned and slain by Lalitāditya Muktāpīda of Kashmir.[3] In the history of Sanskrit literature Yasovarman's name holds an honoured place as that of the patron of Bhavabhūti, the famous author of the *Mālatīmādhava*, and of Vākpatirāja, a less renowned author, who wrote in Prākrit. The next occupant of the throne of Kanauj apparently was Vajrāyudha, who, like his predecessor, suffered the fate of defeat and dethronement by Lalitāditya's son, Jayāpīda.[4] Similar ill-luck attended his successor, Indrāyudha, who is known to have been reigning in A. D. 783, and was dethroned, about A. D. 810, by Dharmapāla, king of Bengal and Bihār. The eastern monarch, while probably insisting on a right to homage and tribute, did not keep the administration of Panchāla in his own hands, but entrusted it to Chakrāyudha, presumably

[1] Cunningham, *Archaeol. S. Rep.*, xi, 11.

[2] Stein, transl. *Rājatar.*, Bk. iv, v. 134, note, with reference to Pauthier.

[3] Stein, transl. *Rājatar.*, Bk. iv, vv. 133–46; Lévi and Chavannes, 'Itin. d'Oukong' (*J.A.*, 1895, p. 353). They fix the date as lying between A. D. 736 and 747.

[4] Konow and Lanman, *Karpūramañjarī*, iii, 5², p. 266; 'to the capital of Vajrāyudha, the king of Panchāla, to Kanauj.' Stein, transl. *Rājatar.*, Bk. iv, 471, records the defeat and dethronement of the king of Kanauj by Jayāpīḍa. The king of Kanauj apparently must have been Vajrāyudha.

a relative of the defeated rāja. The new ruler was consecrated with the consent of the kings of all the neighbouring states.[1] His fortune was no better than that of his predecessors. About A.D. 816 he was deprived of his throne by Nāgabhata, the ambitious king of the Gurjara-Pratihāra kingdom in Rājputāna, the capital of which was at Bhilmāl.[2]

Nāgabhaṭa and Rāmabhadra.

Nāgabhata presumably transferred the head-quarters of his government to Kanauj, which certainly was the capital of his successors for many generations, and so again became for a considerable time the premier city of Northern India. During the reign of Nāgabhata the chronic warfare between the Gurjaras, descendants of foreign invaders, and the Rāshtrakūtas (Rāthōrs) of the Deccan, representing the indigenous ruling races, continued, and the southern king, Govinda III, claims to have won a victory over his northern rival early in the ninth century.[3] Nothing particular is recorded about Nāgabhata's successor, Rāmabhadra (Rāmadeva), who reigned from about A.D. 834 to 840.

Mihira Bhoja.

The next king, Rāmabhadra's son Mihira, usually known by his title Bhoja, enjoyed a long reign of about half a century (*c.* 840–90), and beyond question was a very powerful monarch, whose dominions may be called an 'empire' without exaggeration. They certainly included the Cis-Sutlaj districts of the Panjāb, most of Rājputāna, the greater part, if not the whole, of the present United Provinces of Agra and Oudh, and the Gwālior territory. The next two kings being known to have held the remote province of Surāshtra, or Kāthiāwār, in the extreme west, the possession of which implies control over Gujarāt and Mālava or Avanti, it is highly probable that these distant regions also were

[1] A. D. 783, Jain *Harivaṁśa* in *Bomb. Gaz.* (1896), vol. i, pt. i, p. 197 note; Bhāgalpur copperplate (*Ind. Ant.*, xv, 304; xx, 188); Khālimpur copperplate (*Ep. Ind.*, iv, 252, note 3).

[2] Gwālior inscription, *Nachr. d. k. Gesellsch. d. Wiss. Göttingen*, 1905, 'Epigr. Notes,' No. 17; *Archaeol. S., Annual Rep.*, 1903–4, p. 277. A. M. T. Jackson, 'Bhinmāl,' *Bom. Gaz.* (1896), vol. i, pt. i, App. See Watters, *On Yuan Chwang*, ii, 250; D. R. Bhandarkar, *A. S. W. I., Prog. Rep.*, 1907–8, pp. 36–41; and J. Wilson, *Indian Caste* (1877), vol. i, p. 109.

[3] Unpublished inscription in possession of Prof. D. R. Bhandarkar ('Gurjaras,' p. 4, in *J. Bo. Br. As. Soc.*, vol. xx).

subject to the sway of Bhoja. On the east his dominions abutted on the realm of Devapāla, king of Bengal and Bihār, which he invaded successfully; on the north-west his boundary probably was the Sutlaj river; on the west the lost Hakrā or Wahindah river separated his territories from those of his enemies, the Muhammadan chiefs of Sind; on the south-west his powerful Rāshtrakūta rival, the ally of the Muhammadans, kept his armies continually on the alert; while on the south his next neighbour was the growing Chandēl kingdom of Jejākabhukti, the modern Bundelkhand, which probably acknowledged his suzerainty.[1] Bhoja liked to pose as an incarnation of Vishnu, and therefore assumed the title of *Ādi Varāha*, 'the primaeval boar,' one of the incarnations of the god. Base silver coins inscribed with this title are exceedingly common in Northern India, and by their abundance attest the long duration and wide extension of Bhoja's rule.[2] Unfortunately no Megasthenes or Bāna has left a record of the nature of his internal government, and it is impossible to compare the polity of Bhoja with that of his great forerunners.

Mahendrapāla. Bhoja's son and successor, Mahendrapāla (Mahendrāyudha) (*c.* A.D. 890–908) preserved unimpaired the extensive heritage received from his father, and ruled all Northern India, except the Panjāb and Indus valley, from the borders of Bihār (Magadha) to the shore of the Arabian sea. Inscriptions of his eighth and ninth years found at Gayā seem to prove that Magadha was included in the Parihār (Pratihāra) dominions for some time. His teacher (*Guru*) was the celebrated poet Rājasekhara, author of the *Karpūra-mañjarī* play and other works, who continued to reside at the court of Mahendrapāla's younger son.[3]

[1] These facts are collected from a series of inscriptions, Nos. 542, 544, 710 of Kielhorn's List (*Ep. Ind.*, vol. v, App.), and others. For the relations of the native powers with the Muhammadans see Al Masūdī in Elliot, i, 23–5; *Bom. Gaz.* (1896), vol. i, pt. i, pp. 506, 511, 526.

[2] *Catal. Coins I. M.*, vol. i, pp. 233, 241. The coins are rude degradations of the Sassanian type, such as the Huns issued, and suggest a connexion between the Gurjara-Pratihāras and the Huns.

[3] Konow and Lanman, *Karpūra mañjarī*, p. 178. But the remark (op. cit., p. 179) that Mahendrapāla of Mahodaya must be distinguished from the king of that name in the Dighwa-Dubauli

The throne was occupied for two or three years by Bhoja II, elder son of Mahendrapāla, who died early, and was succeeded by his half-brother, Mahīpāla (*c.* A.D. 910–40).[1] The beginning of the decline and fall of the empire of Kanauj dates from his reign. In A.D. 916 the armies of the Rāshtrakūta king, Indra III, once more captured Kanauj, and gave a severe blow to the power of the Pratihāra dynasty.[2] Surāshtra, which was still subject to Mahīpāla in 914,[3] probably was then lost along with other remote provinces, in consequence of the successes gained by the southern monarch. Indra III not being in a position to hold Kanauj, Mahīpāla recovered his capital with the aid of the Chandēl king, and probably other allies.[4]

Bhoja II and Mahīpāla.

The waning power of Kanauj and the waxing strength of Jejākabhukti are shown by the incident that king Devapāla of Kanauj (*c.* 940–55) was obliged to surrender a much-prized image of Vishnu to the Chandēl king, Yasovarman, who enshrined it in one of the finest temples at Khajurāho.[5] Yasovarman had established his power by the occupation of the strong fortress of Kālanjar, and no doubt became absolutely independent of Kanauj. In the reign of Dhanga, the successor of Yasovarman, the Jumna is known to have formed the boundary between the territories of Panchāla and those of Jejākabhukti.

Devapāla.

Devapāla was succeeded by his brother, Vijayapāla (*c.* A.D. 960–90),[6] whose reign is marked by the loss of Gwālior, the ancient possession of his house, which was captured by a Kachchhwāha (Kachchhapaghāta) chief named

Vijayapāla.

copperplate has been proved to be erroneous. Rājasekhara also wrote a treatise on the art of poetry (*Kāvyamīmāṁsa*), published in the Gaekwar's Oriental Series.

[1] Inscription No. 544 of Kielhorn's *List*.

[2] Cambay plates (*Ep. Ind.* vii, 30, 43).

[3] Inscription No. 353 in Kielhorn's *List*.

[4] *Ep. Ind.*, i, 121.

[5] Ibid., 134.

[6] A stone inscription at Bayana of A.D. 955 records the erection of a temple by a queen named Chitralekha during the reign of a Mahārājādhirājā Mahīpāla, who appears to have belonged to the Kanauj dynasty. If this is so, this Mahīpāla must have succeeded Devapāla and have reigned for a very brief time, as another inscription of A.D. 960 shows that Vijayapāla had gained the throne four or five years after the date of the Bayana inscription (*Prog. Rep. A. S. W. Circle*, 1919, p. 43).

Vajradāman,[1] the founder of a local dynasty which held the fortress until A.D. 1128. The establishment of the Solankī (Chaulukya) kingdom of Anhilwāra in Gujarāt by Mūlarāja, about the middle of the tenth century, shows that the king of Kanauj no longer had any concern with Western India.[2] The Gwālior chieftain became a feudatory of the Chandēl monarchy, which, under Dhanga (*c.* 1000–1050), evidently was stronger than its rival of Kanauj.

Muhammadan invasions. At this period the politics of the Hindu Rājpūt states of Northern India became complicated by the intrusion of Muhammadan invaders. The Arab conquest of Sind, in A.D. 712, did not seriously affect the kingdoms of the interior. The Arabs maintained friendly relations on the whole with their powerful Rāshtrakūta neighbours on the south, and their attacks on the dominions of the Gurjara kings of Rājputāna and Kanauj do not seem ever to have exceeded the proportions of frontier raids. But now the armies of Islam began to appear in more formidable fashion through the north-western passes, the gates which had so often admitted the enemies of India.

Sabuktigīn and Jaipāl. In those days a large kingdom comprising the upper valley of the Indus and most of the Panjāb to the north of Sind, extending westward to the mountains and eastward to the Hakrā river, was governed by a Rāja named Jaipāl, whose capital was at Bathindah (Bhatinda), the Tabarhind of Muhammadan histories, now in the Patiālā State, and for many centuries an important fortress on the military road connecting Mūltān with India proper.[3] Sabuktigīn, the Amīr of Ghaznī, made his first raid into Indian territory in

[1] Inscription No. 47 of Kielhorn's *List*.

[2] Three inscriptions of Mūlarāja, ranging in date from Aug. A. D. 974 to Jan. 995, are known. According to the Gujarāt chronicles his reign extended from A. D. 942 to 997. He is described as the son of Rāji, king of Kanauj. Rāji is probably one of the many designations of king Mahīpāla, who reigned from about A. D. 910 to about 940. Mūlarāja presumably was his viceroy, and finding an opportunity, threw off his allegiance. See *Ep. Ind.*, x, 76, 77, and *J. R. A. S.*, 1909, pp. 269–72. The date, A. D. 961, which I formerly assigned for the establishment of the Anhilwāra kingdom, does not seem to be right. Mūlarāja was killed by a Chauhān Rāja, named Vigraharāja (II), who was alive in A. D. 973 (*J. R. A. S.*, 1913, pp. 266, 267, 269).

[3] *J. Panjab Hist. Soc.*, ii, p. 109, and iii, p. 35.

A.D. 986–7 (A.H. 376). Two years later Jaipāl retaliated by an invasion of the Amīr's territory, but, being defeated, was compelled to accept a treaty binding him to pay a large sum in cash, and to surrender a number of elephants and four fortresses to the west of the Indus. Jaipāl having broken the compact, Sabuktigīn punished him by the devastation of the frontier and the annexation of Lamghān (Jalālābād). Soon afterwards (c. A.D. 991) Jaipāl made a final effort to save his country by organizing a great confederacy of Hindu princes, including Ganda, the Chandēl king, Rājyapāla, then the king of Kanauj, and others. The vast host thus collected was disastrously defeated in or near the Kurram (Kurmah) valley, and Peshāwar was occupied by the Muhammadans. Jaipāl, who was again defeated in November, 1001, by Sultan Mahmūd, committed suicide, and was succeeded by his son, Anandpāl,[1] who, like his father, joined a confederacy of the Hindu powers under the supreme command of Vīsaladeva, the Chauhān Rājā of Ajmēr. In spite of assistance from the powerful Khokhar tribe of the Panjāb, the Hindus again sustained a heavy defeat.

Rājyapāla; Sultan Mahmūd.

At Kanauj, Vijayapāla had been succeeded by his son Rājyapāla, who took his share in opposing the foreign invader. A few years later (A.D. 997) the crown of Sabuktigīn descended, after a short interval of dispute, to his son, the famous Sultan Mahmūd, who made it the business of his life to harry the idolaters of India, and carry off their property to Ghaznī. He is computed to have made no less than seventeen expeditions into India. It was his custom to leave his capital in October, and then three months' steady marching brought him into the richest provinces of the interior. Early in January, A.D. 1019, he appeared before Kanauj. Rājyapāla made no serious attempt to defend his capital, and the seven forts which guarded it all

[1] This summary statement, so far as it differs from current accounts, rests upon the authority of Raverty, *Notes on Afghanistan*, p. 320. Alberūnī (*India*, transl. Sachau, i, 135) tells us that Jaipāl's son, 'Shāh Ānandapāla, who ruled in our time,' had as teacher a grammarian named Ugrabhūti, whose book was made fashionable in Kashmīr by liberal donations from the royal pupils to the pundits.

fell into Mahmūd's hands in a single day. The conqueror plundered the forts but seems to have spared the city, and quickly returned to Ghaznī laden with booty. Rājyapāla made the best terms that he could obtain, abandoned Kanauj, and retired to Bārī on the other side of the Ganges.[1]

Ganda and Mahmūd.

The pusillanimous submission of Rājyapāla incensed his Hindu allies, who felt that he had betrayed their cause. His fault was sternly punished by an army under the command of Vidhyādhara, heir-apparent of the Chandēl king, Ganda, supported by the forces of his feudatory, the chief of Gwālior, which attacked Kanauj in the spring or summer of A.D. 1019, soon after the departure of Sultan Mahmūd, and slew Rājyapāla, whose diminished dominions passed under the rule of Trilochanapāla. The Sultan was furious when he heard of the punishment inflicted on a prince whom he regarded as a vassal, and in the autumn of the same year (A.H. 410) started again from Ghaznī to take vengeance on the Hindu chiefs. Early in A.D. 1020 he captured Bārī, the new Pratihāra capital, without much difficulty, and then advanced into the Chandēl territory, where Ganda had assembled an apparently formidable force to oppose him. But the heart of the Chandēl king failed him, and, like Rājyapāla, he fled from the field without giving battle. His camp, munitions, and elephants were left a prey to the Sultan, who returned as usual to Ghaznī with heaps of spoil.[2]

Successors of Rājyapāla.

Nothing is known about Trilochanapāla except that he ineffectually resisted Mahmūd's passage of the Jumna at the

[1] The name Rājyapāla is obtained from the Jhūsī copperplate (*Ind. Ant.*, xviii, 34, Kielhorn's *List*, No. 60) and the Dūbkund inscription (*Ep. Ind.*, ii, 235). Hitherto it has been misread as 'Rāi Jaipāl' in Al Utbi (Elliot, ii, 45), with the result that much confusion has occurred. Elliot (ibid., pp. 425–7, 461) mixes up the dynasty of Bathindah with that of the Shāhiyas of Ohind, commonly called 'of Kābul', and so renders the whole story unintelligible. The inscriptions were not known when he wrote, and all subsequent writers have perpetuated his error. The version of the *Ṭabaķāt-i-Akbari* is given by Elliot (ibid., 460). The retirement to Bārī is recorded by Alberūnī and Rashīd-ud-dīn. The subject is discussed more fully in my second paper on 'The Gurjaras of Rājputāna and Kanauj' (*J. R. A. S.*, 1909, pp. 276–81).

[2] The history is obtained from the Chandēl inscriptions in *Ep. Ind.*, i, 219; ii, 235, combined with the Muhammadan accounts in Elliot, vol. ii, pp. 464–7. The dates are often stated erroneously by English authors.

end of 1019 or the beginning of 1020, and made the grant of a village near Allāhābād in A.D. 1027.[1] A Rāja named Yasahpāla, who is mentioned in an inscription of A.D. 1036, may have been his immediate successor.[2] Other obscure chiefs continued to be recognized as Rājas of Kanauj, and governed a considerable territory, no doubt in subordination to Muhammadan kings, even after the reduction of Kanauj in 1194. The names of some of these chiefs have been preserved. They seem to have resided at Zafarābād near Jaunpur. But these later chiefs did not belong to the old Gurjara-Pratihāra dynasty, which disappeared utterly. Kanauj had been conquered and occupied, a little before A.D. 1090, by a Rāja of the Gaharwār clan, named Chandradeva, who established his authority certainly over Benares and Ajodhyā, and perhaps over the Delhi territory.[3] The city of Delhi had been founded about a century earlier, in A.D. 993–4.[4]

Gaharwār dynasty of Kanauj.

The Gaharwār dynasty, subsequently known as Rāthōr,[5] thus founded by Chandradeva, lasted until the subjugation of the Kanauj kingdom by Shihāb-ud-dīn, in A.D. 1194

[1] Inscription No. 60 of Kielhorn's *List*. Cunningham (*Coins of Med. India*, p. 61) confounds Trilochanapāla of Kanauj with the prince of the same name who was the last of the Shāhiyas of Ohind.

[2] Colebrooke, *Essays*, ii, 246.

[3] Inscription No. 75 of Kielhorn's *List*; *Ind. Ant.*, xviii, 13. Copperplate grant of Rāja Chanradeva, dated A.D. 1090 (1148 V.E.), found at Chandrāvatī in Benares District, and now in Lucknow Museum (*A. S. Prog. Rep.*, *N. Circle*, 1907–8, pp. 21, 39). Another grant of the same Rāja was executed two years later at Ajodhyā (*Lucknow Prov. Mus. Rep.*, 1911–12, p. 3), as was a third grant dated A.D. 1156.

[4] *Notes on Afghanistan*, p. 320. Raverty informed me that his authority for the date was the *Zain-ul-Akbar* by Abū S'aīd-i-Abū-l Hakk, who wrote his history in the time of Sultan Mahmūd and his sons, not many years after the date stated. Another more modern writer dates the foundation in the year 440 of Bikramajit, which of course is absurd; but if the figures are taken as referring to the Harsha era, the date would be A.D. 1045, about the time of Ānangapāla. Tieffenthaler was told that Delhi had been founded by a Tomar Rāja named Rāsena in A.H. 307 = A.D. 919–20 (*Géogr. de l'Indoustan*, Fr. transl., Berlin, 1791, p. 125). In certain inscriptions and popular verses Delhi is called Yoginīpura (*Ind. Ant.*, 1912, p. 86, and *Ep. Ind.*, xii, 45).

[5] The 'Rāthōr dynasty of Kanauj' commonly mentioned in books is a myth. The Rājas belonged to the Gahaḍavāla or Gaharwār clan, as is expressly affirmed in the Basāhi copperplate grant of Govindachandra dated 1161 V.E. = A.D. 1104 (No. 77 of *List*; *Ind. Ant.*, xiv, 103), and recognized by the traditions of the Gautam clan (*J. A. S. B.*, part i, vol. liv (1885), p. 160). The appellation 'Rāṭhōr' applied to the Kanauj Rājas is due solely to

(A. H. 590). Govindachandra, grandson of Chandradeva, enjoyed a long reign, which included the years A. D. 1104 and 1155. His numerous land grants and widely distributed coins prove that he succeeded to a large extent in restoring the glories of Kanauj, and in making himself a power of considerable importance.[1]

The grandson of Govindachandra was Jayachchandra, renowned in the popular Hindī poems and tales of Northern India as Rāja Jaichand, whose daughter was carried off by the gallant Rāi Pithōra of Ajmēr. He was known to the Muhammadan historian as the king of Benares, which, perhaps, may be regarded as having been his capital, and was reputed the greatest king in India. It is alleged that his territory extended from the borders of China to the province of Mālwā, and from the sea to within ten days' journey of Lahore, but it is difficult to believe that it can have been really so extensive. Shihāb-ud-dīn met him at Chandāwar in the Etawah District near the Jumna, and having defeated his huge host with immense slaughter, in which the Rāja was included, passed on to Benares, which he plundered, carrying off the treasure on 1,400 camels.[2] Thus ends the story of the independent kingdom of Kanauj. When the rājas of the Gaharwār line died out, their place was taken by chiefs of the Chandēl clan from Mahoba, who became the local rulers of Kanauj for eight generations.[3]

Chauhāns of Sāmbhar and

Inscriptions record the genealogy of a long line of Rājpūt kings belonging to the Chauhān (Chāhumāna) clan who governed the principality of Sāmbhar (Sākambharī) in

the claim made by the 'Rāṭhōr' chiefs of Jodhpur to be descended from Rāja Jaichand (Jayachchandra, *Ind. Ant.*, xiv, 98–101) through a boy who escaped massacre. Stories of this kind are commonplaces of family traditions and historically worthless. No Tomara dynasty of Kanauj ever existed.

[1] Nearly sixty grants made by the dynasty are known, most of which belong to Govindachandra's reign. One of Govindachandra's grants from Oudh, dated 1186 (=1129 A. D.), mentions *turushka daṇḍa*, a special tax levied to meet the cost of resisting the Muhammadan invasion (*Lucknow Museum Report*, 1914–15, pp. 4, 10). For the coins, see *Catal. Coins I. M.*, vol. i, pp. 257, 260.

[2] *Kāmilu-t-Tawārīkh*, Elliot, ii, 251.

[3] *J. A. S. B.*, part i, vol. i (1881), pp. 48, 49.

Rājputāna, to which Ajmēr was attached. Only two of these chiefs demand notice. Vigraha-rāja, in the middle of the twelfth century, extended his ancestral dominions considerably, and is erroneously alleged to have conquered Delhi from a chief of the Tomara clan. That chief was a descendant of Ānangapāla, who, a century earlier, had built the Red Fort, where the Kutb mosque now stands, and thus given permanence to the city, which had been founded in A.D. 993–4.[1] Europeans are so accustomed to associate the name of Delhi with the sovereignty of India that they do not easily realize the fact that Delhi is among the most modern of the great Indian cities. Vague legends, it is true, irradiate the lands along the bank of the Jumna near the village of Indarpat with the traditional glories of the prehistoric Indraprastha, and these stories may or may not have some substantial basis. But, as an historical city, Delhi dates only from the time of Ānangapāla in the middle of the eleventh century. The celebrated iron pillar, on which the eulogy of a powerful king named Chandra, who lived in the fourth century, is incised, was removed by the Tomara chief from its original position, probably at Mathurā, and set up in A.D. 1052 as an adjunct to a group of temples, from the materials of which the Muhammadans afterwards constructed the great mosque.[2] Ajmēr; Delhi.

Vigraha-rāja (IV) was a man of considerable distinction. Some years ago, during the progress of repairs executed at the principal mosque of Ajmēr, six slabs of polished black marble were discovered bearing inscriptions in Sanskrit and Prākrit, which on examination proved to be large portions Vigraha-rāja.

[1] For the genealogy, see Kielhorn in *Ep. Ind.*, viii, 'Supplement to Northern List,' p. 13. Ajmēr was founded about A.D. 1100 by Ajayadeva Chauhān. Coins of him and his queen, Somaladevī, are extant (*Ind. Ant.*, 1912, p. 209).

[2] The traditional story of the foundation of Delhi by an imaginary Ānangapāla I is fictitious. The earliest remains, excepting the transported iron pillar, date from the eleventh century (*J. R. A. S.*, 1897, p. 13). For the Red Fort (Lālkot), see Cunningham, *Reports*, i, 153. For Indarpat, see Carr Stephens, *Archaeology of Delhi* (8vo ed., 1876), pp. 1–8; Fanshawe, *Delhi Past and Present* (1902), p. 228. There was no Tomara dynasty of Kanauj. Cunningham's argument (*Reports*, i, 150) rests mainly on the misreading of Rāi Jaipāl for Rājyapāl in Al Utbi.

of two unknown dramas. One of these, the *Lalita-Vigraha-rāja-nāṭaka*, was composed in honour of Vigraha-rāja, while the other, the *Harakali-nāṭaka*, professes to be the composition of that prince himself.[1]

Prithivī-rāja, or Rāi Pithōra.

His nephew was Prithivī-rāja, Prithīrāj, or Rāi Pithōra, lord of Sāmbhar and Ajmēr, famous in song and story as a chivalrous lover and doughty champion. His fame as a bold lover rests upon his daring abduction of the not unwilling daughter of Jaichand, the Gaharwār Rāja of Kanauj, which occurred in or about A. D. 1175. His reputation as a general is securely founded upon his defeat of the Chandēl Rāja, Parmāl, and the capture of Mahoba in 1182, as well as upon gallant resistance to the flood of Muhammadan invasion. Indeed, Rāi Pithōra may be described with justice as the popular hero of Northern India, and his exploits in love and war are the subject of rude epics and bardic lays to this day.[2]

[1] Kielhorn, *Bruchstücke indischer Schauspiele in Inschriften zu Ajmere* (Berlin, 1901).

[2] The best-known work dealing with Prithīrāj is the *Chand-Rāisā*, or *Prithīrāj-Rāisā*, a Hindī epic, extremely popular in the United Provinces. The authorship is attributed to Chand Bardāi, who was the court poet of his hero and patron. A descendant of the poet still lives in the Jodhpur State on the income of the lands granted to his ancestor by Prithīrāj. He has the MS. of the original poem, consisting of only 5,000 verses. Additions were made by descendants until Akbar's time, enlarging the work to 125,000 verses. Copies of part of the original have been made, and it is hoped that the whole may be published (*J. & Proc. A. S. B.*, Feb. 1911, *Ann. Rep.*, p. xxx). The supposed chronological errors in the *Rāisā* are explained by the discovery that the author used the Ananda variety of the Vikrama era, equivalent roughly to A. D. 33, and so 90–1 years later than the ordinary Sananda Vikrama era of 58–57 B.C. (*J. R. A. S.*, 1906, p. 500). Chand gives the date of Prithīrāj's birth as 1115 of *ananda*, which means '*nanda-rahit*', devoid of nine, 'nine' being one of the submeanings of *nanda*. *A-nanda* therefore means (100–9) 91 or 90. Possibly the high-caste Rājpūts declined to recognize the low-caste Nanda kings, to whose dynasty they may have assigned a period of 91 years. Another explanation is that Prithīrāj founded an era of his own on account of his jealousy of Jaichand, who claimed descent from Vikrama, dating the era perhaps from the time of Prithīrāj's ancestor Chandra Deva (Syam Sundar Das in his *Annual Report on the Search for Hindi MSS.* for 1900, pp. 5–10). See also Hoernle in *J. R. A. S.*, 1906, p. 500. Both eras were current in Rājputāna in the twelfth century.

The Sanskrit work from Kashmīr, entitled *Pṛithivīrāja vijaya*, discovered and made known by Bühler, is of higher authority and great historical value. It was composed between A. D. 1178 and 1200, probably later than 1191. Its genealogical statements are

Battle of Tarāīn or Talāwarī.

The dread inspired by the victorious Musalman army under the command of Shihāb-ud-dīn or Muhammad of Ghōr, who was now undisputed master of the greater part of the Panjāb, constrained the jarring states of Northern India to lay aside their quarrels and combine for a moment against the foreign foe. At first fortune smiled on the Indians ; and in A.D. 1191 (A. H. 587) Prithivī-rāja succeeded in inflicting a severe defeat upon the invaders at Tarāīn or Talāwarī between Thānēsar and Karnāl, which forced them to retire beyond the Indus. A year later, in A. D. 1192 (A. H. 588), the Sultan, having returned with a fresh force, again encountered on the same field Prithivī-rāja, who was at the head of an immense host, swollen by contingents from numerous confederate princes. A vigorous charge by twelve thousand well-armed Musalman horsemen repeated the lesson given by Alexander long ages before, and demonstrated the inability of a mob of Indian militia to stand the onset of trained cavalry. Prithivī-rāja, having been taken prisoner, was executed in cold blood, and the wretched inhabitants of his capital Ajmēr were either put to the sword or sold into slavery.[1]

supported by the inscriptions. The correct lineage of Pṛithivīrāja according to the *Pṛithivīrāja-vijaya* is:—

Arṇorāja

Unnamed son, parricide (Jugdeva) — Pṛithivī-rāja I

Vigraha-rāja

Somesvara, m. princess of Chedi — Pṛithivī-rāja II or Rāi Pithōra; Hari-rāja

Chand's statement that Rāi Pithōra (Prithīrāj) was the son of the daughter of Ānangapāla, king of Delhi, is doubtful. The single imperfect MS. of the *Pṛithivīrāja vijaya* has been described and summarized by Har Bilas Sarda in *J. R. A. S.*, 1913, pp. 259–81, with references to earlier notices of the work. He uses the spelling *Pṛithvī*. The truth of the assertion that Vigraha-rāja wrested Delhi from the Tomaras is extremely doubtful (Bühler, *Proc. A. S. B.*, 1893, p. 94). It seems to be contradicted by verse 22 of the Bijoli inscription (*J. A. S. B.*, part i, vol. lv (1886), p. 31).

[1] Raverty, transl. *Ṭabaḳāt-i-Nāṣirī*, pp. 456, 459, 467, 468, 485, 486, and App. A. Most English books give the dates inaccurately and miscall the battle-field Tirauri. A. H. 587, 588, and 589, are almost exactly equivalent to the years A. D. 1191–3, extending from 29th

Conquest of Hindustan.

In A. D. 1193 (A. H. 589), Delhi fell. Kanauj does not seem to have been molested, but must have come under the control of the invaders. Benares, the holy citadel of Hinduism, in A. D. 1194 became the prize of the victors, who could now feel confident that the final triumph of the arms of Islam over 'the land of the Brahmans' was assured. The surrender of Gwālior in 1196, the capture in 1197 of Anhilwāra the capital of Gujarāt, and the capitulation of Kālanjar in 1203 completed the reduction of Upper India, and when Shihāb-ud-dīn died in A. D. 1205–6 (A. H. 602), he—

> 'Held, in different degrees of subjection, the whole of Hindustan Proper, except Mālwā and some contiguous districts. Sind and Bengal were either entirely subdued, or in rapid course of reduction. On Gujarāt he had no hold, except what is implied in the possession of the capital (Anhilwāra or Nahrwāla). Much of Hindustan was immediately under his officers, and the rest under dependent or at least tributary princes. The desert and some of the mountains were left independent from neglect'.[1]

Migration of Gaharwārs.

An important consequence of the Muslim conquest of Kanauj was the migration of the bulk of the Gaharwār clan

January, 1191, to 26th December, 1193. A Hindu tale that Pṛithivirāja was taken to Ghaznī, where he shot the Sultan, and was then cut to pieces, is false. Sultan Shihāb-ud-dīn was assassinated at the halting-place of 'Damyck', in the year 602 (A. D. 1205–6), by a fanatic of the Mulāḥidah sect. The exact spot, the scene of the surprise, has been visited by Mr. G. P. Tate and identified at Dhamiāk in the Jhelum District, Panjāb (*J. R. A. S.*, 1909, p. 168). The phrase attributed to Firishtah by his translator that 'this prodigious army, once shaken, like a great building tottered to its fall, &c.', is not in the Persian.

[1] Elphinstone, *Hist. of India*, 5th ed., p. 338. Shihāb-ud-dīn is designated by an inconvenient variety of names and titles, as Muhammad the son of Sām, Muhammad Ghorī, or Muizz-ud-dīn. Similarly, his elder brother and colleague, who was also named Muhammad, is known as both Shams-ud-dīn and Ghiyāṣ-ud-dunyā wa ud-dīn (Raverty, *J. A. S. B.*, vol. xlv, part 1, p. 328). The article cited fully justifies the chronology adopted in the text. Rājā Jaichand was defeated and killed at Chandāwar in the Etāwah District near the Jumna. Mr. Banerji rightly points out that there is no evidence that Kanauj was then sacked. The Musalman army passed on to Benares. But the Kanauj territory, including the city, must have then passed under Muhammadan control. The army probably did not visit Kanauj, which is on the Ganges. The city certainly was taken by Iltutmish (Altamsh) in or about A. D. 1226 (*J. & Proc. A. S. B.*, 1911, pp. 761, 765, 769). It would seem that in 1194 Kanauj was treated as an unimportant place which could be left aside without danger.

to the deserts of Mārwār in Rājputāna, where they settled and became known as Rāthōrs. The state so founded, now generally designated by the name of its capital, Jodhpur, is one of the most important principalities of Rājputāna.[1] Similar clan movements, necessitated by the pressure of Muhammadan armies, which were frequent at this period, account to a large extent for the existing distribution of the Rājpūt clans.

VI

The Chandēls of Jejākabhukti and the Kalachuris of Chedi

Jejāka-bhukti and Chedi.

The ancient name of the province between the Jumna and Narmadā, now known as Bundelkhand, and partly included in the United Provinces of Agra and Oudh, was Jejākabhukti.[2] The extensive region, farther to the south, which is now under the administration of the Chief Commissioner of the Central Provinces, nearly corresponds with the old kingdom of Chedi. In the mediaeval history of these countries two dynasties—the Chandēls of Jejākabhukti and the Kalachuris of Chedi—which occasionally were connected by marriage, and constantly were in contact one with the other, whether as friends or enemies, are conspicuous. From the beginning of the eleventh century the Chedi country was divided into two kingdoms, Western Chedi, or Dāhāla, with its capital at Tripura, near Jabalpur, and Eastern Chedi, or Mahākosala, with its capital at Ratanpur.

Predecessors of the Chandēls.

The Chandēls, like several other dynasties, first come into notice early in the ninth century, when Nannuka Chandēl, about A. D. 831, overthrew a Parihār chieftain, and became lord of the southern parts of Jejākabhukti. The Parihārs of Bundelkhand, like their brethren of Bhinmāl, must have belonged to the Gurjara or Gūjar group of tribes which had

[1] *Imp. Gaz.*, xiv, 183. Real Rāṭhōrs had been settled at Bāli in Māṛwār as early as the tenth century (ibid., vi, 287).

[2] i. e. the province of Jejāka; the name Jejāka or Jejā occurs in the inscriptions (*Ep. Ind.*, i, 121). Compare Tīrabhukti, Tirhūt. The name of the ruling clan is Chandēl in Hindī, Chandella in Sanskrit. It is better to use the Hindī form.

entered India in the sixth century. The Parihār capital had been at Mau-Sahaniya, between Nowgong (Naugāon) and Chhatarpur.[1] The predecessors of the Parihārs were Gaharwār Rājas, members of the clan which afterwards gave Kanauj the line of kings commonly miscalled Rāthōrs.

Chandēl temples and lakes. The Chandēl princes were great builders, and beautified their chief towns, Mahoba, Kālanjar, and Khajurāho, with many magnificent temples and lovely lakes, formed by throwing massive dams across the openings between the hills. In this practice of building embankments and constructing lakes the Chandēls were imitators of the Gaharwārs, who are credited with the formation of some of the most charming lakes in Bundelkhand.

Yaśovarman. The Chandēls, who appear to have been Hinduized Gonds, closely connected with another autochthonous tribe, the Bhars, first acquired a petty principality near Chhatarpur, and gradually advanced northwards until the Jumna became the frontier between their dominions and those of Kanauj. The earlier Rājas may have been subject to the suzerainty of Bhoja and Mahendrapāla, the powerful kings of Panchāla, but in the first half of the tenth century the Chandēls certainly had become independent. Harsha Chandēl, aided perhaps by other allies, helped Mahīpāla to recover the throne of Kanauj from which he had been driven by Indra III Rāshtrakūta in A. D. 916. Harsha's son and successor, Yasovarman, whose power had been greatly enhanced by the occupation of the fortress of Kālanjar, was strong enough to compel Mahīpāla's successor, Devapāla, to surrender a valuable image of Vishnu, which the Chandēl king wanted for a temple built by him at Khajurāho.

A. D. 950–99. Dhanga. King Dhanga, son of Yasovarman (A. D. 950–99), who lived to an age of more than a hundred years, was the most notable of his family. Some of the grandest temples at Khajurāho are due to his munificence, and he took an active part in the politics of his time. In A. D. 989 or 990 he joined the league formed by Jaipāl, king of the Panjāb, to resist Sabuktigīn, and shared with the Rājas of Ajmēr and

[1] *J. A. S. B.*, 1881, part i, p. 6.

Kanauj in the disastrous defeat which the allies suffered between Bannū and Ghaznī, in or near the Kurram (Kurmah) valley.[1]

A. D. 999–1025. Ganda.

When Mahmud of Ghaznī threatened to overrun India, Dhanga's son Ganda (999–1025) joined the new confederacy of Hindu princes organized by Ānand Pāl, son of Jaipāl, king of the Panjāb, in 1008–9 (A. H. 399), which also failed to stay the hand of the invader. Ten years later, as already narrated, Ganda's son attacked Kanauj and killed the Rāja, Rājyapāla, who had made terms with the Muhammadans; but early in 1023 (A. H. 413) was himself compelled to surrender the strong fortress of Kālanjar to Mahmūd,[2] who, however, did not retain it or any of his conquests in the interior of India beyond the Panjāb.

A. D. 1015–70. Gāngēyadeva and Karṇadeva Kalachuri.

Gāngēyadeva Kalachuri of Chedi (*circa* 1015–40), the contemporary of Ganda and his successors, was an able and ambitious prince, who aimed at attaining the position of paramount power in Upper India, and succeeded to a considerable extent. In 1019 his suzerainty was recognized in distant Tirhūt.[3] His projects of aggrandizement were taken up and proceeded with by his son Karnadeva (*circa* 1040–70), who joined Bhīma, king of Gujarāt, in crushing Bhoja, the learned king of Mālwā, about A. D. 1060. He had attacked the Pāla king of Magadha at an earlier date, about A. D. 1035.

A. D. 1049–1100. Kīrtivarman Chandēl.

But some years later Karnadeva was taught the lesson of the mutability of fortune by suffering defeats inflicted by several hostile kings, and notably one at the hands of Kīrtivarman Chandēl (1049–1100), who widely extended the dominion of his house. The earliest extant specimens of the Chandēl coinage were struck by this king in imitation of the issues of Gāngēyadeva of Chedi. Kīrtivarman is also memorable in literary history as the patron of the curious

[1] Raverty, *Notes on Afghanistan*, p. 320.

[2] *Ṭabakāt-i-Nāṣirī* in Elliot, ii, 467, where A. D. 1021 is wrongly stated to be the equivalent of A. H. 413.

[3] Bendall, 'Hist. of Nepāl' (*J. A. S. B.*, 1903, part i, p. 18 of reprint). Sylvain Lēvi rejects Bendall's interpretation (*Le Népal*, ii, 202, note), but without sufficient reason. See R. D. Banerji in 'The Palas of Bengal' (*Memoirs A. S. B.*, 1915).

allegorical play entitled the *Prabodha-chandrodaya*, or 'Rise of the Moon of Intellect', which was performed at his court in or about A. D. 1065, and gives in dramatic form a clever exposition of the Vedānta system of philosophy.[1]

A. D. 1165–1203. Parmāl. The last Chandēl king to play any considerable part upon the stage of history was Paramardi, or Parmāl (1165–1203), whose reign is memorable for his defeat in 1182 by Prithivīrāja Chauhān, and for the capture of Kālanjar in 1203 (A. H. 599) by Kutb-ud-dīn Ībak.[2] The Chauhān and Chandēl war occupies a large space in the popular Hindī epic, the *Chand-Rāisā*, which is familiar to the people of Upper India.

A. D. 1203 (spring). Capitulation of Kālanjar. The account of the death of Parmāl and the capture of Kālanjar, as told by the contemporary Muhammadan historian, may be quoted as a good illustration of the process by which the Hindu kingdoms passed under the rule of their new Muslim masters :—

'"The accursed Parmār," the Rai of Kālanjar, fled into the fort after a desperate resistance in the field, and afterwards surrendered himself, and placed "the collar of subjection" round his neck ; and, on his promise of allegiance, was admitted to the same favours as his ancestor had experienced from Mahmūd Sabuktigīn, and engaged to make a payment of tribute and elephants, but he died a natural death before he could execute any of his engagements. His Dīwān, or Mahtea, by name Aj Deo, was not disposed to surrender so easily as his master, and gave his enemies much trouble, until he was compelled to capitulate in consequence of severe drought having dried up all the reservoirs of water in the forts. "On Monday, the 20th of Rajab, the garrison, in an extreme state of weakness and distraction, came out of the fort, and by compulsion left their native place empty ; . . . and the fort of Kālanjar, which was celebrated throughout the world for being as strong as the wall of Alexander," was taken. "The temples were converted into mosques and abodes of goodness, and the ejaculations of the bead-counters and the voices of the summoners to prayer ascended to the

[1] A full abstract of the play is given by Sylvain Lévi (*Théâtre Indien*, pp. 229–35). See plate of coins, fig. 13.

[2] There is a variant reading A. H. 597 (A. D. 1200–1201) in the text of the *Tāj-ul-Maāsir* (Raverty, transl. *Ṭabaḳāt*, App. D).

highest heaven, and the very name of idolatry was annihilated. . . . Fifty thousand men came under the collar of slavery, and the plain became black as pitch with Hindus." Elephants and cattle, and countless arms also, became the spoil of the victors.

'The reins of victory were then directed towards Mahobā, and the government of Kālanjar was conferred on Hazabbar-ud-dīn Hasan Arnal. When Kutb-ud-dīn was satisfied with all the arrangements made in that quarter, he went towards Badāūn, "which is one of the mothers of cities, and one of the chiefest of the country of Hind." '[1]

The last of the Chandēls.

Chandēl Rājas lingered on in Bundelkhand as purely local chiefs until the sixteenth century, but their affairs are of no general interest.[2] The Chandēl clan was scattered, and its most notable modern representative is the Rāja of Gidhaur, near Mungir (Monghyr) in Bengal.

The last of the Kalachuris.

The Kalachuri or Haihaya Rājas of Chedi are last mentioned in an inscription of the year A.D. 1181, and the manner of their disappearance is not exactly known; but there is reason to believe that they were supplanted by the Baghēls of Rēwā. The Hayobans Rājpūts of the Baliyā district in the east of the United Provinces claim descent from the Rājas of Ratanpur in the Central Provinces, and probably are really an offshoot of the ancient Haihaya race. The later kings of Chedi used an era according to which the year 1 was equivalent to A. D. 248–9. This era, also called the Traikūtaka, originated in Western India, where its use can be traced back to the fifth century.[3] The reason of its adoption by the kings of Chedi is not apparent.

[1] *Tāj-ul-Maāsir*, as abstracted by Elliot, *Hist. of India*, vol. ii, p. 231; Raverty, transl. *Ṭabaḳāt*, p. 523. The learned translator, usually so accurate, has made an unlucky slip in this passage by rendering the personal name Parmār as 'of the Pramārah race'. Kālanjar is in the Bānda District, N. lat. 25° 1′, E. long. 80° 29′; Mahobā is in the Hamīrpur District, N. lat. 25° 18′, E. long. 79° 53′.

[2] The subject is exhaustively treated (with a bibliography), in my monograph entitled 'The History and Coinage of the Chandel (Chandella) Dynasty of Bundelkhand (Jejākabhukti), from A. D. 831 to 1203' (*Ind. Ant.*, 1908, pp. 114–48). One inscription of Paramardi has been discovered since the publication of that essay (*Ep. Ind.*, x, 44).

[3] For Kalachuri history, see Cunningham, *Reports*, vols. ix, x, xxi; and many inscriptions in *Ep. Ind.* For the era, see Fleet (*J. R. A. S.*, 1905, p. 566), and Kielhorn (*Ep. Ind.*, ix, 129). For

VII

Paramāras (Pawārs) of Mālwā

c. A. D. 820. Paramāra dynasty of Mālwā.

The Paramāra dynasty of Mālwā, the region north of the Narmadā, anciently known as Avanti, or the kingdom of Ujjain, is specially memorable by reason of its association with many eminent names in the history of later Sanskrit literature. The dynasty was founded by a chief named Upendra or Krishnarāja, early in the ninth century, when so many ruling families attract notice for the first time, and it lasted for about four centuries. Upendra appears to have come from Chandrāvatī and Achalgarh, near Mount Ābū, where his clan had been settled for a long time.

A. D. 974–95. Rāja Muñja.

The seventh Rāja, named Munja, who was famous for his learning and eloquence, was not only a patron of poets, but himself a poet of no small reputation, as attested by the anthologies, which include various compositions attributed to his pen. The author Dhanamjaya and his brother Dhanika were among the distinguished scholars who graced his court. His energies were not devoted solely to the peaceful pursuit of literature, much of his time being spent in fighting with his neighbours. Six times the Chalukya king, Taila II, was defeated by him. The seventh attack failed, and Munja, who had crossed the Godāvarī, Taila's northern boundary, was defeated, captured, and executed about A. D. 995.[1]

A. D. 1018–60. Rāja Bhoja.

Munja's nephew, the famous Bhoja, ascended the throne of Dhārā, in those days the capital of Mālwā, about A.D. 1018, and reigned gloriously for more than forty years. Like his

the Hayobans Rājputs, see Crooke, *Ethnographical Handbook* (Allāhābād, 1898), p. 156; *Tribes and Castes of the North-West Provinces and Oudh*, vol. ii, p. 493. In connexion with the Rājas of Ratanpur see C. V. Wills, 'The territorial system of the Rājput kingdoms of mediaeval Chhattisgarh', in *J. and Proc. A. S. B.*, N. S., vol. xv, No. 5, pp. 198–262.

[1] Muñja had an embarrassing variety of names—Vākpati (II), Utpalarāja, Amoghavarsha, Prithivīvallabha, and Śrīvallabha. His accession took place in A. D. 974, and his death about twenty years later, between 994 and 997 (*Bühler*, in *Ep. Ind.*, i, 222–8, 294, 302; Fleet, 'Dynasties of Kanarese Districts,' 2nd ed., p. 432, in *Bom. Gaz.*, 1896, vol. i, part ii; Bhandarkar, 'Early Hist. of Dekkan,' ibid., p. 214). The attacks were six, not sixteen, as erroneously supposed by Bühler (Haas, *Daśarūpa*, p. xxii, note 4; Columbia Univ. Press, 1912).

uncle, he cultivated with equal assiduity the arts of peace and war. Although his fights with the neighbouring powers, including one of the Muhammadan armies of Mahmūd of Ghaznī, are now forgotten, his fame as an enlightened patron of learning and a skilled author remains undimmed, and his name has become proverbial as that of the model king according to the Hindu standard. Works on astronomy, architecture, the art of poetry, and other subjects are attributed to him, and there is no doubt that he was a prince, like Samudragupta, of very uncommon ability. A mosque at Dhārā now occupies the site of Bhoja's Sanskrit college, which seems to have been held in a temple dedicated appropriately to Sarasvatī, the goddess of learning.[1]

Bhōjpur lake. The great Bhōjpur lake, a beautiful sheet of water to the south-east of Bhopāl, covering an area of more than 250 square miles, formed by massive embankments closing the outlet in a circle of hills, was his noblest monument, and continued to testify to the skill of his engineers until the fifteenth century, when the dam was cut by order of a Muhammadan king, and the water drained off. The bed of the lake is now a fertile plain intersected by the Indian Midland Railway.[2]

Later history of Mālwā. About A. D. 1060 this accomplished prince succumbed to an attack by the confederate kings of Gujarāt and Chedi; and the glory of his house departed. His dynasty lasted as a purely local power until the beginning of the thirteenth century, when it was superseded by chiefs of the Tomara clan, who were followed in their turn by Chauhān Rājas,[3]

[1] *Archaeol. S. Annual Rep.*, 1903–4, pp. 238–43. The most complete list of the works ascribed to Bhoja is said to be that in Aufrecht's *Catalogus Catalogorum*, vol. i, p. 418, vol. ii, p. 95. For Bhoja's date and the history of his predecessor, Sindhurāja, see *Ind. Ant.*, 1907, pp. 170–2. Two inscriptions of his are known, dated respectively in A. D. 1019 and 1021 = V. E. 1076 and 1078 (*Ind. Ant.*, 1912, p. 201).

[2] Malcolm, *Central India*, i, 25; Kincaid, *Ind. Ant.*, xvii, pp. 350–2, with map of the bed of the lake. Further details are given in Major Luard's article, 'Gazetteer Gleanings in Central India': the great dam and temple at Bhojpur in Bhopal State, *J. R. A. S.*, 1914, pp. 309–16, with map and photo of the remains of the dam. The king who cut the dam was Hoshang Shāh of Mālwā (1405–35). The lake, while it existed, probably modified the climate and tended to prevent famine.

[3] Malcolm, *Central India*, i, 26.

from whom the crown passed to Muhammadan kings in 1401. Akbar suppressed the local dynasty in 1562, and incorporated Mālwā in the Moghal empire.

VIII

Pāla and Sena Dynasties of Bihār and Bengal

A. D. 650. History of Bengal unknown.

Harsha, when at the height of his power, exercised a certain amount of control as suzerain over the whole of Bengal, even as far east as the distant kingdom of Kāmarupa, or Assam, and seems to have possessed full sovereign authority over western and central Bengal. After his death, the local Rājas no doubt asserted their independence; but, except for the strange story of Arjuna and Wang-Hiuen-tse, related in the thirteenth chapter, no particulars are known concerning the history of Bengal for nearly a century. Bengālī tradition traces the origin of many notable families to five Brahmans and five Kāyasths imported from Kanauj by a king named Ādisūra in order to revive orthodox Hindu customs, which had fallen into disuse during the time when Buddhism was predominant. But no authentic record of this monarch has been discovered. There is, however, no reason to doubt the actual existence of Ādisūra, who belonged to a local dynasty of Rājas ruling Gaur and the neighbourhood. He may be dated approximately in A. D. 700, perhaps a little earlier, or possibly later.[1]

[1] 'Up to date no authentic account of Ādisūra has been obtained. The oldest writers on Brahmanical genealogy whose writings have come down to us—I refer particularly to Hari Miśra and Ēru Miśra—place Ādisūra shortly before the Pālas; and they state that shortly after the arrival of the five Brāhmaṇas from Kanauj, the kingdom of Gauṛ became subject to the Pālas' (U. C. Batavyal in *J. A. S. B.*, part i, vol. lxiii (1894), p. 41).

'Raṇaśūra of southern Rāḍha [*scil.* the Burdwan Division] seems to have belonged to the Śūra dynasty of Bengal who are said to have brought the five Brāhmaṇas from Kanauj. That they were dispossessed of the greater part of their dominions by the Pālas is also asserted by the Bengal genealogists.' Ranaśūra was one of the chiefs who helped Mahīpāla to repel the invasion of Rājendra Chola, king of Kānchī, about A. D. 1023 (H. P. Sastri, *Mem. A. S. B.*, vol. iii, No. 1 (1910), p. 10). H. P. Sastri places Ādisūra in the eighth century, and declares that the story about the importation of Brahmans is neither foolish nor imaginary. It was rather part of the Brahmanical movement set on foot by Kumārila a generation

Early in the eighth century (c. A. D. 730–40) a chieftain named Gopāla was elected king of Bengal, which had been suffering from anarchy. Towards the close of his life he extended his power westwards over Magadha or South Bihār, and is said to have reigned forty-five years. He suffered defeat at the hands of Vatsarāja, the Gurjara king of Rājputāna.[1] He was a pious Buddhist, and founded a great monastery at Uddandapura, or Otantapuri, the existing town of Bihār, which seems to have been at times the capital of the later Pāla kings. Inasmuch as the word *pāla* was an element in the personal names of the founder of the family and his successors, the dynasty is commonly and conveniently designated as that of the 'Pāla kings of Bengal'. **c. A. D. 730–40. Rise of the 'Pāla dynasty'.**

The second king, Dharmapāla, who is credited with a reign of sixty-four years, is known to have reigned for at least thirty-two years. The Tibetan historian Tāranāth expressly states that his rule extended from the Bay of Bengal to Delhi and Jālandhar in the north and to the valleys of the Vindhyan range in the south. This ascription of wide dominion is supported by the certain fact that Dharmapāla dethroned Indrāyudha, or Indrarāja, king of Panchāla, whose capital was Kanauj, and installed in his stead Chakrāyudha, with the assent of the neighbouring northern powers, enumerated as the Bhoja, Matsya, Madra, Kuru, Yadu, Yavana, Avanti, Gandhāra, and Kīra kings. This event took place soon after A. D. 800, and prior to the thirty-second year of Dharmapāla's reign, as recorded in two grants.[2] It is noticeable that the grant of four villages in the province of Paundravardhana was issued from the **Dharmapāla, *flor.* A. D. 800.**

earlier (*J. & Proc. A. S. B.*, 1912, p. 348). On the other hand, the tradition is discredited by Radha Govinda Basak, who thinks that he can prove the existence of learned Brahmans in Bengal from 'time immemorial', or at any rate from the fifth century (*Ep. Ind.*, xiii (1916), p. 288). The site of the palace of Ādisūra is pointed out at the northern end of the ruins of Gaur, outside the walls of Lakhnauti (*E. India*, iii, 72).

[1] Rāshtrakūta grants (*Ind. Ant.*, xi, 136, 160; xii, 164; *Ep. Ind.*, vi, 240). Mr. R. D. Banerji places the accession of Gopāla forty or fifty years later, but I am not satisfied that he is right.

[2] Bhāgalpur copperplate (*Ind. Ant.*, xv, 304; xx, 308); Khālimpur copperplate (*Ep. Ind.*, iv, 252).

royal head-quarters at Pātaliputra.[1] When Hiuen Tsang visited the ancient imperial city in the seventh century he had found the buildings of Asoka in ruins, and the inhabitants limited to about a thousand persons occupying a small walled town on the bank of the Ganges in the northern portion of the site.[2] Apparently the city had recovered to some extent when Dharmapāla held his court there about A.D. 810. The famous monastery of Vikramasīla, which is said to have included 107 temples and six colleges, was founded by Dharmapāla. It stood on a hill overlooking the right bank of the Ganges, but its position has not been conclusively determined.[3]

Devapāla, ninth century.

Devapāla, the third sovereign of the dynasty, is regarded by the oldest writers on Brahman genealogy in Bengal as having been the most powerful of the Pālas.[4] His general, Lāusena or Lavasena, is said to have conquered Assam and Kalinga. A grant dated in the thirty-third year of his reign was issued from the court at Mudgagiri, or Monghyr.[5] Like all the other kings of his house, he was zealous in the cause of Buddhism, and is reputed to have waged war with the unbelievers, destroying forty of their strongholds. He is said to have reigned for forty-eight years.[6]

The Kāmboja rule.

During the latter part of the tenth century the rule of the Pāla kings was interrupted by the intrusion of hillmen, known as Kāmbojas, who set up one of their chiefs as king. His rule is commemorated by an inscribed pillar at Dinājpur, erected apparently in A.D. 966.[7]

Mahīpāla I, c. A.D. 978–1030.

The Kāmbojas were expelled by Mahīpāla I, the ninth sovereign of the Pāla line, who is known to have been reigning in A.D. 1026, and may be assumed to have won

[1] The term *jayaskandhāvāra* does not necessarily mean a camp only (D. R. Bhandarkar).

[2] Watters, ii, 87, 88; Beal, ii, 82, 86.

[3] The site may be at Pathar-ghāṭa in the Bhāgalpur District (*J. & Proc. A. S. B.*, 1909, pp. 1–13).

[4] *J. A. S. B.*, vol. lxiii, part i (1894), p. 41.

[5] *Ind. Ant.*, xxi, 254.

[6] Schiefner, *Tāranāth*, pp. 208–14. Tāranāth adds that Devapāla subdued Varendra, i.e. the Mālda District, &c., which is hard to understand, for that province, apparently, must have been under Pāla rule earlier.

[7] 'Dinājpur Pillar Inscription' (*J. & Proc. A. S. B.*, 1911, p. 615). The date is 888, which, if referred to the Saka era, is equivalent to A.D. 966.

back his ancestral throne about A.D. 978 or 980. He is credited with a long reign of 52 years, a statement which cannot be far wrong, as there is epigraphic evidence that his rule endured for 48 years.[1] Of all the Pāla kings he is the best remembered, and songs in his honour, which used to be sung in many parts of Bengal until recent times, are still to be heard in remote corners of Orissa and Kūch Bihār. He was attacked by Rājendra, the Chola king of Kānchī, about A. D. 1023. His reign is marked by the revival of Buddhism in Tibet, which had been weakened by the persecution of Langdarma a century earlier. Pundit Dharmapāla and other holy men from Magadha accepted an invitation to Tibet in A. D. 1013, and did much to restore the religion of Gautama to honour in that country. A subsequent mission dispatched in 1038, during the reign of Mahīpāla's successor, Nayapāla, and headed by Atīsa, from the Vikramasīla monastery in Magadha, continued the work and firmly re-established Tibetan Buddhism.[2]

The Kaivarta rebellion.

The son of Nayapāla, king Vigrahapāla III, who defeated Karna, king of Chedi, and died about A. D. 1080, left three sons, namely Mahīpāla II, Sūrapāla II, and Rāmapāla.

[1] Sārnāth inscription of 1083 (V. E.) in *Ind. Ant.*, xiv, 140. Two groups of bronze figures found in the Muzaffarpur District of Tirhūt or North Bihār bear inscriptions dated in the forty-eighth year of Mahīpāla (Hoernle in *Ind. Ant.*, xiv (1885), p. 165, note 17. The readings in *Proc. A. S. B.*, 1881, p. 98, are imaginary. Cunningham quoted the date correctly in *A. S. Rep.*, xv, 153). Mahīpāla I seems to have used Samataṭa as his base. The Bāghaura inscription of his regnal year 3, found at Bāghaura in Samataṭa in the Comilla Subdivision of the Tipperah District, indicates that, and also shows that Comilla was included in Samataṭa. The town of Comilla (Kumillā) is on the main road from Dacca to Chittagong. See *J. & Proc. A. S. B.*, 1915, p. 17. The subject is further elucidated by N. K. Bhattasali in 'A Forgotten Kingdom of Eastern Bengal' (ibid., 1914, pp. 85–91). Good reason from inscriptions is shown for holding that Karumanta is the modern Kamta, 12 miles west of Comilla town, where numerous ruins and Buddhist images exist. That was the capital of the Samataṭa kingdom, which seems to have included the Districts of Tipperah, Noakhali, Barisal, Farīdpur, and the eastern half of the Dacca District. In the tenth century the country probably was under the overlordship of the Chandra kings of Arakan.

[2] Sarat Chandra Dās (*J.A.S.B.*, vol. i, part i, pp. 236, 237). Tāranāth says that the date of Mahīpāla's death coincided approximately with that of the Tibetan king, Khriral, whom I cannot trace in the lists (Schiefner, p. 225). For the chronology, see *J. A. S. B.*, vol. lxix, part i (1900), p. 192.

When Mahīpāla succeeded to the throne he imprisoned his brothers and misgoverned the realm. His evil deeds provoked a rebellion, headed by Divya or Divyoka, chief of the Chāsi-Kaivarta tribe or Māhishya caste, which at that time was powerful in Northern Bengal. Mahīpāla II was killed by the rebels, who took possession of the country. Divyoka's place was taken by his nephew Bhīma, who became king of Varendra. Prince Rāmapāla, having escaped from confinement, travelled over a large part of India in order to obtain help in the recovery of his kingdom. After much effort he collected a strong force, including contingents from the Rāshtrakūtas, to whom he was related by marriage, and many other princes. Bhīma was defeated and killed, and Rāmapāla regained the throne of his fathers.[1]

Reign of Rāmapāla, c. A. D. 1084–1130.

Rāmapāla is described by Tāranāth as possessing a vigorous understanding and widely extended power. After defeating the Kaivarta usurper, he conquered Mithilā or North Bihār, the modern Champāran and Darbhanga Districts, and it is clear that his dominions also included Kāmarūpa or Assam, because his son Kumārapāla conferred the government of that country, with kingly powers, upon a valiant minister named Vaidyadeva. Buddhism, although then declining in Hindustan, flourished in the Pāla dominions during the reign of Rāmapāla, the monasteries of Magadha being crowded with thousands of residents. Tāranāth and certain Bengal authors treat Rāmapāla as the last of his dynasty, or at any rate, the last who exercised considerable power, but the inscriptions prove that he was followed by five kings of his family.[2]

[1] The killing of Bhīma and the conquest of Mithilā are recorded in the Kamauli grant of Vaidyadeva (*Ep. Ind.*, ii, 355). The details are supplied by the contemporary historical poem entitled *Rāmacharita*, by Sandhyākara Nandi, discovered in Nepāl and published in *A. S. B. Memoirs*, vol. iii, No. 1 (1910).

[2] The chief authority for the period is R. D. Banerji's elaborate article, 'The Pālas of Bengal', in *Mem. A. S. B.*, vol. v, pp. 43–113, 1915, with a separate fasciculus of plates. See also M. Haraprasad Sastri's 'Literary History of the Pāla Period' in *J. B. & O. Res. Soc.*, vol. v, part ii, pp. 171 ff.; and Benoy Kumar Sarkar, *The Folk-element in Hindu Culture* (Longmans, 1917). The latter lays stress on the power and importance of the Pālas and Cholas, long after Harsha's death, and suggests that India became

King Govindapāla is known to have been on the throne in A. D. 1175; and, according to tradition, the ruler of Magadha at the time of the Muhammadan conquest, in A. D. 1197, was Indradyumna[-pāla]. Forts attributed to him are still pointed out in the Mungir (Monghyr) District.[1] Latest Pāla kings.

The Pāla dynasty deserves remembrance as one of the most remarkable of Indian dynasties. No other royal line in an important kingdom, save that of the Āndhras, endured so long, for four and a half centuries. Dharmapāla and Devapāla succeeded in making Bengal one of the great powers of India, and, although later kings had not the control of realms so wide or possessed influence so extensive, their dominion was far from being contemptible. The Pāla authority was considerably shaken by the Kāmboja usurpation in the latter part of the tenth century, and again by the Chāsi-Kaivarta or Māhishya revolt in the eleventh century, which prepared the way for the encroachments made by the Sena kings. The Pālas seem to have held Magadha or South Bihār, and Mungir in North Bihār, almost throughout to the end, with little interruption, but during the last century of their rule they lost nearly the whole of Bengal to the Senas.[2] The details of the local history need to be worked out. Importance of the Pāla dynasty.

The reigns of Dharmapāla and Devapāla, extending over more than a century, from about A. D. 780 to 892, were a period of marked intellectual and artistic activity. Two artists of that time, Dhīmān and his son Bitpālo (Vitapāla), acquired the highest fame for their skill as painters, sculptors, and bronze-founders. Some works of their school are believed to be extant.[3] No building of Pāla age Intellectual and artistic activity.

really the school of Asia by supplying faith, literature, arts, and material necessities to Nepāl, Tibet, China, Japan, Java, Burma, and other lands beyond the seas.

[1] Buchanan, *Eastern India*, ii, 23; Cunningham, *Rep.*, iii, 135, 159, 162. See also J. N. Samaddar's 'Raja Indradyumna' in *J. B. & O. Res. Soc.*, vol. v, part ii, pp. 295–7. The author suggests that, after his defeat by the Muhammadans, the king fled to Orissa and there rebuilt the temple of Jagannāth in 1198.

[2] Mahendrapāla Gurjara-Pratihāra of Kanauj (*c.* A. D. 850) seems to have annexed Magadha for a few years.

[3] *History of Fine Art in India and Ceylon*, pp. 305–7. The Varendra Research Society at Rājshāhi has devoted special study to the schools of Dhīmān and Bitpālo.

appears to survive, but the numerous great tanks in the central districts of their territory, especially in Dinājpur, testify to the interest taken by the kings in the execution of undertakings intended for the public benefit.

Patronage of Buddhism.

All the Pāla kings without exception were zealous Buddhists, ready to bestow liberal patronage on learned teachers and the numerous monastic communities. Dharmapāla, clearly a man of exceptional capacity, is credited with the merit of having been an ardent reformer of religion. His successors in the eleventh century, who were devoted to Tantric forms of Buddhism, enjoyed the services of many pious men, among whom Atīsa, already mentioned as a missionary in Tibet, was the most eminent.[1]

The beginning of the Senas.

The Sena dynasty was founded by a chief named Sāmantadeva, who came from the Deccan. About the middle of the eleventh century he, or his son Hemantasena, founded a principality at Kāsīpurī, which has been identified with the modern Kasiārī in the Mayūrabhanja State. Neither of those chiefs seems to have acquired extensive power.

Vijayasena (c. A. D. 1070–1108).

But Sāmantasena's grandson, Vijayasena, certainly raised himself to the rank of an independent sovereign in the latter part of the eleventh or early in the twelfth century, and wrested a large part of the Bengal province from the Pālas, thus firmly establishing the Sena dynasty. He also carried on successful wars with other powers, and enjoyed a long reign of about forty years, more or less. He kept on terms of friendship with Choraganga of Kalinga, who ruled that kingdom for the extraordinary term of seventy-one years, and who about the time of the Chāsi-Kaivarta rebellion (c. A. D. 1080) extended his conquests to the extreme north of Orissa.

Vallālasena or

The dominions acquired by Vijayasena were transmitted

[1] See the learned Introduction by Mahā. Haraprasad Shastri to Mr. N. N. Vasu's work on *Modern Buddhism and its Followers in Orissa*, Calcutta, 1911, which is in part a reprint from the *Archaeological Survey of Mayūrabhanja*, vol. i, and the same author's article on the Literary History of the Pāla Period in *J. B. & O. Res. Soc.*, vol. v, part ii, pp. 171 ff. According to him Atīsa was the Tibetan name of Dīpānkara Srījñana, who was the son of the Rāja of Vikramanipura, east of Magadha.

(*c.* A. D. 1108) to his son Vallālasena, famous in Bengal tradition as Ballāl Sen, who is credited with having re-organized the caste system and introduced the practice of 'Kulinism' among Brahmans, Baidyas, and Kāyasths. Some accounts allege that he founded Gaur or Lakhnautī, but there is reason to believe that the city was in existence at an earlier date. The site of a palace attributed to him is pointed out at Rāmpāl near Bikrampur in the Dacca District.[1] All the Sena kings were Brahmanical Hindus, and so had a special reason for hostility to the Buddhist Pālas, and a keen interest in the maintenance of caste. The Hinduism of Ballāl Sen was of the Tantric kind. The Brahman genealogists assert that he sent numerous missionaries, all Brahmans, to Magadha, Bhotan, Chittagong, Arakan, Orissa, and Nepāl.[2]

Ballāl Sen (*c.* 1108–19).

Ballāl Sen was succeeded in A. D. 1119 by his son Lakshmanasena.

Lakshmaṇasena (*c.* 1119).

In Bihār and Bengal both Pālas and Senas were swept away by the torrent of Muhammadan invasion at the end of the twelfth century, when Kutb-ud-dīn's general, Muhammad the son of Bakhtyār, stormed Bihār in or about A. D. 1197, and surprised Nūdīah (*vulgo* Nuddea) a year or two later. The Musalman general, who had already made his name a terror by repeated plundering expeditions in Bihār, seized the capital by a daring stroke. The almost contemporary historian met one of the survivors of the attacking party in A. D. 1243, and learned from him that the fort of Bihār was seized by a party of only two hundred horsemen, who boldly rushed the postern gate and gained possession of the place. Great quantities of plunder were

Muhammadan conquest of Bihār.

[1] *J. A. S. B.*, part i, vol. xlvii (1878), p. 400; *Imp. Gaz.*, s. v. Rāmpāl. According to Mahā. Haraprasad Shastri, Ballāl Sen 'conquered Northern Bengal with the help of the Kaivartas, and tried his best to make a clean caste of them' (Introd. p. 15 to N. N. Vasu, *Modern Buddhism and its Followers in Orissa*). The Māhishyas or Chāsi-Kaivartas deny this and claim that they were a clean caste from time immemorial. They declare themselves to be quite distinct in origin from the Kewats (Jaliya-Kaivartas, &c.), and state that the Pāla kings belonged to their caste. They are hostile to the memory of Ballāl Sen. See also the same writer in *Proc. A. S. B.*, 1902, pp. 2–7.

[2] *Arch. S. Mayūrabhanja*, vol. i, p. lxiv, note.

obtained, and the slaughter of the 'shaven-headed Brahmans', that is to say the Buddhist monks, was so thoroughly completed, that when the victor sought for some one capable of explaining the contents of the books in the libraries of the monasteries, not a living man could be found who was able to read them. 'It was discovered', we are told, 'that the whole of that fortress and city was a college, and in the Hindī tongue they call a college Bihar.'[1]

Destruction of Buddhism.

This crushing blow, followed up, of course, by similar acts of violence, destroyed the vitality of Buddhism in its ancient home. No doubt, a few devout, though disheartened, adherents of the system lingered round the desecrated shrines for a few years longer; and even to this day traces of the religion once so proudly dominant may be discerned in the practices of obscure sects; but Buddhism as an organized religion in Bihār, its last abode in Upper India south of the Himalaya, was destroyed once and for all by the sword of a single Musalman adventurer.[2] Many monks who escaped death fled to Tibet, Nepāl, and Southern India. Their advent produced an important effect upon the Hindu revival in Southern India. In Tibet the arrival of the learned refugees enabled Buton, the Grand Lama appointed by Kublai Khan, to enrich the Tibetan language by translations from Sanskrit sources, which were included in the *Tangyur* encyclopaedia at the close of the thirteenth century. The preservation of the fruits of the joint labours of the Indian Pundits and the Tibetan Lamas was secured by the practice of the art of block-printing, which had been introduced into Tibet from China in the seventh century.[3]

A. D. ? 1199. Overthrow of the Sena dynasty.

The overthrow of the Sena dynasty was accomplished with equal or even greater ease. The ruler of eastern Bengal in those days was Lakshmanasena, described by the Muhammadan writer as an aged man and reputed, though erro-

[1] Raverty, transl. *Ṭabaḳāt-i-Nāṣirī*, p. 552.

[2] See papers by H. P. Çāstrī, 'Buddhism in Bengal since the Muhammadan Conquest'; '*Çrīdharma mangala*; a distant echo of the *Lalitavistara*' (*J. A. S. B.*, vol. lxiv, part i, 1895, pp. 55-68); and N. N. Vasu's work, *Modern Buddhism and its Followers in Orissa*, already cited.

[3] *J. & Proc. A. S. B.*, Feb. 1911, *Address*, p. xliii.

neously, to have occupied the throne for eighty years. The portents which were said to have attended his birth had been justified by the monarch's exceptional personal qualities. His family, we are told, was respected by all the Rāis or chiefs of Hindustan, and he was considered to hold the rank of hereditary Khalīf (Caliph), or spiritual head of the country. Trustworthy persons affirmed that no one, great or small, ever suffered injustice at his hands, and his generosity was proverbial.

Nūdīah, the capital.

This much-revered sovereign held his court at Nūdīah, situated in the upper delta of the Ganges, on the Bhāgīrathī river, about 60 miles north of the site of Calcutta. The town still gives its name to a British district (Nuddea, Nadiā), and is renowned as the seat of a Hindu college organized after the ancient manner.

Capture of Nūdīah, A. D. 1199.

Probably in A. D. 1199, not long after his facile conquest of Bihār, Muhammad the son of Bakhtyār equipped an army for the subjugation of Bengal. Riding in advance of the main body of his troops, he suddenly appeared before Nūdīah with a slender following of eighteen horsemen, and boldly entered the city, the people supposing him to be a horsedealer. But when he reached the gate of the Rāi's palace, he drew his sword and attacked the unsuspecting household. The Rāi, who was at his dinner, was completely taken by surprise,

> 'and fled barefooted by the rear of the palace; and his whole treasure, and all his wives, maidservants, attendants, and women fell into the hands of the invader. Numerous elephants were taken, and such booty was obtained by the Muhammadans as is beyond all compute. When his (Muhammad's) army arrived, the whole city was brought under subjection, and he fixed his head-quarters there.'

Lakhnautī, the Muhammadan capital.

Rāi Lakhmaniya, as the author calls him, fled to Bikrampur in the Dacca district,[1] where he died; and the conqueror presently destroyed the city of Nūdīah, establishing the seat of his government at the ancient Hindu city

[1] Raverty, transl. *Ṭabaḳāt-i-Nāṣirī*, p. 557: Elliot, *Hist. of India*, ii, 309.

of Lakhnautī, or Gaur. Mosques, colleges, and Muhammadan monasteries were endowed by him and his officers in all parts of the kingdom, and a great portion of the spoil was judiciously sent to his distant chief, Kutb-ud-dīn.

Dishonoured end of the Hindu kingdoms.

Such was the dishonoured end of the last Hindu kingdoms of Bengal and Bihār, which would have made a better fight for life if they had deserved to exist.[1] The administration must have been hopelessly inefficient to permit a foreign army to march unobserved across Bengal, and to allow of the surprise of the palace by an insignificant party of eighteen horsemen.

Literature.

The reign of the earlier king Lakshmanasena was remarkable for considerable literary activity and for his liberal patronage of Sanskrit literature. An imitation of Kālidāsa's *Meghadūta* by Dhoyi, or Dhoyīka, court-poet of Lakshmanasena, has been published. Jayadeva, the famous author of the *Gītagovinda*, seems to have lived in the reign of Lakshmanasena, who wrote verses himself. His father, Ballāl Sen, also was an author.

IX

The Rājpūt Clans

Apparent dominance of the clans.

Ethnological speculations, or discussions about facial angles, thick or thin noses, long skulls or broad skulls, the mystery of the origin of caste, and so forth, are foreign to the purpose of this work, and cannot be even lightly handled in these pages.[2] But the narrative sections of this chapter

[1] The Senas continued to exist as a local dynasty in Eastern Bengal subordinate to the Muhammadans for four generations after the capture of Nūdīah. Their eastern capital is believed to have been Rāmpāl in the Dacca District (*Ep. Ind.*, xii, 136). It is in the Bikrampur *pargana*, and Ballāl Sen is said to have held his court there (*I. G.* s. v. Dacca Dist.). See also ibid. s. v. Rāmpāl. The authorities for the history of the dynasty are discussed in App. O, but the chronology is not yet finally settled. The chief difficulty lies in the determination of the duration of Ballāl Sen's reign. For minor dynasties not noticed in this work, see Duff, *The Chronology of India*, Constable, 1899.

[2] See Risley and Gait, *Census of India*, 1901, vol. i; Rose, *Census Report for the Panjāb*, 1901; the other *Census Reports*; Ibbetson, *Outlines of Panjab Ethnography*, 4to, Calcutta, 1883; and Baden-Powell, *Notes . . . on the Rājpūt Clans*, *J. R. A. S.*, 1899, pp. 533–63.

dealing with the political fortunes of many Rājpūt clans can hardly fail to suggest to the thoughtful reader inquiries which seem to demand with urgency some sort of answer. Who were these Rājpūts—Parihārs, Pawārs, Chandēls, and the rest—and why do they and their affairs make such a confused stir during the centuries intervening between the death of Harsha and the Muhammadan conquest? The dominance of the Rājpūt clans is at first sight the conspicuous fact differentiating the mediaeval from the ancient period in the history of Northern India, and the mind craves for an explanation. It is proverbially easier to ask questions than to answer them, and in this case the facts are far too complex and imperfectly known to admit of concise satisfactory explanations. Still it may be worth while to make a few observations on the subject, designed to help the weary reader in his endeavour to find some sort of clue to guide him through the maze of dynasties.

Kshatriyas.

The apparently sudden introduction of Rājpūt states on the stage during the eighth and ninth centuries is in part an illusion. Hardly anything is known about the caste or tribal position of the ancient ruling families. Nobody can tell exactly the rank of Hindu society to which the family of Asoka or Samudragupta belonged, and nothing is on record to indicate how far the kings whose names appear prominently on the scene were merely successful personal adventurers or how far they were the heads of dominant clans. In later times all Rājpūts have considered themselves to be Kshatriyas—members of the second of the four groups of castes according to the familiar Brahman theory.[1] So far back as the time when the *Dialogues of the Buddha* were composed the Kshatriyas were recognized as an important element in society, and in their own estimation stood higher

[1] The four *varṇas* of the theory are Brahmans, Kshatriyas, Vaiśyas, and Śūdras. The Brahmans appear to be as much mixed in blood as the Rājpūts. The Vaiśyas are a very indefinite group, and Śūdras, as such, are hardly recognized in Northern India. For the true explanation of *varṇa* as meaning 'a group of castes (*jāti*)', and not 'a caste', see Ketkar's valuable *History of Caste in India*, esp. vol. i (1909), p. 77. Vol. ii appeared in 1911.

than the Brahmans.[1] The fact probably is that from very remote days ruling clans of Kshatriyas, essentially similar to the Rājpūts of later days, existed and were continually forming new states, just in the same way as in the mediaeval period. But their records have perished, and only a few exceptionally conspicuous dynasties are at all remembered, and so stand out on the page of history in a manner that does not fully represent the truth. The term Kshatriya was, I believe, always one of very vague meaning, simply denoting the Hindu ruling classes which did not claim Brahman descent. Similarly all persons performing priestly functions could be regarded by Hindus only as Brahmans. Occasionally a Rāja might be a Brahman by caste, but the Brahman's natural place at court was that of minister rather than that of king.[2] Chandragupta Maurya presumably was considered to be a Kshatriya—his minister Chānakya or Kautilya certainly was a Brahman.

Break in tradition.

The real difference between the ancient and mediaeval periods is that the living tradition concerning the former has been broken, while that concerning the latter survives. The Mauryas and Guptas belong to a dead and buried past, remembered only through books, inscriptions, and coins, whereas the clans whose ruling families came into notice during the mediaeval period are still very much alive, and in many cases form numerous and influential sections of the existing population.

The 'Scythian' element.

Tod and the other older writers perceived long ago that the Rājpūt clans are in large part of foreign, or, as they called it, 'Scythian' descent. The more exact researches of recent times have fully confirmed this opinion, and it is now possible to indicate with a considerable degree of precision the source of the foreign blood in several of the

[1] Rhys Davids, *Dialogues of the Buddha* (1899), pp. 59, 119; *J. R. A. S.* (1894), p. 342.

[2] See the brilliant paper by K. P. Jayaswal, 'Revised Notes on the Brahman Empire' (*J. B. & O. Res. Soc.*, iv, pp. 257–65). The Sungas, as well as the Kānvas, were Brahmans, anti-Greek and anti-Buddhist. Hiuen Tsang mentions several Brahman Rājas, e. g. of Ujjain, Jijhoti, and Maheśvarapura (Beal, ii, 270, 271). See the explanation of *Brahmakshatra* in App. O *post*.

principal clans, and at the same time to recognize the closeness of their relationship with castes which occupy a social position lower than that of the Rājpūts.

The Sakas and Yüe-chi.

The earliest foreign immigration within the limits of the historical period which can be verified is that of the Sakas in the second century B. C. (*ante*, pp. 240, 265); and the next is that of the Yüe-chi or Kushāns in the first century after Christ (*ante*, p. 267). Probably none of the existing Rājpūt clans can carry back their genuine pedigrees nearly so far. I have no doubt that the ruling families of both the Sakas and the Kushāns when they became Hinduized were admitted to rank as Kshatriyas in the Hindu caste system, but the fact can be inferred only from the analogy of what is ascertained to have happened in later ages—it cannot be proved.

The Hūnas.

The third recorded great irruption of foreign barbarians occurred during the fifth century and the early part of the sixth. There are indications that the immigration from Central Asia had continued during the third century (*ante*, p. 289), but, if it did, no distinct record of the event has been preserved, and, so far as positive knowledge goes, only three certain irruptions of foreigners on a large scale through the northern and north-western passes can be proved to have taken place within the historical period anterior to the Muhammadan invasions of the tenth and eleventh centuries. The first and second, as above observed, were those of the Sakas and Yüe-chi respectively, and the third was that of the Hūnas, or White Huns. These names, Saka, Yüe-chi, and Hūna, merely indicate the predominant elements in the invading swarms, which included many various races. The tradition of descent from the first and second swarms has been lost for ages. The Turkī Shāhiya kings of Kabul, who were displaced by the Hindu Shāhiyas in the ninth century, boasted their descent from the great Kushān king, Kanishka, but I do not know of any later claim on the part of an Indian ruling family to relationship with the Yüe-chi.

The break in tradition seems to be due in large measure

Effects of Hūna invasions.

to the far-reaching effects of the third barbarian irruption, to which the name of Hūna is given. The meagre literary record of the Hun invasion is supplemented by so many miscellaneous observations in the domains of ethnology, archaeology, and numismatics, that a strong impression is produced on the mind of the student that the Hun invasions disturbed Hindu institutions and polity much more deeply than would be supposed from perusal of the *Purānas*, and other literary works. The Hindu writers display great unwillingness to dwell upon 'barbarian' invasions, uniting in 'a conspiracy of silence'. They never allude to the existence of Alexander the Great, and the Gujarāt historians similarly ignore the sack of Somnāth by Mahmūd of Ghaznī.[1] If Muhammadan authors had not related in detail the story of that famous raid, no record of it would have been found in Indian literature or inscriptions. There is, therefore, no reason for surprise that the Hindu record of the Hun deluge is meagre, and that recognition of its importance has had to be won laboriously by the patient researches of modern archaeologists. It is impossible to set forth the complicated evidence in this place, and the reader must be asked to accept the assertion that the series of invasions by the Huns and associated foreign tribes in the fifth and sixth centuries shook Indian society in Northern India to its foundations, severed the chain of tradition, and brought about a rearrangement of both castes and ruling families. The effects of the Hun cataclysm are obscured partially by the brilliant achievement of Harsha in establishing for thirty-five years (612–47) a strong paramount power able to control the conflicting interests of the various races, clans, and creeds subject to his temporary sway.[2] When his heavy hand was removed all those elements broke loose,

[1] *Bom. Gaz.*, vol. i, part i (1896), p. 164, note 5. The sack of Somnāth or Prabhāsa Pattan on the coast of Kāthiāwār was the object of Mahmūd's sixteenth raid. He left Ghaznī in December, A. D. 1023, and appeared before Somnāth about March, A. D. 1024. He spent about a year in Gujarāt and returned through Sind to Ghaznī, which he reached about April, 1026.

[2] Harsha's reign began in 606, but his paramount power dates from A. D. 612 and continued until his death in 647.

and, after a period of unrecorded anarchy, produced in the domain of politics the new grouping of states described in its leading features in this chapter.

The Gurjaras.

It seems to be clearly established that the Hun group of tribes or hordes made their principal permanent settlements in Rājputāna and the Panjāb. The most important element in the group, after the Huns themselves, was that of the Gurjaras, whose name still survives in the spoken form Gūjar as the designation of a widely diffused middle-class caste in North-Western India. The Gūjars, primarily a pastoral people, are, of course, like almost all Indian castes, largely engaged in agriculture. The Jāts or Jats, more exclusively agricultural, are recognized universally to be akin to the Gūjars, although it is impossible to define the relationship. Neither Jats or Gūjars are accounted to rank as Rājpūts or Kshatriyas, but most of the Panjāb Jats claim Rājpūt descent.[1]

Gurjara kingdoms.

The prominent position occupied by Gurjara kingdoms in early mediaeval times is a recent discovery. The existence of a small Gurjara principality at Bharōch (Broach), and of a larger state in Rājputāna, had been known to archaeologists for many years, but the recognition of the fact that Bhoja, and the other kings of the powerful Kanauj dynasty in the ninth, tenth, and eleventh centuries were Gurjaras is of recent date. Certain misreadings of epigraphic dates had obscured the true history of that dynasty, until the correct readings were established. It is now definitely proved that Bhoja (*c.* A. D. 840–90), his predecessors and successors, belonged to the Pratihāra (Parihār) clan of the Gurjara tribe or caste, and, consequently, that the well-known clan of Parihār Rājpūts is a branch of the Gurjara or Gūjar stock.[2]

[1] *Jāt* in United Provinces, *Jat* in Panjāb. *Panjāb Census Rep.*, 1901, pp. 324, 326.

[2] The discovery is the work of Messrs. A. M. T. Jackson (*Bom. Gaz.*, vol. i, part i (1896), esp. p. 467); D. R. Bhandarkar, 'Gurjaras' (*J. Bo. Br. R. A. S.*, vol. xx); 'Epigraphic Notes' (ibid., vol. xxi); and Prof. Kielhorn, 'Epigraphic Notes,' No. 17, 'The Gwālior Inscription of Mihira Bhoja' (*Nachr. d. k. Gesellschaft d. Wissensch.*, Göttingen, 1905). This important inscription has been edited also by Hīrānanda in the

The 'fire-born' clans.

A familiar legend appearing in the *Chand Rāisā* and other late documents in variant forms groups together four Rājpūt clans—the Pawār (Pramāra), Parihār (Pratihāra), Chauhān (Chāhumāna), and Solankī or Chaulukya—as being *Agnikula*, or 'fire-born', originating from a sacrificial fire-pit at Mount Ābū in Southern Rājputāna. The myth seems to express the historical truths that the four clans named are related, and all arose in Southern Rājputāna; and further, as Mr. Crooke justly observes, it 'represents a rite of purgation by fire, the scene of which was in Southern Rājputāna, whereby the impurity of the foreigners was removed and they became fitted to enter the Hindu caste system'.[1]

The Parihārs.

The fact that one of the four clans, namely, the Parihār, undoubtedly is of the Gūjar stock, raises a strong presumption that the three others also are descended from Gurjaras or similar foreign immigrants. In this way the origin of some of the most notable of the Rājpūt clans is accounted for. The Gurjaras are believed to have entered India either along with or soon after the White Huns, and to have settled in large numbers in Rājputāna; but there is nothing to show what part of Asia they came from, or to what race they belonged.[2] The Pawār head-quarters were at Chandrāvatī and Achalgarh, near Mount Ābū, and in the seventh century the Parihārs ruled a large part of Rājputāna from Bhinmāl, some 50 miles to the north-west of Mount Ābū. About A. D. 800 Nāgabhata, king of the Gurjara country, conquered Kanauj on the Ganges, to which city he shifted his capital, and so founded the long line of Kanauj kings who ruled there until the advent of Mahmūd of Ghaznī at the beginning of A. D. 1019 (*ante*, p. 404). The discovery that the Rājas of Kanauj

Archaeol. S. India, Annual Rep., 1903–4, p. 277. Dr. Hoernle has laid stress on the discovery in his small *History of India*, and in articles in *J. R. A. S.*, 1903–5.

[1] 'Rajputs and Mahrattas' (*J. Roy. Anthrop. Inst.*, 1911, p. 42).

[2] Sir J. M. Campbell identified the Gūjars with the Khazars (Ghusars, &c.), 'part of the great horde of which the Juān-Juān or Avārs, and the Ephthalites, Yetas, or White Hūnas were leading elements' (*Bom. Gaz.* 'Hindus of Gujarāt,' App. B, 'The Gūjars,' quoted in *Tribes and Castes of the C. P.*, 1916, vol. iii, p. 168). The Khazars included a Black and a White section.

from 800 to 1018, some of whom enjoyed the rank of paramount sovereigns of Northern India, really were the descendants of 'barbarian' foreign immigrants into Rājputāna in the fifth or sixth century and cousins of the Gūjars, though recognized as high-class Rājpūts, is one of the most notable additions made to Indian historical knowledge for many years past. Although the history of the other Rājpūt clans of the north has not been worked out with equal fullness, a fair presumption arises that many of them were of similar origin. The truth seems to be that when a foreign clan or tribe became Hinduized the ruling families were readily recognized as Kshatriyas or Rājpūts, while the rank and file gradually lost their tribal organization, and developed into an Indian caste not regarded as aristocratic.

Indigenous origin of the southern clans.

Some of the principal clans farther south spring from a different source, and apparently are descended from the so-called aboriginal tribes, Gonds, Bhars, Kols, and the like, whom Sir Herbert Risley designated by the singularly inappropriate generic name of 'Dravidians', one of the most misleading terms ever introduced.[1] The evidence of a close connexion between the Chandēls and the Gonds, who, again, were associated with the Bhars, is particularly strong; and the inference is fully justified that the Chandēl Rājpūts were originally Hinduized Bhars or Gonds, or both, who attained recognition as Kshatriyas or Rājpūts, when they acquired power and took up the business of kingship for which the Kshatriya group of castes was appropriated. The Gaharwārs similarly are associated with the Bhars; the Bundēlas and the northern Rāthōrs are offshoots of the Gaharwārs, and so on. The name of the great Rāshtrakūta clan of the Deccan, the political history of which will be treated in the next chapter, is etymologically identical with

[1] Dravidian is the English form of the adjective *Drāvida*, with the meaning 'belonging to Draviḍa, or the Tamil country.' It is applied with propriety to the territory, people, or language of the extreme south, but is wholly inapplicable to the Goṇḍs, Kols, Bhars, and other so-called 'non-Aryan' tribes of Central India and the North. The word *Drāviḍa* is said to be an Aryanized form of *Tamil*, meaning 'nice' or 'sweet', as applied to the language (*Ind. Ant.*, 1912, p. 229).

Rāthōr, but there is not, so far as I am aware, evidence of any racial connexion between the Rāshtrakūtas of the Deccan and the Rāthōrs of Hindustan. The former seem to have originated among some one or other of the indigenous tribes of the Deccan in much the same way as the Chandēls became differentiated from the Gonds of the territory which is now the Chhatarpur State.[1]

Struggle between northern and southern clans.

The unceasing wars of the mediaeval period become a little more intelligible and interesting when they are regarded as being in large part a secular struggle between the foreign Rājpūts of the north and the indigenous Rājpūts of the south. Of course, this arrangement of the sides did not always hold good, and powers normally at feud sometimes made friends and contracted alliances one with the other, or all parties momentarily combined against the Muhammadans. But I think it is true that, as a general rule, the Rājpūts formed by the social promotion of 'aborigines' were inimical to the Rājpūts descended from 'barbarian' immigrants. In the northern group the clans most conspicuous in the historical field are the Chauhāns, Parihārs, Tomaras, and Pawārs; in the southern group the principal clans are the Chandēls, Kalachuris, or Haihayas, Gaharwārs, and Rāshtrakūtas. The origin of the Solankis or Chalukyas (Chaulukya, &c.) is disputed. They claim to come from Oudh, but it is more probable that they are really of foreign origin, like the three other clans with which they are associated in the 'fire-pit' story.[2]

Summary.

The main points to remember are that the Kshatriya or Rājpūt group of castes is essentially an occupational group, composed of all clans following the Hindu ritual who actually

[1] For the origin of the Chandēls, see my paper in *J. A. S. B.*, vol. xlvi, part i (1877), p. 233; and my monograph, 'The History and Coinage of the Chandēl (Chandella) Dynasty of Bundelkhand (Jejākabhukti) from A. D. 831 to 1203' (*Ind. Ant.*, 1908, pp. 114–48). For Gaharwārs, see Beames and Elliot, *Races of the N.W. Provinces*, and for all northern castes Mr. Crooke's work in four volumes, *Tribes and Castes of the N.W. P.* For speculations about the Rāshṭrakūṭas, see *Bom. Gaz.*, vol. i, part i (1896), pp. 119–34; ibid., part ii, pp. 178, 384.

[2] *Bom. Gaz.*, vol. i, part i (1896), p. 465, &c. *Contra*, Ojha, *Early History of the Solankis* (in Hindī), pp. 12–14.

undertook the work of government [1]; that, consequently, people of most diverse races were and are lumped together as Rājpūts; and that most of the great clans now in existence are descended either from foreign immigrants of the fifth or sixth century of the Christian era, or from indigenous races such as the Gonds and Bhars. This finding will, I fear, be displeasing to many families of Indian gentry, who naturally prefer to believe in orthodox Brahman-made pedigrees going back to the sun, moon, or fire-pit; but I am convinced that it is substantially true, although the evidence is of a kind difficult to grasp, and incapable of brief presentation. The references in the note will enable the curious reader to pursue the subject further.[2]

APPENDIX O

The Origin and Chronology of the Sena Dynasty

The strong interest taken by many of my readers in the early history of Bengal induces me to devote considerable space to the justification of the statements in the text concerning the Sena dynasty, which differ widely from those made in the second Interest in the subject.

[1] 'It may be assumed as certain that had the conquering Moghuls and Puthâns been without a vivid belief and an organized priesthood, they would have adopted Vedism and have become enrolled among the Kshutrees or ruling races' (Cunningham, *Hist. of the Sikhs* (1853), p. 347, App. IV).

[2] Further references are: V. A. Smith, 'The Gurjaras of Rājputāna and Kanauj' (*J. R. A. S.*, 1909, Jan. and April); 'White Hun (Ephthalite) Coins from the Panjāb' (ibid., Jan., 1907); 'White Hun Coin of Vyāghramukha' (ibid., Oct., 1907); 'The Outliers of Rājasthānī' (*Ind. Ant.*, 1911); and D. R. Bhandarkar, 'The Gurjaras' (*J. Bo. Br. R. A. S.*, vol. xxi). The same author's paper 'Guhilots' (*J. & Proc. A. S. B.* (N.S.), vol. v, 1909), is most suggestive and valuable. He demonstrates that the Rāṇās of Mewār or Udaipur, admittedly the premier chiefs in Rājputāna and the leaders of the Rājpūt chivalry, are descended from Nāgar Brahmans; that their ancestors, after they became chiefs, were known as Brahmakshatrīs, and that they were closely associated with the kings of Valabhī, who belonged to the Hūna-Gurjara group.

Bhandarkar's views about the descent of the Rāṇās are disputed at great length by Pandit Mohaulal Vishnulal Pandia, who criticizes his documents and upholds the tradition that the Rāṇās are descended from the kings of Valabhī (*J. & Proc. A. S. B.*, 1912, pp. 63–99). He does not, however, seriously shake Bhandarkar's close reasoning. There is no real proof of the descent of the Rāṇās from the Valabhī kings, but, as Bhandarkar shows, both parties, i. e. the Rāṇās (= Nāgar Brahmans) and the Valabhīs, seem to have been Maitrakas, and closely associated with the Gurjaras.

edition, when much material now available was not at my disposal.

The succession of the Sena kings.

The Sena kings succeeded one another from father to son. The names and order of succession are established by inscriptions beyond dispute as being (1) Sāmantasena, (2) Hemantasena, (3) Vijayasena, (4) Vallālasena or Ballāl Sen, (5) Lakshmaṇasena, (6) Viśvarūpasena. Nos. 1 and 2 were merely local chiefs in Orissa, and No. 6 was a ruler of small power in Eastern Bengal. The general history of India is interested only in Nos. 3, 4, 5, who governed dominions of large extent and took rank among the greater powers.

Matters no longer in dispute.

In supersession of the view adopted in the third edition of this work, it now seems desirable to accept the hypothesis that there were two Lakshmaṇasenas, and that Lakshamaṇasena of the inscriptions is to be distinguished from Rāe Lakhmaneya who was driven out of Nūdīah (Nuddea) by Muhammad the son of Bakhtyār, as described in the *Ṭabaḳāt-i-Nāṣirī*. Another matter definitely settled by the labours of the late Professor Kielhorn, as confirmed by subsequent researches, is the beginning of the era known by the name of *Lakshamaṇasena*. The first day of that era was October 7, A. D. 1119, and the first current year as reckoned from that era was A. D. 1119–20. It is also clear that a Sena king who bore the name of Lakshmana, or perhaps the epithet Lakshmaneya, a descendant of Lakshmana, and who was posterior to the three sons of Lakshmaṇasena of the inscriptions, was driven out of Nūdīah by Muhammad the son of Bakhtyār at some date subsequent to the taking of Delhi by the Muhammadans in A. H. 589, which is practically equivalent to A. D. 1193, and prior to Muhammad's expedition into the hills of the NE. frontier, called Tibbat (Tibet) by the author of the *Ṭabaḳāt*, which took place in A. H. 601 (Aug. 1204–Aug. 1205).

Disputed date of the raid on Nūdīah.

But considerable difference of opinion exists as to the exact date of the raid on Nūdīah, which is not stated in the *Ṭabaḳāt*, our only authority for the details. That work, it may be noted, was closed in A. H. 658, practically equivalent to A. D. 1260. The author, commonly called Minhāj-i-Sirāj, expressly states that in A. H. 641 (June, A. D. 1243–June, 1244) he obtained an account of the operations of Muhammad the son of Bakhtyār against Bihār town from two of his surviving soldiers (Raverty, *transl.*, p. 552). His account, therefore, has almost the authority of a contemporary narrative so far as that event is concerned. But he does not seem to have been so well informed about the raid on Nūdīah.

Narrative in the Ṭabaḳāt-i-Nāṣirī.

In the briefest possible summary, the historian's narrative is as follows. Muhammad, son of Bakhtyār, a man of the Turkish Khalj tribe, failed to obtain employment from Kutb-ud-dīn after the capture of Delhi in A. H. 589. When some time, apparently a considerable interval, had elapsed, he acquired a certain amount of military power and obtained a fief in the Mirzāpur district from which he was 'in the habit of making incursions into Manēr (in the north-west of Patna District)[1] and Bihar', until he collected 'ample resources in the shape of horses, arms, and men'. We are further told that he 'used to carry his depredations into those parts' until he organized a final attack upon the fortified city of Bihār. He captured the city, as related in the text, and brought great booty to the presence of Kutb-ud-dīn, who was, perhaps, then at Mahobā in Bundelkhand. The favour with which he was received excited jealousy, which was not allayed until Muhammad justified himself by defeating a furious elephant. After that incident he departed for Bihār. Meantime, many of the inhabitants of Nūdīah became alarmed and deserted their king, Rāe Lakhmaniya, or Lakshmaṇasena. 'The following year after that, Muhammad-i-Bakhtyār caused a force to be prepared, pressed on from Bihār, and suddenly appeared before the city of Nūdīah', as described in the text.[2]

True date must be about A. H. 595.

Now, on reconsideration of the evidence, I agree with Blochmann that it is impossible to date the attack on Nūdīah, as Raverty did, in A. H. 590. The operations of Muhammad above detailed must have occupied several years after A. H. 589, when Delhi was taken. On the other hand, Minhāj-i-Sirāj tells us (Raverty, p. 560) that 'after some years had passed away', Muhammad organized his expedition to 'Tibbat'. That disastrous operation took place in A. H. 601 (Aug. A. D. 1204–Aug. 1205). The capture of Nūdīah, therefore, must be dated several years after A. H. 589, and 'some years' before A. H. 601, say in or about A. H. 595 (Nov. A. D. 1198 to Oct. 1199).

Rāe Lakhmaniya's alleged reign of eighty years.

But the story told by Minhāj-i-Sirāj enables us to fix the date with a little more precision. He was informed that Rāe Lakhmaniya had then been on the throne for eighty years, reckoned from his birth. That assertion, which is supported by an anecdote, manifestly legendary, is in itself highly improbable. The longest recorded Indian reign is that of Choṛaganga of Orissa, which extended to seventy-one years complete (A. D. 1076–1147); and, so far as I know, a reign of eighty years cannot be traced in the history of any country. Raverty supported his belief in the eighty years' reign by quoting a statement made by Munshi Shiām Parshād in an account of Gaur, written for Major Francklin, that Lakshmaṇasena reigned from A. H. 510–590, eighty lunar

[1] *J. B. & O. Res. Soc.*, iv, 266.

[2] Since the passage above was written, Mr. S. Kumar has published the opinion that the testimony of the *Ṭabaḳāt* should be disregarded. He is inclined to believe that Lakshmaṇasena ascended the throne about A. D. 1119 and was dead long before the Muhammadan raid (*Ind. Ant.*, 1913, p. 188). This is also the opinion of R. D. Banerji, as briefly stated in *Ep. Ind.*, Oct. 1917, vol. xiv, p. 157. After further consideration their view has been adopted. The two systems of chronology differ by just fifty years.

years. But it does not appear what authority the Munshi had for his statement. Another argument on the same side is that Muhammad died in A. H. 602, and according to certain historians had reigned or ruled for twelve years in Lakhnautī or Gauṛ. Twelve years back from A. H. 602 bring us to A. H. 590. It is possible, however, as Bābū Monmohan Chakravarti suggests, that the rule of Muhammad may have been reckoned from a time prior to the attack on Nūdīah. On reconsideration, I agree with Blochmann in rejecting both the alleged eighty years' reign and the date A. H. 590 for the attack on Nūdīah.

Attack on Nūdīah in the year 80 of Lakshmaṇasena's era.

I now accept the suggestion made long ago by Professor Kielhorn (*Ind. Ant.*, vol. xix (1890), p. 7) that the legend of the eighty years' reign is due to a misunderstanding, the Nūdīah raid having really taken place in the year 80 of the Lakshmaṇasena era. Dates in that era were usually calculated as expired years, but occasionally as current years. On the supposition that the year was 'expired', the year 80 would be A. D. 1119–20 plus 80 = A. D. 1199–1200 (October to October). If the current year should be understood, the date would be A. D. 1198–9 (November to October). Probably the event took place during the cold season of 1199–1200, that is to say, late in A. D. 1199, early in A. H. 596. We may be confident that it occurred in either A. H. 595 or 596, not in A. H. 590, as I formerly believed.

Kielhorn's view that the conquest of Nūdīah must have taken place in the eightieth year of the Lakshmaṇasena era is supported by the Jānibīghā inscription of the year 83 (A. D. 1202) of the same era.[1] It is tolerably clear that the era commenced with the reign of the king whose name it bears, and who, as shown in the text (pp. 421, 422 *ante*), was a widely respected king and patron of literature.

Recorded Sena dates and synchronisms.

For Vijayasena we have three synchronisms. He is described as 'the friend of Choṛaganga (*Choṛaganga sakhaḥ*)'. Choṛaganga had an exceptionally long reign of more than seventy-one years, from A. D. 1076 to 1147. The earlier part of it coincides with thirty-eight years of the reign of Vijayasena, according to the chronology followed by R. D. Banerji, which seems to me now to be correct. The other two synchronisms are vague and imperfect. An inscription records that Vijayasena made captive four kings, namely, Nānya, Vīra, Rāghava, and Vardhana. We are also told that he 'impetuously assailed the lord of Gauḍa, put down the prince of Kāmarūpa, and defeated the Kalinga'. Unluckily, the record does not join the names of the kings and the countries. Nānya may mean Nānyadeva of Tirhūt, who, according to tradition, founded Simraun in A. D. 1097 and afterwards established the Karṇāṭaka dynasty in the valley of Nepāl.[2] I cannot positively

[1] *J. B. & O. Res. Soc.*, vol. iv, part iii (1918), pp. 266 ff. and pp. 273–80.

[2] Nānya certainly was a Karnāta king of Mithilā and contemporary with Vijayasena in the

identify either Vīra or Vardhana. One of them presumably must have been the Rāja of Kāmarūpa or Assam.

The Sena kings' family from the Deccan.

¶ I conclude this dissertation by a notice of the origin and rise of the Sena royal family.[1] The ancestors were of southern origin, from the Deccan, and are described both as Karṇāṭa Kshatriyas, and as Brahmakshatras. The meaning of the latter term, misunderstood by Professor Kielhorn, has been elucidated by Mr. D. R. Bhandarkar. His observations, which throw much light on the history of caste, deserve to be quoted textually :—

Meaning of the term Brahma-kshatra.

> ' We have already seen that a Chāṭsū inscription speaks of a Guhilot king Bhartṛibhaṭṭa as *Brahma-Kshatr-ānvita*, which I have translated by " possessed of both priestly and martial energy ", but a footnote has been added below saying that what is also implied is that Bhartṛibhaṭṭa was a Brahmakshatrī, i. e. belonged to the Brahmakshatrī caste. Bhartṛibhaṭṭa is not the only ancient king of India who is so called. In the Deopārā inscription of Vijayasena, of the well-known Sena dynasty of Bengal, Sāmantasena is described as *Brahma-kshatriyānāṁ kula-śiro-dāma*, which expression was rendered by Prof. Kielhorn by " head-garland of the clans of the Brahmans and Kshatriyas ", but which ought to have been rendered, I think, by " head-garland of the Brahma-kshatrī family ". That the latter is the correct translation is shown by the term *Brahma-kshatra* used with reference to the Sena kings in the *Ballāla-charita* [*Bibl. Ind.*].
>
> Now, there is a caste called Brahmakshatrī, corresponding to this *Brahmakshatra*, the members of which are found all over the Panjāb, Rājputānā, Kāthiāwāṛ, Gujarāt, and even the Dekkan. In my opinion, as already stated, they were originally the Brāhmaṇa classes of new tribes afterwards turned Kshatriyas, before their final mergence into the Hindu society.'

The author then cites the case of the Bandhārā weavers and

eleventh and beginning of the twelfth century, and probably also with Jayachchandra of Kanauj (Monmohan Chakravarti in *J. & Proc. A. S. B.*, 1915, pp. 409–11).

[1] The genealogy of the Sena dynasty given by R. D. Banerji is :—

Vīra
|
Sāmanta
|
Hemanta
|
Vijaya
|
Ballāla
|
Lakshmaṇa
|
Mādhava — Viśvarūpa — Kéśava

(*J. & Proc. A. S. B.*, 1914, p. 98).

The *lakshana*, or emblem of the dynasty, was then *Sadāśiva-mudrā*, a seal with a seated figure of the 10-armed form of Śiva, called Sadāśiva (ibid., p. 99).

dyers in the Jodhpur State, who originally were Nāgar Brahmans, and proceeds :—

'Here then we have an instance of a Brahmakshatrī caste, the people of which say that they were originally Nāgar Brāhmaṇas. This clearly explains how the Guhilots, who were also originally Nāgar Brāhmaṇas, became Brahmakshatrīs or Khatrīs, and also strengthens my theory that the various castes of the Brahmakshatrīs were originally the Brāhmaṇa classes of foreign tribes, which after the process of fusion had set in, but before it was complete, exchanged their priestly for martial pursuits.'[1]

The Sena royal family originally Brahman.

Mr. Bhandarkar is perfectly right. Consequently, the ancestor of the Sena kings must have been a Brahman from the Deccan, probably employed in the natural office of a Brahman as a minister. When he passed from ministerial to ruling functions, he became a Brahmakshatrī, his descendants being accepted as full Kshatriyas, capable of intermarriage with other ruling families reckoned as Kshatriyas. Most likely Sāmantasena had been in the service of the king of Kalinga or Orissa. The establishment of Sāmantadeva as a semi-independent chief in northern Orissa may have occurred somewhere about the middle of the eleventh century. Possibly he may not have been a ruling chief. His son, Hemantasena, may have been the first to act as Rāja.

Earliest seat of the Sena family.

According to the authority quoted below, the earliest actually known seat of the Senas was at Kāśīpurī, the modern Kasiāri, on the Suvarṇarekhā river, in the Mayūrabhanja State, the most northerly of the Orissan Tributary States, adjoining the Midnapore District. I quote from the admirable *Archaeological Survey Report* of Bābū Nagendranāth Vasu.

'We have read in the genealogical history of the Paśchātya Vaidika of Bengal, written on palm-leaves and about three hundred years old, that the royal Sena dynasty reigned in a place called Kāśipurī and situated on the banks of the Suvarṇarekhā. Two sons were born to Vijayasena, one of the rulers of this place ; the elder being named Malla and the younger Śyāmala. It was the latter that conquered eastern Bengal and made the city of Vikramapura his capital. According to the Paśchātya Kulamañjarī, Śyāmalavarma's sway in Vikramapura commenced in Śaka 994, i. e. 1072 A. D. . . . There is no doubt that the ancient name of Kāśipurī has now degenerated into Kāsiārī.

The matter, however, is not free from doubt.[2]

[1] Note that the Kanaujiya Brahmans, who supplied many sepoys to the old army, used to say, if irritated, *Ham kshatriya-Brahman hain*, as a boast (J. Wilson, *Indian Caste*, ii, 151).

[2] See 'Earliest Seat of the Senas' by S. Kumar (*Ind. Ant.*, Dec. 1915, p. 270 ff.), and also by the same author, 'The Inscriptions of Asokashalla' (ibid., p. 215). It is not easy to see how Kāśipurī could become Kāsiārī. An alternative synonymous name, Kāśiwārī, may have existed.

'The Senas, who replaced the Pālas in the twelfth century, are believed on acquiring Varendra, to have made their capital at Bijayanagar near Godāgārī in the south-west of the tract, and to have subsequently moved to Lakshmaṇāvatī, the town which afterwards took the name of Gauḍa' (*J. R. A. S.*, 1914, p. 101). Varendra, also spelt Varendrī, the modern Barind,

I cannot follow out the problems of local history suggested by that passage, and the observations which follow in the work cited.

In order to save the necessity of a multitude of foot-notes the principal references are appended in a classified form.

References

The following classified list gives the authorities on which the statements in the text and appendix concerning the Senas are based. Obsolete publications are not cited. **Authorities.**

It is difficult to interpret the account of 'the four Senas' by Tāranāth (Schiefner, pp. 252–7). He gives the names of the kings as (1) Lavasena, (2) Kāśasena, (3) Maṇitasena, (4) Rāthikasena; observing that although he was unable to fix the duration of each reign, all four together ruled for not more than about eighty years. His account of the Turushka king Chandra, who conquered all Magadha, destroyed Vikramaśīla, and slew many clergy in Otantapurī (Bihār town), seems intended to describe the raid of Muhammad the son of Bakhtyār, but why that personage should be described as Chandra I cannot say. He proceeds (p. 256) to enumerate the later Senas, viz. (1) Lavasena II, (2) Buddhasena, (3) Haritasena, and (4) Pratītasena, princes of small power, subordinate to the Turushkas or Muhammadans. **General.**

In the third edition the identity of Lakshmaṇasena of the inscriptions with Rāe Lakhmaniya of the *Ṭabaḳāt-i-Nāṣirī* was assumed. Fresh light has now been thrown on the subject by K. P. Jayaswal in *J. B. & O. Res. Soc.*, vol. iv, pp. 266–72 and by H. Panday (ibid., pp. 273–80, with facs.). It seems reasonable to suppose that Lakshmaṇasena of the era was dead long before Muhammad's raid, and that Lakshmaṇasena II, the Lavasena of Tāranāth, came to the throne after the three sons of Lakshmaṇasena I, shown in the genealogy on p. 435 *ante*. This thesis is supported by the copper-plates of Viśvarūpa-Sena and Keśava-Sena, whose capital was at Gaur. They must have preceded Muhammad, who made the same place his capital. The dates of the plates are respectively the 14th and 3rd regnal years. Lakshmaṇasena therefore was dead before A. D. 1182 (1199 less 17), and a good deal before that date, as the elder brother reigned first. The victory over the Muhammadans claimed by the sons of Lakshmaṇasena must have occurred *before* the raid of 1199, i. e. it must have been won against the Ghorī armies, which had advanced as far as Benares.

may be defined as 'comprising the Districts of Rājshāhi, Māldā, Dinājpur, Rangpur, Bogra, and part of Pabna—in fact almost the whole of the Rājshāhi Division' (*Ep. Ind.*, xiii (1916), p. 285). Godāgāri is a busy mart on the Ganges, where the Calcutta and Mālda road crosses the river. Gauḍa is the Sanskrit way of writing Gaur.

Date of capture of Nūdīah.

Blochmann, *J. A. S. B.*, part i, vol. xliv (1875), p. 275 ; Raverty, in reply, ibid., vol. xlv (1876), p. 320, and transl. *Ṭabaḳāt*, App. D ; Monmohan Chakravarti, 'Appendix on Sena Kings', *J. & Proc. A. S. B.* (N.S.), vol. i, 1905, pp. 45–50 ; and 'Certain Disputed or Doubtful Events in the History of Bengal, Muhammadan Period', ibid., vol. iv, 1908, p. 151.

Era of Lakshmaṇasena, and chronology.

In addition to the above papers—Nagendranāth Vasu, *J.A.S.B.*, part i, vol. lxv (1896), pp. 6–38 ; Babu Akshay Kumar Mitra, ibid., vol. lxix (1900), p. 61 ; Kielhorn, *Ind. Ant.*, xix (1890), p. 6 ; and *Ep. Ind.*, i, 306 ; Beveridge, *J. A. S. B.*, part i, vol. lvii (1888), pp. 1–7 ; R. D. Bandyopādhyāya, 'Mādhāinagar Grant of Lakshmaṇasena', *J. & Proc. A. S. B.*, vol. v (N.S.), 1909, p. 467 ; and Prof. N. K. Bhattasali, 'King Lakshmaṇa Sena of Bengal and his Era' in *Ind. Ant.*, vol. xli (July 1912), pp. 167–9.

Literature in Sena period.

Monmohan Chakravarti, '*Pavana-dūtam*, or Wind-Messenger, by Dhoyīka, a court poet of Lakshmaṇa-sena, king of Bengal,' *J. & Proc. A. S. B.* (N.S.), vol. i (1905), p. 41 ; 'Supplementary Notes on the Bengal Poet Dhoyīka and the Sena Kings,' ibid., vol. ii (1906), p. 15 ; 'Sanskrit Literature in Bengal during the Sena Rule,' ibid., p. 157.

Choḍaganga and Vijayasena.

Monmohan Chakravarti, 'Chronology of the Eastern Ganga Kings of Orissa,' *J. A. S. B.*, part i, vol. lxxii (1903), p. 14, quoting *Vallāla-charitaṁ* of Ānanda Bhaṭṭa.

Synchronisms.

For Rāghava, Monmohan Chakravarti, *J. & Proc. A. S. B.* (N.S.), vol. i (1905), p. 49. For Nānya, S. Lévi, *Le Népal*, t. ii, p. 198 ; Kielhorn, *Ep. Ind.*, i, p. 313, note 57. For kings of Assam named Vīra, Gait, *Report on the Progress of Historical Research in Assam*, Shillong, 1897, pp. 11, 19.

Early seat of the Senas.

Nagendranāth Vasu, *Archaeological Survey of Mayūrabhanja*, published by the Mayūrabhanja State, 1911, p. 122.

Meaning of *Brahmakshatra.*

D. R. Bhandarkar, 'Guhilots,' *J. & Proc. A. S. B.* (N.S.), vol. v, 1909, pp. 167–87, especially p. 186 ; an exceptionally valuable and original essay.

CHAPTER XV

THE KINGDOMS OF THE DECCAN

THE term Deccan, a convenient and familiar corruption of the Sanskrit word (*dakshina*) meaning the South, may be, and sometimes is, extended so as to cover the whole of India south of the Narmadā; but is usually understood as designating a more limited territory, in which Malabar and the Tamil countries of the extreme south are not included. Thus limited, the term connotes the whole region occupied by the Telugu-speaking populations, as well as Mahārāshtra, or the Marāthā country. Certain dynasties of Mysore, which had more concern with the Deccan than with the extreme south, are noticed in this chapter more conveniently than they could be in connexion with the Tamil powers. With reference to modern political divisions, the greater part of the Deccan in the restricted sense is occupied by the territories of the Nizam of Hyderabad. **The Deccan.**

Physically, the country is for the most part a dry, hilly table-land, traversed by two great rivers, the Godāvarī[1] and the Krishnā (Kistna), the latter of which receives on the south an important affluent, the Tungabhadrā.

In this region the dominant power for four centuries and a half, up to about A.D. 225, was the Āndhra, the history of which has been discussed in Chapter VIII of this work. **A.D. 225–550. Blank in history.**

Sir R. G. Bhandarkar, writing in 1896, observed that for some three centuries after the extinction of the Āndhra dynasty 'we have no specific information about the dynasties that ruled over the country'. Although since that date some additional knowledge has been acquired concerning the rulers of the southern part of the table-land, especially the Kadambas,[2] who governed Kanara and the

[1] The Godāvarī is also called Gautamī (Madras, *Epigraphy*, Aug. 10, 1917, p. 121).

[2] The Kadamba dynasty, of Brahman descent, was displaced by the Chalukyas about the middle of the sixth century. The Sangoli plates of Harivarman Kadamba are dated in a year equivalent either to A.D. 526 or

northern districts of Mysore between the third and sixth centuries, the particulars gleaned by archaeologists are not of sufficient general interest to justify detailed notice of them in this work. Mahārāshtra, the western portion of the territory, seems to have been under the rule of princes belonging to the Rāshtrakūta or Ratta clan, which, long afterwards, in the middle of the eighth century, became the ruling power in the Deccan for a time.

Rise of the Chalukyas.

It is still true to say that practically the political history of the Deccan begins in the middle of the sixth century with the rise of the Chalukya dynasty. The Chalukyas claimed to be a race of Rājpūts from the north, who imposed their rule upon the Dravidian inhabitants of the Deccan table-land, which had already been largely influenced by the Aryan ideas of the northerners before the appearance of the Chalukyas on the scene.[1] The statements in the later Chalukya inscriptions, which profess to trace back the clan to its origin in Ajodhya, and provide the royal family with an orthodox mythological pedigree, are of no historical value. There is some reason for believing that the Chalukyas or Solankīs were connected with the Chāpas, and so with the foreign Gurjara tribe of which the Chāpas were a branch, and it seems to be probable that they emigrated from Rājputāna to the Deccan.[2]

545; most probably the latter, as Harīvarman came to the throne in 538 and may have been the last Kadamba (*Ep. Ind.*, xiv (Oct. 1917), p. 166). Copper-plates of King Ravīvarman and of Kṛishṇavarman II have been discovered in North Kanara (*Prog. Rep. A. S. W. C.*, 1918, p. 35).

For the Kadambas, see Rice, *Mysore and Coorg from the Inscriptions*, London, Constable & Co., 1909.

[1] Except as otherwise stated, this chapter is based upon the second editions of Fleet's 'Dynasties of the Kanarese Districts' and R. G. Bhandarkar's 'Early History of the Dekkan', in *Bombay Gazetteer* (1896), vol. i, part ii. Full references to original documents will be found in both works. Kielhorn's 'Supplement to the List of Inscriptions of Southern India' (*Ep. Ind.*, vol. viii, App. ii) gives the most trustworthy dynastic lists and the results of epigraphic studies, up to Jan. 1906. The names of Pulakēśin and many other persons mentioned have numerous variants or equivalents. The spelling Pulakēśin is now generally approved. The name occurs in a Chāpa genealogy, which is the only instance known to Fleet of its occurrence outside the Chalukya family. This fact supports Jackson's view that the Solankīs or Chalukyas were connected with the Gurjaras, of whom the Chāpas were a branch (*Bomb. Gaz.* (1896), vol. i, part i, pp. 127 note 2, 138, 463 note 2, 467). See *ante*, pp. 339, 340.

[2] D. R. Bhandarkar (*Ind. Ant.*, xl) suggests that their original

The dynasty was founded by a chieftain named Pulakēsin I, who made himself master of the town of Vātāpi, the modern Bādāmi in the Bijāpur District, about A.D. 550, and established a principality of modest dimensions. He aimed, however, at more extended power, and is said to have asserted his claim to a paramount position by celebrating an *aśvamedha*, or horse-sacrifice. A.D. 550. Pulakēśin I.

His sons, Kīrtivarman and Mangalesa, extended the possessions of the family both eastward and westward. The clans more or less completely subjugated by the former include the Mauryas of the Konkan—the strip of coast between the Western Ghāts and the sea—who may have been descended from the ancient imperial Maurya dynasty. Kīrtivarman and Mangalēśa.

The succession to Mangalēsa was disputed between his son and one of the sons of Kīrtivarman. The latter, having overcome his rival, ascended the throne of Vātāpi as Pulakēsin II in A.D. 608, and was formally crowned in the following year. For the space of twenty years or more this able prince devoted himself to a career of aggression directed against all the neighbouring states. On the west and north, the kings of Lāta, or Southern Gujarāt; Gurjara, or Northern Gujarāt and Rājputāna; Mālwā, and the Mauryas of the Konkan felt the weight of Pulakēsin's arm. A.D. 608. Pulakēśin II.

In the east he made himself master of Vengī, between the Krishnā and Godāvarī, and established his brother Kubja Vishnuvardhana there as viceroy in A.D. 611, with his capital at the stronghold of Pishtapura, now Pithāpuram in the Godāvarī District.[1] A few years later, about A.D. 615, this prince set up as an independent sovereign, and founded the line of the Eastern Chalukyas,[2] which lasted until A.D. 1070, when it was absorbed into the Chola dynasty. A.D. 611. Conquest of Vengī.

habitat in India was Ahichchatra, the capital of the Sapādalaksha country in the Siwālik mountains ('The Life and Times of Chalukya Vikramāditya,' by A. V. Venkatarama Aiyar, *Ind. Ant.*, xlviii (1919), pp. 112 ff.).

[1] *Report on Epigraphy*, Madras G. O. No. 574, July 17, 1908. For the date (611) see 'The Kopparam Plates of Pulakēśin II', by K. V. Lakshmanrao in *Annals, Bhandarkar Institute*, vol. iv, part i, Oct. 1922.

[2] A grant of Jayasimha I, Sarvasiddhi (A. D. 633–63), refers to places in Guntūr District (*Epigraphy*, Madras, Aug. 10, 1917).

Southern wars.

All the southern kingdoms, the Chola, Pāndya, and Kerala, as well as the Pallava, were forced into conflict with the ambitious king of Vātāpi, who undoubtedly was the most powerful monarch to the south of the Narmadā in A.D. 630.

A.D. 620. Repulse of Harsha.

About ten years before that date he had successfully repelled the attack on his dominions led in person by Harsha, the lord paramount of the north, who aspired to the sovereignty of all India; but was foiled by the watchfulness and military skill of Pulakēsin, by whom the line of the Narmadā as the frontier between the southern and northern empires was successfully maintained.[1]

A.D. 625. Intercourse with Persia.

The fame of the king of the Deccan spread beyond the limits of India, and reached the ears of Khusrū II, king of Persia, who, in the thirty-sixth year of his reign, A.D. 625–6, received a complimentary embassy from Pulakēsin.[2] The courtesy was reciprocated by a return embassy sent from Persia, which was received with due honour at the Indian court. A large fresco painting in Cave No. 1 at Ajantā, although unhappily mutilated, is still easily recognizable as a vivid representation of the ceremonial attending the presentation of their credentials by the Persian envoys.

Ajaṇṭā school of painting.

This picture, in addition to its interest as a contemporary record of unusual political relations between India and Persia, is of the highest value as a landmark in the history of art. It not only fixes the date of some of the most important paintings at Ajantā, and so establishes a standard by which the date of others can be judged; but also suggests the possibility that the Ajantā school of pictorial art may have been derived directly from Persia, and ultimately from Greece.[3]

[1] *Ante*, p. 353.

[2] The authority is the Muhammadan historian Tabari, as translated and quoted in Mr. Fergusson's paper in *J. R. A. S.*, April 1879, and Burgess's 'Notes on the Bauddha Rock Temples of Ajaṇṭā' (*Arch. S. W. I.*, No. 9, Bombay, 1897), pp. 90–2. For the frescoes, see Plate IV of that work; Plates II, III, IV in *J. A. S. B.*, part i, vol. lxvii (1878); the India Office atlas of the Ajaṇṭā paintings; and *Hist. of Fine Art in India and Ceylon*, p. 290, fig. 210.

[3] See *History of Fine Art in India and Ceylon*, p. 388.

On date of the Ajaṇṭā Caves see V. A. Smith's essay 'The Vākāṭaka Dynasty of Berar' (*J. R. A. S.*, April, 1914).

The wonderful caves in the Ajantā valley were duly admired by Hiuen Tsang, who visited the court of Pulakēsin II in the year A.D. 641. The king's head-quarters at that time were not at Vātāpi, but at another city, which has been identified for good reasons with Nāsik. The pilgrim was profoundly impressed by the military power of Pulakēsin, who was obeyed by his numerous subjects with 'perfect submission'.

A.D. 641. Visit of Hiuen Tsang.

But his prosperity was not destined to last much longer. In A.D. 642, the long-continued war, which, since the year 609, had been generally disastrous to the Pallavas of Kānchī, took a new turn, and brought ruin and death upon Pulakēsin. The Pallava king, Narasimhavarman, captured and plundered his capital, and presumably put him to death. Then for thirteen years the Chalukya power, which Pulakēsin had laboured so hard to exalt, remained in abeyance; while the Pallavas dominated Southern India.

A.D. 642. Defeat of Pulakēśin by the Pallavas.

In A.D. 655, Vikramāditya I, a son of Pulakēsin, restored the fallen fortunes of his family, inflicting in A.D. 674 a severe defeat upon the Pallavas, whose strongly fortified capital, Kānchī, was captured. The struggle with the southern power long continued, and victory inclined now to one side and now to the other. During this reign a branch of the Chalukya dynasty succeeded in establishing itself in Gujarāt, where in the next century it offered vigorous opposition to the Arabs.

A.D. 655. Vikramāditya I.

The main feature of the succeeding reigns was the never-ending conflict with the Pallavas, whose capital was again taken by Vikramāditya II, about A.D. 740.

A.D. 740. Vikramāditya II.

In the middle of the eighth century, Dantidurga, a chieftain of the ancient, and apparently indigenous, Rāshtrakūta clan, fought his way to the front, and overthrew Kīrtivarman II Chalukya, the son and successor of Vikramāditya II. The main branch of the Chalukyas now became extinct, and the sovereignty of the Deccan passed to the Rāshtrakūtas, in whose hands it remained for nearly two centuries and a quarter.

A.D. 753 (?). Rāshṭrakūṭa conquest.

A. D. 550–750. State of religion. During the two centuries of the rule of the early Chalukya dynasty of Vātāpi, great changes in the religious state of the country were in progress. Buddhism, although still influential, and supported by a considerable section of the population, was slowly declining, and suffering gradual supersession by its competitors, Jainism and Brahmanical Hinduism. The sacrificial form of the Hindu religion received special attention, and was made the subject of a multitude of formal treatises. The Purānic forms of Hinduism also grew in popularity; and everywhere elaborate temples dedicated to Vishnu, Siva, or other members of the Purānic pantheon, were erected; which, even in their ruins, form magnificent memorials of the kings of this period. The orthodox Hindus borrowed from their Buddhist and Jain rivals the practice of excavating cave-temples; and one of the earliest Hindu works of this class is that made at Bādāmi in honour of Vishnu by Mangalesa Chalukya, at the close of the sixth century. Jainism was specially popular in the Southern Marāthā country.[1] The religion of Zoroaster was introduced into India during the eighth century. The first colony of Parsee emigrants from Khurāsān which settled on the Indian mainland was established at Sanjān in the Thāna District, Bombay, in A. D. 735.[2]

c. A. D. 760. Krishṇa I. Dantidurga Rāshtrakūta, after his occupation of Vātāpi, effected other conquests. He was succeeded by his uncle, Krishna I, who completed the establishment of Rāshtrakūta supremacy over the dominions formerly held by the Chalukyas. A branch of his family founded a principality in Gujarāt.

The reign of Krishna I is memorable for the execution of

[1] 'For more than a thousand years after the beginning of the Christian era, Jainism was the religion professed by most of the rulers of the Kanarese people. The Ganga kings of Talkād, the Rāshtrakūta and Kālachūrya kings of Mānyakheta, and the early Hoysalas were all Jainas.' The Brahmanical Kadamba and early Chālukya kings were tolerant of Jainism. 'The Pandyan kings of Madura were Jainas; and Jainism was dominant in Gujarat and Kāthiāwār. On the other hand, the Pallavas of Kānchī and the Cholas of Uraiyūr and Tanjore, were strongly Hindu and hostile to Jainism' (Rice, *Hist. Kanarese Lit.*, p. 16).

[2] *Ind. Ant.*, 1912, p. 174. The authority for the date is weak (*Ind. Ant.*, 1914, p. 151). See J. J. Modi, *A Few Events in the Early History of the Parsees and their Dates*, Bombay, Fort Printing Press, 1905.

THE ROCK-CUT KAILĀSA TEMPLE AT ELŪRA

(from the north-west)

the most marvellous architectural freak in India, the Kailāsa monolithic temple at Elūra (Ellora), now in the Nizam's dominions (N. lat. 20° 21′, E. long. 75° 10′), which is by far the most extensive and sumptuous of the rock-cut shrines. It has been fully described and illustrated by many writers, among whom Burgess and Fergusson possess most authority.[1] Kailāśa temple.

Krishna I was succeeded by his son Govinda II, who, after a short reign, was followed, and apparently superseded, by his brother Dhruva or Dhora, an able and warlike prince, who continued with success the aggressive wars so dear to the heart of an Indian rāja.[2] He prided himself especially on his defeat of Vatsarāja, the Gurjara king of Bhinmāl, whom he despoiled of two white umbrellas taken by Vatsarāja from the king of Gauda, or Bengal.[3] Govinda II and Dhruva.

Govinda III, son of Dhruva, may justly claim to be the most remarkable prince of his vigorous dynasty. He extended his power from the Vindhya mountains and Mālwā on the north to Kānchī on the south; while his direct rule was carried at least as far as the Tungabhadrā. He created his brother Indrarāja viceroy of Lāta, or Southern Gujarāt. c. A. D. 793–815. Govinda III.

The long reign of the next king, Amōghavarsha, who occupied the throne for not less than sixty-two years, was largely spent in constant wars with the Eastern Chalukya Rājas of Vengī. He transferred his capital from Nāsik to Mānyakheta, the Mānkīr of the Arab writers, now Mālkhed in the Nizam's dominions (N. lat. 17° 10′, E. long. 77° 13′).[4] Amōghavarsha was the long-lived Balhāra of the merchant Sulaiman (A. D. 851), who reckoned him to be fourth of the c. A. D. 815–77. Amōghavarsha; Jain progress.

[1] *Cave Temples* and *Arch. S. W. I.*, vol. v. The correct early form of the name is either Vellūra or Elāpura, with variants.

The record of the building by Krishṇa Rāja is in the Baroda plates of Karkarāja (*Ind. Ant.*, xii (1883), p. 229). The work was intended to rival the temple of the same name at Kānchī (*Ep. Ind.*, xiii (1916), p. 277). The two known inscriptions of Krishṇa's reign are dated 690 and 694 Saka = A. D. 768 and 772.

[2] The accession of Govinda II took place between A. D. 770 and 779 (Saka 602 and 701) (*Prog. Rep. A. S. W. I.*, 1903–4, p. 60). For Dhora, see *Rep. A. S.*, Mysore, 1913–14, p. 37. Dhruva appears under the name Nirupama in a recently discovered copper-plate grant of the Śilahāra Mahāsāmanta Chhadvaideva (*Prog. Rep. A. S. W. I.*, 1919–20, p. 55).

[3] *J. R. A. S.*, 1909, p. 255.

[4] Deoli plates (*Ep. Ind.*, v, 193, l. 18). Fleet erroneously ascribes the foundation of Mānyakheṭa to Govinda III.

great kings of the world, the other three being the Khalīfa of Baghdad, the emperor of China, and the emperor of Constantinople. In his old age Amōghavarsha abdicated in favour of his son, Krishna II, and devoted the brief remainder of his life to ascetic practices.[1] The Digambara, or naked, sect of the Jains was liberally patronized by Amōghavarsha. The rapid progress made by Digambara Jainism late in the ninth and early in the tenth century, under the guidance of various notable leaders, including Jinasena and Gunabhadra, who enjoyed the favour of more than one monarch, had much to do with the marked decay of Buddhism, which daily lost ground, until it almost wholly disappeared from the Deccan in the twelfth century.

A. D. 914–16. Indra III.

The brief reign of Indra III (A. D. 914–16) is signalized by his successful attack upon distant Kanauj, and the consequent temporary dethronement of Mahīpāla, king of Panchāla, the most considerable prince in Northern India. This war probably deprived Mahīpāla of Surāshtra and the other western provinces which were still under his control at the time of the accession of Indra III.[2]

A. D. 949. Choḷa king killed.

The war with the Cholas in the reign of Krishna III Rāshtrakūta, was remarkable for the death of Rājāditya, the Chola king, on the field of battle in A. D. 949. Much bitterness was introduced into the wars of this period by the hostility between the rival religions, Jainism and orthodox Hinduism.

A. D. 973. Restoration of the Chalukyas.

The last of the Rāshtrakūta kings was Kakka II, overthrown in A. D. 973 by Taila, or Tailapa II, a scion of the old Chalukya stock, who restored the family of his ancestors to its former glory, and founded the dynasty known as that of the Chalukyas of Kalyāni ; which lasted, like that which it superseded, for nearly two centuries and a quarter.

Pre-eminence of the Rāshṭrakūṭas.

The conquest of Sind by Muhammad son of Kāsim, early in the eighth century, firmly established the political predominance of Islam in that province, which was separated from India proper by the 'lost river', the Hakrā or Wahindah. The Gurjara kingdom of Bhinmāl to the east of that

[1] Amōghavarsha had another son, Duddaya, hitherto unknown, whose name appears in a recently discovered lithic record (*A. S. I.*, 1912–20, p. 34).

[2] Cambay plates (*Ep. Ind.*, vii, 36 ; *List*, No. 91) ; *ante*, p. 395.

river was united with that of Kanauj from the beginning of the ninth century, and maintained relations of chronic hostility with its Muslim neighbours on the west of the great stream. But the Rāshtrakūta princes found their interest to lie in the pursuit of a different policy, and kept up friendly intercourse with the Arabs, while continually engaged in war with the Gurjaras. In consequence of this policy many Muhammadan merchants and travellers visited the western region of India, of whom some, beginning with the merchant Sulaiman in the middle of the ninth century, have left a record of their observations. All these writers agree in stating that they regarded the Balharā as the greatest sovereign in India. They called the Rāshtrakūta kings 'Balharā' because those princes were in the habit of assuming the title Vallabha ('Beloved,' *Bien aimé*), which, in combination with the word Rāi (prince), was easily corrupted into the form of Balharā.[1] The tribute of honour paid to the Rāshtrakūta kings by their Muhammadan visitors was justified by the achievements of their period. Although the art displayed at Ellora may not be of the highest kind, the Kailāsa temple is one of the wonders of the world, a work of which any nation might be proud, and an honour to the king under whose patronage it was executed. Many other temples were the outcome of the royal munificence, and Sanskrit literature of the artificial type then in fashion was liberally encouraged.

A. D. 995. Execution of Munja.

Taila, the restorer of the Chalukya name, reigned for twenty-four years, and during that time succeeded in recovering all the ancient territory of his race, with the possible exception of the Gujarāt province.[2] Much of his time was spent in fighting Munja, the Pawār (Paramāra) Rāja of Dhārā, who claimed the victory in six conflicts. Towards

[1] The epithet or title *vallabha*, used either singly or in composition with a noun like *śrī* or *prithivī*, was borrowed by the Rāshṭrakūṭas from the preceding dynasty, the Chalukyas of Vātāpi. Muhammadan authors usually describe a Hindu king as *Rāi* or *Rāe* (*Bom. Gaz.* (1896), vol. i, part ii, p. 209). The accounts of the early Arab geographers and the historians of Sind are translated in Elliot, *Hist. of India*, vol. i. Sir R. G. Bhandarkar was the first to explain the meaning of 'Balharā'.

[2] A. V. V. Ayyar (*Ind. Ant.*, xlviii, p. 116) states that Lata (South Gujarāt) was also under Taila's control, and that he ordered Bārappa, ruler of Lata, to attack Mūlarāja, founder of the Anhilwāra dynasty in Gujarāt.

the close of his reign Taila enjoyed the luxury of revenge. His enemy, having crossed the Godāvarī, which then formed the boundary between the two kingdoms, was defeated, taken captive, and for a time treated with the courtesy due to his rank. But an attempt to escape was visited with cruel indignities, the captive Rāja being forced to beg from door to door, and ultimately beheaded. These events may be dated in A.D. 995.[1]

c. A.D. 1000. Invasion by Rājarāja Choḷa.

Two years later Taila died, and transmitted the crown to his son Satyāsraya, during whose reign the Chalukya kingdom suffered severely from invasion by the Chola king, Rājarāja the Great, who overran the country with a vast host, said to number nine hundred thousand men, pillaging and slaughtering in a fashion so merciless that even the women, children, and Brahmans were not spared.

A.D. 1052. Death of Rājādhirāja Choḷa.

In A.D. 1052, Somesvara I, who was called Āhavamalla, fought a battle at Koppam, on the Krishnā, in which Rājādhirāja, the then reigning Chola king, lost his life.[2] Somesvara also claims the honour of having stormed both Dhārā in Mālwā and Kānchī in the south, and of having defeated Karna, the valiant king of Chedi.

A.D. 1068. Suicide of Someśvara Chalukya.

In A.D. 1068, Somesvara, being seized by an incurable fever, put an end to his sufferings by drowning himself in the Tungabhadrā river, while reciting his faith in Siva. Suicide in such circumstances is authorized by Hindu custom, and more than one instance is on record of Rājas having terminated their existence in a similar manner.

A.D. 1076 to 1126. Reign of Vikramāṅka.

Vikramāditya VI, or Vikramānka, the hero of Bilhana's historical poem, who deposed his brother Somesvara II, and was formally crowned or anointed in A.D. 1076, reigned for

[1] *Ante*, p. 410.

[2] Fleet, apparently in error, dates the battle of Koppam 'shortly before the 20th January, 1060' (*Kanarese Dyn.*, p. 441). The date 1052 is determined by Kielhorn. The site of the battle was Khidrāpur, 30 miles east by south from Kolhāpur, where there is a notable temple of Koppeśvara on the bank of the 'great river' or Krishnā (Fleet, *Ep. Ind.*, xii, 298). This identification seems to be correct. Rice (*Coorg Inscrip.*, revised ed., 1914, p. 15) identifies Koppam with Kopana-tīrtha, or Kopal or Koppal, in the Rāichur District of the Nizam's Dominions, and applies the epithet 'big river' to the Tungabhadrā, while admitting that it usually means the Krishnā.

half a century in tolerable, though not unbroken, peace. He is recorded to have captured Kānchī, and late in his reign was engaged in a serious struggle with Vishnu, the Hoysala king of Dōrasamudra in Mysore. Vikramānka considered his achievements sufficiently notable to justify him in establishing a new era, running from A. D. 1076, called after his name, but it never came into general use.[1] His capital Kalyāna, the modern Kalyāni in the Nizam's Dominions, which had been founded by Somesvara I, was the residence of the celebrated jurist Vijnānēsvara, author of the *Mitāksharā*, the chief authority on Hindu law outside of Bengal.[2]

A. D. 1156. Usurpation of Bijjala.

After the death of Vikramānka, the Chalukya power declined; and in the course of the years A. D. 1156–62, during the reign of Taila III, the commander-in-chief, Bijjala or Vijjana, Kalachurya, revolted and obtained possession of the greater portion of the kingdom, which was held by him and his sons until A. D. 1183, when the Chalukya prince, Somesvara IV, succeeded in recovering his ancestral dominions from the successors of Bijjala. But he was not strong enough to resist the attacks of encroaching neighbours; and in the course of a few years the greater part of his kingdom had been absorbed by the Yādavas of Devagiri on the west, and the Hoysalas of Dōrasamudra on the south. The end of the Chalukya dynasty of Kalyāna may be dated in A. D. 1190, after which time the Rājas of the line ranked merely as petty chiefs.

A. D. 1190. End of Chalukya dynasty.

A. D. 1167. The Lingāyat sect.

The brief reign of Bijjala, the usurping rebel, which terminated by abdication or death in A. D. 1167, was marked by a religious revolution effected by a revival of the cult of Siva and the foundation of a new sect, the Vīra Saivas, or Lingāyats, which is a power to this day.[3] Bijjala was a Jain,

[1] The date is confirmed in *Ind. Ant.*, 1918, p. 290. See A. V. V. Ayyar, 'The Life and Times of Chalukya Vikramāditya' (*Ind. Ant.*, xlviii (1919), pp. 114–20, and 133 ff.).

[2] See Introduction to Bühler's edition of the *Vikramānkadeva-charita*, Bombay Sanskrit Series. 1875.

[3] A good summary account of the Lingāyat sect and literature will be found in *A History of Kanarese Literature*, by E. P. Rice (Heritage of India Series), 1918, chaps. iv, v. Fleet (*Bom. Gaz.*,

and, according to one version of the legend, he wantonly blinded two holy men of the Lingāyat sect, and was assassinated in consequence in the year A.D. 1167. The blood of the saints proved, as usual, to be the seed of the church, which had been founded by Basava, the Brahman minister of Bijjala. But in other legends the tale is told quite differently, and the truth of the matter seems to be past finding out. There is, however, no doubt that the rise of the Lingāyats dates from the time of Bijjala. The members of the sect, who are especially numerous in the Kanarese districts, worship Siva in his phallic form, reject the authority of the Vedas, disbelieve in the doctrine of re-birth, object to child-marriage, approve of the re-marriage of widows, and cherish an intense aversion to Brahmans, notwithstanding the fact that the founder of their religion was himself a Brahman.

Decay of Jainism and Buddhism. The growth of this new sect, which secured numerous adherents among the trading classes, up to that time the main strength of both Buddhism and Jainism, checked the progress of the latter religion, and drove another nail into the coffin of Buddhism, the existence of which in the Deccan is rarely traceable later than the first half of the twelfth century.[1]

The Hoysala dynasty of Dōrasamudra. During the twelfth and thirteenth centuries, chiefs belonging to a family or clan named Hoysala, or Poysala, attained considerable power in the Mysore country. The first notable prince of this line was Bittideva, or Bittiga (about A.D. 1111 to 1141), who established his capital at Dōrasamudra, the modern Halebīd, famous for the fine temple which excited Fergusson's enthusiastic admiration. During the early years of his reign the Jain religion enjoyed high favour under the protection of his minister Gangarāja, and the Jain temples, which had been destroyed by the orthodox Chola invaders, were restored; but the king himself was converted to Vishnuism, under the influence of the cele-

p. 477) notes that 'it is due almost entirely to them that this beautiful, highly polished, and powerful [Kanarese] language has been preserved'.

[1] There are many references to Buddhism in the *Āchārasāra*. 'This clearly shows that in the Kanarese country there were numerous followers of Buddha in Śaka 1076' (A. D. 1154) (Pathak, *Ind. Ant.*, 1912, p. 89).

brated reformer, Rāmānuja, and the magnificent buildings at Belūr and Halebīd testify to the zeal and good taste which he devoted to the serving of his new religion.[1] On his conversion he assumed the name of Vishnu-vardhana, or Vishnu, by which he is best known. Vishnu boasts in his records of numerous conquests, and claims to have defeated the Rājas of the Chola, Pāndya, and Chera kingdoms in the south. About the year A.D. 1223, one of his successors, Narasimha II, who was then in alliance with the Cholas, actually occupied Trichinopoly.[2]

Vishnu's grandson, Vīra-Ballāla, in the course of a long reign extended his dominions widely to the north of Mysore, and was specially proud of having defeated the Yādavas of Devagiri, whose kingdom lay to the north, in A.D. 1191–2. His conquests made the Hoysalas fully independent and the dominant power in Southern India, including the southern parts of the Deccan table-land. **A.D. 1173–1220. Vīra-Ballāla.**

The dynasty continued to be powerful until A.D. 1310, when the Muhammadan generals, Malik Kāfūr and Khwāja Hājī entered the Hoysala kingdom, laid it waste, captured the reigning Rāja, and despoiled his capital, which was finally destroyed by a Muslim force in A.D. 1326 or 1327. The Rāja's son is mentioned as a local chief in records a few years later in date. **A.D. 1310. End of Hoysala dynasty.**

The Yādava kings of Devagiri were descendants of feudatory nobles of the Chalukya kingdom. The territory which they acquired, lying between Devagiri (Daulatābād) and Nāsik, was known as Sevana or Seuna. The first of the Yādava line to attain a position of importance was Bhillama, who was killed in battle by the Hoysala chief in A.D. 1191. **Yādava dynasty of Devagiri.**

The most powerful rāja was Singhana (*acc.* A.D. 1210), who invaded Gujarāt and other countries, and established **A.D. 1210.**

[1] Fergusson and Meadows Taylor, *Architecture in Dharwār and Mysore*, atlas folio (Murray, 1866). For much detailed information about Vishṇu's reign and buildings, see Rice's Introduction to *Ep. Carn.*, vol. v, p. i, especially p. xxxvi. S. K. Aiyangar has given a good account of the Hoysalas in his lecture 'The Making of Mysore' (Madras, 1905), reprinted in *Ancient India*, 1911.

[2] *Ep. Ind.*, vii, 162.

Rāja Singhana. a short-lived kingdom almost rivalling in extent the realms of the Chalukyas and Rāshtrakūtas.

A. D. 1294. Attack by Sultan Alā-ud-dīn. The Yādava dynasty, like that of the Hoysalas, was destroyed by the Muhammadans. When Alā-ud-dīn, Sultan of Delhi, crossed the Narmadā, the northern frontier of the Yādava kingdom, in 1294, the reigning Rāja, Rāmachandra, was obliged to surrender, and to ransom his life by payment of an enormous amount of treasure, which is said to have included six hundred *maunds* of pearls, two *maunds* of diamonds, rubies, emeralds, and sapphires, and so forth.

A. D. 1309. Malik Kāfūr. When the Sultan's incursion was repeated by Malik Kāfūr in A. D. 1309, Rāmachandra again refrained from opposition, and submitted to the invader. He was the last independent Hindu sovereign of the Deccan. In wide territories to the south of the Krishnā (Kistna), the kingdom of Vijayanagar, founded in A. D. 1336, maintained the traditions of Hindu polity in unsurpassed splendour until 1565, when it was overwhelmed by a coalition of Muhammadan princes.

A. D. 1318. End of Yādava dynasty. After Rāmachandra's death, his son-in-law, Harapāla, stirred up a revolt against the foreigners in 1318, but, being defeated, was flayed alive and decapitated. Thus miserably ended the Yādava line.[1]

Hemādri, or Hemādpant. The celebrated Sanskrit writer, Hemādri, popularly known as Hemādpant, flourished during the reigns of Rāmachandra and his predecessor, Mahādeva. He devoted himself chiefly to the systematic redaction of Hindu religious practices and observances, and with this object compiled important works upon Hindu sacred law. He is alleged, although erroneously, to have introduced a form of current script, the Modī, from Ceylon;[2] and has given a valuable historical sketch of his patrons' dynasty in the introduction to one of his books.

[1] Further information about the Hoysala and Yādava dynasties will be found in Rice, *Mysore and Coorg from the Inscriptions*, 1909.

[2] The Moḍī script really was invented or introduced by Bālājī Avajī, Secretary of State to Śivājī, the celebrated Marāṭhā chieftain, who died in 1680 (B. A. Gupte, *Ind. Ant.*, 1905, p. 27. Grierson gives the alphabet in *Linguistic Survey*, vol. vii, p. 20).

APPENDIX P

The Principal Dynasties of the Deccan [1]

I. *The Chalukya Kings of Vātāpi (Bādāmi)*, A. D. 550–753.

Serial No.	*Name.*	*Approximate date of Acc.* A.D.	*Known epigraphic dates.*
I	Pulakēśin I (Satyāśraya, Raṇavikrama, Vallabha)	550	Nil. (The title or epithet *vallabha* is used sometimes alone, sometimes in composition with *Śrī*, &c.)
II	Kīrtivarman I (Vallabha, Raṇaparākrama, &c.)	566–7	578
III	Mangalēśa (Vallabha, Raṇavikrānta, &c.)	597–8	601–2
IV	Pulakēśin II (Vallabha, Satyāśraya, &c.)	608	612, 634; crowned 609
		[Interruption from 642 to 655]	
V	Vikramāditya I (Vallabha, Satyāśraya, &c.)	655	659
VI	Vinayāditya (Satyāśraya, Vallabha, &c.)	680	689, 691, 692, 694
VII	Vijayāditya (Satyāśraya, &c.)	696	699, 700, 705, 709
VIII	Vikramāditya II (Anivārita, &c.)	733	735 (?)
IX	Kīrtivarman II (Nṛipasiṃharāja, &c.)	746	754, 757. (In 753 the Rāshtrakūta conquest occurred, and Kīrtivarman sank to the level of a local Rāja)

[1] Only the main lines are shown, collateral and local branches being omitted. The lists now given are abstracted from those published by Kielhorn in *Ep. Ind.*, viii, App. ii (1906), and begin with the real founder of each dynasty, not with the semi-mythical names heading the genealogies.

II. The Rāshṭrakūṭa Kings of Mānyakheṭa (Mālkheḍ), A.D. 753–973.

Serial No.	*Name.*	*Approximate date of Acc.* A.D.	*Known epigraphic dates.*
I	Dantidurga (Khaḍgāvaloka, &c.)	753	753
II	Kṛishṇa I (Akālavarsha, &c.)	760	770 (Govinda *yuvarāja*)
III	Govinda II (Prabhūtavarsha, &c.)	775	779
IV	Dhruva (Nirupama, Śrīvallabha, borrowed from the Chalukyas, &c.)	780	783 (Jain *Harivaṃsa*)
V	Govinda III (Prabhūtavarsha, &c.)	793	794, 804, 808, 813
VI	Amōghavarsha I (Nṛipatuṅga, &c.)	815	817–77
VII	Kṛishṇa II (Kṛishṇavallabha, &c.)	880	902–11
VIII	Indra III (Nityavarsha, &c.)	912	914, 916
IX	Amōghavarsha II	916–7	Nil
X	Govinda IV (Gojjiga, Suvarṇavarsha, &c.)	917	918–33
XI	Amōghavarsha III (Baddiga, &c.)	935	Nil
XII	Kṛishṇa III (Kannara, &c.)	940	940–61
XIII	Khoṭṭiga (Nityavarsha, &c.)	965	971
XIV	Kakka II (Kakkalla, &c.)	972	972, 973. (Restoration of Chalukyas by Taila in 973)

III. The Chalukya Kings of Kalyāṇi (Kalyāṇa), A.D. 973–1190 [1]

Serial No.	*Name.*	*Approximate date of Acc.* A.D.	*Known epigraphic dates.*
I	Taila II (Tailapa, Āhavamalla, &c.)	973	993–7
II	Satyāśraya (Sattiga, &c.)	997	1002, 1008
III	Vikramāditya V (Tribhuvanamalla)	1009	1009
IV	Jayasiṁha II (Jagadekamalla I)	1016	1017 (?)–1040
V	Someśvara I (Āhavamalla, &c.)	1042	1044–68
VI	Someśvara II (Bhuvanaikamalla)	1075	1071–5
VII	Vikramāditya VI (Vikramārka, &c.)	1075–6	1077–1125
VIII	Someśvara III (Bhūlokamalla)	1125–6	1128, 1130
IX	Perma-Jagadekamalla II	1138	1139, 1149
X	Taila III (Tailapa, Trailokyamalla, &c.)	1149	1154, 1155
XI	Someśvara IV (Tribhuvanamalla, &c.)	1162	1184, 1189. (Usurpation of Bijjala Kalachurya in 1156–62 ; he abdicated in 1167, his descendants continuing until 1183 as rivals of Someśvara IV)

[1] A. Venkatasubbiah in 'The Chronology of the Western Chalukyas', (*Ind. Ant.* xlvii, 1918, and xlviii, 1919) gives the following dynastic list:

1.	Taila II	A. D. 973–97	
2.	Satyāśraya	,, 997–1008	
3.	Vikramāditya V	,, 1009–14	
4.	Ayyana II	,, 1014	
5.	Jayaśiṁha II	,, 1015–42	
6.	Someśvara I	,, 1042–68	
7.	Someśvara II	,, 1068–76	
8.	Vikramāditya VI	,, 1076–1127 (?)	
9.	Someśvara III	,, 1127 (?)–36 (?)	
10.	Perma-Jagadekamalla II	,, 1136 (?)–51	
11.	Taila III	,, 1151–63	(Kalachurya usurpation lasted 1156–1183. Taila continued ruling over such part of his kingdom as remained until 1163).
12.	Jagadekamalla III	,, 1163–84	
13.	Someśvara IV	,, 1184–*c.*1200	(he ruled at different times at Annigere, Kalyāṇi and Banavāsi).

CHAPTER XVI

THE KINGDOMS OF THE SOUTH

SECTION I

The 'Three Kingdoms'

The Tamil country.

SOUTHERN India, as distinguished from the plateau of the Deccan, from which it is separated by the Krishnā (Kistna) and Tungabhadrā rivers, has a character of its own, and a history generally independent of that of the rest of India. This extensive region may be described in modern terms as consisting of the Madras Presidency, excluding the 'Northern Circars' Districts of Vizagapatam and Ganjām, and with the addition of the native states of Mysore, Cochin, and Travancore. It is essentially the land of the Tamil race and speech, and accordingly the greater portion of it was known in ancient times as Tamilakam, or the Tamil country. The earliest tradition fixed the northern boundary of Tamilakam on the east coast at Pulicat, a little above Madras, and on the west coast at the White Rock near Badagara, to the south of Mahé, the frontier line between those two points passing round the hill of Venkata or Tirupathi, 100 miles to the north-west of Madras, and then inclining southwards to Badagara.[1] Later traditions extended the north-eastern boundary as far as Nellore on the N. Pennār river,[2] and the north-western limit to the Chandragiri river south of Mangalore.[3] This chapter is concerned only with the Tamil states and the Pallava dynasty. The dynasties of Mysore have been treated in Chapter XV, being closely connected with the kingdoms of the Deccan plateau.

Damirikē of Ptolemy.

The Greek geographer Ptolemy, who wrote his treatise about A.D. 140, was well acquainted with Southern India,

[1] *The Tamils Eighteen Hundred Years Ago*, pp. 10, 17.

[2] Elliot, *Coins of Southern India* p. 108.

[3] The Chandragiri is the boundary between Kerala and the Tuluva country.

which he called Damirikē, a good transliteration of Tamilakam, *r* and *l* being interchangeable, but unfortunately corrupted in the manuscripts into the unmeaning form Limyrikē, owing to the frequent confusion between Λ and Δ.[1] In his time one language only, the Tamil, was spoken over the whole area; Malayālam, now the speech of Malabar, not having been developed as a separate tongue until some centuries later. The population comprised various elements, of which the Villavar, or bowmen (Bhīls), and Mīnavar, or fishermen (Mīnas), are supposed to have been the most ancient. The Tamils seem to be later immigrants.

The early Tamil poetical literature, dating, according to competent expert opinion, from the first three centuries of the Christian era, gives a vivid picture of the state of society at that period. The Tamils had developed an advanced civilization of their own, wholly independent of Northern India.[2] Immigrants from the North, who had settled at Madura and some other cities, sought to introduce Hindu notions of caste and ceremonial, but met with much opposition, and the caste system, which for many centuries past has been observed with special strictness in the South, was then inchoate and imperfect.[3] The prevailing religion was a form of 'demon-worship', which still survives under new names. For example, the most powerful demoness of the southern races, Kottavai, 'the Victorious,' has now taken her place in the Hindu pantheon as Umā or Durgā, the consort of Siva.[4]

Ancient state of society.

In addition to the three principal kingdoms, which will be described presently, about a hundred and twenty more or

Internecine warfare.

[1] Ptolemy, bk. vii, ch. 1, 85; transl. McCrindle, *Ind. Ant.*, xiii, 367. The Peutingerian Tables correctly give the name as Damirikē (*Ind. Ant.*, viii, 144). Possibly, as S. Krishnaswāmi Aiyangar suggests, Damirikē was the transliteration of a Sanskrit form *Dramidaka*.

[2] See M. Srīnivāsa Aiyangar, *Tamil Studies*, Madras, Guardian Press, 1914, which professes to give 'a complete bird's-eye view of Tamil culture and civilization'.

[3] *The Tamils Eighteen Hundred Years Ago*, pp. 3, 10, 39.

[4] Pope, 'Extracts from the Tamil *Purra-poruḷ Veṇba-Mālai*, and the *Purra-nānnūrru* (*J. R. A. S.*, 1899, p. 242). Pope was not so decided in opinion concerning the early date of the literature as South Indian scholars are, but subsequent discussion seems to establish the high antiquity of the great classical works in Tamil.

less independent chieftains shared the government of the country, and indulged in unceasing internecine wars, waged with exceptional ferocity by the agency of the aboriginal tribesmen, whose representatives, the Maravar, Kallar, and others, still form an important and turbulent element in the population. 'These desolating wars', Dr. Pope observes, 'account for the multitudes of deserted strongholds whose ruins are yet to be seen, and for the comparative sparseness of the population at the period when authentic history begins.'

Religion. The aboriginal 'devil worship', exposed to the persistent attacks of the three northern religions—Jainism, Buddhism, and Hinduism—was gradually forced into the background, and constrained to veil itself behind the names and forms of the more respectable faiths. Jainism. The introduction of Jainism into the South was effected, according to Jain tradition, by a body of emigrants who were driven out of the North from their homes by the pressure of a twelve years' famine, in the reign of Chandragupta Maurya. The event is assigned by some authorities to 309 B.C. The strangers settled at Sravana Belgola in Mysore, where their sainted leader, Bhadrabāhu, starved himself to death in the approved Jain manner. The present head of the ancient Jain settlement at Sravana Belgola claims to be the successor of Bhadrabāhu and is recognized as the pontiff of all the Jains of Southern India. The story is associated, as we have seen (*ante*, p. 154), with statements concerning the last days of Chandragupta Maurya which are discredited by some and accepted by other critics. Whatever may be the truth concerning the alleged abdication and suicide of the Maurya emperor, no sufficient reason seems to exist for rejecting the tradition of the Jain immigration, which brought the religion of Mahāvira to the South half a century before Buddhist missionaries appeared. Samprati, a grandson of Asoka, is said to have been converted by Suhastin, and to have sent many missionaries to preach Jainism in the Peninsula, where his creed undoubtedly secured such wide acceptance that Mr. Rice is justified in affirming that during the first millennium of the Christian era Jainism may be regarded as having been the predominant religion of Mysore. Nor was it confined to Mysore; it spread everywhere more or less.[1] In the Pāndya country the decline of Jainism began in the seventh century, but the religion continued to flourish in Mysore and the Deccan for ages after that time.

Buddhism. The effective importation of Buddhism undoubtedly was the work of Asoka's brother Mahendra and the other missionaries sent out by the great proselytizing emperor in the middle of the third century B.C. (*ante*, p. 193). The imperial religion does not seem to have become at any time the dominant creed of the South, although it attained a considerable amount of popularity during several centuries. In the seventh century of the Christian era it was dying out, overshadowed by both Jainism and Hinduism. After that date those two faiths almost exclusively disputed the field, often with great bitterness and ferocity. The early southern Buddhism ignored caste, but the mysterious and insidious power of the Brahmanical organization was too much for it, and won the day. The rules of caste are now enforced in the South with far greater rigour than in the North. It is not possible to follow the subject farther in this place, but it is safe to affirm that there is room for a very interesting book on the history of the conflict of religions in the Tamil and Kanarese country.

No slavery; the five great assemblies. Slavery is said to have been unknown among the ancient Tamils. The statement of Megasthenes that 'it was a great thing that all Indians were free, no slave existing in India' (*ante*, pp. 105 *n.*, 187 *n.*), probably was based on a rash generalization made from information which may have been strictly true for parts of the South.[2] His strange enumeration of the seven classes of the population, usually mistranslated 'castes', as being (1) philosophers, (2) agriculturists,

[1] For Jain historical traditions, with varying systems of chronology, see Jacobi in *S. B. E.*, vol. xxii, and many articles in the *Indian Antiquary*, vols. ii, ix, xi, xiii, xvii, xx, and xxi, by Hoernle and other writers; also Rice, *Mysore and Coorg from the Inscriptions*.

[2] The statement is not true if applied to Malabar or Keraḷa (Dubois, *Hindu Manners, Customs, and Ceremonies*, by Beauchamp, third ed. (1906), p. 56).

(3) herdsmen, shepherds, and graziers, (4) artisans and traders, (5) the military, (6) the overseers, and (7) the councillors (*ante*, pp. 140, 141 *n.*), may be compared with the list of the 'five great assemblies', which checked the autocracy of Tamil kings, and comprised the people, priests, astrologers, physicians, and ministers.[1]

War and peace.

The frequency and savagery of the internecine wars described in the old literature might seem to justify the opinion that the arts of peace and the amenities of civil life must have been wholly neglected in the ancient Tamil states. But such an inference would be erroneous, for there is no doubt that poetry and other refined arts were carried to a high degree of excellence, and that the dwellers in the cities, at all events, enjoyed all the luxuries which wealth could purchase. In this matter, too, an observation of Megasthenes helps us to understand the apparent contradiction between a state of incessant war and the existence of a rich trading and agricultural community of peaceful citizens.

'The second class', the Greek ambassador noted, 'consists of the husbandmen, who form the bulk of the population, and are in disposition most mild and gentle. They are exempted from military service, and cultivate their lands undisturbed by fear. They never go to town, either to take part in its tumults, or for any other purpose. It therefore not unfrequently happens that at the same time, and in the same part of the country, men may be seen drawn up in array of battle and fighting at the risk of their lives, while other men close at hand are ploughing and digging in perfect security, having these soldiers to protect them.'

This pretty picture may be a little overdrawn, although we may accept as true the statement that in the India known to Megasthenes the fighting ordinarily was done by professional soldiers, who interfered little with the work of the harmless and necessary peasant. The fortified towns too, as a rule, were protected by their gates and walls from the injuries of war, and only on rare occasions suffered the horrors of a sack. Thus it was possible for the Tamils, like the mediaeval Florentines and Pisans, to have their fill of fighting and still

[1] *The Tamils Eighteen Hundred Years Ago*, pp. 108, 114.

pay a close attention to careful farming and lucrative trade.

Pepper, pearls, and beryls.

Tamil Land had the good fortune to possess three precious commodities not procurable elsewhere, namely, pepper, pearls, and beryls. Pepper fetched an enormous price in the markets of Europe, and was so highly prized that when Alaric the Goth levied his war indemnity from Rome, in A. D. 409, his terms included the delivery of 3,000 pounds of pepper.[1] The pearl fishery of the southern sea, which still is productive and valuable, had been worked for untold ages, and always had attracted a crowd of foreign merchants. The beryl or aquamarine gem, which, as Pliny truly observed, is closely related to the emerald, was highly esteemed by both Indians and Romans, and often furnished material for the choicest achievements of the engraver's art. Its scarcity, except in India, tempted clever Indian forgers to fabricate imitations made from rock-crystal. Three Indian mines are recorded, namely, (1) Punnāta, where Ptolemy noted that beryl was found, close to Kittūr on the Kabbani river, a tributary of the Kāvirī (Cauvery) in the south-west of Mysore; (2) Padiyūr or Pattiāli, 40 miles ESE. from the town of Coimbatore, where a mine was worked successfully as late as 1820; and (3) Vāniyambādi, in the north-eastern corner of the Salem District, not far from the Kolar gold-field. The large and numerous hoards of Roman gold coins found in the districts where the mines were situated, testify to the activity of ancient commerce in the gems of Southern India. The fact that the mineral corundum, a variety of the ruby and sapphire, found abundantly in Salem and Coimbatore, bears a purely Tamil name (*kurrandam*), affords another indication of the familiarity of ancient Europe with the products of the Indian gem mines.[2]

[1] Gibbon, ch. xxxi.

[2] References for the beryl trade are: Πουννάτα ἐν ᾗ βήρυλλος, Ptolemy, *Geogr.*, Bk. vii, ch. i. 86, transl. in *Ind. Ant.*, xiii, 367; Pliny, *Hist. Nat.*, Bk. xxxvii, ch. v; Walhouse, 'Aquamarina Gems, Ancient and Modern', *Ind. Ant.*, v, 237, with a full account of the Paḍiyūr mine. The mine at Vāṇiyambādi rests on the authority of Sewell (*J. R. A. S.*, 1904, p. 595). The correct identification of Πουννάτα, which in the second edition I wrongly identified with Paḍiyūr, following Sewell, is due to Lewis Rice. Ptolemy's name, *Pounnata*, is an accurate transcrip-

Maritime commerce; foreign settlements.

The Tamil states maintained powerful navies, and were visited freely by ships from both east and west, which brought merchants of various races eager to buy the pearls, pepper, beryls, and other choice commodities of India, and to pay for them with the gold, silver, and art ware of Europe. The Roman *aureus* circulated in Southern India as freely as the English sovereign passed on the continent of Europe before 1914, and Roman bronze small change, partly imported and partly minted at Madura, was commonly used in the bazaars.[1] There is good reason to believe that considerable colonies of Roman subjects engaged in trade were settled in Southern India during the first two centuries of our era, and that European soldiers, described as 'powerful Yavanas, dumb Mlechchhas [barbarians], clad in complete armour,' acted as bodyguards to Tamil kings, while 'the beautiful large ships of the Yavanas' lay off Muziris (Cranganore) to receive the cargoes of pepper paid for by Roman gold. It is even stated, and no doubt truly, that a temple dedicated to Augustus existed at Muziris. Another foreign (Yavana) colony was settled at Kāviripaddanam, or Puhār, a busy port situated on the eastern coast at the mouth of the northern branch of the Kāviri (Cauvery) river. Both town and harbour disappeared long since, and now lie buried under vast mounds of sand.[2] The poems tell of the importa-

tion of Punnāṭa (al. Punāḍu or Punnāḍu), an ancient principality mentioned in an early inscription, perhaps of the fifth or sixth century, and also in the *Bṛihatkathākośa* of Harisheṇa, dated A. D. 931. Kittūr, a village on the Kabbini (Kapini) river, a tributary of the Kāviri (Cauvery), in the south-west of Mysore, represents Kitthipura or Kīrtipura, the ancient capital of the Punnāṭa State (Rice, *Mysore and Coorg from the Inscriptions* (1909), pp. 4, 10; *Ind. Ant.*, xii, 13; xviii, 366). The Mamballi copper-plates from Yelandūr taluk, Mysore, of Rāshtravarma, Rāja of Pumrāshtra [=Punnāṭa], mention the Kāvēri and Kapini rivers, and show that the capital Kittūr (Kīrtipura) was on the Kapini in Heggaḍadēvankōt taluk. The plates, written in the Hale-Kannaḍa script, are clearly genuine and date from about A. D. 550 (*Mysore, A. S. Rep.* for 1917, pars. 87–9). Full details about the mines of corundum in Balfour *Cyclop.*, s.v.

[1] Sewell, 'Roman Coins found in India,' *J. R. A. S.*, 1904, pp. 591–637, a valuable article. See especially pp. 609–13.

[2] According to S. K. Aiyangar, the destruction took place in the first quarter of the third century after Christ at the latest. The Tamil tradition is that the city was 'overwhelmed by the sea' as stated in the *Epic of the Anklet* and the *Jewel-Belt*, referred to in S. K. Aiyangar's *Ancient India*, p. 352. M. Srīnivāsa Aiyangar in

tion of Yavana wines, lamps, and vases, and their testimony is confirmed by the discovery in the Nīlgiri megalithic tombs of numerous bronze vessels similar to those known to have been produced in Europe during the early centuries of the Christian era, and by the statements of the *Periplus*.[1]

Early literature and art.

So far as I can judge, the scholars who maintain the early date of the best Tamil poems are right, and the 'Augustan age' of Tamil literature may be placed in the first three centuries of the Christian era. One authority would assign it to the first century, but the wider limits indicated may be accepted with some confidence.[2] Other arts besides poetry were cultivated with success, including music, the

Tamil Studies, p. 60, puts the date of its 'destruction' in the second century A. C. This theory of the ruin of the city does not accord with the view held by C. P. Venkatarāma Ayyar (*Town Planning in Ancient Dekkan*, Madras, 1916) that 'this ancient sea-port, which had an extensive commerce, has ceased to be of importance owing to the silting-up of the Kavery'.

[1] *The Tamils Eighteen Hundred Years Ago*, pp. 16, 25, 31, 36, 38. Puhār is also written Pugār or Pukār. The 'Peutingerian Tables', a collection of ancient maps believed to date from about A. D. 226 (ed. Scheyb, 1733; Mannert, Leipzig, 1824; Charles Ruelens, Brussels, 1884; Walker, *On the Tabula Peutingeriana*, Cambridge, 1883, in *Cambridge Antiquarian Society's Communications*, vol. v, p. 237), are the authority for the temple of Augustus at Muziris, which is indicated on the map by a rough sketch of a building marked 'templ. augusti' inserted beside 'Muziris'. The identification of Muziris with Cranganore is well established. Kāviripaddanam = Puhār; = Kākanthi (Kākandī of Bharhut inscription, No. 101, *Ind. Ant.*, xxi, 235); = Kamara (*Periplus*, ch. 60, *Ind. Ant.*, viii, 149); = Khabēris (*Ptolemy*, Bk. vii, ch. 1, 13, *Ind. Ant.*, vii, 40; xiii, 332). For the bronze vessels see the collection in the British Museum, and the labels on the specimens; *Ind. Ant.*, 1905, p. 229; Breeks, *An Account of the Primitive Tribes and Monuments of the Nīlagiris*, London, 1873; Foote, *Catal. Prehist. Antiq. Madras Museum*, 1901, pls. x–xiii. The *Periplus* (ch. 56), states that 'ships which frequent these ports are of a large size, on account of the great amount and bulkiness of the pepper and malabathrum of which their lading consists'. A full list of exports and imports is then given. Malabathrum (μαλάβαθρον) was not 'betel', as McCrindle erroneously supposed, but the leaves of different species of *Cinnamomum*, especially *C. Zeylanicum* (Schoff, transl. of *Periplus* p. 84; with references). The massacre at Alexandria, perpetrated in 215 by Caracalla, stopped most of the direct trade between that port and India (*J. R. A. S.*, 1907, p. 954).

[2] Gover was of opinion that Tiruvalluva, the famous author of the *Kural* (*Cural*), 'probably flourished about the third century of our era' (*The Folk-songs of Southern India*, 1872, p. 217). Gover penetrated into the Hindu mind perhaps more deeply than any other European writer, and any one desirous of understanding Southern India should read, if possible, his admirable book, which, unfortunately, is now scarce.

drama, painting, and sculpture; but the statues and pictures apparently were executed in perishable materials, and have wholly vanished. The plays are said to have been of two kinds—the Tamil or indigenous, in numerous varieties, which permitted the insertion of love scenes; and the Aryan or northern, which were more formal, and restricted to eleven stock subjects.

The 'Three Kingdoms'.

Such was the state of civilization in the three Dravidian or Tamil kingdoms of the South during the early centuries of the Christian era, when they are disclosed dimly to view in the pages of the ancient native literature and the scanty notices of Greek and Roman authors, as supplemented by a few archaeological and numismatic observations. With the exception of the Asoka edicts, the Bhattiprolu casket inscriptions, and a small number of other records, epigraphic testimony does not go back so far. General tradition recognized the existence of three important kingdoms, and only three, in the Tamil country—namely, the Pāndya, Chola, and Chera or Kerala. The poet sings:

> The pleasant Tamil lands possess
> For boundary the ocean wide,
> The heaven, where tempests loud sway not,
> Upon their brow rests as a crown.
> Fertile the soil they till and wide:
> Three kings with mighty hosts this land divide.[1]

Asoka calls the Chera realm by the name of Keralaputra, 'son of Kerala', which appears in corrupt forms in Pliny's work and the *Periplus*, and he adds a fourth name, Satiyaputra, not recorded elsewhere.[2] Mangalore is the centre of the Tuluva country, in which Tulu, a language allied to Kanarese, is spoken.

Position of the Pāṇḍya kingdom.

The Pāndya kingdom, as defined by tradition, extended north and south from the Southern Vellāru river (Pudukottai) to Cape Comorin, and east and west from the Coromandel coast to the 'great highway', the Achchhankōvil Pass leading into Southern Kerala, or Travancore; and thus

[1] *Pura-nannūṛu*, No. 35, in *Tam. Ant.*, vol. i, No. 6, p. 50.
[2] See *ante*, pp. 171, 194.

was nearly co-extensive with the existing Districts of Madura and Tinnevelly, with part of Travancore in which Cape Comorin is now included.

Position of the Choḷa kingdom.

According to the most generally received traditions, the Chola country (*Choḷamaṇḍalam*) was bounded on the north by the Pennār, and on the south by the Southern Vellāru river; or, in other words, it extended along the eastern, or Coromandel, coast from Nellore to Pudukottai, where it abutted on the Pāndya territory. On the west it extended to the borders of Coorg. The limits thus defined include Madras and several other British districts on the east, as well as the greater part of the Mysore State. But the ancient literature does not carry the Tamil Land farther north than Pulicat and the Venkata or Tirupathi Hill, 100 miles to the north-west of Madras. On the other hand, in the seventh century, the Chola country, as known to Hiuen Tsang, was a small territory, nearly coincident with the Cuddapah District, and did not extend to the south. Cholamandalam, or the Coromandel coast, called Dravida by the pilgrim, was then in the hands of the Pallava kings, whose capital was at Kānchī (Conjeeveram) 45 miles WSW. from the city of Madras.

Position of the Chera or Keraḷa kingdom.

Scholars are now agreed that Chera and Kerala are only variant forms of the one word.[1] The name of Kerala is still well remembered, and there is no doubt that the ancient kingdom so called was equivalent to the Southern Konkans or Malabar coast, comprising the present Malabar District with Travancore and Cochin. The southern portion of Travancore, known as Ven or Venādu, was attached to the Pāndya kingdom in the first century after Christ. In later times the Chera kingdom included the Kongu country, the modern Coimbatore District with the southern part of Salem, but it is doubtful whether or not such was the case in early days. Generally, Kerala means the rugged region

[1] *Keraḷa* is the Kanarese form of the Tamil *Cheraḷa*. The country was anciently called Cheraḷam or Cheraḷa-nāḍu, and the kings were Cheraḷ-ādan or Cheraḷ-Irum-Porrai, *Cheraḷam* means 'mountain-range', and so is equivalent to Malabar (Pundit D. Savariroyan in *Tamilian Antiquary*, No. 1, pp. 69–71).

of the Western Ghāts south of the Chandragiri river. Of course, the boundaries of the three kingdoms varied much from time to time.

The Pallavas.

From about the fourth to the eighth century the Pallava dynasty plays a great part in the history of Southern India. But there was no Pallava country with traditional limits. The Pallava domination, while it lasted, extended in degrees varying from time to time over all the three ancient kingdoms, the extent of such domination being in proportion to the vigour of the Pallava chiefs and the weakness of their rivals. This fact has been held to indicate that the Pallavas, like the Marāthās, were a predatory clan, tribe, or caste, which rose to power by violence, and superimposed its authority upon the Rājas of the territorial kingdoms. It is, however, possible that the Pallavas were not one distinct tribe or class, but a mixed population, composed partly of foreigners and partly of south Indian tribes or castes, differing in race from the Tamils, and taking their name from the title of an intruding foreign dynasty, which obtained control over them and welded them into an aggressive political power.[1] The tradition of the Pallava rule is faint, and the existence of the dynasty was unknown to European scholars until 1840, when the discovery of a copper-plate inscription drew their attention to the subject.[2] Since then many similar discoveries have been effected, and much progress has been made in the reconstruction of the dynastic framework of Pallava history.

General view of southern history.

In the following sections of this chapter an attempt will be made to give an outline of the political history, so far as it is known, of the three Tamil kingdoms, the position and character of which have been described, and also of the intrusive dynasty of the Pallavas. But the time for writing in brief the history of the southern kingdoms in a satisfactory manner has not yet come, and at present any sketch such as that now offered must be tentative and incomplete. In its revised form it is less imperfect than the account in the earlier editions of this work, but, until

[1] See pp. 491–3, *post.* [2] Elliot, *Coins of Southern India*, p. 39.

specialists intimately acquainted with the languages and local conditions shall have worked out detailed monographs for each dynasty, it will not be possible to compile an adequate early history of the southern kingdoms in a form suitable for inclusion in a volume dealing with India as a whole. Still, notwithstanding the inevitable defects incident to the attempt, it is worth while to make it. I do not know of the existence of any book which professes to give the student or general reader a view of the history of Southern India before the Muhammadan conquest, as it has been partially recovered by the patient labours of modern scholarship.[1] I feel assured, therefore, that my effort to supply the want, however imperfectly executed, will not be wasted, and that expert critics who know the difficulties of the subject will be the most ready to pardon my shortcomings. *Tout connaître c'est tout pardonner.*

Difficulties.

Those difficulties are great. The sources of southern history prior to the ninth century are far scantier than those available in the north. The eighteen *Purānas* pay small attention to the south, early inscriptions are extremely rare, the coinage gives little help, the publication of archaeological investigations in a finished form is backward, and the exploration of the ancient literature is incomplete.[2] On the other hand, from the ninth century onwards, the mass of epigraphic material is so enormous as to be unmanageable. The southern princes and peoples have bequeathed to posterity many thousands of inscriptions, which often attain portentous length. Eight volumes of Mr. Rice's *Epigraphia Carnatica*, which are concerned with both the Deccan and the Tamil kingdoms, give notices of 5,800 inscriptions. The staff of the Archaeological Survey in Madras during a single year copied more than 800 inscriptions, none of which, probably, are included in Mr. Rice's work ; and every year makes a huge addition to the unwieldy accumulation of

[1] The volume of collected essays by Mr. S. Krishnaswāmī Aiyangar, entitled *Ancient India* (Luzac, 1911), although valuable, and freely utilized in the following pages, does not profess to be the desired book.

[2] Southern India has *Purāṇas* of its own.

historical material. The length of individual documents is illustrated by the fact that one important record is engraved on thirty-one sheets of copper, fastened together on a massive ring. It is obvious that the thorough examination of the epigraphic sources alone of the early history of Southern India must be the work of specialists for many years to come, and that additions to knowledge of the subject must continue to be made from day to day. With these preliminary explanations I proceed to give the best account that I can of the three Tamil kingdoms, and of the intruding Pallava dynasty which for a time overshadowed them all.

SECTION II

The Pāndya, Chera, or Kerala, and Satiyaputra Kingdoms

The 'five Pāṇḍyas.' The Pāndya kingdom, approximately equivalent to the modern Madura and Tinnevelly Districts, with part of Trichinopoly and sometimes also of Travancore, is supposed to have been divided into five principalities, the chiefs of which were known as the 'five Pāndyas'. Details as to the jurisdiction of the several chiefs are unknown, and the evidence for the existence of 'the five kings' is of doubtful value.[1]

Korkai, Κόλχοι. As early as the time of Pliny, in the first century after Christ, the capital was Madura or Kūdal; but there is reason to believe that in still more ancient days Korkai was the chief place of the kingdom, and there is some evidence that a place called South Maṇalūr on the east side of the Madura District had been the capital of Pāndya chiefs in prehistoric times.[2] All native traditions indicate Korkai or Kolkai, the

[1] See Sewell in *Ind. Ant.*, Aug. 1915, vol. xliv, p. 176. He holds that the monarch was always single and that the belief in the 'Five Kings' grew out of the legend of the Five Pāṇḍavas.

[2] Pliny, *Hist. Nat.*, Bk. vi, ch. 23 (26). He describes Becarē, the harbour on the Malabar coast, the Bakarai or Barkarē of Ptolemy (Bk. vii, ch. 1, 8), which is Vaikkarai, the landing-place for Kottayam; and adds that 'there Pandion used to reign, dwelling at a great distance from the mart, in a town in the interior of the country, called Modura'. At the time he was writing Caelobothras (Keralaputra) was sovereign of the Malabar coast. The *Periplus* (ch.

Greek Κόλχοι, as the cradle of South Indian civilization, and the home of the mythical three brothers who were supposed to have founded the Pāndya, Chera, and Chola kingdoms. The city, now represented by an insignificant village on the bank of the Tāmrāparni river [1] in Tinnevelly, was a great seaport in the days of its glory, and the head-quarters of the trade in pearls and conch-shells (*Turbinella rapa*), which constituted the special source of wealth enjoyed by the Pāndya kings. Even when the royal court was established at Madura, the Crown Prince resided at Korkai in order to control the important revenue and commercial interests centred there. In the course of time the slow elevation of the coast [2] rendered Korkai inaccessible to ships, and the city gradually decayed, like the Cinque Ports in England.

Its commercial business was transferred to the new port, which was founded at Kāyal,[3] 3 miles lower down the river, and continued for many centuries to be one of the greatest marts of the east. Here Marco Polo landed late in the thirteenth century, probably more than once, and was much impressed by the wealth and magnificence of both prince

Kāyal.

54, 55) shows clearly that while Muziris belonged to the kingdom of Keralaputra, Bakarē, farther south, was included in the Pāṇḍya dominions; which, therefore, must have comprised the southern parts of the modern Travancore State. This tract was called Venāḍu or Ven. For identification of Becarē and many other places, see *The Tamils Eighteen Hundred Years Ago*, pp. 17–20. Pliny's work was published in A. D. 77, as is proved by the dedication to Titus, before his accession. The *Periplus* may be dated about A. D. 70, and Ptolemy about A. D. 140. For Mañalūr see *Ind. Ant.*, 1913, pp. 66, 72. North Mañalūr, of which the position is not known, is supposed to have been the earliest Choḷa capital.

[1] The river was also called Porundam and Muḍigonḍaśōlapperāru (*Ep. Ind.* xi (1914), p. 295). It is mentioned in Rock Edicts ii and xiii of Asoka and in chap. xi of the Arthaśāstra of Kautilya. Caldwell (*Tinnevelly*, p. 5) points out the great commercial importance of the river. See also the author's article in *Ind. Ant.*, vol. xlvii (1918), p. 48.

[2] The gradual elevation of the land is proved specifically by a piece of pottery resembling modern ware being found in grit stone at Kulasēkhara paṭṭanam, a mile from the seashore. Caldwell concludes that the grit stone which contains recent shells is of comparatively modern formation (*Hist. of Tinnevelly*, Madras, 1881, p. 5).

[3] This Kāyal is now Old Kāyal, and is not to be identified with Kāyal-paṭṭanam (Caldwell, ibid., p. 38). For alteration in the eastern coast-line, see *The Tamils Eighteen Hundred Years Ago*, p. 236.

and people.[1] But the same process which had ruined Korkai caused the abandonment of Kāyal, and compelled the Portuguese to remove their trade to Tuticorin, where a sheltered roadstead, free from deposits of silt, offered superior convenience. The site of Kāyal is now occupied by the miserable huts of a few Muhammadan and native Christian fishermen.[2]

Early notices; Megasthenes.

It is impossible to name a date for the abandonment of Korkai as a port, but the coins of that mint are supposed to extend up to about A. D. 700. The special crest or cognizance of the princes of Korkai was the battle-axe, often associated with the elephant. The kings of Madura adopted a fish, or a pair of fishes, as the family crest.[3]

The capital of the country, as already mentioned, was at Madura in Pliny's time, but the kingdom had existed from much earlier days. The Pāndyas were known to the Sanskrit grammarian Kātyāyana, whose date probably is not later than the fourth century B. C.;[4] and in the same century, Megasthenes, the ambassador of Seleukos Nikator at the court of Chandragupta Maurya, was told strange tales about the southern realm, which was supposed to be under the regimen of women. He was informed that 'Herakles begat a daughter in India whom he called Pandaia. To her he assigned that portion of India which lies to the southward and extends to the sea, while he distributed the people subject to her rule into 365 villages, giving orders that one

[1] Medlycott, *India and the Apostle Thomas*, pp. 85 and 87. The first visit seems to have been made in 1288 and the second in 1293.

[2] Bishop Caldwell, *Ind. Ant.*, vi, 80–3, 279.

[3] Loventhal, *The Coins of Tinnevelly* (Madras, 1888), p. 9.

[4] Bhandarkar, *Early History of the Dekkan*, 2nd ed., in *Bomb. Gaz.* (1896), vol. i, part i, p. 139. I accept the view of Professors Goldstücker and Bhandarkar concerning the antiquity of Pāṇini and Kātyāyana as necessarily resulting from the ascertained date of Patañjali, 150 B.C. In an essay, *Systems of Sanskrit Grammar*, published Poona, 1915, with the permission of the University of Bombay, Shripad Krishna Belvalkar, M.A., Ph.D., remarks (p. 18) that there is nothing in Pāṇini's Ashṭadyāyi inconsistent with his having flourished in the seventh century B. C. He believes in this early date, while admitting that none of the arguments are decisive when taken singly, and on p. 15 gives 700 to 600 B. C., 'as near an approximation to Pānini's time as, in our present state of knowledge, or rather want of knowledge, we are likely to get.'

village each day should bring to the treasury the royal tribute, so that the queen might always have the assistance of those men whose turn it was to pay the tribute in coercing those who for the time being were defaulters in their payment.' This female potentate was credited with having received from her hero father 500 elephants, 4,000 cavalry, and 130,000 infantry. She possessed a great treasure in the fishery for pearls, which, as Arrian observes, had been eagerly sought by the Greeks, and in his time were equally prized by the Romans.[1]

Relations with Rome.

We hear of a mission sent by 'King Pandion' to Augustus Caesar in 20 B.C.;[2] and both the author of the *Periplus of the Erythraean Sea* (*c.* A.D. 80) and Ptolemy the geographer (*c.* A.D. 140) were well informed concerning the names and positions of the marts and ports of the Pāndya country. Caracalla's massacre at Alexandria in A.D. 215 checked, or perhaps put an end to, the direct Roman trade between Southern India and Egypt,[3] so that for long ages the history of the Pāndya realm is hidden from our eyes.

Ancient kings.

The ancient Tamil literature, now being vigorously explored by many patriotic students in Southern India, mentions numerous kings by their clumsy names or titles, of whom some may be referred to an extremely early period. But the first Pāndya king who can be placed in a chronological position at all definite is Nedum-cheliyan, who lived in the second century of the Christian era, and was more or less contemporary with Nedumudi Killi, grandson of Karikāla Chola, with Chenkuttuvan, a powerful Chera king, and with Gajabāhu I of Ceylon. As is usually the case in Indian history, the key is obtained by the synchronism with a foreign prince. Although it cannot be said that the chronology of the early kings of Ceylon has been settled definitely, Pro-

[1] Megasthenes, Fragm. I, lvi B, lviii, in Schwanbeck's text and McCrindle's translation; Arrian, *Indika*, ch. viii. The story may have been suggested by distorted reports of the Malabar system of succession through females. Mr. F. Fawcett informs me that at the present day the Laccadive islands are administered by the women while the men are at sea.

[2] Strabo, Bk. xv, ch. 4, 73; Merivale, *History of the Romans under the Empire*, iv, 118, 175.

[3] *J. R. A. S.*, Oct., 1907, p. 954.

fessor Geiger's dating of the reign of Gajabāhu between A.D. 173 and 191 may be accepted as a close approximation to the truth.[1]

The Madura Academy.

The most remarkable characteristic of the Pāndya state in those times was the maintenance at Madura of a flourishing literary academy or Sangam, the members of which produced much literature of the highest quality. The famous *Kural* of Tiruvalluva—which lives in the hearts of the Tamil people—may be assigned to a time a little before or after A.D. 100. The interesting 'Epic of the Anklet' and the 'Jewel-belt' are a century or so later. It is impossible at present to write out a 'connected relation' of the story of the Pāndya kings during the early centuries of the Christian era, and the reader must be content with these few observations.[2]

Hiuen Tsang's account.

When Hiuen Tsang visited Southern India, in A.D. 640, he spent a considerable time, doubtless including the 'rest' during the rainy season, at Kānchī (Conjeeveram), then the capital of the Pallava king Narasimhavarman, the most considerable potentate in the South at that period. The pilgrim did not personally visit the Pāndya country farther south, and was content to record notes from descriptions supplied by his Buddhist friends at Kānchī. He gives the name of Malakūta, or Malakotta, to the country, but fails to indicate the name or position of the capital, which presumably was Madura, and is silent on the subject of the mode of government. It is probable that the Pāndya Rāja at that time was a tributary of the powerful Pallava king of Kānchī. In Malakūta Buddhism was almost extinct, the ancient monasteries being mostly in ruins. Temples of the Hindu gods were numbered by hundreds, and the nude (Digambara) Jains were present in multitudes. The inhabitants were re-

[1] K. G. Sankara Aiyar, in 'The Age of the Third Tamil Sangam' (*J. Mythic Soc.*, 1917) prefers A.D. 154–76—anyhow the second half of the second century A.C. The same author puts the third Sangam about the same time, which seems reasonable.

[2] *The Tamils Eighteen Hundred Years Ago*, pp. 80, 81, 88. Gover dated Tiruvallava in the third century (*Folk Songs of Southern India*, p. 217). See *Ancient India*, by S. K. Aiyangar, ch. xiv; 'The Augustan Age of Tamil Literature'; Dr. J. Lazarus on the *Kural* in *Tam. Ant.*, vol. ii (1913), pp. 53–72, and various other papers in vol. i of the same periodical.

puted to care little for learning, and to be wholly immersed in commercial pursuits, especially the pearl trade.[1]

Eighth to tenth centuries.

An inscription furnishes a list of Pāndya kings who reigned from about the middle of the eighth to the beginning of the tenth century, but they are little more than names. Arikesarin, who lived in the eighth century, is said to have defeated the Pallavas, and there is reason to believe that the accession of Varagunavarman, who was defeated by the Pallava, Aparājita, at the battle of Srī Purambiya, may be assigned to the definite date A. D. 862–3.[2] During this period the Chola kingdom, ground between the Pallava and the Pāndya millstones, was weak and unimportant, and the business of resisting Pallava aggression seems to have devolved chiefly on the Pāndyas. The defeat of Nandivarman by Vikramāditya Chalukya, in A. D. 740, had greatly weakened the Pallava power, which was still further reduced by the victories of Aditya Chola at the close of the ninth century.[3] From the beginning of the tenth century the

[1] Beal, ii, 228–30; Watters, ii, 228–33. See remarks by Hultzsch, *Ind. Ant.*, xviii, 242. What has happened to the ruins of the Hindu and Buddhist buildings anterior to the seventh century? It seems tolerably certain that some of them were converted at a later date to Brahmanical use. This is clearly the case with the Buddhist apsidal *chaitya* hall at Chazarla in Guntūr District, converted into a Saiva temple of late Pallava style (*A. S. Ann. Rep. S. Circle*, 1917–18, p. 35). See 'Bouddha Vestiges in Kānchīpura', by T. A. Gopinatha Rao, M.A., Trivandrum (*Ind. Ant.*, 1915, pp. 127–9) with plates. In twelve hours the author discovered five images of Buddha, two being inside the Kamākshī Temple, which probably occupies the site of a Buddhist Tārā temple, the image inside at A being 7′ 10″, including pedestal, which is not likely to have been moved far. All five images are of considerable size. See also Wilson in Introduction to Mackenzie Coll. (ed. 1882), p. 40.

[2] *Progress Report, Epigraphy*, 1906–7, in *Madras G.O., Public*, No. 503, June 27, 1907, pp. 62–70. That report by the late Rai Bahadur V. Venkayya Avargal gives a summary of the few known facts about the early Pāndya kings, as ascertained to date. Additions have been made by T. A. Gopinatha Rao in the *Travancore Archaeol. Series*, especially No. 7 (1911).

[3] *Progress Report, Epigraphy*, 1905–6, in *Madras G.O., Public*, No. 492, July 2, 1906, paras. 10, 16. 'The Chōḷa king who extended his sovereignty over the Tōṇḍaināḍu was, as we know from other sources, Rāja Kēsarivarman Āditya, the first. He allied himself with the Pāṇḍya king, Varaguṇa Pāṇḍya, and uprooted the Pallava dynasty, and extended his dominions over the whole of the Tōṇḍaināḍu. Therefore, Āditya ought to have lived about the second half of the ninth century, for we know Varaguṇa Pāṇḍya reigned from A. D. 862–3 upwards' (*Travancore Archaeol. Series*, vol. ii, p. 77). Jouveau-Dubreuil (*Pallavas*, p. 66) dates Varaguṇa's accession about A. D. 854.

Pāndya kings were constrained to acknowledge the ever-growing power of the Cholas. Whether independent or tributary, the Pāndya dynasty continued to exist throughout the ages, and its conflicts with neighbouring powers are noticed in inscriptions from time to time, but few of the events recorded are deserving of remembrance.[1]

Chola ascendancy.

The Pāndya state, in common with the other kingdoms of the South, undoubtedly was reduced to a condition of tributary dependence by the Chola king, Rājarāja the Great, about the year 994, and continued to be more or less under Chola control for nearly two centuries ; although, of course, the local administration remained in the hands of the native Rājas, and the relations of the two states varied from time to time. Some revival of the Pāndya power took place in the first half of the thirteenth century.

Persecution of Jains.

When Hiuen Tsang, the Chinese pilgrim, visited Southern India in A.D. 640, Digambara Jains and Jain temples were numerous in both the Pallava realm (Dravida) and the Pāndya kingdom (Malakoṭṭa).[2] His account does not offer the slightest indication of religious persecution. We must hold, therefore, that the persecution which certainly occurred about that time was subsequent to the pilgrim's visit. It is well established that king Kūna, Sundara, or Nedumāran Pāndya, who had been brought up as a Jain and was married to a Chola princess, was converted about the middle of the seventh century, by his consort and the famous saint Tirujnānasambandar, to the faith of Siva, which was warmly supported by the Chola dynasty. King Sundara displayed even more than the proverbial zeal of a convert, and persecuted his late co-religionists, who refused to apostatize,

[1] The Pāṇḍyas could never be completely subdued. They continued in a state of chronic revolt against the Choḷa yoke during the whole period of Choḷa supremacy. For about fifty years in the eleventh century Choḷa-Pāṇḍya kings governed the Pāṇḍya country, i. e. Choḷa princes acting apparently as viceroys under the Choḷa suzerain at Tanjore. The first Choḷa-Pāṇḍya was the son of Rājendra-Choḷa I (A. D. 1011–44). Two others are recorded, and there are inscriptions of two out of the three (K. V. Subrahmanya Aiyar, *Ep. Ind.*, xi (1914), p. 293). For further details, see *Epigraphy* (*G.O.*, No. 1035, Home (Education), Aug. 10, 1917, pp. 106, 107.

[2] Hultzsch, *Ind. Ant.*, xviii, 240.

with the most savage cruelty, inflicting on no less than eight thousand innocent persons a horrible death by impalement. Certain unpublished sculptures on the walls of a temple at Trivatūr (Tiruvattūr) in Arcot record these executions, and are regarded as confirmation of the tradition.[1] The position of the Jain religion in the South was much shaken by the persecution, which evidently was a reality, although possibly exaggerated.

Wars with Ceylon.

Wars between the Pāndya kings and the rulers of Ceylon frequently occurred. The most notable incident in this protracted conflict was the invasion of the Pāndya territory, in or about A. D. 1166, by a powerful force under the command of two generals in the service of Parākrama-bāhu, the ambitious king of Ceylon. Two detailed accounts of this event, written from different points of view, are extant. The story, as told in the island chronicle, the *Mahāvaṁśa*, naturally represents the victorious career of the invaders as unbroken by defeat; but the rival account, preserved in a long Chola inscription at Arpakkam near Kānchī, which is the more trustworthy record, proves that the invading army, having gained considerable success at first, ultimately was obliged to retire in consequence of the vigorous resistance of a coalition of the southern princes. The occasion of the Sinhalese intervention was a disputed succession to the Pāndya throne of Madura, contested by claimants bearing the oft-recurring names of Vīra and Sundara.[2] This recurrence of names is

[1] The date of Tirujñānāsambandar and Kūna Pāṇḍya was settled by Hultzsch in 1894–5 (*Ep. Ind.*, iii, 277). See also *Tam. Ant.*, vol. i (1909), No. 3, p. 65. The approximate date thus determined is one of the most important fixed points in the early political and literary history of the South. The event took place at Madura, where it is celebrated as 'the impalement of the Jains' on the 7th day of the *mahōtsava* of Siva, and is treated as an *utsava* (T. A. Gopinatha Rao, *Elements of Hindu Iconography*, 1914, Introd., p. 55).

The persecution is described in the 62nd and 63rd *Tiruvalliadal* (Wilson, *Mackenzie MSS.* 2nd ed., Calcutta, 1828, p. 41). The story is repeated in Rodriguez (*The Hindu Pantheon*, Madras, 1841–5), illustrated by a plate depicting the horrid tortures of the victims; also by Gribble in *Calc. Rev.*, 1875, p. 70; and by Elliot, *Coins of Southern India* (1885), p. 126. The Pāṇḍya king is named Neḍumāṛan in the *Periyapurāṇa* (*Ind. Ant.*, xxii, 63). All the southern kings had many names and titles, which cause much confusion. For the sculptures, see Sewell, *Lists*, vol. i, p. 167.

[2] Full details will be found in the article appended to *Madras*

one of the difficulties which hinder the reconstruction of the dynastic framework of Pāndya history.

The later Pāṇḍyas.

Prof. Kielhorn has succeeded in working out the dates of seventeen Pāndya rājas who ruled a territory more or less extensive during the long period between A. D. 1100 and 1567, but the list of names is believed to be incomplete, and most of the princes were merely local chiefs of slight importance.[1] By far the most powerful of the mediaeval Pāndya Rājas was Jatāvarman Sundara I, who reigned from A. D. 1251 to at least 1271, and made himself master of the whole eastern coast from Nellore to Cape Comorin. Some of his coins can be identified.[2] The partial Muhammadan conquest effected by Malik Kāfūr and other leaders in A. D. 1310 and subsequent years, did not destroy the local dynasties, although it marks a change in political conditions which has been taken as the limit of this history.

Earliest references to the Chera or Kerala kingdom.

The earliest reference to the Kerala or Chera kingdom is that made in the edicts of Asoka under the name of Keralaputra, which was known in slightly corrupted forms to both Pliny and the author of the *Periplus* as still used in their time, the first century after Christ. The ancient Tamil literature, dating approximately from the same period, or a little later, proves that the Chera kingdom comprised five *nādus* or districts, namely : (1) Pooli, 'the sandy,' extending from Agalappula to the mouth of the Ponāni river, about 10° 50′ N. lat. ; (2) Kudam, 'the western,' extending from the Ponāni to the southernmost mouth of the Periyar river near Ernakulam, about 10° N. lat. ; (3) Kuddam, 'the land of lakes,' about Kottayam and Quilon ; (4) Ven,[3] from below Quilon nearly to Cape Comorin ; and (5) Karkā,

G. O., *Public*, Nos. 922, 923, dated Aug. 19, 1899, pp. 8–14. See also Hultzsch, 'Contributions to Singhalese Chronology' (*J. R. A. S.*, 1913, pp. 517–31).

[1] 'Supplement to the List of Inscriptions of Southern India,' in *Ep. Ind.* viii, App. ii, p. 24. In the second half of the sixteenth century the Pāṇḍyas 'became more or less Polygars, and had to wait, like vassals, on the proud Telugu Kartas' ('The History of the Naik Kingdom of Madura,' *Ind. Ant.*, 1915, p. 39).

[2] *Ind. Ant.*, 1911, pp. 137, 138.

[3] The *Periplus* and Pliny assign the southern province or district to the kingdom of Pāṇḍya. No doubt the Pāṇḍyas always did their best to obtain control of some ports on the western coast, and sometimes succeeded in securing their object.

'the rocky,' the hill country to the east of No. 2. Pliny's Cottonara or Kottanara, the pepper coast, corresponds with No. 3.

Ports.

In the early centuries of the Christian era, two of the principal ports at which the trade in pepper and other rarities was carried on were Muziris, the modern Cranganore, at the mouth of the Periyar, and Bakarei, or Vaikkarai, the landing-place for Kottayam. With a favourable south-east monsoon, the voyage from Arabia to Muziris occupied forty days during July and August, and traders were able to return in December or January after transacting their business.

These notices, recorded by the Greek and Roman authors, concerning the extent and methods of commerce are no doubt extremely interesting, but they give little help towards the reconstruction of the political history of Kerala. In fact, next to nothing is known on that subject until Kerala was forced into contact with the aggressive Chola power in the tenth century, from which time the Chola inscriptions throw some sidelights on the history of the western kingdom.

The capital.

The most ancient Chera capital is said to have been Vanji, Vanchi, or Karūr, now represented by the deserted village Tiru-Karūr, high up the Periyar, about 28 miles ENE. of Cochin. Tiruvanji-kalam, near the mouth of the Periyar, was a later capital. Some writers have erroneously believed Karūr in Coimbatore to have been the Chera capital, but there is no doubt that that opinion is mistaken.[1]

The Kongu country.

In the earliest times of which we have any knowledge the Kongu country, comprising Coimbatore and the southern part of Salem, is believed to have been distinct from Kerala, whereas in later days both Kerala proper and the Kongu country seem to have been comprised in a single kingdom;

[1] *The Tamils Eighteen Hundred Years Ago*, p. 15; *Ind. Ant.*, xvii, 259; xxxi, 343; *Ep. Ind.*, iv, 294; *S. I. Inscr.*, vol. iii, part i, p. 30. A few names of early Chera kings have been ascertained: e. g. Sthānu Ravi was contemporary and friendly with Āditya Choḷa, the father of Parāntaka I ('Epigraphy,' p. 61, in *Madras G. O., Public*, No. 919, July 29, 1912). Three inscriptions of Sthānu Ravi have been published and discussed. He made the famous grants to the Syrian Christians of Koṭṭayam, the only Christian documents of the pre-Portuguese period. The inscriptions are about 40 or 50 years later than the date of the Kollam Era, A. D. 825, which perhaps marks the foundation of Ko am (Quilon) by Sapīr Īśō, who built the church at Quilon.

and subsequently again the Kongu country alone was known as the Chera kingdom, while Kerala was separate. Apparently it is not possible at present to assign these changes to definite dates. Kerala itself has not always formed a single kingdom, and it now comprises the British District of Malabar, as well as the native states of Cochin and Travancore.

An early king.

Tamil literature represents, as already observed (*ante*, p. 452), that Chenkuttuvan, an exceptionally powerful Chera king, was contemporary more or less with Nedum-cheliyan, the Pāndya, and Nedumudi Killi Chola, the grandson of Karikāla, as well as with Gajabāhu I of Ceylon. The authentic political history of the Chera or Kerala kingdom, therefore, like that of the other Tamil monarchies, cannot at present be carried back farther than the first two centuries of the Christian era. Even about the events of that period very little is recorded.

Travancore, or South Keraḷa.

A learned writer, the late Mr. P. Sundaram Pillai, who was a native of Travancore, rightly claimed that his country possesses claims to exceptional interest, and may be regarded as an epitome of India. Having never been affected seriously by the Muhammadan conquest, it 'plays in Indian anthropology the part of a happy and undisturbed fossiliferous stratum'. To vary the metaphor, the state may be regarded as a museum in which are preserved alive survivals of nearly all the ancient Indian peoples, religions, laws, customs, and manners. The old and new can be studied together within that limited area in a way which is not possible elsewhere. I have already invited attention (*ante*, p. 8) to the view that the scientific study of the history of Indian institutions should begin with the South, rather than with the North.

Rājas of Travancore.

The political history of Travancore was seriously investigated for the first time by the scholar named above, who collected over a hundred inscriptions, mostly recorded in the ancient Vatteluttu alphabet,[1] by the aid of which he was able to trace back the royal family to A.D. 1125, and to compile a nearly complete list of the Rājas for two centuries from

[1] According to M. M. Haraparshad Sāstrī, the Vatteluttu alphabet is the sole descendant of Kharoshṭhī (*J. B. & O. Res. Soc.*, vol. i, p. 58).

that date.[1] The records published show that at the beginning of the twelfth century Travancore, or Southern Kerala, formed part of the Chola empire of Rājendra Chola-Kulottunga,[2] and to all appearance was well governed and administered. The details of the working of the ancient village associations or assemblies are especially interesting, and prove that the government was by no means a mere centralized autocracy. The village assemblies possessed considerable administrative and judicial powers, exercised under the supervision of the Crown officials.

Chera coins. The crest or cognizance of the Chera kings was a bow. Their coins are very rare, and only two late types, characterized by the bow device, are known. They are found in the Kongu country of Salem and Coimbatore, and I do not know any record of the coinage of Kerala, the Malabar coast.[3]

Lack of material. The above disjointed notes are all that I am in a position to offer as a contribution to the early history of the Chera or Kerala kingdom. One of the most important of the later Chera kings was Ravivarman, born in A.D. 1266–7 (Saka era, 1188), who conquered both the Pāṇḍyas and Cholas in 1299 and was crowned at Quilon in 1312. During the first quarter of the fourteenth century he seems to have been the leading power in South India and he played a prominent part in the organized resistance offered to Malik Kāfūr.[4] The story of the Zamorins of Calicut falls outside of the limits of this work. Professor Kielhorn has compiled a list of the inscriptions of the later kings and chiefs of Kerala, being mostly those collected by Mr. Sundaram Pillai,[5] but has not attempted to draw up a dynastic list.

[1] 'Some Early Sovereigns of Travancore,' *Ind. Ant.*, vol. xxiv (1895), pp. 249, 277, 305, 333; ibid., vol. xxvi, p. 109; 'Miscellaneous Travancore Inscriptions,' ibid., vol. xxvi, pp. 113, 141. Later information will be found in V. Nagam Aiya, *The Travancore State Manual*, 3 vols., Trivandrum, 1906, and in the *Travancore Archaeological Series*, commencing in 1910.

[2] Kerala had been annexed at an earlier date by Rajendra-Choḷa I.

[3] *Ante*, plate of coins, fig 17; Tufnell, *Hints to Coin Collectors in Southern India* (Madras, 1889), p. 17.

[4] See *Ep. Ind.*, iv, 145 ff.

[5] *Ep. Ind.*, vol. vii, App. O, Nos. 939–66. The inscriptions generally are dated in the Kollam or Malabar era of A.D. 824–5, which marks the date of the foundation of Kollam or Quilon (*J. R. A. S.*, 1916, p. 156). Much further information will be found in the works above cited, but the details are not of general interest.

SECTION III

The Chola Kingdom

Traditional limits of the Chola country.

According to tradition, the Chola country (*Cholamaṇḍalam*) was bounded on the north by the Pennār, and on the south by the southern Vellāru river; or, in other words, it extended along the eastern coast from Nellore to Pudukottai, where it abutted on the Pāndya territory. On the west it reached to the borders of Coorg. The limits thus defined include Madras, and several other British districts on the east, as well as the greater part of the Mysore state.[1] The most ancient historical capital was Uraiyūr, or Old Trichinopoly, so far as is known with certainty.[2] A town called North Mañalūr, of which the position is not known, is said to have been the Chola capital in prehistoric times.[3]

Variation of political boundaries.

The existence of well-known traditional boundaries must not be taken to justify the inference that they always agreed with the frontiers of the Chola kingdom, which latter, as a matter of fact, varied enormously. The limits of the Chola country, as determined by tradition, mark ethnic rather than political frontiers on the north and west, where they do not differ widely from the lines of demarcation between the Tamil and the other Dravidian languages—Telugu, Kanarese, Malayālam, and Tulu. Tamil, however, is as much the vernacular of the Pāndya as of the Chola region, and no clear ethnical distinction can be drawn between the peoples residing north and south of the Vellāru, the southern limit of the traditional Chola territory.

Earliest notices of Choḷa kingdom.

The kingdom of the Cholas, which, like that of the Pāndyas, was unknown to Pānini, was familiar by name to Kātyāyana,

[1] *Coins of Southern India*, p. 108. *Choḷa* is also written *Chora*, *Śola*, or *Śora*. Coromandel is a corruption of *Choḷamaṇḍalam* (Yule & Burnell, *Anglo-Indian Glossary*, s. v. 'Coromandel'). The name Choḷa means a people as well as a dynasty, but nothing is known about the Choḷas as a people. They have become merged in the existing population without leaving a trace.

[2] Uraiyur is also spelt Woraiyur. 'Woraiyur, which is two miles from Trichinopoly, was a city newly planned and built by the great Choḷa king, Karikāl Peruvaḷattān' (*Town Planning in Ancient Dekkan*, by C. P. Venkatarama Ayyar, Madras, 1916, p. 11).

[3] *Ind. Ant.*, 1913, pp. 70, 72.

and recognized by Asoka as independent. Inasmuch as the great Maurya's authority unquestionably extended to the south of Chitaldūrg in Mysore, and down to at least the fourteenth degree of latitude, the Pennār river probably was the northern Chola frontier in the Maurya age. In later times that frontier on both north and south was much advanced, while, on the contrary, at an intermediate date, it was greatly contracted during the period of Pallava supremacy.

Trade in ancient times.

Ancient Tamil literature and the Greek and Roman authors prove that in the first two centuries of the Christian era the ports on the Coromandel or Chola coast enjoyed the benefits of active commerce with both West and East.[1] The Chola fleets did not confine themselves to coasting voyages, but boldly crossed the Bay of Bengal to the mouths of the Ganges and Irrawaddy, as well as the Indian Ocean to the islands of the Malay Archipelago. All kinds of goods imported into Kerala or Malabar from Egypt found a ready market in the Chola territory; while, on the other hand, the western ports drew a large part of their supplies of merchandise from the bazaars of the eastern coast, which produced great quantities of cotton goods. The principal Chola port was Kāviripaddinam, situated at the northern mouth of the Kāvēri (Cauvery) river. This once wealthy city, in which the king maintained a magnificent palace, and foreign merchants found residence agreeable and profitable, has vanished, and its site lies buried under deep sand-drifts.[2]

Karikāla.

The first historical, or semi-historical, Chola king is Karikāla (Karikkāl), who is represented by the early poets as having invaded Ceylon and carried off thence thousands of coolies to work on the embankments of the Kāvēri river, a hundred miles in length, which he constructed. He founded Kāviripaddinam, transferring his capital from Uraiyūr to the new port. He enjoyed a long reign, which was much

[1] Schoff holds that 'the eastern sea-trade of India exceeded its western trade' (*J. A. O. S.*, 37, p. 242).

[2] For Kāviripaddinam, see *ante*, p. 462. *The Tamils Eighteen Hundred Years Ago*, pp. 25, 26, 38. The full Tamil name of the town is *Kāvēripūmpaṭṭinam.*

occupied by fighting with his neighbours, the Pāndyas and Cheras. He seems to have lived in the second half of the first century of the Christian era, or perhaps in the second century. Karikāla was succeeded on the throne by his grandson, Nedumudi Killi, in whose reign Kāviripaddinam is supposed to have been destroyed by the sea. Nedumudi Killi was contemporary with Chenkuttuvan Chera and Gajabāhu I of Ceylon. The Chera king appears to have then become the leading power in the South for a short time, while the glory of the Cholas departed, not to be renewed until ages had passed.

Rise of the Pallavas.

Literary references indicate that, in the second or third century after Christ, the power of the Chola and other Tamil kings declined, and was superseded by the rise of the Aruvalar and similar tribes, apparently distinct in race from the Tamils.[1] The earliest known Pallava inscriptions, dating from about the beginning of the fourth century, show that at that time a Pallava prince was reigning at Kānchī in the middle of the traditional Chola country ; and it may well be that the opposition of the tribes alluded to was organized and directed by the foreign or semi-foreign dynasty of the Pallavas, who, as hereafter stated, may perhaps have been connected by descent with the rulers of Maṇi-pallavam or the Jaffna peninsula in Ceylon.[2] However that may be, a Pallava king certainly was established at Kānchī when Samudragupta raided the South, about A. D. 350 (*ante*, p. 300), and the Chola dominions at that time must have been much diminished in consequence.[3] Nothing further is known about Chola history until the seventh century.

Hiuen Tsang.

The observations of Hiuen Tsang give an interesting

[1] *The Tamils Eighteen Hundred Years Ago*, pp. 64–78 ; S. Krishnaswāmī Aiyangar, 'Some Points in Tamil Literary History,' *Malabar Quarterly Review*, 1904. The dates in Kanakasabhai's book seem to be placed too early, Chap. vi of S. K. Aiyangar's book, *Ancient India*, 1911, is the best history of the Chola kingdom. In the article entitled 'Karikala and his Times' (*Ind. Ant.*, 1912, p. 146), K. V. S. Aiyar unsuccessfully tries to prove that Karikāla lived in the earlier half of the sixth century after Christ. That view seems to me to be wholly untenable, and to involve a false chronology of Tamil literature.

[2] See p. 491, *post*.

[3] *The Tamils Eighteen Hundred Years Ago*, p. 44.

notice of the Chola kingdom in the first half of that century, the significance of which has not been fully appreciated by commentators on his travels. His visit to the South, when he penetrated as far as Kānchī, the Pallava capital, may be dated with certainty in the year A.D. 640. At that time the kingdom of Chola (Chu-li-ya) was a restricted territory estimated to be 400 or 500 miles in circuit, with a small capital town barely 2 miles in circumference. The country was wild and mostly deserted, consisting of a succession of hot marshes and jungles, occupied by a scanty population, of ferocious habits, addicted to open brigandage. The few Buddhist monasteries were ruinous, and the monks dwelling in them as dirty as the buildings. The prevailing religion was Jainism, but there were a few Brahmanical temples. The position of the country is indicated as being some 200 miles or less to the south-west of Amarāvatī. It must, therefore, be identified with a portion of the Ceded Districts, and more especially with the Cuddapah District, which possesses the hot climate and other characteristics noted by the pilgrim, and was still notorious for brigandage when annexed by the British in 1800. The pilgrim speaks merely of the 'country' of Chola, and makes no mention of a king; doubtless for the reason that the local Rāja was a person of small importance, subordinate to the reigning Pallava king of Kānchī, the powerful Narasimhavarman, who two years later destroyed the Chalukya power.[1] The correctness of this interpretation of Hiuen Tsang's notice of the Chola principality is demonstrated by the discovery in the Cuddapah District of stone inscriptions of local Chola Rājas engraved in characters anterior to the eighth century.[2]

Decline of the Pallavas.

During the early part of that century the struggle for predominance in Southern India was waged between the Chalukyas of the Deccan and the Pallavas of Kānchī, the Cholas not counting for much. But the severe defeat suffered

[1] Beal, ii, 227-30, Watters, ii, 224.

[2] *Reports on Epigraphy* in *Madras G. O., Public*, No. 518, dated July 18, 1905, p. 48, and No. 503, dated June 27, 1907, para. 43. For the state of Cuddapah in 1800, see Hamilton, *Description of Hindostan*, 4to ed., 1820, vol. ii, p. 323.

by the Pallavas at the hands of the Chalukya king, Vikramāditya, in 740, weakened the power of the kingdom of Kānchī, and gave the Cholas, who had been reduced to insignificance by the pressure of the Pallavas on the north and the Pāndyas on the south, an opportunity of recovering their position. We hear of a Chola Rāja named Vijayālaya, who came to the throne about the middle of the ninth century, and reigned for thirty-four years. His son Āditya (c. A. D. 880–907) conquered Aparājita Pallava, and so finally put an end to the Pallava supremacy.

Parāntaka I. From the date of the accession of Āditya's son and successor, Parāntaka I, in A. D. 907, the historian stands on firm chronological ground, and is embarrassed by the plethora rather than by the lack of epigraphic material. More than forty stone inscriptions of Parāntaka I were copied during the single season of 1906–7, ranging in date from his third to his forty-first year, i. e. from A. D. 909–10 to 947–8. This ambitious prince, not content with the overthrow of the Pallava power, pushed on to the extreme south, captured the Pāndya capital, Madura, drove its king into exile, and invaded Ceylon.

Chola administration. Certain long inscriptions of Parāntaka I are of especial interest to the students of village institutions by reason of the full details which they give of the manner in which local affairs were administered by well-organized local committees, or panchāyats, exercising their extensive administrative and judicial powers under royal sanction. It is a pity that this apparently excellent system of local self-government, really popular in origin, should have died out ages ago. Modern governments would be happier if they could command equally effective local agency. The subject has been studied carefully by several Indian scholars, whose disquisitions are well worth reading. Whenever the mediaeval history of Southern India comes to be treated in detail, a long and interesting chapter must be devoted to the methods of Chola administration.[1]

[1] S. Krishnaswami Iyenngar, The Chola Administration, 900–1300 A. D.' (*Madras Review*, 1908), and *Ancient India*, pp. 158–91.

Parāntaka I died about A.D. 953 or possibly later.[1] His son, Rājāditya, seems to have predeceased him, having been killed in battle at Takkola about A. D. 947–8 by the Rāshtrakūta king, Krishnarāja III. Parāntaka was followed by five obscure successors, who had short and troubled reigns. Successors of Parāntaka I.

The accession in 985 A.D. of a strong ruler, Rājarāja-deva the Great, put an end to dynastic intrigue, and placed at the head of the Chola state a man qualified to make it the leading power in the South. In the course of a busy reign of about twenty-eight years, Rājarāja passed from victory to victory, and, when he died, was beyond dispute the Lord Paramount of Southern India, ruling a realm which included nearly the whole of the Madras Presidency, Ceylon, and a large part of Mysore. Rājarāja the Great, *acc.* A. D. 985.

He began his career by the conquest of the Chera country,[2] and in the fourteenth year of his reign his acquisitions on the mainland comprised the Eastern Chalukya kingdom of Vengī, formerly held by the Pallavas, Coorg, the Pāndya country, and extensive regions in the table-land of the Deccan. During the next three years, Quilon (Kollam) on the Malabar coast, and the northern kingdom of Kalinga were added to his dominions. Protracted campaigns in Ceylon next occupied Rājarājā, and resulted in the annexation of the island in the twentieth year of his reign. In or about A. D. 1005 he sheathed the sword and spent the rest of his life in peace. From 1011 his son Rājendra became his colleague, in accordance with Chola custom. Conquest of Ceylon, &c.

The ancient enmity between the Chalukyas and the Pallavas, inherited by the Chola power, which had succeeded to the premier rank formerly enjoyed by the Pallavas, led to War with Chalukyas.

The author sometimes spells his name Aiyangar. V. Venkayya, 'Irrigation in Southern India in Ancient Times' (*Archaeol. Survey Annual Rep.*, 1903–4, pp. 203–11). R. D. Mukharji, *Local Government in Ancient India*, 1919; and R. C. Majumdar, *Corporate Life in Ancient India*, Calcutta, 1918.

[1] *Ep. Ind.*, vol. xii, July, 1913, pp. 123, 124.

[2] T. A. Gopinatha Rao (*Travancore Archaeol. Series*, vol. ii, pp. 3–5) shows that the earliest inscriptions of Rājarāja are of the 8th and 10th regnal years, and imply the conquest of the Chera country. The Chera king was Bhāskara Ravivarman, who ruled for at least 58 years, from A. D. 978 to about 1036 (ibid., p. 33).

a four years' war, ending in the defeat of the Chalukyas, who had not been long freed from subjection to the Rāshtrakūtas.

Naval operations.

Rājarāja possessed a powerful navy, of which he made full use, and his last martial exploit was the acquisition of a large number of unspecified islands, meaning, perhaps, the Laccadives and Maldives, in his twenty-ninth year.

Temple at Tanjore.

The magnificent temple at his capital Tanjore (Tanjūvūr), built by his command, the walls of which are engraved with the story of his victories, as recorded in the twenty-sixth year of his reign, stands to this day as a memorial of Rājarāja's brilliant career.[1]

Buddhism.

Although himself a worshipper of Siva, he was sufficiently liberal-minded to endow a Burmese Buddhist temple at the port of Negapatam, where two such temples continued to be the object of foreign pilgrimages until the fifteenth century. One of them, probably that endowed by Rājarāja, survived in a ruinous condition until 1867, when the remains of it were pulled down by the Jesuit Fathers, and utilized for the construction of Christian buildings.[2]

Rājendra I, Gangai-konda, *acc.* A. D. 1018.[3]

Rājendra-Choladeva I, surnamed Gangai-konda, son and successor of Rājarāja, continued his father's ambitious career, with added vigour and even more conspicuous success. His fleet, crossing the Bay of Bengal, attacked and captured Kadāram (Kidāram), the ancient capital of the kingdom of Prome or Pegu, and also the seaports of Takkolam and Matama, or Martaban, on the same coast. The fall of these towns involved the temporary annexation of the whole kingdom of Pegu to the Chola empire.[4] Two granite pillars still

[1] A characteristic specimen of his coinage is shown in Fig. 15 of the plate of coins.

[2] *Ind. Ant.*, vii, 224, with plates; *Madras G. O.*, *Public*, Nos. 922, 923, dated Aug. 19, 1899.

[3] Diwan Bahadur L. D. Swamikannu Pillai Avagal works out astronomically a number of Choḷa and Pāṇḍya dates in *Prog. Rep. Epigraphy*, *Madras G. O.*, No. 1260, dated 25 Aug. 1915, pp. 72 ff. He makes the reign of Rājendra-Choḷadeva I begin between May 6 and July 7, 1012. But this may be his conjoint reign, as the writer makes his successor, Rājādhirāja I begin between May 9 and Dec. 3, 1018 (see next page), reducing Kielhorn's limits by two months.

[4] V. Kanakasabhai, 'The Conquest of Bengal and Burma by the Tamils' (*Madras Review*, 1902, p. 251). Kidāram or Kadāram is supposed to be Tharekhettra, 8 miles west of Prome (*Ind. Ant.*,

THE GREAT TEMPLE AT TANJORE

(from outside the fort wall)

standing at the town of Pegu are believed to have been set up by the Chola king to commemorate his conquest, which was effected in the years A. D. 1025–7.[1] The annexation of the Nicobar (Nakkavāram) and Andaman islands followed on the conquest of Pegu.

His wars and capital.

During the earlier years of his reign Rājendra-Choladeva had occupied himself with a succession of wars against the northern powers. About A. D. 1023 he came into collision even with Mahīpāla, king of Bihār and Bengal, and brought his army to the banks of the Ganges. In memory of this exploit he assumed the title of Gangaikonda,[2] and built a new capital city, which he called Gangaikonda-Cholapuram. Near the city he constructed a vast artificial lake, with an embankment 16 miles long, fully provided with the necessary sluices and channels for the irrigation of a large area. The city was adorned by a magnificent palace and a gigantic temple, enshrining a *lingam* formed of a black granite monolith 30 feet high. The ruins of these structures, sadly defaced by the ravages of modern utilitarians in search of building material, still stand in lonely grandeur in a desolate region of the Trichinopoly District. The sculptures in the temples are of singular excellence.[3] The Pāndya dominions continued to be subject to the Chola domination during the reign of Rājendra Gangaikonda, and were administered by his son as Viceroy, with the title of Chola-Pāndya.[4]

xxii, 6, 160). Takkolam = Takōla of Ptolemy (Bk. vii, ch. 2, 5; *Ind. Ant.*, xiii, 372), and is now called Ayethema (ibid., xxi, 383), some miles from the present coast. On Takkolam and Kadāram (or Kālagam), see Taw Sein Ko in *Burma A. S. Prog. Rep.*, 1909–10, pp. 14–16 and 1916–17, para. 57. It is Taikkula to SE. of Pegu. It is suggested that Pegu was under foreign Indian domination for 500 years. Kadāram seems to mean Pegu. Yet the position of Ptolemy's Takōla really is uncertain. See articles by St. John and Blagden in Actes xi, Congrès Or., Paris, 1898, Deuxième Section.

[1] *Archaeol. S. Burma, Progr. Rep.*, 1906–7, p. 19.

[2] Rice interprets the title differently: 'His son Rājendra Coḷa, in command of his father's forces, advanced against Talekād, the Ganga capital, and this ancient city fell in 1004, and with it the Ganga line came to an end as a sovereign power. The event was marked by Rājendra Coḷa assuming the title of Gaṅgaikoṇḍa Coḷa, "the Coḷa who took Gangai"' (*Bh. Comm.*, vol. 1917, p. 247).

[3] *Hist. of Fine Art in India and Ceylon*, figs. 159–61. A detailed survey and description of the site, fully illustrated, would be of much interest.

[4] *Report on Epigraphy*, in *Madras G. O., Public*, No. 503, dated June 27, 1907, para. 25.

Rājādhirāja; *yuvarāja* A.D. 1018; king A.D. 1035.

Rājādhirāja, eldest son of Rājendra, who had been his father's colleague since 1018, succeeded him in A.D. 1035, and continued the never-ending fight with all the neighbouring powers.[1] He fell in the fierce struggle with the Chalukya army at the battle of Koppam (*ante*, p. 448) in A.D. 1052 or 1053, which determined that the Tungabhadrā river should be the frontier between the rival Chola and Chalukya empires. Notwithstanding the death of Rājādhirāja, the fortunes of the day were retrieved by his brother Rājendra Parakesarivarman, who was crowned on the battle-field as his successor.

The customary wars went on during the reigns of this king and three kings who succeeded him, but few of the details are worthy of remembrance. A notable incident was the battle

Battle of Kūdal Sangamam.

of Kūdal Sangamam, fought at the junction of the Krishnā and Panch Ganga rivers,[2] in which the Chalukyas suffered a severe defeat at the hands of Vīrarājendra Chola (acc. A.D. 1062–3). In the civil war between the brothers and rival claimants to the Chalukya throne—Somesvara II and Vikramāditya—Vīrarājendra took the side of the latter, and gave him his daughter in marriage.

A revolution: Adhirājendra.

The death of Vīrarājendra (A.D. 1070) was followed by a disputed succession and civil war. Vikramāditya Chalukya, having established himself on the throne of the Deccan, came to the aid of his brother-in-law, Adhirājendra, and succeeded in making him king of the Chola realm (1072). But the new sovereign proved to be unpopular, and was assassinated two years later (1074). With him the direct line in male succession of the great mediaeval Cholas came to an end.

Chalukya-Chola dynasty;

Adhirājendra appears to have left no issue capable of ruling, and so was succeeded by his relative Rājendra, subsequently known as Kulottunga I. Rājendra, whose mother

[1] The practice of appointing the Crown Prince, or *yuvarāja*, as his father's colleague causes the regnal years to overlap. The chronology has been settled by Prof. Kielhorn (*Ep. Ind.*, viii, App. ii, 26). The references in detail to inscriptions can be traced through the paper cited. Later discoveries will be found in the *Reports on Epigraphy* in *Madras G. O., Public*, No. 492, dated July 2, 1906, and No. 503, dated June 26, 1907, and subsequent issues, as well as in *Ep. Ind.* to date.

[2] Fleet, *Ep. Ind.*, xii, 298.

Kulottuṅga I, A. D. 1070–1118.

was a daughter of the famous Gangaikonda Chola, was the son of the Eastern Chalukya prince of Vengi who had died in 1062. But Rājendra had preferred to remain at the Chola court, and had allowed his uncle to rule Vengi for some years. In 1070 [1] Rājendra was crowned as lord of Vengi, and four years later, when Adhirājendra was murdered, he assumed the government of the whole Chola territory. He thus founded a new Chalukya-Chola dynasty, taking the title of Kulottunga Chola. He was worthy of his position and ruled his extensive dominions successfully for forty-nine years. He reconquered Kalinga, defeating the Eastern Ganga king, Anantavarman Choda. His internal administration was distinguished by the execution of an elaborate revision of the revenue survey in A. D. 1086, the year of the survey for Domesday Book.

Rāmānuja.

The celebrated philosopher, Rāmānuja, the most venerated teacher of the Vaishnava Hindus in the south, received his education at Kānchī, and resided at Srīrangam near Trichinopoly during the reign of Adhirājendra ; but, owing to the hostility of the king, who professed the Saiva faith, was obliged to retire into Mysore territory until Adhirājendra's death freed him from anxiety. The holy man then returned to Srīrangam, where he remained until his decease.[2]

Vikrama Choḷa, acc. A. D. 1118.

Vikrama Chola, the son and successor of Kulottunga, continued to fight with his neighbours according to precedent, and seems to have succeeded in maintaining the predominant position of his dynasty.[3] The next three kings, who had short reigns, were not notable in any way.

The last Chola king of any importance was Kulottunga

[1] L. D. S. Pillai says that Kulottuṅga I's 'reign must have commenced before 28 June 1070'—as shown by inscriptions (*G. O.*, No. 920, Aug. 4, 1914, *Epigraphy*, p. 59). See also ibid., No. 1260, Aug. 25, 1915, p. 73, where he says that the limits of the reign are now established beyond doubt.

[2] For the history of Adhirājendra, Kulottuṅga, and Rāmānuja, I follow Bhaṭṭanātha Svamin, 'The Cholas and the Chalukyas in the Eleventh Century' (*Ind. Ant.*, 1912, pp. 217–27). His article is based on a contemporary metrical chronicle, entitled *Divyasūricharita*, of which he is about to publish a critical edition. The text was printed in Mysore in 1885. The title Kulottuṅga means 'highest in his family'.

[3] The exploits of Vikrama Choḷa are the subject of a Tamil poem of some merit, entitled *Vikrama-Choḷan-Ulā* (*Ind. Ant.*, xxii, 142).

Kulottunga III, *acc.* A. D. 1287.

Chola III, who reigned for about forty years from A. D. 1287. The succession was then disputed, and the Chola princes sank into a position of insignificance. For a time the Pāndyas in the south reasserted themselves and gained the upper hand, until 1310, when the power of all the Hindu states in Southern India was broken by the successes of Malik Kāfūr's Muhammadan army in that year and following years. The rapid development of the Vijayanagar kingdom during the fourteenth century again restored Hindu authority in the Peninsula. The extreme South passed under the rule of Vijayanagar about A. D. 1370.[1]

SECTION IV

The Pallavas

Origin of the Pallavas.

Who were the Pallavas? Whence did they come? How did they attain the chief place among the powers of the South? To these questions no complete answer can be given at present, although considerable progress has been made in solving the problem.

The name Pallava resembles Pahlava so closely that some writers have been disposed to favour the hypothesis that Pallavas and Pahlavas were identical, and that consequently the Southern Pallava dynasty of Kānchī should be considered as ultimately of Persian origin. But recent research has failed to adduce any historical facts in support of that notion.

A close study of ancient Tamil literature has recently led to the suggestion that the Pallavas were originally connected with Ceylon. An examination of the Tamil poems, *Maṇimēkalai* and *Chilappatikāran*, seems to indicate that the destruction by the sea of the Chola capital, Puhār or Kāviripaddinam, must have occurred before the close of the third quarter of the second century A. D., when Gajabāhu's reign in Ceylon came to an end, and that Kiḷḷi Vaḷavan

[1] The coins of the Muhammadan Sultans of Madura range from A. D. 1329–30 to 1377–8 (Hultzsch in *J. R. A. S.*, 1909, p. 682).

or Nedumudi Kiḷḷi, the Chola king, then moved his capital to Uraiyūr.[1] Quite recently, Mr. Mudaliyar C. Rasanayagam of Colombo,[2] on the strength of a further study of these Tamil epics, asserts that this Chola king had a *liaison* with a Nāga princess, daughter of Vaḷaivānam, the Nāga king of Maṇipallavam, which can be identified with the Jaffna peninsula, at that early date an island off the coast of Ceylon. Of this union was born a son, known as Toṇḍaimān Iḷantirāyan,[3] who some time in the latter half of the second century A. D. was created by his father (Kiḷḷi Vaḷavan) king of *Toṇḍaimandalam*, as distinct from *Cholamandalam*, with his capital at Kānchī. The dynasty, of which Toṇḍaimān Iḷantirāyan thus became the first representative, took its title from the second half of the word Maṇipallavam, the home of his Nāga mother, who was regarded as inferior in rank to his Chola father. According to this view, therefore, the Pallavas, who were a dynasty rather than a tribe or clan, were descended on one side from the Chola family of Uraiyūr and on the other from the Nāga rulers of what is now the Jaffna peninsula in Ceylon.[4] The persistent hostility of the Pallavas to the territorial Tamil states and the fact that tradition does not assign any recognized territorial

[1] *Ind. Ant.*, xxvii, 235.

[2] 'The Origin of the Pallavas' (*Ind. Ant.*, lii, April, 1923, pp. 75–80). But see S. K. Aiyangar's 'Origin and Early History of the Pallavas of Kānchī', mentioned in Preface *ante*.

[3] So named, according to the article (ibid.), because on his way from Maṇipallavam to Puhār he was shipwrecked and washed ashore on a *toṇḍai* creeper. The name probably indicates the totem of the tribe or community.

[4] According to M. C. Rasanayagam, the name Maṇipallavam occurs only in the *Maṇimēkalai*, the island or peninsula being elsewhere called *Maṇipuram*, and by the Sinhalese *Maṇi-Nāgadīpa*, owing to its being populated by Nāgas and governed by Nāga kings. The Tamils retained the word *Maṇi* and added *pallavam*, meaning in Tamil, 'a sprout' or 'shoot', in allusion to the appearance of the isle, which to persons sailing from India to Ceylon would have looked very like a sprout or branch from the parent island. It is noteworthy also that the Pallava kings called themselves *Pōt-rāyar*, from the Tamil word *pōttu*, which is a synonym of *pallavam*. The later Pallavas adopted Sanskritic titles ending in *ankūra*, which also signifies a 'sprout', and may indicate memories of their origin. Though the derivation of the name is tentative, it seems to me quite as plausible as Mr. Rea's derivation from Tamil *pal*, 'milk', and the masculine termination, *-avan* (sing.), or *-avar* (pl.), which would make the name equivalent to that of the Gwālas and Āhirs of Hindustan.

limits to the Pallava dominion[1] are indications that the Pallavas were distinct in race from the Tamils, and that their rule was superimposed upon that of the Rājas of the Pāndya, Chola, and Chera countries, the three states which together covered the whole area of the south, according to constant tradition. The possible origin of the Pallavas, as suggested by ancient Tamil poetry, does not appear to conflict with known facts and may perhaps offer an additional reason for the enmity which unquestionably existed between the Pallavas and the Tamil kingdoms. Professor S. K. Aiyangar holds that the historical Pallavas were feudatories of the Satavahanas of the Deccan and belonged to the Naga family.

Castes connected with Pallavas. The rāja of the Pudukottai tributary principality, who is the recognized head of the Kallar tribe, still styles himself Rāja Pallava, and claims descent from the ancient royal family. The Kallars, as Sir Walter Elliot observes, 'belong to what have been called the predatory classes,' and their 'bold, indomitable, and martial habits' agree well with the characteristics of the ancient Pallavas as known from history. Until recent times the Kallars exercised a formidable control over the peaceable inhabitants of the Carnatic, from whom they levied blackmail in return for protection, just as the Marāthās levied similar contributions under the name of *chauth*. It seems to be highly probable that the political power of the Pallavas was exercised in a similar manner, its extent varying according to the variations in the relative strength of the ancient Tamil states and that of the usurping tribesmen. The Palli caste and certain sections

[1] The monuments, as distinct from the copperplates, show that 'the Pallava kingdom extended all along the Coromandel coast from Kālahasti in the north to Pudukottai in the south, and was bounded on the west by the Eastern Ghāts' (Jouveau-Dubreuil, *Pallava Antiquities*, vol. viii, p. 43). Kālahasti town is in N. Arcot District, in 13° 45′ N. and 79° 42′ E. The limits from north to south include N. Arcot, Chingleput, S. Arcot, Trichinopoly and Tanjore Districts. Pudukottai town is in 10° 23′ N. and 78° 49′ E. in the State of the same name. Traditionally the northern part of the State belonged to the Cholas and the southern to the Pāṇḍyas; so the Pallava dominion evidently extended over the Chola country to the Pāṇḍya boundary. Pudukottai is near the centre of the State.

of the Vellāla agricultural caste, which is proverbially associated with the Kallar and Maravar robber tribes, also claim a connexion with the Pallavas.[1] It may well be that the so-called 'predatory classes', whom the Pallava dynasty may once have governed and welded into an aggressive force, belong to a section of the population distinct from and more ancient than the Tamils.

Earliest Pallava kings.

The earliest known documents of the dynasty, certain copperplate grants found in the Guntūr District, tell us of a king reigning at Kānchī (Conjeeveram), whose dominions included Amarāvatī, and so extended to the Krishnā (Kistnā) river. Those grants, which date from about the third century or the beginning of the fourth, and are written in Prākrit, give no indication of the manner in which the kingdom was acquired. It seems to be safe to date its origin not later than the beginning of the third century. All authors are agreed in regarding as a Pallava the Rāja Vishnugopa of Kānchī, who was defeated by Samudragupta about A.D. 350; and Hastivarman, the contemporary Rāja of Vengī, also must have been a Pallava. The names Vishnugopa and Hastivarman both occur in Pallava genealogies. Simhavarman, king of Kānchī (*acc.* A.D. 437), was a Buddhist.[2]

Simhavishṇu.

From the second half of the sixth century, when Chalukya history begins, until the overthrow of the Chalukya power by the Rāshtrakūtas, in A.D. 753, the Pallavas and Chalukyas, who regarded each other as 'enemies by nature', remained

[1] Elliot, *Coins of Southern India*, pp. 42–4. 'The caste of *Kullars*, or robbers, who exercise their calling as an hereditary right, is found only in the Marava country, which borders on the coast, or fishing, districts. The rulers of the country are of the same caste. They regard a robber's occupation as discreditable neither to themselves nor to their fellow castemen, for the simple reason that they consider robbery a duty and a right sanctioned by descent. They are not ashamed of their caste or occupation, and if one were to ask of a *Kullar* to what people he belonged, he would coolly answer, "I am a robber". This caste is looked upon in the district of Madura, where it is widely diffused, as one of the most distinguished among the Sudras' (Dubois, *Hindu Manners, Customs, and Ceremonies*, by Beauchamp, 3rd ed., p. 17).

[2] The date is deduced from the colophon of a Jain work, which gives Śaka 380 = A.D. 458 as the 22nd year of Simhavarma, king of Kānchī. The date, which is genuine, is the earliest date recorded in the Śaka era so far (*Arch. S. of Mysore, Report*, 1908–9, p. 31; 1909–10, para. 115).

constantly in touch and generally at war, each power striving to acquire for itself the mastery of the South. During this period of about two centuries the Pallava royal genealogy for nine reigns, beginning with Simhavishnu (acc. *c.* A.D. 575,) is well ascertained.[1] Simhavishnu claims to have inflicted defeats on the kings of Ceylon and the three Tamil states.

Mahendravarman I; his public works.

Mahendravarman I, son and successor of Simhavishnu (*c.* A.D. 600 to 625), has immortalized his name by the excavation of many rock-cut temples in the Trichinopoly, Chingleput, North Arcot, and South Arcot Districts. His fame is also preserved by the ruins of the city of Mahendravādi, between Arcot and Arkonam, and of a great reservoir, the Mahendra tank, near the same. A cave temple dedicated to Vishnu exists on the bank of the tank.[2]

His wars.

In war Mahendravarman encountered a formidable rival in the person of the ambitious Chalukya monarch, Pulakēsin II, who boasted of having inflicted a severe defeat on the Pallava king about A.D. 609 or 610. At or about the same time the Chalukya king annexed the province of Vengī, the northern portion of the Pallava dominions, and made it over to the government of his younger brother, the founder of the Eastern Chalukya dynasty. It is probable that the loss of Vengī stimulated the Pallavas to push forward their southern frontier, and it is certain that Mahendravarman held Trichinopoly. He appears to have been a Jain originally,

[1] Full details given by Prof. Kielhorn (op. cit., p. 20). The following observations, except as otherwise stated, are based on three publications, namely (1) Venkayya, 'The Pallavas' (*A.S.I., Ann. Rep.* 1906–7, pp. 217–43); (2) Hultzsch, 'The Pallava Inscriptions of the Seven Pagodas' (*Ep. Ind.*, vol. x (July, 1909), pp. 1–14); and (3) Rea, *Pallava Architecture*, 1909, with cxxiv plates, being vol. xxxiv of the 4to Imperial Series of the Archaeol. Survey.

[2] *Report on Epigraphy* in *Madras G. O., Public*, No. 518, dated July 18, 1905, p. 47; *Archaeol. S. Annual Rep.*, 1903–4, p. 203. In 1882, when Mr. Sewell inserted a note on Mahendravāḍi in his *Lists of Antiquities, Madras*, vol. i, p. 162, the Pallava origin of the remains was not known. Three gold coins, ascribed to Mahendravarman, are mentioned in *A. S. Prog. Rep.* W. I., 1917–18, pp. 17, 18. Jouveau-Dubreuil (*Pallava Antiq.*, vol. ii (1918)) distinguishes three styles of Pallava building, with sharply marked characteristics, viz. (i) Mahendra, (ii) Māmallapuram (Narasiṅha), (iii) Rājasiṅha. One example of a fourth style belongs to the period of Aparājita, *c.* A.D. 850–900.

and to have been converted to faith in Siva by a famous Tamil saint. The king, after his conversion, destroyed the large Jain monastery at Pātaliputtiram in South Arcot, replacing it by a Saiva fane. It is interesting to find the name of the old imperial capital brought down to the neighbourhood of Madras, presumably by the Jains.

Narasiṁha-varman. c. A. D. 625–45.

The Pallava power and art attained their highest point in the reign of Mahendravarman's successor, Narasimha-varman I (*c.* A. D. 625–45). In A. D. 642 he enjoyed the satisfaction of taking Vātāpi, the capital of his enemy, Pulakēsin II, who presumably then lost his life. It is certain that the reverse was so crushing that the Chalukya power remained in abeyance for thirteen years, while the Pallava king became beyond dispute the most influential sovereign in the South, and extended his jurisdiction far into Mysore and the Deccan. The Pallava monarch received effective help in his enterprise from a Sinhalese prince named Mānavamma, who was subsequently enabled to seize the island crown by means of an army equipped by the grateful Indian king.[1]

Hiuen Tsang at Kānchī, A. D. 640.

Hiuen Tsang, who visited Kānchī (Conjeeveram) in A. D. 640, during the reign of Narasimha-varman I, and stayed there for a considerable time, calls the country of which Kānchī was the capital by the name of Dravida, and describes it as being about 1,000 miles in circuit. It corresponded, therefore, very closely with the traditional 'Chola country' between the Northern Pennār and the Southern Vellāru rivers. The soil was fertile and regularly cultivated, producing abundance of grain, flowers, and fruits. The capital was a large city 5 or 6 miles in circumference. In the kingdom the pilgrim found more than a hundred Buddhist monasteries,[2] occupied by a large number of monks, estimated at above ten thousand, all attached, like

[1] *Mahāvaṁsa*, part ii, chap. xlvii.

[2] One large building, 'a rendezvous for the most eminent men of the country,' stood to the south of Kānchī, and a *stūpa* built by Asoka, 100 feet high, adjoined it. As stated in note on page 473 *ante*, some of these Buddhist buildings were later converted to Brahmanical uses. Jain buildings were similarly utilized.

the majority of the Ceylonese, to the Sthavira school of the Mahāyāna. The Hindu, including the Jain, temples numbered about four-score, and, as in other parts of Southern India, the sect of nude, or Digambara, Jains had many adherents. In the Pāndya country farther south Buddhism was almost extinct. Kānchī, which is reckoned among the seven Hindu sacred cities, enjoyed special fame among the Buddhists as having been the birthplace of Dharmapāla, a celebrated metaphysician, who was the predecessor of Hiuen Tsang's teacher Sīlabhadra in the headship of the great monastery at Nālandā.[1]

Monuments. The earliest of the remarkable monolithic temples known as the Seven Pagodas at Māmallapuram, namely that now called the Dharmarāja Ratha, was the work of Narasimha-varman, who bore the title of Mahāmalla, or 'great champion', from which the name of the place is derived.[2] The other similar shrines were wrought under the orders of the same king and his successor down to about the time when Kānchī was taken by its hereditary enemies.[3] That calamity probably explains the fact that some of the shrines were never completed.

The noble temple now called Kailāsanātha at Kānchī, and the 'Shore Temple' at the Seven Pagodas were built by Narasimha-varman II, also named Rājasimha, late in the seventh century.

Parameśvara-varman. In or about A.D. 655 Vikramāditya I Chalukya, a son of Pulakēsin, retrieved the fortunes of his family, and recovered his father's dominions from Paramesvara-varman, who had succeeded to the Pallava throne. During this war Kānchī,

[1] Beal, *Records*, ii, 228–30; *Life*, pp. 138–40; Watters, ii, 226–8; I-tsing, *Records of the Buddhist Religion*, transl. Takakusu; pp. lvii, lviii, 179, 181.

[2] The name of the place assumes many forms—such as Māvalivaram, Mahābalipur, Mahavellipore, &c., but the true name is that given in the text. The forms which include the word *bali* in one spelling or another are based on a false etymology.

[3] It is probable that all the rocks of the Seven Pagodas were carved during the reigns of the two princes, Narasiṁhavarman I (*c.* A.D. 625–50) and Parameśvaravarman I (*c.* 655–90). The style is intermediate between the cave style of Mahendravarman I and the structural temples of Rājasiṁha (Jouveau-Dubreuil, *Pallava Antiquities*, Probsthain, London, 1916, vol. i, p. 60).

THE GAṆĒSA RATHA AT MĀMALLAPURAM

(one of the 'Seven Pagodas')

the Pallava capital, was taken and occupied for a time by the Chalukyas. On the other hand, the Pallavas claimed the gain of a victory at Peruvalanallūr.

Nandivarman.

The perennial conflict continued during succeeding reigns. In about A.D. 740 Kānchī was captured once more by Vikramāditya II Chalukya, who inflicted on Nandivarman Pallava a defeat so decisive that the event may be regarded as the beginning of the end of the Pallava supremacy. Nandivarman, who had succeeded Parameśvara-varman II about A.D. 720, was a distant relative of that prince, being descended from a brother of King Simhavishnu. The change in the line of succession is stated to have been the result of a popular election; and a curious series of sculptures, accompanied by unfinished labels apparently intended to have been explanatory, still extant in a mutilated form at the Vaikuntha Perumāl temple in Conjeeveram (Kānchī), seems to have been designed as a contemporary record of the dynastic revolution.[1]

Aparājita.

Nandivarman reigned for about sixty-two years, and was succeeded by several princes ending with Aparājita Pallava, who vanquished the Pāndya king, Varaguna II, at the battle of Srī-Purambiya, but was himself overcome by Āditya Chola about the close of the ninth century.[2] From that time the Pallava supremacy, which had been severely shaken by the Chalukya successes in 740, finally passed away and was transferred to the Cholas, who, as already narrated, brought all the southern kingdoms under their control more or less completely during the tenth and eleventh centuries.

Wars with Rāshṭrakūṭas.

During their period of decline the Pallava chiefs managed to do some fighting on their own account. When the Rāshtrakūtas supplemented the Chalukyas in the middle of the eighth century, the traditional hostility between the leading power of the Deccan and its southern enemy was not abated, and the new rulers took up the old quarrel with the Pallavas. King Dhruva, a cousin of Dantidurga, who

[1] *Report on Epigraphy* in *Madras G. O., Public*, No. 492, dated July 2, 1906, paras. 2–4.

[2] *Reports on Epigraphy* in *Madras G. O., Public*, No. 492, dated July 2, 1906, paras. 9, 25; and No. 502, dated June 27, 1907, paras. 8, 19–24.

had overthrown the Chalukya dynasty, inflicted a defeat on the Pallavas about A.D. 775; and his son, Govinda III, levied tribute from Dantiga, Rāja of Kānchī, in A.D. 803.

The Gaṅgas.

During the tenth century we hear of wars between the Pallavas and the ancient dynasty of the Ganga kings of Gangavādi, or Mysore, who are now commonly known as the Western Gangas, in order to distinguish them from the family of the same name which ruled Kalinga in the east, and held court at Kalinganagaram, the modern Mukhalingam in the Ganjām District. Various inscriptions of the Western Gangas, which are certainly genuine, date back to about the close of the fifth century A.C.;[1] and the dynasty appears to have reached the zenith of its power during the long reign of Srīpurusha (A.D. 725–776), whose territory was known as the Fortunate Kingdom.[2] The most notable king of the Eastern Gangas of Kalinga was Anantavarman Chodaganga, who reigned for seventy-one years from A.D. 1076 to 1147, and carved out for himself a considerable kingdom, extending from the Ganges to the Godāvarī. He built the temple of Jagannāth at Puri.[3]

The last of the Pallavas.

The later Pallava chiefs sank into the position of mere feudatory nobles and officials in the service of the territorial kingdoms; and it is on record that the Pallava Rāja took the first place among the feudatories of King Vikrama Chola early in the twelfth century.[4] The Rājas can be traced as in possession of limited local power down to the thirteenth century, and Pallava nobles are mentioned as late as the close of the seventeenth century. After that time all trace of the Pallavas as a distinct race or clan disappears, and their blood is now merged in that of the Kallar, Palli, and Vellāla castes.[5]

[1] *Mysore A. S. Rep.*, 1917, paras. 73–82.

[2] *Bhandarkar Comm. Vol.*, p. 244.

[3] Monmohan Chakravarti, 'Chronology of the Eastern Gaṅga kings of Orissa,' an excellent monograph in *J. A. S. B.*, vol. lxxii, part i (1903). For Mukhalingam, about 20 miles distant from Parla-Kimedi, see *Ep. Ind.*, iv, 183–93, and *Madras G. O., Public*, Nos. 827–9, dated Aug. 25, 1902. The history of the Western Gaṅgas has been discussed by Dr. Fleet in *Kanarese Dynasties.*

[4] *Ind. Ant.*, xxii, 143.

[5] The contents of the Pallava inscriptions as known up to 1896 are summarized by Fleet in *Bomb. Gaz.* (1896), vol. i, part ii, 'Dynasties of the Kanarese Districts,'

Religion. The earliest Pallava king who can be precisely dated, Simhavarman, in the fifth century, presented an image at Amarāvatī and is expressly described as being a lay worshipper of Buddha. Probably other members of the dynasty also were Buddhists.[1] Several princes were specially devoted to the cult of Vishnu.[2] Mahendravarman, who was a Jain in early life, at first persecuted the followers of Siva, but was converted to the Saiva creed and turned against his former co-religionists, whose principal monastery he destroyed.[3]

Usually, however, the adherents of rival creeds seem to have lived together in peace and to have enjoyed the impartial protection of the government. The narrative of Hiuen Tsang implies that such was the case in A. D. 640.[3] All the later Pallava kings, apparently, were worshippers of Siva, whose emblem, the bull, was adopted as the family crest. Two of the kings were so zealous for religion that they have been included in the list of sixty-three Saiva saints.[4]

Epilogue. This is the fourth edition of Dr. Vincent A. Smith's work, the second edition having appeared in 1908, and the third in 1914. In commending the third edition to the public, the author wrote :—' My task—a labour of love—is now ended, and this book goes forth once more in its new form which, so far as the author is concerned, is not unlikely to be final. Planned twenty-five years ago, it appeared for the first time sixteen years later in a very imperfect shape.

2nd ed. Later discoveries are described in *S. I. Inscriptions*, the annual *Progress Reports* of the Madras Archaeol. Survey ; Kielhorn's *List* and *Supplement* (*Ep. Ind.*, vii, viii, App.), and the publications of Prof. G. Jouveau-Dubreuil, of the College, Pondicherry, namely (i) *Archéologie du Sud de l'Inde* ; Tomes I and II, Paris, Geuthner, 1914 ; (ii) *Pallava Antiquities*, vol. i, London, Probsthain, 1916 ; (iii) *Dravidian Architecture*, Madras, S. P. C. K. Press, 1917 ; (iv) *The Pallavas*, Pondicherry, sold by author, 1917.

[1] Amarāvatī inscr. No. 39 (*S. I. Inscr.*, vol. i, p. 25). This record is to be read from the bottom upwards. I assume the identity of the Buddhist Siṁhavarman with the king who came to the throne in A. D. 437 (Śaka 359). The inscription may be a copy of an older document (Venkayya, op. cit., p. 240, note 9).

[2] Hastivarman (Attivarmā), Vijayaskandavarman, and Vishṇugopavarman.

[3] Venkayya, op. cit., p. 235, notes.

[4] Ibid., p. 229, note 11.

The generous reception accorded to that faulty pioneer attempt encourages the hope that this much improved edition may be of still greater service in guiding and stimulating the study of the early history of India, now pursued with laudable ardour by a multitude of her sons as well as by foreigners.' The reviser can only re-echo the hope that the present work, based as it is upon the further investigations and discoveries of scholars during the last few years, will prove as acceptable to students of India's early history as the earlier editions, and that the work of revision will be adjudged to have been performed in a manner worthy of the late author and of the great theme with which his name is so closely and so honourably associated.

The volume deals with the political history of Hindu India, the land of the Brahmans, which is the real India; a land the fascination of which is largely due to the unique character of its civilization. That quality of strangeness makes the history of Hindu India less attractive to the European or American general reader than the more easily intelligible story of the Muslim and British conquerors, but anybody who desires to understand modern India must be content to spend some labour on the study of ancient India during the long ages of autonomy.

The political history of India cannot vie with that of Greece, Rome, or modern Europe as illustrating the evolution of constitutions in city or state. Indians, like other Asiatic peoples, usually have been content with simple despotic rule, so that the difference between one government and another has lain in the personal characters and abilities of the several despots rather than in the changes consequent upon the gradual development of institutions. The regulations devised by able individual autocrats, such as Chandragupta Maurya, Asoka, and Akbar, have mostly perished with their authors. The nascent Indian constitution now in course of construction is a foreign importation, imperfectly intelligible to the people for whose benefit it is intended, and perhaps will never be thoroughly acclimatized.

The most important branch of the history of India is the

history of her thought.[1] For the adequate presentation of the story of Indian ideas in the fields of philosophy, religion, science, art, and literature, a chronological narrative of the political vicissitudes of the land is the indispensable foundation. Readers who may find such a narrative dry, or at times even repellent, may take comfort in the conviction that its existence will render possible the composition of more attractive disquisitions, arranged with due regard to the order of time.

[1] See R. W. Frazer, *Indian Thought, Past and Present* (Unwin, 1915)—an attempt to give 'a history of the underlying thought of India, in so far as that Thought has influenced the aspirations, religious beliefs, and social life of all thinking and orthodox Hindus.'

INDEX